The Child with a Handicap

The Child with a Handicap

D. M. B. Hall
MB, BS, BSc, MRCP
Consultant and Senior Lecturer in Paediatrics
Department of Child Health
St George's Hospital Medical School
London

With a Foreword by

Hugh Jolly
MD, MRCS, FCRCP, DCH
Consulting Paediatrician
Charing Cross Hospital
London

Blackwell Scientific Publications
OXFORD LONDON EDINBURGH
BOSTON PALO ALTO MELBOURNE

© 1984 by
Blackwell Scientific Publications;
Editorial offices:
Osney Mead, Oxford, OX2 0EL
8 John Street, London, WC1N 2ES
9 Forrest Road, Edinburgh, EH1 2QH
52 Beacon Street, Boston
  Massachusetts 02108, USA
706 Cowper Street, Palo Alto
  California 94301, USA
99 Barry Street, Carlton
  Victoria 3053, Australia

First published 1984

Printed in Great Britain at
the Alden Press, Oxford

DISTRIBUTORS

USA
  Blackwell Mosby Book Distributors
  11830 Westline Industrial Drive
  St Louis, Missouri 63141

Canada
  Blackwell Mosby Book Distributors
  120 Melford Drive, Scarborough
  Ontario M1B 2X4

Australia
  Blackwell Scientific Book
  Distributors
  31 Advantage Road, Highett
  Victoria 3190

British Library
Cataloguing in Publication Data

Hall, D.M.B.
  The child with a handicap
  1. Handicapped children
  I. Title
  362.4'088054   HV888

ISBN 0-632-01011-8

Contents

v

Foreword

Dr David Hall has wisely chosen the title *The Child with a Handicap* rather than *The Handicapped Child* for this new and excellent book. This change emphasises that he is writing about ordinary children who have to contend with a disability rather than a special breed of children. To understand the effect of this disability requires a detailed understanding of normal development which is admirably reviewed at the start.

The book is written primarily for those working with children who are handicapped, whether doctors, therapists, teachers, psychologists or social workers. However, since little technical language is used, the author hopes that parents will find it of use for obtaining further information about their own child and his problems.

The Consultant in Community Paediatrics will increasingly be the doctor responsible for these children and he or she should be competent to undertake auditory and visual testing. These are fully described by a paediatrician who is obviously experienced in this field.

In this connection the chapter on behaviour problems and their modification is particularly helpful. The child with a handicap is not an ill child who can be cured by medicines or surgery but someone with educational and social problems. His needs must be assessed so that a plan of management can be worked out to help him achieve the optimum of his capabilities. Parents are vital members of the team undertaking this task and to illustrate their involvement Dr Hall has included a sample letter sent to the parents of a child at the conclusion of his first period of assessment.

The second part of the book covers the neurological disorders causing children to be handicapped. This section is particularly valuable as a reference to the causes of mental handicap, the types of cerebral palsy, the reasons for visual or hearing loss and why children fail to communicate normally.

This is a scholarly book written for readers coming from a wide range of disciplines. It fills a gap in our understanding of the needs of children who are handicapped.

Hugh Jolly
Charing Cross Hospital
London

Introduction

The first edition of *The Handicapped Child*, by Dr Grace Woods, was published in 1976. At that time it was, to the best of my knowledge, the only single-author British book to offer a comprehensive introduction to the medical aspects of childhood disability and handicap, and it has retained this unique position.

During the eight years since publication of *The Handicapped Child* there have been rapid advances in knowledge and a more gradual evolution in the philosophical aspects of handicap. More attention is now devoted to the child's needs as a person and to the development of his assets and abilities instead of emphasising his disability. This shift in emphasis was recognised in the Warnock Report on Special Education and subsequently in the 1981 Education Act.

The change in title of this book from *The Handicapped Child* to *The Child with a Handicap* reflects these changing attitudes. Although it retains links with Grace Woods' book, and was conceived as a second edition, it has been completely revised and rewritten with much new material, to take account of recent advances in our knowledge of child development, assessment and related subjects.

The Child with a Handicap will be of particular value to doctors who, having undertaken some training in acute paediatric medicine, wish to expand their knowledge of developmental paediatrics as practised both in Child Development Centres, and outside the hospital in general practice, clinics, nurseries and schools. Students in related specialties such as speech therapy, psychology, special education and social work may also find it useful. As plain English has been used in preference to technical language wherever possible, I hope that parents of handicapped children will also find it a helpful source of information.

It is difficult to decide what to include and what to omit in a book on handicap. I elected to concentrate on neurological handicaps, and have not discussed disorders such as juvenile arthritis or haemophilia, which are well described in standard text books and monographs. Some may object to the inclusion of epilepsy and non-accidental injury, and to my suggestion that the paediatrician should undertake basic audiological testing; but I believe that these aspects of paediatrics will increasingly be managed by the new breed of paediatrician, the Consultant in Community Paediatrics. The contents of this book reflect my views as to the work and breadth of knowledge required of this new specialist, and the circumstances in which he will call on the greater expertise of the paediatric audiologist or neurologist.

The inevitable apology must be made for the deficiencies of the English language which lacks a unisex pronoun and has forced me to use the male pronoun for both doctor and child. The latter at least can be justified; liberated female readers can take comfort from the fact that in all studies of developmental problems there is a preponderance of boys!

I am grateful to many friends and colleagues who have helped me in various ways. I owe my interest and training in handicap to J.A.M. Martin, the paediatricians and neurologists at Baragwanath Hospital, Soweto, Johannesburg and to Dr Hugh Jolly, Nancie Finnie and the staff at the Child Development Centre at Charing Cross Hospital. In particular I value the enthusiasm and skill of my colleagues, both medical and non-medical, at St George's Hospital and in the community we serve.

I would like to thank all those who read portions of the manuscript and/or made valuable suggestions: Mike Berger, Peter Hill, Tony Martin, Alison Hutchinson, Peter Depla, Dorothy Klein, Andrea Pugh, David Taylor, Heather Hunt, Sheila Henderson, Joan Bicknell, Marion Levick, Michael Baraitser, Nick Carter, June Lloyd, Krystina Summers, Matgorzata Borzyskowski, and my wife Sue. Needless to say, the opinions expressed and any errors that remain are my own.

The manuscript was typed by Sandra Garrett, Mary Mitchell, Christine Ryan and Pat Baldwin; Shirley Wheeler prepared the excellent illustrations; Per Saugman provided moral support and J. Russell guided the book through its production stages. I thank them all. Lastly I thank my family for their patience while this book was written. Without their love and support, the task would certainly not have been completed; it might not even have been started.

David Hall
Department of Child Health
St George's Hospital, London

PART ONE

Chapter One
The Nature of Handicap

Tolstoy opened his novel *Anna Karenina* with the provocative observation that 'Happy families are all alike; every unhappy family is unhappy in its own way.' He might have gone on to remark that every handicapped family is handicapped in its own way. All who have any professional contact with childhood handicap must have noticed how remarkably well some families cope with the most distressing problems, whereas others are devastated by handicaps that in purely medical terms are far less severe. The differences are to be found in the personalities and life experiences of the child and his parents, the functioning and strength of the family unit and the effectiveness of their network of support among relatives, friends, and professional services. Of course, these remarks are relevant not only to neurological handicap but also to other chronic disorders of childhood, and many paediatricians have expressed doubts, privately or publicly, about the need to regard the study of child development and handicap, often called 'developmental paediatrics',[1,2] as a separate sub-specialty, believing that every doctor who deals with children should be capable of diagnosing and managing chronic neurological disorders. Certainly this is a desirable goal of paediatric training, for these problems form an ever increasing proportion of the total case load of most paediatricians in developed countries. Nevertheless, there are some important differences between developmental paediatrics and other branches of the specialty.

Firstly, the problems of the handicapped child are often complex and multiple. No single profession can have the requisite knowledge and skill to deal with all of them. Child development, like other aspects of paediatrics, is a rapidly advancing subject, but many of the most relevant new ideas and concepts originate in disciplines such as psychology, child and family psychiatry, education, linguistics, sociology and epidemiology, and are not easily accessible to the paediatrician unless he has the opportunity to collaborate with workers in these fields. Developmental paediatrics is therefore essentially a multidisciplinary specialty, and the paediatrician must be able to understand the techniques and terminology used by his colleagues, both medical and non-medical. Furthermore, in contrast to most other medical specialties, the developmental paediatrician will often find that his role, though vital, is subsidiary to that of his colleagues; for example, the diagnosis and management of a child with a language disorder or learning disability might be largely the responsibility of the speech therapist, psychologist, or teacher. He will also observe that in these disciplines there is less emphasis on, or expectation of, a unitary diagnosis and more emphasis on defining problems that are amenable to intervention; in fact there are many situations in which the medical diagnosis is of little relevance and is of considerably more interest to the doctor than to the child, his family, or his teacher! Nevertheless, exact diagnosis and delineation of disorders must not be neglected and one of the major problems of developmental paediatrics has been the lack of clear definitions and consistent usage of terms such as cerebral palsy, speech delay, or clumsiness.

Another important distinction between paediatric patients and children with handicaps is that the latter are not sick. They come to medical attention because they are recognised to be different from other children, and their parents hope for a medical explanation and cure, which sadly are seldom available. Their subsequent progress is determined mainly by social and educational factors; their problems arise because of the complexities (and prejudices) of modern society. An increasingly vocal body of opinion, particularly among those working with the adult mentally handicapped, believes that handicap is not a medical problem at all and that treating it as such merely increases disability. Most developmental paediatricians will regard this as an extremist view but it cannot be ignored and accounts for some of the difficulties and tensions experienced in communicating with parents and other professionals.

The power of medical 'labels' is easily forgotten.[3,4] When parents are told that their child is handicapped, their perceptions of him and of themselves are changed.[5] There is still a profound stigma attached to the notion of handicap; Goffman in his classic study[6] described the concept of stigma thus:

> 'the Greeks, who were apparently strong on visual aids, originated the term stigma to refer to bodily signs designed to expose something unusual and bad about the moral status of the signifier. The signs were cut or burnt into the body and advertised that the bearer was a slave, a criminal, a traitor—a blemished person, ritually polluted, to be avoided, especially in public places . . . today the term is widely used in something like the original literal sense, but is applied more to the disgrace itself than to the bodily evidence of it'

Society has stereotyped ideas about the handicapped; for example, the deaf are pictured as communicating with grunts and signs, the blind as being musical and kind to dogs, and epileptic or mentally handicapped people as potentially violent or even insane! The parents may therefore resist a label of handicap and refuse offers of therapy at a hospital-based clinic, with almost superstitious fervour; it seems that medical labels and therapy stigmatise the child as much as his actual disability. An opposite phenomenon may also occur; parents may seek eagerly for a medical label, since our society has come to believe that modern medicine is powerful enough to have an answer for all problems. Nevertheless, doctors can take comfort in the knowledge that the effects of labelling are not all bad. Without a medical

diagnosis, parents often remain confused and bitter about the cause, natu
and prognosis of their child's handicap (*see also* p. 135). Accurate diagnosis
is also essential for genetic counselling. The paediatrician will continue to
make full use of his diagnostic skills, but must use medical and technical
words with great care if he is to avoid the creation of unnecessary secondary
social handicaps.

Lastly, it follows from the previous points that the handicapped child
does not need to be treated as a hospital patient. For logistic and historical
reasons most services, notably Child Development Centres, are in hospital
premises, but most management problems arise in the community, either at
home or at school. The paediatrician must therefore be peripatetic and will
expect to spend much of his time away from the hospital. There are obvious
implications for the planning of paediatric services. The developmental
paediatrician of the future will regard himself as a Consultant in
Community Paediatrics, as described in the Court Report,[73] and his
training[7] will need to cover all the diverse disciplines and problems referred
to in this book.

SOME DEFINITIONS

A *defect* is any abnormality of anatomical structure or physiologic process. A
disability is a lack or impairment of a particular capability or skill. A *handicap*
is any condition which prevents or hinders the pursuit or achievement of
desired goals.[8,9] Whether or not a defect or disability becomes a handicap
depends not only on the severity of the problem, but also on the attitudes
and ambitions of the child and family, and the prejudices of society. These
definitions are valuable since they emphasise an important philosophical
point, but for the purposes of this book it is more useful to separate three
main groups of clinical problems as they present in practice. The first
contains those *major handicapping conditions* which are likely to have a
substantial and permanent effect on the child's future development.
Blindness, sensorineural deafness, cerebral palsy, and mental handicap fall
into this group. Almost without exception these are of organic origin and
are caused by lesions of the central or peripheral nervous system. They are
commonly apparent to the parents very early in the child's life and it is most
often the parents who first seek professional advice. The second group
includes *minor defects* which are also of organic origin but do not usually
have a profound effect on the child's future. Examples include squint,
myopia, and conductive hearing loss due to otitis media. Although these
conditions may be suspected by parents, they are easily overlooked unless
specifically sought, and are often detected as the result of developmental
surveillance programmes. The third group consists of conditions known
variously as *developmental* or *neurodevelopmental disorders*, *developmental
delays*, or *learning disabilities*. Examples include speech delay, clumsiness,

and reading difficulties. These seldom fit neatly into precise diagnostic categories and there is no proven organic basis for them, although there is much speculation in the literature. There may be contributory environmental factors but it is often difficult to decide whether a particular problem should be attributed to these.

A few children with 'developmental disorders' or minor defects have more severe functional problems than some of those with 'major handicaps' and there is inevitably some overlap between the three categories. In general, however, the distinction is of some practical value and in order to retain consistency, the terms *major handicap*, *minor defect*, and *developmental disorder* will be used throughout this book to distinguish the three groups.

Chapter Two
Intelligence, Development and Assessment

When intelligence tests were first introduced, around the turn of the century, they were thought by many to be measuring an innate and inherited quality, determined by the genes received from one's parents. In the late 1920s and early 1930s it was realised that substantial changes in intelligence could sometimes occur in response to changes in the environment. This discovery provoked intense speculation on the relative importance of heredity and environment in determining intelligence; this 'nature v. nurture' debate still continues today, though it has become very much more sophisticated. It is now clear that there are both genetic and environmental contributions to intelligence, personality, and temperament, and that there is a lifelong interaction between them.

Those readers who require a detailed and erudite analysis of this problem should consult other sources such as the comprehensive volumes edited by Rutter.[10,11] For the developmental paediatrician, the following issues are of immediate clinical relevance.

1   Is the genetic contribution the major determinant of development and intellect? If it is, a child's developmental progress would be expected to follow a predetermined trajectory which could not be easily altered by environmental factors, by therapy or by teaching.

2   How much do biological influences such as intrauterine malnutrition or birth trauma affect development?

3   If environmental factors are important, what aspects of the environment are most closely related to development?

4   How can the clinician assess a child's development and the interactions between the factors which affect it?

5   How should the results of this assessment be summarised and presented to the parents and to other professionals?

6   Is intervention effective, and in which form, and for what indications?

Much of the following discussion will focus on intelligence, since this has been more extensively studied than other parameters; however, similar points could be made about the development of language, personality, temperament, etc. The issues listed above will be briefly examined in turn.

The genetic contribution

There is no doubt that heredity makes a significant contribution to intellect and also to other qualities such as temperament and personality. It would be surprising if this were not so, since heredity has important effects on most other biological parameters. It is the exact extent of the genetic contribution that is controversial.

The inheritance referred to here is biological, that is, it is carried on the genes rather than transmitted socially through the quality of the environment created by the parents. The distinction between biological and social inheritance has always presented difficult research problems. Data which show a relationship between the I.Q. of parents and that of their offspring could indicate either biological transmission, or the effects of social and environmental variables. The most favoured solution to this difficulty has been the study of identical and non-identical twin pairs reared separately and together. Data from numerous studies have been interpreted to mean that up to 80% of the variance in intelligence in a given population can be attributed to genetic transmission. It must be emphasised that this is a *statistical* statement about a population selected for study. It does not preclude the possibility that in one particular subject or subpopulation at a particular point in time, the environment may be of overwhelming importance in determining intelligence.

Biological influences on intelligence

Brain development, and therefore neurological and intellectual function, are influenced by intrauterine and postnatal biological factors such as malnutrition and cerebral damage, which must be regarded as environmental influences. Biological factors which affect the physical structure and growth of the nervous system could be responsible both for developmental disorders and for at least a part of normal variation. For example, some developmental problems might result from subtle perinatal brain damage, which could either be focal or diffuse.

The literature relating problems of intellect, learning and behaviour in children can be summarised as follows:[467,468]

1   There is no doubt that organically based psychological sequelae of brain damage can occur in the absence of neurological physical signs.

2   Behavioural and psychiatric disorders are more commonly seen in children with brain pathology than in those without, and this is in part a

function of the pathology itself, rather than any functional disability which it may have caused.

3   There is no distinctive pattern of behavioural or psychiatric disorder which can be attributed to brain pathology. All patterns of disturbance can be found in children with and in those without brain pathology. The exception is the syndrome of gross social disinhibition which may be associated with frontal lobe damage.

4   Primate experiments suggest that the functions of damaged areas of the brain (excluding motor areas and vital centres) are not immutable and the intact areas can often make up for any deficiencies, though at the cost of a slight reduction in overall intellectual capacity.[14] Head injury studies support the idea that, in children, brain injury is more likely to result in a global intellectual deficit than in a specific developmental or learning disability. Nevertheless, although the young child's brain shows considerable plasticity of function, some hemisphere specialisation is present very early in life (p. 311).[474]

5   Disturbances in psychological functioning are probably more likely to result from abnormal brain activity (e.g. epilepsy) than from loss of brain substance.

6   A threshold phenomenon appears to govern the relationship between the severity of brain damage and the sequelae; the damage must reach a certain degree of severity before sequelae become detectable.[12,13]

7   Severe intrauterine malnutrition is associated with mild reduction in all parameters of intelligence and particularly motor function; possibly this is due to reduction of neuronal numbers and connections, notably in the cerebellum. Similar effects may result from prolonged postnatal malnutrition.[16,17]

8   Whatever the nature of the biological insult to the brain, psychosocial factors strongly affect the outcome by interacting with the child's intrinsic problems and become an increasingly important influence as the child grows older. An adverse environment greatly exaggerates the effects of brain damage, whereas a good one minimises them.[15,18]

9   Severe perinatal brain damage can undoubtedly result in cerebral palsy and mental handicap but rarely causes severe mental retardation *without* any evidence of cerebral palsy.[470]

10   If one excludes cases of *severe* perinatal brain damage associated with obvious neurological abnormality in the neonatal period, some relationship still exists between perinatal disorder and intellectual and learning deficits, but the correlations are weak and it is far from certain that the relationship is causal. In studying such relationships it is vital to control for the numerous psychosocial factors which contribute both to the occurrence of perinatal disorder (e.g. incidence of prematurity) and also to the outcome.

In summary, it is clear that although brain pathology affects learning, intellect and behaviour, the relationships are very complex. It is naive and misleading to attribute developmental disorder to 'brain damage' without also examining the child's psychosocial background;[19] furthermore it is only the latter which might be amenable to change.

Environmental influences

In some circumstances intelligence is clearly related to environmental factors. For example, Rutter noted that, 'there is abundant evidence that mild mental retardation is extremely common among children brought up in city slums . . . intelligence develops and is not a 'given capacity'. Its development is a social process strictly dependent upon the quality and organisation of the human environment in which it evolves.'

In extreme circumstances, environmental manipulation can lead to substantial gains in intelligence: some relevant studies are described later in this chapter. It is more difficult to discover if this is also true in families where the parents are of normal intelligence, material conditions are adequate, and family life is stable. Environmental measures such as social class, income, or quality of housing are no more than crude indicators of child-rearing styles and are too insensitive to be useful in unravelling this problem. It seems likely that the skill of the parents in encouraging and extending their child's development throughout childhood is the key factor. The term 'micro-environment' is useful to describe the innumerable small details of daily child-rearing and experience.

Analysis of this micro-environment is exceptionally difficult. Furthermore, there is always the possibility that any correlation found between the quality of the micro-environment and the child's abilities may simply indicate that parents find it more rewarding to teach a child who is good-natured and intelligent! Nevertheless, there is some evidence that micro-environmental factors do influence intellect, personality and temperament.

Many researchers have looked specifically at the development of language and the factors which affect it, since in Western culture competence in the use of language is one of the most highly valued of all skills. These studies, which are discussed in more detail in the next chapter, suggest that the development of language and play can indeed be accelerated, though this does not necessarily mean that the child's ultimate abilities are significantly altered; the consolidation of any gains which might be achieved depends on whether the improvements in the environment continue throughout childhood.

ASSESSMENT

What is assessment? To many people the word has come to mean administration of a developmental or psychological test, but this is only a small part of the assessment process, and in many cases it may even be

Table 2.1   Reasons for assessment.

---

1. There is parental or professional concern over the development of a child previously thought to be normal
2. A child is under regular supervision because he is 'at-risk', e.g. because of a family history of a handicapping disorder or a previous cerebral insult
3. A child with a known handicap attends for routine review
4. A child with a known handicap attends because his parents wish to discuss a new problem
5. A child believed to be normal is invited for a developmental screening examination

---

irrelevant to the presenting complaint. Assessment has been defined[11] as 'the systematic collection, organisation and interpretation of information about a person and his situation'. Table 2.1 summarises the various circumstances in which assessment may be undertaken. It is clear that a very different approach is needed in each of these situations. The performance of a test procedure can easily become a ritual substitute for identifying and dealing with the real problem. For example, parents may have made their own accurate assessment of their child's handicap and the request for referral may be precipitated by a conflict over the most appropriate management.

A complete assessment might include the following components: definition of the main problem(s); evaluation of the genetic, biological, environmental and pathological factors which contributed to the problem; an estimate of the child's present developmental status—this may vary from a rough approximation to a detailed set of measurements using a psychometric test battery; tests of hearing and vision; evaluation by speech therapist, physiotherapist, or occupational therapist; the organisation of an intervention programme; and periodic review of progress.

Methods of assessment

The most appropriate approach to assessment of a child's development can only be selected when the problem has been clearly defined. For the paediatrician, the most usual approach would be an interview with the parents, followed by involvement of the child in simple play and/or observation of his spontaneous activities. The information obtained in this way is interpreted using a developmental scale, together with one's general knowledge of child development. A developmental scale is simply a means of arranging information about the mean ages at which children achieve various milestones. The way in which information is elicited about the items in the scale is left to the discretion of the clinician, and the extent of normal variation is indicated only in the most general terms. The most widely used and convenient scale in this country is probably the one prepared by Dr Mary Sheridan.[20] In this scale the various items are classified into the following convenient, though arbitrary, categories; (1) posture and large movements, (2) vision and fine movement, (3) hearing and speech, (4) social behaviour and play.

There are many clinical situations in which it might be quite sufficient for the paediatrician to state, for example, that a child aged 3 years is functioning at the level of an 18-month-old. Parents find it easy to understand this concept and can state whether or not they agree with the doctor's estimate. This information can also be expressed as a developmental quotient:

$$\frac{\text{developmental age}}{\text{chronological age}} \times 100.$$

However, this practice has some disadvantages; it has an aura of accuracy which is not justified by the precision of the test procedures used, it conceals variations between different aspects of development, and it is mistaken by parents and sometimes other professionals for an I.Q., and is interpreted accordingly.

USING PARENTS AS A SOURCE OF INFORMATION

There is a widespread belief that, to parents, 'all their geese are swans', and that therefore their report of the child's abilities is likely to be hopelessly exaggerated and quite unreliable. As a result, excessive reliance is placed on the small and often unrepresentative sample of behaviour which can be elicited during a brief assessment session, and the parents' vast store of knowledge about their child is ignored.[21] Yet only the parents can know whether the child's performance is representative of his true abilities or can explain the history of individual items of behaviour; why for example a word is used in a particular way or why the child shows an unexpected reaction to a task. Furthermore, the way in which they describe the child and his activities gives some insight into the quality of his micro-environment.

There are several reasons for the apparent unreliability of developmental information obtained from parents. Firstly, retrospective recall of the times at which milestones were achieved in the past is known to be unreliable.[22] Secondly, where the child's current abilities are concerned, the questions put to the parents are often ambiguous and their replies are not subjected to further critical probing. Thirdly, it is usually the parents' *interpretation* of what they observe which is unreliable; their observations, though unstructured, are usually remarkably accurate.[23] Much confusion and resentment is generated by the failure of doctors and other professionals to recognise this latter distinction. Agreement must be established first with the parents on what the child can and cannot do. Only then can the significance of his abilities be discussed.

Occasionally, parental accounts do seem to substantially over- or underestimate a child's abilities, by comparison with what is seen during assessment. This discrepancy is itself of considerable diagnostic importance, for their lack of understanding may explain many management problems and might be a contributing cause in some developmental disorders. A few parents are manipulative and their description is distorted in order to obtain the opinion they desire. Even more rarely, they may deliberately try to mislead the doctor, perhaps for medicolegal reasons. All of these situations must be recognised if the family is to be helped. The parents' view of the child's problem is every bit as important as an 'objective' assessment of his development.

PSYCHOLOGICAL TESTS

Many doctors regard assessments based on interview and observation as crude and inaccurate, and feel that 'proper' tests, using more structured procedures, are essential for diagnostic precision. It is therefore worth noting that psychologists define a test as 'any systematic procedure for observing a person's behaviour and describing it with the aid of a numerical scale or a category system'.[11] A systematic interview or an observation session constitutes a test in terms of this definition. The important question to ask is not 'Is this test accurate enough?' but 'Will this procedure provide information relevant to the problem in hand?'

When it does seem necessary to quantify one's observations accurately, a formal test procedure may be used. For example, it may be useful to decide whether a deaf child has normal intelligence when confronted with non-verbal tasks, or to exclude a low I.Q. as a cause of a learning problem in school. The mechanics of test administration are not difficult to master; the skill lies in the interpretation of the results, which calls for a knowledge of the psychological literature. For this reason, the supply of many test kits is quite rightly restricted to qualified clinical or educational psychologists, and it is the psychologist who will normally be responsible for the detailed assessment of these more complex problems.

Psychometric tests have been devised to examine almost every aspect of human behaviour. An important feature of psychological tests is that they are designed to make systematic observations and quantify them. The results are then related to normative data: in other words, they are compared either to the individual's own previous performance or, more often, to the results obtained by a group of similar individuals. The first of these approaches is useful in, for example, planned teaching programmes for the mentally handicapped, as a means of evaluating progress. The majority of the psychometric tests used in clinical assessment are of the second type, and the most familiar are those used to measure intelligence (I.Q. tests) and language development. Procedures are also available for the examination of personality, behaviour, brain damage, and many other

Table 2.2   Psychometric tests and scales in common use (with age range in brackets).

Tests of mental ability
Bayley Scales of Infant Development (2 months–$2\frac{1}{2}$ years)
British Ability Scales ($2\frac{1}{2}$–17 years)
Wechsler Preschool and Primary Scale of Intelligence (WPPSI) (4–$6\frac{1}{2}$ years)
Merrill–Palmer Preschool Performance Tests ($1\frac{1}{2}$–$5\frac{1}{4}$ years)
McCarthy Scales of Infant Development ($2\frac{1}{2}$–$8\frac{1}{2}$ years)
Wechsler Intelligence Scale for Children (WISC) ($6\frac{1}{2}$–16 years)
Stanford–Binet Intelligence Scale (2 years–adult)
Griffiths Scales (0–8 years)
Gesell Developmental Schedule (4 weeks–6 years)
Vineland Social Maturity Scale (3 months–30 years)
Stycar Developmental Sequences (1 month–5 years)

Specialised tests and applications
Illinois Test of Psycholinguistic Abilities (speech and language problems) (2–10 years)
Hiskey–Nebraska Test of Learning Aptitude (hearing defects) (3–17 years)
Snijders–Oomen Non-verbal Intelligence Scale ($2\frac{1}{2}$–7 years) (all forms of verbal communication handicap)
Leiter International Performance Scale (communication defects and multiple handicap) (2–16 years)
Raven's Progressive Matrices (non-verbal abilities)
Williams Intelligence Test (vision defects) (5–15 years)
Reynell–Zinkin Scales (vision defects) (0–5 years)
Columbia Mental Maturity Scale (verbal and physical handicaps) (3–10 years)
Frostig Developmental Test of Visual Perception (learning disabilities) (4–8 years)
Bender Gestalt Test (visual motor perception) (4 years and over)
Stott–Moyes–Henderson Test of Motor Impairment (motor disability, clumsiness) (5–14 years)

Language and vocabulary tests
Reynell Developmental Language Scale ($1\frac{1}{2}$–6 years)
British Picture Vocabulary Scale ($2\frac{1}{2}$–18 years)
Peabody Picture Vocabulary Test ($2\frac{1}{2}$–18 years)
Stycar Language Test (up to 7 years)
Edinburgh Articulation Test
Renfrew Articulation Test
Lowe–Costello Symbolic Play Test (1–3 years)

Attainment tests
Neall Analysis of Reading Ability (6–12 years)
Wide Range Achievement Test (5 years–adult)
Schonell Reading Test
Holborn Reading Test

Assessment scales linked to remedial programmes
Behaviour Assessment Battery
Parent Involvement Project
Portage Project

factors. Table 2.2 summarises some of the tests in common use. An important distinction is made between tests of I.Q. and tests of attainment, such as reading or writing.

Many psychometric tests are *standardised*, that is they require a specified set of materials, and the instructions and mode of presentation are precisely stated. The tester may of course use his discretion to depart from the specified procedure but the more he does this, the less accurate the result will be.

Before they are introduced for general use, tests are checked for *reliability*, to ensure that comparable results would be obtained by different observers or on different occasions. The most important characteristic of a test procedure is its *validity*. Validity is concerned with questions such as, what is this test actually measuring?; does this test give a true measure of the child's abilities in this particular area?; what deductions can be made from the results?; and do these results imply that the child has a problem which can be expected to interfere with future progress and prospects?

In general, any assessment of a young child should be regarded primarily as a measure of current functioning, a method of quantifying what the child has learnt up to the present moment. Prediction of future progress or ultimate intellectual capacity from measures made in early childhood is unwise, unless the child's abilities are repeatedly found to be in the severely handicapped range. Many factors contribute to the difficulties of prediction including the intrinsic deficiencies of the test; variations in the skill of the tester; anxiety, shyness, lack of motivation, or undiagnosed hearing loss in the child; and unusual patterns or temporary setbacks in development. The tester has to make a subjective judgement of the extent to which these factors might invalidate the results. Also, since the child's ultimate abilities depend to a considerable extent on experiences yet to come, it is intrinsically unlikely that one could predict his future on the basis of his performance in the first few years of life.

Several studies have shown that by $2\frac{1}{2}$ years of age there begins to be some correlation between test scores and later intelligence, but throughout childhood the increasing predictive value of I.Q. conceals substantial individual fluctuations. For example, in one study 58% of children showed an I.Q. change over the years of more than 15 points, and 9% more than 30 points. Given the right conditions, intellectual growth can continue well into adult life.

Tests available to doctors.   The Griffiths' test deserves particular mention because it is the most readily available formal test for the paediatrician. It is a standardised scale for children aged 0–8 years. It requires a special test kit, which is only supplied when a training period has been completed. The results are presented as a developmental profile (Fig 2.1) which is undoubtedly preferable to a single score. The Griffiths' test is a

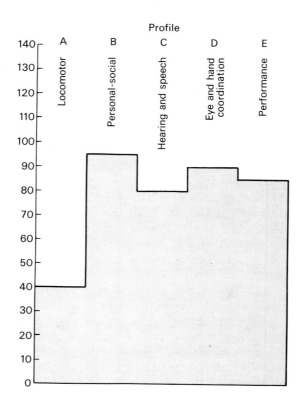

Profile

Fig. 2.1 The Griffiths' test. Profile of a child aged 3.5 years with 'delayed motor development'. Diagnosis: muscular dystrophy (Duchenne).

valuable tool if correctly used, but the doctor who can use only this test is at a definite disadvantage compared to the psychologist who can select the most appropriate procedure from an extensive repertoire. Furthermore, there are some aspects of this test which are open to criticism on technical grounds. A revised and improved version is in preparation.

Other tests which are supplied to doctors include the Lowe and Costello Symbolic Play Test (p. 49), the Reynell Language Test (p. 259), and a variety of developmental scales (Appendix 7).

INFORMATION FROM OTHER SOURCES

Whenever one doubts that the child has been seen at his best or when there is a serious degree of conflict between the parents' view and that of the referring professional, a definite opinion should be deferred until further information can be obtained from playgroup or nursery leaders, speech therapists or others who know the child. Conversation with the health visitor may be very revealing, particularly where the quality of parental care is suspect. Serious diagnostic errors may result from neglecting to cross-check information in this way.

In many cases, there will still be doubt as to the extent of the child's problems even after the most meticulous assessment. Placement in a suitable playgroup or nursery, preferably with experienced and well trained staff, provides an opportunity for more prolonged assessment, and the child's progress in this new environment may throw further light on his problems. Indeed, the response to specialised and expert teaching is of such diagnostic importance, that it may be unwise to venture any final opinion until this has been undertaken.

Misconceptions about developmental assessment

An estimate of a child's level of development, however expertly performed, is only one part of assessment and seldom leads *directly* to the diagnosis of major physical handicaps, defects of vision and hearing, or developmental disorders. There are several reasons for this. Firstly, many errors in developmental assessment are made through failure to consider the reasons for, and diagnostic implications of, the child's failure on a particular item. For example, drawing is classified as a fine motor skill, but inability to draw a recognisable figure of a man at the appropriate age could be due to mental handicap, poor vision, ataxia, or lack of previous experience with drawing materials. Inability to climb stairs might indicate immature motor development or Duchenne muscular dystrophy; observation and physical examination would be essential in differential diagnosis.

Secondly, there is a very wide range of both ability and cooperation among normal young children, and the limits of normality are so wide that children with major handicaps may achieve important milestones within the normal time; for example, a child with spastic hemiplegia may walk well before 18 months; conversely many children whose milestones fall outside the 'normal' range (i.e. the 97th percentile) are normal.

Thirdly, developmental scales make no provision for describing children whose behaviour patterns are deviant rather than immature, as for example in autism. Lastly, no developmental tests will reveal minor defects of vision or hearing.[24] Specific tests must be done to detect these.

Summary

It is vital that the paediatrician appreciates the limitations of developmental assessment, however it is performed. Detailed measures of development should not be undertaken in situations where an approximation would suffice, and should be treated as an index of current competence, not as a predictor of the future. A test score should never be considered in isolation from the context in which it was obtained.

DIAGNOSIS OR FORMULATION?

A doctor is trained to approach clinical problems with what is known as 'the medical model' of disease (Fig. 2.2). This has proved to be a highly effective model where organic disease is concerned, but has been criticised as inappropriate to the problems of chronic disability and handicap. There is some truth in this view, but the 'medical model' can make a substantial contribution in this field; obvious examples include the discovery and prevention of the causes of congenital rubella and kernicterus. Nevertheless, the concept of a single diagnosis and specific treatment does have serious limitations in the care of the handicapped person. Often the diagnosis is uncertain; even if an exact diagnosis can be made, the condition is unlikely to be susceptible to medical treatment.

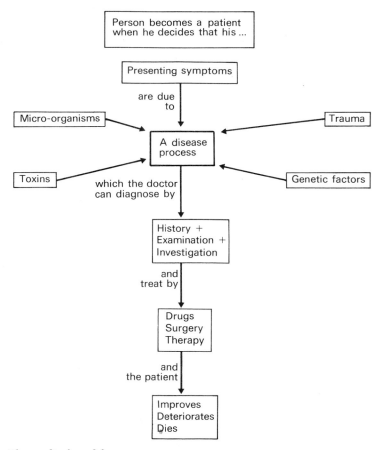

Fig. 2.2   The medical model.

It is often more useful to explain a child's handicap to the parents at three separate diagnostic levels. The first is the *type of problem*—for example, hearing loss or mental handicap. The second is the *cause or causes*—for example, congenital rubella or tuberose sclerosis. The parents may have to be told that the cause cannot be determined even after extensive investigation, but they must at least be clear about the distinction between the type of problem and its cause (*see also* p. 135). The third level of diagnosis is the *severity and functional effects* of the handicap. These three levels are useful in the preparation of written reports for parents; an example is provided in Appendix 9.

When dealing with 'developmental disorder', the limitations of the medical model become much more apparent. In most of these clinical problems, no organic pathology can be detected except perhaps minor contributory defects, such as secretory otitis media or squint. The cause of concern is the child's failure to perform in one or more areas of development at the level expected for his age. The response dictated by the medical model is to diagnose a disorder, for example 'speech delay' or 'clumsiness'. Sometimes other titles, which make unjustified assumptions about the cause of the difficulty, may be used, for example 'minimal brain dysfunction'. These terms are really no more than circular definitions (Fig. 2.3) and add nothing to the understanding or management of the problem.

The questions which must be asked about the child with a 'developmental disorder' are different from those relevant to major handicap. Firstly, why has this particular child been brought for consultation at this point in

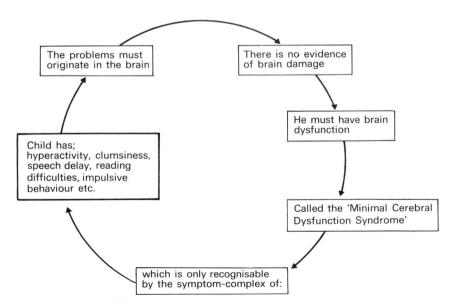

Fig. 2.3   Circular definitions.

time, whereas the parents of others with identical levels of ability may never seek professional advice? For example, a child may present with a parental complaint of speech delay, but the parents may really be more concerned about an associated behaviour disorder (as discussed in Chapter 9), or a parent may complain about a boy's clumsiness, but the real problem may be depression which makes it hard to cope with the child's natural exuberance.

Secondly, how does one *define* a developmental disorder? The mere fact that a child performs poorly on assessment measures is not necessarily a problem in itself, since this finding has many possible causes as discussed previously (p. 15). A child might be said to have a developmental disorder if he scored below 2 standard deviations (i.e. below the 3rd percentile as an approximation) on a particular measure, for example a language test such as the Reynell; but by definition 3% of the population score below this level and this finding does not necessarily predict future problems. The variations in normal development are such that a developmental disorder is almost impossible to define with any degree of precision.

Thirdly, it is commonly assumed that a child who comes from a poor environment and performs poorly is slow because of his genetically determined low intellect. The parents of these children make less effective use of available services than more fortunate families, yet it is in precisely this area of 'subcultural deprivation' that efforts to improve the environment may be most beneficial.

Fourthly, when faced with a child whose development and behaviour are deviant one has to consider to what extent these observations are explained by an interaction between inborn temperamental factors in the child, and the responses of his family; it must not be assumed that the parents are the sole cause of his problem!

Lastly, there is the question of labelling; will it be helpful or detrimental to the family and to the child to use terms such as specific language delay or mild mental handicap? The advantages and disadvantages of labelling have already been mentioned.

There is no final solution to these difficulties, but a change of orientation may help. Instead of thinking in terms of diagnosis and treatment, it may be more profitable to adopt an 'educational model' (Fig. 2.4); this approach also has much to offer in major handicaps. The multidisciplinary team can formulate the child's problems in such a way that, while the question of diagnosis is not ignored, the emphasis is on setting goals and working towards them.

INTERVENTION

The term 'intervention' is preferable to therapy or treatment, which have strictly medical connotations. It encompasses speech therapy, occupational

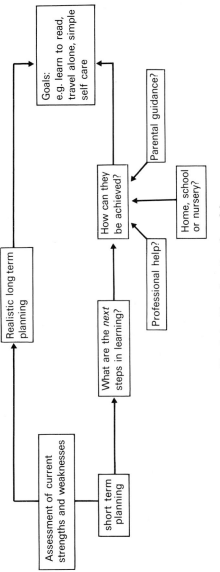

Fig. 2.4 The educational model.

therapy, physiotherapy and nursery experience, specialised education, behavioural or psychotherapeutic management by a psychologist or a psychiatrist, and social support of all kinds. Most intervention programmes for children with handicaps or developmental disorders have more in common with education than with the medical tradition of a specific treatment for a particular disease.[25] Sometimes an assessment is in itself a useful intervention even if no further help is needed. A good intervention programme should consist of four stages:

1   Definition of the problem and of the child's current developmental status.
2   The setting of realistic goals.
3   Devising and executing a means of achieving these goals.
4   Evaluation of the result.

Is intervention effective?

The effectiveness of intervention programmes has been studied more extensively by educators and psychologists than by therapists or paediatricians. This may be explained by the differences between the medical and educational models which generate different research questions. Four aspects of intervention will be considered here: (1) the possibility of making major increases in the low intellectual capacity of children from a poor environment ('subcultural deprivation'); (2) the potential for improving the development of mentally handicapped children; (3) the effects of nursery education; and (4) the effects of therapy.

SUBCULTURAL DEPRIVATION

The most important studies on intervention are the series of 'Head Start' programmes in the USA, which began in the Kennedy era.[26] The motivation for these programmes was a belief that poor unintelligent parents would produce children who would follow the same pattern—the 'cycle of disadvantage'. Many of the early Head Start programmes found that the improvement produced by interventions such as enthusiastic nursery teaching was poorly sustained, although there were some small long term gains in motivation and parental attitudes.

The designers of the 'Milwaukee project' recognised that earlier intervention programmes for poor children had done too little too late. Heber and his colleagues selected children of socially disadvantaged mothers with I.Q.s of less than 80, and in the first year of life embarked on an intensive programme of daily infant stimulation, while simultaneously arranging instruction for these mothers in child care and home making, and also providing training for more satisfactory and lucrative employment. By school entry age, the 'treated' group had gained about 30 points on the I.Q. scale by comparison with the controls. The Milwaukee programme was massive in conception, very expensive, and clearly not feasible for the whole nation but is widely quoted as evidence that, at least at the lower end of the socioeconomic scale, low intelligence is a potentially reversible disability. Unfortunately, the results of this important study are not readily available for scrutiny and subsequent events have cast doubt on their validity.[448]

There is no other published study which provided such prolonged and intensive early intervention and, except in cases of extreme deprivation, substantial gains in I.Q. are disappointingly difficult to achieve.

MENTAL HANDICAP

The famous Brooklands experiment[27] showed that mentally handicapped children made dramatic gains in intellect and personality when removed from a featureless institutional routine and placed in a normal stimulating household environment. This classic study laid the foundation for modern ideas on mental handicap by demonstrating that, even in the most severely handicapped child, important gains can be made by providing appropriate experiences. Less ambitious stimulation programmes seem to produce smaller but measurable improvements.[475]

THE BENEFITS OF PRESCHOOL NURSERY EXPERIENCE

Placement in nursery or nursery school is often prescribed as a means of overcoming early social disadvantage. Nursery education provides valuable experience and enjoyable social contact for the children and is a great help to parents. These benefits alone are reason enough to regard universal nursery education as a desirable goal. However there is no evidence that it will have a significant *long term* effect on the child's development or intellect, nor will it reduce social inequalities. The benefits of nursery education apply to fortunate children as much as or perhaps more than to disadvantaged children, and in any case they largely disappear after 3–4 years in school. The benefits are greater and more persistent if parents are involved in a planned programme of nursery education.[28,29] Nevertheless the gains made in this way are quite small unless the parental involvement is on the massive scale of the Milwaukee project. The stimulation of language development is primarily the task of parents and nursery education does not compensate for their inadequacies.[466]

As with all research studies on large groups, these findings may conceal important individual differences. Anecdotal clinical experience strongly suggests that some children do in fact benefit very significantly from nursery placement. It would be very foolish to discount these observations, but there are few documented case studies to support them. It is seldom possible to predict which children will benefit, or to be certain that they would not eventually have made the same progress without their nursery experience.

THE EFFECTIVENESS OF THERAPY

It is doubtful whether rigorous controlled comparisons of therapeutic methods in major handicaps such as aphasia or cerebral palsy will ever be accomplished, because it is almost impossible to find enough similar cases.[30,31] Evidence of efficacy in this field is likely to be based mainly on single case experimental designs rather than between-group studies.[473] There is, however, a great need for further research on the effects of intervention in the much commoner developmental disorders. Only a handful of good studies are available and these indicate some benefit from language stimulation programmes and from the treatment of 'clumsiness'.

Although the literature of speech therapy, occupational therapy and physiotherapy is rather deficient in carefully designed evaluative studies,[475] the educational research discussed previously does suggest two basic principles. Firstly, if the child's developmental disorder appears to be related to environmental factors, intervention needs to be intensive and prolonged if sustained progress is to be achieved. Secondly, whatever the child's problem may be, programmes which involve the parent are much more likely to be effective. These findings suggest that professional time may often be better spent on counselling, instructing and demonstrating than on direct treatment of the child. If the parents are incapable of cooperating because of low intelligence or indifference, the child may still be helped but the long term gains will probably be very much smaller.

Is there a 'critical period' for intervention?

One striking feature of developmental paediatrics has been the emphasis on the preschool child. This has come about for two reasons. Firstly, children with handicaps come to the attention of paediatricians at an early age, whereas educational services until recently have only been available from the age of 5 onwards. The second and more fundamental reason for concentrating attention on preschool children arises from an implicit assumption about the development of intelligence; that not only are environmental influences important in determining a child's intelligence, but that these influences are of overriding importance and have an irreversible effect in the first few years of life.

The early work of John Bowlby in the 1950s dealt specifically with mother–infant attachment but had a profound effect on ideas about all aspects of child development. His researches seemed to imply that inadequate or adverse early experiences inevitably lead to irreversible intellectual and emotional damage and therefore services for the young child should have a major impact on performance through the school years into adult life. A parallel concept was the 'critical period'. This meant that if a child failed to acquire a particular ability or level of development by a certain age, he might never do so. These ideas have been challenged by many authors since Bowlby. Two recent reviews[32,33] concluded that, while the first few years of life are of great importance, they are not substantially more important than the rest of childhood. Several lines of evidence support this view. Firstly, further research has shown that early separation is not necessarily damaging and can even be beneficial.[34] The effects depend on the circumstances and handling of the separation, the previous experiences of the child, and perhaps his temperament and adaptability. Secondly, there are at least two reports of children adopted in mid-childhood (7–9 years) from orphanages in Korea and Vietnam. These children showed substantial gains in both intellect and emotional maturity. Although the outcome was probably not quite as favourable as with very early adoption the results show that the damage caused by early adversity is not irreversible.

A further line of evidence is the progress made by the Koluchova twins, who were discovered at the age of 7 years imprisoned in a cellar in a house in Czechoslovakia. The parents had kept these children concealed from the neighbours and the authorities throughout their lives and had treated them like animals. When found, they had no social skills or language and were extremely retarded. After placement with a normal family they steadily improved and by their mid-teens performed within normal limits on all standard psychological test batteries. The extent of their adjustment to marriage, work and adult life in general remains to be seen, but evidently an enormous change in intelligence could be attributed solely to a change of environment.

There seems very little justification for the fear that a critical period of development might be missed, with disastrous consequences. The apparent importance of early experience may be largely an artefact. Most children who start life in a poor environment remain in that environment throughout childhood, and there is therefore a built-in correlation between early childhood adversity and ultimate outcome, but nevertheless the environment can be changed with good effects at any point in childhood.

Conclusion

It is probable that *all* children would benefit from the increased involvement of parents in their preschool education. No parent has the time or resources to help the child explore all the avenues of human activity and there are many who would welcome expert guidance in encouraging their child's development. Professional skills are scarce and it is reasonable to devote them to the children who lag behind the majority, but in the long run the universal availability of a preschool educational system which encourages parents' involvement, would greatly reduce the need to make arbitrary judgements about developmental disorders. Similarly, where remedial teaching for school age children is adequate in quantity and quality, the temptation to diagnose 'learning disabilities' as if they were specific neurological entities is much reduced.

All intervention programmes cost time and money, both for professional time, and also frequently in terms of parental travel and time off work. Furthermore, the prescription of some therapy or specialised educational management sometimes carries for the parent the unspoken message that they have failed in the task of child rearing, and this can most certainly be harmful. A decision as to whether a child needs specialised help, and if so in what form, must always be made in cooperation with the parents and never on an isolated assessment of the child outside the context of the family.

Chapter Three
A Review of Normal Development

The development of the normal child has been described in detail by a number of authors.[67] For assessment purposes, numerous scales and tests are available and every developmental paediatrician must have access to one or other of these, as discussed in the previous chapter.[20] It would be superfluous to duplicate these here and no attempt will be made to provide a detailed list of developmental milestones or a comprehensive review of normal development. The purpose of this chapter is to consider, in the light of recent advances in psychology and linguistics, some of the numerous influences on and variations in normal development which account for many of the differences between children. It will be apparent that developmental paediatrics and child psychiatry are inseparable, since a child's development can only usefully be measured and altered within the context of his family environment.

THE DEVELOPMENT OF SOCIAL BEHAVIOUR

The child's place in the family

There are many clinical situations in which parental behaviour only makes sense when the significance of the child within the family is understood. The notion that all children are wanted and are planned at times of social and economic convenience for the family unit is a Western middle class ideal which is seldom realised. Numerous factors influence the decision to embark upon or continue with, a pregnancy.[36] At least a part of the urge to reproduce derives from cultural pressures. For example, some couples are often made to feel peculiar or deficient if they announce their intention of remaining childless. Would-be grandparents in particular are powerful persuaders! In other families, conception may be deliberately planned to save a deteriorating relationship or to manipulate the partner. In poor communities, the birth of a child sometimes brings status to a young woman, the chance of obtaining accommodation of her own and acceptance as an adult by other women. Children are seen in some cultures as an inevitable part of family life, necessary to the family economy and bringing security in old age.

Some children are conceived for special reasons or come to assume a special significance in the family. A baby conceived after the death of a previous child or after a stillbirth may be expected to take on the attributes, real or imagined, of the deceased child. Lewis has suggested[37] that these 'replacement' children are at special risk of emotional and developmental problems, particularly if conceived while the parents are still mourning their loss. In some families, one child, usually the first son, is expected to fulfil the family's academic or financial ambitions or to compensate for his parents' failure in those fields. Conversely, the youngest child of a large family may be encouraged to remain as a baby for as long as possible.

The concept of 'bonding'

This term has been applied to the development of a loving relationship between a human parent and a newborn baby.[35] In man, bonding is an extremely complex process which develops over a period of months or years, both before and after the birth of the child. It is not purely a matter of instinct; both in the higher primates and in man, it is often deficient in parents who have themselves had negative or inadequate experiences of mothering in their own childhood.

During pregnancy, much thought is devoted to the infant's future personality and needs. Sometimes this period of mental preparation is disrupted, for example by complications of pregnancy, or unavoidable iatrogenic anxieties such as abnormal ultrasound scan results, which strengthen parental fears that the infant may be abnormal. It is very common for parents to have ambivalent feelings about pregnancy, and the influence of the baby on their lifestyle. Where the pregnancy was not desired, or was undertaken for reasons no longer valid, the mother may sometimes even refuse to admit to herself that she is pregnant. She may reveal her state of mind by adverse comment on the unborn baby, or on babies in general. Difficulties in child-rearing and non-accidental injury can sometimes be traced to disturbances in the normal process of mental preparation which occurs in pregnancy.

PARENTAL RESPONSES TO THE INFANT

The antenatal mental preparation for the infant's arrival normally equips the parents to weather any crisis that may occur. There may be disappointments, for example in the sex of the infant, his appearance or his premature arrival. Most of these are rapidly overome, although on occasion they may continue to be a source of distress and resentment. When the infant's survival or normality is in doubt, many parents deliberately distance themselves from him, sometimes to the extent of not handling or visiting him. They feel that they dare not allow themselves to love the infant, for fear that they would be unable to tolerate his loss. If he then survives, it may be very hard to reverse these inhibitions. Any of these events may have a profound effect on the child's development, and may be manifest in disturbances of behaviour and relationships.

A stable union is generally strengthened by the birth of a child, but in a poor relationship the mother's preoccupation with the infant often makes the father jealous and eventually the parents may separate. The mother may feel bitter towards the infant for this reason, particularly if additional problems such as handicap or illness have contributed to the father's departure.

THE EFFECT OF HANDICAP ON ATTACHMENT

During pregnancy, most parents consider the possibility that the child might be abnormal, and may mentally rehearse their reactions to such an event in advance. For example, mothers in their 40s are well aware of the high risk of Down's syndrome and may explain their apparently bland reaction to the birth of a Down's syndrome child on the basis that they 'half expected it'. Conversely some conclude during pregnancy that under no circumstances could they tolerate an abnormal child, and in these rejection may be all but inevitable, even before the child is born.

Not surprisingly, a handicapped child is more easily accepted if the parents have other normal children, if the child was wanted, and if there is a supportive extended family. Handicaps associated with obvious external deformity are initially hardest to accept, but sometimes this external marker makes adjustment easier. Conversely, the parents find it hard to believe that their child is handicapped when his external appearance is totally normal, as may be the case in mental handicap or deafness. Problems which only become apparent at a later date, seem likely to be associated with more intense grief, but much less likelihood of rejection (*see* Chapter 7).

THE INFANT'S CONTRIBUTION TO BONDING

In the first hour after birth, the neonate exhibits a peaceful wide-eyed alertness, gazing intently at his mother's face. This behaviour is universal, though it is readily disrupted by obstetric interventions such as sedative medication, and is presumably a neurologically 'programmed' aid to attachment or bonding.

An ability known as 'turn-taking' appears very early, within the first weeks or even days.[38,39] It can be demonstrated most easily when the baby is in a peaceful and relaxed state. The mother makes a sound to the baby; in response the baby reduces his gross, random movements, and instead makes small movements of the limbs synchronously with the mother's voice. When the mother stops, the baby vocalises and increases bodily movement. Trevarthen noted that 'if the mother stops responding and just makes a blank face at the baby, the infant is clearly puzzled by the change in the mother and makes exaggerated solicitations as if to get her attention back. Some quickly become dejected-looking and withdrawn, a state of acute depression that takes minutes to abate'.[40] Turn-taking appears to be a very fundamental behaviour pattern and is a reassuring sign of normal development,[41] while its absence would suggest either severe neurological disorder or perhaps gross deprivation.

Turn-taking is normally developed through both auditory and visual channels but it can certainly occur in both blind and deaf babies. The extent, range and persistence of this behaviour may well be as important a factor in development as the mothering skill of the parent. A study of babies in an orphanage showed how much more skilful were some babies than others in obtaining mothering from the nurse in charge. It seems likely that the more skilful parent can provide increased stimulation for a baby who is relatively sluggish or unresponsive. Conversely an immature or uncertain mother with an unresponsive infant is an unpromising combination.

Differences in temperament can be recognised in the early days of life and these cannot be attributed solely to differences in obstetric practice or maternal handling.[42, 43] There are variations in sleep requirements, irritability, and the speed at which feeding routines are developed. These temperamental differences are of great importance in determining parental responses; not everything that goes wrong with child development is due to bad management by the parents!

Attachment behaviour

Between 6 and 12 months a number of 'attachment behaviours' appear. The development of the relationships between the infant and his family is a two-way affair. Smiling, and the increasing ability to discriminate between familiar and unfamiliar people actively elicit loving and care-taking responses by his parents. In most family groups the first attachment is to the mother, although there is no evidence that this is essential or that the first attachment is intrinsically different from any other. Fathers and other familiar adults may also be the object of early attachment behaviour and many small children also display similar responses to an inanimate 'comfort' object. It is convenient to use 'mother' as shorthand for 'the main attachment object'.

When a young child is relaxed and feels secure he may enjoy the company and attention of other strangers, indeed he may temporarily prefer them to his mother, but anxiety, stress, pain and fear invariably demonstrate his need for the security provided by her, revealed by anxious glances and clinging in infancy, and active seeking, following, and sometimes pestering in the mobile toddler or older child. The mother is used as a secure base from which to make exploratory forays and to embark on play activities, and it is her presence rather than her active involvement which provides the necessary security. Enforced separation of the child from the mother causes intense distress or 'separation protest'. Provision of this secure base is a vital part of the mother's task. If she is unable to do this, because of depression, inadequate comprehension of the child's needs, or inability to love him,[44,45] he may become depressed and withdrawn and may fail to thrive or develop, sometimes to the extent that hospitalisation is necessary (*see also* p. 411).

The strength and frequency of attachment behaviour patterns and the vigour of separation protest are not proportional to the quality of parenting, the degree of parent/child empathy or the amount of time spent in each other's company; nevertheless, misinterpretation of attachment behaviours is commonplace among inexperienced medical and nursing staff. For example, a tendency to make indiscriminate casual attachments with any available adult is often seen among children in care who have been unable to make strong bonds with a permanent caregiver; it is not a sign of a pleasant friendly nature nor an indication of the adult's personal charm! Strong attachment behaviours are not inhibited by punishment or physical abuse. Excessive clinging and separation protest are not necessarily a sign of an intensely loving relationship, indeed they are more likely to be a sign of insecurity and are often seen in unhappy and unstable families. Conversely, a strong attachment to a comfort object is not as one might imagine a sign of insecurity; rather surprisingly, it is unusual in institutionalised children.

In young families, changes of job or housing, the birth of siblings, temporary absence of one parent, marital breakdown and death of a grandparent are all common life events. It is often tempting to attribute a whole variety of clinical problems to these events, but there is substantial evidence that they are not in themselves damaging to young children. What is important is the circumstances which surround them and the way in which the situation is managed. In a normal family environment, the infant is generally protected to some extent from these disruptions by the continuation of his normal routine. A variety of behavioural changes may occur at such times, but these are usually transient and are readily understood by the parents.

Many young children react to separation with intense distress, followed by a period of apathy and despair (often mistaken by hospital staff for 'settling down'). This is followed by indifference to, and rejection of the parent when the separation is over. If the parent recognises what is happening and does not overreact, normal affectionate behaviour is soon restored. The parent who responds with anger and disappointment may unwittingly perpetuate a prolonged and mutual antagonism which may eventually present as a behavioural or developmental disorder. If separation is unavoidable, as may happen if the child is hospitalised, it is essential to encourage free and regular contact between parent and child, and to warn the parent of the likelihood of temporary behaviour disturbances when the child is discharged.

With increasing age and emotional maturity, the child becomes better able to tolerate separation. As language develops, concepts of time and place are established and enable the child to maintain the bond with the absent parent. With the approach of adolescence he will often actively seek and relish the independence offered by temporary separation. Marital discord, the fear of family disintegration, parental illness, or emotional immaturity in one or other parent may all inhibit this process of maturation so that the child is fearful of even brief separations, resulting in social inhibitions, school phobia and a variety of other psychological problems.

A child who is brought up in care has no opportunity to develop normal attachment behaviours. The end result of such deprivation has been described as affectionless psychopathy, the features of which include emotional immaturity, failure to learn social rules, inability to tolerate and maintain close relationships, a lack of guilt feelings, and antisocial behaviour. Individual components of this picture are very common though the complete syndrome is rare.

An understanding of attachment behaviour is vital in the interpretation of many developmental and behavioural disorders, and particularly in the management of non-accidental injury (Chapter 19).

Learning the rules of social behaviour

Although children are born with the ability to initiate social attachments, the complex rules which govern social behaviour have to be learnt. The child has to extract these rules from his observations of everyday life by a process which is presumably very similar to that described for language, later in this chapter.

Certain patterns of social behaviour are regarded as typical of particular age groups. For example, the 13-month infant is often rather suspicious of strangers; the 18-month toddler is shy and clinging, perhaps hiding his face against the adult; whereas the 3 year old is much more easily involved in games and has acquired considerable social poise. These are of course generalisations and social behaviour is determined by numerous environmental and temperamental factors such as the social class and attitudes of the parents, their own degree of introversion and extroversion, and the extent to which the child has met adults other than his parents or been cared for by them. Advanced language development tends to be associated with more mature and outgoing social behaviour, but the social poise of some non-speaking deaf children suggests that this is a case of parallel development rather than cause and effect. Parental attitudes to authority are also significant, both in general development, and in the particular context of a consultation with a doctor or other professional person. Lower social class families tend to be more aware of hierarchies of authority and their children develop more acquiescent attitudes to instruction and information, whereas in middle-class families self-confidence and a critical faculty are encouraged. These differences are often very apparent in the ways in which both children and adults behave when using professional services.

For professional people such as doctors and psychologists, the standard of 'normal' social behaviour is that seen in the happy, well adjusted child of their own social class. He is vocal, open and friendly after a brief period of initial shyness. He has learnt, by the age of $2\frac{1}{2}$, and often very much earlier than this, to sit down, listen carefully to instructions, and await the next item in a game or test without fidgeting. He is eager to please. This behaviour pattern certainly makes clinical assessment easier! It is doubtless also an enormous advantage to the child when he starts school, and middle-class parents are well aware of this and try to develop an organised attitude to learning from a very early age. Originality is encouraged and indeed highly prized. Small games are extended and developed, and creative efforts with bricks or paint are proudly displayed. It is almost impossible for any child-minder or nursery to recreate this atmosphere for the child who lacks it at home, and it may be that this is one of the fundamental problems of most intervention programmes for disadvantaged children.

Many other behaviour patterns are seen in the course of developmental assessment. Although they are different from the one described above, and often make the clinician's task more difficult, they are not necessarily abnormal. The child may be excessively shy, perhaps because he has little contact with other adults, or because the atomsphere of a clinic is so unfamiliar. He may be extremely active, incapable of sitting and awaiting instructions and comprehending a sequence of events. He may only enjoy destructive games, or his play may be fragmentary, lacking in originality and perhaps limited to lining up and pushing toy cars. Some children are incapable of any normal social exchange, as in the case of pseudo-autism (p. 250).

The relative contributions of genes and child-rearing styles in creating social behaviour is uncertain but clinical observation and some research evidence suggests that micro-environmental factors are as important here as with global intelligence or language. Although temperamental characteristics observed early in life do persist to some extent, behaviour patterns are very dependent on the situation in which the child is seen. For this reason teachers' and parents' assessments of behaviour problems differ to a remarkable extent,[46] while minor changes in a play setting can lead to dramatic changes in activity levels.[47] For this reason it is very unwise to draw firm conclusions or to use words like 'hyperactivity' or 'distractable' on the basis of behaviour seen only in the very artificial surroundings of a clinic.

Lastly, there are sex differences both in child behaviour and in child-rearing practices. These arise both from inherited behaviour patterns and from social attitudes. Even when parents deliberately try to minimise these distinctions in the interests of sex equality, temperamental differences can still be observed.

DEVELOPMENT FROM 1 TO 5

Between the 1st and 2nd birthdays the child makes rapid strides in understanding. He recognises and comprehends in considerable detail the daily routine of life at home, and becomes increasingly aware of his own rights and identity as an individual. Clashes of will with his parents are frequent. When placed in unfamiliar surroundings his behaviour may be more diffident, and he may still cling to his mother, but will gradually make increasingly daring forays into unfamiliar territory—a behaviour pattern which is very typical of the middle of the second year. Evidence of the extent of his understanding begins to be seen in his play, both in imitation of domestic activities and in the use of toys and symbolic play.

In the 3rd year, the child firmly establishes his identity. He sees himself as distinct from the world around and uses the pronoun 'I'. He is completely mobile and can explore where he will; he has worked out all the important relationships and functions of his surroundings and familiar adults, and has the language to describe them. This feeling of understanding gives him confidence to deal with new situations much more readily than the 18-month-old child. By the age of 4 a child has often acquired such confidence in his own abilities and importance, that he becomes somewhat exuberant and bumptious. He is nevertheless still vulnerable in new situations, subject to sudden changes of mood and inexplicable fears, but in familiar surroundings is able to join in complex games and activities with other children.

Most parents actively foster this growing independence in their child, in preparation for school. They may provide nursery experiences or other opportunities to play with young children. Some parents (the socially isolated, depressed, or agoraphobic) are unable to help their children to learn to mix and play with others, or master the social rules which govern play and peer activities. A warm relationship with an adult may be lacking, or alternatively the child may have to take on the role of an adult companion to the parent. In such circumstances, the child may present with a variety of developmental or behavioural problems, and later is likely to show considerable difficulties of adjustment in school.

Some parents have very unrealistic expectations; for example they may imagine that speech appears as if by magic without any contribution from them. The child comes to be regarded as a chronic disappointment and is neglected or harshly disciplined.

THE EARLY SCHOOL YEARS

At school the child is introduced to a new world of learning and discipline, and the previous typical exuberance of the 4 year old may disappear as he becomes rather more sober and subdued. Provided that his initial experiences are happy, his innate capacity and enthusiasm for learning enable him to master numerous new areas of intellectual and physical skill. Fear of failure and of disappointing the adults around him, and difficulties in adjusting to the demands of his peers may be apparent in the less fortunate child. A degree of neuroticism, minor obsessions, episodes of lying and stealing, and moodiness due to quarrels with friends or dislike of teachers are all commonplace. Most of the problems experienced by children in this age group are transient, and should be seen as part of normal development.

With increasing maturity, there is more awareness of major events such as marital discord or the death of a near relative, but the effects on the child's behaviour, personality and performance are unpredictable, and apparent links between life events and clinical problems often turn out to be spurious. In the school years, the peer group becomes rapidly more influential, but the stability, interest and support of the family remain as essential as ever.[48] Children expect their parents to listen to their news from school, and to champion them when in difficulties. The ability of parents to respond in this way appears to correlate with progress in school. It probably also determines whether many of the commonplace problems mentioned above are self-limiting, or escalate to the point of requiring professional intervention.[49]

THE DEVELOPMENT OF LANGUAGE

The science of linguistics now encompasses the whole of human communication, by words, gestures, signs, and social behaviour. Fig. 3.1 summarises the terminology used in describing spoken language. For the clinician, the distinctions between 'speech' and 'language' and between expression and comprehension, are of particular significance.

Chomsky is acknowledged as the leader of the modern revolution in linguistics, but much of his work is difficult to apply to the everyday problems of paediatrics. Crystal has made a major contribution to the exposition of linguistic theory and its application to clinical work, and his books should be consulted for an authoritative analysis of the subject.[50,51]

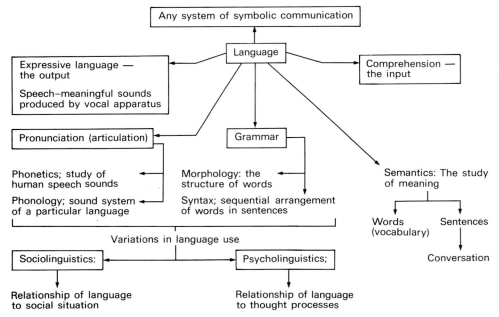

Fig. 3.1   Linguistic terminology.

Speech sounds

From early infancy the baby produces an ever-increasing range of sounds. At first only vowel sounds are made, but from about six months onwards consonants can be recognised. Individual sounds are repeated and strung together and variations in intonation, volume and pitch gradually come under voluntary control.[52] It is important to distinguish between the random sounds made by the baby's early experimenting and the increasing voluntary control over production of specific consonants. This natural progression sometimes worries parents because they notice that some sounds, for example 1 and r, have disappeared from the child's repertoire.

Consonant sounds are made in a variety of ways and places. Some are made by the sudden release of air pressure, producing a single sound called a plosive (e.g. p), others are made by the passage of air through a narrow space producing a continuous hissing noise, called a fricative (e.g. s). The place of articulation may be the lips (labials) the teeth (dentals) or the palate (palatals). Air may be allowed to pass at the side of the tongue (laterals) or through the nose (nasals). There are wide variations in the rate at which children acquire the various sounds of speech, and the order is also unpredictable, although certain generalisations can be made. Firstly, sounds made at the front of the mouth appear before back sounds (p, b, m before k, g). Secondly, plosives usually appear before fricatives. Thirdly, oral sounds seem easier to make than nasal sounds. Fourthly, consonant

Table 3.1 Acquisition of consonants.

Achieved by age (years)						
2	p	b	m	n	w	
2½	t	d	k	g	ng	
3	f	s	l	y (as in 'you')		
4	sh	v	z	r	ch	j
5	th					
6	s (as in 'mea<u>s</u>ure')					

clusters appear at the end of words before the beginnings. Correct articulation of all sounds may not be achieved until after the child starts school (*see* Table 3.1) and the mastery of intonation patterns (rise and fall in pitch, changes of stress, etc.) may take even longer.

Long strings of 'jargon' talk are frequently heard and these take on the intonation patterns of the child's native language, so that by one year an observer can distinguish the babble of an English from that of a Chinese baby. Jargon varies greatly in quantity and complexity and some babies seem very silent until they start to use true words. Deaf babies produce jargon which is less complex, has fewer intonational changes, and tends to be rather harsh; also the total amount of jargon may be less than normal and is decreasing by the first birthday. However, very careful observation is needed in order to recognise these differences.

The origins of communication

The behavioural pattern known as turn-taking (Fig. 3.2) undoubtedly provides the framework within which language can develop. The capacity to listen to and discriminate between sounds is present at birth. Very young babies can copy facial gestures, such as tongue protrusion, and it can be shown that they make efforts to imitate sounds long before their imitations are easily recognisable. By 6 or 7 months the primitive turn-taking capability has developed into more sophisticated reciprocal vocal games between parent and child. It is a simple matter for the parent to select sounds produced by the baby and to develop them in these auditory games.

REFERENTIAL LOOKING

The phenomenon of referential looking may partly explain the emergence of the first words.[53] When a baby's gaze falls on an interesting object or person the mother glances at him and follows his line of sight, to see what has caught his attention (Fig. 3.3). She then describes and comments on the

Fig. 3.2   Turn-taking
behaviour.

Fig. 3.3   Referential looking. The child looks at the cat, the mother follows his line
of gaze and says, 'Yes, that's a cat'.

object of his interest. In this way the child learns to associate word labels with the object or person they describe.

BABY TALK

The use of baby words is frowned upon by many standard baby books, but they are widely used in other cultures.[54] Baby words are usually simple stressed two-syllable pairs (e.g. tum tum, gee gee) which are easy for the child to learn, so that he rapidly masters the link between words and objects. Even if baby words are avoided, deliberate simplification of language, clear voice, slower speed of delivery and a raised pitch (register) are so widely adopted by adults and even young chldren talking to babies that the term 'motherese' has been suggested to describe these features.

ACQUISITION OF GRAMMAR

It is often impossible to decide at what point the infant's utterances can be called words. Probably parental enthusiasm is the main determinant of when the first word is recognised. The first few words are often used in a variety of ways (Table 3.2); they do not have a single specific meaning or

Table 3.2 Overgeneralisation of word meanings. (From work by Eve V. Clark of Stanford University.)

Child's lexical item	First referents	Other referents in order of occurrence	General area of semantic extension
MOOI	Moon	Cake Round marks on windows Writing on windows and in blocks Round shapes in books Tooling in leather book-covers Round postmarks Letter O	Shape
KOTIBAIZ	Bars of cot	Large toy abacus Toast rack with parallel bars Picture of building with columns	Shape
VOV-VOV	Dog	Kittens Hens All animals at zoo Picture of pigs dancing	Shape
KOKO	Cockerel's crowing	Tunes played on a violin Tunes played on a piano Tunes played on an accordion Tunes played on a phonograph All music Merry-go-round	Sound

Table 3.3   Crystal's seven stages in expressive language development.[51]

Stage 1 9–18 months	Single-element: e.g. dada, there, no, gone, more
Stage 2 18–24 months	Two-element: e.g. dada there, all gone car
Stage 3 24–30 months	Three-element: e.g. daddy kick ball, where man gone
Stage 4 30–36 months	Four or more elements: e.g. Where my mummy's bag gone
Stage 5 36–42 months	Complex sentences: use of 'and' and 'but', multiple clauses, comparisons. e.g. Daddy gone in the garden and he felled over—and he hurted his knee
Stage 6 42–54 months	Refinement of grammar: irregular verbs and plurals, passive structures, etc., e.g. I just been stung by a wasp.
Stage 7 Beyond 54 months	Increasing sophistication of language use: continues at least until puberty

use. The joining of words to make two-element sentences usually occurs at around 18–24 months but it is doubtful whether grammatical terms like subject or verb are appropriate at this stage. These can only be applied with confidence when three-element sentences appear. Crystal has neatly summarised these and subsequent stages of grammatical development (Table 3.3). Comprehension of language develops along similar lines but is generally some months in advance of expressive ability.

At one time it was thought that language development was dependent on the parent reinforcing, by praise and encouragement, the random utterances of the infant, whenever he utters a word-like sound. Modern linguists have rejected this simple explanation for language development for many reasons, of which the most compelling is the fact that so many early utterances of young children are clearly invented by them. The child extracts the rules of grammar from adult speech and builds on them himself. He does this so successfully and so universally that Chomsky proposed that the brain must be programmed to carry out this analytic feat; he called this hypothetical brain circuit the 'language acquisition device'. Alternatively, it may be that the need for the basic classes of word, names (nouns) and actions (verbs) is so fundamental that no other system of symbolic communication is conceivable,[55] and this discovery is made afresh by every child in every culture. Certainly the distinction is recognised by mentally retarded children learning to communicate by sign systems, where the noun–verb distinction is equally essential.

Children frequently learn a word without fully understanding its

Table 3.4 Learning the rules about plurals.

1	Boy	Cat	Man	House	Foot
					Feet
2			Men		
3	Boys	Cats	Mans	House	Foots
					Feets
4	Boysez	Catsez	Mansez	House	Footsez
			Mensez		Feetsez
5	Boys	Cats	Mans	Houses	Feets
6	Boys	Cats	Men	Houses	Feet

significance. They overgeneralise its meaning and then refine it as their knowledge of the world develops.[56] The same process can be recognised with grammatical rules (Table 3.4). In clinical assessment of language development, overgeneralisation often accounts for the apparent 'errors' made by children in labelling objects or describing pictures. Often the parent can explain how the particular use of the word came about.

CHARACTERISTICS OF PARENT–CHILD CONVERSATION

Correction of the child's statements is usually related to content and factual accuracy more than grammatical style or pronunciation, e.g. 'Grandad are a lady' would be corrected to 'No, grandad is a *man*'. Paraphrase and expansion give the child a correct model to copy, without being discouraged by constant correction or negative responses: (child) 'Car . . . red car', (mother) 'Yes, it's a big red car'. Competent parents manage to interpret many utterances that would be incomprehensible to a stranger, and feed these back to the child in the corrected form.

Imitation plays a part in the rapid acquisition of vocabulary and syntax. Many children pass through a phase of repeating much of what is said to them, as if this helped them to understand the meaning and rehearse the use of the word. This is known as 'echolalia'; it seldom persists much beyond the 3rd birthday.

HIGHER LEVELS OF LANGUAGE LEARNING

The essentials of basic grammar are generally mastered by the end of the 4th year but the more sophisticated constructions and the ability to remember and integrate a series of ideas, as in a story, continue to develop throughout the school years.[57] The child also has to learn about the more subtle aspects of communication; sarcasm, understatement, the concealment of orders within questions (e.g. 'would you like to . . .'), the difference between formal and informal conversation, the rules for addressing important adults such as teachers and so on.

Factors affecting language development

The number of verbal exchanges between parent and child is likely to affect progress. It would be surprising if the child of a depressed, uncommunicative parent progressed as fast as one who is constantly talked to by parents, siblings and relatives. In many societies children do not acquire language from their parents, but from contact with their siblings and peers. This does not seem to cause any disadvantage in their normal surroundings, but when such families are transplanted to an unfamiliar society and children are deprived of much contact with their peers, they may be in serious difficulty.

Bernstein described some interesting differences in the usage of language between social groups (although the distinction is not as sharp as his original description suggested). Middle class families were said to use language extensively to discuss, plan, argue and describe—'the extended code'.[58] The lower social classes limited the use of language only to conveying instructions and essential information—'the restricted code'. It is a characteristic of Western middle class culture that children are encouraged in critical questioning and abstract thought. A high value is placed on imagination, creative thought and play. Nevertheless, the class distinctions described by Bernstein were later realised, both by him and other workers, to be partly artefactual. It is probable that the social circumstances in which professional assessments of language are made are more inhibiting to lower class children than to those from the middle classes.[456]

The importance of empathy, putting oneself in the other's shoes, is revealed in numerous daily exchanges, e.g. 'How would you feel if I pulled *your* hair?' Empathy facilitates the function of the close-knit nuclear family, and probably makes for greater success in business and professional life, but it is not necessarily so highly prized by other cultures, where there may be more emphasis for example on conformity to group behaviour, or on independence and strength.[59] It is foolish to apply Western norms to children from other cultures without recognising these differences. At the same time, they inevitably put the child at a disadvantage if he has to compete in the educational system and later the labour market in Western society.

Some parents, particularly professional people, overestimate their child's intelligence and language ability and their conversation with him is pitched at too high a level of complexity. This seems particularly likely to occur with a child with less intrinsic ability than his older siblings. Conversely, parents may persistently underestimate a child's expressive language, refusing to credit him with saying a word unless the pronunciation is clear. Such parents fail to recognise that the conveying of meaning is the most vital aspect of communication and they make repeated attempts to make him speak more clearly. The child may react with stubborn silence;

this negativistic behaviour is quite normal in the young child, although it is seldom an adequate explanation on its own for severe delay in language development.

Non-verbal communication

Humans communicate by numerous non-verbal signals, involving auditory, visual and tactile channels. A speaker conveys information not only by his words, but by tone of voice, intonation, and the use of pauses and 'punctuation' noises (er, um, you see, etc.). Visual signals include gestures such as pointing, changing facial expressions, body posture or movement (Fig. 3.4). 'Turn-taking' behaviour is learned both by auditory and visual channels, and can also be mastered by the deaf-blind, using tactile cues. Much has been written about non-verbal communication in adults,[60] but less is known about the way that this is learned in childhood;[61] presumably the same processes are at work as in spoken language.

Fig. 3.4   Non-verbal communication—caught red-handed!

Summary

Linguistic knowledge is expanding very rapidly and the clinical applications are not yet finally established. The features highlighted in this chapter are those which already seem to have some clinical value. Thus, turn-taking and referential looking provide valuable evidence of a satisfactory parent–infant relationship. Observation that a parent uses language teaching strategies such as expansion and paraphrase might suggest that a poor linguistic environment is not primarily responsible for a child's difficulties in language acquisition. An apparently bizarre use of words or grammar may sometimes be explained by the principle of overgeneralisation. A child's familiarity with the social rules of language use—making a request, awaiting instructions, or recounting an experience—is an encouraging sign when his grammar or articulation seem deficient. The close relationship between language usage and the social situation means that interpretation of assessment results must be very circumspect.

Recent research has emphasised the need to consider communication in the context of the environment. Measures of language development such as the vocabulary count and sentence length are not adequate in themselves. It must be remembered, however, that substantial differences in the genetic endowment of intelligence and of language skills still remain. It would be a serious error to explain all disturbances of language development purely in terms of an inappropriate linguistic environment.

COGNITIVE DEVELOPMENT

This term is used to describe the understanding of concepts about functions and relationships. Under normal circumstances cognitive and linguistic development are intimately related.[62] Some theorists argue that language is a necessary tool for the acquisition of concepts, others believe that language can only advance when the necessary concepts have already been formed. It seems more likely that the two usually develop simultaneously, but they may be dissociated in conditions such as deafness or aphasia. Whatever the exact learning process may be, the presence of a particular language skill can be taken as evidence that the underlying concept is present; thus, if a child says, 'This doll bigger 'n that one', he clearly understands the concept of size. A severely deaf child with no spoken language might also understand the concept of big and little, but this would need to be demonstrated by non-verbal means. For example, the child could be given a set of dolls and chairs of differing sizes; if he selects the appropriate size for each, it may be assumed that he has some understanding of the concept of size.

Learning in infancy

The infant's ability to learn is demonstrated by his preference for novel and interesting stimuli, and his decreased interest in repeated presentations of the same stimulus. This latter phenomenon is known as habituation.[63] For example, if a bell is rung gently behind a resting baby, he responds with a startle, but each successive repetition elicits a decreasing response. After the third or fourth presentation he may ignore it all together, but will respond again to a new and different sound. By presenting test stimuli which are similar but not identical, it is possible to determine how fine a discrimination can be achieved by the baby. Habituation has also been used as a clinical measure of nervous system integrity in the newborn.

THE IMPORTANCE OF VISION

The visual channel is of great significance to the infant, long before he is mobile, in the construction of his own mental map of his surroundings. It is vision which later provides the main spur for the infant to reach, creep, crawl and walk. Even in the first months, the infant's behaviour towards inanimate objects is different from that reserved for humans. Inanimate objects are inspected with detached interest. The infant attempts to grasp and explore them by hand and mouth. Objects which make a noise are of particular importance. By three months an infant has learnt to pay attention and turn to a noise 'in the expectation of seeing a spectacle', as Piaget put it.

In contrast, humans elicit the complicated behavioural pattern called turn-taking, described previously. Facial patterns and contours arouse the infant's interest at a very early age. By $2\frac{1}{2}$ months, a human face regularly elicits a smile. During the next 3 months the infant learns to distinguish his mother from other adults, and familiar people from unfamiliar. Certain additions to a familiar face, such as spectacles, may alarm and upset him. Distinction between male and female faces and awareness of strangers can be demonstrated by 7 months of age. The increasing recognition of human voice patterns parallels that of faces and the infant learns to associate his mother's voice with her facial appearance, and sounds with the objects that make them.

The importance of vision in social and cognitive development is best illustrated by the responses of blind babies, and the problems experienced by their parents in developing normal attachments to them. This is discussed on p. 297.

Acquisition of concepts and skills

A child does not learn to speak unless he is exposed to spoken language, but however poor the environment may be, he can acquire some understanding of his surroundings, of spatial relationships, and of his own abilities to influence the world around him, by observation and experimentation. The opportunity to explore and manipulate objects helps intellectual development but, given a suitably structured task, even a severely physically handicapped child may reveal a surprisingly advanced level of understanding gained entirely by observation.

The Swiss psychologist, Piaget, has had a major influence on modern ideas about cognitive development. His theories were based on observation of the spontaneous activities of his own children. Piaget realised that the infant is not merely the passive recipient of auditory and visual sensations; he has to organise and make sense of them. This is achieved in a series of developmental stages characterised by increasing sophistication of logical thought.

Piaget's work has stimulated a vast amount of research, which in turn has generated alternative explanations for his original observations. Some of the tasks used in his studies have been incorporated into various psychometric scales,[64] and two examples of Piagetian concepts which are of immediate value to the clinician are mentioned below. In general, however, Piaget's work in its original form is not easily adapted to clinical assessment.

Object permanence means that objects continue to have an existence of their own even when they cannot be seen. This is a concept of fundamental importance, discovered by each normal infant for himself in the first year of life. In the first few months any object which is out of sight, is out of mind. The evolution of the concept of object permanence is illustrated in Fig. 3.5. This is the concept underlying many familiar milestones and assessment tasks, including peek-a-boo games, searching for a fallen object, retrieving a pellet covered by a box or cup, and (at a more advanced level) having a regular place for storing toys and searching systematically for one that is missing. It is also a necessary concept for language development; before an object can be labelled, it must be recognised to have an independent existence. Emotional security and maturation are dependent on the child's discovery that his parents continue to exist even when not immediately visible.

Causality.   This refers to the child's ability to deduce the link between an action and its consequence. Between 4 and 8 months, a baby observing an interesting spectacle will indicate his desire for a repeat performance by what Piaget called 'procedures'—for example, generalised excitement, vocalisation, or banging his hands on his table (Fig. 3.6). Procedure games help the infant to learn that his actions influence the world around him, and make things happen. From 8 to 12 months, he becomes more certain of the link between spectacle and performer and his procedures become more complex—for example, touching the adult's hand. Between 12 and 18 months, if presented with an interesting toy, he is likely to explore it, but will not be able to operate it and will therefore return it to the adult with an

Fig. 3.5 Development of object permanence. **a** Adult shows baby the toy so he wants it; **b** adult hides toy under a cloth; **c** baby can retrieve toy if only partly covered; **d** baby can retrieve toy even if fully covered; **e** if it is hidden several times under the same cloth, then under a second cloth, the baby searches under the first cloth; **f** baby searches under correct cloth even with a choice of three.

eloquent unspoken request for the toy to be reactivated. From 18 months onwards, he is likely to make a more prolonged, determined and systematic effort to solve such problems on his own.

Attention and attention control

Advances in play, logical thought and in language skills are associated with increasing maturity of attention control. Attention, the ability to focus only

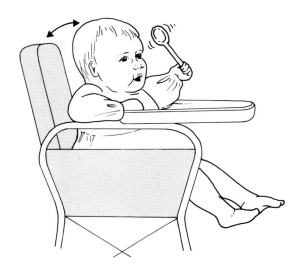

Fig. 3.6 Example of a procedure. An 8-month-old baby banging his spoon on a high chair and shouting/rocking to regain attention.

on selected stimuli, is a difficult function to measure and it certainly cannot be adequately described in terms of duration alone. Even very young babies sometimes show intense and prolonged concentration on an object or a social game. The young child has difficulty retaining and processing information from auditory and visual channels simultaneously. He cannot await sequential instructions or switch his attention easily back and forth between for example a play activity and an adult's comments; these abilities gradually develop, in the 3rd and 4th years. With increasing maturity, the child becomes less readily distracted by irrelevant stimuli. There is good reason to believe that attention is a skill which is to some extent determined by environmental factors and can be taught. In clinical practice, observations of attention control are invaluable and are easily made during the course of hearing and language assessments. The clinical problems of hyperactivity (p. 399) are regarded by some authors as, at least in part, an impairment of selective attention control.

Play

Play enables the child to experiment with objects and ideas, and to rehearse various activities, real or imagined, without any external pressure to achieve a particular goal.[65,66] There are conflicting views on whether adults should intervene and help a child with his play. Some authorities feel that this robs him of the satisfaction of making discoveries for himself. However there is some evidence that judicious help from an interested adult can accelerate the child's mastery of ideas and methods of reasoning:

> 'Some parents show a superb capacity to break tasks down so that they are always offering the child problems to solve as he tries to learn something, but problems which are neither too difficult nor too easy.

When the child starts to experience difficulty, they immediately step in and structure the situation more tightly; as he shows signs of success they back off, leaving him greater scope for initiative. In simple laboratory situations at least, this performance by the parent correlates with the child's ultimate ability to solve the problem alone. The strategy of teaching does have a causal influence on the child's learning . . .' (D.J.Wood[10])

Adult interventions in play may involve spoken instructions and suggestions but are probably more effective if the point at issue is also demonstrated, since young children appear to have some difficulty in learning by purely verbal instruction. Pictures, story books, and toys all stimulate parent–child interactions with both visual and auditory components. In a favourable environment, play becomes increasingly complex and imaginative in the early years of life, as summarised in Table 3.5. The Lowe and Costello Symbolic Play test offers a standardised method of assessing play in children under the age of 3.

Play is not synonymous with toys and in many cultures children invent their own games without any purpose-designed props. Indeed, there are some cultures where play hardly exists. Neither is it dependent on internal verbalisation, although it is sometimes said to require 'inner language'. The

Table 3.5   Development of play. (Adapted from Rutter,[10] work of Rosenblatt.)

1 Year	3 Years
Indiscriminate response to all toys (e.g. mouthing, handling, banging)	Actions which demonstrate understanding of properties (e.g. balls roll, cars can be pushed)
Random series of actions	Sequential investigation (touching, manipulating, activating)
Items used one at a time	Use of toys as a group (building bricks; cup and saucer; toy cars and garage)
Brief episodes of attention	Organised game with a theme and time sequence
Imitates adult actions on self (pretends to eat) then on doll (feeds doll)	Objects interacting, e.g. doll feeds another doll
Functional use of toy (brick used to build)	Toy can represent something else (e.g. brick becomes a car)
Dependence on adult for ideas	Can invent a game and direct its execution

play of a totally deaf child may reveal an extensive understanding of everyday events and ideas, even though he has no verbal language.

Summary

Developmental scales indicate mean ages at which various skills are achieved, but clinical experience shows that there is wide variation in the responses of different children to the tasks used for assessment in the early years of life. Table 3.6 illustrates why it is naïve to score a child's response simply as 'pass' or 'fail'. His behaviour will depend not only on his innate

Table 3.6   Two examples of variations in behaviour of normal children. (Adapted from Gesell.[185])

			Age			
	52wks	80wks	2yrs	3yrs	4yrs	5yrs
Spontaneous drawing: percentage of cases displaying various behaviours						
No combination of paper and crayon	46	5	6	3		
Bangs crayon on paper	31	35	3	3		
Linear marks	10	65				
Scribbles	0	57	62	39	9	16
Horizontal marks		16	6			
Vertical marks		16	18			
Marks at an angle		24	35			
Circular marks		3	15			
Marks in all directions		38	21			
Lines go off page		41	9	13		
Names drawing		0	6	77	64	95
Draws a person				26	14	23
Draws a building				7	23	25
Spontaneous block play						
Leaves table or shows no interest		18	6	4	7	10
No constructive spontaneous play		69	47		6	10
Builds a tower		26	25	25	13	12
Puts blocks in row		5	23	75	10	6
Names construction				50	70	82
Builds two-dimensional structures				0	80	27
Builds three-dimensional structures					6	55

intellect, but also on motivation, attention control, previous experience at the task, the skill of the parent as a teacher, and the way in which the task is presented (*see also* p. 394). Detailed analysis of children's thought-processes and of the strategies used by successful teachers and parents should provide better intervention techniques for children whose development seems unduly slow.

The motivation to explore and learn seems to be inborn. This can be encouraged and reinforced by the parents, so that the child discovers that learning is a pleasurable experience. Not all motivation is dependent on reinforcement from other people or by material rewards; discovery and problem-solving bring their own satisfaction.

MOTOR DEVELOPMENT

The movement patterns of normal infants show a remarkable uniformity, implying that some neural pathways are 'preprogrammed'. A number of 'primitive' reflexes can be demonstrated (Fig. 3.7) and these gradually disappear as the baby matures and develops cortical mastery of movement.[67] The biological importance of these reflexes is uncertain and the rate at which they disappear is variable, so they are of limited usefulness in clinical assessment. Because his movements appear at first glance to be random, uncoordinated and purposeless, the neonate was for many years regarded as a 'purely reflexive being'. It is now known that purposeful movement does occur even in the early weeks of life, for example visually-guided reaching for an object is present as early as 11 days, although a carefully contrived experimental situation is needed to demonstrate this.

The development of posture and movement is dependent on two physiologic functions, tone and reciprocal innervation.[68] Postural tone is the degree of muscular tension at a particular point in time; it is constantly altering in response to movement and changes in posture. Reciprocal innervation means that whenever a movement is performed, there is a change in the tone not only of the muscles performing the movement but also in opposing muscle groups and in those that provide fixation for the active part of the body, for example stabilisation of the shoulder while performing a skilled movement with the fingers. Both the early motor development of infancy and the later acquisition of complex motor skills depend on increasingly refined cortical control of tone and reciprocal innervation.

The righting reactions and equilibrium reactions are reflex postural mechanisms which are believed to be essential to normal motor function. Righting reactions are active responses which maintain normal alignment of the head and face with the body, trunk and limbs. They are dependent on sensory information through visual, labyrinthine, tactile and propriocep-

Fig. 3.7 Motor development—the primitive responses of the first two weeks. **a** Placing and stepping; **b** Moro; **c** grasp; **d** head-lag.

tive stimuli. Equilibrium reactions are complex responses to changes in posture and involve continuing changes in muscle tone to maintain posture and balance. When handling a young infant these are often better felt than seen. Sudden changes in posture elicit the saving or parachute reactions.

While there is no doubt that complex reflex mechanisms of movement do develop as the infant matures, it should be remembered that much of the experimental work on which their original description was based was carried out on animals. After extensive brain lesions have been created in experimental animals, the reflex patterns which can be elicited are stereotyped and the normal control of movement is totally abolished. In contrast, motor development in the normal infant is smooth and integrated.

The value of describing it in terms of discrete reflex patterns must be questioned.

THE FIRST SIX MONTHS

The flexed posture of the neonate gradually changes over the first few months to one of predominant extension. There is increasing control of head and trunk as the postural reflexes develop (Fig. 3.8). In the prone position, he pushes himself up on his hands and by 4 or 5 months shows eager but usually ineffectual attempts to crawl towards desired objects. He learns to pivot round in this position and gradually discovers the creeping posture. At 5–7 months the protective reflexes appear (Fig. 3.9) and these remain for life. Independent safe sitting is only possible when these are present.

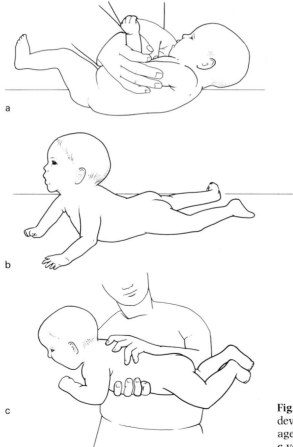

a

b

c

Fig. 3.8 Motor development—5 months of age. **a** Pull to sitting; **b** prone; **c** ventral suspension.

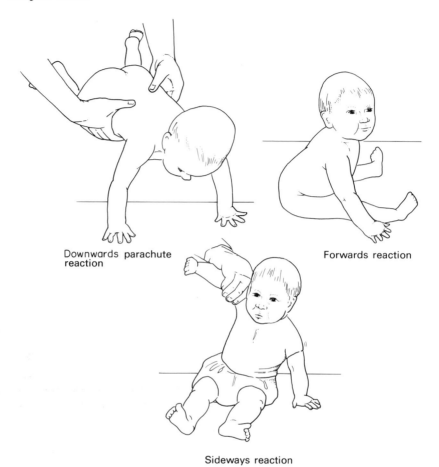

Downwards parachute
reaction

Forwards reaction

Sideways reaction

Fig. 3.9   Protective reflexes at 10 months old.

In the early weeks, the hands are often fisted, but extension of the wrist and fingers occurs in periods of activity. The asymmetric tonic reflex posture (Fig. 3.10), in which the head and eyes turn towards the extended arm, encourages the infant to view his hands and he becomes fascinated by the movements of his fingers, using vision to supply feedback in the development of more complex manual skills.

By 3 months he is examining the fingers of both hands together in the midline (Fig. 3.11) and by $4\frac{1}{2}$ months he can control them enough to pick up objects. He then learns to hold two objects simultaneously and to transfer from one hand to the other. By 7–8 months he acquires the skill to oppose finger and thumb but, when presented with a small object, a raking movement of all four fingers may be used, a movement which is characteristic of this stage of development. Manual dexterity improves

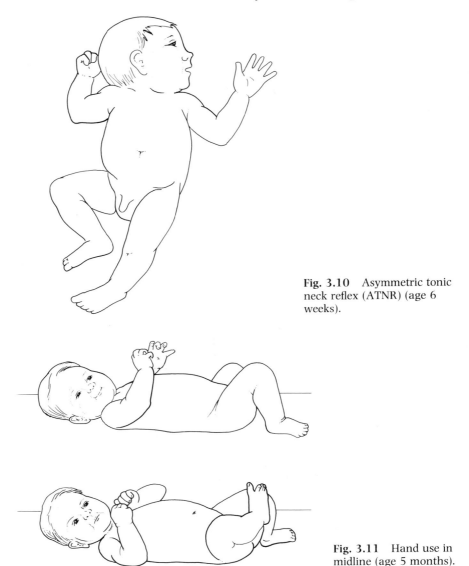

Fig. 3.10 Asymmetric tonic neck reflex (ATNR) (age 6 weeks).

Fig. 3.11 Hand use in midline (age 5 months).

throughout the 2nd year with increasing control over delicate finger/ thumb movements.

In the early years, initiation of fine movements in one limb causes similar movements in the opposite limb and other associated movements, such as tongue protrusion and facial grimacing, also occur during the performance of skilled motor tasks. With increasing competence movement becomes more concise and economical and associated movements diminish, but they may still be observed at times even in adult life. Motor control depends not only on the level of maturity but also on emotional status at the time of examination.

Hand skills and the suppression of unwanted associated movements continue to mature throughout childhood, and this can be demonstrated using the neurodevelopmental examination techniques described on p. 80.

Motor learning

In the early stages of learning a motor task performance is slow, jerky and inaccurate and is monitored by visual and proprioceptive feedback as the results of the movement are observed. With mastery of the task, the execution becomes smooth, continuous and organised and is no longer dependent on feedback. Specific examples such as learning to play a musical instrument or mastering a sport like skating are familiar to everyone. Undoubtedly the same learning process increases the economy and efficiency of movement in all motor development. One striking feature of motor learning is that, once a skill has been mastered, it can be executed in a variety of ways. For example, when a child has acquired the skill of signing his name, this unique signature can be reproduced in an endless variety of ways, with a pencil on paper, a paint brush on a wall, or a stick in the sand. The muscles used are different, but the pattern is the same. Probably the effects of encouragement and opportunity to practise motor skills are cumulative and become more evident as motor activity becomes more complex, as with language and cognitive development. Some children, however, appear to have exceptional difficulties in organising their movement patterns and making the transition from the jerky to the smooth level of performance, as seems to be the case in 'clumsy' children.

Factors affecting motor development

There are wide variations between individuals in the rate of motor maturation, and examples of this are shown in Fig. 3.12. There are probably also racial differences in the speed of maturation which are only partly explained by different methods of child rearing. Certainly there are familial differences. Many of the children with isolated motor delay show a particular pattern of motor development known as bottom-shuffling (Fig. 3.13) which runs in families, providing good evidence for the existence of genetically determined variations in development.[69,70] Some children walk as early as 7 months, whereas shufflers may not walk until 30 months, yet subsequently no difference can be found between the early and the later walkers, either in motor competence or in intelligence.

As with other aspects of development much of the variation in motor progress must be attributed to genetic factors affecting both specific motor

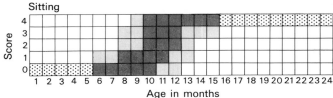

Score:
0. The infant was unable to sit without support
1. The infant was able to sit free for some seconds
2. The infant was able to sit free for about 30 seconds
3. The infant was able to sit free for about one minute
4. The infant was able to sit free for longer than at least one minute

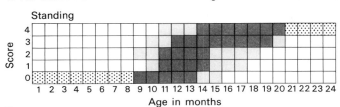

Score:
0. The infant was unable to stand up
1. The infant was able to get into a kneeling position while supporting himself with one or both hands
2. The infant was able to get into a standing position while supporting himself during standing. He was not able to sit down without help
3. The infant was able to get into a standing position while supporting himself during standing. He was able to sit down without help
4. The infant was able to stand free

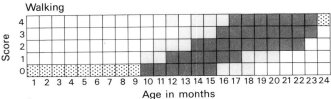

Score:
0. The infant was unable to walk
1. The infant could walk if his mother held him by both hands
2. The infant could walk if his mother held him by one hand
3. The infant walked free for a few paces
4. The infant walked free for at least seven paces consecutively

Key   100% of infants score at this level
       80% or more of infants score at these levels
       20% or less of infants score at these levels

Fig. 3.12 Variations in the motor development of normal infants. (From Touwen[480] by permission.)

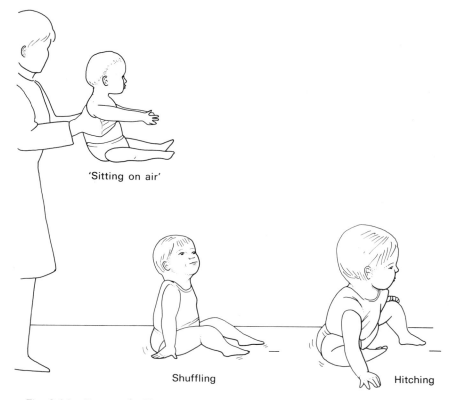

'Sitting on air'

Shuffling   Hitching

Fig. 3.13   Bottom-shuffling.

pathways and temperamental characteristics of curiosity and drive. Under normal circumstances environmental influences do not seem to have much effect on the rate of early motor development, although teaching of specific motor skills is certainly possible even in infancy. In cases of extreme emotional deprivation, for example when a child has been left unattended in a cot for hours at a time, there may be an apparent marked delay in motor development associated with general apathy. The motor development of blind babies is also delayed, probably because the motivation for movement is reduced (p. 297).

Anatomical variations affecting motor development

There are marked variations in the degree of internal and external rotation of the femur and tibia in early childhood.[71] There may be an extreme degree of external rotation at the hips, so that the feet can be turned 90° outwards. In femoral internal torsion the femoral neck points slightly anteriorly, causing the feet to point inwards. The tibia may show medial torsion with similar results.

Bow-legs (genu varum) are normal in the infant but should correct by 18 months of age. At this age there should not be more than 4 cm between the femoral condyles when the ankles are placed together. Knock-knees (genu valgum) are common in childhood, but also rarely need treatment. (*Anterior* bowing of the tibia is abnormal and is associated with bone defects which predispose to fracture.) With the exception of the last, most of these deformities correct spontaneously. Their importance to the paediatrician is that, although they are normal variants, they may present with an 'awkward' gait or a complaint of excessive falling.

Chapter Four
Practical Aspects of Assessment

CHILD DEVELOPMENT CENTRES

In 1968 the Sheldon Working Party recommended the creation of comprehensive Child Assessment Centres, where handicapped children could receive diagnostic and therapeutic services. Over the succeeding years, as it became clear that child handicap is an evolving problem which can be influenced by adequate intervention, the emphasis moved from diagnosis to management[77] and the notion of a once-and-for-all assessment, so alarming to parents, has been discarded. For these reasons the term 'Child Development Centre' (CDC) is now preferred. Most CDCs are located on a hospital campus in close proximity to specialist services.

The Court Report[73] on paediatric services recommended that the professionals involved in the care of handicapped children should organise themselves into District Handicap Teams. The suggested composition of the team was: paediatrician, social worker, educational psychologist, senior nurse and teacher. The Report failed to clarify whether the same team members should be responsible for clinical care, organisation and supervision of services, or both. In inner cities, health districts, hospital catchment areas, social services units and educational divisions seldom share the same boundaries, causing considerable administrative difficulties. Most districts have solved these problems by their own modifications of the Court proposals.

A close working relationship between general practitioners, Community Child Health Services, and the Paediatric Consultant is essential, since most of the services needed by the handicapped child and family are based outside the hospital. The concept of a Consultant Community Paediatrician was proposed to bridge the gap between the CDC and the Community Services, and has much to recommend it (p. 5). Many professions contribute to the work of a Child Development Centre (Table 4.1). Much has been written about the need for multidisciplinary assessment since many children have more than one handicap, and in such a broad field no profession has a monopoly of wisdom in assessment or

Table 4.1   Child Development Centre personnel.

Regular CDC staff	Referrals or joint clinics	Liaison with community staff
Secretary/organiser	Paediatric neurologist	GP
Paediatrician	Geneticist	Community paediatric services
Social worker	Audiologist	Health visitor
Therapists	Ophthalmologist	District Social Services
Teacher	Orthoptist	Education office
Clinical psychologist	Orthopaedic surgeon	Voluntary societies
Liaison health visitor	Neurosurgeon	Mental handicap team
	Paediatric surgeon	
	Orthotist	
	Educational psychologist	
	Dentist	
	Dental hygienist	
	Orthodontist	
	Plastic surgeon	

remediation.[74] Multidisciplinary team work is difficult, demanding, and time-consuming. Mutual professional respect, flexibility in allocating tasks, familiarity with each other's abilities and interests, and adequate time for discussion are essential ingredients for success. The diagnosis and management programmes which originate in the Centre are of little value unless they are communicated to those who run the services used by the child outside the hospital. Communication is greatly simplified if appointments for CDC staff are made jointly between hospital and community.

The organisation of the CDC depends on the facilities available and on the personal styles of the staff. There is no evidence that any one method of assessment is superior. Several authors have described their personal approach and shown how their resources have been adapted to meet the particular needs of their patients.[72,75,76] One essential, on which all authors agree, is an efficient secretary and organiser for the Centre. The vital importance of this post is seldom appreciated by hospital administrators.

In some units, assessment of a handicapped child may last for three weeks, whereas in others it is completed in a few hours. Hardly any information is available on the relative efficiency or value of varying styles of assessment. It is not possible to outline any one approach which can be used as a recipe for every clinical problem, and flexibility and imagination are essential if time and skill are to be used economically.

Organising the assessment

Assessment of developmental problems is time consuming. The initial consultation can seldom be completed in less than 30 minutes and may often require an hour or more. Failed appointments are therefore both irritating and very expensive in terms of wasted professional time. The paediatrician should encourage his colleagues who refer children for assessment to write directly rather than use a hospital or clinic appointment system, since only by knowing the details of referrals in advance can he make optimum use of time and resources. All available details about the child should be collected in advance. A letter outlining practical details of the assessment is sent to the parents with the appointment. Sometimes, if the family is socially incompetent or disorganised, the health visitor or social worker may help to ensure that the appointment is kept. An interpreter may be needed for immigrant families.

Introduction to the family

The doctor should usually collect the parents and the child from the waiting area himself, as much can be learnt about the child by discreet eavesdropping while casually strolling in the waiting area. Older children should of course be greeted by name. It is easy to be seduced by the charm of a smaller normal sibling and to ignore the handicapped child if he is not very active or vocal. This mistake commonly irritates parents, since it reflects the attitudes of society in general to the disabled, and parents feel that doctors specialising in this field should know better!

If a behavioural or emotional problem seems to be the main cause for concern, older children may sometimes conveniently be left in the waiting area to play or read, so that the parents feel less inhibited in explaining their worries. The child should always be recalled and given a résumé, appropriately edited, of what has been discussed.

Parents should sit in comfortable chairs, beside the doctor rather than on the far side of the desk (Fig. 4.1). Colleagues should be introduced, and permission obtained beforehand for the presence of non-essential observers such as professional visitors or students. Young children are often shy and clinging on arrival in a strange place. Social overtures should not be made too soon; even looking at some children may provoke tears. The production of a few interesting toys, particularly wind-up clockwork items, often works wonders, but they should be handed casually to the child without comment or eye contact. Nothing should be said to a young child that demands a reply until confidence is established.

'DIFFICULT CHILDREN'

It is frequently valuable to share the first consultation with one colleague, most commonly a speech therapist or physiotherapist. The therapist concentrates on involving the child in relevant activities while the doctor interviews the parents. It is then possible to compare notes immediately and

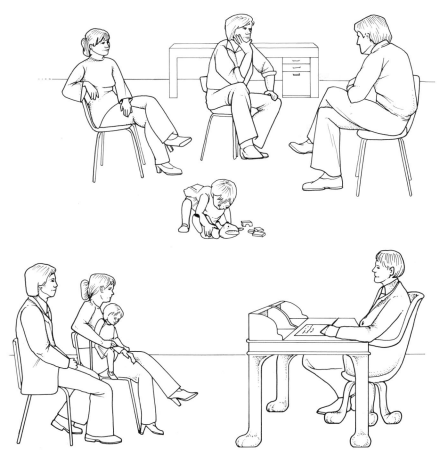

Fig. 4.1. (Above) Relaxed interviewing aids communication; (below) excessive formality can be intimidating.

to proceed to physical examination, hearing testing, etc., so that a preliminary combined opinion on diagnosis and management can be offered.

Observation facilities consisting of a large playroom and a smaller room separated by a one-way mirror are often useful. Good sound transmission is essential, and a portable radio-microphone which can be worn by the child or carried by the therapist gives better results than all but the most expensive fixed ceiling microphone systems. These facilities can be used in two ways. A child may happily separate from the parents, indeed may perform better in their absence, and his play and language abilities can be demonstrated by a therapist or psychologist, while the doctor and parents watch from the observation room. This system enables the parents to comment on the significance of the child's activities, and on whether they are representative. It has an additional unexpected advantage; many parents find that the one-way mirror enables them to take a more objective view of their child's handicap than has hitherto been possible.

Alternatively, one or both parents may be asked to play with the child in the playroom, while the doctor and his colleagues watch from the observation room. This is sometimes the only way of assessing an extremely shy child, and is invaluable in cases of severe language disorder or selective mutism. It is surprising how well most parents cope with this experience.

Overactive, restless and fidgety children can be very distracting and may make interviewing impossible. It is helpful to fix a bolt high on the door of the consulting room to prevent the child from absconding every few moments. Cupboards should be locked, shelves high, and taps isolated by stopcocks! When the paediatrician fails dismally in attempts to control the child, he can say to the parents 'How would you normally deal with this at home?' This gives them freedom to carry out any course of action and may, at the same time, throw more light on behaviour problems. When all else fails, one must either find an alternative child-minder while the interview is completed or make another appointment to see the parents unencumbered.

Sometimes a restless or fretful child may be used by the parents as a 'prop' to pace the interview. If the discussion is distressing, for example at the time of diagnosis of a handicap, they may welcome opportunities to comfort the child or intervene in his bad behaviour or play, while they regain control of their emotions and digest each item of information.

VIDEO- AND TAPE-RECORDING

Video facilities are invaluable for making a permanent record of motor and language disorders. A portable camera is sometimes helpful for the analysis of puzzling behavioural problems which only occur in specific situations. Video is also a powerful tool in some training regimes, for example social skills training. The bizarre language and behaviour of autistic children can also be captured in this way. A tape-recorder may be loaned to parents of children who refuse to talk in a clinic, for example in selective mutism.

ASSESSMENT AT HOME

Children are seldom seen at their best in unfamiliar clinic surroundings and there is much to be said for assessing children at home, at their playgroup or in nursery school. The extra time spent may be justified by the additional information gained and the reduced need for further consultations. On the other hand, hearing and vision tests are more difficult to perform at home, and some parents feel that an opinion delivered in a hospital consulting room is more authoritative than one given at home.

Non-attendance and non-compliance

Parents may fail to attend because they are unconvinced that there is anything wrong with their child; they only agreed to visit the paediatrician to placate their general practitioner or clinic doctor! Others fear that something really is wrong, but cannot face the possible bad news. Follow-up appointments are often failed for different reasons.[78] Parents may need time to adjust to the bad news before facing the doctor again, or they may feel dissatisfied with the opinion given, or may be despondent about the limited ability of medical knowledge to help their child. It should not be forgotten that there are other genuine reasons for non-attendance, such as muddled appointments and long delays in clinics.

For people of limited means, without transport of their own, the usual social orbit is very restricted, and a visit to a paediatric unit only a few miles away may require a great personal effort of organisation, enquiries about bus routes, etc., which may be more than the inadequate parent can manage. The paediatric team must be sufficiently flexible that it can respond to such cases in the most appropriate way, for example by visiting the child at home or at school. Contact may be made via the health visitor or social worker. There is clear evidence from the Black Report that often those who most need professional health care are those least competent at obtaining it.[79]

Some parents are criticised by therapists for not complying with the recommended treatment programme, either by non-attendance or by not following instructions at home. Often this is interpreted as a form of non-acceptance or rejection of the child. While this may be so, other reasons include the demands of other members of the family, doubt about the effectiveness of the measures recommended, and inadequate instruction or explanation.

STRUCTURE OF THE INTERVIEW

A consultation for a developmental problem can be divided into the following stages: (1) definition of the problem, (2) background history, (3) present developmental abilities and problems, (4) physical and neurological examination, (5) preliminary exposition of the findings to the parents. These may be followed by: (6) further assessment by members of the multidisciplinary team, (7) investigations, if indicated, and (8) further discussion and/or case conference with parents. Most readers of this book will be familiar with routine paediatric interviewing and physical examination. It would be superfluous to describe these in detail and the following discussion is confined to points of particular relevance in developmental problems.

DEFINITION OF THE PROBLEM

The first questions to ask are: 'Why have the parents brought the child?'; 'Who is worried, and about what?' and 'Why has the child been referred at this particular time?' It is not always the parents who are most worried; it may be the teacher, school doctor or grandparent. For example, the main object of an assessment is sometimes to reassure other professionals that they are managing the child's handicap correctly. The parents should be asked where they have been for previous advice, whom they have consulted, who is currently responsible for the child's care, and what they understand of the child's problems. Often the parents' view of the situation is remarkably different (and sometimes more accurate!) than that of the referring professional. Whatever the problem may be, it is essential to establish whether it is improving, deteriorating, or merely becoming more obvious as the child gets older. In all forms of major handicap, the distinction between progressive and non-progressive or static disorders is a vital and early stage in differential diagnosis.

THE BACKGROUND HISTORY

In developmental problems it is often easier and more logical to begin the history in the past and work forwards. This gives an immediate understanding of family background, attitudes and function; crucial information such as a family history of an inherited disorder or severe maternal depression emerges early in the interview; and parents are less likely to suspect that this detailed family history means that the doctor attributes their child's problems to bad management.

Family structure. A family tree should be constructed, using the conventional symbols (p. 169). This clearly defines family relationships, at the same time providing the basis for recognising inherited disorders. Now that there are so many one-parent families, it may be diplomatic to ask an unaccompanied parent 'Who else is there in the family?'; it is important to know about both parents, both to avoid embarassing mistakes in relation to genetic aspects and also to understand the family reactions to handicap. Other children with their dates of birth are listed. The question 'Any other pregnancies?' will elicit details of babies who have died, miscarriages, and stillbirths. This information may not otherwise be volunteered, but is often relevant in the genesis of parental depression and conflict, and may also help in aetiological diagnosis of the handicap.

Consanguinity should be noted, particularly among Asian families. The question 'Are you related to your husband?' usually causes some confusion or amusement and should be supplemented 'For example, are you cousins or second cousins?' The point may need to be pursued still further, e.g. 'Do you come from quite separate families?' There are often distant relationships which may be thought insignificant by the family.

The parents' occupations are recorded. Specific enquiries should be made of their health, and about relevant familial disorders including muscle disease, backwardness or learning problems in school, fits, delay in speech or motor development, and a history of bottom-shuffling in parents or siblings.

Social background. The parents' geographic and ethnic origins and religion should be established as they are of importance in understanding both child-rearing practices and attitudes to handicap.[80] Isolation from family support makes it harder for parents to cope with handicapped children. Religious beliefs may explain unexpected response to bad news; Catholics, Moslems, Hindus and non-believers may react in very different ways to the birth of a handicapped child.

Family relationships.   It is sometimes relevant to explore family dynamics and the parent–child relationship. For example, many of the common developmental disorders, notably speech and language delay, are associated with behavioural disturbances—indeed it may be largely chance which determines whether the child is first seen by a paediatrician, speech therapist or child psychiatrist. In cases of major handicap, some insight into family function is essential for optimal counselling. It is not always necessary or desirable to ask explicit questions. One can often 'read between the lines' and the doctor may do better to keep his insights to himself rather than alienate the parents by probing too deeply, before they feel ready to discuss private matters. Some psychopathology can be found is most families and it may be tempting to exaggerate the parental contribution to a disturbed relationship and to ignore deviant language development or difficult temperamental characteristics in a child.

Obstetric history. In addition to the usual medical information, the obstetric history can provide an opportunity to probe parental attitudes to the child. For example, 'What was pregnancy like?', 'How did you feel about being pregnant?', 'How did his father feel about it?' The usual enquiry about viral illnesses, drugs and smoking should include alcohol and exposure to any other drugs or noxious substances.

The birth history should include the parents' recollection of the early minutes of the baby's life. Minor obstetric interventions and abnormalities such as forceps delivery may acquire an exaggerated importance to the layman, but details must be carefully recorded so that misconceptions can be eliminated later. Abnormal birth and neonatal behaviour are of great diagnostic importance, but the parents' recollections are often hazy and inaccurate, and a report from the place of birth is usually essential to evaluate the significance of perinatal events. Puerperal depression is common and well known, and many mothers will admit to having been depressed, though they may disguise its severity. Sometimes the nature of the clinical problem makes it unlikely that perinatal events are relevant. In these cases, the history may be curtailed by asking 'screening' questions such as 'Were the doctors worried about him?', or 'Did you go home with him at the usual time?'

Past medical history.   Specific questions should be asked about fits, faints and funny turns, head injuries, and pertussis immunisation. The doctor may well consider these events irrelevant, but the family often regard them as highly significant.

Important events.   Life-events such as births, deaths, marital breakdown, or moving house should be noted. They may well not be relevant to the child's handicap but sometimes account for management problems and may seem to the parents to have aetiologic significance. A convenient question is 'Did anything important happen in the family around this time; for example, serious illnesses, moving, a death in the family and so on?'

In cases where the life-events affecting the child are complex, and seem related to the onset of the problem, for example in some cases of 'late-onset' autism (p. 251), a rough diagram may clarify the situation (Fig 4.2).

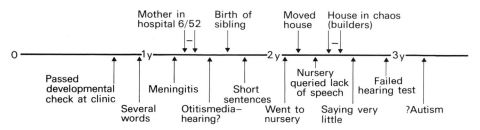

Child: M.V. ♀ age 3.3

Referral ⎱ by grandmother : emotional disturbance   Final diagnosis: degenerative CNS
Diagnosis ⎰ by GP   ?Autism   disease

Fig. 4.2   A life-event diagram.

Developmental history.   Retrospective recall of the ages at which milestones were achieved is known to be unreliable, so little time should be spent on this unless it seems likely to be useful, as may be the case when a progressive disease is suspected. One can enquire about the child's progress at specific points, e.g. his 2nd birthday, Christmas, or a period of hospitalisation. Comparisons with siblings or children of relatives or neighbours may also jog the memory.

Though parents may rapidly forget dates and ages, they never forget the growing feeling of anxiety that something was wrong. Useful questions are, 'Were you, or anyone else, ever worried about his development at that time?', or 'If you look back over his early months now, do you think there was any problem at all?'

Interview with the child.   In appropriate cases the child should be interviewed, either alone or with his parents. Suitable topics for conversation include: his family and pets; whether he likes school, ever wishes he need not go to school, and what he likes most and least at school; the names of his friends; what he does at home; what he worries about; what makes him happy and sad; what other people think of him; and what he would wish for if he had three wishes. Often a brief conversation along these lines will enable the developmental paediatrician to recognise situations where the help of a child psychiatrist might be useful. Conversely, it can be reassuring when a parent is desperately worried about the effects of a handicap or disability on the child's emotional wellbeing.

DEVELOPMENTAL EXAMINATION

In developmental assessment an initial profile of the child's abilities is obtained by combining information obtained from the parents, with observations of the child's behaviour as discussed in Chapter 3. A guide to normal attainments and milestones is essential, such as the developmental scale produced by Dr Mary Sheridan (*see* p. 11).[20,81]

The information obtainable from the parents is limited only by the ingenuity of the interviewer. Examples of suitable questions are given in Tables 4.2, 4.3 and 4.4. Some equipment is needed for assessment; most of this can be purchased very cheaply,[82] and there is no need to buy expensive test kits. Some suggestions for equipment will be found in Appendix 7.

Children under 1 year of age will usually respond quickly to friendly overtures. In this age group, most developmental scales overemphasise

Table 4.2   General questions about development.

How does he compare with other children of the same age?
How much do you think he is behind other children in his development?
Do you think he is getting further behind as he gets older?
Is he losing the ability to do things he could do before?
Is this what he is like at home?
Have I seen a fair picture of what he can do?
What do you think is his biggest problem?
Is he able to concentrate when he is interested in something?
How does he spend his time at home?
Does he pretend or show any imagination?

Table 4.3   Questions about expressive language.

How much can he say?
  any sounds that you understand?
  any words that you recognise?
  how many words: a few, up to 10, 10–20, or too many to count?
  does he join words; if so how many?
  can he make up long sentences?
  does he tend to copy what you say?
Are you worried because
  he doesn't say very much?
  his speech is hard to understand?
  both?
Does he try to make you understand what he wants; if so how?
What language(s) do you speak at home; which does he speak and understand best?
Which language do you use most of the time?
Does he ask for things?
Does he ask questions?
Can he tell you what he has been doing, e.g. at playgroup?

Table 4.4   Questions about comprehension.

Does he understand everyday noises? e.g. his bottle being shaken, dinner being prepared, bath water running, dog barking
Does he understand pat-a-cake, wave bye-bye or similar instructions?
How much does he understand when you talk to him?
Does he understand better if he can see your face or if you point to the thing you are talking about?
Does he understand:
  names of objects, people or pets?
  simple instructions e.g. shut the door, get your coat?
  two part instructions e.g. go and get your coat from the kitchen?
  more complicated instructions?
Can you make a bargain with him? e.g. let me finish this and I will play with you
Can you tell him what is going to happen? e.g. we are going out in the car to the hospital
Can you tell him a story; does he follow it?

---

motor development and it is essential to look carefully at social and communicative behaviour as well. Demonstration that the child understands object permanence and causality (p. 46) is particularly useful.

In the 12–21 months age group, the child can initially be presented with four or five familiar items, such as a cup, spoon, brush and shoe. He is more likely to demonstrate his understanding by appropriate action ('definition by use') than by speech (Fig 4.3). The child is then asked to point out the items, using a normal voice level. If his cooperation can be sustained, a very simple hearing test can be attempted (p. 97) but many toddlers become

Fig. 4.3   Definition by use.

engrossed in one or two objects and ignore all further spoken instructions. Patience and skill are needed to divert attention to new tasks.

Beyond 21 months of age, even a shy child can usually be persuaded to respond to instructions, though it may be a long time before he will speak and even longer before the speech produced is representative of his competence. No pressure should be put on the child to talk, and parents who try to do so must be asked to desist. When toys are offered to him he is told the name of each, but is *not* asked to say the word. Once he seems relaxed and interested, he can be casually asked 'What is this one?', but if he does not reply he should be told at once, or he may well dissolve into tears or retreat to the parent. A game can often be developed using, for example, doll's-house furniture or a toy garage, and this will reveal the extent of his understanding and symbolic play. Alternatively, books and pictures can be used as a stimulus for conversation (Table 4.5).

When the parents are questioned about the child's language abilities, it should be remembered that they often *under*estimate the extent of his speech output, because they do not credit his unclear utterances with meaning. The opposite error may occur when parents are exceptionally astute at interpreting the child's attempts at speech. Comprehension is usually *over*estimated and parents often reply 'everything' when asked how much the child understands, because they automatically keep their conversation with him within the limits of his understanding. More searching questions are needed to define the true extent of his comprehension (Tables 4.3 and 4.4).

When verbal comprehension is age appropriate, non-verbal skills are usually also normal. On the other hand, if verbal comprehension is significantly delayed, assessment of performance or non-verbal skills is invaluable (p. 259). An approximate assessment of these can be made using familiar tests such as the copying of models built from bricks; copying a line, circle, cross, square and triangle; colour matching; the 'draw a man test'; a

Table 4.5   Using simple toys, pictures and books to detect impaired comprehension.

Age	Comprehension level
12–18 months	Recognition of objects by name: 'Show me the . . .'
2–2½ years	Relating two ideas: 'Put the . . . in the . . .' 'Give the . . . to mummy' Understanding action words: 'Show me someone sweeping'
2½–3 years	Recognition of objects by function: 'Which one is for eating/kicking/drinking with?' The beginnings of negatives and concepts of size and colour: 'Show me a big/little . . .' 'Show me a round/long . . .' 'Find a red one'
3–3½ years	More complicated ideas: 'Which one is the same as that one?' 'Show me a different one?' 'Are you a boy or a girl?' 'Which one is behind/underneath . . .?'
4 years +	Abstract questions involving concepts of time, place, reasoning etc.: 'How did you come here today?' 'What did you have for breakfast?' 'What is . . . doing—why?'

three-piece form board, or a more complex board with up to a dozen pieces. Toys which can be activated in various ways often produce more cooperation and interest. Simultaneously the attention control and social maturity are estimated.

Hearing tests.   A hearing test is a routine part of developmental assessment. For descriptive convenience however, the techniques are discussed in Chapter 5. There are several reasons why the developmental paediatrician should assume responsibility for most diagnostic hearing testing. Firstly, he has the necessary skills in handling young children. Secondly, the differential diagnosis of abnormal language development includes deafness; conversely the assessment of suspected deafness includes an evaluation of language development. Furthermore, the child's reactions to a hearing test are in themselves a useful developmental test. Thirdly, paediatric audiology is a shortage specialty in Britain and there are not nearly enough consultants in this field to see all children who need a hearing test. It seems logical therefore to refer to the paediatric audiologist only those children in whom diagnostic testing is exceptionally difficult, and those who have a significant previously undiagnosed sensorineural loss.

Motor development.   Delayed motor milestones are usually obvious even to unsophisticated parents. Motor development and the disorders which affect it are easier to assess than language or intellect, because they can be analysed by means of the classical neurological examination and investigations. Because of the wide variations of normality, developmental assessment can never be a substitute for the neurological evaluation. The distinction between gross and fine motor function, recognised in all developmental scales, has no *neurological* validity. Both may be, and usually are, affected by any disorder of the central or peripheral nervous system. Nevertheless, the motor items found in these scales offer useful ways of eliciting and documenting motor behaviour.

Generalisation.   A normal child can use previous experience to solve unfamiliar problems. For example, he can recognise a hairbrush or a cup even though it may be of a different shape, size, colour and material from the one he has at home. The parents of a mentally handicapped infant often report that he recognises such objects, and are surprised that he obviously does not recognise the item presented to him in the clinic. Similarly, the parent may teach him to complete a difficult jigsaw, but when he is asked to complete a slightly different puzzle it becomes clear that he has not generalised this learning and that he has no idea of the significance of the task or of the picture on the puzzle. It is important to recognise this situation, since it is a common source of confusion among parents of mentally handicapped children.

Deviant behaviour.   Some children exhibit patterns of development and behaviour which are not merely delayed, but qualitatively abnormal. In extreme cases, the presenting complaint may be of deafness or blindness, yet they may well turn out to have mental handicap or a communication disorder. These children seem unable to relax or enjoy being cuddled and fail to adapt their body posture to the parent's body when held. Responses to sound may be inconsistent and localisation poor, so that one has difficulty in capturing the baby's attention by voice alone. Exaggerated movements and gestures are needed. His vocalisations may be abnormal in quality or lacking in modulation or variety, and he may show no appreciation of 'turn-taking'. Eye contact, which should be direct and intent, is often deficient in abnormal infants. The baby may seem to avoid eye contact, or look past the examiner, or he may simply have a vacant expression. In such cases, it is not possible to interpret the baby's 'feelings' with changing facial expression as one can do so easily in a normal child.

Any unusual features of the child's language should be noted. There may be bizarre grammatical constructions; difficulties in word selection; echolalia of whole sentences irrelevant to the situation; obsessional concentration on one theme; or inability to deal with abstract ideas. Any or all of these may suggest a diagnosis of language disorder or autism. Parents are often well aware of their child's abnormal behaviour patterns and if asked appropriate questions can provide some useful information.

Persistence of immature behaviour patterns.   It is normal for an infant to mouth objects, but this does not usually continue much beyond 18 months, except for comfort or in moments of boredom. Similarly, 'casting' or throwing objects away as soon as they have been inspected briefly, is common at 1 year, but by 18–21 months should have more or less disappeared, except perhaps as part of a temper tantrum. Shaking a toy is a normal response at 9–12 months, but also is unusual by 18 months, except with rattles and noise-makers where the behaviour is appropriate. The repeated occurrence of such activities in a child over the age of 2 is cause for concern.

A normal child of 2 and upwards can concentrate on an activity or toy and explore its possibilities methodically. Flitting rapidly from one toy to another, constant opening of cupboards or fiddling with taps and light switches in spite of reprimands are disturbing behaviour patterns that are often associated with mental handicap, autism or severe emotional disturbance. It may be tempting to describe these children as 'hyperactive' but this is a much abused term which is best avoided (p. 400).

PHYSICAL EXAMINATION

Physical examination is often deferred until the developmental assessment is completed. Measurement and charting of height, weight and head circumference, and a general examination should be routine. More comprehensive accounts of physical and neurological examination will be found elsewhere.[77,83]

Physical anomalies.   So many dysmorphic syndromes have now been described that no one can or should try to remember them all. In many cases, the features are so striking that they immediately prompt further enquiry, but this is not always the case. It is therefore essential to cultivate the habit of careful observation; all minor anomalies, however trivial, should be recorded and if their significance is uncertain, the excellent reference works by Smith,[84] McKusick[85] or Königsmark[86] should be consulted. These books should be available in every Child Development Centre. The fact that an anomaly is trivial in appearance does not always imply that its significance is also trivial; for example, ear pits may be a genetic marker of severe deafness. Some defects can occur either as isolated anomalies or as part of a more serious disorder, for example pes cavus may be the first sign of Friedreich's ataxia.

Single minor anomalies such as those listed in Table 4.6 occur in 14% of infants and are seldom significant. They are often also present in other

Table 4.6   Minor anomalies. (These may be indications of more serious malformations and suggest a prenatal origin for a child's problems.)

Large fontanelle (particularly posterior fontanelle) (suggestive of delay in ossification)
Third fontanelle
Wide spaced eyes (hypertelorism)
Slanted palpebral fissures
High palate and prominent lateral palatal ridges (suggestive of hypotonia with weakness of tongue)
Pre-auricular tags and pits
Prominent, slanted or low-set ears
Clinodactyly (curved finger)
Camptodactyly (bent finger)
Syndactyly
Hypoplasia of nails
Abnormal skin creases
Anomalous hair patterns
Dimples over bony points
Shawl scrotum (scrotum extends above and around base of penis)
Scalp defects

Variants not classed as anomalies
Capillary haemangiomata on head, face or lumbosacral area
Minor variations in folding of ear
Shallow sacral dimple
Syndactyly of 2nd and 3rd toes

---

family members. However, only 0·5% of babies have three or more minor defects and 90% of these have a major defect as well.[87] Thus, though they may not suffice to make an exact diagnosis, minor dysmorphic features are a useful pointer to a prenatal origin of a child's problems. There is also evidence that minor physical anomalies are associated with 'hyperactivity' (see p. 392). Abnormal dermatoglyphics (fingerprints) are found in some conditions but as a diagnostic aid have proved to be very disappointing.

Neurological examination.   Neurological assessment is intended to answer two questions: firstly, where is the lesion? and, secondly, what is the lesion? Traditionally, it is said that the first of these is more likely to be answered by the physical findings, and the second by the history. The principles underlying the adult neurological examination are applicable to children of all ages but with two additional complications: the young child's inability to cooperate and the need to distinguish between signs due to organic nervous system disease and those associated simply with immaturity. A distinction is sometimes made between hard and soft signs. Hard signs are those which would provide unequivocal evidence of damage to neurological pathways at any age. Soft signs are more subjective and their interpretation more variable.[88,89] They indicate immaturity rather than disease of the nervous system[90] and they largely disappear by the age of 9 or 10 years. The neurodevelopmental examination[91,92] is designed to demonstrate these signs (Appendix 4).

Preliminary observations.   Abnormalities of posture, poverty of movement, and unwanted movement patterns can be recognised simply by watching the infant. Hemiplegia, ataxia and athetosis are demonstrated by presenting him with a toy at arm's length. Building a tower with bricks is a poor test of intellect but a good way of demonstrating unwanted movements. If old enough, the child is asked to walk, run, climb on a chair, hop, walk heel-to-toe, and rise from the supine position (Fig. 4.4). These can all be done before the child is touched, and if they are made into a game subsequent examination is simplified. If these manoeuvres show no weakness or abnormality of posture, gait or fine hand function, the child is unlikely to have any major neuromuscular disease.

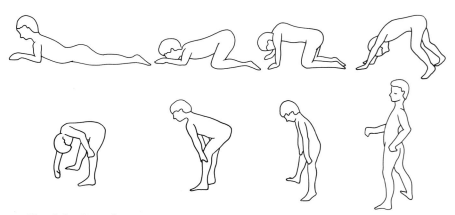

Fig. 4.4   Gower's manoeuvre. To rise from supine, the child turns into the prone position, and 'walks' the hands up the thighs. The manoeuvre indicates proximal muscle weakness. (Courtesy of Dubowitz[370].)

Cranial nerves.   Examination of the eyes, eye movements and visual fields is described on pp. 108–33, and hearing testing on pp. 83–107. Facial movements and asymmetry can be recognised when the child smiles or cries. In upper motor neurone lesions, the forehead movements are spared. Facial involvement and asymmetry may be seen in hemiplegia but surprisingly are often minimal or undetectable. In lower motor neurone lesions the whole face is involved. The asymmetric crying facies syndrome, which is due to congenital absence of the depressor anguli oris muscle (Fig. 4.5), is often mistaken for a lower motor neurone lesion. Bilateral facial weakness occurs in myopathies and in the Moebius syndrome. A brisk jaw-jerk (Fig. 4.6) is found when upper motor neurone lesions affect the

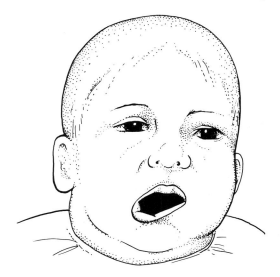

Fig. 4.5 Asymmetric crying facies syndrome.

Fig. 4.6 Eliciting the jaw-jerk.

facial and oral musculature. Neurological examination of facial sensation, tongue, lips and palate rarely reveals hard signs in developmental problems but soft signs are common.

Primitive reflexes.   Assessment of the primitive reflexes is usually included in the routine examination of infants under 6 months of age, though their value is limited. Prolonged persistence of these reflexes is seen in severe cerebral palsy, but is rarely if ever the first or main clue to the diagnosis. The age at which they disappear is very variable even in normal babies. Minor asymmetries of movement, posture and reflexes are often detectable in the first weeks of life. Some authors consider that these 'hemisyndromes' are often followed by developmental problems, but the physical signs are very subtle and errors are easily made.

Protective and postural reflexes.   The positive supporting reaction, and the sideways- and forwards-saving reactions appear around 6–8 months as weight-bearing and independent sitting become established. The feel of the baby as he attempts to correct his posture during the sideways-saving reaction should be noted. The forwards response is a sensitive way of demonstrating sluggish and asymmetric hand function in cerebral palsy. The Landau reaction may be abnormal in any neurological or muscular disorder which impairs muscle strength or control of the trunk postural reflexes. These reflexes are often difficult to demonstrate if the child is very tense, fearful or screaming and, in these situations, the hands may be fisted and the arms flexed, even in the normal baby.

Examination of the limbs.   The limbs are inspected for muscle bulk, texture, pseudohypertrophy, fasciculation, and equality of size and length. Asymmetry may be recognised by a need for different size shoes (half a size difference is common and is not necessarily significant), unequal wear, or unequal size of the feet and hands, often best demonstrated by comparing the finger or toe nails and if necessary by measuring limb circumference.

Tone can be assessed by flapping the limb, by flexing and extending at the elbow and knee, and abducting the hip, and by pronating or supinating the forearm while holding the child's hand as in a handshake. The characteristic catch of spasticity (the claspknife phenomenon) and continuous rigidity through the full range of movement (leadpipe rigidity) may be distinguished by these manoeuvres.

Power in the major muscle groups can be examined even in very young children with a little ingenuity. Observation of spontaneous activity is usually adequate to rule out gross weakness. Trying to take a toy away from the child, or tickling his feet while holding them still, may help to assess muscle power in toddlers and babies. By the age of 3, many children will try to cooperate with detailed muscle testing, but their limbs often need to be moved passively to demonstrate each action, rather than relying on verbal instructions. Little boys in particular will often cooperate better if the examination is made into a 'trial of strength' game.

Tendon reflexes can be difficult to evaluate in small children. Muscle tone and reflexes depend very much on the child's state of mind. These may appear to be markedly increased in a hungry crying baby or in a frightened young child. Even very brisk reflexes and a few beats of ankle clonus may be within normal limits. Babinski responses are unpredictable and of little clinical value before the second birthday. Even if one is extensor and the other flexor, this may be of no significance. Asymmetry of tendon jerks is more likely to be clinically important, but is usually only unequivocally present when other physical signs are also obvious. Complete areflexia is found in some neuromuscular disorders such as Werdnig–Hoffman disease, but tendon reflexes may be difficult to elicit in some normal babies. The presence of brisk reflexes does not rule out the possibility of muscle disease. In very severe spasticity or rigidity it may be difficult to elicit any reflexes at all.

Problems of movement control.   A mild symmetrical tremor is quite commonly seen in 2 and 3 year olds, but does not seem to cause much functional difficulty. In the absence of any other signs or complaints, a long-standing but non-progressive tremor in this age-group is unlikely to indicate either ataxic cerebral palsy or any other serious neurological disorder.

A broad-based gait with exaggerated balancing movements of the arms is normal when a child first begins to walk, but in an older child may be evidence of ataxia. In children old enough to cooperate, a poor performance on classical tests such as the 'finger nose test' and rapid alternating hand movements, is more commonly associated with 'clumsiness' (*see* below) than with cerebellar disease.

Excessive choreiform movement is best revealed by the manoeuvre shown in Fig. 4.7. It may be very marked, particularly in boys of around 4 or 5 years of age. The suggestion that choreiform movements have an association with reading disability is probably incorrect. These movements gradually resolve with increasing maturity and, unless the history suggests unusual severity, recent onset or progression, they should not be regarded as evidence of nervous system disease.

Sensation.   In young children, major sensory deficits may be delineated by watching for changing facial expression or withdrawal reactions when unpleasant stimuli such as tickling, pin prick or pinch are applied. Even with cooperative older children, sensory examination is tedious, and several attempts are usually needed. Situations where this is necessary are uncommon in general paediatric practice.

Children with hemiplegic cerebral palsy often have a deficiency in cortical sensation, best assessed by 'writing' shapes and letters on the palm,

Fig. 4.7 Demonstration of
choreiform movements.

(graphaesthesia), or by placing objects in the hand for tactile recognition
(stereognosis).

Orthopaedic examination.   The full length of the spine must be exposed to
reveal short neck syndromes, midline cutaneous anomalies, and scoliosis.
Limbs are inspected for deformities such as syndactyly. Rotational deformities of the lower limbs, and normal variations in posture of the feet are easily
mistaken for neurodevelopmental disorders (p. 59).

The neurodevelopmental examination.   This is designed to reveal the 'soft
signs' sometimes found in young children with learning disabilities,
clumsiness, etc. It is not a substitute for conventional neurological
examination. Soft signs are rarely indicative of neurological disease, neither
do they reliably predict educational progress. The main value of the
neurodevelopmental examination is in demonstrating to parents and
teachers the reasons why a child is having so much difficulty with certain
tasks, particularly those involving motor functions. Many versions of this
examination have been described.[88,91] Selected test items are listed in
Appendix 4.

Head circumference.   Measurement of the head circumference is always
included in the developmental examination but as small children dislike it,
this may be left until last. It is essential to record the *maximum*
occipito-frontal circumference (Fig. 4.8) and the measurement should be
taken twice to ensure accuracy. Paper and steel tapes do not stretch but

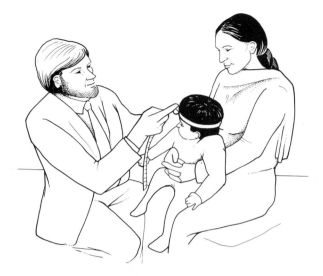

Fig. 4.8 Measuring the head circumference.

they have sharp edges, and cloth tapes lengthen with prolonged use. Fibreglass tapes are best. The measurement is meaningless unless it is plotted on a head circmference chart and is related to the child's height and weight. One commonly used chart includes only the 10th and 90th centiles rather than the 3rd and 97th, and this often leads to unnecessary concern (p. 212).

Conclusion

It is a relatively simple matter to record a child's responses to a variety of developmental tests and convert these to a developmental quotient or profile, but what the parents want is a diagnosis and an opinion as to whether the child really does have a problem that will significantly effect his and their lives. It must never be forgotten that assessment is only the means by which this question may be answered. It has no intrinsic therapeutic merits!

The success of the consultation depends not only on the accuracy of the assessment and diagnosis, but also on the way in which the results are presented to the parents. This topic is discussed in more detail in Chapter 6. When the child has been seen and assessed by those members of the multidisciplinary team whose skills are relevant to the problem, a further consultation is arranged so that the conclusions can be discussed with the parents. This may be arranged in a variety of ways. In some areas, with well developed services, the parents' biggest problem may be the proliferation of professionals who are all eager to help their child. It may sometimes be useful to hold a 'case conference' to plan management and to decide on the most appropriate professional involvement.[77] One person should be named as the 'key' worker and the contact for the parents in case of queries as recommended in the Warnock Report.

Follow-up consultations

When the early crises of diagnosis, adjustment and preschool placement are over, the need for regular attendance at the Child Development Centre should be reviewed. Some parents may prefer to be left to request appointments only when new problems arise. If a parent feels that regular visits to the paediatrician are not necessary, they may instead wish to keep in touch with some more accessible person, for example their GP, school doctor, or health visitor. Whatever arrangement is adopted, parents should always be able to write or telephone for a new appointment, if some new problem arises.

Telephone consultations are widely used in the United States, but are less popular in Britain. For some patients, particularly those on long-term medication, regular appointments are made, so that the child's notes are available; but the family is invited to telephone during the clinic time to report progress. By this means, one keeps in regular contact with the family, without requiring them to travel all the way to the hospital simply to report that a child has no new problems or is having no convulsions.

Chapter Five
Hearing Tests

Acoustics is the science of sound and its properties;[93] audiology is the clinical study of hearing and its disorders.[94,95] The developmental paediatrician cannot hope to acquire a complete understanding of these subjects without specialised training, but if he is to diagnose communication disorders, recognise children with hearing loss and undertake hearing tests himself as recommended in Chapter 4, some familiarity with the basic principles of acoustics is essential.

ACOUSTICS

Sounds can be divided into two main types—tones and noises. A *tone* is a periodic sound with a waveform showing regularly repeating patterns. A *noise* is a sound in which pressure changes are random and do not show repeated patterns. Noises may be continuous, like hissing steam, or discrete, like the crack of a rifle.

Most clinical hearing tests in paediatrics require the child to respond by some means either to speech, familiar non-speech sounds (for example rustling paper) or pure tones. In acoustic terms, the first two of these are complex sounds since they may contain many components, including tones, noises, or both, whereas a pure tone is a simple sound consisting of a single tone of fixed intensity, frequency and duration. The concepts of intensity and frequency and the units in which they are measured merit a detailed description, since these are the two parameters which are estimated in the technique of pure tone audiometry and they are also essential in describing the characteristics of complex sounds.

INTENSITY AND LOUDNESS

The intensity of a soundwave refers to the transmission of sound energy, measured either as a pressure or as a flow of power. Loudness refers to the

Intensity

0dB	Audibility threshold
20–30dB	Whisper
40–50dB	Background noise in average home/office
60dB	Conversational voice
75–80dB	Cocktail party voice
90–100dB	Discotheque
105–110dB	Shout
110–120dB	Low-flying aircraft
120–140dB	Jet engines, heavy machinery
140dB	Threshold of pain

Fig. 5.1 Sound intensities related to everyday experiences.

subjective experience of the intensity of a sound. The human ear is sensitive to a wide range of intensities: the loudest tolerable sound (the pain threshold) has about one hundred million million (10^{14}) times the intensity of the softest sound audible to the average person (the audibility threshold) (Fig. 5.1). Because this range is so wide, it is inconvenient to measure sound intensity in absolute units of pressure or power. It is customary to describe intensity as a ratio between the pressure of the sound and a reference pressure which corresponds approximately to the audibility threshold. The logarithm of this ratio is the number of bels. One bel is divided into ten decibels. Thus, 0 db is the audibility threshold; it does *not* mean the absence of sound. Some people have better than average hearing and their threshold might well be − 5 or even − 10 dB. An increase in intensity from 0 to 10 dB or from 30 to 40 dB represents a tenfold increase. Intensity decreases in inverse proportion to the square of the distance from the sound source.

FREQUENCY AND PITCH

Frequency of a soundwave is measured in cycles per second or Hertz (Hz). Pitch is the subjective impression of frequency. The human ear is able to perceive frequencies of between 16 Hz and 20 000 Hz (20 KHz). The very low frequencies may be perceived partly as vibration. The ear is not equally sensitive to all frequencies. The greatest sensitivity is in the middle of the frequency range, around 1000 Hz. Higher sound pressure levels are needed in the low and high frequencies to exceed the audibility threshold (Fig. 5.2).

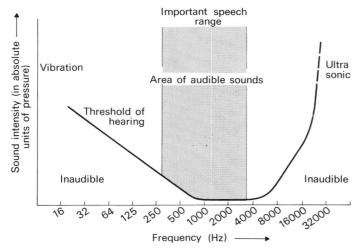

Fig. 5.2 Absolute threshold of hearing depends on frequency. (Redrawn from Newby[94] by permission of the publishers.)

However, at *each frequency*, 0 dB is taken as the normal person's threshold of hearing for that frequency, and audiometers are calibrated accordingly, so the clinician does not normally need to make any adjustments for the differences in absolute sensitivity.

Speech sounds

Speech contains both tones and noises.

Tones are generated in the larynx by the vibration of the vocal cords. The waveform contains a fundamental frequency, and many harmonics. The pharyngeal space and oral cavity act as resonators to reinforce certain harmonics which are determined by the position of the palate and tongue (Fig. 5.3).[95] The resultant sound can be analysed and displayed graphically to show the intensity of sound at each frequency. Vowel sounds, such as oo, aa, and ee, are tonal and their frequency spectrum contains peaks called formants, known respectively as F1, F2, etc. Each vowel sound has characteristic formants and it is the relationship of these to each other that the ear recognises, rather than their absolute frequency and intensity. Consonant sounds modify the shape of the vowel formants so that the ear can detect not only the noise of the consonant itself but also the subsequent effect on the vowel.

The laryngeal tone may be regarded as a high-energy, low-frequency carrier wave. The fundamental frequency is lower in men than in women and is around 100–200 Hz. There is no laryngeal tone in a whisper, which has a higher frequency spectrum and is therefore acoustically different from a quiet voice.

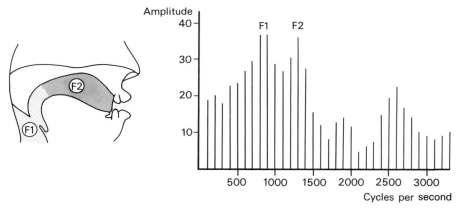

Fig. 5.3 Oral cavities: formants of 'a' as in 'Bard'. (From Whetnall & Fry[95] by permission.)

Noises. In speech, hissing noises such as the 's' sound (fricatives) and sudden noises like the 'b' sound (plosives) are superimposed on the basic laryngeal tone. Consonant sounds in general have a lower energy content but a higher frequency than vowels (Fig. 5.4). Analysis of connected speech shows that the intensity is not constant but varies over a 30–40 dB range (Fig. 5.5).

Most of the information content of speech is carried in the consonants. Even a modest degree of hearing loss impairs the perception of consonants and therefore causes difficulties in the comprehension of speech. A child who has a high-frequency hearing loss may seem to respond normally to speech and other sounds in infancy because of their low-frequency components, and his handicap may only be diagnosed when he is old enough for the impaired speech comprehension to be recognised. The diagnosis of high-frequency hearing loss will inevitably be overlooked unless hearing tests always include high-frequency sounds.

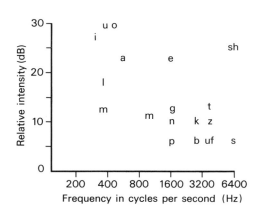

Fig. 5.4 Intensity and frequency of some common English sounds. (From Whetnall & Fry[95] by permission.)

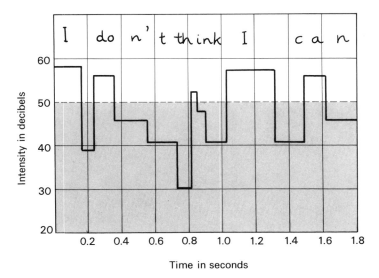

Fig. 5.5. Changes in mean intensity during the sentence 'I don't think I can'. Only the sounds whose intensity is above the shaded area would be audible to a child with an overall hearing loss of 50 dB. (Redrawn from Whetnall & Fry[95] by permission.)

Characteristics of non-speech sounds

Most everyday sounds, including those made by sound-producing toys and musical instruments, are complex mixtures of many components and harmonics.[96,97] Responses to such sounds are useful in detecting hearing loss in young children, although they give no information about the hearing loss at different frequencies. Sounds commonly used for hearing tests include the rustle of paper, the scraping of a spoon on a cup, bells, musical boxes, rattles and drums. Two rattles, the Manchester and Nuffield,

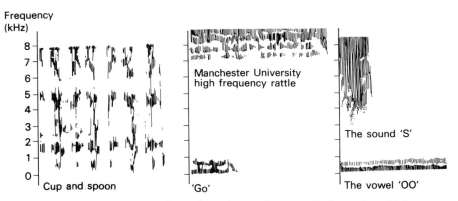

Fig. 5.6 Frequency spectrum of sounds used to test hearing. (Redrawn from Nolan and Tucker[97] by permission.)

are specially designed to produce only high-frequency sound, but with these exceptions all sound-making toys must be assumed to produce mixed frequencies, however high-pitched they may sound to the listener (Fig. 5.6).

Measurement of intensity

Subjective estimates of sound intensity are very unreliable even when made by an experienced observer. It is essential to measure intensity of the speech and other sounds used in audiological testing of young children by using a sound-level meter (Fig. 5.7). This instrument measures sound pressure

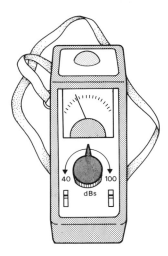

Fig. 5.7 A sound-level meter.

levels, usually in the range between 40 and 100 dB. The calibration which is known as the dBA scale is designed to take account of the fact that the sensitivity of the ear varies according to the frequency of the sound.

Sound-level meters do not respond instantaneously to sound and therefore significantly underestimate the intensity of sounds whose duration is very brief, for example 'impact' sounds like the clink when a spoon is tapped against a cup, a bell, and some musical boxes.

Sound intensity falls off with the square of the distance, so when the intensity of test sounds is checked, the meter must be placed at the same distance from the source as was the child during the test. It should also be in the same position since, even in the best sound-proofed room, there may be variations in sound intensity at different points.

HEARING LOSS

A person with impaired hearing will only hear sound when the intensity is raised beyond the normal audibility threshold. The sound intensity required to reach the threshold of the impaired ear is the threshold hearing level or *hearing loss* for that ear. Thus a person who cannot hear any sound quieter than 30 dB has 30 dB hearing loss. *Sensation level* is the intensity of a sound above the threshold of the individual observer. For example, a person with 30 dB hearing loss hears a sound of 60 dB intensity at a sensation level of 30 dB.

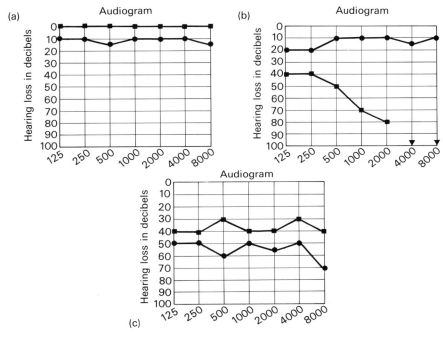

Fig. 5.8   Examples of audiograms. **a** Normal audiogram (left ear) and insignificant hearing loss (right ear); **b** minimal hearing loss in right ear, severe high-frequency loss in left ear; **c** bilateral hearing loss, averaging 40 dB in left ear and 50 dB in right ear. ● Right ear, ■ Left ear.

The adult or older child will cooperate in establishing his threshold by means of an audiometer, which generates pure tones, each having a single fixed frequency and known intensity. The sounds are delivered via headphones to exclude extraneous noise and this technique is called pure tone audiometry. The results are plotted graphically, as an audiogram. At each frequency, one records the quietest sound which the subject can hear. By definition the average normal person can hear a sound of 0 dB intensity at each frequency. The normal audiogram and audiograms of two subjects with hearing loss are shown in Fig. 5.8.

Hearing tests in preschool children

Until the age of 3 or 4 years, a child cannot be expected to cooperate in determining his threshold of hearing by pure tone audiometry, and it is therefore not usually possible to establish the exact extent of a hearing loss. Nevertheless, a reasonably accurate estimate of hearing can be made by a variety of techniques using human voice and other familiar sounds. The physical characteristics of these must be understood before they can safely be used to test hearing.

Hearing tests in this age group are performed in 'free field', i.e. without headphones. The child indicates that he has heard the sound by a variety of behavioural responses, such as turning to locate the sound or selecting the named toy. The object is to determine, and to measure on a sound level meter, the quietest sound level at which an unequivocal response can be obtained. This level exceeds the threshold of hearing by a variable amount, which depends on the testing conditions and developmental maturity of the child. It is probable that the child's previous auditory experiences are also important. Psychosocial deprivation or prolonged exposure to loud meaningless sound may raise the sensation level needed to obtain a response.

It is usual to assume that, if hearing responses can be obtained at levels of 30–35 dB, there is unlikely to be a hearing loss of major clinical significance, though middle-ear disease may still be present. If responses are only obtainable at 40–45 dB or above, a hearing loss must be suspected.

BACKGROUND NOISE

When free field tests are performed no response can be expected from the child if the test sounds are obscured by background noise. The child can only be assumed to have normal or near-normal hearing if he responds to speech or sounds of 30–35 dB intensity, but in most clinics and general practice premises, background noise levels are much higher than this, and there is then an almost irresistible temptation to raise the intensity of the test sounds to 50 db or more. Unfortunately, the child may then respond at this level, yet still have a significant hearing problem. The diagnosis of hearing loss is too important for casual testing in bad conditions and a quiet room is essential.

PRACTICAL ASPECTS OF HEARING TESTS

The purpose of the diagnostic hearing tests described below is to establish the presence, severity, significance and probable location of a child's hearing loss.[98,99] Diagnostic tests should not be confused with the screening tests which are used in developmental surveillance and which are intended only to separate children into two categories: the normally hearing and those with possible hearing loss. This topic is discussed separately on p. 106.

THE HISTORY

The reason for the consultation should be established. Children with hearing loss usually present with one of the following: parental suspicion, family history of deafness, delayed speech development, failed screening test, symptoms of middle-ear disease, or behaviour disturbance. The parents are asked about family history of hearing loss and, if this is positive, further details must be obtained if possible. Minor illnesses in pregnancy, perinatal problems, and a history of viral illness, meningitis or head injury may all be relevant.

Whatever the age of the child, the most valuable of all hearing tests is to ask the parents, 'What do you think about his hearing?' *If the parents think that their child has a hearing defect they are right until proved otherwise.* Sometimes their diagnosis is incorrect; for example, mental retardation may be the correct explanation of their observations, but when the parents suspect a hearing loss there is usually something wrong with the child. Conversely, if they are sure that he can hear, he is most unlikely to have a severe hearing loss, though the parents may easily overlook a mild or high-frequency impairment. The lack of external stigmata of hearing defects and the child's ability to make sense of visual clues and behave in a socially normal fashion, together deceive many parents and doctors into doubting that the child has a hearing problem.

The next question should be, '*Why* do you think he can/cannot hear?'. The parents' observations should be noted in detail; if they are hesitant, questions such as those listed in Table 5.1 may be used to prompt them.

Table 5.1   Useful questions about hearing.

What do *you* think about his hearing?
Why do you think he can/cannot hear?
  e.g. listens and turns to voices
  wakes when bedroom door opens
  hears dog bark, father's keys in lock, etc.
  hears rustling of sweet or biscuit paper
  responds to name
  carries out instructions when called from another room
  hears loud noises, such as aircraft, sirens, etc.
  turns TV up loud
Can he tell where a sound is coming from?
Does he respond better if you raise your voice?
Does he try to see your face when you speak to him?
Does he watch your lips when you speak?
Does he say 'eh', 'what' or 'pardon' frequently?
Does he sometimes seem to deliberately ignore you?
Does his hearing seem to vary from day to day?

Beyond infancy, assessment of the child's comprehension of spoken language also provides much information about hearing (*see also* p. 69). If the child has age-appropriate comprehension, without the aid of raised voice level, lip reading or gestural clues such as pointing, he is unlikely to have any serious hearing problem.

Time spent on a detailed history of the child's hearing behaviour is never wasted, but if one senses that the child will be responsive to conversational advances and that the hearing test will be straightforward, the history may reasonably be curtailed. On the other hand, if the child seems disturbed, mentally handicapped, electively mute, autistic or unusually shy, as much information as possible should be obtained from the parents before embarking on clinical testing.

Techniques of hearing testing

THE BLINK REFLEX

This is also known as the acoustico-palpebral reflex (APR). The blink is produced by a sudden loud noise. A positive response to a noise of 80–90 dB is good evidence that the child has considerable hearing, but the reflex is influenced by too many variables to be useful in establishing the hearing level.

FREE FIELD TESTS

Free field tests are capable of producing an estimate of hearing loss which correlates remarkably well with the results obtained when the child is old enough to cooperate with audiometric testing. The apparent simplicity of the equipment and techniques used in free field testing disturb many parents and they may feel that the results should be confirmed with 'proper' tests using more sophisticated equipment. They can best be reassurred that the findings are valid by an explanation of the principles underlying free field testing.

DISTRACTION TESTS

These tests rely on changes in behaviour and activity in response to a sound whose source is outside the child's visual field.[100] From the moment of birth, an infant can hear and sound will elicit behavioural changes. In the early months of life the responses are often transient and fragmentary. Five factors influence the infant's response to a distraction test. The first of these is of course the existence of a hearing loss. The other four are: (1) the infant's attention at the moment of testing; (2) development of the ability to localise sound; (3) the emergence of object permanence; and (4) the level of motor development. A common difficulty in distraction testing is to decide whether poor responses are due to a hearing loss, or to these developmental factors.

1   In the early weeks of life, testing is only possible when the baby is in a relaxed, alert state which may be of very brief duration. By 6 months of age, the baby is likely to be alert and responsive for longer periods, but testing may be impossible if he is tired, hungry or unwell. Responses to sound may be difficult to demonstrate in the baby who is very sociable and visually alert to his surroundings, or in the retarded baby who cannot attend consistently to either auditory or visual stimuli.

2   The ability to localise sound can sometimes be demonstrated even in the first weeks of life, by a gradual head turn towards human voice. Localisation becomes increasingly accurate during the first year. By 8 months the baby can turn his gaze directly and precisely to a sound source in any position, except immediately above or behind his head. This behaviour is not observed in the visually handicapped (p. 297). A baby who can hear the sound, but cannot turn to localise it because of visual or motor handicap, developmental immaturity or asymmetric hearing difficulty, may respond in other ways; for example, by cessation of motor activity or vocalisation, or widening of the palpebral fissure. These responses are genuine indicators of hearing but are more easily misinterpreted than a head turn.

3   As the concepts of object and person permanence develop, the baby becomes increasingly aware of the tester's presence behind him (Fig. 5.9)

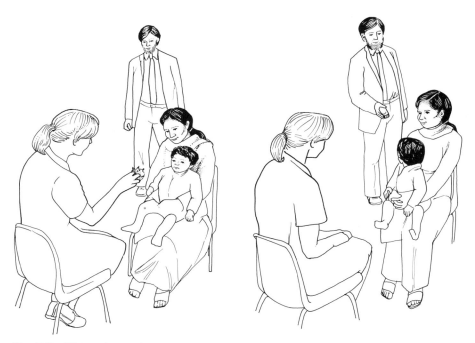

Fig. 5.9   Distraction testing.

and he may decide to ignore further stimuli; or else he regards the whole performance as a game, and tries to out-guess the tester by turning before the sound stimulus is presented. From about 15 months onwards, the child is increasingly likely to become so engrossed in play that he may ignore even very loud sounds, making distraction testing difficult.

4 Lastly, motor competence and localisation ability normally develop in parallel. The ability to localise a sound depends not only on auditory processing but also on sitting balance, head posture and the control of eye movements. Since most babies have adequate localising and motor abilities by 8 or 9 months of age, but do not yet have a sophisticated concept of object permanence, this is regarded as the ideal age for distraction testing; however, the techniques can be applied throughout infancy or indeed at any age and are particularly useful in testing mentally handicapped children.

Technique.   The participants are arranged as shown in Fig. 5.9. The aim is to produce head-turning responses to sound, since these are more reliable than subtle activity changes. False-positive head-turn responses can easily be produced, by intrusion into the baby's visual field (Fig. 5.10), shadows, a draught created by shaking a noise-making toy, or even perfume or aftershave. The distractor is in the best position to recognise these artefacts. The skill of the distractor is crucial. The baby's visual attention is built up by means of interesting toys, amusing facial expressions, talking, or any other available means.[101] This stimulation is then abruptly withdrawn, creating a sudden 'sensory vacuum'. The baby looks surprised at the sudden cessation of entertainment, and waits tensely for its restoration. This tension reaches

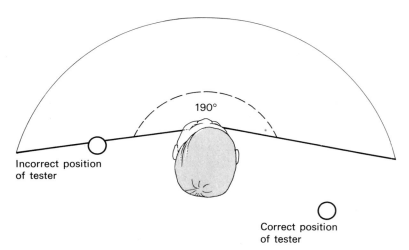

Fig. 5.10   Visual fields. Because they extend beyond 180°, it is easy to produce false-positive turning responses due to vision rather than hearing.

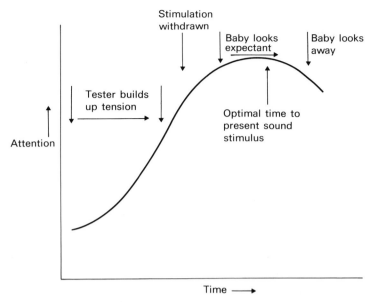

Fig. 5.11 Distraction testing; timing is crucial. (Redrawn from Taylor[101] by permission.)

a plateau, and the tester must then present the sound stimulus, before the baby begins to look around for new interests (Fig. 5.11). When he turns to look for the sound source, he is immediately rewarded with brief praise. The tester then turns away and the distractor regains the baby's attention. A useful refinement in difficult cases is the 'double act'. The distractor gains the baby's attention with loud sounds made by a noise-making toy. The tester then uses an identical toy but produces a much quieter test sound. Because the baby's attention is already tuned to this particular sound spectrum, the technique often produces a response where others have failed.

It is customary to present test sounds on each side, but free field testing does not yield reliable estimates of hearing in the individual ears unless one is occluded; this is seldom tolerated by young children. There is a 'head-baffle' effect, of around 10–15 dB* (Fig. 5.12). Consider a child with no hearing in the left ear but normal hearing in the right. He responds to a sound presented on the right at 35 dB, but because of the baffle effect, he responds at 45–50 dB when the sound is presented on the left. Having heard the sound with his right ear, he initially searches for the sound source on the right. Identical results would be obtained with a hearing loss of only 20 or 30 dB in the left ear. Thus, incorrect localisation is very suggestive of an

* The exact figure is frequency-dependent.

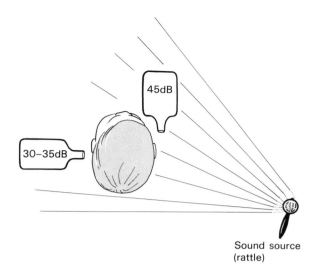

Fig. 5.12   The head-baffle
effect.

Sound source
(rattle)

asymmetric hearing loss, but gives no indication of its severity in the worse
ear. The value of distraction tests is that they indicate the level of functional
hearing and, in a hearing-impaired child, may show which is the better ear.

Testing should begin with mixed frequency, interesting sounds. If the
infant is responsive and the history does not suggest any hearing loss, the
intensity of these should be at minimal levels, i.e. 30–35 dB. When
responses are not easily obtained, a variety of louder sounds may be used to
gain the baby's interest. The intensity is then progressively reduced until
responses become inconsistent or cease. The test is then repeated with
high-frequency sounds, such as an 'S' sound, a Nuffield rattle shaken gently
about 45 cm from the ear, or a Manchester rattle rotated about 90 cm from
the ear. Lastly, low-frequency sounds are used, for example 'ooh' or 'baba'.
A portable free field audiometer can be used in distraction testing, but
because pure tones are uninteresting and are hard to localise, a level of 45
dB may be needed to obtain responses. Audiometers producing warble tones
or other complex sounds are more satisfactory for this purpose.

Some audiology rooms are equipped with loudspeakers through which
a variety of electronically controlled signals can be played, in a sophisticated
version of distraction testing.[102]

COOPERATIVE TESTING

Hearing tests which require the cooperation of the child are occasionally
possible in children as young as 18 months; others are unable to perform
these tasks reliably until the age of $2\frac{1}{2}$ or even 3. Cooperative tests are
themselves a valuable means of general developmental assessment. The
tests fall into two groups: those that make use of the child's ability to

discriminate speech, and those that demand a response to other sounds. If possible, one test of each type should be performed. The history and preliminary distraction tests indicate whether a major hearing loss is likely. Errors are commonly made because the tester begins with the assumption that the child can hear his instructions and test sounds. To the hearing-impaired child, the tasks required of him are meaningless, but he tries to cooperate making full use of any visual and situational clues and may well succeed in misleading the tester. The only safe approach is to begin with a 'null hypothesis' that the child has no hearing. The estimate of his hearing threshold is then progressively revised as evidence is collected from the history and examination.

Hearing can sometimes be assessed for each ear separately by occluding one ear, but many children will not tolerate this. Unless this can be done, there is very little value in attempting to test the ears separately by presenting signals from either side.

Cooperative tests can often be completed even if the child is physically handicapped. He can respond by eye pointing, or by any motor response which is under his command. Satisfactory results may also be obtained in the mentally handicapped, provided that the mental age is about $2\frac{1}{2}$ years or more.

Speech tests.   It is not possible to use a standardised procedure for speech testing in very young children and the results cannot be directly compared with those obtained by methods appropriate for older children and adults.[103] Both the choice of words and the structure of the test depend on the child's vocabulary and behaviour. The test materials can be pictures or toys. Pictures are preferable; toys are useful to gain attention and overcome shyness in the less mature child, but he may then become too involved in play to cooperate with the test. A list of suitable items is given in Appendix 7; usually 6–12 items are used for any one test.

The child should preferably be seated at a table (Fig. 5.13) but if he prefers he can sit on his mother's lap or on the floor, or even under the table! Each object or picture is shown in turn. The parent is asked to indicate if an unfamiliar item is presented. Neither tester nor parent should ask the child to name the items himself: he is *told* the name of each item in a loud clear voice. Often, he will then start to name them himself, but for the purposes of the hearing test it does not matter if he remains silent throughout. The tester then says, 'Show me the. . . .'. Once the child understands the task, the tester reduces his voice intensity and covers his mouth with a hand or card, so that the child cannot lip-read. In a quiet room, with the tester and the child separated by a small table, the child should be able to correctly identify the toys or pictures with the tester's voice at minimal intensity, around 30–40 dB. Voice intensity may be further reduced by moving 8–10 feet away from the child, but the loss of rapport seldom justifies the small gain in sensitivity of the test.

Fig. 5.13 A hearing test using picture identification.

Certain behaviour patterns provide useful preliminary clues to the presence of a hearing loss. The child may keep looking at the tester's face with a puzzled expression, instantly replaced by enlightenment when the word is repeated at higher intensity. He may ignore the tester and play when he cannot hear him, or become tearful and retreat to the parent. He may make a few errors when the items are not sufficiently familiar but this can usually be distinguished from errors due to hearing difficulty. The child with a hearing loss may also be very alert to visual clues, and the tester must be careful not to stare at the item he is about to name. When the voice intensity is raised, the child often repeats the word after the tester, yet does not respond by selecting the correct item. It can sometimes be established that the difficulty lies with the hearing, rather than with the child's understanding of the task, by asking for items using mime instead of words. The normally intelligent but hearing-impaired child will respond instantly to such signals.

Conditioning tests.   In these tests, the child is asked to make a specific response each time he hears a sound.[103] The sound stimulus may be pure tones, warbled tones or narrow band noise, produced by a free-field audiometer (Fig. 5.14), or speech sounds of known frequency composition such as 'go' (low frequency) and 's' (high frequency). The response may involve placing a brick in a basket, a marble in a pot, or any other simple response which the child's play and the tester's ingenuity may suggest.

The child is gently guided through the response required of him, using as stimulus either a loud 'Go' or the loudest tone on the audiometer, at a frequency of 1 KHz. When it is certain that he is hearing this loud sound, he is given generous encouragement for each correct response, however tentative. As he gains confidence the tester gives less and less assistance until the child has mastered the game. He then reduces the intensity of the sound stimulus by small increments, usually of 10 dB, until a point is reached where the child will no longer respond.

Fig. 5.14   Using the free-field audiometer.

It is essential to avoid visual clues, for example, the movement of a tendon in the arm when pressing the button or switch of the audiometer, a raise of the eyebrows, a nod of the head, or a glance at the child (*see* Fig. 5.14). The presentation of the stimuli must be at irregular and random intervals, but not so far apart that the child gets bored. If attention is lost, sound intensity is immediately raised again. Positive reinforcement techniques (p. 156) using rewards such as quartered Smarties are sometimes useful in gaining the cooperation of a reluctant child.

Initially the aim is to obtain a reliable response at 35 dB at each frequency, but in good testing conditions many children will respond at 25 dB. If it can be shown unequivocally that the child hears 35 dB at all frequencies, it can be assumed that he has adequate hearing to acquire speech. Nevertheless, with this type of testing the threshold of hearing is not measured and exact comparisons with pure tone audiometry results are not possible. The child could still have a mild hearing loss and respond at 35 dB, and it is common to find children with conductive hearing loss who respond hesitantly to the 35 dB sound, but only become confident at 45 dB. This behaviour is characteristic of a modest conductive hearing loss which may nevertheless be clinically significant.

PURE TONE AUDIOMETRY

Pure tone audiometry (PTA) using headphones is the standard audiometric technique for children of 5 years and upwards.[94] Below this age, a child will often refuse to wear the headset, but may nevertheless cooperate if the earphone is held to his ear by the parent (Fig. 5.15). By this means a PTA may sometimes be obtained in children under the age of 3 years. With preschool children a PTA should only be attempted when some information has been obtained by the methods described above and one has established some rapport with the child. Usually, the child is asked to make a similar response using headphones as with the free-field test.

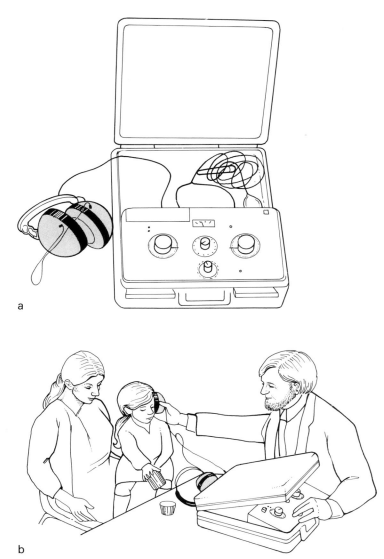

Fig. 5.15   **a** An audiometer; **b** introducing a young child to pure-tone audiometry.

It is usually best to start with an easily audible tone at 1 KHz; the signal intensity is reduced by 10 dB increments until the child fails to respond and is then increased by 5 dB until the threshold is 'bracketed'. As attention span may be short, it is sometimes preferable to obtain readings at only three frequencies initially (500, 1 K and 4 K), then to test the opposite side. Pure tone audiometry is subject to the same potential errors as free field audiometry, particularly a rhythmic presentation of signals, and unintentional visual or facial clues by the tester or some other person in the room. Excessively anxious children sometimes will not admit to hearing a sound until it is very loud, and bizarre and improbable audiograms may then be obtained.

Air and bone conduction.   Sound is normally transmitted most efficiently to the middle ear and cochlea by air conduction, but if there is middle-ear dysfunction, sound transmission to the cochlea via bone may be more efficient. This is the basis for the classical tuning fork tests of Rinne and Weber, but these are difficult to perform and interpret in preschool children.

When there is a conductive hearing loss, bone conduction thresholds are significantly better than air conduction and there is said to be an air–bone gap (Fig. 5.16). Bone conduction is tested by placing the sound source on the mastoid process, behind the pinna. When this is done, sound is transmitted with almost equal efficiency via bone to the test ear and to the opposite ear. The result of a bone conduction test is therefore the threshold of the better ear, not necessarily the side under test.

With air conduction tests via headphones, transmission of sounds to the ear opposite the one being tested is less efficient and the intensity falls by 40–50 dB. However, if the ear under test is severely deaf, the *opposite* ear will start to hear the tone at 40–50 dB, and the subject will respond.

The technique of masking is used to overcome these problems. This involves presenting continuous white noise or a narrow band noise to the opposite ear to the one under test, thereby preventing the subject from using the hearing in the masked ear. A true measure of hearing in the test ear can then be obtained. Masking is needed whenever there is a substantial difference in air conduction thresholds between the two ears and should be used whenever possible for bone conduction tests.

Many children will perform a bone conduction test, with the examiner holding the vibrator against the mastoid (Fig. 5.17) even though they may

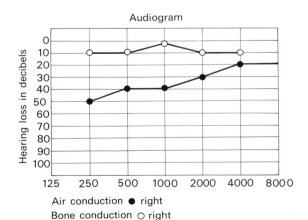

Air conduction ● right
Bone conduction ○ right

Fig. 5.16   The air-bone gap in conductive hearing loss.

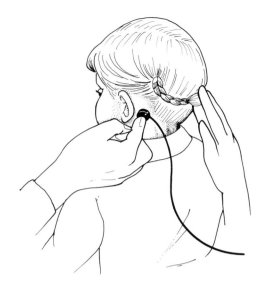

Fig. 5.17 Bone conduction can be tested even in young children.

be too young to cope with masking. In spite of the problem outlined above, this is useful, particularly when combined with otoscopy and impedance testing; if free field testing reveals a hearing loss and secretory otitis is suspected, normal bone conduction responses confirm that a conductive loss is present. Without masking, however, it is impossible to rule out the remote possibility that there is a conductive loss on one side and a sensorineural loss on the other, or to distinguish between conductive losses of differing severity on the two sides.

The vibrator used in bone conduction testing may produce sufficient vibration to elicit a tactile response at higher intensities, particularly with

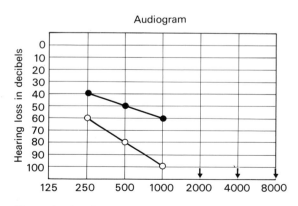

Fig. 5.18 A spurious air–bone gap, caused by tactile response to the bone conduction test.

Air conduction ○ = left
Bone conduction ● = left

low frequencies. This may lead to the incorrect diagnosis of an air–bone gap in children with a severe sensorineural hearing loss (Fig. 5.18). Another problem is that, because of anatomical variations, bone conduction thresholds vary between subjects by 10–15 dB, so that if the bone conduction is better than air conduction threshold by this amount, it does not necessarily indicate an air–bone gap.

Most children old enough to cooperate with masking will be tested by, or with the assistance of, an audiometrician who is likely to have more experience of this technique than the developmental paediatrician. For this reason, details of masking technique are omitted here and should be obtained from standard audiological texts.

SPEECH TESTS—5 YEARS AND UPWARDS

In the older child and adult, speech audiometry is an accurate and sophisticated technique. Speech tests using standard word lists or sentences can be used both as a primary diagnostic aid, and also as a means of assessing the effectiveness of amplification in children using hearing aids. Presentation may be via an audiometer, or in free field, with the intensity monitored by a sound-level meter. Another useful, though less precise, measure is the distance at which the subject can understand words and sentences spoken in an ordinary conversational voice.

ELECTRICAL RESPONSE AUDIOMETRY

These 'objective' methods of measuring hearing may be invaluable where there is serious doubt about a child's responses, for example in autism, mental retardation, and some cases of aphasia.[103] A few milliseconds after a sound reaches the ear, action potentials are propagated along the auditory pathways to the brainstem and cortex. It is possible to detect these potentials and use them to find a patient's threshold of hearing. They may also add information about the site of the lesion.

Electrocochleography (ECoG). A needle electrode is inserted through the tympanic membrane, on to the promontory of the middle ear, and the action potentials produced by the cochlea are recorded. The stimulus is normally a train of clicks. A general anaesthetic is needed in children for this technique.

Brainstem-evoked response (BSER). The BSER is recorded from three surface electrodes (usually scalp, earlobe and forehead). It represents transmission of the auditory signal from the cochlea to the cortex. The complex waveform is demonstrated by computer analysis of the EEG as a number of peaks, which may correspond to brainstem nuclei in the auditory pathway. The BSER can be recorded with the child awake, asleep or under anaesthetic.

Crossed acoustic reflex. This reflex is also known as the post-auricular myogenic response.[104] It relies on the contraction in response to sound of the post-auricular muscle, and is measured via surface electrodes. The technique is less sensitive than the other tests but does not require sedation. The apparatus is now available in a simplified form which could be used for screening purposes (*but see* p. 181).

Both ECoG and BSER are invaluable and rapidly advancing techniques, which can be of great help in solving difficult problems, but they are not infallible. These investigations will generally only be requested, and the results interpreted, with the guidance of a paediatric audiologist.

IMPEDANCE

The measurement of impedance gives an objective assessment of the mobility of the tympanic membrane and ossicular chain.[105,106] The middle ear presents some resistance to vibratory motion, in response to a sound stimulus. Some of the acoustical energy is accepted by the middle ear and the remainder is reflected back into the external canal. The ratio of acceptance to reflection is dependent on the middle-ear resistance, which in turn is affected by the presence of fluid or other abnormalities. An ear which absorbs a large amount of sound energy has low impedance. The inverse of this measure is compliance.

The measurement is made via a probe inserted in the external ear canal to form an airtight cavity (Fig. 5.19). The probe contains a sound source

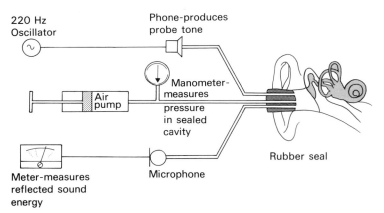

Fig. 5.19 Measurement of acoustic impedance. A probe tip with three apertures is sealed in the external meatus with a rubber cuff. An oscillator and phone deliver the 'probe' tone into the meatus and a microphone monitors the sound level. An air pump is used to place varying loads on the tympanic membrane. (Courtesy of Fria[106].)

and a microphone to measure reflected sound energy. An air pump attached via a tube to the probe is used to vary the pressure in the ear canal. Under normal conditions, compliance is maximal when the pressures on either side of the ear drum are equal. Thus, if the pressure in the middle ear is below atmospheric, compliance will be greatest when external canal pressure is correspondingly reduced.

The results are plotted as a graph of compliance against external canal pressure. In the normal ear, compliance is maximum at atmospheric pressure (Fig. 5.20, type A). The type B curve shows low compliance at all pressures, with no peak, and is strong evidence of secretory otitis media. The type C curve implies negative pressure in the middle ear, suggestive of eustachian tube dysfunction. This curve is sometimes, but not always, associated with fluid in the middle ear.

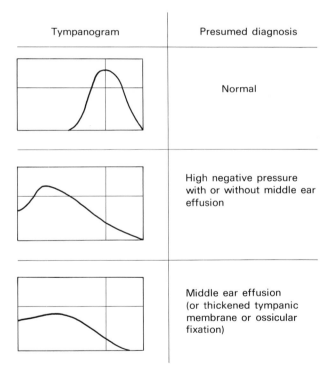

Tympanogram	Presumed diagnosis
	Normal
	High negative pressure with or without middle ear effusion
	Middle ear effusion (or thickened tympanic membrane or ossicular fixation)

Fig. 5.20 Impedance measurement. Interpretation of the three commonest tympanogram curves.

The stapedial muscle contracts reflexly in response to loud sound, reducing the compliance of the middle ear. The reflex can be observed and measured with the impedance meter. The pure tone sound stimulus can be presented to the ear ipsilateral or contralateral to the probe ear. The reflex threshold is at a sensation level of 70–90 dB in the normal ear. An absent reflex may indicate either conductive impairment in the probe ear, or reduced hearing level (from any cause) in the stimulated ear. These reflexes can be useful indicators that hearing is present but they may be reduced or abolished even by minimal middle-ear pathology. This problem limits the value of a useful additional technique of measuring hearing loss.

SCREENING FOR HEARING DEFECTS

Sensorineural hearing loss of 50 dB or worse occurs in approximately 1 per 1000 births. In a substantial proportion of these babies, deafness is first suspected by the parents. In the EEC Survey, this often happened in the first year of life,[107] but delays of a year or more before diagnosis were commonplace. When parents do not recognise the problem, it is likely that the hearing loss is less severe, unilateral, or predominantly affects the high frequencies. Careful testing is essential if these are to be detected by screening.

Neonatal screening using the 'auditory response cradle' is now possible and from the logistic point of view is ideal, since virtually all babies are born in hospital and the total population can be screened. Unfortunately, there is concern both about the specificity and sensitivity, and also the follow-up of cases diagnosed so early; but neonatal screening may be useful for high risk babies (i.e. special care admissions, familial deafness, etc).[108]

Distraction and cooperative testing can be used for screening purposes by doctors or health visitors.[109] The optimum age for a distraction test is about 8–9 months. If the infant fails to respond at minimal levels (30–35 dB) on two consecutive occasions, he is deemed to have failed and requires a diagnostic hearing assessment. For older children, cooperative speech tests are generally employed. The Stycar pictures are widely available but are too small and somewhat dated, and the materials suggested in this chapter are more convenient.

Whereas most other developmental screening tests are inevitably non-specific however expertly they are performed, the techniques of hearing tests described in this chapter are potentially specific and sensitive. Unfortunately they are often badly performed, in noisy conditions, with test sounds that are too loud, and are then useless. With distraction testing, better results are undoubtedly obtained when two people work regularly together. If training and supervision are adequate, health visitors can maintain very high standards of screening testing, and not only sensorineural losses but also mild conductive defects can be detected. As part of the screening process it is vital that the parents are asked their opinion about the child's hearing. The use of a simple checklist (Appendix 8) by parents facilitates early detection.[457]

All school entrants undergo a screening test of hearing, known as the Sweep test. This is a simplified pure tone audiogram performed at a fixed intensity, usually 20–25 dB, though sometimes the level is fixed at 30 dB to reduce false positives caused by inattention or background noise. Children who fail have a complete audiogram and, if necessary, are then referred for detailed assessment in the audiology clinic. A failure rate of between 5 and 10% is expected in school audiometric testing; about half of these children have normal hearing on retest. Of the remainder, most have secretory otitis media. Although bilateral sensorineural hearing loss has usually been detected by school age, new cases are still found, at least in inner city areas among the socially deprived, and in recent immigrants. Severe unilateral hearing loss is also detected, often for the first time, since free-field audiometry rarely identifies this. Although treatment is rarely possible or necessary, the child's teacher should be aware of this disability.

Conductive hearing loss due to secretory otitis media is by far the commonest finding in children who have failed screening tests of hearing at any age. There is still very little reliable data on the significance or natural history of this condition, or the indications for, and long term effectiveness of, surgery (p. 286). Also, unlike other developmental problems, secretory otitis media is an intermittent disorder and a single screening test only identifies those children affected at the time of testing, but it is not established whether, or how often, screening ought to be repeated.

Some authorities have suggested that impedance measurements might be more efficient than audiometry for screening school children,[110] but this view assumes that secretory otitis media is the disorder for which screening is needed, rather than the hearing loss which it may cause. The 'Acship' committee[98] observed that screening by impedance audiometry would reveal many cases of mild and often transient secretory otitis which would overload ENT and audiology clinics and they felt that further research is needed before impedance screening could be recommended.

Chapter Six
Vision Tests

Serious visual handicap is rare, but because it is often caused by obvious abnormalities of the globe, and is accompanied by abnormal visual behaviour, recognition of the handicap does not usually present great difficulties. In contrast, minor visual defects, in particular squints, amblyopia and refractive errors, are not always obvious even to the most observant parent, and a deliberate search for these is often needed. Nevertheless, they are among the commonest defects found in otherwise normal children,[111] while up to 50% of handicapped children may have some visual defect.[112]

The paediatrician does not need a detailed knowledge of ophthalmology, but should understand the principles underlying the diagnosis of the commoner visual defects and handicaps in childhood and the limitations of standard methods of ophthalmic examination.[113,114]

Early development of vision

Animal experiments have advanced our understanding of the neurophysiology of vision and its early development. Kittens temporarily deprived of vision do not develop normal visual acuity since the cortical neurones responsible for vision do not acquire the ability to discriminate and process the stimuli which reach them from the retina.[116] It has been suggested that the cat's visual system is programmed to perform as a 'feature detector' to recognise significant objects against the background, but for this system to develop normally, adequate visual stimuli must be available during the 'critical period' of neuronal maturation. The critical period is brief and well defined in the kitten. Human visual development is probably equally dependent on visual stimuli; the timing and duration of the critical period is not yet certain, but is thought to be from birth up to about 18 months of age.

The immediate practical application of these discoveries is in the management of cataract and squint, as discussed below.[117]

VISUAL ACUITY (VA)

This is a measure of the ability to separate visual stimuli, i.e. to distinguish the details and shapes of objects. This ability is dependent on the cerebral cortex as well as the eyes, and VA can therefore only be assessed if the subject is able to give a response to what he sees. (Recent electrophysiological methods[115] allow VA measurement without the subject's direct cooperation but the technique is not yet widely available (p. 129).)

The Snellen letter chart is the criterion against which all other visual acuity measures are standardised. It is used at a distance of 6 metres to give a measure of distant vision. Similar charts with reduced type are used to assess near vision. The VA for distant vision is expressed as a pseudo-fraction, e.g. 6/60 means that the subject can see at 6 m, a letter that can be seen by the normal person at 60 m. Thus 6/6 is normal vision, 6/5 better-than-average vision; 6/18 a moderate loss of acuity and 6/60 very poor vision. Near vision is expressed either as a Snellen pseudo-fraction or by type size (N5 = normal VA). Visual acuities should always be stated both with and without spectacle corrections.

Exact measures of VA are not meaningful in infants, since VA depends not only on the clarity of the retinal image but also on the brain's interpretation of what is seen. The infant's preference for interesting stimuli (p. 45) can, however, be used to give some estimate of his vision in terms of the Snellen chart (Fig. 6.1). In the first week of life, black and white strips of 3.5 mm width can be perceived, corresponding to a visual acuity of 3/60. There is rapid development of visual discrimination, and adult levels of acuity are probably reached before the age of 6 months. Binocular vision is thought to be present by the sixth week of life.

Refraction and refractive error

The eye is an optical system in which rays of light are brought to a focus on the retina. A sharp image is obtained, whatever the distance of the object being viewed, by changes in the curvature and therefore the power of the lens. The accommodation reflex enables near objects to be viewed; to do this the eyes converge and the curvature of the lens is increased. For distance vision, the reverse occurs.

The power of a lens is measured in dioptres*. Convex lenses are recorded

---

* Dioptres $= \dfrac{1}{\text{Focal length in metres}}$

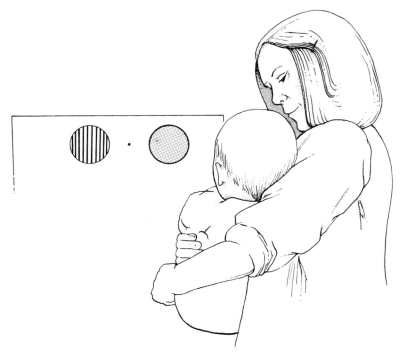

Fig. 6.1   Preferential looking: the baby prefers to look at a stripe or grid pattern rather than a plain surface. An observer watches through a peephole and patterns of varying size are presented randomly to right or left. (Courtesy of Robb[114].)

as plus and concave as minus. By convention, the refractive error of an eye is stated in terms of the lens needed to correct it.

An eye with normal refraction is said to be *emmetropic* (Fig. 6.2). Parallel light rays from a distant object are brought to a focus on the retina without any increase in the curvature of the lens. The light rays from a near object are divergent and the curvature of the lens and therefore the refractive power is increased by the accommodation reflex in order to focus the image on the retina.

The long-sighted or *hypermetropic* eye is usually smaller than normal. There is no difficulty in viewing distant objects. Children with hypermetropia seldom complain directly of problems with near vision but the increased accommodative effort needed to maintain a focused image predisposes to convergent squint. A convex lens is needed to correct hypermetropia.

The short-sighted or *myopic* eye is usually larger than normal. There is no problem with near vision but light rays from distant objects are brought to a focus in front of the retina and the image is therefore blurred. A concave lens is used to correct myopia.

The lens of the eye may not have the same refraction in all meridia,

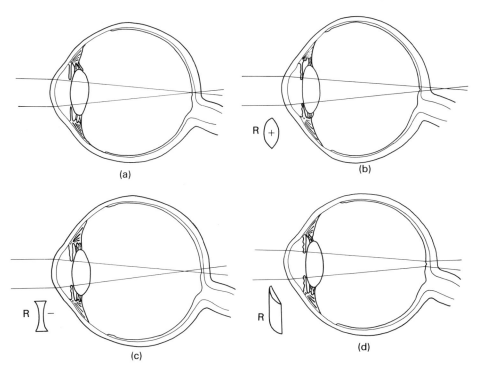

Fig. 6.2   (a) The emmetropic eye; (b) the hypermetropic eye; (c) the myopic eye; and (d) the astigmatic eye. (Courtesy of Robb[114].)

resulting in a distorted image. This is known as *astigmatism*. The lens needed to correct it is cylindrical rather than spherical in section.

A significant difference between the refractive error of the two eyes is known as *anisometropia*. In this situation the differing power of the two lenses produces images of different sizes. The brain can correct for this difference to a limited degree but a difference in refraction of 2.5 dioptres results in a 5% difference in image size, beyond which fusion becomes difficult and one image may then be suppressed, causing amblyopia (*see* below).

Few eyes are perfect optical systems.[118] Measurements of refraction in a population form an approximately normal distribution curve (Fig. 6.3). However there is evidence that even mild and apparently asymptomatic hypermetropia, anisometropia and astigmatism may predispose to squint and amblyopia. This has important implications in screening for visual defects (p. 132). There is no precise point on this distribution curve at which it can be assumed that symptoms will appear and it is therefore impossible to define the degree of refractive error which should be regarded as pathological.

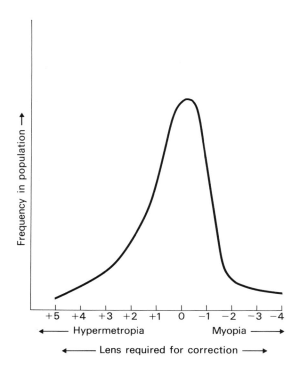

Fig. 6.3   Measurement of refraction—the distribution curve.

Measurement of refractive error

In young children who cannot cooperate by fixating a distant target, the amount of accommodation is constantly changing and therefore the refractive power of the eye can be measured only when this reflex has been paralysed (cycloplegia). Atropine or cyclopentolate are used for this purpose; these agents also dilate the pupil (mydriasis).

Refraction is measured objectively using a retinoscope. The technique of retinoscopy is not difficult in principle, although considerable practice is required to obtain reliable results. In older children and adults, the refractive power of the lens can be assessed by determining, with the cooperation of the subject, the power of spectacle lens which gives the clearest vision of a distant or near target, usually a Snellen chart. This is called subjective refraction. Subjective refraction provides a measure of visual acuity; in other words, it defines how much the subject can see. In contrast, objective refraction by retinoscopy describes the eye as an optical system and determines whether spectacles would produce a sharper retinal image; it provides no information about visual acuity. An eye could have normal refraction yet be blind.

In clinics and schools where ophthalmic reports are often not immediately available, the type of refractive error may usefully be deduced by examination of the child's glasses. An object is viewed through the lens, and the glasses are moved from side to side. If the lens is convex (hypermetropia, aphakia) the object appears to move in the opposite direction to the movement of the spectacles, but in the same direction if the lens is concave (myopia). When the spectacles are rotated, changes in refractive power between the two meridia of each lens are immediately obvious giving a 'scissoring' effect and the child may be assumed to have astigmatism.

SQUINT—STRABISMUS, HETEROTROPIA

This is a condition in which the visual axis of one eye (the squinting eye) is not directed to the object being looked at by the other eye (the fixing eye). The *visual axis* is the line from the fovea to the point of fixation. A *micro-squint* is a squint of very small angle which is not detectable by observation alone. A *concomitant* squint is one in which the angle is the same in all directions of gaze, and whichever eye is fixing; it is by far the commonest type in children. A *paralytic* (incomitant) squint is one in which the angle alters with different positions of gaze and with a change of fixation between the eyes. It results from paralysis of one or more of the extraocular muscles or from damage to the cranial nerves supplying them. An important example is Duane's retraction syndrome, which is easily mistaken for a sixth nerve palsy. In its usual form, there is failure of abduction and widening of the palpebral fissure with protrusion of the globe on attempted abduction; attempted adduction is accompanied by retraction of the globe and narrowing of the palpebral fissure. A *uniocular* squint is one in which one eye is habitually the squinting eye; an *alternating* squint is one in which either eye squints alternately.

The direction of the squint may be convergent (esotropia) or divergent (exotropia), or vertical (hyper- or hypotropia). There may be divergence on depression and convergence on elevation (the A phenomenon) or the reverse (the V phenomenon). A *latent* squint (heterophoria) is one in which an underlying tendency to squint is controlled by fusional mechanisms except under conditions of fatigue or illness. The cerebral fusion mechanism can be disrupted by rapidly covering the eyes alternately (the cover–uncover test), and the latent squint may then become manifest.

A *pseudosquint* is the illusory appearance of a convergent squint (Fig. 6.4). It occurs when a wide nasal bridge or broad epicanthic fold hides part of the sclera.

Binocular single vision (BSV) is the fusion into a single perception of the slightly disparate images from the two eyes. In addition to achieving single vision, this synthesis gives perception of depth or stereoscopic vision. BSV will not develop unless there are reasonably clear and similar images in the two eyes, functioning cerebral fusion mechanisms, and precise coordination of eye movements.

Fig. 6.4   Pseudosquint.

Causes of squint

Defective cerebral fusion.   There is little direct evidence about this but it may be the explanation for the high prevalence of squint in children with mental retardation or cerebral palsy. Squints seem to occur more commonly in children who are clumsy, poor readers, etc., though it should not be assumed to be the cause of these problems.

Defective visual stimulation.   BSV is needed to maintain alignment of the eyes. The brain is unable to control the alignment of an eye that does not receive a clear image. Squint is therefore commonly seen in infants with cataract, and congenital eye defects, due to poor visual stimulation in the critical period. Refractive errors which produce blurred or unequal images may also cause squint.

Refractive error.   Hypermetropia is commonly associated with squint because the child has to accommodate excessively to obtain a clear image of near objects. The excessive accommodation is reflexly associated with excessive convergence activity which may lead to a convergent squint. This may often be treated simply by the appropriate convex spectacle lens. Much less commonly, myopia may be associated with a divergent squint, particularly when looking at distant objects.

Genetic Factors.   There is a hereditary element in the aetiology of many cases of squint. In the best available study, a family history of squint was found in 25% of squinting children compared to 12% of controls.[119] This study did not confirm the widely held belief that squint is more common as one descends the social scale, although it may be less effectively treated due to lack of patient cooperation.

Management of squint

Any child with a suspected squint should be seen by an ophthalmologist. Squint is most commmonly detected first by a parent or relative, but delays in referral are common, due to the widespread myths firstly that squints are normal in the first six months of life and secondly that treatment is impossible or unnecessary until the child is older. Babies frequently show dissociated eye movements in the early months but any squint is abnormal after 6 months of age. A persistent uniocular squint is abnormal at any age and should be investigated, for two reasons; firstly, treatable defects (cataract, retinoblastoma) can cause squint, and secondly the prevention (as opposed to the treatment) of amblyopia probably depends on early diagnosis.

Treatment depends on the cause. Sometimes correction of the refractive error is all that is needed. Exercises may be used for older cooperative children. Surgical correction is often necessary. Although in many cases the main benefit is cosmetic, the considerable stigma of a squint justifies surgery. It is worth correcting squints even in very young handicapped children. Parents who have difficulty in loving a very unattractive handicapped baby may find the appearance of the squint more than they can tolerate. Sometimes a child with severe cerebral palsy makes considerable progress after squint surgery for reasons which are not clear.

AMBLYOPIA

An amblyopic eye can be defined as one which, even after correction of any refractive error with a spectacle lens, shows a defect in VA which cannot be explained by structural disease of the eye. It can only develop in a child under the age of about 7 years, and is due to defective development of vision during the critical period of rapid brain maturation. It is not yet clear either what is the peak age for development of amblyopia, or how early the predisposing factors need to be recognised if treatment is to result in the development of normal visual acuity and BSV.

The severity of amblyopia ranges from one line on the Snellen chart (i.e. the best vision attainable with optimal spectacle correction is 6/9) to near blindness. An amblyopic eye frequently has better vision for single letters than for a line of adjacent letters. This is known as the crowding phenomenon[120] and has important implications for vision tests in young children (p. 128).

Amblyopia[121] may result from:

1   Structural lesions that obscure vision, such as corneal opacity, cataract (p. 291) or ptosis (if the eyelid covers the pupil).
2   A blurred image due to refractive error, particularly where there is a marked degree of anisometropia and/or astigmatism.[116]
3   An image displaced by squint away from the fovea (much the most sensitive part of the retina). Amblyopia does not usually occur with alternating squints, because each eye in turn receives normal retinal stimulation.

SIGNIFICANCE OF AMBLYOPIA

Unilateral amblyopia is common and is not a major handicap for most people. Nevertheless it has the following effects: in severe cases the child is effectively one-eyed and loss of vision in the good eye would leave him with a significant visual handicap; depth vision will never be perfect so performance in ball games and in tasks requiring good depth vision (e.g. connecting electronic components) will be impaired; and some careers such as the armed forces, flying and crane operating may be closed to him.

TREATMENT OF AMBLYOPIA

The aim is to restore visual acuity in the amblyopic eye. Any refractive error is corrected. Various methods are used to blur or obscure the vision in the good eye, in order to stimulate use of the amblyopic eye. Some children, particularly if they have other handicaps, may find the temporary impairment of vision very disturbing and the potential gains may not always justify this. The long term results of treatment are sometimes disappointing and the initial gains in vision may be lost in later years.

Ptosis

Unilateral or (less frequently) bilateral ptosis is a common isolated anomaly. Much more rarely ptosis is associated with other disorders, e.g. Horner's syndrome, muscle diseases and a variety of dysmorphic syndromes. If the eyelid occludes the pupil amblyopia may result, but otherwise correction is needed only for cosmetic reasons.

EPIDEMIOLOGY OF VISUAL DEFECTS

Prevalence in normal children

Minor anomalies of visual function are among the commonest defects found in children. Estimates of the exact prevalence vary widely, due both to different criteria of abnormality and variable thoroughness of case finding: but perhaps 10% of schoolchildren have some visual defect.

Around 7% of 5-year-olds have a squint[119] and between 3 and 5% have amblyopia.[121] The prevalence of refractive error is difficult to measure for reasons discussed above. Mild degrees of astigmatism and hypermetropia sufficient to predispose to squint occur in 10–15% of infants. Myopia is rare in the first few years but becomes increasingly common in the school years.[122]

Published figures for the prevalence of eye defects among handicapped children vary between 20% and 50%, but all authors agree that, since they are so common, an eye examination is essential.[112,123] If possible, every handicapped child should first be examined by an orthoptist, and should then have a refraction and fundoscopy by an ophthalmologist.

ASSESSMENT

A complete assessment of a visual defect or handicap includes relevant medical history, the parents' observations, systematic inspection of the eyes, examination of eye movements and visual fields, and measurement of visual acuity.

Information from parents

Most congenital disorders of vision present either as an anomaly obvious to inspection or as abnormal visual behaviour, both of which are likely to be noted first by the parent. Most parents are certain that their baby can see from a very early age, and in infancy normal visual behaviour provides better evidence of functionally adequate vision than any test readily available to the paediatrician. Even when the child is old enough to cooperate with visual acuity testing, useful information can be obtained from the parents' observations of the child's spontaneous activity and play. The question, 'Have you any worries about his eyesight?' should be asked as part of any developmental assessment. Some further useful questions are suggested in Table 6.1.

A complete developmental assessment is mandatory in any infant whose parents suspect a significant visual impairment, firstly because abnormal visual behaviour is sometimes a manifestation of mental handicap or autism rather than an ophthalmic disease, secondly because eye defects are commonly associated with other handicaps and lastly because visual handicap impairs other aspects of development. The

Table 6.1 Useful questions about vision.

Do you think he can see—why/why not?
Does he recognise you/strangers?
Does he look at toys or pictures?
Does he reach for objects/take them?
Does he feel for objects?
Does he pick up tiny things, e.g. pieces of fluff, biscuit crumbs?
Does he look at windows/bright lights?
Does he look at his hands?
Do you think his vision has got better/worse recently?
Does he bump into things?
Does he go up close to objects, e.g. toys, TV?
Does he complain of difficulty with vision?
Have you ever noticed a squint (cast, turn, lazy eye)?

---

development of the visually handicapped infant is discussed in Chapter 15.

Squint also is most commonly detected first by a parent or relative[124] but, with the exception of severe myopia, refractive errors are not usually clinically apparent unless they cause a squint. In early childhood, the majority of refractive errors cause only a minor impairment of visual acuity, which is not readily detected even by the standard preschool tests (see below).

Systematic examination

The eyelid, cornea, iris and anterior chamber of each eye are inspected and compared. It is easy to overlook differences in the size of the eye or cornea, or variations in pigmentation. An eye which is too small (or microphthalmic) often has poor vision. Minor differences in pupil size are common in infancy but, in the absence of other anomalies, are usually of no significance.

If the infant does not respond normally to visual stimuli, an attempt is made to elicit visual attention with a slowly moving bright light.[125] If there is still no reaction, an attempt should be made to produce a startle reaction with a photographic flashgun. A careful examination of the pupil with a lens (an otoscope without speculum is convenient) should be made before concluding that pupil reactions to light are absent. When there is a little vision in one eye, changing accommodation may produce alteration in size of the other pupil which can be mistaken for a light response.

Detailed ophthalmoscopy is difficult in the young infant. He is more likely to open his eyes when sitting upright. No attempt should be made to forcibly hold the eyes open, but his attention should be distracted by an assistant so that he does not look directly into the light of the instrument.

Fig. 6.5   Detection of cataract.

Children old enough to cooperate can be asked to look at a target such as a small picture fixed on the wall or ceiling of the consulting room. For the detection of opacities such as cataract, the ophthalmoscope is set on $+1$ to $+3$ and the pupil is viewed from a distance of about 30 cm.[117] Opacities show clearly against the red reflex from the retina (Fig. 6.5). Adequate fundoscopy is difficult without dilating the pupils and it may only be possible to obtain a fleeting glimpse of the optic disc. This often appears somewhat pale in early infancy.

Any child presenting with a suspected abnormality of vision must have a detailed examination, including refraction, by an ophthalmologist, with the pupils dilated, and perhaps with sedation or even anaesthesia; there is therefore little point in wasting much time on fundoscopy without these advantages.

Tests for squint

Squint and other abnormalities of eye movement can be detected by the methods described here. The tests sound simple, but orthoptists spend three years mastering them! It is well worth spending a few sessions in an eye clinic with an orthoptist, acquiring some practical instruction in these techniques.

Corneal reflections.   A bright torch producing a narrow beam is held at 30 cm from the child. If the eyes are straight, the reflection in the two corneas

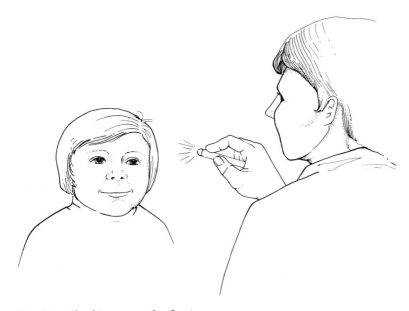

Fig. 6.6   Checking corneal reflections.

Fig. 6.7   Head-tilt as a
presenting feature of squint.

will be symmetrical. This is best judged by comparing the positions of the
reflexes in relation to the pupils (Fig. 6.6).

A head-tilt.   This is often adopted by the child to compensate for a squint
(Fig. 6.7).

Eye movements are examined by moving an interesting small target within
the child's visual field. Young children move the whole head as well as the
eyes in tracking an object, but this can be overcome by moving the target
very slowly while gently restraining the head with one hand. Both
horizontal and vertical movements are examined. The target must not be
too close to the eyes nor should it be moved too far laterally, as both errors
are liable to evoke jerking movements of the eyes. These are commonly
recorded as 'nystagmoid jerks' and wrongly interpreted as minimal
nystagmus.

Most nystagmus seen in children is either associated with eye disease, is
congenital, or is of the 'gaze paretic' type ('cerebellar' in some texts). The
commonest cause of the latter is probably anticonvulsant medication, but it
occurs in many forms of neurological disorder. Vestibular nystagmus is
uncommon. The reader is referred elsewhere for a detailed discussion of
nystagmus.[77]

Random wandering eye movements or nystagmus in early childhood are usually indicative either of very poor vision dating from early infancy or occasionally of profound mental handicap.[77] Congenital nystagmus without other eye disease is often familial. It is apparent even in the primary (straight ahead) position of gaze. Nystagmus in one eye only may be a manifestation of severe uniocular visual impairment. Some other, less common, abnormal eye movements are described on p. 293.[126]

Cover tests. The correct technique for these is illustrated in Figs. 6.8 and 6.9. If the child objects or struggles when one eye is covered but not the other, he is probably dependent on vision from one eye only. In the absence of obvious eye disease, this behaviour is very suggestive of amblyopia.

Stereo tests. The presence of BSV or 'stereo' vision indicates that both eyes are healthy and are functioning as a pair. Young children can be tested using the Wirt 'fly' test. This is a picture of a large and somewhat repulsive fly which is seen in 3-D when stereo spectacles are worn. A positive result is indicated by the child reaching out to grasp the fly's wings, or by a look of

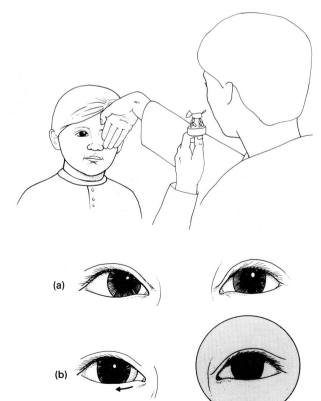

Fig. 6.8 The cover tests. These should be performed with a near and a distant target.

(a)

(b)

Fig. 6.9a The cover test. (*Top*) Is there a convergent squint in the right eye? (*Bottom*) When the left eye is covered, the right eye moves outwards to assume fixation. Diagnosis: Right manifest convergent squint.

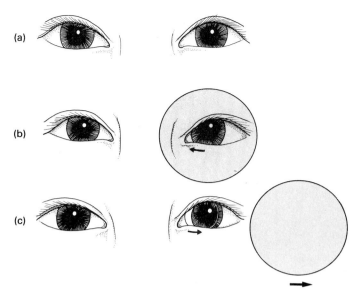

Fig. 6.9b   The cover-uncover test for latent squint. (*Top*) No squint is apparent. (*Middle*) Left eye covered; unable to maintain fixation, it deviates medially behind the cover. (*Bottom*) The outwards recovery movement to resume fixation is observed *as the cover is removed*. Diagnosis: Left latent convergent squint. Note that this test may need to be repeated several times on each eye.

horror! For older cooperative children, more sophisticated tests of stereo vision are used by orthoptists, for example, the TNO screen test, the Randot and the Frisby.

Visual fields

In children too young to cooperate, visual fields can be examined as shown in Fig. 6.10, although only extensive defects can be detected in this way. Some mentally handicapped and autistic children often behave as though they have field defects, but they are usually inconsistent and turn out to be a behavioural feature associated with variable attention. From about 3 years of age upwards, confrontation testing can be used. It must be remembered that the visual fields normally extend beyond 180°. In hemiplegia, the suspected field defect would be homonymous hemianopia, which can be detected with both eyes open together. When a bitemporal defect is suspected (as in craniopharyngioma), the eyes must be tested separately.

Very young children can rarely manage the classic method by which the examiner introduces a target progressively into the visual field. They often do not admit to seeing the target until it is in front of the nose, resulting in a spurious diagnosis of tunnel vision. The most successful method is to

Fig. 6.10 Testing visual fields.

ask the child to point at whichever finger is moving (Fig. 6.11). Older children can count the number of fingers displayed.

Measurement of visual acuity

Subjective refraction requires the child's intelligent cooperation and is seldom possible under the age of 4 years, and often not until much later than this, whereas the technique of objective refraction can be used at all ages but does not measure VA. Measurement of VA by clinical techniques presents great difficulties under the age of about $2\frac{1}{2}$ years and, although many ingenious methods have been devised, none can compare in precision with the Snellen. Three groups of tests can be distinguished (Table 6.2):

1 The simplest tests are those that attempt to establish the size of the smallest object visible to the child—the 'minimum observable'. Tests of this type can be performed even with very young or handicapped children. If presented under carefully controlled conditions they can provide an objective, though approximate, measure of VA in children with visual or intellectual impairment; however, they are not sensitive enough to be useful in detection of minor VA defects such as those caused by mild refractive errors. Attempts have been made to calculate the Snellen

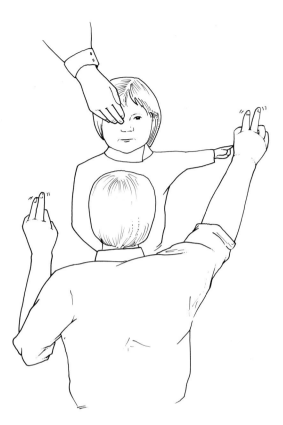

Fig. 6.11 Confrontation
testing of visual fields.

equivalent of 'minimum observable' tests but this exercise is of dubious
validity, since the visual discrimination and separation of objects is a much
more complex function than their detection; it is easy to overestimate
functional vision if Snellen equivalents are extrapolated from these tests.
Furthermore, movement of the target object considerably enhances its
visibility and, when recording results, a note should be made of whether the
target was moving or stationary.

2   Precise estimates of VA as previously defined can only be obtained by
tests that measure the ability to separate visual stimuli—the 'minimum
separable'. These tests require a greater degree of subject participation.

3   The presence of normal visual function and the severity of impairment
in the mentally or visually handicapped can often be determined best by
qualitative methods which make no pretence of giving an accurate VA
measure.

Those who undertake developmental surveillance of 'normal' children
should recognise that, although all three approaches have a part to play,
only 'minimum separable' tests are sufficiently precise to detect the minor
defects of VA which are associated with most refractive errors and

Table 6.2 Classification of vision tests.

Minimum observable
Hundreds & thousands
Silver sweets
Smarties
Cubes
Stycar graded balls

Minimum separable
Snellen charts
Stycar letter tests
Stycar toy test
Sheridan–Gardiner letter tests
Illiterate-E
Silhouettes
Stycar Panda test

Qualitative tests
Play observations
Person recognition
Object recognition, e.g. toys of graded sizes
Pictures; lifesize, miniature, stylised
Responses to TV
Observe effects of distance, lighting, contrast, colour

---

predispose to squint and amblyopia. Satisfactory performance of a 'minimum observable' test is not adequate reason to reassure and dismiss a parent who is worried about any aspect of a child's vision.

Stycar tests. A useful contribution to vision testing was made by Sheridan, who developed the 'Stycar' series (Sheridan tests for Young Children and Retardates).[127,128] Detailed descriptions of the equipment and technique will be found in the Manual which accompanies each test kit.

Testing the eyes separately. Whichever method is used, each eye should be tested separately if the child's cooperation can be secured. This may be possible in babies up to 8 or 9 months old, but is less readily tolerated thereafter until the child is over 2 years old. The eye not being tested is covered with the parent's hand or preferably an elasticated or adhesive patch. The child's own hand is not adequate and he is bound to peep through his fingers, particularly if vision is defective in the test eye. If the eyes are not tested separately, a useful estimate of functional vision can still be obtained but a serious uniocular defect could easily be missed.

MINIMUM OBSERVABLE TESTS

Stycar Graded Balls Test.   There are two versions of this (Figs. 6.12 & 6.13). Both are normally performed at a distance of 3 m from the child. Visualisation of even the smallest ball (3 mm in diameter) does not require perfect vision; subjects old enough to cooperate can frequently locate a target of this size even when able to read only the top line (6/60) of the Snellen chart. If the child is observed carefully, these tests can also provide information about possible field defects, and the rolling balls test examines the child's eye tracking ability.

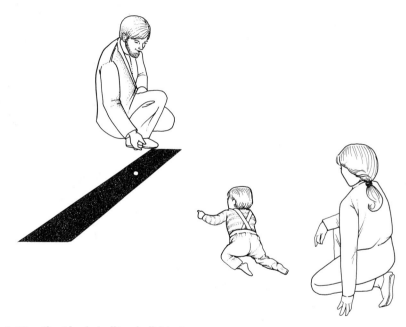

Fig. 6.12   Sheridan's 'rolling balls' test.

Near Vision.   Small sweets, about 1.5 mm in diameter (hundreds and thousands), saccharine tablets (2 mm), cake decoration balls (3 mm), and Smarties (15 mm) are useful in assessing the near vision of the mentally or visually handicapped. Snellen equivalents are of little significance in this situation, but inability to locate and pick up the small sweet suggests that the near vision is 6/36 or worse and other signs of abnormal visual behaviour would then usually be evident. Even infants with high degrees of hypermetropia can perform this task without difficulty, but it may elicit a squint and, if the eyes are tested separately, severe amblyopia may be detected.

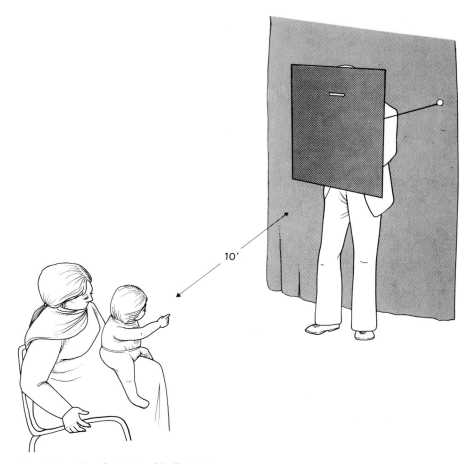

Fig. 6.13   Sheridan's 'fixed balls' test.

MINIMUM SEPARABLE TESTS

Stycar miniature toys test.   In this test the child is required to distinguish between a toy knife, fork and spoon at a distance of 3 m. Other toys are included to add interest. A visual acuity of 6/18 or better is needed for success. Most normal children who can do this test reliably will, within a few months, be able to perform the much more accurate five-letter test, but it is occasionally useful in assessing handicapped children.

Letter-matching tests.   These require the child to recognise differences between letters, but the ability to name them is not necessary. He is asked to look at a single letter held 3 m away from him (for the Stycar tests) or 6 m (for Sheridan-Gardner single letters), and to match it by pointing to the same letter on a key card held by the parent (Fig. 6.14). A specialised

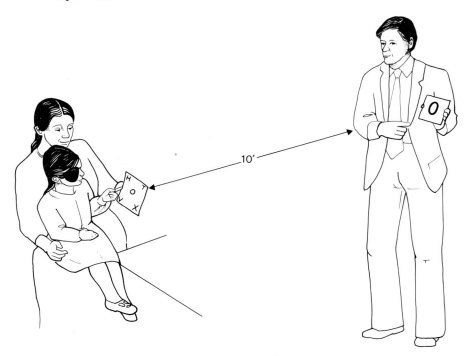

Fig. 6.14   A single-letter test of visual acuity.

single-letter test (the 'Panda') is available for assessing the visual acuity of children with severe visual handicap.[128]

Snellen chart.   A full line of letters should be used to test vision as soon as possible, because amblyopia is associated with the 'crowding phenomenon', in which vision for single letters is often much better than that for a line of letters. By using the matching letter technique of the Stycar test, children can cope with a line of letters on a standard chart long before they can name them. Lower case letters are preferable. The Snellen test is performed at a distance of 6 m.

Other chart tests.   The illiterate E and shape recognition tests (animal silhouettes etc.) are still used in some clinics but, by the time the child can perform these reliably, he can usually cope with a letter-matching test.

FUNCTIONAL TESTS

Observations of visually directed behaviour and the child's response to play activities are an essential part of assessment; examples are given in Tables 6.1 and 6.2.

OTHER METHODS OF MEASURING VISUAL ACUITY

Optokinetic devices rely on the alternating refixation and following movements induced by repetitive stimuli, such as spots or stripes on an oscillating or revolving drum (the Barany drum). The Catford drum (Fig. 6.15) is widely used and is similar, though not strictly an optokinetic device. These techniques may be useful in detecting a marked difference in acuity between the two eyes and provide a useful way of demonstrating the presence of some visual function in the severely handicapped, but very misleading results are occasionally obtained[130] and sometimes a child who is almost blind seems to respond.

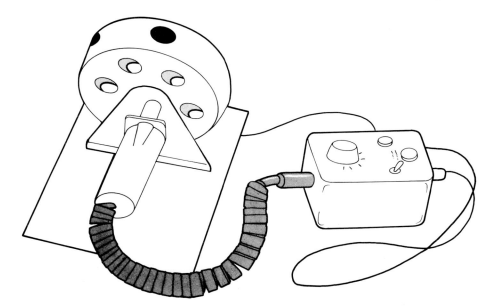

Fig. 6.15   The Catford drum.

Newer methods of measuring VA include some ingenious tests for confirming the presence of stereoscopic vision;[131] techniques which make use of the infant's preference for novel visual stimuli (Fig. 6.1);[132] and visual evoked responses elicited by chequer-boards of varying square size. None of these techniques is readily available for routine clinical use.

SPECIALISED TECHNIQUES OF OPHTHALMIC INVESTIGATION

Electrophysiological techniques.   These are useful in the investigation of some visual disorders, particularly the inherited retinal degenerations, cerebral storage disorders, and demyelinating disease.[134] The electroretino-gram (ERG) is derived from the superficial or outer layers of the retina and may therefore be normal even when there is obvious optic atrophy; a normal result does not imply that the child can see. Conversely the ERG may be grossly abnormal in children with retinitis pigmentosa long before the defect is clinically apparent. The visual evoked response (VER) represents the EEG activity generated when nerve impulses travel from the eye to the cortex, and is used to assess the integrity of the visual pathways. It is obtained by computer analysis of the EEG activity evoked by visual stimulation, using a flashing light or chequer-board pattern. The VER is a valuable complementary investigation to the ERG, although in cases of suspected cortical blindness with non-progressive mental handicap, results are often equivocal and their main value is in ruling out other disorders.

CT Scan.   This investigation is useful where structural lesions of the ocular pathways or occipital cortex are suspected.

VA assessment in the visually handicapped child

This presents considerable difficulties and exact measures may not be possible for some years; similar problems occur with mentally handicapped children.[129] The 'visual world' of the normal infant is limited and he pays attention only to his immediate close surroundings, for reasons which are probably more related to psychological development than to optical factors.[112] His visual world expands rapidly so that by 8 or 9 months, tests such as those shown in Figs. 6.12 and 6.13 will hold his attention at a distance of 3 or even 6 m. In the visually or mentally handicapped child, the visual world expands more slowly, and it is often impossible to obtain any response to tests at more than 60 or 90 cm from the infant. The 'minimum observable' tests can, however, be modified according to the child's handicap; for example, the rolling balls test can usefully be performed on a table top about 45 cm from the child (Fig. 6.16) and, if necessary, a large brightly coloured ball can be added to the series.

Functional tests provide the most relevant information, but limitations in the child's ability to respond are sometimes due to impaired intellectual or language development rather than poor vision. Visual handicap so reduces the child's experience of objects, faces and pictures that he may show little interest in them, and therefore estimates of VA made prior to any intervention or training may be unduly pessimistic (an analogous situation occurs with the newly diagnosed deaf child). Conversely, the child's familiarity with his own possessions may deceive his parents into overestimating his VA and his responses should be checked with unfamiliar examples of the same objects.

Further essential information is obtained by an objective refraction, and optokinetic devices and electrophysiological methods may also be useful,

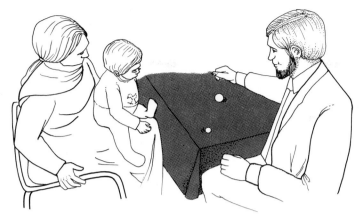

Fig. 6.16 A modification of Sheridan's test for examination of a multiply-handicapped child.

but none are a substitute for functional assessment. Furthermore, if the assessment is performed in the presence of the parents and the teacher, it provides an invaluable demonstration of the child's handicaps, and helps them to construct a mental picture of the child's visual experiences and perceptions.

Colour vision

Impaired colour vision usually affects red-green discrimination and other defects are very rare. It is much commoner in boys (8%) than girls (0.5–1%). Although colour-coded educational materials are widely used, in practice impaired red-green discrimination does not often seem to result in serious classroom difficulties.[135,136] It may be important for older pupils to be aware of their disability, which may affect their choice of career.[137] If a colour vision defect is found and this threatens to interfere with the pursuit of a desired career, expert advice should be obtained, as these defects vary widely in severity and significance, and some can be helped with coloured filters.[138]

The Ishihara plates are the standard method for testing for red-green colour defects. Most 5-year-olds can perform this test if the tester has enough time and patience. It is probably more efficient to concentrate attention on only those primary school children who have learning problems, and then to screen all male secondary school entrants for colour defects.

The City University test is useful for older children, but too difficult for 5-year-olds, and the Guy's test has proved disappointing in practice. The simple test devised by Bacon[136] probably has a very low specificity. The

Farnsworth–Munsell 100-hue test is the most accurate colour vision test, but needs a mental age of at least 7–8 years.

SCREENING FOR VISUAL DEFECTS

Serious visual handicaps are rare, occurring in only about 3–4 children per 10 000 births. They are usually apparent to the parents at an early stage, either because of obvious external abnormalities of the eyes, or from the infant's abnormal visual behaviour. The Stycar visual acuity tests can demonstrate the presence of severe vision defects but in practice they are very rarely *first* detected in this way. Unfortunately the skills included in developmental scales under the heading 'fine visuomotor coordination' give *no* information about minor visual defects, though they may reveal abnormal behaviour associated with severe visual loss.

Minor visual defects occur in about 10% of children. Squints are most often recognised first by parents; those that are not may only be detectable by careful application of the orthoptic techniques described on p. 119. Refractive errors and amblyopia are often not detected until the age of $2\frac{1}{2}$–3 years, since the 'minimum observable' tests used in the under-2s are too insensitive to reveal any but the most severe defects of visual acuity. This deficiency is intrinsic to the design of the tests and is not related to the competence of the tester.

Although there is as yet no proof that earlier treatment would improve outcome, animal studies imply that the detection and correction of squint and refractive error in the first year may be desirable. If this is so, the association between refractive error, squint and amblyopia together with the high prevalence of these defects might justify VA screening of all infants if a sufficiently sensitive test could be found. There are several promising reseach methods by which minor VA defects could be detected at an early stage.[139,140] The most direct approach, adopted by Ingram as a research study, is the refraction of all infants,[121] but this is hardly a practical proposition. At present screening for VA defects in children too young to cooperate with 'minimum separable' tests should perhaps be limited to cases where there is parental concern or a risk factor such as family history of eye disease or another handicap; however, in these situations, a complete examination is usually needed.

One solution to the problem of screening the under-2s for minor visual defects is the use of a community orthoptist, who is usually based at a hospital ophthalmology clinic, but spends much of her time visiting community clinics and nurseries. Although orthoptic techniques do not provide a direct measure of VA in this age group, they do establish whether the eyes are healthy and are working together as a pair. Ease of access to the community orthoptist facilitates the prompt referral and investigation of any child suspected of having a visual defect and reduces the burden of unnecessary outpatient visits both for parents and for the ophthalmologist. It is not yet certain whether the screening of *asymptomatic* infants by the orthoptist is justified since the yield appears to be very small.

School vision testing.   At school, visual acuity testing is performed regularly by the school nurse. Most 5-year-old children can manage a Snellen test if a matching card is used and this is preferable to single letter tests which underestimate the severity of amblyopia. The prevalence of myopia increases with age; repeated checks throughout the school years are therefore desirable.

Chapter Seven
Reactions to Handicap

COUNSELLING

To the parents, a consultation about their child's suspected handicap is a major event. Although the details may later be forgotten, the overall impression will remain for many years, perhaps for a lifetime. The consultation is not merely a diagnostic assessment. It should be the first stage in the therapeutic process of helping the family to cope with a handicap which may affect their entire lifestyle. This is a task which cannot be rushed; far more parental unhappiness and dissatisfaction with their medical advisers can be traced to difficulties in communication[141] or to lack of information, than to clinical ignorance or incompetence.

Research studies based on interviews with parents of children with Down's syndrome, deafness and many other handicaps provide abundant evidence that parents wish to be informed as soon as there is any suspicion that their child is abnormal.[143,145] Adequate information must be provided as soon as possible and in language appropriate to their educational background, so that they know what problems may face them. Stock phrases which carry a wealth of meaning to doctors are meaningless to the parents, e.g. 'invasive investigation', 'conservative management', 'progressive lesion', etc. Scientific terms such as 'chromosome disorder', 'cell metabolism' or 'nerve fibre' mean very little to those who have never studied biology, and words like 'chronological' and 'environment' are not part of the everyday vocabulary of ordinary people. Unpleasant facts must not be disguised in medical jargon, though this is often done by the doctor to spare the parents and himself from the pain caused by everyday words which he knows will have a more devastating impact. It is often tempting to defer an explanation of the most distressing aspects of the diagnosis (such as the progressive deterioration and early death, or the fact that a disorder is inherited) until the parents have recovered from the shock of hearing that their child is handicapped. The necessity to explain these additional facts at a subsequent interview will make some parents very angry and diminish trust, because they wonder what further information is being withheld from them. Deliberate withholding of the facts is quite different from genuine uncertainty, which must be acknowledged.

Parents do not remember all the information they are given. Even when calm, they may retain less than a third[141]—which is often incorrect! If upset by bad news, they may well 'switch off' and absorb nothing further except the fact that their child is abnormal. Rather than delivering a lecture, the doctor should involve the parents in the conversation from the beginning, for example 'What do you think about him yourself?' or 'What have you been told so far by other people?' Their comprehension of a problem can be checked by asking how they would themselves explain the child's handicap to an enquirer such as a grandparent. Further feedback on the success of communication can often be obtained from the health visitor, GP or social worker, and this information is invaluable in correcting misconceptions.

Every parent who is told that their child has a significant handicap must be offered a follow-up appointment within a few weeks of the first visit, and it may be useful to invite the parents to prepare a list of questions which are worrying them. Most parents appreciate a written report;[142] it is remarkable that the people who usually have the least information about the doctor's opinion are the ones who have the most personal interest! The report is written in non-technical language; a copy is sent to the GP and, with the parents' permission, to other professionals involved with the child, so that they know not only what is wrong with him, but also what the parents have been told. (An example is provided in Appendix 9.) This procedure can still be followed when one suspects a strong environmental component in the child's problems, and it is an excellent discipline to formulate the diagnosis in a constructive way that will be acceptable to the parents.

Three levels of diagnosis

Parents are easily confused by the terminology used to describe handicaps and developmental disorders. The exposition of the child's problem should focus on three levels of diagnosis: the type of handicap, the cause, and the effects.

WHAT KIND OF HANDICAP?

There is seldom much difficulty in answering this question when there is an obvious major handicap, for example cerebral palsy or severe mental retardation, although there may be a period of doubt if the child is very young when first seen. The diagnosis of developmental disorders is much more difficult. The term 'developmental delay' is commonly used. It includes the various patterns of slow language development (Chapter 13) and motor development (Chapter 3). The term is legitimate while there is genuine doubt, but it must not be used as a euphemism for more specific terms such as mild mental handicap or language disorder. Words like 'slow' or 'delayed' imply to the parents that the child will 'catch up' and it must be made clear that this cannot be guaranteed. The point at which words like 'handicap' or 'retardation' are introduced needs delicate judgement. The parents can be told that these words might apply to their child unless his current slow rate of development accelerates, but that it is impossible to predict what effect his future experiences may have on his ultimate intelligence.

The starting point for discussion has to be the parents' own perceptions of the child's abilities and problems. This is why developmental assessment must be done in the presence of the parents and with the help of their information about the child. The extent of their anxiety and their own explanations for his slow development must be considered. Nothing will be gained by urging them to accept the diagnosis before they are ready. Many parents recognise that their child is 'developmentally delayed' but feel that he should be given every opportunity to progress before he is 'labelled' as handicapped. This attitude is perfectly reasonable. They should be assisted in arranging whatever intervention is most appropriate and encouraged to observe their child carefully, aided perhaps by a PIP chart (p. 232) or by observing other children of the same age at a nursery or playgroup. If the child makes rapid progress, everyone is pleased; if he turns out to be handicapped, the parents have had time to recognise it for themselves.

WHAT IS THE CAUSE?

An exact medical diagnosis is not always possible, even in major handicap, and is rarely achieved in cases with developmental disorders or mild mental handicap. It is important for parents to understand the distinction between the *type* of handicap and the underlying *cause*, even when the latter cannot be determined. They may be helped by an outline of the main causes of handicap which are relevant to their child and should be told which of these might merit further investigation. Even if no exact diagnosis is possible it is desirable to establish whether the child has a progressive or a static disorder. The presence of minor dysmorphic features is a useful pointer to a prenatal and usually non-progressive cause of handicap.

The possibility of overlooking a specific disease process should always be remembered but should not be allowed to dominate clinical judgement. It may be difficult to decide whether, when and how much investigation is justified, but (with the possible exception of hypothyroidism which needs urgent treatment, and muscular dystrophy where genetic advice is occasionally urgent) there are few situations where a delay of a few months in establishing a diagnosis will have a significant effect on the child or his family. A short delay may allow time for the existence of handicap to be accepted before investigation is undertaken.

WHAT ARE THE FUNCTIONAL EFFECTS OF THE HANDICAP?

Parents want to know whether the child is likely to walk and talk. They usually enquire about prospects for education in a normal school, and for an independent adult existence. Some may be particularly worried about epilepsy, either because of a family history or because of general background knowledge about the association between brain lesions and epilepsy. Others have intense anxieties about adolescence. Boys may be seen as potential rapists, a fear that surfaces surprisingly often at a very early age and is often disguised as a general anxiety about 'growing up'. There are parallel fears about girls becoming promiscuous or pregnant.

It is seldom easy to give a prognosis in childhood handicap, but one way of dealing with uncertainty is to suggest some limits—the best and the worst that might happen. These limits should be broad in the early years and will become narrower as one watches the child's progress. For example, with mental handicap of moderate degree one could suggest that the limits might lie somewhere between non-skilled labour on the open market with community support, and a need for sheltered workshop accommodation and regular supervision.

THE PROBLEM OF UNCERTAINTY

Months or even years may elapse before a definite diagnosis and prognosis can be established. This period of uncertainty is difficult both for parents and for the professionals who advise them. No doctor or other professional should embark on child assessment unless he is prepared to take the responsibility of guiding the family through any problems that may be revealed. In chronic disorders, it is impossible to overemphasise the importance of continuity of care by one person.

THE BEREAVEMENT REACTION

The response of parents to the diagnosis of a serious handicap in their child has many parallels with the reaction to bereavement.[143] The main difference is that the child's handicap is a permanent source of sorrow throughout his life, whereas bereavement marks a crisis point beyond which readjustment can begin (Fig. 7.1). Although it is convenient to describe the bereavement reaction as if it occurred in a sequence of definable stages, human emotions are not so tidy and elements of several stages can often be discerned at any particular time.

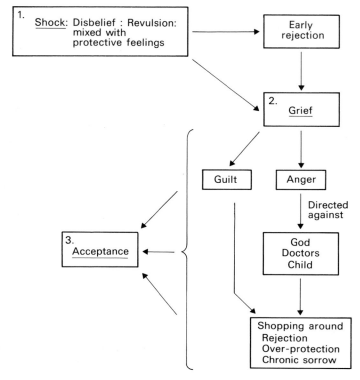

Fig. 7.1   Parental reactions to handicap.

Shock

When told that their child is handicapped most parents experience a sense of shock, panic and disbelief. The reaction is usually more severe when the handicap is caused by a sudden unanticipated catastrophe, such as birth asphyxia or a road accident, or in cases where the parents have not suspected or acknowledged that their child is not developing normally. Conversely, it is not uncommon for parents to realise the extent and nature of the child's handicap long before any professional will believe them, and they may actually greet the diagnosis with a smile of relief. This response may be puzzling or irritating to the doctor if it is not correctly interpreted. These parents are already reaching the point of acceptance and their apparent failure to experience shock or grief should not be mistaken for denial.

It is common and natural for parents to feel revulsion for the abnormal child, particularly if there are obvious external deformities such as cleft lip or eye anomalies. Revulsion is a mixed emotion, often tinged with guilt and simultaneous protective feelings aroused by the child's helplessness.

Grief

An intense grief reaction occurs immediately after diagnosis. This is followed by a period of mourning, which may be regarded as grieving the loss of the perfect child who has now been replaced by one who is handicapped. The sadness caused by handicap never disappears, but the intensity of the grief diminishes with time as the parents adjust to the child's problems. The period of mourning is likely to be prolonged or suspended if the parents do not know the extent and details of the problem which confronts them.

Grief may be projected inwards, resulting in feelings of guilt, despair and isolation, or outwards, when it is manifest as anger. It is thought that some people do not complete the process of mourning[144] and instead develop a variety of maladaptive behaviour patterns, which may limit their own happiness and inhibit their child's development.

GUILT

The notion that a damaged child is a punishment for past sins might be thought rather archaic, but it is a widespread and deepseated reaction. Parents often ask themselves, 'Whose fault is this?' Often there are anxieties about psychiatric or neurological disorders in the family tree, guilt about smoking, drug usage, alcohol, previous termination of pregnancy, or deliberate delay in childbearing for social and financial reasons. 'Whose fault?' is a question of particular significance in some ethnic and religious groups where any defects in the child are automatically regarded as being caused by some defect in the wife or her family. Nevertheless, many parents report that guilt is not a dominant emotion at any point in their response to handicap and are irritated when well-meaning counsellors repeatedly return to this issue.

THOUGHTS ABOUT DEATH

In cases of very severe handicap, it is natural for the parents to wonder if the child will survive. They may well hope that he will not, but feel that this might horrify the doctor. Lack of opportunity to confess these feelings intensifies the guilt which they cause. They may ask, 'What happens to babies like this?' and 'How long do children like this usually live?'

It is sometimes necessary to discuss the policy to be followed if the child's condition should deteriorate. Life-threatening medical problems in the severely handicapped should, if possible, be managed by the same doctor who has previously been responsible for the child's general care. If he knows the family well, he is more likely correctly to gauge their feelings as to the appropriate management.

The ethical issues surrounding the maintenance of life in severe handicap cannot be avoided, but I do not think it is desirable to have rigid rules derived from one's own personal beliefs. The medical responsibility is to determine what course of action is most acceptable in terms of the family's personal beliefs and then to share the burden of that decision. It may sometimes be right for the doctor to continue active treatment of the child who in his view has no useful future. However a doctor should not succumb to pressure to discontinue treatment, or actively to hasten death, against the dictates of his own conscience.

When a handicapped child dies in hospital the parents should of course be permitted all the time and privacy they desire, and should be encouraged to touch and hold him. The mourning which naturally follows is complicated by relief—and by guilt at feeling relieved. An opportunity should be offered for a further discussion after the funeral, and in some cases contact may need to be continued for a long time.

ANGER

A sense of frustrated anger and bitterness is a normal part of the bereavement response. The anger may be directed against God or against the child who has caused them so much sorrow. Anger may be very intense in a middle-class couple whose careful planning of their life and reproduction has been disorganised, or where there has been ambivalence about the pregnancy in the first place; in contrast, the philosophical attitude to life taught by some religions may virtually eliminate anger and bitterness.

Anger is frequently directed at doctors or other professionals, either for medical errors or more often because of difficulties in communication. Where the child's survival is or has been an achievement of modern medical care, there may be resentment against the doctors for keeping the child alive. Other common genuine grievances are that the child is seen as an interesting case; that little interest is shown in minor intercurrent problems such as infections, because the child is 'too handicapped to be worth the trouble'; that detailed diagnosis is offered but no treatment plan is made; and that major behaviour problems are ignored.

The paediatrician is in a difficult position when the parents wrongly believe that poor obstetric care is responsible for the child's handicap. The general public knows that doctors are reluctant to criticise their colleagues and for this reason assurances about obstetric competence are seldom believed. Some obstetricians are prepared to meet the family and discuss the matter with them. On the rare occasions when it seems that there really has been obstetric negligence, the problem is even more delicate. If it cannot be resolved by informal discussion, the parents' initial course of action should be to write to the Hospital Administrator. If their complaints are side-stepped or dismissed, they are likely to become aggressive and alienate all those who could help them, and the child's care may suffer as a result.

THE 'SHOPPING AROUND' SYNDROME

Some parents collect numerous opinions about their handicapped child. The motives for their behaviour need careful analysis. Sometimes the reason is genuinely that the initial counselling or diagnosis has been inadequate; questions that could have been answered were ignored or side-stepped. There are many parents who accept the facts of the handicap but want specific advice on what they themselves can do to help the child; they may be dissatisfied with the available educational facilities.

In some cases, however, people who shop around are very distressed and disturbed, and extremely difficult to help. They may still be angry or suffering from guilt feelings, usually with an overlay of chronic sorrow and depression; this is sometimes associated with organic symptoms but, not surprisingly, fails to respond to antidepressants or tranquillisers. The paediatrician should not regard these parents as an irritating nuisance nor as a challenge to prove his superiority over those previously consulted. A detailed assessment of the child's abilities is usually superfluous in such cases. It will have been done before—many times! A careful life history of parents and the child and an attempt to define the source of their confusion and despair are more likely to be profitable.

One feature of the 'shopping around' syndrome is that a certain person or place is idealised and seen as a potential miracle worker. If the goal seems inaccessible, due to distance, cost or the reluctance of a family doctor to refer the child, it merely becomes more desirable. However, a pilgrimage of a religious nature is not necessarily a manifestation of this syndrome. It may indicate the parents' acceptance that the child is handicapped because it is the will of God. For those who have a religious faith, a pilgrimage, for example to Lourdes, may be an invaluable experience and one that should be encouraged.

OVERPROTECTION AND REJECTION

These two apparently opposite attitudes are not mutually exclusive; indeed both can be identified to some degree in the majority of parents of handicapped children in Western society. Present-day attitudes to the disabled dictate that it is the duty of parents to provide for their children even if severely handicapped. This is reinforced by professional counselling which is almost invariably directed towards home-based care and barely admits of any alternatives such as fostering or institutional placement. Doctors must recognise how much pressure there is on parents to prove that they can cope and can live up to the expectations of society. It is not surprising that some parents devote excessive care and zeal to their handicapped child while others reject him totally.

Overprotective parents often have sound reasons for their behaviour. Some children with severe handicaps are very difficult to handle or feed, or there may be anxiety about medical emergencies such as fits. The parents may learn by bitter experience that it is not possible to leave the child with a babysitter. Overprotection can easily become a maladaptive response that inhibits the development of independence. The parents' fear of what the child will be like when adult, encourages them to keep him as a baby for as long as possible; one mother explained to me, 'Everybody loves a handicapped child but nobody loves a handicapped man'. The handicapped child may provide a purpose for living, without which the parents would be lost. One or other parent, commonly the father, oftens becomes an enthusiastic and vociferous member of voluntary societies and charities. In some cases this seems to indicate a subtle form of rejection, releasing the parent from the chore of caring for the child, because he is so busy with charitable work.

A very useful service can be performed by the Handicap Team in helping the parents to separate from the child before these maladaptive patterns become established. Because they are professionals, they will often have the parents' confidence sooner than relatives or friends.

Acceptance

Acceptance has been defined as 'the death of an imaginary perfect child and the redirection of parental love to the newly perceived child as he is in reality'. It may take many years for the parents to realise the extent of a handicap. The pace of realisation should not be forced to fit the professional's notion of acceptance, unless the child is being deprived of appropriate management. The wealth and variety of preschool services now available makes it easier to provide adequate help for the child while allowing parental understanding to evolve at a natural speed.

For many parents, the care of a handicapped child does become rewarding and they are able to make some sense of the experience, and perhaps to offer sympathy and guidance to new parents of children in similar circumstances. An opportunity to meet such parents who have a positive attitude to handicap does much to bring back a sense of proportion to those suffering the first shock of diagnosis.

THE EFFECTS OF HANDICAP ON FAMILIES AND INDIVIDUALS

Family differences in reactions to handicap

Parents do not necessarily recognise or acknowledge the existence of handicap at the same speed. These differences are not abnormal in themselves but are a potential source of conflict and disharmony.[146] Differences of opinion and insight may be exacerbated if both parents are not seen and counselled together. In a mutually supportive marriage, the relationship can be strengthened following the diagnosis, but unstable relationships often collapse under the strain. Other members of the family may take much longer to accept the situation.[148] In particular grandparents cause much distress by their often prolonged insistence that the child is normal, forcing parents continually to emphasise the child's deficiencies.

The siblings of a handicapped child reflect their parents' emotions but also have some problems unique to themselves.[146] They may feel neglected and ignored, and may display neurotic or antisocial symptoms. Their own social life may be disrupted and often they are embarrassed to bring friends home. The handicapped person's future care after the parents' death is an additional worry. Lastly, as teenagers, they may become anxious about the genetic risks to their own offspring.

Feelings of the handicapped person

All but the most profoundly handicapped children gradually develop some insight into the fact that they are different.[147] This process often begins in early childhood, accelerating in adolescence as sexual feelings emerge. Successful adaptation to the personal predicament of being handicapped is dependent on the attitudes of family, professional staff and society in general. Misdirected kindness and failure to treat a handicapped person as a responsible and sensitive individual in his own right together encourage him to unnecessary dependence, adoption of the 'sick role'[4] and manipulative behaviour. He may retreat into fantasy, become selfish or self-centred. These undesirable characteristics are not an inevitable part of being handicapped and modern attitudes to the early care of handicapped children are likely to produce more positive personality characteristics in adult life.

Further crises

Following the initial shock of diagnosis, there are a number of situations in which parents who have apparently come to terms with their child's handicap may show a renewal of the grief reaction, though usually less intense than at the time of diagnosis. These crisis points include: the child's failure to walk and talk at the usual time; realisation that the child will not be able to attend normal school; the need for residential care if the family breaks up; times when behaviour or management problems become intolerable; realisation that the child is never going to walk unaided; the problems of early adolescence; and the time of school leaving.

An unexpected crisis is sometimes caused by the use of a new and unexpected word; for example, I have seen an apparently well adjusted family use the terms 'retarded' and 'backward' in connection with their child without any distress; but become very disturbed at the use of the words 'mentally handicapped'. For this reason, it is essential to present parents with all the relevant words at the time of initial diagnosis, preferably in writing. Adjustment and acceptance cannot be completed until the parents are clear about the facts and the terminology which will be used to describe their child.[149]

Residential care

Requests for residential care of a handicapped child may be made during the acute early grief reaction, when they may be seen as evidence of rejection, or later, after the stage of acceptance has been reached. A few years ago, recommendation for institutional care was the normal reaction of professionals faced with any handicapped baby, but public and professional opinion is now strongly in favour of keeping these children at home. It is much better both for the progress of the child and the psychological health of his family, that he should become an accepted part of a family unit, even if only for a few years. Although still distressing for the parents, the decision to place him in some form of residential care is usually then made after much thought, and for good reason, such as the needs of other normal children.

The pendulum has probably swung too far in favour of keeping handicapped children at home at all costs. It must be recognised that, for many families, residential care will be the right answer and every possible help should be given in finding a suitable placement. Modern units are run on compact family lines and have little in common with the old style of purely custodial care in large hospital wards.

Professional reactions to handicap

Doctors and their professional colleagues are not immune from the reactions described above. Feelings of sorrow, revulsion, therapeutic inadequacy and anger are natural responses of sympathetic people to the tragedy of childhood handicap. Difficulties in communication may arise when these feelings are deliberately stifled in the cause of 'professionalism' instead of using them to empathise with the parents; or when the professional is unable to distinguish between his own private reactions and those of the parents. Some knowledge of counselling techniques is invaluable for those who have to manage these distressing problems.[472]

UNORTHODOX MEDICINE

Unorthodox systems of treatment for handicap have a powerful attraction for many parents, for several reasons. Their proponents have an enthusiasm which is sometimes lacking among professional staff. They provide new opportunities to meet other parents who are facing similar problems. The fact that they are not available on the National Health Service and have to be obtained privately is also, for some people, clear evidence of superiority. A trial of 'fringe' medicine is often seen as evidence that parents have not yet accepted the handicap but there may be other explanations. Since the history of medicine includes many examples of major advances being ignored or dismissed by the profession, it is not altogether surprising that some parents feel that they should investigate new 'unscientific' ideas, for fear of overlooking something that may later turn out to be valuable. Parents who take this view will not be impressed by talk of controlled trials or of the implausible nature of the claims made for these treatments. They should be given whatever factual information or advice they request, together with a balanced opinion. Even if they do decide to adopt an unorthodox system, they should be invited to remain in touch with the paediatric team. Certain systems arouse such anger in some doctors and therapists that parents who adopt them may be banned from the Child Development Centre! This is of course inexcusable; it is the parents' right to try whatever form of medicine they choose, particularly in conditions which are so obviously incurable by orthodox means.

THE DOMAN–DELACATO METHOD

This is a very intensive method of treatment, devised at the Insitute for the Achievement of Human Potential in Philadelphia, USA, and recommended by its originators for many forms of handicap.[150] It includes a variety of manoeuvres whose rationale does not stand up to detailed examination in the light of modern neurophysiology. The individualised programme which is prepared for each child may occupy most of the child's waking hours. For its execution, the parents have to gather a circle of helpers. The attraction of this system probably lies in its intensity. Parents who have felt impotent to help their child are made to feel that his recovery and future are in their hands. In the early stages, some improvement may be seen, but there is no evidence that more orthodox treatment (physiotherapy, education, etc.) would not be just as effective if applied with similar intensity, and the Institute has not published its long term results in any scientifically acceptable format.

VITAMIN, TRACE ELEMENT AND MINERAL SUPPLEMENTS

Massive vitamin supplementation is currently popular for the treatment of mental retardation. There is no evidence of its efficacy (except in a few extremely rare inborn errors of metabolism). It is, however, unlikely to be harmful provided that the supplement excludes vitamins A and D. Hair analysis to obtain a 'profile' of mineral deficiencies is also fashionable, although there is very little scientific evidence on the subject.

The Feingold diet and other approaches to 'hyperactivity' are described on p. 406.

CONCLUSION

No two families or individuals react to the problems of handicap in the same way. The professional's task is to understand these reactions; there is no place for criticism or derogatory comment.

Chapter Eight
Services for Handicapped Children

Assessment is only one of the functions of a Child Development Centre (CDC). It should also be a place where parents can obtain advice and information on all aspects of their child's handicap and, by coordinating the many services needed by the child, can reduce the burden of frequent visits to a variety of hospital clinics and departments.

MEDICAL SERVICES

Information

An important function of the CDC is to provide an information resource. The CDC secretary should maintain files on all the various facilities mentioned in the following paragraphs.

Individual reports (p. 135), developmental charts, and written suggestions on management, are appreciated. A reference library of books suitable for the layman can be provided at little cost (Appendix 11). Intensive workshops, and residential 'teach-ins', though time consuming, are undoubtedly worthwhile. Parents should be encouraged to join the society appropriate for their child's handicap, in order to obtain further information and literature and to meet other parents (Appendix 10). In addition, many like to contribute financially, recognising that the voluntary societies are a valuable pressure group and can help to improve facilities for the future.

Helping the child's development

Parents often feel that they have no special expertise for aiding their child's development and that all the work must be done by professionals. This belief is all-too-easily reinforced by professional attitudes. To combat this it is vital for parents to be involved in all therapeutic and teaching activities, and a written programme which can be carried out by the parents at home each day is also helpful. An introduction to the nearest toy library may be arranged. Numerous specialised activities are available, for example horse-riding, swimming, skiing, adventure playgrounds, and music, art, drama and dance therapy. These can be invaluable in developing the child's coordination, confidence and independence.

Using child psychiatry services

Developmental and behavioural problems, atypical parental reactions to handicap, and failure of attempts to improve behaviour can often be traced to a disturbance in the parent/child relationship or in family dynamics. A modern eclectic department of child psychiatry can contribute to the care of these families but, since many people are very wary of psychiatrists and psychologists, a little care is needed in setting up a successful referral. A psychiatric consultation should seldom be offered until the parents themselves recognise the possibility of a psychological problem and acknowledge that they need expert guidance. It is often helpful to make a personal introduction and an initial joint consultation may be invaluable. Alternatively, a 'one-off' interview with the psychiatrist can be arranged and the parents are told that this is to be regarded as another investigation.

Psychiatric referral is easily misconstrued by parents to mean that they are either mad or bad, and must be beyond the help of ordinary medicine. The offer of a further appointment with the paediatrician helps to avoid such misconceptions, and guarantees that continuity of follow-up will be maintained if the psychiatric intervention is unsuccessful.

DENTISTRY

Cavities and periodontal disease are more likely to occur in the handicapped child because of the difficulty in maintaining oral hygiene. In addition, abnormalities of tooth structure and other orthodontic problems occur in many dysmorphic syndromes. These should be treated if possible, to improve the social acceptability of the handicapped person. Dentistry for the handicapped is 'special' not because of any particular technical problems, but because of the need for quiet surroundings, an unhurried approach, and the availability of sedation or anaesthesia.[152] Fluoride treatment (Table 8.1) should be recommended from the time of diagnosis.

IMMUNISATION

There is no reason to withhold diphtheria, tetanus and polio immunisation from handicapped infants. The DHSS recommend that pertussis vaccine should not be administered to infants with a history of convulsions and that other neurological disorders should be regarded as a relative contraindication.[153] This advice is based on the logical premise that, since the vaccine

Table 8.1 Fluoride supplementation.

| Age in years | Concentration of fluoride in drinking water (in parts/10^6) | | |
	0.0–0.3	0.3–0.7	>0.7
0–2	0.25 mg F/day	—	—
2–3	0.50 mg F/day	0.25 mg F/day	—
3–12	1.0 mg F/day	0.50 mg F/day	—

Notes   (1) Supplements should begin as early as possible.
(2) Once-daily dose is adequate.
(3) Only one source of fluoride should be given (excluding toothpaste).
(4) Higher doses may cause fluorosis.
(5) Fluoride is toxic in overdosage.
(6) Details of local fluoride concentrations are obtainable from the local Water Board.

can rarely precipitate fits and brain injury (p. 229), it is best avoided in infants in whom these problems already exist. However, there is no firm evidence that these complications are more likely to occur in such children. Severe pertussis has afflicted many handicapped infants in the epidemics of the last few years and it seems likely that the risks arising from the disease are now substantially greater than those of the vaccine (*see* Appendix 5). Many parents are reaching this conclusion for themselves and request pertussis immunisation.[458] If, after discussion with them, the vaccine is given to a handicapped child, the reasons should be clearly recorded in the child's notes, for medico-legal protection.

Measles immunisation probably should be recommended even in severe neurological handicaps, for the risk of contracting measles at a playgroup, nursery or hospital waiting room is very high. The use of specific measles immunoglobulin to reduce the reaction is recommended if the child is epileptic or has ever had febrile fits.[154] Occasionally anticonvulsant cover is offered as well. The parents should be told that the risk of a febrile fit occurring with the vaccine is much less than that with natural measles. 'Allergy' is not a contraindication unless there is severe, proven sensitivity to egg protein.

None of these vaccines is contraindicated by a history of asthma, eczema or hay fever in the child or his relative. An adverse reaction (excessive screaming or a febrile convulsion) following pertussis vaccine is a contraindication to further doses.

PRACTICAL HELP

Respite care

An occasional break from the tiring routine of caring for a handicapped child may help to preserve the parents' health and the stability of their marriage, and allows them to spend more time with their normal children. Some social service departments run a hostel for this purpose, or organise voluntary short term fostering or baby sitting schemes. Many societies and charities offer special holidays for handicapped children. Day nursery facilities provide valuable experiences for the child as well as relief for the parents. For the most severely handicapped, and those who have severe epilepsy or other medical problems, relief care may be provided in the paediatric ward. Parents should be encouraged to use this and told that this is a legitimate use of a hospital bed.

Financial help

Parents who have to devote substantially more time to the handicapped child than would be required by a normal child may be entitled to the attendance allowance when the child reaches his second birthday. The mobility allowance is payable for children over the age of 5 who are physically disabled. There have been many problems in the interpretation of this legislation and changes are likely in the near future.[151] DHSS literature outlines the exact criteria for payment but, regrettably, many parents are not informed about these allowances for months or even years.

The 'Family Fund' (*see* Appendix 10 for address) will sometimes be able to help parents with special needs which cannot be met by any statutory provision; for example, a washing machine may be provided for the parents of an incontinent child with spina bifida.

Long term care

The use of long-stay beds for the handicapped in children's hospitals has fallen steadily in recent years from 7100 in 1969 to 3900 in 1977. There will always be some children who cannot be managed at home (p. 144) but most of these can be cared for in small children's homes which provide a family atmosphere. The number of places in these units is not adequate to meet the demand and long delays may be experienced in placing a child. For the adolescent and young adult, various forms of hostel and sheltered accommodation are being developed and in the future, if adequate funds are made available, these should cater for most handicapped people. Even the most profoundly handicapped, for whom it is likely that nursing care will always be needed, can be cared for in small homely units.

Adoption or long term fostering of handicapped children is a desirable alternative to placement in a children's home. Several organisations now specialise in finding adoptive parents for 'hard-to-place' children (*see* Appendix 10 for addresses). If the adoption of these children is to be successful, detailed counselling and adequate family support are essential. There is always some anxiety about the adoption of children whose natural parents are psychotic, psychopathic, or alcoholic.[155] The evidence suggests that, although all these disorders have a genetic component, a good environment in childhood has some protective effect, and adoption therefore seems particularly desirable for such children.

The handicapped teenager

Handicapped teenagers have frequently lost contact with the paediatric services, and quite rightly most of their needs are met through the educational system; nevertheless teenagers, particularly those with handicaps which affect mobility, will often benefit from a realistic reassessment. These youngsters often have social difficulties in developing independence. Many of the voluntary societies provide clubs and holiday activities which can boost self-confidence and morale. Social skills training is helpful to shy, awkward teenagers with mild mental handicap, for example, they may practise buying something in a shop or entering a room full of people. This work is usually done in small groups and a video system is very useful, providing immediate feedback as social competence improves.[156,157]

The sexual problems of many handicapped teenagers and adults are self-evident. Several groups, notably SPOD (Sexual Problems of the Disabled), have devoted much attention to these in recent years. Physical handicaps may directly affect sexual function, as in spina bifida, or may inhibit sexual activity by making the person totally dependent on others, as for example in severe athetosis. In mental handicaps of mild degree the main problems are likely to be social rather than biological; for example, the development of stable relationships, the control of fertility and the avoidance of exploitation. In the severely handicapped, it is unlikely that sexual relationships will develop (*see also* p. 166).

EDUCATION

After the family, school is the biggest influence in the life of a handicapped child. All children, however handicapped, have a right to receive education from the age of 5. Many local authorities now make provision for handicapped children to start school at 3, or even earlier in some cases.

Early school placement has many advantages. All the necessary services are available under one roof, and a coordinated programme of management is easily arranged. The child is weaned away from excessive dependence on his parents and given valuable social experiences. The atmosphere of the school is a more normalising influence than a Child Development Centre sited in a hospital and encourages the parents to see handicap as an educational and social problem rather than a medical one. Many special schools run coffee mornings and other social events, which enable parents to meet others who have similar problems. Parents are kept informed about

Table 8.2 Children in special schools. (Figures from Statistics of Education 1977 (HMSO).)

Blind	0.7
Partially sighted	1.4
Deaf	2.4
Partially deaf	3.4
Physically handicapped	9.1
Delicate	3.5
Maladjusted	11.9
Educationally subnormal (moderate)	45.7
Educationally subnormal (severe)	19.3
Epileptic	0.8
Speech Defect	1.3
Autistic	0.5
Total	100% (177 117 children)

their child's progress by means of a notebook which travels to and from home with him.

Most handicapped children until recently have been educated in special schools (Table 8.2). The education services in the UK have a distinguished record in providing these specialised and expensive schools. For those children too young to attend school, there are peripatetic teachers specialising in hearing or vision defects, or in severe mental handicap.

Decisions about special school placements are the responsibility of the educational psychologist, but the paediatrician is often in the best position to know when and how to introduce the topic of special education. The parents must be told that the doctor has no authority to decide about school placement and it is usually unwise to name a particular school as potentially suitable for the child until the educational psychologist has been consulted. Once his agreement has been obtained, the parents may like to visit an appropriate school; they often have fantasies about special schools which are far more alarming than the reality.

Placement in a special school has always been a potential source of conflict between parents and professionals. Parents feel that special education stigmatises the child; that he will learn 'bad habits' from other retarded children; and that he would have more chance of learning social skills in a normal school. These misgivings are by no means unjustified and should be acknowledged, but the high quality of special education, the advantages of small classes, and the depressing effects on a child of being unable to keep up with his peers in a normal class should also be mentioned. It may reassure parents to know that special school placements are regularly reviewed and that there is no bar to transferring to a normal school.

Psychological assessment commonly provokes parental anxiety and anger, particularly when decisions about school placement appear to be based on formal I.Q. tests. In the past these were frequently thought to be 'unfair', particularly when the stopwatch was much in evidence, and there are still many misconceptions about them. At home, where daily routines can be mastered over the years, a handicapped child may appear much more intelligent than he really is. His handicap is only revealed when he is expected to generalise what he has learnt to an unfamiliar situation (*see* p. 73). Failure to appreciate this rather subtle point sometimes leads parents to doubt the competence of the educational psychologist, and they may even suspect him of distorting the results for the administrative convenience of the education authority! However, most educational psychologists now incorporate informal observations, teachers' reports and parental information into their assessment, cross-checking their findings with tests which the parents are usually allowed to observe. It is essential that the parents feel that the tester has seen a true picture of the child. Only then can discussion proceed to the interpretation of the findings and the future management.

The Warnock Report and the 1981 Education Act

The Warnock Report presented an outstanding study of the educational needs of handicapped children.[158] Among its most significant recommendtions were (1) the concept of 'handicap' should be replaced by that of 'special educational needs'. (2) The statutory designation of handicapped children by a single 'label' should be abolished. (3) Parents should have more say in the education of their children. (4) The Report took a balanced view on the question of integrating handicapped children into normal schools, recognising that for some this is desirable and possible, but for others integration could be detrimental both to the handicapped child and the normal classmates.

The Education Act (1981) is intended to implement the recommendations of Warnock.[159] The sharp distinction between handicapped and non-handicapped children will be abolished. Any child who is experiencing difficulties in school may need special help and this may be true of 20% of children at some point in their school career. The Act defines a child with special educational needs as one with a learning difficulty; he has 'significantly greater difficulty in learning than the majority of children of his age, or has a disability which prevents or hinders him from making use of the educational facilities generally provided for children of his age'. The local education authority must make this special educational provision available; furthermore, they must do so in ordinary school *provided that* firstly the parents agree; secondly it is in the best interests of the child *and* that the education of other children will not be adversely affected; and thirdly resources are thereby used efficiently. The authority must also identify and assess children who may need special help, and must review them annually and reassess them between 14 and 15 years of age.

Most children with severe handicaps will be known to a paediatrician long before they are of school age. It will be the duty of the doctor to notify the education authority of the possibility that the child may need special education. The parents should certainly be told before this is done, and careful judgement will be needed over the timing; however, in districts where there is already mutual respect between the paediatric and educational services, this provision of the new Act should make little difference.

Children will initially be assessed informally but those who have more complex or severe problems will need a more detailed multidisciplinary assessment. Section 5 of the new Act describes the assessment procedures. The local authority must notify parents of their intention to assess the child. Appropriate professional advice and opinions are to be submitted in written form, in language intelligible to the layman. The child's strengths and weaknesses, and his needs for special resources or equipment, should be summarised. Having collected this information the authority may decide that the child's problem is complicated or severe, and will then make a 'statement' (Section 7 of the Act). This includes summaries of professional opinions (but not the records on which they are based); the educational provision proposed; and the views of the parents, who must themselves receive a copy of the complete statement. This document will be the foundation of record-keeping, review and reassessement.

At all stages of this procedure, parents have statutory rights to be consulted and informed, and they have a right of appeal, ultimately to the Secretary of State. This new legislation is complex and undoubtedly some difficulties will be encountered as it is implemented, but the underlying philosophy appears to be sound.

Integration

Although very desirable in principle, the trend towards integration has revealed a number of problems.[160] Children may be physically present in a normal class, but are not necessarily integrated socially. Alternatively, the handicapped child may become a classroom 'pet' with possibly detrimental effects on emotional development. Successful integration depends both on the physical environment of the school and the enthusiasm and skill of the head and the teachers. The paediatrician and his colleagues, together with the school doctor, have a vital role to play in supporting the staff, explaining the implications of the handicap, and sharing the inevitably increased responsibility for the child's safety and progress.

Taking a long term view, integration must be seen as a powerful way of increasing society's awareness and acceptance of handicap, and for this reason alone justifies the extra effort and cost involved.

Chapter Nine
Behaviour Problems and Behaviour Modification

BEHAVIOURAL PSYCHOLOGY

In behavioural psychology, the term 'behaviour' includes all the observed abilities and activities of a living organism—movement, eating, speaking, and so on. For the behaviourist, the starting point is the behaviour actually observed; diagnoses such as mental retardation or 'developmental delay' and speculation about either the neurological basis or the long forgotten origins of the behaviour are largely irrelevant. The goal is to identify specific areas of behaviour which might be amenable to useful change or improvement.

Behaviour modification originated in the USA as a result of basic research first in animal psychology and later on human subjects. In the past 15 years it has developed into a powerful and effective tool for changing the behaviour of both normal and handicapped people of all ages. The following account is intended only to outline the scope of the subject and illustrate some practical applications in the field of childhood handicap. The paediatrician cannot expect to master the principles and techniques of behavioural psychology without training and practice. Several excellent reviews and manuals are recommended for more detailed study.[161,162,163,164]

There are four steps in the use of a behavioural technique. It will be apparent that these steps reflect the general principles of the scientific method. Each problem is seen as an experiment with a definite end result. Behaviour modification is a method of approaching problems; it does not provide a series of prescriptions for specific behaviour disorders.

Stage 1—Definition of the Problem.   Three types of behavioural problems are recognized (Fig. 9.1). A detailed analysis is essential. For example, if the complaint is of unwanted behaviour, the analysis would include time, place

155

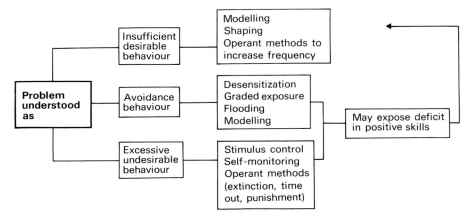

Fig. 9.1 Basic techniques in behaviour modification with children. (Reproduced from Hill[163] by permission.)

and frequency, preceding events, reaction of other people, etc. Often it is helpful to ask the parents to keep a diary which will clarify these points, and provide a baseline to estimate the effectiveness of intervention. It is also necessary to decide what change in the behaviour would constitute an acceptable solution.

Stage 2—Setting Up a Hypothesis.   There may be many possible explanations for the persistence of an unwanted behaviour or the failure to develop desired behaviour. Selection of the most plausible is based on the information gained by interview, direct observation, experience with previous similar cases, and a knowledge of child development.

Stage 3—Testing the Hypothesis.   The intervention programme is designed in such a way that results can be measured. If the hypothesis was correct, improvement should follow intervention.

Stage 4—Evaluating the Results.   The outcome of the programme is assessed to decide whether the object was achieved, whether the improvement was permanent and whether it could have been achieved with greater economy of effort.

Increasing wanted behaviour

REINFORCEMENT

A reinforcer is any consequence of a behaviour which increases the likelihood that the behaviour will be repeated. Reinforcers may be an item of food or drink, attention, a cuddle, praise, or tokens that may be exchanged for desired items. Among the handicapped, reinforcers may be bizarre; for example, being allowed to twiddle a piece of silver paper might be reinforcing to an autistic child. The fact that a child seems to like something very much suggests that it might be a reinforcer (*see* Stage 2 above) but it must then be shown to actually increase the frequency of the behaviour in question (Stage 3). If it does not, it is not a reinforcer.

Reinforcement is used to increase wanted behaviour. The way in which the reward is delivered is crucial. The interval between the behaviour and the reinforcement must be as short as is practical. It should be provided every time the behaviour occurs in the early stages, although later it can be provided intermittently. Intermittent reinforcement tends to be more effective. In the case of reinforcers which may satiate the child very rapidly, such as food, the quantity must also be carefully defined.

SHAPING, PROMPTING, CHAINING AND MODELLING

These techniques are of particular value in building up complex skills, for example dressing or feeding. Having defined the desired behaviour, it is broken down into very small steps. Reinforcement is given for completion of each step. In shaping, the child has first to produce an approximation to the required skill before he receives his reinforcer. Prompting means that the child is guided, verbally or manually, to produce the required behaviour which is then immediately rewarded; this is quicker than waiting for the child to perform spontaneously. If the skill consists of multiple small steps, each of which has to be acquired in sequence, the operation is known as chaining. It is usual to start with the last step, and work backwards. In modelling, the child learns by imitating the behaviour of other children or adults.

Example.   G was an 8-year-old boy with a mental age of around 18 months. He made no effort to feed himself. The therapist held a spoon loaded with ice-cream against his lips, his hand was placed around the handle, and the spoon guided into his mouth. On each successive day, his hand was placed on the spoon at a greater distance from his mouth, until he was able to complete the entire sequence of movements himself. There were two reinforcers here; the ice-cream itself, and the praise which accompanied each success.

A similar approach is used to bring about gradual changes in undesirable behaviour patterns and replace them with more acceptable ones. 'Scene setting' is a useful addition to these techniques; a routine sequence of events is established and the child learns to recognise this routine as a cue that a specific series of responses is expected. An example is described in the section on sleep disturbance (p. 163).

TOKEN ECONOMIES

A token may be used as a reinforcer. When sufficient tokens have been accumulated they are exchanged for a reward. The Star Chart (commonly used in the treatment of enuresis) and the award of house points by school teachers provide familiar examples. Sometimes the token itself may be desirable; for example, Batman transfers or coloured beads. The reward may be tangible (a visit to the swimming bath) or may be limited to the praise and approval of adults or peers.

Token economies have numerous uses in encouraging desired behaviour. With a little more ingenuity they can also be useful in eliminating undesirable behaviour, for example by giving a token for *not* producing the behaviour during a specified period of time.

If this method is to succeed, the child and parents must be quite clear as to what behaviour is required in order to earn a token and both parties must adhere to the agreement. They must decide whether tokens are to be deducted for bad behaviour. The reward must not appear massive and unattainable (like a bicycle); it should be modest but desirable and within realistic reach in relation to the child's capabilities. It is better to arrange for the reward to be earned *when* a certain number of tokens has been collected rather than *if* they are collected by a certain time, since with the former method there is no prospect of ultimate failure to discourage the child. Tokens can be exchanged for a variety of rewards during the course of one programme. This flexibility helps to maintain enthusiasm for long enough to consolidate the 'cure' before the system is finally phased out.

Example.   P was a mildly retarded 12-year-old boy. His parents complained about his outbursts of temper, usually in the evening, and his refusal to get up in the morning. A token economy was designed in which he earned stars on a chart for arriving at breakfast on time, and for each evening in which he had no tantrums. It was linked to his pocket money so that with good behaviour he could buy a new pop single about once a fortnight.

Eliminating unwanted behaviour

Undesirable or intolerable behaviour is often the biggest problem faced by parents of a handicapped child and is often assumed to be an inevitable consequence of brain injury or retardation. However, although behaviour problems are certainly commoner in handicapped children,[165,166,167] there is no evidence that any particular pattern of behaviour is associated with any specific handicap.[10,11] Probably several factors contribute to the reported high prevalence of behaviour disorder in handicap.

1   Regular contact with medical services provides an opportunity for reporting these problems, which is not so readily available to parents of normal children.

2   Parents may be less optimistic that behaviour problems will resolve spontaneously if the child is handicapped.

3   Many parents lack confidence in managing a child who is handicapped, and their feelings of inadequacy are easily increased by the well-meaning help offered by numerous and highly competent professionals. Some people feel unable to apply even the most gentle discipline in managing their handicapped child, feeling that his bad behaviour is beyond his control. As a result they may tolerate appalling problems for months or years before seeking help.

4   There is sometimes a particular reluctance to discipline children who have fits, because of a fear that a tantrum may lead on to a fit.

5   The handicapped child's inability to generate his own ideas and activities often results in unwanted behaviour when the parents cannot give him unlimited attention.

In many cases the undesirable behaviour only occurs in specified situations, most often at home. Parents often feel distressed by this apparent discrimination and should be reminded that most people reserve their worst behaviour for situations in which they feel safe. In addition, the fact that the child can behave well in other situations is good evidence that the behaviour disorder is not an inevitable consequence of his neurological handicap.

Bad behaviours develop and become established because they produce a reward for the child; in other words they are reinforced, usually unwittingly, by the response of someone or something in their environment. For the handicapped child in particular, adult attention is often a potent reinforcer and it does not necessarily matter whether the attention is of a pleasant or punitive nature. Parental compliance with the child's demands is an additional reward of undesirable behaviour; as emphasised previously, *anything* that perpetuates a behaviour is a reinforcer.

The prevention of behaviour disorder in the handicapped child has not received as much study as its treatment. Parents should be warned at an early stage that even very handicapped children are quite capable of developing manipulative behaviour patterns if permitted to do so. Advice should be readily available so that any problems can be dealt with before they become entrenched.

RESTRUCTURING THE ENVIRONMENT

If the unwanted behaviour only occurs in certain circumstances it is likely to be dependent on some preceding event or on some aspect of the surrounding environment. It is often possible to either remove the stimulus, alter it, or change the situation so that the problem either resolves or becomes more manageable.

Example. A severely retarded 8-year-old girl at boarding school persistently got out of bed every night and wandered in the corridor. She did no damage and always returned happily to bed, but the staff were afraid that sooner or later some accident might happen. They felt that they could cope with the problem if they could be alerted as soon as she was out of bed. This was easily accomplished by the construction of a simple alarm system.

EXTINCTION

If an unwanted behaviour is maintained by regular reinforcement, it can be eliminated by discontinuing that reinforcement. The predictable consequence is an initial increase in the unwanted behaviour which had previously been effective in securing the reinforcer. When the child realises that the rewards are no longer forthcoming, there is a rapid decline in the frequency of the behaviour. Before embarking on a programme based on extinction, one must be certain that firstly the responsible adults are aware of and can tolerate the expected initial increased severity and frequency, and secondly the increase will not be dangerous to the child. If these conditions are not met, other approaches must be used.

Example. A 5-year-old mildly retarded boy reacted to any instruction or reprimand from his teacher by banging his head with his hands. As he had arrested hydrocephalus, the teacher always gave in at once, fearing that he might injure himself. She was advised that this would not occur and that she should not respond to his head banging. After the predicted initial increase, it rapidly disappeared.

PUNISHMENT

The concept of retribution is not popular in our present society and the term punishment has therefore to be used with some care. In behavioural terms it is the opposite of reinforcement; it is any consequence of a particular behaviour which decreases the likelihood that the behaviour will be repeated. As with reinforcement, the hypothesis that something is a punishment is dependent on the demonstration that it reduces the behaviour in question. Several forms of punishment are recognised.

Time-out means the removal of the child from the reinforcement which maintains the behaviour. Often the reinforcement is found on careful analysis to be social attention, sometimes of an apparently unpleasant kind (e.g. scolding or even a smack). A short period of time-out (1–2 minutes) is as effective and probably more effective than a longer period. The child may be removed from the room, for example to the hall or bedroom; it is essential to first establish that the suggested place is safe, and also that it really does represent an undesirable experience to the child. Sometimes, sitting on a particular chair or standing in a corner may be just as effective. Release from time-out depends only on good behaviour at the moment of release; he does not have to repent or apologise. The adult must know how to respond if the child does not stay in his time-out situation. Time-out is often used by parents but is rejected as ineffective because they have neglected one or more of these principles. Properly used, it is often a highly effective way of eliminating undesirable behaviour.

Token Economy.   Where this is used, fines can easily be imposed for inappropriate behaviour.

Restraint.   Firm physical restraint, for example with the arms held firmly by the sides, is an effective punishment for many mentally handicapped children. The adult should either hold the child from behind or avert his gaze so that there is no eye contact. Periods of restraint need only last for a matter of seconds. This method can be combined with a shout of 'no' in tones of controlled anger.

It is surprising how some parents and teachers are afraid to apply this technique, often reporting that a child 'is much stronger than I am'. Possibly there is a fear that restraint may damage the child in some way, either physically or psychologically, but there is no justification for this anxiety.

Restitution.   This means that the child has to make amends for inappropriate behaviour by a directly relevant action, such as cleaning up food which he has deliberately spilt. If necessary he is guided through this task by the adult. Sometimes this is extended so that the child has to perform the act of restitution several times or carry out several related tasks.

REINFORCEMENT OF DESIRABLE BEHAVIOUR

Differential reinforcement of other behaviour (DRO) may be used instead of, or as well as, methods to reduce unwanted behaviour. For example, the problem of a girl who bangs her head with her fists could be approached by punishment for the head banging, or by reinforcement for keeping her hands by her sides. Development of desirable activity such as play or communication is often the only permanent solution to behaviour problems in the severely handicapped. If all therapeutic efforts are directed towards removal of an unwanted behaviour without encouraging an alternative repertoire of skills, new and equally undesirable behaviour problems will inevitably emerge.

TREATMENT OF LIFE-THREATENING BEHAVIOUR DISORDER

Occasionally severely retarded people develop potentially lethal habits, such as severe self-mutilation or persistent rumination and vomiting.[168,169] In cases where other methods have been ineffective, intensely adversive stimuli, such as electric shock, the smell of ammonia, or the taste of lemon juice, have been used. There are both ethical and practical difficulties in these cases, and advice should be sought from someone with experience in this field, since an intensive behavioural programme in a specialised unit may be the only solution.[476]

Behaviour modification—summary

1   Behaviour modification offers a scientific method of approaching behaviour problems, but it does not provide a single prescription for a particular type of behaviour disorder.

2   The skills which are taught to the mentally handicapped do not always generalise. For example, toilet training may be taught successfully in school, but the child may still be incontinent at home and has to be taught the necessary steps there as well.

3   Some parents are incapable of applying a behavioural programme, because of limited intellect or emotional and ethical objections.

4   Many adults are uneasy about manipulating a child's behaviour in this way, feeling that the child should be 'good' without such 'artificial' methods. Token systems are often confused with bribery, although bribery is correctly defined as a 'reward offered to a person to induce him to act contrary to what is just and right'. All parents use behaviour modification techniques; the skill of a psychologist lies in using them effectively.

5   Complaints about a child's behaviour commonly mask more fundamental problems. For example, a sleep disturbance is sometimes used as a marital weapon by a husband or wife. Parents may quietly sabotage behaviour modification programmes designed to eliminate hyperactivity or other undesirable behaviours, because they have reached a point where they can no longer tolerate the burdens of caring for a handicapped child, yet feel unable to ask for him to be taken into residential care. Family problems are often revealed when a serious attempt is made to tackle a behaviour disorder and some form of family therapy or counselling may then be indicated (p. 142).

6   The shortage of clinical psychologists trained in behaviour modification techniques is hindering their wider application in childhood handicap. Although professional time is indeed expensive, anything which keeps mentally handicapped people out of residential care is likely to be cost effective as well as humane.

COMMON BEHAVIOUR PROBLEMS

Sleep disturbances

These are among the commonest of all behaviour problems. Waking at night is in itself quite normal, but most children settle themselves to sleep again without waking the rest of the household.[170,171,174] Problems arise when the child refuses to go to bed, insists on falling asleep in the parent's arms, wakes repeatedly and demands attention each time, or transfers to the parent's bed. Prolonged sleep disturbance is exhausting to the parents and sometimes makes the child irritable; possibly it is one cause of 'hyperactivity', since fatigue may reduce attention span.

Sleep disturbances have many causes, some of which may be organic (pp. 354, 400) but most of which are environmental. The natural anxieties of parents responsible for the care of a young child are magnified when he is handicapped and they often unwittingly perpetuate and reinforce undesirable bedtime behaviour and night waking, by responding patiently and caringly to the child's every demand.

Sedative medication such as trimeprazine (Vallergan) 2–4 mg per kg, 1–2 hours before bedtime may help, but although it induces sleep it seldom rectifies the total pattern of sleep disturbance. Parents can, however, be assured that it can safely be used for long periods without side-effects.

Behavioural methods are now known to be an effective way of eliminating sleep disturbances even in handicapped children.[170] A careful preliminary analysis is essential. Better bedtime habits can be achieved by 'scene setting'; for example, a regular quiet period before bed in which the child has a game, story or a cuddle. For children who refuse to settle until their parents go to bed, 'graded change' is used to achieve an earlier bedtime, since it is usually easier to adjust the bedtime by small increments than by several hours in a single step. A token economy can be used to reinforce desirable behaviour such as staying in his own bed all night. Extinction, by leaving the child to cry is effective, if carried out ruthlessly, but is seldom acceptable to parents; but all positive reinforcements such as cuddles or drinks during episodes of night waking must be eliminated.

Pica

This is the ingestion of substances not normally considered edible.[172,173] The name is derived from the scientific name of the magpie, a bird noted for its habit of collecting useless material. Sucking and mouthing of inedible objects is a normal developmental stage, but pica is not merely a prolongation of this phase; it is a specific maladaptive behaviour pattern which is commoner in, but not confined to, severely mentally handicapped children. It most often develops as a response to deprivation and an unstimulating environment.

Virtually any substance may be ingested but there is particular concern about lead-containing materials such as old paint and some imported toys (now banned), and also over fibrous materials like hair or cloth which can cause intestinal obstruction. Children with pica often have elevated blood lead levels but it is not usually possible to trace any particular behaviour disturbance to this and, except for cases which present with encephalopathy, the lead intoxication is not the cause of the child's mental handicap (*see also* p. 229). Iron deficiency is also common; it has been suggested that this is the stimulus which prompts the child to eat mineral substances in search of iron, but more probably the iron deficiency is only the result of the distorted eating habit. There is, however, some evidence that iron deficiency can cause irritability and mood changes which could initiate behaviour problems, and an improvement in mood sometimes results from iron therapy before any rise in haemoglobin is detectable.

Pica will usually respond to changes in the environment, for example provision of stimulating play opportunities, the development of a method of communication, and the differential reinforcement of more appropriate activities. The blood lead and haemoglobin levels should be checked and a course of oral iron therapy may be beneficial.

Nocturnal enuresis (bed wetting)

This is an extremely common problem among handicapped children.[162,164] The acquisition of continence in the handicapped is governed to some extent by neurological factors and by mental age, but enuresis can be eliminated even in the severely handicapped. As in normal children, a distinction is made between primary enuresis, in which the child has never been dry, and secondary enuresis, meaning that the child has become enuretic again after achieving night-time continence. Organic causes, notably infection and spinal cord lesions such as occult dysraphism (p. 369) should be excluded but enuresis is very rarely the only feature of these conditions.

After an initial period of diary recording, a token economy system should be introduced and is often remarkably effective. The buzzer and pad method is reserved for those who do not succeed with the token system, and also works well provided that the child is woken by the alarm and has to get out of bed to disconnect it. Extra loud buzzers and vibrating devices are available for heavy sleepers and for hearing-impaired children. Imipramine is used occasionally, but has only modest effectiveness, a high relapse rate and serious toxicity if accidentally ingested by younger siblings.

An intensive behavioural programme called 'Dry Bed Training' is claimed to produce outstanding results. The programme has several components including a buzzer, hourly toileting during the first night, and a series of aversive procedures such as helping to change the bed and 'practice toileting' if the person wets the bed.

Day-time wetting

Like nocturnal enuresis, this seldom has a detectable organic cause. In addition to those causes mentioned above, the rare possibility of an ectopic ureter opening into the urethra or vagina must be excluded if the child is never dry even for a few minutes. In most cases of day-time wetting, the history suggests that because of 'immaturity' signals from the full bladder do not impress themselves on the child's consciousness until it is too late to reach the toilet. Sometimes the adult attention gained while the child is cleaned and changed reinforces the pattern.

A diary record of the child's wetting and toileting should be kept for a few days. The problem often responds to a token system, in which rewards are earned for appropriate use of the toilet and/or remaining dry for a specified period. This may be combined with a graded programme of regular toileting under supervision, perhaps starting hourly or half hourly, according to the initial frequency of wetting and the interval is then gradually lengthened. Imipramine is used occasionally in day-time wetting, but its effectiveness is limited.

Faecal soiling

Soiling in the handicapped child is often associated with chronic constipation to which poor diet, low tone in abdominal muscles, and occasionally anal fissures may contribute. An improved bowel habit can often be achieved with a stool softener such as lactulose, combined with a laxative such as Senokot, given at night. If necessary a glycerine or 'Dulcolax' suppository is given in the morning to initiate regular toileting. At the same time, reinforcement (e.g. using a token system) is introduced. Tokens are awarded for opening the bowels in the toilet rather than for having clean pants since, if the latter is made the main goal, faecal retention may unwittingly be encouraged.

Faecal smearing is a less common complaint. It may occur in the severely retarded, particularly when inadequately stimulated and poorly supervised; or in children with milder handicaps, when it may be suggestive of some emotional or environmental disturbance. Whatever the circumstances, the furore created by this activity is often reinforcing to the child. Approaches to management might include a manipulation of the situation in which it occurs, for example a change of toilet routine or use of clothing which the child cannot remove himself so that he does not have access to his soiled nappy or pants. Any positive reinforcement which seems likely to perpetuate the habit, such as the attention involved in cleaning up the mess, is identified and eliminated as far as possible, and punishment such as 'time-out' or restitution may be used.

Self injurious behaviour (self-mutilation)

Mild forms of self injurious behaviour, such as head-banging, may occur in normal children but they are usually transient and need no specialised management. In the mentally handicapped child, self mutilation may be serious and even life-threatening and poses a most distressing problem to those who care for him.[168] It takes many forms: head-banging, self-biting, eye-poking, etc. The aetiology is not certain. Self injury is particularly common in the Lesch-Nyhan syndrome (p. 469), suggesting that there may be a specific neurological cause in some cases. It may possibly begin as a response to pain, for example from middle-ear disease or toothache. The child sometimes seems to gain some pleasurable sensation from the activity in spite of its apparently painful consequences but in other cases there seems to be some inner compulsion which distresses him. Undoubtedly, whatever the original cause of the behaviour, the child often learns to use it either to gain attention or to avoid some unwanted task or activity.

Many behavioural approaches have been designed to eliminate self injury. It is no longer acceptable to treat such cases with padded restraints and sedatives, except perhaps as a short-term measure. Most important is a restructuring of the child's daily routine to include more stimulating activities. Extinction may be used when the behaviour is maintained by attention, but only if the predicted initial increase in frequency will not be dangerous. Punishment by means of restraint and a shout may be used. Rarely, more extreme aversive measures are needed (p. 162).

Sexual problems in adolescence

Severe brain damage is a recognized, though rare, cause of precocious puberty. If this occurs, menstruation can be suppressed by injectable medroxyprogesterone acetate, but such cases should be discussed first with a paediatric endocrinologist, since further investigation may be needed.

Sexual behaviour may cause problems in the retarded adolescent. These are due to the lack of normal social inhibitions rather than to a pathologically increased sex drive, as is sometimes imagined by the layman in his fantasies about mental handicap. Attempted intercourse is relatively rare and masturbation in public places is the commonest cause for concern. This can usually be dealt with by a simple behavioural programme in which the person is taught that this is done only in private.

In girls, the main fears of parents are promiscuous behaviour and the management of menstrual hygiene. Education is as important for the handicapped girl as for the normal population, and useful literature is available.[176] Advice on contraception may be appropriate for the mildly handicapped girl. Menstruation can, if necessary, be suppressed by continuous administration of a low-dose oestrogen–progesterone combination. Sterilisation and hysterectomy are both drastic measures which should only rarely be necessary.[175]

Sexuality in the handicapped is a difficult subject and arouses intense and often irrational emotions. The excellent review by Craft and Craft of the medical, legal and ethical aspects is recommended for further study.[197]

Chapter Ten
Genetic Aspects of Handicap

A consultant in clinical genetics is not only trained to advise parents on the recurrence risks of genetic diseases, but is also better equipped than most paediatricians to recognise the unusual dysmorphic syndrome or a rare variant of a familiar disorder. Nevertheless, the paediatrician will often need to deal (at least in general terms) with such questions as the relevance of a family history of neurological disorder or the recurrence risk of a handicapping condition, and a knowledge of basic principles enables better use to be made of the genetic service.[177,178]

Some commonly used genetic terms are defined in Table 10.1.

Diagnosis

Genetic counselling can only be as accurate as the diagnosis. If a child has a recognisable disorder, risk factors can be accurately defined; but in many handicaps, particularly mental retardation, it may be difficult to establish a diagnosis that is specific enough to be useful in genetic counselling. It is essential for parents to understand that often no precise explanation can be found for a handicap, and risk factors are then necessarily empiric; that is, they are based on observed recurrence risks in numerous similar situations, rather than derived from basic genetic principles.

Nothing is gained by attributing a child's problems to perinatal events when the clinical history does not support this. Many parents have been advised that their child's handicap was caused by 'birth trauma' with a negligible recurrence risk, and have subsequently produced another child with an identical handicap. Not only is this mistake disastrous for the parents, but it also has possible medico-legal consequences. Mistakes can also be made even when a diagnosis seems obvious, since there may be several subgroups within one clinical category, each with a different inheritance but a similar clinical picture (e.g. achondroplasia and similar dwarfism syndromes); this is known as genetic heterogeneity. Conversely, there may be wide variation in the severity of the disorder between family members, as for example in tuberose sclerosis (p. 217). This clinical

167

Table 10.1   Terminology in genetics.

Term	Meaning
Allele	Alleles are genes which are located at the same locus of the same chromosome, and which are concerned with the same category of information
Barr body (sex chromatin)	A small oblong heterochromatic particle near the nuclear membrane which represents the inactivated chromosome X during interphase
Banding	Technique for distinguishing individual regions of a chromosome
Clone	Cell population with the same karyotype
Deletion	Part of a chromosomal arm broken off and lost
Dysmorphic	Deviating from the normal morphology, e.g. mongoloid slant of the eyes, shawl scrotum.
Gamete	Mature germ cell of either sex (ovum or sperm) with a haploid set of 23 chromosomes (in normal circumstances)
Isochromosome	Chromosome with two identical halves: ip = chromosome consisting of two identical short arms; iq = chromosome consisting of two identical long arms
Karyotype	Chromosomal complement arranged and analysed according to size and banding patterns
Meiosis	Consists of two cell divisions by which a haploid gamete originates from a diploid gametic stem-cell. Meiosis I = reduction division; meiosis II = equational division
Mitosis	Division of a cell resulting in two daughter cells with the same chromosomal complement as mother cell
Monosomy	One chromosome is missing; complement of 45 chromosomes
Nondisjunction	Failure of bivalent in meiosis I and of chromatids in meiosis II and mitosis to segregate
Proband	Individual with a genetic disorder who is the first member of a family to be diagnosed
Translocation	Transfer of a piece of one chromosome to a non-homologous chromosome. If two non-homologous chromosomes exchange pieces the translocation is balanced
Zygote	The product of fusion of sperm and ovum

Nomenclature   + or − before chromosome number = additional or missing whole chromosome, p = short arm of chromosome, q = long arm of chromosome, + or − *after* p or q = additional or missing portion of chromosome, figure after p or q = region and band number.

variability, particularly common with autosomal dominant traits, is attributed to variable penetrance of the gene.

Variation in age of onset of an inherited condition may also be misleading, when advice has to be based on the apparently normal status of siblings or relatives. For example, a person may develop Huntington's chorea, which is dominantly inherited, before signs of the disease appear in his parent. In this situation it might easily be assumed that, since no other relative was affected, a new mutation had occurred, and other family members would be reassured that they were not at risk. Another common difficulty when faced with an unfamiliar disorder is to decide whether it has occurred as a result of a new mutation, or is recessively inherited (p. 171). When no siblings or other family members are affected, this distinction may be difficult or even impossible.

HISTORY

Particular attention should be paid to the points listed in Table 10.2. The family tree is recorded; the accepted conventions for this are summarised in Fig. 10.1.

Table 10.2   Genetic counselling: four important points in the history.

Details of all children of both parents, including previous relationships
Exact details of disorders affecting other members of the family
All miscarriages and stillbirths, and whether any investigation or post mortem done
Exposure to teratogens in pregnancy, including alcohol, drugs, tobacco and radiation

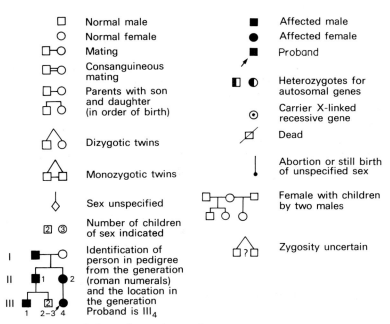

Fig. 10.1   Symbols used in pedigree charts.

TYPES OF GENETIC DISORDER

There are three major groups of genetic disorders: single gene disorders, chromosome abnormalities, and multifactorial conditions.

Single gene disorders

AUTOSOMAL DOMINANT DISORDERS

These are caused by a single gene defect. They are commonly associated with the presence of structural or anatomical abnormalities. Autosomal dominant conditions are transmitted vertically from parents to child and the ratio of affected-to-normal offspring from an affected parent is 1:1 (Fig. 10.2). An affected child has a 50% chance of passing the mutant gene to his

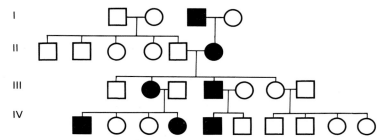

Fig. 10.2   Pedigree showing transmission of an autosomal dominant disorder.

offspring. In some cases, particularly in severe disorders such as achondroplasia, the mutant gene usually appears as a new mutation, but because of the variation in severity between the generations, it is essential to examine both the parents carefully for minor stigmata of the disorder before assuming that a new mutation has occurred.

AUTOSOMAL RECESSIVE TRAITS

These are expressed only in the presence of a double dose of the mutant gene (Fig. 10.3) and usually involve enzyme deficiencies. The parents are heterozygotes and are clinically normal. The ratio of clinically affected to normal children is 1:3, but two of the three normal children are carriers. Where there is inbreeding, recessive disorders may appear in more than one siblingship, usually as a result of first-cousin marriage. An individual affected by a recessively inherited disorder will not normally pass the disease to his offspring unless he marries a heterozygote; this is of course much more probable if he marries a close relative. There is a high risk of recessive

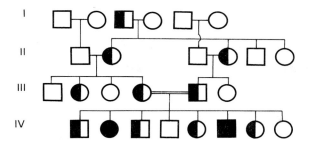

Fig. 10.3 Pedigree showing transmission of an autosomal recessive disorder in a cousin marriage.

disorders in the offspring of incestuous relationships,[155] and mental retardation is common in such cases. Detection of the heterozygote carrier state is now possible in some disorders and is important when the gene is common, as in Tay–Sachs disease among Jews.

X-LINKED RECESSIVE DISORDERS

These are due to a defective gene located on the X chromosome, which is expressed only in the absence of a normal allele on another X chromosome (Fig. 10.4). The trait is transmitted by carrier females to half their sons, who will have the disorder, and to half their daughters, who will be carriers.

Females are not usually affected by X-linked recessive disorders, but this can happen in three ways:
1   She receives a double dose of the defective gene (i.e. one from each parent).
2   She has only one X chromosome (Turner's syndrome).
3   Random inactivation. The Lyon Hypothesis postulates that, in any cell, only one X chromosome is active. The other is inactivated and is visible in the cell as the nuclear chromatin or Barr body. One would expect half the normal and half of the defective X chromosomes to be inactivated, but because X inactivation is random it is possible for an individual to have predominantly defective X chromosomes active in her cells and therefore to have clinical evidence of the disorder. Conversely if, by chance, most of the defective chromosomes are inactivated, even the most sensitive test for the carrier state is likely to be falsely negative.

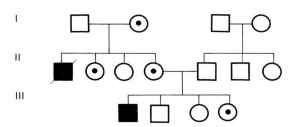

Fig. 10.4 Pedigree showing transmission of an X-linked recessive disorder.

These are due to mutant genes on the X chromosome which are expressed even in a single dose. The heterozygous female is affected as well as the male, who has only the mutant X chromosome (hemizygous). The female is likely to be less severely affected.

Chromosome disorders

Disorders of chromosomes are conveniently divided into structural and numerical abnormalities. Translocations have features of both.

The technique of banding has made it possible to recognise many more subtle chromosome defects. When chromosomes are stained with a variety of agents, a pattern of transverse bands becomes visible. This pattern is a specific property of each chromosome and therefore small deviations from the normal can be recognised. With the aid of specialised culture techniques, it is also possible to demonstrate the existence of fragile sites at which chromosome breakage may occur.

Progress in this field is very rapid. It is possible that older children and young adults who were thought to have a normal chromosome karyotype when first investigated some years ago, might now be found to have subtle defects demonstrable only with the new methods. A further consequence of technical advance is that adequate clinical information is more important than ever, so that the laboratory staff can select the most appropriate techniques.

STRUCTURAL ANOMALIES

These are likely to occur at interchange or crossing over. Segments of chromosome may be lost or rearranged (Table 10.1). Not every minor structural anomaly is clinically significant. It may be found not only in the handicapped child, but also in the normal parent, and this finding would cast doubt on its relevance to the clinical problem.

NUMERICAL ANOMALIES

Errors of number occur at the time of disjunction when the chromatids move apart (Fig. 10.5). When homologous chromosomes fail to separate, one cell receives an extra chromosome and is trisomic; the other (which is deficient in one chromosome) is monosomic. A monosomic fetus is usually non-viable. The only known viable monosomy affecting autosomal chromosomes is that involving chromosomes 21/22.

The reason for the failure in separation of the chromosome ('non-disjunction') is not understood, nor is the association with maternal age. There is probably a pre-existing tendency for this to happen in certain people,

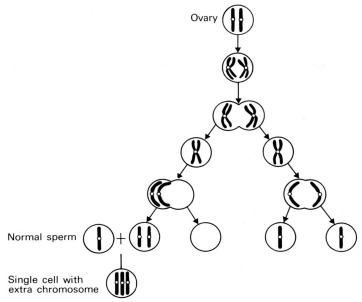

Fig. 10.5   Abnormal cell division resulting in one cell with an extra chromosome.

since there is an increased risk of non-disjunction of both autosomal and sex chromosomes among siblings of Down's syndrome children.

Mosaicism is explained by the occurrence of non-disjunction in a cell line subsequent to zygote formation (Fig. 10.6). There are therefore two cell lines, one trisomic and one normal. The proportions of each may vary in an individual between tissues and may change with time.

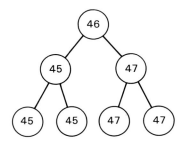
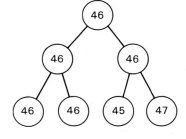

A. Non-disjunction at first division of zygote

B. Non-disjunction after first division of zygote

Fig. 10.6   Mosaic formation.

TRANSLOCATION

This is usually a transfer of material from one chromosome to another non-homologous (different number) chromosome, although in Robertsonian translocation, there is transfer of genetic material between two homologous chromosomes. If there is no net loss or gain of genetic material, the translocation is said to be balanced, and there is no phenotypic abnormality. If the offspring inherits the chromosome with deficient material or the one with extra material, the translocation is said to be unbalanced (Fig. 10.7). This situation can also be described as partial monosomy or partial trisomy, respectively.

   If an abnormal child is found to have an unbalanced translocation, the parents' chromosomes should be examined. In a majority of cases these will be normal and the translocation is assumed to have arisen *de novo*. The recurrence risk is then low. In a minority, a balanced translocation is found in the parent and there is a distinct risk of recurrence. This may be around 10–20% if the mother is the carrier, but only 2–5% if the father carries the rearrangement. The balanced translocation can also be passed to normal offspring whose children are then at risk. Their chromosomes should be examined and appropriate counselling given.

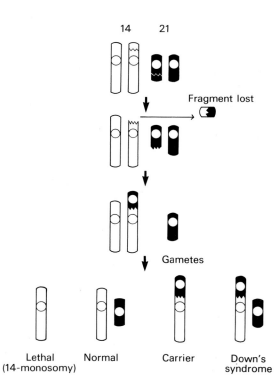

Fig. 10.7 Mechanism of formation of a translocation. (Reproduced from Carter 1980 by permission.)

Polygenic inheritance

There are many disorders which appear more commonly in some families than one would expect from the frequency in the general population. In other words, an individual is more likely to be affected by a particular disorder if he has a relative with the same condition. It seems probable that these disorders are produced by the interaction of a genetic predisposition involving more than one gene with one or more adverse environmental factors, but the exact mechanism by which this happens is unknown.

The inheritance of these conditions may well be determined by many genes. The larger the number of adverse genes, the greater the genetic predisposition to the disease. This 'polygenic' model generates some specific mathematical predictions which are fulfilled better in some cases than in others. For clinical purposes, empiric risks are available from large population studies and these figures are used in genetic counselling. Accurate definition of the disorder is essential, since many defects which are usually inherited in polygenic fashion, may also occasionally occur as part of a specific syndrome with simple dominant or recessive inheritance. Cleft palate and neural tube defects (pp. 243 & 367) provide examples.

INVESTIGATIONS

Chromosome analysis

Suggested indications for chromosome analysis are summarised in Table 10.3. Even though it is usually possible to diagnose the classic chromosome syndromes clinically, confirmation is essential if only to detect the occasional translocation case. Multiple anomaly syndromes associated with retardation justify chromosome study, except in the case of a recognisable and well described syndrome which has repeatedly been associated with normal chromosomes (e.g. Apert's syndrome).

Mental retardation, even in the absence of dysmorphic features, is an indication for chromosome study. The yield is small, but the discovery of the fragile X syndrome certainly justifies this investigation in boys.

Table 10.3   Indications for chromosome analysis.

---

1. Confirmation of a classic chromosomal syndrome
2. Two or more dysmorphic features
3. Moderate or severe mental retardation of undetermined aetiology (with or without dysmorphic features)
4. Parents of children with duplications, deletions or translocations
5. All children of a parent with a balanced translocation or structural anomaly
6. Malformed stillborns and unexplained stillborns
7. Endocrine and genital disorders, and females with unexplained short stature

---

X and Y bodies

The chromatin of the inactivated X chromosome can be seen in cells by light microscopy and is known as the Barr body. The number of Barr bodies is one less than the number of X chromosomes. The Y chromosome can also be visualised since part of this chromosome can be seen readily with fluorescent staining. The number of Y bodies equals the number of Y chromosomes. The X and Y bodies can be examined in buccal smears, cultured fibroblasts, and in cells from amniotic fluid. However, X and Y body counts are not now thought to be sufficiently reliable to be used in the diagnosis of sex chromosome disorders and it is more usual to proceed directly to a chromosome investigation.

PRENATAL DIAGNOSIS

AMNIOCENTESIS

This is best performed at about 16 weeks' gestation.[179] If it is deferred much beyond this, termination of the pregnancy might have to be performed at a very late stage, which is undesirable for many reasons. Alpha-fetoprotein measurement should be routine on all specimens. The desquamated fetal cells in the fluid are cultured and, if a successful growth is obtained, the relevant cytogenetic and biochemical tests are performed.

The indications for amniocentesis include advanced maternal age, a previous child with a chromosome abnormality, a balanced translocation carrier state in one or other parent, and elevated blood alpha-fetoprotein measurement, or a previous sibling with a metabolic disease which can be diagnosed prenatally. The parents should be warned that the logical outcome of amniocentesis may well be a recommendation to terminate the pregnancy, and if they find this morally unacceptable the procedure is usually contraindicated.

Amniocentesis is a safe procedure in terms of maternal morbidity, fetal loss, and premature labour. The risk of fetal loss should not be greater than 1:200. The risk of incorrect results is low, but an occasional error with such technically difficult procedures is almost inevitable. There may also be moral dilemmas; for example, it may be difficult to decide whether to abort a fetus who has an abnormal sex chromosome complement such as XXY.

ULTRASOUND

Ultrasonic examination of the fetus uses no ionising radiation and early fears about its effects on chromosomes appear to be groundless. Many fetal defects, in particular neural tube disorders, can be diagnosed in this way.

FETOSCOPY

This involves the percutaneous insertion of a small fibreoptic telescope into the amniotic cavity.[178] The fetus can be visualised directly, although the field of view is very narrow. Blood samples can be drawn from the fetal vessels on the placental surface. The technique is in its infancy, and its main application to date has been in the diagnosis of haemoglobinopathies; however, haemophilia and Duchenne muscular dystrophy are possible indications for its use.

RADIOGRAPHY

Many inherited syndromes are characterised by skeletal anomalies, and some of these can be recognised by prenatal radiography.[180]

GENETIC COUNSELLING

The concepts of genetics are not easy for the average layman to understand. The parents may find it hard to understand the difficulties of making a precise diagnosis, and may be bewildered by the mathematical ideas of chance and probability. The counsellor should provide facts and delineate the options available to the parents. Numerical risk factors are often less useful than a simple statement that the risk of recurrence of a particular condition is high, moderate or low. These risks should be put into perspective by comparing them with the risk of congenital abnormality in the population at large—around 1 in 40.

Genetic counselling should not be forced on parents who do not desire it since it can have damaging effects. The knowledge that one carries a recessive gene, or a dominant with incomplete penetrance, may be very distressing and can lead to guilt, depression, marital or family dishar-mony,[181] and even to suicide. In cultural groups where the woman is traditionally assumed to be responsible for any defects in the children, the concepts of modern genetics may be unacceptable or incomprehensible.

When a condition is known to have a high recurrence risk and prenatal diagnosis is not feasible, the couple should be reminded of other options including adoption and, in the case of recessive disorders, artificial insemination by donor (AID).

Chapter Eleven
Developmental Screening and Surveillance

PRINCIPLES OF DEVELOPMENTAL SCREENING

The approach to developmental assessment outlined in Chapter 4 is designed for children whose development is suspect. Usually, the parents are worried, and the search for an expert opinion is initiated by them. In contrast, developmental screening examinations are generally initiated by professionals and the goal is to examine the entire population of infants and young children, to detect those who merit a detailed assessment.

Screening was defined by the American Commission on Chronic Illness in 1957 as 'the presumptive identification of unrecognised disease or defect by the application of tests, examinations, and other procedures, which can be applied rapidly. Screening tests sort out apparently well persons who have a disease from those who probably do not. A screening test is not intended to be diagnostic.'

Criteria for screening programmes

Wilson and Jungner suggested ten principles of early disease detection.[182]
1   The condition being sought should be an important health problem for the individual and for the community.
2   There should be an acceptable form of treatment for patients with recognisable disease or some other form of useful intervention should be available, such as genetic advice.*
3   The natural history of the condition, including its development from latent to declared disease should be adequately understood.
4   There should be a recognisable latent or early symptomatic stage.
5   There should be a suitable test or examination for detecting the disease at an early or latent stage, which should be acceptable to the population.

    * Author's addition.

6 Facilities should be available for diagnosing and treating the patients uncovered by this programme.

7 There should be an agreed policy on whom to treat as patients.

8 The treatment at the presymptomatic stage of the disease should favourably influence its course and prognosis.

9 The cost of case finding (which should include cost of diagnosis and treatment) should be economically balanced in relation to (1) possible expenditure on medical care as a whole, and (2) the cost of treatment if the patient does not present until the disease reaches the symptomatic stage.*

10 Case finding should be a continuing process, not a once-and-for-all project.

Rose added an additional criterion for a screening programme, that it should provide a high yield of newly diagnosed, previously unsuspected true positives.[183] He defined yield as:

$$\text{Yield (y\%)} = \frac{\text{number of significant new cases}}{\text{total number screened}} \times 100.$$

This criterion is not fulfilled in cases where the parents are the first to suspect a defect, even though the programme facilitates its correct management and referral.

Screening tests

However desirable it may be to screen for a condition, there is no point in attempting to do so unless a suitable test is available. Cochrane and Holland[184] suggested six criteria for a good screening test (Table 11.1). The concept of sensitivity and specificity (Table 11.2) is important in evaluating screening tests. A perfect test would have 100% specificity and sensitivity.

Table 11.1 Criteria of Cochrane and Holland for a satisfactory screening test.

---

1. *Simple, quick, easy to interpret*; capable of being performed by paramedical or other personnel
2. *Acceptable* in order to encourage participation in screening programmes which is, by definition, voluntary
3. *Accurate*, i.e. give a true measurement of the attribute under investigation
4. *Repeatable*. This involves the components of observer variability, both within and between; subject variability; and test variability
5. *Sensitive*. This is the ability of a test to give a positive finding when the individual screened has the disease or abnormality under investigation
6. *Specific*. This is the ability of the test to give a negative finding when the individual does not have the disease or abnormality under investigation

---

* Author's addition.

Table 11.2 The concept of sensitivity and specificity (for an example *see* Table 18.6).

Screening Test	Reference Test (ie. does person have disease) Positive	Negative	Total
Positive	a	b	a+b
Negative	c	d	c+d
Total	a+c	b+d	a+b+c+d

Sensitivity of screening test
= proportion of true cases (diseased subjects) correctly identified

$$= \frac{a}{a+c}$$

Specificity of screening test
= proportion of true negatives (healthy subjects) correctly identified

$$= \frac{d}{b+d}$$

Positive predictive value of screening test
= proportion of positive screening tests that are confirmed by reference test

$$= \frac{a}{a+b}$$

Note Sensitivity and specificity are characteristics of the test, but positive predictive value falls as the number of abnormal subjects in the population declines. Thus a test which looks excellent when applied to a highly selected referral population may turn out to be very disappointing when used for whole-population screening.

In practice it is usually necessary to compromise. If the test is sufficiently sensitive to detect all true positives, inclusion of some false positives is inevitable; conversely, if it is sufficiently specific to exclude all negatives, some positives are likely to be missed. The more rare the condition being sought, the more specific the test must be. This is a matter of simple arithmetic. For example, if a test has a specificity of 98% and a sensitivity of 100% (an outstanding test!) and the condition occurs with a prevalence of 1:1000, there will be 20 false positives for every true case. This large number of false positives does not necessarily matter if further investigation is simple, e.g. a single blood test; but is a serious disadvantage where each case revealed by screening needs extensive follow-up and further study, as in the example of neonatal auditory screening (p. 106). Screening for learning disabilities is a situation where available tests have rather low sensitivity and specificity (p. 407) and therefore their usefulness in educational planning is limited.

The question of sensitivity and specificity can be viewed in another way. Most screening procedures separate children into two groups; those at high risk and those at low risk, of having the disorder in question. Although the prevalence is smaller in the latter group, it contains many more children, and may therefore ultimately contribute as many cases as the high-risk group.

Screening tests are not intended to be diagnostic. When a possible abnormality is detected by screening, further evaluation is needed. The tests or procedures used in definitive diagnosis are the criteria by which the specificity and sensitivity of the screening programme must be judged; these are known as the 'reference tests'. In developmental paediatrics the reference test is usually the opinion formed by a multidisciplinary team, or an audiologist or ophthalmologist, and in some cases the accuracy of this opinion can only be assessed after some months or years have elapsed. With the possible exceptions of retinoscopy for refractive errors and electrical response audiometry, there are no 'absolute' or wholly objective reference tests.

Developmental screening tests are often simplified versions of detailed assessment procedures and the distinction between them is blurred; furthermore, many of the available screening procedures need considerable skill and clinical judgement, although they are within the competence of paramedical personnel, if adequate training and supervision are provided.

DEVELOPMENTAL SCREENING AND SURVEILLANCE

Gesell and Amatruda in the 1940s introduced the concept of developmental diagnosis[185] and suggested that their scheme of examination could detect children with handicaps and neurological disorders. In the UK, Dr Mary Sheridan developed the Stycar tests and these were introduced around 1960. Because there were inadequate staff and facilities to examine all children, special attention was paid to those who had one or more risk factors, for example, perinatal asphyxia. The names of such children were recorded in an 'At-Risk' register.* It soon became apparent that many children with handicaps have no previous risk factors and therefore would not be submitted to a developmental examination. The concept of 'At-Risk' registers has now been abandoned and it is accepted that effective developmental screening must involve *all* children.[186]

* This term is now used for the Non-Accidental Injury Register.

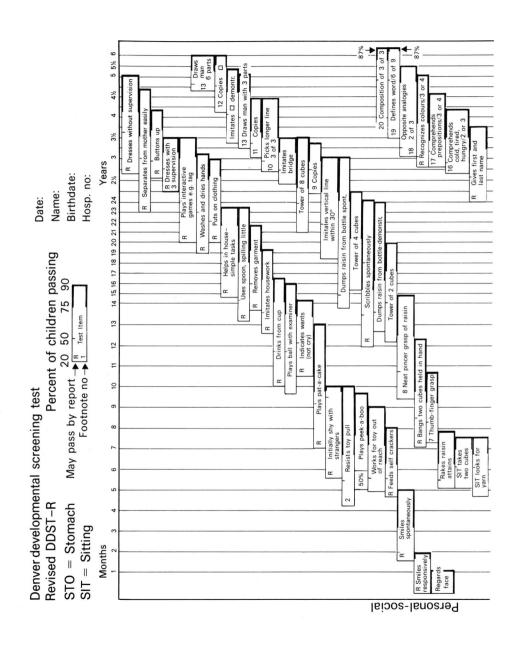

Denver developmental screening test
Revised DDST–R

Percent of children passing

STO = Stomach
SIT = Sitting

May pass by report   20   50   75   90

Footnote no ➞ ┌─┐ Test Item
              │R│
              │1│
              └─┘

Date:
Name:
Birthdate:
Hosp. no:

Personal-social

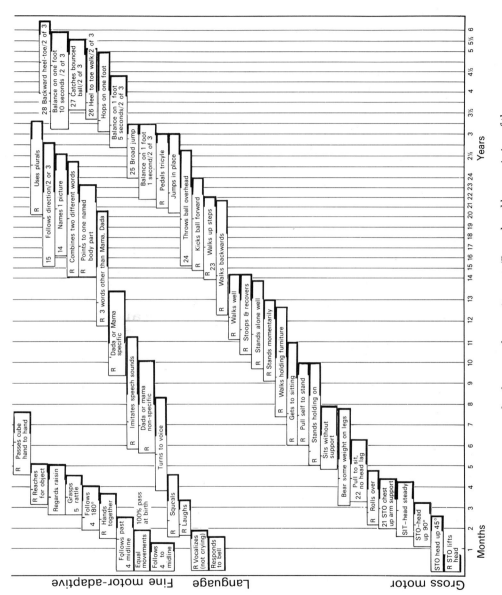

Fig. 11.1 Denver developmental screening test. (Reproduced by permission of the Test Centre, High Wycombe.)

Sheridan suggested that developmental screening has three main functions:

1   To promote optimum physical and mental health for all children.
2   To ensure early diagnosis and treatment for handicapping conditions.
3   To permit the discovery of potentially preventable causes of handicap.

These aims were of course entirely laudable, and in the past decade developmental screening has been widely adopted in Europe and the USA.[187] Children are submitted to between one and six examinations in the preschool years, and a further comprehensive examination is commonly performed at school entry. In spite of the cost in time and money of these procedures, there has been little critical evaluation of developmental screening. As with other screening programmes, the fact that it is possible has been regarded as *prima facie* evidence that it must be good.

The Court Report noted that 'firm evidence does not exist' on the effectiveness of developmental screening and called for evaluation research. The term 'health surveillance' was proposed as an alternative to developmental screening. Health surveillance implies continuity of care, and constant vigilance over all aspects of a child's health and development, rather than a single or several screening examinations. Although this concept seems good, any unsolicited inspection of an apparently normal child is a form of screening (even if renamed 'surveillance') and may be examined in the light of the criteria suggested for screening.

The most successful paediatric screening procedures are the biochemical tests for phenylketonuria and hypothyroidism, since although the yield is low, they fit the criteria for screening admirably. There is little doubt that the routine neonatal and six-week examinations are justified by the yield of minor and major anomalies, recording of growth parameters, and the opportunity to review early feeding and management problems. However, only gross developmental defects are likely to be recognised at this age, for example, apathy, hypotonia, cranial enlargement and obvious external eye defects. There is no universal agreement about the ages at which further developmental examinations should be performed. Eight months is a convenient age for hearing tests (p. 92) and the recognition of motor disorders, and 28–30 months for the detection of language delay. A school entrance examination, at age 5 years, is routine in the UK. Many schools have abandoned regular medical inspections beyond this age, but vision is usually rechecked at intervals. Recently there has been much interest in screening adolescent girls for scoliosis.[188]

A major difficulty in the planning and evaluation of developmental surveillance beyond the neonatal period is that there are many types of developmental problems, so that the effectiveness of the screening programme as a whole cannot be easily studied. It is more profitable to examine its effectiveness in detecting one specific disorder, or group of disorders.

The remaining chapters in this book will describe some of the many unanswered questions and clinical problems in developmental paediatrics.[189] These include the lack of agreed diagnostic criteria for communication disorders, the uncertainty about the value of early intervention and the natural history of many developmental defects and disorders, and the difficulties of assessment when the child is disturbed or uncooperative. Because of these problems, it is doubtful whether developmental screening fulfils many of the criteria suggested by Wilson and Jungner. Nevertheless, many benefits have resulted from the increasing interest in child development. Certainly, earlier diagnosis does at least seem to reduce secondary emotional and behavioural handicaps in both child and family, and may also, on rare occasions, allow earlier genetic counselling, thereby preventing the birth of further affected children. There is no doubt that most parents prefer to know of their child's handicap as soon as possible, and early diagnosis spares them the trauma of suddenly discovering a serious problem at school entry—a shattering experience which was common in the past, but now is quite unusual. Whether these improvements can be attributed to developmental screening or whether they are due mainly to increasing public and professional awareness and easier access to services, is a separate and undecided issue.

SCREENING IN GENERAL PRACTICE

Although many doubts remain about developmental screening programmes, they are now firmly established. General Practitioners will undoubtedly be responsible for much of this work in the future,[190] and they should consider the following points in the design of new surveillance programmes.

1 Parents are the most efficient detectors of childhood handicap. They must always be asked for their opinion and their concerns must be taken seriously. Reassurance by inexperienced staff is one of the main causes of delay in the diagnosis of handicap. When this is allowed to happen, developmental screening is not merely useless, it is positively harmful.

2 When professionals do find a handicap unsuspected by parents, it is usually subtle—for example, high frequency deafness, impaired language comprehension, or small angle squint. The standard of developmental surveillance must be high if such defects are to be detected.

3 The children who are most at risk of developmental disorders are those who use Child Health Clinics the least. Although 80% of children are seen in clinics during the first year, this figure drops rapidly thereafter. Careful records and energetic pursuit of non-attenders are desirable and can best be achieved by an efficient health visitor network. The children whose parents voluntarily attend clinics are those who least need to be seen. However, non-attendance and non-recognition of handicap are not confined to low

Table 11.3 Screening in general practice; the problem of inadequate experience. New cases of childhood handicap, assuming a group practice of 4 or 5 partners with 200 births per annum.

Handicap	Approximate number of years between each new case
Severe mental handicap (all causes)	1.2
Down's syndrome	3.5
Cerebral palsy	2.0
Sensorineural deafness	5.0
Congenital blindness	14.0
Autism	12.0
Duchenne muscular dystrophy	30.0

social classes. Sophisticated and intelligent people also overlook or ignore defects in their children and often resent the 'interference' of health visitors.

4   Major handicaps are rare at primary care level (Table 11.3) and it is difficult for GPs, clinic doctors and heath visitors to maintain their vigilance. Furthermore, many staff may never have seen cases of cerebral palsy, mental handicap or deafness, and fail to recognise the behaviour and developmental patterns of these children which are so obvious to the specialist. No amount of teaching about development can substitute for experience of the conditions for which screening is performed; but videotaped case demonstrations offer a partial solution to this problem.

5   Most of the problems detected will be in the categories of minor defect and developmental disorder. Networks of referrals should be clearly defined for these cases. Contacts should be established and maintained with the speech therapist, physiotherapist, and educational psychologist. A peripatetic orthoptist facilitates the management of suspected visual defects. Policy for the management of secretory otitis media should be agreed with the ENT consultant.

6   A programme of child health surveillance may have benefits other than the recognition of developmental problems.[191] Regular contact between the doctor and the family, without the anxiety of acute illness, offers opportunities for health education and advice on problems of child rearing. Many doctors are enthusiastic about these benefits,[192] although detailed evidence is lacking. Health education needs very careful planning and delivery if it is to be effective.[452] Interested readers should study the history of unsolicited professional advice on child rearing, which is long and murky![193]

7   A surveillance programme provides opportunities for parents to seek help for behavioural problems, but there is no point in encouraging this or

in 'screening' for behaviour disorders unless one has the skills to deal with them.

8 Developmental screening is by no means harmless; it can result in prolonged and often unjustified parental concern, time-wasting consultations, and unnecessary therapy. The benefits only outweight the potential damage when the service is well organised and supervised, and continuity of care and responsibility is assured.

Who should do developmental screening?

This task may be undertaken by GPs, community child health doctors or health visitors. Non-medically qualified persons can learn to administer screening tests almost as effectively as doctors, but training, supervision and feedback are vital. An enthusiastic health visitor will certainly screen more efficiently than a bored doctor. Many screening tests have been devised. Of these the Denver Developmental Screening Test (DDST), which has been recently revised and presented in a new form (Fig. 11.1), is the most extensively used and the most carefully standardised.[194] Although developed in the USA, it can be used for British children with only minor modification.[195] It has some deficiencies, and includes no specific tests of hearing or vision but was specifically designed for use by non-medical personnel.[196] Alternatively, the Stycar sequences and tests can be adapted and taught to health visitors, but they require a more extensive understanding of child development. Lists of 'indications for referral' (Table 11.4) are somewhat crude, but at least provide a quick method of rote instruction for non-medical staff. Parent administered check lists provide another economic means of developmental surveillance and deserve wider use. An example of a hearing checklist is provided in Appendix 8.

Table 11.4 Simple indications for referral for non-medical staff.

Parental concern—any age
Strong hand preference in first year
Unable to sit at 10 months
Abnormal tone or movements
Not walking at 18 months
Clumsy or weak (especially boys) beyond 18 months
No words at 2 years
Not joining words at 3 years
Speech unintelligible to strangers at 4 years
Persistence of casting, continuing beyond 2 years
Brevity of concentration span beyond 2 years
Unilateral squint—any age
Any squint—beyond 6 months
Not looking at mother's face or at objects
Diminished response to sound

PART TWO

Chapter Twelve
Mental Handicap

There is no completely satisfactory definition of mental retardation. The old terminology of mental defective, imbecile and idiot has quite rightly disappeared from the professional vocabulary. The Mental Health Act of 1959 (Section 4) set out four categories of mental disorder:
1. Mental illness
2. Subnormality
3. Severe subnormality
4. Psychopathic disorder.

The definitions in this Act were as follows.

'Mental disorder means mental illness, arrested or incomplete development of mind, psychopathic disorder, and any other disorder or disability of mind.'

'Severe subnormality means a state of arrested or incomplete development of mind which includes subnormality of intelligence and is of such a nature or degree that the patient is incapable of living an independent life or guarding himself against serious exploitation or will be so incapable when of an age to do so.'

'Subnormality means a state of arrested or incomplete development of mind (not amounting to severe subnormality) which includes subnor-

191

mality of intelligence and is of a nature or degree which requires or is susceptible to medical treatment or other special care or training of the patient.'

It is worth noting that these definitions assumed a medical view of handicap, in the use of the words 'patient' and 'medical treatment'. Furthermore, mentally handicapped persons, like patients suffering from other forms of mental disorder, were liable to compulsory admission to and detention in hospital.

The Mental Health Act of 1983 replaced the term 'subnormality' with 'impairment'. Severe mental impairment is now defined as 'a state of arrested or incomplete development of mind which includes severe impairment of intelligence *and* social functioning *and* is associated with abnormally aggressive or seriously irresponsible conduct on the part of the person concerned.' Mental impairment is defined in the same way; the word 'significant' is substituted for 'severe' impairment of intelligence and social functioning. This new legislation recognises the clear distinction between psychiatric illness and mental handicap. Thus the mere fact of being mentally handicapped will not now be enough to justify a prolonged compulsory admission for treatment; there must also be evidence of a serious disturbance of conduct.

Although the detailed legal implications of the new Act are of more interest to those dealing with adults than to paediatricians, it marks important advances in the attitudes of society to the mentally handicapped; increasingly the problems of these people are seen as social rather than medical or psychiatric.[198,199,200]

Until 1971 children who had an I.Q. below 50 and were designated severely subnormal were generally considered to be ineducable, and were therefore the responsiblity of the health authority. The Education Act of 1971 transferred responsibility for the education of all children to the local education authority, and this was a major step forward in improving educational facilities for the severely handicapped.

The terms Educationally Subnormal (ESN) Mild (M) and Severe (S) are used to describe children with I.Q.s in the range 50–75 and under 50, respectively, and separate schools cater for these two groups. In practice, many factors other than I.Q. are considered in selecting the most appropriate school for a child. Although the Education Act (1981) recognises the increasing reluctance to 'label' handicapped children and encourages the trend towards integration of the less severely handicapped into normal school, the terms ESN(M) and (S) are likely to remain in use for many years because they recognise some real distinctions which are of practical significance.

1   Children with I.Q. below 50 frequently show some evidence, either in the history or on clinical examination, of some form of brain pathology. This is much less common among the ESN(M).

2   Because severe mental subnormality is usually due to organic pathology, it is likely that the child will have other physical defects.
3   Children with I.Q. under 50 generally have little success in academic tasks. Reading and writing at a very simple level may be achieved.
4   As adults they are unlikely to be able to lead independent lives.
5   Mild mental handicap is more common in the lower social classes whereas severe mental handicap is more evenly distributed across all social classes.
6   Mild mental handicap is most commonly due to a combination of genetic and environmental factors rather than a biological disorder.

Epidemiology

The prevalence of severe mental handicap is approximately 3.7 per 1000 children. Because education is universal and compulsory, virtually all handicapped children are identified and therefore this figure is reasonably accurate. Case finding is less complete among adults but the prevalence is probably slightly lower, since the mortality rate among the severely handicapped is higher than for the normal population.

Figures for the prevalence of mild mental handicap are necessarily less precise. If mild mental handicap is defined on the basis of I.Q. alone, then around 3% of the population have an I.Q. more than two standard deviations below the mean, but this is a purely statistical definition, and neglects the important factors of social competence, educational management, and family support—which together ultimately determine whether the person will need special education at school and supporting services in adult life. For these same reasons case finding is incomplete at all ages. Because of the relationship between mild mental handicap and social class, prevalence figures are dependent on the social class structure of the population under study.

Presentation of mental handicap

The age at which mental handicap presents is dependent upon the severity, the presence of recognisable specific disorders, the alertness of the parents, and the quality of the paediatric services. Most mental handicap is caused by non-progressive lesions. A few cases are acquired as a result of a cerebral catastrophe. Progressive disorders are found in a tiny minority of children with mental handicap, and may present at any age.[201,202] Clues to progressive disease include family history, loss of previously acquired skills, intractable convulsions, gait disturbance, and the specific features listed in Table 12.7.

1. PRESENTATION AT BIRTH

Babies with recognisable malformation patterns, such as Down's syndrome, are usually diagnosed at birth and often mental handicap can be predicted with confidence.

2. FIRST YEAR OF LIFE

Recognition of mental handicap is often possible in the first year of life. Slow motor development is sometimes the most obvious feature, although some mentally handicapped babies have little or no motor delay. Mental handicap is an important cause of hypotonia or 'floppiness' (p. 333). Children with severe cerebral palsy are often mentally handicapped but it is usually the motor disorder which first brings them to medical attention.

The mother may detect that 'turn-taking' behaviour and play are absent or deficient, and in some cases unresponsiveness leads to a suspicion of deafness or blindness. The baby is often described as 'too good' because he does not demand entertainment and stimulating company as does the normal infant; he is quite content to sleep or gaze vacantly at his hands. These behavioural features are more difficult to quantify than motor development, but they are often the first clue to the parents that something is wrong and their fears should always be taken seriously.

3. SECOND AND THIRD YEARS OF LIFE

The child may present at this age with developmental delays in one or more areas, most commonly in speech development. This is invariably associated with impairment of language comprehension, which is not always immediately obvious (Chapter 13). There may also be delay in walking, but this is rarely the sole presenting feature because by this age the parents usually suspect that the child also has an intellectual deficit. Some cases present because of disturbing social behaviour, such as head-banging, casting of objects, excessive mouthing, temper tantrums, aimless hyperactivity, or destructiveness.

In a few cases, there is clear evidence from a retrospective history and from previous developmental assessments, that early development was within normal limits. The child begins to use single words and may even begin to join words. Gradually his language and general development slow to a halt and may even regress. In a proportion of these there is also increasing social impairment and the terms 'disintegrative psychosis' or 'late-onset autism' may be applied (*see* p. 251); however in other cases social skills are retained and the ultimate picture is of sociable mental handicap. This sequence of events may suggest a progressive disorder, but usually none is found.

4. FOURTH AND FIFTH YEARS OF LIFE

Mild mental handicap may be detected during assessment for speech delay but some cases may not be recognised until the child begins to fail in school. Indeed, if his behaviour and social skills are satisfactory, he may survive two years of schooling before his handicap is revealed, or may be thought to simply have a 'learning disability'.

CAUSES OF MENTAL HANDICAP

Introduction

A biological cause is more commonly found in severe mental handicap than in those with I.Q.s in the 50–75 range. Familial and environmental causes predominate in the latter,[203,204] as discussed in Chapter 2. Mild retardation can, however, be caused by the many syndromes and disorders which have variable effects on intelligence, ranging from normality to severe retardation. A careful search for a biological cause of mild retardation is particularly indicated when the child's parents are highly intelligent, but the possibility of an organic cause should always be considered however low the parents' I.Q. may be.

Among the severely handicapped, chromosome disorders account for 20–25% and, of those, 80–90% have Down's syndrome. Another 20–25% have identifiable disorders or syndromes; only a small minority of these have progressive metabolic or degenerative diseases. Mental handicap in association with severe cerebral palsy, microcephaly, or infantile spasms, accounts for another 10–20% and postnatal cerebral insults (meningitis, trauma, etc.) for perhaps 10%.[205,206] There are many cases in which defects of growth or dysmorphic features clearly indicate that the mental handicap originated in the prenatal period, even though no recognised syndrome can be identified.

In most series a substantial number of cases remain unexplained. Some authors have claimed that a cause can be found for most cases of severe mental handicap,[207,208] but this is usually achieved by attributing many cases to non-specific or even spurious events such as 'perinatal problems'. However, it is true that in most cases a distinction can be made between progressive and non-progressive and between pre- and postnatal causes. A classification based on the time at which the handicap occurs is convenient, although this gives no guide as to when the condition presents clinically. The more important causes of mental handicap are summarised in Table 12.1.

CHROMOSOME DISORDERS

Down's syndrome

This is the commonest and most familiar of mental handicap syndromes.[209] It is also known as mongolism but this term is now regarded as obsolete and offensive by many parents. The incidence is around 1 in 660 of all live births. The risk of Down's syndrome is also related to maternal age; it rises

Table 12.1   Classification of the causes of mental handicap.

Prenatal
Chromosome disorders
    autosomes, e.g. Down's syndrome
    sex chromosomes: XYY, XXY, XO, etc.
Single-gene defects
    dominant inheritance, e.g. neurocutaneous syndromes: tuberose sclerosis,
        neurofibromatosis
    recessive inheritance, e.g. disorders of metabolism: aminoacids, carbohydrates,
        lysosomal storage diseases, etc.
Dysmorphic syndromes of uncertain and variable inheritance
Intrauterine infections: toxoplasmosis; cytomegalovirus, rubella
Intrauterine insults: placental insufficiency(?), alcohol, other teratogenic agents,
    hypothyroidism

Perinatal
Severe asphyxia
Complications of extreme prematurity
Meningitis
Kernicterus
Hypoglycaemia
Hydrocephalus

Postnatal
CNS infection (meningitis/encephalitis)
Non-accidental injury
Accidental trauma
Severe convulsions
Lead poisoning
Reye's syndrome
Environmental: severe deprivation, malnutrition

---

from less than 1 in 1000 in young mothers, to 1 in 800 in the early 30s, and greater than 1 in 100 in the over 40s. Paternal age is probably much less significant, although this point is still undecided. Although the *risk* of having a Down's syndrome baby is higher for older women, a large majority of women have had their babies before they are 30, and therefore most Down's syndrome babies are born to mothers in this age group.[210] (For this reason a significant reduction in the *overall* incidence of Down's syndrome will never be achieved by any amniocentesis programme that concentrates on the over 35s.)

    Down's syndrome is usually caused by an additional chromosome 21, i.e. trisomy 21, which is caused by non-disjunction during meiosis; this is related to maternal age. A minority of cases (about 3–4%) are caused by translocations, with about equal occurrence of D/G and G/G transloca- tion.[250] Nearly half of the former but less than 10% of the latter arise from a balanced translocation carrier parent. Translocation is unrelated to maternal age; it accounts for a higher proportion of cases in young mothers, although even in these the figure is only about 6%. Mosaicism (p. 173) accounts for 2–6% of cases, and a few other rare chromosomal variants also occur.

When one parent is a translocation carrier the risk of recurrence in subsequent pregnancies is high (p. 174). Mothers who have had a baby with trisomy 21 have approximately twice the risk of Down's syndrome occurring in a subsequent pregnancy, compared to other women of the same age. Although this risk is still small except for the over 35s, most couples accept the offer of amniocentesis for chromosome analysis in subsequent pregnancies.

CLINICAL FEATURES

The diagnosis is usually easy in the full-term baby, though it is readily overlooked in sick premature infants. The main features are summarised in Table 12.2.

Table 12.2   Features of Down's syndrome.

Hypotonia	Simian crease
Small stature	Distal palmar axial triradius
Awkward gait	Wide gap between first & second toes
Mental handicap	Cardiac defect:
Flat occiput and short neck	AV canal defect
Upslanting palpebral fissures	VSD
Small nose and low nasal bridge	PDA
Chronic rhinitis	ASD
Middle ear disease	aberrant subclavian artery
Conjunctivitis	Hyperkeratotic skin, fine soft hair
Brushfield spots (speckled iris)	Male hypogonadism
Lens opacities	Cryptorchidism
Refractive error	High incidence of:
Small middle phalanx of 5th finger	leukaemia
Clinodactyly	thyroid disorders
	atlantoaxial subluxation[211]

Cardiac defects are of special significance in Down's syndrome, since they are the main factor that determines life expectancy. Some of these (notably atrioventricular canal defects) are clinically rather unimpressive in the early months. Cyanosis, cardiomegaly, and murmurs may be trivial or absent. An ECG is often helpful since it may reveal left axis deviation (vertical axis), which is always abnormal. The parents should not be told that the heart is normal until careful clinical evaluation, ECG, chest X-ray, and preferably an echocardiogram, have been performed. The unexpected discovery of heart disease later in the first or second year, often causes intense parental bitterness and distress at a time when they are just getting over the shock of the original diagnosis.

Large left-to-right shunts in Down's syndrome seem to progress to pulmonary hypertension more quickly than in normal children and severe cyanosis and shunt reversal may be seen very early.[212] All children with heart defects should be assessed by a paediatric cardiologist. The decision not to operate on an operable lesion must be a positive one made with the parents' full agreement. If the defect is inoperable or the risks are unacceptable, the parents must understand that the reasons are technical; they should not be left with the impression that the child has been refused surgery simply because he has Down's syndrome.

Eye defects and conductive hearing loss due to 'glue ear' are both very common in Down's syndrome. These sensory handicaps, which may be of small significance to the normal child, are undoubtedly important when superimposed on mental handicap. An eye examination and regular vision and hearing checks are essential.

Behaviour.   Traditionally, Down's syndrome children are said to be often musical and of a placid and friendly personality, but there is really little evidence for this and behavioural problems are certainly not unknown. Possibly the early recognition and understanding of their handicap does aid their parents in management so that, in contrast with other handicaps, slow development does not lead to excessive parental pressure and anxiety. Social withdrawal of 'autistic' type is rare in Down's syndrome, but does occur occasionally.

Development.   These children are all retarded but the degree of retardation is variable (Table 12.3). Intelligent parents tend to have more intelligent Down's syndrome children. Environmental factors undoubtedly influence ultimate intelligence. In the first few years, development is sometimes remarkably good, and may even approach the normal range. Retardation becomes gradually more evident after the age of 3 or 4 years. Educational placement should be decided on the basis of the child's abilities, not his diagnosis. Some Down's children benefit from a few years of ESN(M) or even

Table 12.3   Milestones in Down's syndrome. (Compiled from several authors.)

	Mean (months)	Range (months)
Sitting	13	6–30
Standing	22	9–48
Walking	30	12–60
Single words	34	12–72

normal schooling though most will eventually require an ESN(S) placement.

Puberty and adult life.   Precocious puberty occurs only rarely. Most females start to menstruate at the normal time. Females are potentially fertile but there is no known case of a male fathering a child. Down's syndrome adults are always retarded but their potential ability may be greater than has been realised in the past, and they certainly benefit from modern attitudes to mental handicap. Life expectancy is reduced by congenital heart disease. Those who escape this problem may live to middle age but there is a high incidence of presenile dementia due to Alzheimer's disease.

MANAGEMENT

Parents should be told of the diagnosis as soon as it is suspected. Both parents should be informed together if possible. The doctor who breaks the news should not be excessively gloomy or project his own feelings. Parents expect a sympathetic approach, but they should be given a positive attitude to the child. Confirmation by chromosome culture is desirable; apart from the need to recognise translocation cases, it eliminates any doubts in the parents' minds and may thereby help acceptance. In neonatal emergencies, rapid diagnosis is possible using bone-marrow cells and allows informed decision making, but trisomy-21 should not be a reason to withhold necessary treatment.

The parents should be told of the likely development of a Down's syndrome child, as they may have unnecessarily pessimistic expectations.[213] An introduction to the Down's Children's Association may be offered. Several early stimulation programmes and special diets (p. 145) have been devised to accelerate the development of mentally handicapped children.[475] Brinkworth introduced a programme especially designed for children with Down's syndrome. The ultimate benefits of this intensive stimulation are uncertain, but there can be no doubt that these children do far better in a stimulating family environment than in an institution.

Trisomy of other chromosomes

Trisomy 13 (Patau's syndrome) and Trisomy 18 (Edwards' syndrome) are easily recognised (Table 12.4), usually in the neonatal period. Survival is rare so these conditions are not important causes of mental handicap. Recurrence risks are low unless there is an unbalanced translocation. Trisomy 22 is less familiar but can also be suspected clinically.

Partial trisomies and deletions

The best known is the cri-du-chat syndrome in which there is often a typical mewing cry in the newborn. Numerous other conditions can be suspected clinically[77] but individually they are very uncommon (*see also* p. 172).

Table 12.4   Clinical features of trisomies 13, 18 and 22.

Trisomy 13	Trisomy 18	Trisomy 22
Small head	Long head	Small head
Small eyes	Small chin	Low ears
Coloboma of iris	Low ears	Preauricular skin tags
Cleft palate and lip	Small mouth	Cleft palate
Small jaw	Ptosis	Beaked nose
Rockerbottom feet	2nd/3rd fingers overlap	Antimongoloid slant
Polydactyly	Heart defect	Short neck
Heart defect		Heart defect

Sex chromosome disorders

The physical features of the commoner sex chromosome disorders are summarised in Table 12.5. In general these have less severe effects than autosomal disorders. Knowledge of the handicaps caused by sex chromosome defects is incomplete, because chromosomal analysis is usually performed only on children or adults who present with clinical problems such as mental handicap or psychiatric disorder; it is natural that their problems should be attributed to a chromosome disorder if this is found.[214] However, longitudinal studies of children found to have sex chromosome defects as a result of routine neonatal screening reveal that some of these

Table 12.5   Features of sex chromosome anomalies. (Note that clinical findings are variable and may be minimal.

XYY syndrome	XXY syndrome (Klinefelter's syndrome)	XO syndrome (Turner's syndrome)
Rapid growth in mid-childhood	Tall, slim with long limbs	Small at birth
Tall stature	Mild reduction in I.Q.	Small stature
Poor muscle strength and coordination	Behavioural and social problems	Ovarian dysgenesis
Prominent glabella, long ears, long fingers,	Hypogonadism, infertility	Transient congenital lymphoedema
Dull intellect	Gynaecomastia	Widely spaced nipples
Behaviour problems, aggression		Narrow palate and small mandible
Severe acne at adolescence		Short neck, often webbed
(*note* XYY individuals may show *no* abnormalities)		Elbow and knee anomalies
		Renal anomalies
		Coarctation of aorta and other cardiac defects
		Sensorineural deafness
		Mild retardation (performance lower than verbal)

are compatible with essentially normal intelligence, development and behaviour,[215] and therefore the fact that a child has a sex chromosome disorder does not necessarily mean that this is the cause of his problems.

KLINEFELTER'S SYNDROME (47,XXY)

These boys may be recognised in childhood because of their body build, small testes, or slow speech development and learning problems. Many are not diagnosed until they present as young adults at an infertility clinic. Although they may have a slight reduction in intelligence and a delay in the onset of puberty these are not usually major problems. Their small genitalia and lack of social drive gives rise to some personality difficulties in puberty.[215] Assessment of endocrine function and psychiatric advice may be needed at this time. The common and understandable parental fear that the boy is more likely to become homosexual has no basis in fact.[11]

XYY SYNDROME (47,XYY)

This was first recognised among men in institutions. They were tall, mentally handicapped, and had violent and unstable personalities. Although the XYY constitution seems to predispose to personality and intellectual problems, many cases are probably normal and unrecognised, while others have lesser problems such as speech dyspraxia, incoordination, and reading difficulties. Tall stature is not an invariable finding. The XYY karyotype is sometimes found unexpectedly when a chromosome analysis is performed for other reasons. As the clinical problems are so variable, and unnecessary alarm about criminality may be created, this *may* be one of the rare situations where information should be withheld from parents.

TURNER'S SYNDROME (45,XO)

Girls with Turner's syndrome may be diagnosed at birth, during childhood because of short stature (which may be the only feature), or at puberty because of amenorrhoea. The degree of retardation is variable. Usually language development is essentially normal, provided the hearing is not impaired, but spatial and arithmetical problems are prominent, so that there is a large difference between verbal and performance I.Q.s. Girls with Turner's syndrome are unequivocally feminine in psychological adjustment but tend to be passive and lack initiative. These girls require cyclical oestrogen therapy and psychological support when they reach the age of puberty.

Noonan described a syndrome with Turner-like appearance but normal chromosomes occurring both in males and females (Appendix 1).

XXX SYNDROME

Girls with this uncommon disorder have no striking clinical features other than mental retardation of variable degree and they may be apparently normal or even of superior intellect.

X-LINKED MENTAL RETARDATION

This is common and there appear to be several distinct syndromes.[216] Renpenning's syndrome consists of severe retardation often with microcephaly and associated with normal chromosomes. There is another syndrome of X-linked retardation in which the physical appearance is not grossly abnormal but marked testicular enlargement occurs, usually at puberty. Some of these boys have rather large ears, and a prominent supraorbital ridge, nose and chin. Speech dyspraxia is common and there is said to be a characteristic rhythmic intonation known as 'litany speech'. This syndrome is sometimes associated with a fragile site on the X chromosome (Xq27), which is difficult to demonstrate and is only seen when the culture medium is folate deficient. For this reason it is still uncertain how many cases of X-linked retardation have the fragile X, or whether cases with testicular enlargement represent a different entity from those without. The fragile X may be found in young female heterozygotes but seems to disappear with age, adding to the difficulties of unravelling this condition. It seems possible that fragile X may turn out to be as common a cause of mental handicap as Down's syndrome.

SINGLE GENE DEFECTS

As a general rule, inborn errors of metabolism are due to an enzyme defect and are recessively inherited,[217] whereas structural disorders tend to be dominantly inherited. The most important members of the latter group are the neurocutaneous syndromes, which are discussed on p. 217 under the heading of dysmorphic syndromes.[218,84,85,86]

Recessive disorders

This group includes disorders of aminoacid, carbohydrate and uric acid metabolism; a variety of storage disorders due to lysosomal enzyme defects, and some degenerative disorders.

Metabolic disorders are a rare cause of mental handicap. The commonest, phenylketonuria, is usually detected by neonatal screening, and many of the others present early in life with symptoms which demand urgent investigation, for example, coma, hypotonia, convulsions, unusual odour, vomiting, episodic ketosis, megaloblastic anaemia, or gross developmental delay. The number of individual disorders now recognised is so large, and the manifestations so variable, that an aminoacid chromatogram is usually included in the investigation of unexplained mental handicap, although the yield is extremely small. The following account includes only the more common disorders, and even these are rare.

PHENYLKETONURIA (PKU)

The classical form of PKU occurs in about 1 in 15 000 births. It is caused by deficient activity of the enzyme phenylalanine hydroxylase, which converts phenylalanine to tyrosine. Infants with classical PKU are normal at birth. In the early weeks severe vomiting may occur and later seizures and infantile spasms appear. The child is typically blue-eyed and eczema is common. There may be a musty odour. During the first year deterioration continues insidiously and without treatment the ultimate outcome is severe retardation and sometimes mild spastic diplegia.

Untreated PKU is now very rare in developed countries because the disease is usually detected by a screening programme, which has proved highly effective. Blood samples are collected by heel prick and spotted onto a filter paper for analysis by the Guthrie test. This depends on the ability of high phenylalanine levels to overcome growth inhibition of the bacterium *B. subtilis* by 2-thienylalanine. False results are obtained if the baby is not receiving feeds or is on antibiotics. If the screening test is positive, plasma phenylalanine and tyrosine levels are measured. A phenylalanine level of less than 4 mg% (240 μmol/l) is normal.

Detailed study of children with hyperphenylalaninaemia has revealed a number of variant types, some of which are transient and do not need treatment. There is also a rare form, 'malignant' hyperphenylalaninaemia,[219] which is due to defects in the metabolic pathways of a co-factor (tetrahydrobiopterin) needed for normal activity of phenylalanine hydroxylase.

Investigation and treatment of PKU is best carried out at designated centres. The child is reared on a diet which is low in phenylalanine. Vitamin and mineral supplements are needed. The requirement of phenylalanine is 30–35 mg/kg/day and the blood level is maintained between 3 and 10 mg%. Excessive dietary restriction may cause a serious deficiency state. The diet must be continued for some years, and the I.Q. may fall if it is stopped. The age at which the diet may be stopped varies between centres, and is still somewhat controversial.

Maternal hyperphenylalaninaemia in pregnancy may cause microcephaly, retardation, and congenital heart defects. Young women with PKU who have successfully discontinued the special diet and wish to become pregnant should obtain expert advice.

HISTIDINAEMIA

This is one of the more common disorders and neonatal screening has been advocated. Some cases have been associated with mental handicap, fits, and speech disorders, but in others the effects have been mild. Dietary treatment improves biochemical parameters, but seems to have little effect on the clinical problems. The significance of histidinaemia is still uncertain.

HOMOCYSTINURIA

The incidence of this condition is uncertain but may be around 1 in 50 000–200 000. It is caused by deficiency of the enzyme cystathionine B synthetase. The main features are summarised in Table 12.6. The baby appears normal, and developmental retardation is insidious and variable. Some patients have normal intellect. Homocystinuria should always be excluded in children who have strokes, features of Marfan's syndrome, or

Table 12.6　Clinical features of homocystinuria.

Eye
ectopia lentis (3–10 years)
iridodonesis (tremulous iris)
myopia
astigmatism
glaucoma
Skeletal
tall, thin
arachnodactyly
abnormal shape chest
high palate
pes cavus
scoliosis
fractures
concave vertebrae
osteoporosis
Vascular
thromboembolic phenomena
hemiplegia, pseudobulbar palsy, etc.
emboli to other organs
Other
mental retardation
fits (10–15%)
fine hair
malar flush
large liver

dislocated lenses. It may also be found unexpectedly in a handicapped person who lacks the typical features.

Homocystinuria may be detected by the nitroprusside test or by aminoacid chromatography. A diet low in methionine together with pyridoxine supplements is available, but the benefits are uncertain. Homocystinurics are at particular risk of thromboembolic phenomena after surgery. In adolescence, girls should probably be advised to avoid oral contraceptives.

GALACTOSAEMIA

This occurs in about 1 : 50 000 births. Classical galactosaemia is caused by deficiency of the enzyme galactose-1-phosphate uridyl transferase. The child is unable to metabolise galactose which is produced by hydrolysis of lactose in milk. Galactitol, the alcohol derived from galactose, accumulates in the lens (causing cataracts) and in other tissues. Hypoglycaemia may account for some of the cerebral damage in this disease. Affected babies fail to thrive and develop evidence of hepatic dysfunction. Cataracts appear early. Mortality without treatment is high. In some cases, particularly those with variant forms, the child presents later with mental retardation, liver disease, or cataracts.

The urine contains a non-glucose reducing sugar which is identified as galactose on chromatography. Confirmation is by specific enzyme assay. Treatment involves a lactose-free diet and the results are satisfactory, although ultimate I.Q. may be slightly below the norm. The results may be better in subsequent pregnancies if the mother's diet is regulated during pregnancy, so that the infant is not exposed to galactose *in utero*. Deficiency of the enzyme galactokinase causes cataracts without other signs of liver or brain involvement.

Lysosomal storage diseases (LSDs)

These diseases result from a deficiency in one or more acid hydrolase enzymes in the lysosome, which is a membrane-bound organelle found in all cells. Excessive quantities of substrate accumulate, causing cell expansion, disturbed function, and eventually cell death. The clinical effects depend on the concentrations and the functions of the various substrates in different body tissues. At least 40 different conditions are known. They are all very rare, and even collectively they occur with a frequency of no more than 1 in 5000 births. The exact figure depends on the ethnic composition of the population, since two of the commonest diseases are more prevalent in Jews. In spite of their rarity, they are important for several reasons; they provide valuable insights into the physiology of nerve cells; they have genetic and prognostic implications; and in some conditions new methods of treatment are appearing. The inheritance of LSDs is autosomal recessive,

Table 12.7   Features suggestive of lysosomal storage diseases.

Neurodevelopmental features:
  severe failure to thrive in infancy
  microcephaly
  macrocephaly
  hepatosplenomegaly
  gait disturbance—ataxia, spasticity, neuropathy
  abnormal eye movements
  cherry-red spot at macula
  optic atrophy
  fits are rare
  deafness

Dysmorphic features:
  short stature
  coarse facies
  corneal clouding
  large tongue
  airways obstruction
  limitation of joint movements
  X-ray abnormalities of vertebrae, hands etc.
  scoliosis

---

with the exceptions of Fabry's and Hunter's diseases which are transmitted as sex-linked recessives.

The classification of the LSDs together with their main clinical features is provided in Appendix 2. It is, however, more helpful for the clinician to know when to suspect these disorders and initiate investigation (Table 12.7). None of the features listed here is invariable. The recognition of LSDs in their classic and advanced form is seldom difficult, although only laboratory studies can determine the specific metabolic defect. The problem facing the paediatrician who sees predominantly mental handicap of non-progressive type is to recognise the early or atypical case, without overloading laboratory services with requests for complex and expensive tests. Particular difficulties arise in those rare cases in which deterioration is so slow that the child continues to acquire new skills, and dysmorphic features are lacking, so that the child is thought to have non-progressive mental handicap. Indeed, LSDs have occasionally been diagnosed in adults whose retardation has apparently remained static for many years.

DIAGNOSIS

A urine screening test for mucopolysaccharides (MPS) may be justified in all cases of mental handicap. Assays of many specific enzymes are now available and have largely replaced biopsy of the brain, rectum, or appendix as the most direct way to diagnose the LSDs. Other useful investigations include blood film, bone marrow examination (for white cell inclusions), radiological survey, acid phosphatase, EEG, and ERG (p. 129). In 'neuronal ceroid lipofuscinosis' the EEG often reveals a dramatic response to flicker which may provide a valuable diagnostic clue.

MANAGEMENT

In all LSDs accurate diagnosis must precede genetic counselling. Antenatal diagnosis is possible in some cases. In most cases management is supportive. Since the rate of progression of these disorders is variable, the child's care should be based on his current status rather than his expected deterioration. Specific treatment with enzyme replacement has, in general, been disappointing, but recent work with bone marrow transplantation offers an exciting new approach. This is a rapidly changing field and advice must be obtained from a major centre.

Degenerative disorders

There are numerous recognisable inherited syndromes in which progressive mental handicap is the main feature. In some cases there may also be motor and visual disorders, or seizures. Like lysosomal storage diseases, they are all very rare and account for a tiny minority of children with mental handicap. Table 12.8 lists separately those conditions which present early and progress rapidly so that early investigation is inevitable, and those in which presentation is more insidious and progression slow. In addition, mental deterioration may occur in many other disorders but be overshadowed by spasticity, ataxia or weakness (p. 329).

DYSMORPHIC SYNDROMES

There is an enormous and ever-increasing number of conditions characterised by congenital physical abnormalities and in many cases mental retardation which, in contrast to metabolic disorders, is usually non-progressive. Some of these syndromes are inherited, though the mode of inheritance is often uncertain; others occur mainly as sporadic cases.

The nomenclature recommended by Smith[84] for dysmorphic syndromes is summarised in Table 12.9. He suggested that the possessive use of eponymous titles should be discontinued, since 'the author of the original description neither had, nor owned the condition', i.e. 'Down syndrome' would be preferable to 'Down's syndrome'. Although logical, this recommendation has not been generally adopted. Smith's book should be consulted for full details of these syndromes, together with a diagnostic index and standards for a variety of anthropometric data. McKusick's catalogue[85] of inherited disorders is also an essential reference work. The

Table 12.8   Progressive psychomotor retardation.

Early onset and rapid deterioration
Pelizaeus–Merzbacher disease
Canavan's disease
Alexander's disease
Menkes' disease (kinky hair disease)
Leigh's disease (necrotising encephalomyelopathy)
Lowe's syndrome

Later onset and slower progression
Adrenoleukodystrophy
Alpers' disease
Huntington's chorea (juvenile)
Cockayne's syndrome
Lesch–Nyhan syndrome
Familial myoclonus epilepsy
Heller's disease
Tuberose sclerosis

Metabolic disease
(Variable presentation)
Lysosomal storage diseases
Aminoacid and carbohydrate metabolic diseases

Space-occupying lesions
Hydrocephalus

Table 12.9   Terminology for description of dysmorphic diseases.

Term	Meaning
Malformation	A primary structural defect
Deformation	Alteration in shape or structure of a previously normal part
Anomalad	A malformation together with its consequential structural changes
Malformation syndromes	Recognised patterns of malformation presumed to have a common aetiology
Association	A pattern of malformations occurring together more often than expected by chance but not definitely regarded as a syndrome

classification outlined in Table 12.10 is adapted from that of Smith. Only the more common syndromes associated with mental handicap are listed. It should be noted that this classification serves a different purpose from that of Table 12.1: it emphasises structural defects which are clinically recognisable, rather than the cause or causes of each condition.

Table 12.10 Classification of dysmorphic syndromes. Those marked * are discussed in the text; the remainder are summarised in Appendix 1. S = Syndrome.

*Chromosome disorders**

Very small stature
1. Relatively proportionate (i.e. ratio of crown–pubis:pubis–heel measurement within normal limits for age)
   Cornelia de Lange S
   Rubinstein–Taybi S
   Russell–Silver S
   Seckel S
   Hallermann-Streiff S
   Cockayne's S
   Septo-optic dysplasia*
2. Limbs short relative to trunk
   Numerous bone-dysplasia syndromes, many lethal in early life. Mental defect not a major feature

Growth deficiency with abnormal genitalia
Smith–Lemli–Opitz S

Overgrowth
Sotos S
Beckwith–Wiedemann S

Neuromuscular disorders
Sjögren–Larsson S
Marinesco–Sjögren S
Zellweger's S
Myotonic dystrophy*
Prader–Willi S*

Facial defects and limb defects
Moebius S*
Cryptophthalmos*
Blepharophimosis S
Facio-auriculo-vertebral anomalad
Coffin–Lowry S
EEC S

Limb defects
Fanconi's S

Abnormal head size or shape
Craniosynostoses*
Macrocephaly*
Microcephaly*

Table 12.10 (*cont.*)

Hamartomata (an abnormal admixture of tissues)
Sturge–Weber S*
Tuberose sclerosis*
Neurofibromatosis*
Incontinentia pigmenti
Various syndromes with skin naevi, haemangiomata, etc.

Ectodermal dysplasias

Miscellaneous
Intrauterine insults* (alcohol, drugs, infections)
Laurence–Moon–Biedl S
Hypothyroidism*
Klippel-Feil S
Vater association
Noonan S
Williams' S

A few of the more important conditions will be described here; a brief summary of the other conditions listed in the table will be found in Appendix 1.

Prader–Willi syndrome

This condition affects around 1 in 10 000 children, making it one of the commonest birth defect syndromes.[220] The main features are summarised in Table 12.11. In particular, it should be noted that obesity, the best known feature of the disorder, may not be apparent in infancy.

The cause of Prader–Willi syndrome is unknown, although hypothalmic dysfunction is postulated and a few cases have an abnormality of chromosome 15. It is usually sporadic; a few familial cases are reported but the recurrence risk is small. Probably it is not a single entity.

Because of the early failure to thrive, parents become very concerned about feeding, and when the child begins to eat more eagerly they are naturally pleased. Later, however, the child becomes a compulsive eater and may steal and forage for food. Obesity is said to be preventable by strict adherence to a diet. Behavioural measures are also essential: the child should not be praised for eating; food must be locked away; parents and relatives must not use food as a present or reward. These children become obese on lower calorie intakes than normals. For weight loss, restriction to 8.5 kCal/kg is recommended, and 10–11 kCal/cm height for steady growth. Vitamin supplements may be needed. Drug treatment (appetite suppressants and nalozone) has not been helpful. Intestinal bypass has been performed in a few cases of massive obesity, which may be life threatening.[222]

Table 12.11   Features of Prader–Willi syndrome.

Essential features (97% of patients)
Infantile hypotonia
Poor sucking and feeding, failure to thrive
Motor delay (average: sit 13 months, walk 28 months)
Hypogonadism
    undescended testes, micropenis
    small labia minora
Obesity, onset 6 months–6 years
Slow development (average: talking 21 months, sentences $3\frac{1}{2}$ years)
I.Q. range: moderate retardation–low normal
Face
    narrow bifrontal diameter
    almond-shaped eyes
    triangular mouth
Short stature

Common features (50–90% of children)
Small hands and feet
Easy bruising and infection of skin
Skin-picking habit
Sticky saliva, caries
Kitten-like neonatal cry
Scoliosis, may be progressive
Unable to vomit
Hyperphagia, food foraging

Features in 50% of cases
Breech birth
Decreased pain sensation
Diabetes ($\pm 7\%$)
Dislocated hip

Adolescence
Late menarche
Obesity
Not sexually active
Hypoventilation syndrome

Management of the undescended testes is difficult. Measurements of testosterone before and after HCG stimulation may help to determine whether the testes are present and functioning. The small penis may enlarge under the influence of depot testosterone given every three weeks for 3–5 injections.

Children with Prader–Willi syndrome are at particular risk during anaesthesia, both from hypoglycaemia and from reactions to anaesthetic agents.[221]

ABNORMAL SIZE OR SHAPE OF THE HEAD

Large heads

The commonest cause of a large head is normal variation. By definition 3% of the population have a head circumference above the 97th centile. Familial factors account for some of the variation and the parents' and siblings' heads should be measured and compared to the norm. (The normal adult head circumference range (mean $\pm$ 1 s.d.) in males is 55 cm $\pm$ 1.46 and in females is 54.27 cm $\pm$ 1.14.)

Some children have large heads at birth, an excessive rate of head growth, and even some suture separation. CT scan shows a ventricle size at the upper limit of normal but no other pathology and their development and progress are normal. Siblings and one or other parent (usually the father) may also have large heads.[223,224] The condition has been called benign familial megalencephaly but it should be regarded as a normal variant, not a disease. It should not be confused with true megalencephaly (Appendix 1).

Pathological causes of cranial enlargement (Table 12.12) can be divided into those with hydrocephalus and those in which this is usually absent or a minor additional feature.[225] Although hydrocephalus is commoner than all the other conditions put together, the word must not be used as a synonym for a large head.

Table 12.12   Causes of cranial enlargement.

Normal and familial variations
Hydrocephalus
Hydranencephaly
Subdural haematoma
Neurocutaneous syndromes
Storage diseases
Sotos' syndrome
Achondroplasia
Megalencephaly
Thickened skull (rickets, hemolytic anemias, bone dysplasias)

HYDRANENCEPHALY

Hydranencephaly means massive enlargement of the ventricles with little or no remnant of cerebral cortex, and variable head enlargement. The head transilluminates (but this should not be done in the presence of the parents). In the early weeks of life it is surprisingly easy to overlook the diagnosis if the head is not grossly enlarged. Survival beyond a few months is unusual.

HYDROCEPHALUS

Hydrocephalus is a condition in which an imbalance between production and reabsorption of CSF leads to ventricular enlargement. The ventricles can also become enlarged due to atrophy or loss of brain substance, but this situation can usually be distinguished from true hydrocephalus by the clinical and radiological findings.

Hydrocephalus may be caused by an obstruction within the ventricular system, around the exit foramina in the posterior fossa, in the CSF spaces surrounding the brain, or at the sites of reabsorption, which are mainly but not exclusively the arachnoid (Pacchionian) granulations along the superior sagittal sinus. The main causes are summarised in Table 12.13. The terms obstructive, internal, external, and communicating hydrocephalus are no longer popular because they lack precision. The commonest cause of hydrocephalus in children is the Arnold–Chiari malformation in association with neural tube defects (p. 361). Extraventricular obstruction and aqueduct stenosis are the two other common causes.

Progressive enlargement of the head is the usual presenting feature; the head circumference is noted to be crossing the percentile lines. If the head was initially small, severe hydrocephalus can exist long before the head circumference reaches the 97th centile. Other features include irritability, failure to thrive, developmental delay, a large tense, fontanelle, hyper-reflexia in the legs, squint and the 'sunset' sign with loss of upwards gaze. A rim of sclera may be seen above the cornea in normal babies at times, but 'sunsetting' in hydrocephalus is usually more dramatic and persistent. There may be other evidence of oculomotor or visual disturbance.

Table 12.13 Classification of hydrocephalus.

Obstruction within the ventricular system (non-communicating or obstructive)
Malformations of the aqueduct of Sylvius (stenosis, atresia, forking, etc.)
X-linked aqueduct stenosis (may be associated with abnormal thumbs)
Obstruction by mass lesions
Obstruction by inflammation: bacterial meningitis (also? mumps), haemorrhage; congenital infections
Obstruction of the fourth ventricle outlet foramina: inflammation; Dandy–Walker syndrome

Obstruction outside the ventricular system (communicating)
Adhesions in basal cisterns or subarachnoid space: infection or subarachnoid haemorrhage
Developmental abnormality or acquired obstruction of arachnoid villi
Arnold–Chiari malformation (may also be associated with aqueduct lesion)

Excess production of CSF
Choroid plexus papilloma

Papilloedema is rarely seen. The cry is sometimes harsh and high-pitched and rarely stridor occurs. The skull may have a 'crackpot' sound on percussion. Any or all of these signs may be absent, depending on the intracranial pressure and the rate of ventricular enlargement.

Investigations and management.   Skull X-rays may be of some help but the definitive study is the CT scan, which makes it possible to promptly investigate any child with a suspiciously large head instead of causing months of worry by repeated head measurements. The child should, if possible, be referred to a paediatric neurosurgeon for advice on management.

Treatment is discussed in detail on p. 361. The insertion of a CSF shunting system is associated with more complications than any other operation in paediatric surgery, and is not undertaken unless essential.[229] The presence of ventricular enlargement does not automatically mean that treatment is needed; for example, premature babies who have had intraventricular haemorrhage may have large ventricles without evidence of raised pressure; the natural history of this problem is not yet certain but it may resolve without treatment.[226,227] In some children with evidence of impaired CSF reabsorption, stabilisation may occur spontaneously. Marked asymptomatic hydrocephalus is occasionally discovered in older children or adults and has evidently arrested without treatment.

Hydrocephalus may also present at any time in later infancy or childhood, with features of acute raised intracranial pressure, with more insidious disturbances of gait or intellect, or with optic atrophy. A clinical diagnosis of 'arrested hydrocephalus' should *not* however be suggested to the parents of children with minor developmental disorders simply on the basis of a large head circumference.

Sequelae and prognosis.   Whether or not they are treated surgically, children with hydrocephalus often show some degree of early psychomotor retardation. The size and weight of the head probably accounts for some of the motor delay. There is often some spasticity and ataxia, particularly affecting the lower limbs; the legs are believed to be more affected than the arms because of the greater vulnerability of their nerve fibres to stretching by the enlarged lateral ventricles. For practical purposes, these children may be regarded as having a form of cerebral palsy, and managed as such.

Squint, optic atrophy, and varying degrees of visual loss are common. The I.Q. is very variable. There is often mild retardation in the borderline to ESN(M) range, and the verbal ability is often better than performance, with a tendency to inconsequential facile chatter (the 'cocktail party' syndrome), though this may also be seen in other forms of mental handicap.

Shunt surgery substantially decreases mortality and removes the risk of a grotesquely ugly enlarged head. The gains in I.Q. and motor function are less dramatic. Ultimate I.Q. does not correlate with the extent of the ventricular enlargement nor the thickness of the cerebral cortical mantle. It is possible that the outcome is determined by the disorder causing the hydrocephalus rather than the hydrocephalus per se.[228]

Genetic aspects.   It is generally believed that isolated hydrocephalus is not genetically related to neural tube defects. Hydrocephalus has many causes, the majority of which are not inherited. Some cases of aqueduct stenosis are inherited as a sex-linked recessive and the recurrence risk after the birth of one male with this condition is about 1 in 10.

Small heads

Microcephaly is sometimes defined as a head circumference more than 2 standard deviations below the mean—roughly equivalent to the 3rd centile. This is unsatisfactory because, by definition, 3% of the population have head measurements below this figure, and many of them are normal. Although the probability of neurologic and intellectual deficit increases rapidly with decreasing head size below the 3rd centile, no single measurement can define microcephaly. There are marked racial variations in head size, and charts standardised for European use are misleading when used for other races. Asians in particular may have head measurements far below the European 3rd centile, yet be perfectly normal. The head circumference of parents and siblings should be measured as well as that of the patient. It is probably best to reserve the term 'microcephaly' for a *pathologically* small head without attempting to specify numerical criteria.

The main causes of microcephaly are classified in Table 12.14. The importance of ascertaining the head circumference at birth is obvious. Serial measurements are essential in the follow-up of children who have suffered severe cerebral insults. A head circumference which is falling away from the centile lines is an ominous sign in these circumstances. A small head which is growing parallel to the centile lines gives less cause for concern. There may also be some faltering in head growth in any child who is failing to thrive, followed by catch-up growth on recovery.

Investigation.   A careful examination for other anomalies may help in recognition of a specific syndrome. Chromosome studies and tests for congenital infections may be indicated. A CT scan may reveal various malformations although these are seldom useful in management or genetic counselling. Calcification caused by congenital infections may be revealed on a CT scan before it is visible on plain X-ray.

Development and prognosis.   This is very variable, since microcephaly is not itself a diagnosis. In general, the severity of mental retardation correlates with the head circumference. There may be spastic quadriplegia, visual or auditory defects, seizures, and behaviour problems. In some children with

Table 12.14   Causes of microcephaly.

Primary: present at birth
Microcephaly with recessive inheritance
Abnormal neuronal development, cause(s) unknown
    lissencephaly (agyria)
    macrogyria
    polymicrogyria, etc.
Craniosynostosis of all sutures
Numerous chromosomal defects and other dysmorphic syndromes
Severe intrauterine growth retardation*
Insults to previously normal brain*
    fetal alcohol syndrome
    intrauterine infections
    radiation
    maternal phenylketonuria

Secondary: head circumference normal at birth;
insult occurs in infancy or early childhood
Severe anoxia or asphyxia
Meningitis and encephalitis
Non-accidental injury (shaking)
Inborn errors of metabolism
Lysosomal storage diseases
Storage diseases
Vascular accidents

---

* Some authors classify all insults (pre- or postnatal) to a normal
brain as secondary microcephaly.

microcephaly early development seems reasonably normal, motor development proceeds steadily, and several years elapse before the extent of the
intellectual handicap is apparent.

Genetic aspects.   Most cases of microcephaly are caused by pre- or postnatal
insults, or form part of a dysmorphic syndrome. Among the remainder, with
unexplained and often severe microcephaly, a significant proportion is
recessively inherited. Recessive microcephaly is characterised by the
extremely small head, sloping forehead, small chin, large ears, normal-sized
face, and usually the absence of spasticity or seizures.

Craniosynostosis (craniostenosis)

Growth of the skull vault usually occurs along the sutures. In craniosynostosis, one or more of the sutures are inactive, the normal interdigitations are
reduced, and the suture line becomes obliterated, with bony thickening and
the bones become fused prematurely.[229] The brain is unable to expand in
the plane of the closed sutures and the head therefore develops an abnormal

shape. Sagittal craniosynostosis results in a boat-shaped head (scaphocephaly) early in infancy. There are usually no associated anomalies and intellect is normal. Surgical treatment is undertaken for purely cosmetic reasons and the results are good if the operation is performed within the first six months.

In coronal craniosynostosis, the head is broad, and the anteroposterior diameter is reduced (acrocephaly). Growth of the brain may be restricted and there may be retardation, proptosis or optic atrophy. The nasal airway may be restricted resulting in mouth breathing and frequent ear infections. In addition, there may be underdevelopment of the maxilla (Crouzon's syndrome) or limb defects such as syndactyly (Apert's syndrome). Plagiocephaly (asymmetry of the head) may result from asymmetric craniosynostosis, although it is more commonly a simple postural anomaly that corrects itself with time (p. 312).

In all these conditions the shape of the head is obviously abnormal. The only situation in which a normal shaped head can occur with craniosynostosis is when *all* the sutures are involved—total craniosynostosis. In this very rare condition, skull X-ray shows a gross excess of digital markings due to the chronically raised intracranial pressure. The distinction between total craniosynostosis and primary microcephaly causes some unnecessary anxiety; the presence of any suture on the skull X-ray of a baby with microcephaly rules out the diagnosis of craniosynostosis.

Treatment.   A baby with suspected craniosynostosis should be referred to a paediatric neurosurgeon as soon as possible. The sutures can be opened by removing a strip of bone and periosteum—craniectomy. Various manoeuvres are available to prevent premature reunion. The more complex craniofacial malformations can now be repaired using the remarkable techniques devised by the French surgeon, Tessier.

Genetic aspects.   Craniosynostosis, uncomplicated by other malformations, is usually sporadic but cases of both dominant and recessive inheritance have been reported. In familial cases the patterns and severity of suture involvement may not be the same in all family members.

NEUROCUTANEOUS SYNDROMES

Tuberose sclerosis (tuberous sclerosis, Epiloia, Bourneville disease)

This is one of the most important malformation syndromes.[230] Cerebral and skin lesions are the most striking features (Table 12.15). The disorder may present with neonatal fits, infantile spasms, epilepsy, or psychomotor retardation. The degree of mental handicap is very variable and some subjects are of normal intelligence. Retardation is usually static, but in some cases deterioration may occur around puberty.

Table 12.15   Features of tuberose sclerosis.

Skin
White 'ash-leaf' macules, present at birth, size 3 mm–5 cm; best seen with Wood's light
Adenoma sebaceum; yellow, pink or brown papules on cheeks, nasolabial folds, appearing in childhood or adolescence
Shagreen patches: leathery patches over lumbosacral area
Café-au-lait spots
Subungual fibromata: papules between nail and cuticle, appear at puberty

Brain
Hamartomatous malformations with calcification
No specific EEG changes. Seizures: often in first year
Mental handicap—variable
Malignancy
Retinal lesions (flat or elevated)

Bones
Cystic changes in phalanges and skull
Areas of sclerosis

Kidney
Cystic changes
Angiolipomata
Haematuria

Lung
Lymphangiectasis, cystic changes, etc.

Heart
Tumours of heart muscle

A careful search for the cutaneous manifestations of this disease should be included in the examination of all handicapped children. Cerebral calcification on X-ray helps to confirm the diagnosis but it is not always visible. CT scanning shows nodules in the walls of the lateral ventricles, which are virtually diagnostic of tuberose sclerosis (the only other cause of such nodules is heterotopic grey matter). As malignant change in these nodules is not uncommon, the scan should be repeated if new symptoms develop.

Tuberose sclerosis is dominantly inherited, with around 80% of cases occurring as new mutations. A careful inspection of the parents for minor stigmata of the disease is mandatory before deciding that a new mutation has occurred.

Sturge–Weber syndrome

A flat facial haemangioma, often in the trigeminal distribution, is present at birth and does not usually progress. Asymmetrical tonic clonic seizures often begin in the first year of life, and are due to meningeal haemangiomata. Cerebral calcification, visible on X-ray, is not present until late infancy. It follows the contours of the cortical convolutions. The vascular abnormality may cause glaucoma and regular eye inspections are desirable.

Continued uncontrollable epilepsy, hemiparesis, and mental handicap are common, though not invariable. Occasionally neurosurgical treatment for these has been attempted. The condition is usually sporadic and clear evidence of heredity has not been established.

Neurofibromatosis (Von Recklinghausen's disease)

This is among the commonest of all malformation syndromes, affecting around 1 in 3000 of the population, but only a minority of subjects are mentally retarded. The hallmark of the condition is the café-au-lait spot. It is said that the presence of six or more spots, if greater than 1.5 cm diameter, is pathognomonic, as is the finding of freckles or café-au-lait spots in the

Table 12.16   Features of neurofibromatosis.

Skin
Café-au-lait spots
Axillary freckles

Nervous system
Subcutaneous tumours on peripheral nerves
CNS tumours
    optic glioma
    acoustic neuroma
    spinal canal tumours
Macrocranium
Mental handicap
Seizures (especially with CNS tumours)

Bone
Bowing of lower leg
Pseudoarthrosis
Scoliosis
Facial and skeletal asymmetry

Miscellaneous
Hypertension
Eye defects
Malignant change in hamartomata

axillae. Small subcutaneous hamartomatous lesions develop along the peripheral nerves. There are numerous other manifestations (Table 12.16). Neurofibromatosis is dominantly inherited. About 50% of cases arise from a fresh mutation.

CONGENITAL INFECTIONS

The best known of these are rubella, cytomegalovirus (CMV), and toxoplasmosis, but congenital herpes simplex and chicken pox may also occur. These infections have a number of features in common.[232,233,234,237] The organisms normally cause only trivial or subclinical illness, but when a primary or first infection occurs in a susceptible (non-immune) woman during pregnancy, they are liable to cause severe fetal damage. Only a proportion of primary maternal infections result in fetal infections, and only a proportion of fetal infections are symptomatic.

INTERPRETATION OF LABORATORY DATA

The classical clinical features of congenital infection are described below and are easily recognised, but diagnosis may not be so easy when these features are absent. The older the child is when first seen, the more difficult it is to decide whether positive serology indicates that the child's handicap is attributable to congenital infection. The finding of retinopathy is a useful pointer to a congenital rather than acquired infection, and an eye examination is always worthwhile in doubtful cases. The following points should be considered in interpreting laboratory data.

1   The first antibody to appear in response to infection is IgM. This has a high molecular weight and therefore does not cross the placenta. It appears within 7–10 days after the infection has been acquired, reaches a plateau and then slowly declines to undetectable levels over 4–8 months. Measurement of total IgM is of little value in the diagnosis of congenital infection. It is essential to assay IgM specific to the suspected infection. This is technically difficult but more accurate results are now obtainable using the ELISA (enzyme-linked assay) technique.

2   IgG antibody appears slightly later than IgM, and production continues indefinitely, although the titre declines from the immediate postinfection peak to lower levels. IgG has a lower molecular weight, and therefore crosses the placenta from mother to fetus.

3   It follows that if IgM antibody is detected in the newborn infant it is proof that the baby is infected, although, if congenital infection occurs in the first trimester, the baby's IgM may have fallen to undetectable levels by the time he is born.

4   The finding of IgG antibody in the infant's blood may indicate either fetal infection or passive transplacental transfer from the mother.

5   If the infant is congenitally infected, his IgG level will remain high and may rise further in the early months of life.

6   If the infant is not infected, any IgG antibody found in his blood must come only from the mother and the level will decline in the early months of life. The fact that transplacental transfer of IgG antibody has occurred is not proof that the mother has had a primary infection during pregnancy. She may simply have a high antibody level from a previous infection. The finding of specific IgM in her blood would confirm that she has had a primary infection during pregnancy, but if the infection occurred in the first trimester, IgM may be undetectable by the end of pregnancy.

7   The presence of IgG or IgM antibodies after the first few weeks of life may reflect acquired rather than congenital infection.

8   For these reasons diagnosis of congenital infection is difficult unless the infant has all the classical clinical features. In most cases, specific IgM measurement, and often repeat serology on both mother and infant, are necessary to confirm or eliminate the diagnosis of congenital infection.

Cytomegalovirus infection (CMV)

This is widespread and usually asymptomatic. Antibodies are found in between 40 and 100% of adults; the higher prevalence rates are found in poor communities and lower social classes.[237] The virus is frequently present in the genital tract during pregnancy, and around 5% of babies acquire it during the perinatal period. In these cases, the virus is not excreted in urine until 4–8 weeks after birth and IgM antibody is not detectable in the cord blood or in the first few weeks of life. Perinatal infection is probably benign but this is not yet certain.

Congenital (transplacental) infection is less common, and usually results from a primary maternal infection, but it may also occur following reactivation of a latent infection.[231,235] The latter, however, seems less likely to result in severe neonatal disease. The incidence of congenital CMV infection varies in different populations from 0.2% to 2.5%. In a recent American study it was about 0.5%; in the UK it was 0.3%.[479] Only 6% of congenitally infected babies are symptomatic in the neonatal period, and have the classic features of cytomegalic inclusion disease (Table 12.17). The prognosis for these is poor; 90% either die or are severely handicapped.

The remaining 94% of congenitally infected babies are asymptomatic in the neonatal period, but a significant number (around 13%) are found to have sensorineural deafness which may be unilateral or bilateral, is of varying severity, and occasionally appears to be progressive.[235,236] Intellect and neurological function are usually preserved although cerebral palsy and microcephaly occasionally develop during the first year of life. CMV infection is probably now a commoner cause of congenital sensorineural deafness than rubella.

Table 12.17   Features of congenital cytomegalovirus infection.

Low birthweight
Microcephaly
Periventricular intracranial calcification
Spasticity
Retardation
Deafness
Chorioretinitis
Hepatomegaly
Splenomegaly
Anaemia and thrombocytopenia
Pneumonitis
Bone lesions

DIAGNOSIS

The baby presenting with severe disease in the neonatal period will have IgM antibody in the blood and will excrete virus in the urine, sometimes for months and occasionally for up to four years. Diagnosis is more difficult if the child is initially asymptomatic, and only presents at a later age with a handicap such as deafness. Since about 10% of 1-year-old children, and over 20% of 5-year-olds, have been exposed postnatally to CMV and have antibodies, positive serology or viriuria do not prove that the infection is congenital nor that it is the cause of the child's handicap. Unless a retinopathy is found, it may never be possible to confirm the diagnosis.

Prevention of CMV infection is not yet possible. A vaccine was developed some years ago but its efficacy and safety are still not established. Two observations have raised further questions about the nature of immunity to CMV and therefore the effectiveness of vaccination. Firstly, on rare occasions, two consecutive congenitally infected children have been born to the same mother. Secondly, congenital infection may occur following reactivation of a latent maternal infection.

There has been much concern that young female child-care staff and nurses may be at risk of having congenitally infected infants themselves as a result of acquiring CMV from a handicapped infant. Two independent working parties have examined this issue, and both have concluded that there is no substantially increased risk and that therefore there is no reason to exclude infants with congenital CMV from nurseries or other child care facilities.[451]

Congenital rubella

This is still an important cause of handicap; although the incidence is falling and it is potentially totally preventable by immunisation, congenital rubella remains one of the major causes of deafness.[234]

Table 12.18   Congenital rubella: Risk of infection and of defects (Miller *et al*[238]).

	Risk (%)
Risk of congenital infection:	
If mother symptomatic in first trimester	>80
Asymptomatic proven rubella in first trimester	Exact risk uncertain but much less
Maternal infection 13–16 weeks	approx 50
Maternal infection 17–36 weeks	approx 40
Maternal infection 36 weeks–term	approx 100
Risk of defects caused by congenital infection:	
Infection in weeks 2–11	>90
Infection in weeks 12–16	±30
Infection beyond week 17	very low
Type of defect	
Cardiac defects: only if infection occurs before 11 weeks	
Isolated deafness: 13–16 weeks	

There is a serious risk of fetal abnormality or spontaneous abortion if a woman contracts rubella during pregnancy. Authors differ as to the exact risk, but the results of a recent study are shown in Table 12.18.[238] Infections beyond the first trimester more often lead to single defects, particularly deafness. The maternal infection can be so mild that it is overlooked. Reinfection, usually subclinical, following either a primary maternal infection or immunisation, is common but rarely leads to viraemia and the fetal risk is very small. Administration of gammaglobulin to a susceptible woman in contact with rubella cannot be relied upon to protect the fetus against congenital infection.

The multiple systemic features which may occur in congenital rubella are listed in Table 12.19. Hearing loss is the commonest single manifestation. It is sensorineural and varies widely in severity and in the frequencies affected. The hearing loss may become more severe during childhood and repeated testing is essential. A number of rubella children seem to have problems of language acquisition out of proportion to their deafness, and a few show behaviour patterns suggestive of autism.[239] Associated eye disorders include cataract (usually present at, or soon after, birth), microphthalmia, congenital glaucoma, and the characteristic 'pepper and salt' retinopathy which of itself does not seem to impair vision. The brain may be extensively damaged, and microcephaly, mental retardation, and spastic diplegia are frequently seen. Rubella very rarely causes hydrocephalus. A few cases of an illness similar to SSPE (Appendix 1) have been reported following congenital rubella infection. Management of the deaf-blind child is discussed on p. 302.

Table 12.19   Systemic features of congenital rubella infection.

General
Intrauterine growth retardation
Delayed postnatal growth

Heart
Patent ductus
Pulmonary artery stenosis
Aortic stenosis
Renal artery stenosis
VSD
Myocarditis

Other
Thrombocytopenia
Hepatosplenomegaly
Hepatitis and jaundice
Bone lesions
Pneumonitis
Rash
Adenopathy
Hypogammaglobulinaemia
Abnormal dermatoglyphics
Diarrhoea
Diabetes
Growth hormone deficiency
Pancreatic deficiency

DIAGNOSIS

Rubella antibody status is usually checked at the antenatal clinic, and it may be possible to confirm or refute a diagnosis of congenital rubella by examination of the mother's obstetric record. The virus may be isolated from the baby's nasal secretions, stools, or CSF in the first few months of life, and from cataracts for up to two years. An elevated haemagglutination inhibition (HI) titre which falls during the first 4–6 months may be due to passive transfer of maternal antibody, but a persistent or rising titre is suggestive of congenital infection. Detection of rubella-specific IgM confirms that the infant is, or has been, infected. Beyond 3 years of age the diagnosis becomes increasingly difficult. The HI titre may fall to undetectable levels, and a high titre is more likely to result from acquired infection as the child gets older. Immunisation with rubella vaccine does not cause seroconversion in children with congenital infection; this may be a useful diagnostic aid. In all cases of suspected rubella syndrome, an ophthalmic examination and a complete paediatric assessment are essential.

Girls with congenital rubella should be offered immunisation at the usual age as they may not be immune and are therefore at risk of having a rubella-damaged infant themselves.

Congenital toxoplasmosis

This is caused by the protozoan *Toxoplasma gondii*.[241] The organism is found in many animal species. It is thought that human infection is acquired either from cats or from infected uncooked meat, though the exact mode of transmission is still uncertain. Asymptomatic human infection is common and antibody is found in up to half the adult population. Primary infection occurs in pregnancy in about 0.3% of susceptible women, and the risk of transmission to the fetus rises from 20% in the first trimester to 70% in the third. About 10–20% of infected infants show one or more classic features of congenital toxoplasmosis: hydrocephalus, intracranial calcification, chorioretinitis, and hepatosplenomegaly. If the infant survives, severe multiple handicap is usual. Among asymptomatic infected infants there is a very high probability that chorioretinitis will develop and this may present at any time in childhood or even in adult life.[240] Occasionally late progressive psychomotor retardation occurs in a child who appeared normal at birth.

DIAGNOSIS

Diagnosis is suggested by the finding of IgG antibody using the Sabin–Feldman dye test. Detection of IgM antibody confirms that the infant is infected, though there are still some technical problems with this test. Acquired toxoplasmosis in infancy is unusual but not unknown, and is likely to be responsible for the finding of IgM antibody after 8 months of age. As with other congenital infections, interpretation of toxoplasma antibody results is often difficult. Maternal serum and repeat infant sera may be needed. Consultation with the laboratory is essential before deciding whether an infant's handicap can be attributed to congenital toxoplasmosis.[477]

The organism is sensitive to pyrimethamine, which is given with folic acid, and to spiramycin; but the effectiveness of treatment is not known.

OTHER PRENATAL CAUSES

Fetal alcohol syndrome

Exposure to alcohol *in utero* is associated with a consistent pattern of malformations (Table 12.20). The exact degree of alcohol abuse needed to damage the baby is unknown but it seems unlikely that an occasional 'social' drink is harmful. Fetal alcohol syndrome is probably a fairly common cause of mental handicap but its exact frequency is not known.[242]

OTHER DRUGS

Parents often worry about drug ingestion in early pregnancy as a cause of handicap. Table 12.21 lists those drugs known or suspected to have definite adverse effects in pregnancy.[455]

Table 12.20   Fetal alcohol syndrome.

Pre- and postnatal growth deficiency
Psychomotor retardation
Microcephaly
Short palpebral fissures
Ptosis
Maxillary hypoplasia
Joint anomalies

Table 12.21   Drugs with teratogenic effects.

Definite teratogens
Thalidomide
Cytotoxic drugs
Radiation
Probable teratogens
Alcohol
Phenytoin
Trimethadione
Warfarin
Lithium
Quinine
Possible teratogens
Sex hormones
Barbiturates and primidone
Sodium valproate
Chloroquine
Operating theatre environment (?nitrous oxide)
Common drugs with no known teratogenicity
Antibiotics
Anti-emetics
Psychotropic drugs
Sedatives
Clomiphene
Aspirin

Congenital hypothyroidism

This is among the commonest treatable causes of handicap.[243] Prior to the advent of neonatal screening, the incidence was estimated at 1 per 7000–10 000 births, but screening programmes in the USA involving over one million babies have detected one case per 4000 births.[244,245] Most of these have primary hypothyroidism, caused by hypoplasia or aplasia of the gland in two-thirds of the cases, and associated with an ectopic gland, goitrogens, or inborn errors of thyroxine metabolism (dyshormonogenesis) in the remainder. These babies have low thyroxine (T4) levels and raised thyroid stimulating hormone levels (TSH). In some cases the hypothyroidism turns out to be transient. About 7% of babies detected by screening have secondary hypothyroidism caused by hypothalamic or pituitary disease, and therefore have low TSH levels. These babies may also have neonatal hypoglycaemia, small genitalia, or cleft palate.

The classic features of severe hypothyroidism in the neonatal period are well known (Table 12.22) but are recognisable clinically in only about 5% of the cases detected by screening. If not diagnosed at this time, the condition may present at any time in infancy, with slow development in combination with any of the features listed in Table 12.22.

Replacement therapy is commenced immediately the diagnosis is made, using thyroxin 5–10 μg/kg/day (usually 25 μg/day). If the infant has severe clinical disease, the starting dose is smaller (1–2 μg/kg) and increases are made every 4–5 days. Therapy is monitored clinically and by T4 and TSH measurement. Unrecognised overtreatment can cause craniosynostosis.

Table 12.22   Hypothyroidism.

Neonatal features
Characteristic facies (can be mistaken for Down's syndrome)
Macroglossia
Underdeveloped nasal ridge between eyes
Umbilical hernia
Oedema
Goitre
Large fontanelles
Bradycardia
Prolonged jaundice

First few months
Lethargic
Slow to feed
Constipation
Cold peripheries
Respiratory infections
Hypothermia
Deafness

Later
Short stature
Mental retardation
Delayed bone age
Squint
Abnormal gait: pyramidal signs, tremor, skeletal muscle abnormalities, ataxia, 'clumsiness'

Some children remain severely retarded in spite of treatment, but even in those who make good progress, permanent sequelae such as clumsiness, learning disability and squint are common. Several studies have now demonstrated that the earlier the diagnosis is made and treatment is commenced, the better is the prognosis for normal development. These findings were the stimulus for the introduction of neonatal screening programmes, which are now being developed in many parts of the UK, making use of the well established organisational network for PKU screening. Samples are collected on the same card, processed at a central laboratory, using assays of T4, TSH or both, and the results are distributed via the community services. Each laboratory has its own protocol defining the action to be taken when abnormal results are obtained.

There are still a few unsolved problems in screening for hypothyroidism. Permanent sequelae may still be found in cases where treatment was begun very early, perhaps because permanent brain damage is already present at the time of diagnosis. If the screening programme involves the assay of TSH alone and not T4, all cases of secondary hypothyroidism will be missed. Even if both assays are performed, a small proportion of false-negative results is inevitable. For these reasons, the possibility of hypothyroidism must still be considered even in areas where neonatal screening is established.

PERINATAL INSULTS

Serious obstetric complications leading to perinatal asphyxia can cause cerebral palsy with or without mental handicap, but it is rare for these problems to result in mental handicap *without* cerebral palsy. Mentally handicapped children often have a history of abnormal pregnancy or birth, but it is likely that these abnormalities are caused by, rather than the cause of, an intellectual defect. The high incidence of minor and major congenital anomalies is evidence that many cases of mental handicap originate in the early months of fetal life (p. 74). Similarly, handicap is often attributed to breech delivery, but the breech position often occurs *because* of pre-existing abnormality and is common in, for example, Prader–Willi syndrome, Cornelia de Lange syndrome, fetal alcohol syndrome, and many others.

Whatever the perinatal insult may have been, it is unwise to accept it as the sole cause of mental handicap. This is not merely an academic point; failure to appreciate the prenatal origins of handicap can result in incorrect genetic counselling. Furthermore, the implication that better obstetric care might have prevented the handicap causes much unwarranted bitterness and may have medicolegal implications.

The effects of extreme prematurity on intellectual development are difficult to assess. Except for those children with obvious extensive brain damage, in whom cerebral palsy is usually a prominent feature, the outcome in survivors is generally satisfactory. Any reduction in intelligence may partly be attributed to the social or obstetric factors which caused the prematurity. It is likely that hypoglycaemia, apnoeic spells, neonatal fits, and intrauterine growth retardation, are contributory causes of mental handicap. Further study is needed to determine the precise effects of intraventricular haemorrhage on I.Q., behaviour, and learning.

POSTNATAL DISORDERS

Examples of the numerous cerebral insults which may cause mental handicap are given in Table 12.1. Often there are other defects as well, such as cerebral palsy, cortical blindness, and secondary microcephaly. When a cerebral insult occurs after the neonatal period, it is usually possible to determine that previous development was normal and that the insult is the sole cause of any residual handicap. However, parents often attribute mental handicap to a postnatal event such as immunisation, a minor illness, or a convulsion. Careful probing will reveal whether or not there was in fact any change or regression in development after the incident.

Two of the postnatal causes of mental handicap merit further discussion here. Febrile fits are described on p. 438.

Pertussis immunisation

There is no doubt that some children have suffered severe convulsions and permanent brain damage following pertussis immunisation. However, a severe encephalopathy with fits may also occur in babies who have not been immunised. Since immunisation is a common event, it is statistically inevitable that some cases of encephalopathy will coincide with a recent immunisation; it cannot be assumed that the events are necessarily related.[153]

The National Childhood Encephalopathy Study was designed to examine this problem.[246] The results showed that encephalopathic illness is commonest at precisely the peak age for immunisation and that pertussis immunisation could only account for a minority of cases. The risk of permanent severe brain damage is estimated at 1 case per 300 000 immunisations. Pertussis immunisation should not be accepted as the cause of a child's handicap unless there is a close temporal relationship between the procedure and a severe neurological illness, and even then the possibility of another diagnosis should be remembered.

Lead poisoning

This deserves detailed consideration because it is the cause of much public and parental concern.[172,247,248] Lead poisoning may present as a severe encephalopathy with convulsions and cerebral oedema. There is a significant risk of permanent neurological damage. A detailed account will be found in standard paediatric texts.[77]

Chronic lead poisoning is more difficult to recognise and its significance as a cause of handicap is controversial. Children with acute encephalopathy have usually had a heavy exposure to sources such as old paint or batteries. Pica accounts for significant lead consumption in some children (p. 163). The whole population is continually exposed to low levels of lead from many sources, including food, water, air and dust, and much of this occurs naturally. There is undoubtedly a contribution from petrol engines and industrial emissions, both directly through the air and indirectly through soil, food and water, but it is uncertain how much total lead intake or blood lead levels would fall if these sources of pollution were to be removed.

Numerous studies show a correlation between increasing lead levels in blood and other tissues, and poorer performance on measures of intellect and behaviour. The differences between children with low and high lead levels are small in absolute terms, though highly statistically significant. As with all epidemiological studies, there is no proof of a cause and effect relationship and there are several possible explanations for the results. For example, it is possible that less intelligent children indulge in pica more often and therefore have a higher lead level.

At present, the DHSS recommend that efforts should be made to identify and reduce sources of lead exposure if a child's lead level exceeds 25 μg/100 ml (previously the level was 36 μg/100 ml). Few clinicians would consider active treatment unless the level was much higher than this and, at present, it would seem unwise to attribute minor mental handicap or behaviour problems to marginally elevated lead levels. Nevertheless, lead has no known beneficial effects and in view of the damage which lead pollution *may* be causing, many authorities feel that there is a strong case for removing lead from petrol.

Environmental causes of mental handicap, including 'subcultural deprivation' and malnutrition, are discussed in Chapter 2.

MANAGEMENT

Counselling—some common anxieties

Inadequate and confused knowledge of mental handicap probably causes as much sadness and distress as the handicap itself. Many parents do not understand that the terms 'mental handicap', 'mental retardation', 'backwardness' and 'subnormality' have essentially the same meaning. 'Developmental delay' is an acceptable term while the diagnosis is in doubt, but often it is simply a euphemism that allows one to defer the painful task of telling the parents the true diagnosis. It is also necessary in some cases to explain that mental handicap is not the same as mental illness.

Educated parents may read about dysphasia and autism and may consider these labels appropriate to their child. Frequently they are accused of searching for a more socially acceptable label, but this is rarely the primary motivation. More often, they have been led to believe, by voluntary societies or the popular press, that these conditions are more likely to respond to highly specialised teaching than is simple mental retardation. This problem is further discussed on p. 260.

Prognosis for walking and talking is usually requested at an early stage. Unless the child's mental handicap is severe and is associated with cerebral palsy or profound hypotonia, the parents can be told that most mentally handicapped children will walk eventually. The majority also acquire some speech, but, as this may be slow, a sign system such as the Makaton Vocabulary may be suggested (p. 265). Most parents are also concerned about the prospects for the child's education; this topic is discussed in Chapter 8.

The diagnosis of mental handicap raises many alarming fears about the future, even while the child is very young. Boys are seen as potential violent and aggressive rapists, girls as becoming promiscuous or pregnant. These fears cannot be totally dismissed but sexual aggression in boys is seldom a major problem. Promiscuity and unwanted pregnancy are no greater a problem than in normal girls and are easier to avoid because the mentally handicapped teenager is more likely to be under regular close supervision. Sexual relationships and marriage between mentally handicapped people are becoming more widely accepted (although the parents of a young child may not find this fact particularly reassuring!).

Parents who have visited long-stay mental hospitals may be appalled at the thought of their child ending his days in such a place. Some reassurance can be given that the education and care of mentally handicapped adults is improving steadily, and a reasonably normal existence in small units or hostel accommodation can be anticipated. There are now plans to accommodate even the most profoundly handicapped people in ordinary housing.

Investigation

Many parents find it hard to accept that much mental handicap remains unexplained. They should be warned of this fact before investigation is undertaken. It is worth explaining in simple terms the reason for any tests which are performed, since many laymen imagine that blood tests are done only for anaemia and blood grouping.

Intensive investigation of mental handicap can rarely be justified by the hope of finding a treatable disorder, but an exact diagnosis is nevertheless useful to the parents for several reasons. The recognition of a specific syndrome may alert one to search for associated handicaps recorded by previous observers, and allows more accurate genetic advice to be given. Furthermore, parents often feel happier when the child's handicap can be medically explained. There are no 'routine' investigations for mental retardation, but if the history and physical examination suggest no specific diagnosis or line of investigation, the following may be considered:

1   Urine and blood examination for inborn errors of metabolism.

2   Tests for congenital infections.

3   CT scan is often requested by the parents, but has a very low yield of positive findings except in cases of abnormal size or shape of the head, focal neurological damage, or severe epilepsy.[249]

4   An EEG is rarely helpful except for investigation of epilepsy, but there are specific changes in minor epileptic status, SSPE, and Batten's disease.

5   A chromosome study is the one investigation which occasionally yields an unexpected result in a case of mental handicap with no specific features.

Genetic aspects

If single gene disorders, common dysmorphic syndromes and chromosomal abnormalities are excluded, recurrence risks for mental handicap are usually empiric.[250] The presence of identical anomalies in two or more siblings born to normal parents may be suggestive of recessive inheritance, even if no exact diagnosis can be made; this situation is known as a 'provisional private syndrome'.

Mental handicap with multiple congenital anomalies occurring as a sporadic case has a low risk of recurrence, about 1 in 30 to 1 in 50, but it is essential to exclude the many rare single gene malformation syndromes. Mental handicap associated with cerebral palsy has a similarly low risk of recurrence, except in some diplegias (p. 320), as do those cases with idiopathic epilepsy or severe hypotonia.

In pure mental retardation without significant anomalies, microcephaly or severe epilepsy, recurrence risks depend on the sex of the handicapped child. When the proband is a boy the risk is about 1 in 20, if fragile X is excluded and there is no pedigree evidence of X-linkage (p. 202). If the proband is a girl the risk is about 1 in 30.

PRESCHOOL EDUCATION

The parents should be told that most mentally handicapped children are capable of learning even though they are slow. Some people appreciate a detailed programme of activities making use of modern behavioural research (Chapter 9) to teach increasingly complex skills in a series of small steps. The Portage system is one example of a planned programme and is currently very popular (Fig. 12.1). The Parent Involvement Project (PIP) charts provide a useful system of observation-based assessment which is described in a book written specially for parents (Appendix 11). Some schools for severely retarded children now employ a peripatetic teacher who visits preschool children at home or in the playgroup or nursery. This arrangement provides continuity of teaching when the child goes to school.

The occupational therapist (OT) will advise on suitable toys and play activities and can introduce the parents to a toy library. In collaboration with the psychologist, guidance is offered on the development of simple skills such as feeding, washing, and dressing. The speech therapist (ST) will instruct the parents on the principles of language development, and introduce alternative communication systems where appropriate, rather than undertake formal speech therapy. Physiotherapy has a limited role in the care of the mentally handicapped. Advice on positioning, seating and

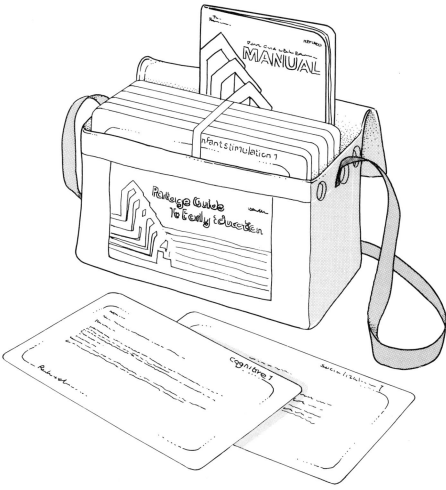

Fig. 12.1 a The Portage Guide—a system of early teaching for the mentally handicapped. (Courtesy of NFER, Windsor.)

self help 93

AGE 5-6

TITLE: Stops at curb, looks both ways, and crosses street without verbal reminders

WHAT TO DO:

1. Remind child how to cross street before going to a friend's house or to the store.
2. Ask child what he should do each time he crosses street.
3. Praise child for crossing street safely and correctly.
4. Walk with child and show him how to cross street. When he demonstrates skill, let him go alone.
5. Role play crossing street safely or use dolls and toy cars to demonstrate.
6. Give child a safety star-shaped badge to wear when he crosses street correctly.

 PortageGuide

© 1976 Cooperative Educational Service Agency 12

Fig. 12.1   b An example from the Portage Guide.

mobility, may be needed. In the profoundly handicapped child, contractures, hip deformities, and scoliosis may develop (p. 351) and their prevention requires constant vigilance.

There is no doubt that planned teaching of mentally handicapped children is worthwhile but it is important to avoid excessive optimism. There are no miracles even with the most modern and sophisticated programmes of teaching. Furthermore there is a danger that family dynamics may be seriously disturbed if excessive attention is devoted to the mentally handicapped child, resulting in marital discord and disturbed behaviour in siblings. The mentally handicapped child may learn to expect constant attention and stimulation and may produce intolerable behaviour problems if this is not provided.

SCHOOL

School placement and education are discussed in more detail in Chapter 8. Education for the severely mentally handicapped must be realistic. Goals might include skills such as personal care, hygiene and safety, development of acceptable social behaviour, and short journeys in a familiar neighbourhood. For the mildly handicapped, the curriculum may be similar to that in normal schools, but the pace is slower and some important skills such as shopping and travel may need special attention. Once the child is established in school, contact with the Child Development Centre often diminishes, but the parents should be told that the Centre's services are available if needed.

LEAVING SCHOOL

The education authority should inform the parents of the available facilities, which may include an adult training centre, a special class in a local college, and a variety of special hostels, communities and vocational training schemes. The formation of Community Mental Handicap Teams (not to be confused with the children's District Handicap Teams (p. 60)) should facilitate the care of the mentally handicapped adult[251] and bring about an improvement in what is at present still an understaffed and underfunded area of the National Health Service and the Social Services. Another recent development is the 'Pathways Officer', whose brief is to place mentally handicapped school-leavers in open employment.

The development and the psychiatric problems of the mentally handicapped adolescent have been sadly neglected by paediatricians, child psychiatrists, and adult psychiatrists, who all feel that these people are somebody else's responsibility. The school medical officer may be in the best position to provide medical advice when needed, but he seldom receives adequate consultant support. Ideally the District Handicap Team should ensure that there is continuity of care through the school years and arrange a formal hand-over to an adult orientated Community Mental Handicap Team at, or before, school-leaving age.

Chapter Thirteen
Disorders of Communication

Disorders of speech and language development are the commonest single reason for referral to a Child Development Centre, with a peak age of presentation between the 2nd and 3rd birthdays. In many of these children, intellect and hearing are normal, and unclear or inadequate speech is the only problem; however, in a minority, failure to develop speech is the presenting feature of a more serious disorder such as mental handicap, hearing loss or autism. These children have problems not only with the use of words and sentences (expressive language) but also with comprehension of language and in some cases are also unable to use or understand social cues and non-verbal communication (pp. 32 & 43). It is surprising how even apparently well informed parents will focus on the lack of speech and fail to recognise the significance of delays in other aspects of their child's development.

In addition to those children in whom speech delay is the predominant and presenting complaint, there are many others with established major handicaps such as cerebral palsy, mental retardation or severe deafness, which cause major difficulties in communication; indeed the parents often regard this as the child's greatest problem.

The concept of a 'communication disorder'

This term can be applied to any child who has difficulties in the use or comprehension of spoken language, either in isolation, or in association with impaired ability to communicate by non-verbal means. It includes the commonest of all developmental problems, 'simple' delay in speech development, together with major handicaps such as the more severe disorders of language development, hearing loss and autism and the physical or mental handicaps insofar as they impede communication. The link between these disparate conditions lies in their functional effects rather than their underlying pathology. The justification for grouping them together is that all require a similar diagnostic process (Fig 13.1).

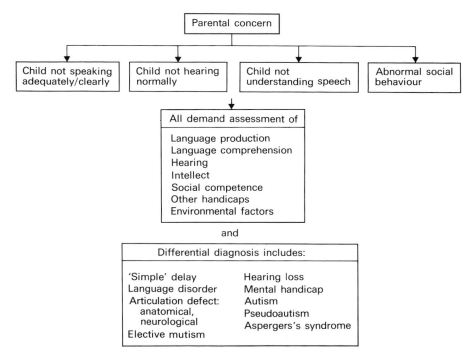

Fig. 13.1   Diagnostic process in communication disorders.

Competent audiological assessment is an essential part of this process; they also have in common many special educational problems and needs. For these reasons, I have argued (p. 72) that the developmental paediatrician should be competent to perform and interpret behavioural tests of hearing as an integral part of developmental assessment.

Hearing loss can be regarded as a particular form of communication disorder but, because of the specific problems of diagnosis and treatment, this subject is discussed in Chapter 14.

Problems of terminology

There is no completely satisfactory classification of communication dis-orders, for the reasons set out below.

1   Many children with language abilities which are below the mean for their age are nevertheless quite normal and it is difficult to know when they should be regarded as 'delayed'. This problem has already been discussed (*see also* p. 19). Furthermore, children with 'delayed language development' are not a homogeneous group. Some have problems only with expressive language, while others also have limited comprehension: the distinction is of considerable diagnostic and prognostic importance.

2   A very small minority of children turn out to have a more serious and prolonged or even permanent impairment of language development. These have been described as having a 'language disorder' or 'developmental dysphasia'*, but there is no agreement on the exact meaning of these terms. Undoubtedly this is a heterogeneous group of disorders but their pathologi-cal basis is unknown. The term 'disorder' implies something more serious than just severe delay, although the validity of this distinction is uncertain. It has been suggested that there are qualitative differences between 'delayed' and 'disordered' language development in the use and/or perception of language, but these are not yet adequately defined for practical use, and take no account of the child whose speech output is so negligible or whose behaviour is so disturbed that no linguistic analysis is possible. Because of the immense difficulty of predicting the future progress of a young child presenting with a communication problem, 'language disorder' is essentially a retrospective diagnosis, which in most cases may be made with confidence only when the child's problems persist after a period of observation or treatment. A practical definition of 'language disorder' is suggested below.

The term 'developmental dysphasia' is often used to describe children with problems of language development. The adult dysphasia literature is complicated but two main types can be distinguished (Fig. 13.2).[252,253] In non-fluent or expressive dysphasia, the patient can understand speech but cannot speak or produces only brief 'telegram' phrases—the lesion is in Broca's speech area. In fluent ('receptive') dysphasia, the patient has impaired understanding of speech, but can speak fluently; however, his speech has little meaningful content and includes bizarre words and constructions—the lesion is in Wernicke's area.

Although problems superficially similar to those of adult expressive dysphasia are sometimes seen in children, there is seldom any evidence for a focal lesion except in those who suffer a 'stroke' (p. 310); these children may

---

* Dysphasia = impairment of language functions; aphasia = absence of language functions.

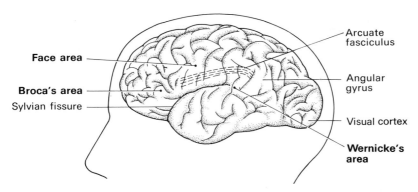

Fig. 13.2   Speech areas of the brain.

have transient total aphasia but recovery of language functions is rapid and usually complete. This suggests that some explanation, other than a focal lesion, must be sought in 'developmental' expressive dysphasia. Receptive dysphasia in childhood is rare, and has different characteristics from fluent dysphasia as seen in adults, which is virtually unknown in children.

To avoid confusion with adult usage, it is suggested that the terms dysphasia and aphasia should not be used as a synonym for 'language disorder' but are reserved for certain specific and recognisable clinical entities described below.

3 Communication disorders are sometimes associated with behavioural problems such as tantrums, shyness, or immature attention and impulse control, and with disturbed family relationships.[254] Indeed, it may be largely chance that determines whether the child is first seen by a speech therapist, paediatrician, or child psychiatrist. Each of these may have different perceptions of how the child's problems interrelate and will describe them in different terms.

4 There is some overlap between severe 'language disorders', mental retardation and autism, and severe communication difficulties occur in all these conditions.

Classification

Since the pathophysiologic basis of communication disorders is unknown, and there is no medical treatment, the 'medical model' (p. 18) is of limited relevance. With few exceptions management of these cases is undertaken by teachers, speech therapists or psychologists and is based on an 'educational model'. Classification should therefore be based on functional aspects. Two basic distinctions are suggested (Table 13.1).

The first recognises the considerable differences between children with isolated expressive language problems, and those who also have difficulties affecting comprehension of spoken language and in some cases non-verbal

Table 13.1   A classification of communication disorders.

Type 1 Impairment of expressive language; comprehension normal or functionally adequate	Type 2 Impairment of expressive language and of comprehension; normal or immature non-verbal communication	Type 3 Impairment of expressive language and of comprehension; deviant or bizarre non-verbal communication and social behaviour

'Delay'
   vocabulary and syntax
   articulation
   both
	'Delay'	Delay and multiple
		behavioural/attentional problems
		'Pseudo-autism'

Expressive language disorders
   vocabulary and syntax
   articulation
      uncertain cause
      definable neurological
        causes
      structural causes
   content and articulation
	Mental handicap (sociable)
	
	Receptive language
	disorders
	   acquired receptive
	     aphasia
	   auditory agnosia
	   undefined
	Hearing loss
		Mental handicap (non-sociable)
		
		Autism
		   'disintegrative psychosis'
		
		Disturbed child with hearing
		loss (usually other handicaps
		or late diagnosis)

Voice disorders Rhythm disorders Transient aphasia		

communication. The division into three types relates to the child's practical difficulties at a particular point in time, and his classification may change as he matures.[258]

The second distinction is between language delay and language disorder. The term 'delay' is used to describe children whose slow language development is causing concern, irrespective of the exact extent of the delay. It is purely descriptive and carries no implications about cause, severity or the need for intervention. The following definition of a 'language disorder' is suggested: 'difficulties in the comprehension and/or production of spoken language such that at the age of 5 years the child cannot communicate adequately with his peers or with adults outside his family circle; or, if he is under the age of 5, it is anticipated that such difficulties will still be present when he reaches that age'. Children whose primary problem is hearing loss or severe mental handicap or autism are excluded, as are children who speak normally in their native language but not in English. In the present state of knowledge no precise *linguistic* distinction can be made between delay and disorder but the concept of language disorder as a deficit requiring specialised educational help probably is valid.

Autism can be regarded as a severe form of type 3 communication disorder (*see* below) in which all modalities of language, both spoken and non-verbal, are impaired, together with a disturbance of symbolic thought.

TYPE 1 DISORDERS

This group incorporates conditions in which the primary problem is in the production of spoken language in the presence of normal or near-normal comprehension.

Expressive language delay

This may predominantly affect vocabulary size and sentence length; or the articulation of speech sounds may be poor so that intelligibility is reduced; or these two problems may coexist. The link between them could result from the same neurological immaturity or defect, or it may be that the difficulty in pronouncing words inhibits the child from developing longer sentences, possibly reinforced by negative responses from adults who cannot understand them. There is a wide variation in the rate at which vocabulary, syntax and articulation develop, and in the ability of adults to understand a child's speech (p. 39). For these reasons, the decision to assess or treat a child is subjective and no exact definition of language delay is possible.

The child who has normal comprehension of language is unlikely to be mentally retarded or to have a hearing loss, other than a mild conductive type. Children with significant hearing impairment are much more likely to present as a type 2 disorder.

Most children with expressive language delay eventually talk normally. There is, however, a statistical association between delayed expressive language development, behaviour disorder and educational problems in school, particularly but not exclusively affecting reading. Children who score in the bottom 3% on measures of language production at age 3 are certainly a high-risk group. Some authors have deduced that speech therapy should be more widely available to preschool and primary school children[255] but there is no evidence that this will have any impact on the educational problems. It seems equally likely that whatever genetic and psychosocial factors account for language delay also explain the academic difficulties which follow.

Expressive language disorder

This implies a severe and persistent deficiency of spoken language in the presence of reasonable, though seldom normal, comprehension.[256,257] It is often impossible to decide whether the problem originates at a word finding or sentence-generating level (i.e. dysphasia) or in the operation of the speech apparatus (dysarthria); therefore the term 'expressive dysphasia' is best avoided. The recognised causes of dysarthria are discussed below, but when these have been excluded there remains a group of children whose limitations of expressive language are unexplained. Detailed analysis of language samples obtained from children with expressive language disorder indicates an enormous variety of problems, and any classification is inevitably an oversimplification.

In some of these cases, the vocabulary at 6 years of age consists of only 100 words or less, often poorly pronounced. These children do not join words or use word endings, tenses and pronouns adequately. There may be a degree of general motor clumsiness (p. 398). Sometimes rapid progress follows over the next few years, leaving only minor residual abnormalities of pronunciation, rhythm or syntax, although often reading difficulties remain. Other children are less fortunate and remain permanently handicapped, often developing a variety of secondary social and behavioural problems.

Dysarthria

This denotes defective articulation, attributable to disordered function or structure of the articulatory organs.

NEUROLOGICAL CAUSES OF DYSARTHRIA

Cerebral palsy is the most important of these. Communication problems are caused by varying combinations of dysarthria and dysphasia,[259] often associated with mental retardation, hearing loss or visual handicap. Spasticity of speech musculature is associated with slow laboured speech, difficulty with precise tongue movements, and tongue thrusting. In athetosis, speech development may be very slow. The speech is jerky and poorly articulated due to impaired control of the speech and respiratory musculature and high-frequency deafness is a common additional problem. Similarly, there is severe speech delay in cases of ataxia, and the intonation pattern is often abnormal.

Congenital pseudobulbar palsy is caused by bilateral upper motor neurone lesions of the motor tracts supplying the lower cranial nerve nuclei.[260] There is gross incompetence of all movements of lips, tongue and palate. Dribbling is a persistent problem. The lesion may predominantly affect the palate, in which case the picture is that of cleft palate speech without a cleft palate. The brisk jaw jerk distinguishes this disorder from those caused by nuclear agenesis or lower motor neurone lesions.

The Möbius syndrome (also spelt Moebius) consists of congenital facial diplegia and bilateral external rectus muscle palsy.[261] There may also be paresis of tongue, palate and larynx, with gross dysarthria. The clinical signs vary considerably. A few cases have also had limb anomalies such as talipes, absence of the pectoralis muscle, deafness, cleft palate, mild pyramidal signs, and mild mental handicap. Although there are at least two recorded cases of familial occurrence, in the vast majority the condition appears to be sporadic.

Verbal dyspraxia is defined as an inability to carry out a series of purposeful movements of speech and facial musculature, becoming more severe as the child attempts more complex phonetic combinations.[262] These difficulties cannot be explained by demonstrable upper or lower motor neurone lesions, since individual movements are intact. This is probably not a homogeneous condition and may be seen in otherwise normal, mentally handicapped and cerebral palsied children. The prognosis is correspondingly variable but the most severe cases may have persisting problems for many years.

Myotonic dystrophy may cause delayed and unclear speech and early feeding problems (p. 375). Very rarely, other neurological disorders may present as speech disturbances.

STRUCTURAL CAUSES OF DYSARTHRIA

Cleft lip and palate.   Within the cleft lip and palate group of defects, there is a wide spectrum of severity ranging from minor deformities such as notching of the lip or bifid uvula to complete unilateral or bilateral clefts of lip, alveolus and palate.[263] The classification of these defects is based on embryological consideration and is described in textbooks of plastic surgery.[264]

The incidence is 2–3/1000 live births. There are genetic, embryological and epidemiological differences between cleft lip with or without cleft palate, and isolated cleft palate. Cleft lip, with or without cleft palate, occurs in about 1.5/1000 births, is more common in boys than girls and in Caucasians than Negroes, and is associated with recognisable malformation syndromes in less than 3% of cases. Isolated cleft palate occurs in 0.5/1000 births, is commoner in girls, has no racial predilection, and is part of a syndrome in around 8% of cases. Median clefts of the lip are rare (less than 1%) but should not be confused with severe bilateral clefts, since they are usually associated with other severe cerebral or facial malformations.

Over 100 syndromes including clefts of lip or palate have been described.[178] Some of these are chromosomal or have a single gene inheritance (notably the Treacher–Collins, Stickler, Apert's and van der Woude syndromes), while others are sporadic or show no clear-cut pattern of inheritance. The most important of these is the Pierre Robin Anomalad.[265] Teratogens such as rubella virus or phenytoin may also cause cleft palate. Details of all these disorders are summarised in Appendix 1. Most cases of cleft lip or palate are not part of a specific syndrome and inheritance

Table 13.2   Recurrence risks (%) in cleft lip and palate.

	Proband has cleft lip ± cleft palate
Frequency in general population	0.1
Normal parents with one affected child— recurrence risk* if there are no affected relatives	4
Normal parents with two affected children— recurrence risk	12
One parent affected; no affected children— risk to next child	4
One parent affected; one child affected— recurrence risk	10

* Risk increases in proportion to the severity of the defect.

is then polygenic. Recurrence risks are summarised in Table 13.2, but before counselling is given it is essential to rule out the numerous syndromes mentioned above, particularly in cases with isolated cleft palate.

In about one-fifth of all children with clefts other anomalies are also found, especially of the limbs, heart, head, back, and genitalia. There is an increased incidence of both growth hormone deficiency and unexplained short stature. The mean I.Q. of children with clefts is some 5–10 points lower than that of normal controls but for several reasons the validity of these findings is uncertain. School achievements do not differ significantly from those of controls.

Management.   Cleft lip is obvious at birth; isolated cleft palate should be detected in the routine neonatal examination. Inspection for other anomalies is essential. An early visit by the plastic surgeon and photographs of previous patients before and after surgery, together help the parents through the initial shock of diagnosis. Advice on feeding techniques may be needed (Fig. 13.3). Primary repair of the lip is most commonly performed at about 3 months of age, and the palate at 12–15 months.

Long term follow-up is essential and these children are best managed in a multidisciplinary clinic. Regular supervision by a speech therapist should begin as soon as possible. Further surgery may be needed to improve the appearance and function of lip or palate. Dental problems are common; fluoride should be introduced early and regular dental supervision is vital. Orthodontic treatment is often needed when the secondary teeth have erupted. Secretory otitis media affects up to 90% of these children, and repeated hearing and ENT checks should be arranged. Adeno-tonsillectomy should be performed only after consultation with the plastic surgeon, since this operation may compromise palatal function.

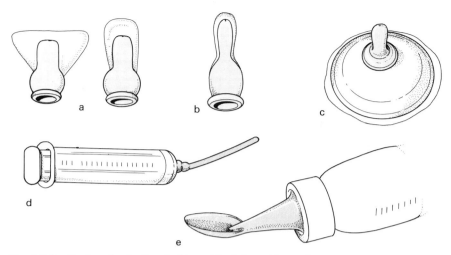

Fig. 13.3 Devices for feeding babies with clefts. **a** Flanged teats, **b** Lamb's teat, **c** special nurser, **d** syringe with rubber tube (Breck feeder), **e** feeding bottle with spoon attachment.

The palate and the posterior and lateral walls of the pharynx together form the 'velopharyngeal sphincter' which controls the flow of air through the nose. Because palatal structure, function and musculature are abnormal in cleft palate, there is an uncontrollable escape of air through the nose, making the speech hypernasal. Articulation of many consonants is defective and there may also be delay in expressive language development. Prolonged speech therapy may be needed to improve these defects, even after a successful surgical repair. The child with persistent nasal escape after primary closure of the palate may benefit from the operation of pharyngoplasty, in which the posterior wall of the pharynx is built forwards to improve the function of the sphincter.

'Cleft palate speech without cleft palate' or 'congenital palatal incompetence' may result from neurological disorders or from anatomic defects. Occasionally the speech problem only becomes apparent when adenoidectomy unmasks an imbalance between the depth of the pharynx and the length of the palate. The most common defect is the submucous cleft, which is easily overlooked. It is recognised by the triad of bifid uvula, notched hard palate and translucent central area. In some cases, nasal escape is due to an anomaly of the palatal musculature (absence of the musculus uvuli).[266,267] Any child with persistent hypernasal speech, whether or not he has had a cleft palate, should be referred to a plastic surgeon. A new endoscopic technique makes it possible to view the palate and pharynx while the child is talking and this allows more accurate diagnosis and treatment.

Macroglossia (enlargement of the tongue) is usually associated with conditions that cause mental retardation (Hunter's, Down's, Beckwith's syndromes; cretinism). Probably the size of the tongue plays little part in the child's speech problems in most cases.

Tongue-tie is widely believed by the layman to be a cause of late talking and defective articulation, but it should only be diagnosed if the frenulum is so tight that the tongue cannot be protruded to the outer margin of the lower lip, in which case there will be a history of feeding difficulties in infancy. Surgery should not be undertaken unless there is genuine tongue-tie, which is rare.

Nasal Obstruction.   Chronic enlargement of the adenoids and obstruction of the nasal airway causes defective articulation, particularly of the nasal sounds 'n', 'm' and 'ng'. The child sounds as if he has 'a cold in the nose' (hyporhinophonia). It is commonly associated with a history of recurrent upper respiratory infections and 'tonsillitis' but adeno-tonsillectomy does not necessarily lead to either dramatic or permanent improvement.

Malocclusion of the jaws is commonly but inconstantly related to articulatory problems.[100] If the lower jaw is underdeveloped, or there is anterior malocclusion (open bite) the tongue may be thrust out during speech causing inter-dental sigmatism or 'lisping' (e.g. 'thing a thong of thickthpenth'). When the mandible protrudes, the lower incisors lie anterior to the uppers and this may cause lateralisation of 's' sounds, making the 's' sound like the Welsh 'll' in Llandudno. Either of these articulatory patterns may also occur without any apparent anatomical cause. Malocclusion and jaw abnormalities may be isolated, and sometimes familial, or may be part of a dysmorphic syndrome. The orthodontist and plastic surgeon will advise on the probability of spontaneous improvement with growth, and may be able to improve appearance and articulation when necessary. Associated handicaps should be carefully considered before recommending treatment. Improving the articulation of speech will not necessarily increase language competence and usage if the child has defective language abilities and is mentally retarded.

Dysphonia

This term implies a difficulty in voice production and most often refers to a hoarse voice. Voice quality may vary with changes in volume and pitch or in different situations. Psychological factors may contribute in some cases. Any child with unexplained persistent voice disorder should undergo a laryngoscopy. Inspection of the vocal cords often reveals chronic inflammatory changes, or more rarely nodules or papillomata. Recurrent laryngeal nerve palsy is occasionally the cause of dysphonia.

Dysrhythmia

This means an incoordination between respiratory and articulatory function, causing prolongation of word sounds, arrest or blocking of speech, or repetitions of one or more words or sounds.[268] Dysrhythmia is so common between the ages of 2 and 4 that it may be regarded as normal non-fluency or physiological stuttering. It is possible, though by no means proven, that undue parental concern over this phase may generate anxiety in the child, leading to a persistent stammer in later childhood. Even if true, this explanation clearly could account for only part of the problem of stammering; but if parents are worried about stammering in a child of this age group, they should be offered an interview with a speech therapist, not for treatment but to alleviate anxiety. This is particularly important when there is a family history of stammer.

Although 3–4% of children stammer at some time during childhood, persistent stammer or stutter affects only around 1% of school-age children. The literature on the aetiology and treatment of the condition is vast and confusing. These cases are rarely seen by paediatricians, and are quite rightly referred directly to speech therapists, since even the most meticulous history and neurological examination contribute little or nothing to further management. Unless there is something very atypical about the dysrhythmia, one can be confident that it is not an indicator of any sinister neurological disease.

Sudden loss of speech

This may occur in the acute infantile hemiplegia syndrome (p. 310) or very rarely in an acquired pseudobulbar palsy, for example in sickle cell disease. Intermittent loss of speech may be a manifestation of either temporal lobe epilepsy or migraine, both of which may occur even in early childhood.

Elective mutism

This condition may be better described as selective mutism. The child is unable or unwilling to talk in certain selected situations, most commonly in school, but talks normally at other times.[269] Unlike most developmental disorders, in elective mutism girls equal or even outnumber boys. About 7 children per 1000 do not speak in school at the age of 5 but often this is a transient problem and persistent elective mutism probably occurs in about 1 child per 1000.

Shyness develops, usually insidiously, in the earliest years of life, but although it may be severe parents often do not consider it abnormal until the child goes to school. The child may be referred before the age of 5 because of mutism in nursery or playgroup, but it is not always easy to distinguish between normal shyness and pathological mutism. Most cases present soon after school entry, although sometimes many months elapse before the teacher realises that the child consistently avoids speaking. Speech may be the only area of concern but some children also avoid all other social contact and activity, and their school work is often poor. Sulkiness, negativism, poor adaptability and problems of bowel and bladder control are often observed.

The disorder is undoubtedly emotional in origin. There is no specific pattern of family disturbance but an increased incidence of parental neurosis and depression is reported. There are probably predisposing temperamental characteristics in the child and, in a significant proportion of cases, a speech defect contributes to the child's reluctance to talk. The I.Q. tends to be in the low-normal or mildly retarded range. To establish the diagnosis it is necessary to confirm that the child is capable of normal speech and play. This may require a home visit. A tape recording can be made by the parents, or they can be asked to play with the child in an observation room with a one-way mirror. The most successful treatments are based on behavioural principles, using a combination of desensitisation to alarming situations, positive reinforcement of every attempt to communicate, and identification and removal of factors such as peer interest and sympathy which reinforce the mutism.

TYPE 2 DISORDERS

Children described in Table 13.1 as having a type 2 communication disorder, show a substantial delay in expressive language but, in contrast to type 1, there is also a severe difficulty in comprehension. In some cases, the delay is approximately the same in expression and comprehension, but in others, the expressive delay is more severe. The ability to communicate by non-verbal means is not qualitatively abnormal, though it may not be age-appropriate.

Many of the children presenting in this way are delayed in other aspects of development, including social competence, attention control and play. A significant proportion have I.Q.s in the borderline or subnormal range; in other words, an important cause of a type 2 communication disorder is mental handicap. Children with impaired comprehension are more likely to have substantial learning difficulties in school than those who have only expressive language deficits,[270,271,272] and most of them need a curriculum that will accelerate all aspects of their development. There is however a subgroup of children who have problems of comprehension often associated with immature attention control, which are out of proportion to the delays in other aspects of their development. These may benefit from teaching oriented more specifically to language. This applies particularly to cases where a longstanding conductive hearing loss is superimposed on low ability and/or environmental deprivation—this situation can be regarded as a form of receptive language disorder.

A severe impairment of expressive language and comprehension in the presence of age-appropriate social competence and cognitive skills is very suggestive of a hearing loss. A child whose congenital sensorineural hearing loss escapes detection in the first year of life is likely to present in this way (*see* Chapter 5).

The other important, though rare, cause of a type 2 communication disorder is the group of conditions known as receptive language disorders.

Receptive language disorders

The specific disorders described here are very rare in comparison to those in the preceding section.[256] They are characterised by a severe inability to comprehend spoken language in spite of normal or near-normal hearing and non-verbal intelligence. In some cases there is mild high-frequency hearing loss and I.Q. assessment using non-verbal tests may reveal a mild degree of retardation, but the language deficit is much too severe to be explained on either of these grounds.[273]

The severity of the comprehension deficit is very variable. In some cases the child does not even respond to simple everyday sounds, and may be thought to be deaf: this is known as auditory agnosia. Others respond briskly, though often unpredictably, to such sounds so that the parents are confident (and often remain so in the face of contrary professional opinion!) that the child can hear. Social behaviour is often a little odd, but the child is able to understand non-verbal signals and communications by gesture. There may also be behavioural problems such as a brief attention span, and an obsessional fascination for mechanical objects. In the most severe cases a diagnosis of autism may be considered; there is inevitably some overlap between type 2 and type 3 communication disorders. Conversely, in mildly affected cases, there is steady improvement with maturation, so that in later childhood careful testing is needed to reveal residual problems in the comprehension of abstract ideas and complex syntax.

In many of these children, language development is abnormal from the beginning. Others initially develop normally but then their language deteriorates, producing a rather dramatic clinical picture known as acquired receptive aphasia, or the epilepsy-aphasia syndrome.[274-6] Similar clinical and EEG abnormalities may be seen in both groups and it is uncertain whether there are two distinct entities. Acquired receptive aphasia is very rare. There is severe and often total deterioration of expressive language and comprehension, so that the child may be thought to have a progressive deafness. Sometimes a few brief fits occur, but the epilepsy is rarely a major problem. There is a corresponding EEG abnormality in the temporal area. No recognisable cerebral catastrophe ushers in this deterioration and the underlying brain lesion has not been established. Neuroradiological studies, though generally unrewarding, are probably justified if only to eliminate parental fears of a tumour.

Prognosis for the recovery of language must be very guarded and special education is usually needed. These children may be capable of mastering language in non-auditory forms, such as sign language and reading. Anticonvulsants are rarely needed for the seizures, which are usually brief and transient, and do not alter the language development, though behaviour problems might possibly be improved by carbamazepine.

Deterioration of speech and comprehension may also occur in various rare progressive neurological disorders, but other features such as severe epilepsy, optic atrophy or motor signs help to differentiate these from acquired receptive aphasia.

TYPE 3 DISORDERS

In type 3 disorders expressive language, comprehension and non-verbal communication skills are all impaired and social behaviour is not merely immature but is deviant and often bizarre. This category includes the classic young autistic child, the most severe cases of receptive language disorder, and some children with a combination of handicaps, such as partial deafness and poor vision, or deafness with mental retardation.

Pseudo-autism

A behaviour pattern superficially similar to autism was described by Pollak as 'pseudo-autism'.[277] The child is referred for language delay usually between the 2nd and 4th birthday but all attempts to assess his language, hearing or non-verbal skills are futile and meet with no cooperation, because he is very active and restless and is unable to sit still or wait for instructions. He makes little or no eye contact or social relationships either with his accompanying parent or with the doctor. Even distraction tests of hearing produce equivocal results, for he does not show normal responses to verbal or non-verbal sounds. Sometimes, items reported by the parent, childminder or nursery nurse, or fleeting moments of play, indicate that the child is not severely retarded. After a period in a good nursery or assessment unit, he will probably behave more normally, though still showing a marked language deficit. A striking feature of 'pseudo-autism' is that the parents are often less concerned about the child than the paediatrician. This seems to be due not to lack of caring but to different perceptions of what constitutes good child-rearing and normal child behaviour (p. 32).

Pseudo-autism appears to be more common in the immigrant population, particularly those from the Caribbean. It is doubtful whether this behaviour pattern really justifies delineation as a specific syndrome, but it certainly exists and is worth recognising because these children do seem to benefit substantially from appropriate placement and teaching. The prognosis may be much better than one might predict at the initial consultation.

Autism

The term 'early infantile autism'[278] was coined by Kanner in 1943. Some authors have regarded autism as a form of childhood psychosis or childhood schizophrenia but this term implies that it is a form of mental illness—a view which is not now generally accepted.[11] True childhood schizophrenia is recognised as a distinct entity with onset in late childhood or the teens and an increased incidence of schizophrenia in family members, whereas in autism there is no evidence of any particular psychopathology or personality type in the parents. There is certainly no support for the outdated notion that the parents of an autistic child tend to be cold, aloof and unloving. There is a relative preponderance of upper social classes among parents of autistic children. This is *not* due to the desire of such parents to use autism as a more socially acceptable label than mental retardation. The observation can be explained by the finding that autism is commoner with advancing maternal age and upper social class mothers tend to have their children later than lower class mothers.

Autism can best be regarded as a severe form of global communication disorder. It is not a single biological entity, but a behaviour pattern that has many possible causes. Though often unknown, these are almost certainly organic. Several authors have listed the salient behavioural features (e.g. Table 13.3) but this 'check-list' approach is purely descriptive and it is essential to distinguish between the fundamental disturbances of communi-

Table 13.3   The 'check-list' approach to autism. Rendle-Short's 14-point list; seven or more points indicate autism.

1. Difficulty mixing with other children
2. Acts as deaf
3. Resists any learning
4. No fear of real dangers
5. Resists routine changes
6. Indicates needs by gesture*
7. Inappropriate laughing and giggling
8. Not cuddly
9. Marked physical overactivity
10. No eye contact
11. Inappropriate attachment to objects
12. Spins objects
13. Sustained odd play
14. Stand-offish manner

* This is actually a point *against* autism.

Table 13.4   The four essential features of autism (Rutter).

---

1. Delayed and deviant language development which has certain defined features and is out of keeping with the child's intellectual level
2. Impaired social development which has a number of special characteristics and is out of keeping with the child's intellectual level
3. Insistence on sameness, as shown by stereotyped play patterns, abnormal preoccupations, or resistance to change
4. Onset before the age of 30 months

---

cation and thought which are now regarded as essential and interrelated criteria for the diagnosis (Table 13.4), and the secondary behavioural consequences of these disturbances.[278] It should be noted that, although the majority of autistic children are mentally handicapped, this is not essential to the definition.

Language and communication.   Impairment of language in all aspects is central to the diagnosis of autism. The child with a receptive language disorder is unable to make use of spoken language, but can communicate by non-verbal means, whereas the autistic child has difficulty with all aspects of communication whether by speech, gesture, facial expression or physical contact.

Autism is not always obvious in infancy, but in some cases parents recognise even in the early weeks of life that normal 'turn-taking' behaviour is difficult or impossible to elicit, and they may be unable to obtain normal eye contact. The baby seems unable or unwilling to respond to the parents' 'baby talk' by vocalisation or facial expression. As he gets older, he seems to be aloof and remote because he does not make eye contact, or demand cuddles or comfort. He is described as 'living in a world of his own'. He makes little or no distinction between familiar and unfamiliar adults, or between people and inanimate objects, and does not resist separation. He may be regarded as abnormally quiet and 'good', being content with his own company for long periods. When he does vocalise, only a very limited range of sounds is used; he may screech and scream intermittently for no apparent reason.

By the first birthday, when most children begin to understand some words, the autistic child is still unresponsive to the parents' speech and shows little or no evidence of comprehension. This impairment of verbal comprehension is very slow to resolve and, in the more severely affected case, is a permanent handicap. Deafness may be suspected, indeed the autistic child is sometimes referred first to an audiology clinic; but the parents can often report occasional unexpected but appropriate responses to sounds such as door bells or sweet papers, and these help to rule out this diagnosis. It should be remembered however that deafness and autism sometimes coexist and, since clinical testing may be extremely difficult, electrical response audiometry is often necessary.

Speech is usually very delayed and in the most severe cases never develops. In the more intelligent autistic child, the stage of labelling, using mainly single nouns, may begin at the usual time, but he fails to progress to the formation of spontaneous two and three word sentences. There is often simple echolalia of the terminal sounds of questions which he cannot understand and this may persist for many years, whereas in normal children the common developmental phase of echolalia usually disappears by the third birthday. Echoed phrases are often used as answers to simple questions, or as requests; for example, the child may say 'Do you want a biscuit?' meaning that *he* wants a biscuit. He has great difficulty in mastering the grammatical rules of sentence construction and transformation, so the use of pronouns, tenses, etc. is frequently bizarre. The intonation pattern is odd and the delivery is stilted and mechanical. 'Yes' and 'No' are used incorrectly or not at all. Although these rules may eventually be mastered, the more subtle aspects of language, such as metaphor or sarcasm, may continue to bewilder him. He finds it hard to read the subtle non-verbal signals which are part of normal communication, lacking the empathy to understand other peoples' feelings and reactions.

Social behaviour.   The autistic child shows a characteristic aloofness and a lack of interest or curiosity in other people. He has a marked lack of empathy which prevents him from sharing his emotions with other people and is solitary, impersonal and apparently preoccupied with his own inner world. Various mannerisms such as tiptoe-walking and hand flapping are commonly seen and add to the impression of 'oddness'.[279]

Rigidity of thought.   The language impairment of autism includes all modalities of symbolic thought and communication. The rules of language and social behaviour are a mystery to the autistic child. He is not able to deduce a general concept from a particular example and is bewildered by exceptions to the rules he has learnt. Only by clinging to his self-imposed rules system can he make sense of a bewildering world and he therefore becomes very distressed by apparently trivial changes. The use of an unfamiliar synonym for a familiar object (for example bucket for pail, dish for plate) may precipitate extreme reaction such as uncontrollable crying or screaming. Changes in clothing, furniture, routes to the shops and so on may elicit similar responses.

The rituals, obsessions and stereotypes which are typical of autism may be regarded as a natural outcome of these difficulties. By retreating into repetitive and predictable cycles of activity the child protects himself against a frightening confusion of stimuli which he does not understand. The complexity of the rituals bears some relationship to intelligence. Elaborate activities related to maps, routes, timetables, mechanical objects or astronomical matters are usually confined to the more intelligent autistic children whereas such rituals as twiddling and twirling of silver paper, picking up fragments of wool or paper, spinning toys or fiddling with light switches are suggestive of severe retardation if they persist beyond early childhood. These obsessions tend to perpetuate the child's handicap since they exclude any more productive activities. They can sometimes be reduced by behavioural techniques.

Age of onset.   Some parents suspect their child is abnormal in early infancy, but often experienced and competent mothers fail to notice any abnormality until the 2nd or 3rd year and it must be assumed that normal communicative ability in infancy is not incompatible with later autistic behaviour. Some autistic children seem to have developed normally in all aspects including language until the age of 18–30 months, and then gradually use fewer and fewer words, becoming mute and withdrawn. At the same time, comprehension seems to deteriorate. The associated loss of all attempts to communicate or play distinguishes these cases from the syndrome of acquired receptive aphasia. The rate of this deterioration is very variable. It may be so dramatic that neurological investigation is undertaken (usually with negative results[465]), or so insidious as to be recognised only in retrospect. The onset may seen to coincide with a family upheaval, but this cannot be the sole cause. These cases probably overlap with those described as having a disintegrative psychosis, although the latter tend to have a slightly later onset, at 3–4 years of age. Very rarely, typical autistic behaviour may result from encephalitis.[280]

Intelligence in autism.   At least three-quarters of autistic children are mentally retarded. The retardation is persistent and must not be attributed to the child's apparent disinterest or poor motivation during assessment. Psychometric testing is often extremely difficult, but results obtained by a psychologist experienced with autism, have a surprisingly good correlation with future progress. Sometimes the parents' ability to understand and interpret their autistic child's bizarre behaviour, together with the preservation of 'islands' of skilled behaviour, such as the ability to solve jigsaw puzzles, lead to their overestimating his abilities. In the mentally handicapped autistic child there is no hidden intelligence needing only the right key for its release, but unfortunately many parents acquire from the popular press the notion that autism is in some way a more hopeful diagnosis than mental handicap.

Autistic behaviour and severe mental handicap.   The extent to which social relationships are impaired in mentally handicapped children varies from normal sociability to severe social impairment (Fig. 13.4). About half of all severely mentally handicapped children have some degree of social impairment[281] with some of the other features listed in Table 13.3, but only

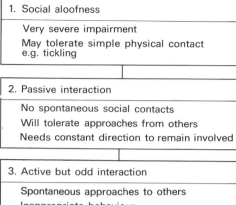

1. Social aloofness

   Very severe impairment
   May tolerate simple physical contact
   e.g. tickling

2. Passive interaction

   No spontaneous social contacts
   Will tolerate approaches from others
   Needs constant direction to remain involved

3. Active but odd interaction

   Spontaneous approaches to others
   Inappropriate behaviour
   No empathy: pursues own preoccupations
   Often rejected by peers as 'peculiar'

4. Appropriate interaction for mental age

   Enjoys social contact
   Indicates interest
   Tries to converse
   Uses non-verbal communication effectively

Fig. 13.4   Quality of social interaction—a rating scale devised by Wing and Gould.[281]

about one-quarter of these have the linguistic idiosyncrasies typical of autism. The more severe the mental handicap, the more likely it is that some autistic behavioural features will be observed but at the same time the exact delineation of autism as a specific syndrome becomes increasingly difficult.

Adolescence and adult life.   Most autistic children remain severely handicapped, totally unable to live an independent existence. An I.Q. below 50, and failure to develop useful speech by the age of 5 are predictive of a very poor outcome, and there is a high incidence of epilepsy which often begins at adolescence. When the non-verbal I.Q. is above 70 the outlook for adult life is more hopeful and epilepsy is less frequent.

At adolescence many autistic children show increasing behavioural disturbances, including unprovoked aggression, inappropriate sexual activity, depression and intense anxiety. Occasionally there may be evidence of frank neurological deterioration. A combination of behavioural methods and drugs may be needed to control these problems. Whenever possible, a psychiatrist specialising in mental handicap, should care for the autistic teenager.

At school-leaving age these unfortunate individuals leave the educational system, with its network of psychologists, devoted teachers and residential facilities. The lucky ones may manage simple work, join a specialised community, or go to a modern residential hostel. Many spend the rest of their lives in long-stay mental hospitals.

The terms 'autistic psychopathy', 'atypical child', 'schizoid personality', and 'Asperger's syndrome' have all been used to describe children who might well be mistaken for intelligent autistics.[282,283] Asperger's syndrome is the preferred designation for this condition which, like autism, appears to be a behavioural symptom-complex rather than a single biological entity. There are many similarities between Asperger's syndrome and autism but also some distinctions. In Asperger's syndrome early language development is not delayed, gestural communication is used, albeit inappropriately, and the typical aloofness of the autistic child is not seen.

The child with Asperger's syndrome is likely to be referred at a slightly later age than the typical autistic. Boys substantially outnumber girls. Speech development is not usually delayed but the use of pronouns is odd and there is a tendency to pedantic speech patterns and lengthy dissertations on sterile subjects. The child is solitary and emotionally detached, disliking rough games with peers and group activities. There is often an odd loping gait. Although he may be superficially imaginative and creative, he is liable to become obsessed with one particular system of ideas which may dominate his activities and thoughts for months or years at a time. If he is fortunate his eccentricities are affectionately tolerated by his peers but more often are the cause of merciless teasing. In the teens he continues to have difficulties with relationships, complex language structures and abstract concepts. He is prone to depression rather than frank psychotic illness. The clinical picture is of a personality type rather than an illness or disorder. There may be a close relative with a similar personality.

Recognition of the condition and the distinction from classical autism is worthwhile, since, although the personality cannot be altered, secondary educational and behavioural problems may be alleviated by adequate counselling and psychological guidance where appropriate; furthermore the child and family can be spared intensive psychotherapy which is of no value in Asperger's syndrome.

EPIDEMIOLOGY OF COMMUNICATION DISORDERS

The prevalence of language delay is entirely dependent on how it is defined (pp. 39 & 241). Language disorders are relatively rare, but because definitions vary so much between authors, there are no reliable prevalence data. Possibly two or three children per 1000 at age 5 might fit the definition on p. 240. Expressive language disorders are undoubtedly commoner than the severe receptive problems. The prevalence of classical autism is 2.5 cases per 10 000, but some autistic features in association with severe mental handicap are seen in around 20 cases per 10 000 children.

CAUSES OF COMMUNICATION DISORDER

In most cases, the cause or causes are unknown; the following discussion is therefore necessarily speculative.

NORMAL VARIATION

Undoubtedly variation within the normal range of genetic endowment and environmental experience is the only possible explanation for many cases of so-called language delay (p. 35).

HEARING LOSS

The importance of hearing in the development of language is self-evident. What is not so clear is why some children should be so much more disabled than others by a relatively mild hearing loss. This point is discussed in the next chapter.

ORGANIC BRAIN DISORDERS

1   Severe delay in speech development is commoner in boys than girls. This may be partly due to differences in child-rearing styles (p. 34). However the X and Y chromosomes have some effect on maturation.[284] Children with XYY, XXY, XXYY and various mosaic patterns of chromosomes all have a higher than expected prevalence of speech and language disorder. In the syndrome of X-linked retardation (p. 202) apraxia of speech may be the main handicap,[285] and autism may be disproportionately common.
2   Twin studies suggest that there may be a genetic predisposition to autism and to language disorders.
3   Disorders of dominance or minor degrees of diffuse brain damage are thought by some to account for speech and language problems and other developmental disorders, but, as with learning disabilities, the evidence is equivocal (p. 391). A few cases are caused by congenital cytomegalovirus infection. Abnormal brain development presumably accounts for the interesting association of language disorder with ectodermal dysplasia. Focal brain damage may be detectable in a few cases of severe language disorders and in autism.[286]

4 Dysfunction at a neurophysiological level may cause receptive language disorders. The occurrence of temporal lobe EEG abnormalities supports this hypothesis. Abnormal and delayed auditory perception and processing have been demonstrated in a few cases.[256,287]

5 There is compelling evidence that autism is caused by an organic brain disorder rather than by psychosocial factors. It is rare, whereas adverse psychological experiences are very common. It is commoner in boys and can be produced by known causes of cerebral damage, such as tuberose sclerosis, phenylketonuria and encephalitis. The incidence of epilepsy is high. The deafness caused by congenital rubella is sometimes accompanied by autistic behaviour patterns, and the double sensory handicaps of deafness and blindness, particularly in association with mental retardation, may give rise to a similar picture.

6. Some cases of autism with onset in the 2nd or 3rd year, and some designated disintegrative psychoses, are found at autopsy to have a neuronal storage disease or evidence of longstanding brain damage.[288]

ENVIRONMENTAL FACTORS

Some communication disorders are associated with a global lack of stimulation and parental interest, while in others the deficit may be more specifically linguistic, as discussed in Chapter 3.

1. Language is said to develop more slowly in twins and in late-born children of large families, but these are statistical correlations and are of little clinical relevance.

2. Most children cope very well with a bilingual environment and this should never be accepted as the sole explanation of language delay. Inappropriate and misguided social usage of the various languages is probably the significant factor. For example, immigrant parents may speak to each other fluently in their mother tongue, but do not use this language when speaking to the child. Instead they use hesitant and poorly articulated English because they want him to learn English as his first language.

Some children hear a sequence of different languages from a succession of 'au-pairs' and suffer a rather sophisticated form of parental neglect. These may show considerable emotional disturbance as well as language delay.

3. The hearing child of deaf parents may acquire sign language as his first language. Provided that he has adequate contact with relatives, friends and other children, spoken language is likely to develop normally.

INVESTIGATION AND MANAGEMENT

Multidisciplinary assessment

Delays in expressive language are very common and most of these cases are managed by the speech therapist alone. Children in whom expressive language disorder is suspected or who have significant deficits in comprehension require a more detailed multidisciplinary assessment, including a developmental and neurological examination and hearing test, and a psychological evaluation.

FORMAL ASSESSMENT PROCEDURES

The Reynell developmental language scale is the most popular of these. It is used by speech therapists to provide a formal measure of language development. There are two sub-scales: expressive language and verbal comprehension. The results can be expressed either as an age equivalent or in terms of standard deviations from the mean. Comprehension is often found to be more advanced than expression. The reverse situation is theoretically improbable; a child cannot meaningfully use a language structure which he cannot understand. Nevertheless, this result is obtained occasionally in the following circumstances: when the child's attention span is so short that his comprehension score (though an accurate statement of his level of function) is an underestimate of his true linguistic ability; when gross echolalia gives a false idea of his ability to construct original sentences; following a sudden severe hearing loss (e.g. after meningitis), before his speech output has declined.

The expressive language scale of the Reynell is not thought to be as reliable as the comprehension scale. A more detailed linguistic analysis of a sample of the child's speech can be undertaken using the procedure known as LARSP (language assessment, remediation and screening procedure), devised by Crystal. This is somewhat time-consuming and is only undertaken in selected cases. Several tests of vocabulary and articulation are also available (p. 14) and provide precise measurements of these aspects when required.

The Illinois Test of Psycholinguistic Abilities (ITPA) analyses language functions into a number of components, for example auditory sequencing and auditory memory; but the theoretical framework on which it is based is now somewhat dated and its clinical value seems to be limited.

If a child is found to have a significant impairment of comprehension, formal assessment of his non-verbal abilities may also be needed. Selected items from standard I.Q. tests may be used. More specialised tests are available, which are specifically designed to bypass the need for auditory communication; many of these tests are also used for deaf children (p. 201).

NEUROLOGICAL EXAMINATION

The majority of children with communication disorders have no 'hard' neurological signs, although there may be an increased number of 'soft' signs on neurodevelopmental examination. However, a detailed neurological assessment should be performed if there is any suspicion of generalised motor dysfunction, muscle weakness, or unusual difficulties with movements of the speech apparatus.

INVESTIGATIONS

Craniofacial and palatal malformations are the province of the plastic surgeon and orthodontist, and may call for radiological and endoscopic studies. An EEG should be performed in cases with receptive language disorder. Electrical response audiometry is sometimes needed when hearing thresholds are hard to define. A CT scan may be justified by the need to accumulate knowledge on these obscure problems, though it is unlikely to help the child and is usually normal. Chromosome studies may be worthwhile.

Explanation to parents

Parents must be told that there is no medical treatment for communication disorders other than the control of epilepsy and behavioural disturbances with drugs when needed, and the appropriate management of hearing loss. In spite of rapid developments in our knowledge of normal language development, little is known about the causes of language delay or disorder. Many laymen find it hard to believe the extent of our ignorance about the neurological basis of language development, and 'shop around' for someone who will give them definite answers. Particular problems occur in the use of the terms 'language disorder' and 'dysphasia', because the lack of standard terminology confuses discussions between doctors and educationists. Parents must be guided away from the search for a label and instead must concentrate on finding the most appropriate educational provision.

In many cases, the process of assessment and the discussion which accompanies it is itself reassuring and therapeutic. Simple measures to encourage language development can be demonstrated to the parents, and strategies which are suspected to be disadvantageous (p. 44) can be corrected. Periodic review is advisable. Genetic advice may be requested; most severe communication disorders are sporadic and have a low recurrence risk, with the exception of those cases of autism associated with a specific mental handicap syndrome. When the index case has global language delay, particularly if male, there does appear to be a significant recurrence risk, but because precise diagnosis is elusive, it is difficult to give exact advice.

Speech therapy

There is little information about the most economic and effective way of using the speech therapist's skills. In the preschool child, it seems unlikely that any intervention occurring for half or one hour per week will have much effect on language development. Only when the child is old enough to practise what he has learnt from the therapist is he likely to benefit from sessional therapy; in practice this applies mainly to children of school age with articulation or rhythm disorders. There is some evidence that more intensive intervention either by regular parental instruction or by attendance at a 'language group' can accelerate language in the preschool child.[289] Several schemes have been devised for the acceleration of language development, but they have not been evaluated against each other or against adequate controls.

Nurseries and schools

Placement in a day nursery is often recommended for children with language delay and certainly many parents believe that this is beneficial, but it is uncertain how much these apparent gains are translated into any long term advantage (p. 24). Nursery staff vary widely in commitment, enthusiasm and training and in practice can seldom devote as much time to each individual child as a parent.[456,466] Strategies used to stimulate language development do seem to be effective[290,291] and possibly speech therapists could use their time more effectively to train nursery staff rather than 'treat' individual children.

More specialised provision is needed for some children. Some do well in the environment of a partially hearing unit even if they have little or no hearing loss. 'Language units' which have both teachers and speech therapists on the staff, usually cater for a small number of children who have exceptional difficulties in learning language. There is still some debate about the value of these units, and it is not yet known how effective they are. For children with severe communication disorders, highly specialised teaching, perhaps using an alternative means of communication (see below) may be essential. Such cases are rare and there are only a few schools in the country which cater for them, so boarding is often necessary.

Management of autism

Where possible, management of the autistic child, should be shared with a modern department of child psychiatry.[292] In the absence of any evidence that family pathology is responsible for autism, child or family psychotherapy is unlikely to have any significant impact on the child's problems. Behavioural techniques are sometimes effective in modifying undesirable behaviour and in teaching new skills, but are very demanding in parental and professional time. Each new step has to be taught, since the autistic child is unable to generalise or extend ideas for himself. The educational gains from individualised structured teaching are modest but worthwhile. Bright autistic children are best educated in a school catering for their special needs.[293] Teaching techniques and skills relevant to autism are used in schools catering for sociable severely retarded children and therefore less intelligent autistic children do not necessarily need to be educated in a separate establishment. Those with severe behaviour problems are very disruptive both to the school and to their family and either regular respite care or a boarding placement is desirable for such children.

In cases where the diagnosis of 'autism' is borderline or in dispute, it is more important to select the most appropriate educational environment than to engage in fruitless debates about diagnostic labels.

ALTERNATIVE MEANS OF COMMUNICATION

The development of speech may be very slow in children with severe cerebral palsy or mental retardation, particularly when complicated by additional handicaps, such as hearing loss or vision. To complicate matters further, the child's environment is often impoverished because his need for communication is not recognised and he is deprived of ordinary baby talk; this is particularly true in cerebral palsy where there is a danger that all therapeutic energies are directed to his physical handicap. Some of these children eventually develop some speech, after several years of frustration, because they can understand speech but cannot respond. The more severely handicapped may never learn to speak and verbal comprehension remains very limited. Without a means of communication they become severely disturbed, frustrated adults who are likely to need institutional care.

Many ingenious systems are now available to bypass the need for speech in communication.[294] The terms 'alternative' or 'augmented' communication are used to describe these systems. The latter term is preferable, because the non-handicapped user always uses speech and the communication system simultaneously, in order to encourage the eventual development of speech in the child.

The introduction of an augmented system of communication should be considered in any handicapped child in whom the acquisition of speech is severely delayed. Careful explanation to the parents is essential and three objections are commonly encountered. Firstly, the parents invariably fear that the child will become lazy so that he will not make any further effort to speak. In fact, experience shows unequivocally that these systems encourage speech development, reduce frustration and often produce a remarkable improvement in personality. Secondly, the parents may point out that the child can understand their speech even if he cannot reply and therefore it is a waste of effort for them to learn the augmented system to communicate with him. They should be told that the acquisition of the new system is like that of speech; the child must gain experience in understanding the system before he himself can use it to respond. Thirdly, parents often become despondent after a brief trial, reporting that the child sees the system only as a game or a tedious academic exercise. The child who has been passive and unable to control his environment in any way needs time to learn that his communication system can be useful and produce rewards.

Assessment

The selection of the most appropriate system is difficult and these children should be referred to a Child Development Centre with experience of such problems. Many parents seem to communicate almost intuitively with their handicapped child and can interpret his apparently meaningless efforts

Table 13.5 Alternative communication: the need for multidisciplinary assessment.

Paediatrician/Audiologist
What is the underlying diagnosis? And the prognosis?
Does he have any hearing loss?
How much can he see?

Speech therapist
Does the child show any wish to communicate?
Does he respond differentially to different stimuli? e.g. auditory, visual, tactile
Can the parents interpret his needs? If so, how? e.g. by his cry, eye pointing, gesture or vocalisation
Can the child confidently indicate any particular need? If so, describe how.
Offered a choice, can he indicate his selection? If so, how?
How much do his parents use spoken language to communicate with him; how much does he understand?
If he can vocalise, how wide a variety of sounds can he make?
If he uses words, is he frustrated because he is not understood? Is there a wide discrepancy between his expressive and receptive abilities?

Psychologist
What are the child's non-verbal abilities?
What strategies can he use to solve problems?
Can he use any form of gestural or verbal communication to indicate answers to questions?

Physiotherapist and occupational therapist
What movements are under his control? Hands, eyes, feet, head, etc.
Is he able to perform better in one position than another; can his posture be adjusted to improve this?
Is he frustrated by spasticity, athetosis, ataxia, etc.?
Are his responses very delayed? How long does it take him to initiate a movement?

---

with confidence. The analysis of the means by which they do this is the first step in the selection and introduction of an augmented communication system. A multidisciplinary assessment is needed to construct a profile of the child's needs, abilities and weaknesses (Table 13.5).

Methods of communication

OBJECT AND PICTURE BOARDS

These are simple and cheap. A few common objects or pictures of them, are attached to a large board; the child is taught to point at these to indicate his wants. Any means of pointing may be used, for example, a head pointer or the direction of gaze.

POINTER BOARDS

These very simple devices are useful for introducing the idea of making a choice between two alternatives by means of a switch, and are the forerunner of more complex systems. These can be introduced before the

Fig. 13.5   Bliss symbols.

second birthday for selected children, usually those with severe physical handicap and relative preservation of intellect.

BLISS

Bliss symbols (Figs. 13.5 & 13.6) can be used on cards, boards, cloth badges sewn on clothing, or electronic systems such as 'Possum'. Some children can master several hundred symbols. Because the word is indicated below

Fig. 13.6   A Bliss board in use.

each picture no specialised knowledge is required by the person conversing with the child. The system is ideal for non-speaking children with cerebral palsy.[295] The Rebus method has many similarities to Bliss but has some advantages, being linked more closely to the teaching of reading.

MAKATON

Makaton is a sign language for the mentally handicapped, based on a selection of the most commonly used signs in British Sign Language for the deaf.[296] Each sign represents a word (Fig. 13.7). Signs require some degree of manual dexterity and therefore it is not always suitable for children with

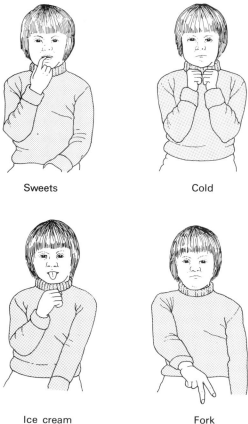

Sweets   Cold

Ice cream   Fork

Fig. 13.7 Examples of signs
from the Makaton vocabulary.

cerebral palsy. It has been very successful with severely retarded children
and adults, with or without hearing loss, and is now widely used in mental
handicap schools, long-stay hospitals, etc.

PAGET–GORMAN

Whereas British Sign Language for the deaf has been developed by the deaf
themselves, Paget–Gorman is an invented language.[297] The signs each
represent a word, and word endings and inflections may be added. It is more
grammatical than Makaton and is claimed to provide a better basis for
language teaching, particularly in children with severe language disorders.
Unfortunately, if these children remain dependent on manual communication by the time they leave school, their natural social grouping will be with
the deaf and they will still need to learn British Sign Language for the deaf. It
is arguable whether the supposed increased grammatical flexibility of

Paget–Gorman justifies its use in the face of this major practical disadvantage.

ELECTRONIC SYSTEMS

'Possum'. Equipment such as a 'Possum' typewriter is needed by a few very disabled children, for example those with severe athetosis. The switch is operated by whatever movement the child has under his control and can be arranged to operate a typewriter (Fig. 13.8), Bliss board or environmental controls. The modern microcomputer is even more versatile than 'Possum', providing word processing, graphics and calculation facilities. Many other possible applications of modern electronics and microcomputers are now being explored (p. 494).

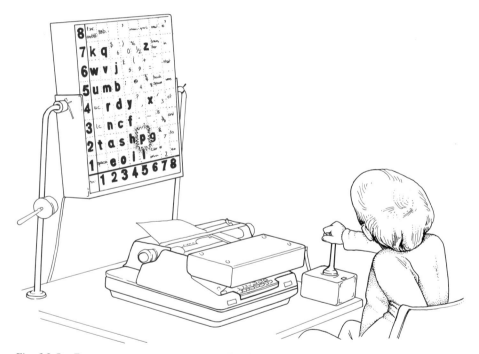

Fig. 13.8 Possum—a typewriter system for the severely disabled.

Canon communicator. This is a portable device, the size of a pocket dictaphone, which is used as a small typewriter (Fig. 13.9). It has been found useful by some older children of good intelligence, with severe dysarthria but reasonable finger control.

'Splink' and Voice Synthesisers. Electronic voice synthesis can be utilised to provide a range of up to 800 words, which can be selected by a touch-board.

Fig. 13.9   The Canon Communicator—an 'ultra-mini electronic typewriter'.

A memory stores enough words to construct a sentence which can be recalled when needed. Splink also uses a word selection board operated by touch; the words are displayed on a TV screen rather than spoken by synthetic voice. Good reading and reasonable finger control are needed for these devices, which have their main application in adult rehabilitation, but they are occasionally useful for older children.

READING

The teaching of reading helps to develop language in selected cases. There is no point in teaching reading as a purely mechanical skill. The child must not only learn to recognise the word but also to associate it with its meaning. Several systems are available; for example, in the Moor House School colour-coded scheme, different colours are used to indicate different parts of speech, for example red indicates nouns, blue verbs, etc.

Chapter Fourteen
Hearing Loss

DEFINITIONS

The terms 'hearing impaired' or 'hard of hearing' are commonly used in preference to 'deaf' which many laymen take to mean total deafness. A hearing loss which is present before speech has been acquired is described as 'pre-lingual'. In 'conductive hearing loss' the lesion is in the external auditory meatus, tympanic membrane or middle ear cavity. In 'sensori-neural hearing loss' the lesion is in the cochlea and/or the neural pathways to the auditory cortex. Most cases of conductive hearing loss in paediatric practice are acquired and are caused by secretory otitis media, whereas most sensorineural deafness is of congenital origin. Both types may be unilateral or bilateral.

There is no universally accepted classification of hearing impairment on the basis of severity. A hearing loss of 20–35 dB in the better ear is generally regarded as mild, though the *effects* may not be mild (p. 285). Between 40 and 60 dB, a hearing loss is moderate; from 70 to 90 dB it is severe; and if greater than 90 dB it is profound. The extent of a hearing loss is only one of the factors which determines the child's use and understanding of spoken language: intelligence, motivation, parental support and education all play a part. The type and location of damage to the auditory pathways are also important, since children with identical hearing losses as determined by pure tone audiometry show substantial variation in their ability to discriminate the complex sounds of speech.

Education authorities distinguish between *partial hearing loss* and *deafness* and make separate provision for these two groups (p. 280). For the reasons outlined above, the distinction is based not on the severity of the hearing loss, but on an assessment of the child's educational needs.

CONGENITAL BILATERAL SENSORINEURAL HEARING LOSS

Epidemiology

The 1977 EEC survey[107] provided comprehensive epidemiological data on hearing loss. The following figures are taken from this study. Approximately one child per 1000 has a hearing loss of 50 dB or more in the better ear, at the age of 8 years and one-third of these have a hearing loss greater than 100 dB. There is a very slight preponderance of affected boys.

Intrauterine rubella was until recently the commonest identifiable cause and only a few years ago accounted for about 16% of cases; however, the incidence of this disease is falling and cytomegalovirus may now be a more important cause.[235,236] Acquired hearing loss due to meningitis, head injury or occasionally a severe conductive loss due to middle ear disease,

Table 14.1   Associated handicaps of hearing-impaired children.

Handicap	% of total
Mental	4.8
Mental and visual	0.6
Mental and other	2.5
Visual	4.8
Visual and other	2.0
Neurological dysfunction (cerebral palsy, etc.)	3.5
Behaviour disorder	1.5
Disorders of other systems (cardiac, renal, etc.)	10.3
Total	30%
No other handicap	70%
	100%

make up another 10%.[103] There is no doubt that perinatal events are potential causes of hearing loss, but their importance is uncertain. The cause is completely unknown in about half of all cases, but this group includes a substantial number of inherited disorders.[85,86] In most of these, hearing loss is an isolated defect, but in a minority it is one feature of an identifiable malformation system. About 30% of hearing-impaired children have other handicaps (Table 14.1).

Causes

These are summarised in Table 14.2.

Table 14.2   Causes of hearing loss in childhood.

Prenatal causes
Genetic hearing loss with
  no other abnormalities
  abnormal external ears
  eye disease
  musculoskeletal disease
  skin, nail or hair disorder
  renal disease
  neurological disease
  miscellaneous abnormalities
Sporadic malformations of inner
or middle ear
Intrauterine viral infections

Perinatal causes
Prematurity
Hypoxia
Kernicterus
Meningitis
Aminoglycoside antibiotics

Postnatal causes
Middle-ear disease
Meningitis
Other childhood fevers
Trauma
Ototoxic drugs

GENETIC HEARING LOSS WITHOUT OTHER DEFECTS

The distinction between genetically determined and non-genetic hearing loss may be impossible if the family history is negative or incomplete, and therefore the exact prevalence of the genetic types is not known. Probably 40% or even more of all cases of congenital hearing loss are genetically determined, and of these the recessive forms are commonest. At least 16 different subgroups are recognised, distinguished by the mode of inheritance, age of onset, and the severity and frequency pattern of the hearing loss.[86] Usually the hearing loss is static but progressive deterioration occurs in a few cases. Genetic sensorineural hearing loss is nearly always bilateral but families are known where some members have a unilateral loss.

GENETIC HEARING LOSS WITH OTHER DEFECTS

Königsmark's monograph[86] lists over 150 syndromes associated with deafness. Only a few of the more common can be mentioned here. Every child with a congenital sensorineural hearing loss should have a complete paediatric assessment and an eye examination. Even apparently trivial anomalies may provide the clue to a specific diagnosis of a syndrome with genetic implications.

Deafness with external ear anomalies.   External ear anomalies, for example malformations of the pinna or cutaneous pits are often associated with a hearing loss which may be conductive, sensorineural or mixed. The Treacher–Collins and Goldenhaar syndromes are familiar examples. The external ear canal may be narrow or atretic, making otoscopy impossible. Tomographic examination of the middle ear is invaluable but requires referral to a centre with the necessary specialised equipment. Plastic surgical repair of the pinna may be undertaken for cosmetic reasons, or a prosthesis may be used. Reconstruction of the atretic ear canal or ossicular anomalies may be possible.

Genetic hearing loss with eye disease.   Usher's syndrome consists of retinitis pigmentosa plus sensorineural deafness. This condition which may contain several subtypes occurs in between 3 and 10% of hearing-impaired children. The hearing loss is usually severe and the vestibular system may also be involved causing poor balance. Night blindness may be noted as early as 5 years and this is followed by progressive loss of vision. There may be an increased incidence of mental retardation. The diagnosis may be confirmed or eliminated by an ERG long before ophthalmoscopy reveals the characteristic pigmentation, and some have argued that an ERG should be performed in all children with unexplained hearing loss.
    There are over 20 other syndromes in which deafness is associated with eye disease including cryptophthalmos, Alström's, Refsum's and Cockayne's syndromes, and the optic atrophy-diabetes syndrome.

Genetic hearing loss with musculoskeletal defects.   This group includes the otopalato-digital, Klippel–Feil anomalad, and Crouzon's syndrome, and osteogenesis imperfecta.

Genetic hearing loss with ectodermal disorder.   Waardenburg's syndrome accounts for about 2% of congenital deafness. Transmission is autosomal dominant but expression is very variable. The features are: deafness (usually but not always severe), abnormal vestibular function, an appearance of widely spaced eyes produced by lateral displacement of the medial canthi, a white tuft of hair, variable iris pigmentation (heterochromia iridis) such as one blue and one brown iris, prognathous mandible, occasional cleft lip and palate, and vitiligo.

Genetic hearing loss with renal disease.   The most important of these is Alport's syndrome which accounts for about 1% of genetic deafness. Inheritance is autosomal dominant, with males more severely affected. Haematuria may occur in the first decade, followed by progressive hypertension and uraemia. The deafness is usually mild and appears in the second decade. Eye anomalies occur in 10% of cases.

Genetic hearing loss with metabolic disease.   Pendred's syndrome (goitre and deafness) is inherited as an autosomal recessive. The goitre is usually soft, diffuse and small and may be present at birth or appear at any time up to puberty. Mild hypothyroidism may occur but most cases are euthyroid and are not readily diagnosed by standard thyroid function tests. The metabolic defect is in the organic binding of iodide and is demonstrated by the perchlorate discharge test. The deafness is usually severe, may be asymmetric, and may progress slightly during childhood. Thyroxine therapy controls the goitre but does not improve the hearing.

Hearing loss may also occur in other rare metabolic disorders, notably in some of the lysosomal storage diseases, for example the mucopolysaccharidoses.

Genetic hearing loss and miscellaneous defects.   In the Jervell–Nielsen syndrome, hearing loss is associated with ECG abnormalities and episodic loss of consciousness due to cardiac arrhythmias. There is an increased incidence of hearing loss in Down's and Turner's syndromes. There are several rare neurological disorders in which progressive nervous system disease is associated with a hearing loss.

INTRAUTERINE INFECTIONS

Maternal infection during pregnancy with rubella or cytomegalovirus may cause deafness alone or in association with other handicaps. These conditions are discussed in detail on pp. 220–5.

PERINATAL CAUSES

Perinatal events, singly or in combination, undoubtedly account for some cases of hearing defects, but their significance is often overestimated and the alternative possibility of genetic hearing loss must always be considered.[298,299]

Prematurity.   Estimates of the risk of hearing loss in premature infants vary so widely as to be of very little value. As with other handicaps, it is probably the problems associated with prematurity rather than the prematurity itself which account for the undoubtedly increased incidence of hearing loss. Earlier fears that incubator noise and the extensive use of gentamicin would damage the hearing do not seem to have been realised. There may be an increased incidence of secretory otitis media in premature infants, and it is essential that research studies distinguish between conductive and sensori-neural deafness.

Hypoxia and Asphyxia.   Sensorineural hearing loss is surprisingly uncommon in children who have cerebral palsy resulting from severe perinatal hypoxia and asphyxia, although a high frequency loss may occur with athetoid cerebral palsy caused by hypoxia. It is uncertain whether these perinatal events in isolation cause hearing loss in the absence of any other neurological handicap.

Jaundice.   The healthy full-term neonate may tolerate bilirubin levels of over 340 μmol/l without any immediate or long term sequelae, but sick or premature babies are susceptible to bilirubin damage at much lower levels. It may not be possible to decide whether neonatal jaundice was the likely cause of a child's hearing loss unless full details of the neonatal period are available; a parental report of jaundice is not sufficient.

Hearing loss can be attributed with more confidence to hyperbilirubinaemia when features of kernicterus or other neurologic dysfunction have been noted in the neonatal period. The end result may be any combination of sensorineural hearing loss (which is usually high frequency in type), mental handicap and athetosis. One-fifth of children with athetoid cerebral palsy caused by kernicterus have a hearing loss.

Development of the hearing-impaired child

The major impact of congenital sensorineural hearing loss inevitably is on language acquisition.[300] The hearing-impaired child uses his vision to acquire social and non-verbal communicative skills and is less likely to develop bizarre behaviour and mannerisms than the visually handicapped child, although behaviour problems may emerge if his handicap remains unrecognised. Unless he has other handicaps, the development of cognitive and performance skills usually progresses normally, except that language deficiency limits his ability to solve problems in which verbal strategies are useful.

Although only moderate in audiological terms, a 50 dB hearing loss may cause a marked delay in language development, and defective speech, and even mild losses of less than 30 dB may be significant in some cases. When the hearing loss exceeds 70 dB, spontaneous acquisition of language is unlikely. Even with optimal amplification by means of a hearing aid, and expert teaching, many children with sensorineural hearing loss have

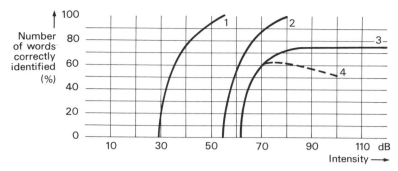

Fig. 14.1 Speech intelligibility with various hearing defects. **1** Normal hearing: 100% of words heard correctly at 50 dB; **2** conductive hearing loss: 100% of words heard correctly at 80 dB; **3** sensorineural hearing loss: some words not heard correctly at any intensity; **4** sensorineural loss with recruitment: increasing intensity may make speech less intelligible. (After Huizing & Reyntjes[453].)

immense difficulty in acquiring spoken language. This is because the ear has a reduced ability to *discriminate* sounds, no matter how loud they may be. Fig. 14.1 illustrates how an increase in intensity of speech beyond a certain point (in this case 80 dB) is of no further help to the subject and he is unable to correctly identify 100% of words at any intensity.

A further problem is the phenomenon of recruitment, which occurs with cochlear lesions. This is an abnormally rapid increase in the sensation of loudness, once the subject's hearing threshold is passed. For example, his threshold of hearing might be at 70 dB, yet he may find a sound of 100 dB intolerably loud. Thus, many people with sensorineural hearing loss, experience increasing distortion and discomfort when using a powerful hearing aid. Recruitment and distortion are difficult to measure, particularly in children, but explain in part why the results of amplification are so often disappointing.

The child with a severe prelingual hearing loss has little or no experience of sound until amplification is provided. He does not associate sound with meaning and has never learned to attend to auditory stimuli, nor can he modulate and control his voice patterns (p. 37). The concept of a word as a group of sounds with a specific meaning has to be learnt. These skills are beginning to be acquired effortlessly by the normal infant before the 1st birthday, but must be specifically taught to the hearing-impaired child. As he learns to listen, his hearing loss may show apparent improvement and he responds to quieter sounds—for this reason the initial assessment of his hearing loss may be unduly pessimistic.

In spite of all their problems, some children learn to make full use of the minimal acoustic information audible to them (p. 85) and, by supplementing this with clues from lip reading, facial expression and the social situation, make excellent progress in listening and speaking. Unfortunately, these are in the minority. In the EEC survey mentioned above, the speech of only half the children was intelligible to strangers, a quarter could only use single word utterances, and less than half could understand normal conversation even with hearing aids *in situ*. Severe retardation in reading was common in this and in several other studies. The written work of hearing-impaired children reflects their impoverished linguistic experience. Sentences tend to be short and contain numerous syntactic errors[301] which follow a distinct pattern (Table 14.3). There is increasing evidence that

Table 14.3   Examples of common syntactic errors made by deaf students. (Adapted from Martin,[103] based on original work of Quigley.)

The cat under the table.
John sick. The girl a ball.
Jim have sick.

Tom has pushing the wagon.
The boy was pushed the girl.

Beth made candy no.
Beth threw the ball and Jean catch it.
Joe bought ate the apple.

For to play baseball is fun.
John goes to fishing.
John goes to fish.
Bill liked to played baseball.
Jim wanted go.

I helped the boy's mother was sick.
John saw the boy who the boy kicked
the ball.

Who a boy gave you a ball?

Who the baby did love?
Who TV watched.

I amn't tired. Bill willn't go.

John chased the girl and he scared.
(John chased the girl. He scared the girl.)

The dog chased the girl had on a red dress.
(The dog chased the girl. The girl had on
a red dress).

these deficiencies can be overcome to some extent by the early use of 'total communication' (*see* below). Other advances which should improve results include neonatal diagnosis with introduction of a hearing aid within the first few months of life, and the rapid improvements in hearing aid technology.

Management

DIAGNOSIS AND INVESTIGATION

The diagnosis of a specific deafness syndrome is possible in only a few cases but a systematic paediatric examination is essential (Table 14.4). In the remainder, serology for rubella and cytomegalovirus should be considered, and an eye examination (p. 108) should be routine. Tomography may be helpful when middle ear malformations are suspected, and can also establish the structural integrity of the cochlea and semicircular canals.

Table 14.4   Paediatric examination of the child with a hearing loss: findings which may suggest a specific cause or syndrome.

External ear
    atresia of canal
    preauricular pits or nodules
    low set ears
    small malformed ears

Eyes
    heterochromia (different colour) of iris
    hypertelorism
    vision defect
    optic atrophy
    retinopathy
    cataract
    corneal clouding

Musculoskeletal
    abnormal length/spacing, of digits
    short neck
    craniosynostosis
    cleft palate
    kyphoscoliosis

Skin and hair
    white forelock
    vitiligo

Miscellaneous
    congenital heart disease
    ataxia
    neuropathy
    goitre
    hepatosplenomegaly
    short stature
    developmental delay
    microcephaly

COUNSELLING·

A diagnosis of congenital hearing impairment can evoke the same parental reactions as any other handicap. They must be told where the lesion is, preferably with the aid of a model or diagram, and why a surgical cure for sensorineural deafness is not possible. Many parents are puzzled by the word 'deaf' particularly in cases of high-tone hearing loss, since their observations confirm that the child has some hearing. A simple explanation of the audiogram helps to clarify this. The possible causes should be discussed. Where relevant, genetic counselling may be offered,[302] since in unexplained congenital hearing loss the risk of having a further affected child may be as high as 1 in 10.

Most parents are distressed at the thought of their child using a hearing aid, fearing that he will be stigmatised or ridiculed, that he will refuse to wear it, or that the aid will be damaged or lost. It is also essential to explain why an aid is not the complete answer to sensorineural hearing loss, for reasons explained above. The parents must understand that, while outstanding results can be obtained even in cases of severe hearing loss, much hard work will be necessary. At the same time, a positive attitude must be encouraged and an early introduction to an enthusiastic teacher helps to achieve this and to avoid early management problems.

HEARING AIDS

A hearing aid is a device to amplify sound. It may be worn behind the ear or in a pocket or harness on the body (Fig. 14.2). A wide variety of hearing aids suitable for children is now available on the National Health Service, but commercial aids may be prescribed by a consultant audiological physician or otologist in special cases. Some aids have special features such as selective amplification of high or low frequencies, and circuits to reduce sudden peaks of intense noise. Most aids provided for school children can be used with the 'loop' wiring system which transmits the teacher's voice, thus bypassing background noise interference. Radio transmission systems such as the 'Phonic Ear' are also widely used in schools and are valued for their increased clarity and range and reduced noise interference.

Selection of the most suitable hearing aid for a young child is usually made by a paediatric audiologist, in consultation with the peripatetic teacher of the hearing-impaired. The latter is responsible for introducing the child to the use of the aid, and teaching the parents about its management and maintenance. The choice of the first hearing aid is based on the severity and pattern of the hearing loss. As soon as the child is old enough to cooperate with detailed testing, clinical tests of speech discrimination are used to select the most effective aid, since it is not possible to do this purely on the basis of the audiogram.

The most powerful modern aids produce a very high output of over 130

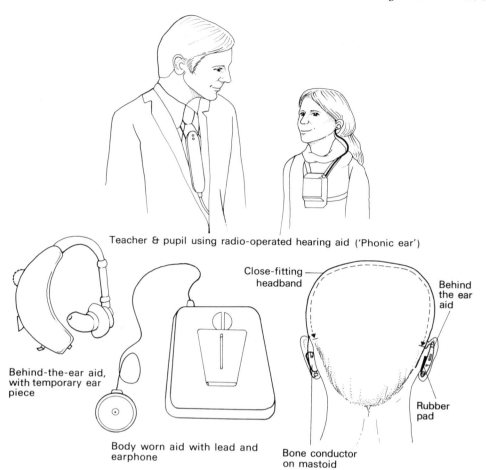

Teacher & pupil using radio-operated hearing aid ('Phonic ear')

Behind-the-ear aid, with temporary ear piece

Body worn aid with lead and earphone

Close-fitting headband

Behind the ear aid

Rubber pad

Bone conductor on mastoid

Fig. 14.2   A selection of hearing aids.

dB. Fears have been expressed that acoustic trauma might cause further damage to the hearing, but there is no firm evidence that this is so, and there should be no hesitation about prescribing a powerful aid when this is indicated. The ear phone of the hearing aid is attached to an ear mould, which is made from an impression of the child's ear taken with a rapid hardening material (Fig. 14.3). The ear mould must be a good fit, otherwise amplified sound escapes from the ear canal, is picked up by the microphone of the aid, and is amplified yet further. The resulting loud whistle is known as acoustic feedback, and prevents the child from making full use of the gain available in the instrument. While children are growing rapidly, new moulds may be needed every few months. The efficient provision of these presents difficult organisational problems and in many areas children are repeatedly deprived of adequate amplification while they wait for new

Fig. 14.3 Taking an impression of the ear. A rapid hardening material is injected gently into the meatus using a syringe.

moulds to be delivered. Other problems associated with ear moulds include occlusion by wax, and chronic otitis externa.

EDUCATION

The peripatetic teacher of the deaf (more recently known as the Adviser to the Hearing Impaired) is employed by the local education authority and is responsible for the child's early education and management. Later, she advises the educational psychologist on school placement, liaises with the school, and provides continuing supervision if the child is placed in a normal school.

About 50% of hearing-impaired children as defined in the EEC survey attend normal schools. The remainder attend either partially hearing units (PHU), which are often attached to normal schools, or schools for the deaf. The distinction between the two is not sharply defined. The children attending at PHU must be able to make good use of their residual hearing, whereas in schools for the deaf, more intensive and individual methods are needed to help children acquire language and there may be a more extensive use of sign language. Educational needs rather than the audiogram determine school placement, but as a generalisation most children with a hearing loss greater than 90 dB will need the type of education provided in a school for the deaf.

There is still intense controversy about the education of hearing-impaired children. Some educators favour a purely oral approach, arguing that the children must eventually live in a world of hearing people. With adequate amplification, lip reading and the use of touch and vibration sense, many children do progress well. Lip reading is limited by the fact that many consonant sounds look identical. The system of 'cued' speech was designed to overcome this problem. Hand signs displayed at chin level are used to differentiate similar-appearing consonants. A more recent development is the use of electronic analysers which convert voice patterns to visual displays, thus enabling the child to compare his articulation and voice patterns with those of his teacher. However, even with all available assistance, the results are often disappointing and many children grow up with a severe communication handicap, complicated by numerous personality and behavioural problems.

For this reason, many educators favour the use of non-verbal communication methods such as British Sign Language (BSL) and finger spelling. BSL is a highly versatile system developed over many years by the deaf themselves. Each sign represents a word (Fig. 14.4). Finger spelling is used to spell out words for which there is no BSL sign. There is increasing evidence that the use of sign language in early childhood encourages language development rather than inhibiting it and for the more severely handicapped children, 'total communication' is recommended; this is a combination of oral and manual methods. This approach is certainly endorsed by many deaf people.

The education of mentally or visually handicapped children who also have a severe hearing loss presents exceptional problems[303,304] and for these British Sign Language, Makaton, or Paget–Gorman are invaluable. The end result of a purely oral approach in such cases is usually a non-communicating, severely disturbed adult.

INTELLIGENCE TESTS FOR HEARING-IMPAIRED CHILDREN

Items selected from standard tests such as the WISC, Merrill–Palmer, or Stanford–Binet can be used to assess non-verbal abilities, although they are not standardised for use with deaf children. The Leiter scale, and the Nebraska and Snijders–Oomen tests are specifically designed for non-verbal presentation, and are very useful for assessing children with any form of communication disorder. Raven's progressive matrices may also be used, though this test may tend to underestimate the abilities of very deaf children (p. 274).

Vocabulary and language tests may be employed to measure progress. A picture vocabulary test can be presented with or without lip reading and hearing aids, and with the aid of mime or sign language. Discrepancies in the child's performance with and without these forms of assistance will sometimes dramatically demonstrate to parents or teachers the differences between a purely oral approach and total communication.

Baby: Slightly rock the arms

Exams: Take 'thoughts' from head down on to paper on desk

Queen (or King)

Apple: Jerk hand slightly forward and down as if biting a crisp apple

Fig. 14.4 British Sign Language for the Deaf. Four examples to show the logical derivation of signs.

ACQUIRED SENSORINEURAL HEARING LOSS

Bacterial or tubercular meningitis may cause deafness at any age. The hearing loss is usually bilateral and varies in severity from moderate to profound. No child should be discharged from follow-up after meningitis until normal hearing has been confirmed. Occasionally, a child may initially appear to be deaf following meningitis, but it gradually becomes apparent that peripheral hearing is intact and the lesion is presumably in the auditory pathways or cortex.

Other causes of acquired hearing loss include trauma, non-accidental injury and ototoxic drugs. Some forms of genetic deafness are progressive and present as acquired defects.

Acquired sensorineural hearing loss is an indication for urgent educational advice and help. The child who has already had some experience of language before losing his hearing has a tremendous advantage over the congenitally hearing-impaired child, but this advantage will be squandered if expert help is not supplied rapidly.

Mumps is generally believed to be the most common cause of the total unilateral hearing loss which is occasionally found during routine hearing testing of school entrants. It is impossible to prove this unless there is a clear history of otological symptoms or vertigo during an attack of mumps. Other childhood fevers, inherited disorders, cytomegalovirus and middle-ear disease may cause unilateral hearing loss. These children should all be seen by an otologist, but further investigation is rarely necessary.

The child seldom benefits from the use of a hearing aid but he should wherever possible sit with his better ear towards the teacher, who should be aware of his disability. An annual check of the hearing in the normal ear is a sensible precaution.

CONDUCTIVE HEARING LOSS

Congenital forms

There may be a conductive component in the hearing loss associated with ear malformations, for example in Treacher–Collins syndrome. Congenital anomalies of the ossicles may also occur in isolation.

Otosclerosis is the most important inherited form of deafness which is predominantly conductive. It is dominantly inherited, with incomplete penetrance. Ninety per cent of cases develop symptoms between the ages of 15 and 45, so it is rarely seen in paediatric practice.

Acquired conductive hearing loss

SECRETORY OTITIS MEDIA (SOM, 'GLUE EAR')

Secretory otitis media is among the commonest of all defects in young children.[305] There is a middle-ear effusion behind an intact drum, without evidence of acute infection. The effusion varies in viscosity from watery to an almost solid rubbery consistency. The viscosity does not correlate closely either with duration of the condition or with severity of the hearing loss. The fluid contains leucocytes, dead bacteria and a number of mucoproteins which are secreted by the middle-ear epithelium. Postulated causes include upper respiratory infections, allergy, inadequate antibiotic therapy of acute otitis media, and Eustachian tube dysfunction. It is particularly associated with cleft palate, and with Down's, Turner's, and craniostenosis syndromes.

The main symptom is hearing loss; this may vary from negligible to 50–55 dB, with an average of 28 dB. All frequencies may be affected but most commonly the hearing loss is more severe in the lower frequencies. Mild pain may occur, perhaps indicated by the young child rubbing or poking his ear. SOM is often found in children who snore, mouth-breathe and have chronic catarrh.

The otoscopic signs are very variable. The drum may look almost normal except for loss of the usual grey translucent sheen; there may be hyperaemia, or the colour may be obviously abnormal, varying from golden to slate blue. The presence of the cone-shaped light reflex is not a reliable indicator of normality. Bubbles or fluid levels may occasionally be seen. Retraction is a difficult but useful physical sign. The pneumatic otoscope (Fig. 14.5) demonstrates reduced mobility. Impedance measurement is invaluable as a confirmatory investigation (p. 104).

Untreated, SOM usually resolves eventually. The commonest pattern is an isolated attack in association with an upper respiratory infection, followed by recovery within 6–8 weeks. Some children have recurrent episodes but recover completely after each episode. In a minority, the SOM persists for months or even years. Serious middle-ear complications such as cholesteatoma are recognised but are very rare.

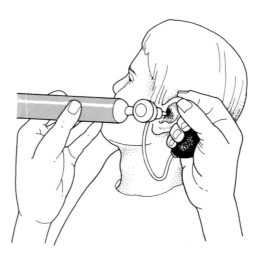

Fig. 14.5 Otoscope with pneumatic speculum.

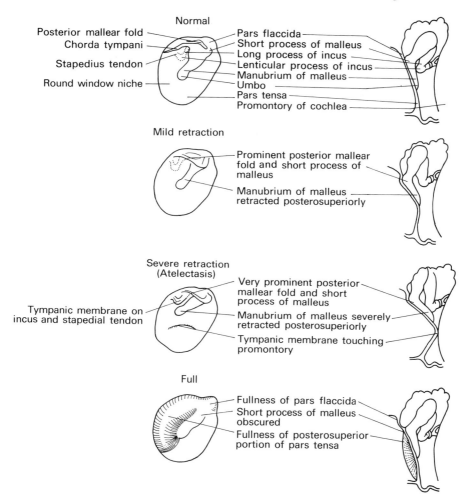

Fig. 14.6 Various positions of tympanic membrane as visualised by the otoscope and a lateral section through the tympanic membrane-middle ear. (Redrawn from Bluestone[106] by permission.)

Clinical importance. SOM may be found in children with delayed language development, behaviour problems or school failure. Because the condition is so common, it must not be assumed that it is always the cause of the child's symptoms.[306] In assessing the need for surgical treatment one should consider the following:

1 Whether it is transient or longstanding. The parents may know how long the child has been hard of hearing. A history of repeated ear infections may help. In the absence of these clues, it is advisable to see the child again

after 6–8 weeks to see if the condition has resolved before deciding about surgery.

2   The severity of the hearing loss. This may fluctuate from day to day.

3   Other handicaps. It seems likely that a mild hearing loss has a much more devastating effect in a child who has little exposure to spoken language or is mildly mentally retarded. Such children are commonly found in the day nurseries of deprived inner-city areas.

4   ENT Problems. One postulated cause of SOM is obstruction of the Eustachian tube orifice by hypertrophied adenoids, thus preventing adequate aeration of the middle ear. SOM is often associated with symptoms of airway obstruction—snoring, mouth-breathing, difficulty in chewing and swallowing, and constant nasal discharge. In some cases intermittent respiratory obstruction caused by large tonsils and adenoids leads to sleep disturbance with repeated episodes of sleep apnoea and tiredness and irritability during the day. Blood CO_2 levels may rise during sleep and occasionally may even cause pulmonary hypertension and right heart failure. There is a clinical impression that SOM is more likely to be chronic in children with symptoms of adenoidal hypertrophy and airway obstruction and therefore these findings would bias one towards earlier operation.

Management.   Conservative treatment consists of a decongestant and antihistamine mixture, with or without a broad spectrum antibiotic such as cotrimoxazole. It is reasonable to try this but it is of dubious efficacy.[307] Surgical treatment consists of drainage of the ear by myringotomy and suction, and ventilation tubes (grommets) may be inserted. Adenoidectomy probably should be done only if there are symptoms of airway obstruction and when performed for this indication, it is a very successful operation. SOM is not an indication for tonsillectomy.

Surgery is dramatically effective in the short term, but the frequency of both spontaneous remissions and relapses makes long term results very hard to assess.[308,309] An additional, though minor, consideration in planning surgical treatment, is that the child with grommets may be banned from swimming: however, some surgeons permit this if cottonwool plugs with vaseline and a tight-fitting bathing hat are used.

A small minority of children with SOM suffer repeated attacks in spite of surgical treatment and have a substantial hearing loss for a large percentage of their early childhood. These may benefit from a hearing aid and/or education for a year or two in a partially hearing unit. Children suffering a combination of environmental language deprivation and mild deafness due to SOM need special attention. Parents and nursery nurses should make a specific effort to teach them to sit still and listen; and should speak in a slow, clear fairly loud voice, using simple language. These measures may have a very gratifying effect on language development.

Hearing must always be retested after surgery, to confirm improvement; the possibility of a coexisting sensorineural loss must not be overlooked.

CHRONIC SUPPURATIVE OTITIS MEDIA

Chronically discharging ears, perforation of the tympanic membrane, and cholesteatoma formation are now relatively rare in developed countries. These problems require long term expert management by an otologist. Surgical reconstruction may be possible, but for various reasons the surgeon may elect to postpone this. The disease may cause a conductive hearing loss which is severe enough to be of educational significance and the child may benefit from the use of a hearing aid of the bone conducting type (Fig. 14.2).

WAX

The production of wax varies widely between children and is partly determined by genetic factors. Wax only causes a hearing loss when it totally occludes the auditory meatus. Contrary to popular myth, middle ear disease can and often does coexist with impacted wax, and it is essential to remove the wax and re-test the hearing before accepting that wax is the sole cause of the hearing loss.

Chapter Fifteen
Visual Handicap

Blindness and partial sight cannot be defined solely on criteria of visual acuity (VA). Visual field defects, colour vision disturbances, intelligence and visual experience prior to the onset of the visual handicap must all be considered. Functional definitions are therefore more practical and useful. A blind child is one who will require education by methods not involving sight and, if of adequate intelligence, will need to learn Braille. Similarly a blind adult is one who is unable to do any work for which sight is essential. In practice this usually means that visual acuity is around 3/60 or less but a person whose visual field is severely constricted may be effectively blind with a better VA than this. A partially sighted child is one with a significant visual handicap who can nevertheless make substantial use of his residual vision. This corresponds to a VA of between 6/18 and 6/60 in most cases, depending on the other factors mentioned above.

Intelligence has an important influence on the child's ability to cope with his handicap. The bright child whose defective vision is his only handicap will do much better than one who is mentally handicapped or who has another disability such as a hearing loss.

Classification of eye disorders

The paediatrician does not need a detailed knowledge of eye disorders.[113,114] He should however be able to recognise the signs of important eye disease, particularly those that need urgent treatment, to detect associated malformations and disorders, and to ensure that adequate arrangements are made for the child's general paediatric and educational care.

For paediatric purposes, a classification based on the presenting problem is of more practical use than a detailed anatomical one (Table 15.1). The three divisions suggested are (1) obvious external abnormality of the eye, (2) mass behind the pupil, (3) normal appearance of eyes but abnormal visual behaviour.

Table 15.1   A classification of the commoner paediatric eye disorders.

Group 1—Obvious external abnormality of the eyes	Group 2—Mass behind the lens	Group 3—Eyes look normal but visual behaviour is abnormal
Cataract	Retrolental fibroplasia	Refractive error
Corneal opacity	Retinoblastoma	Retinal degenerations
Microphthalmos	Toxocara	Optic atrophy
Cryptophthalmos	Norrie's disease	Optic nerve hypoplasia
Glaucoma		Coloboma
Anterior chamber cleavage syndrome		Congenital infections
Albinism		Cortical blindness
Nystagmus		Delayed visual maturation
Oculomotor apraxia		
Aniridia		

Table 15.2   Causes of visual handicap: 1973–74. (From DHSS data presented by S. Fine.[112]) $n = 532$.

Cause	Percentage
Optic atrophy	26
Cataract	14
Diseases of macula, retina and choroid	13
Nystagmus	8
Albinism	7
Coloboma	7
Myopia	4
Retrolental fibroplasia	4
Rubella syndrome	4
Cortical blindness	3
Buphthalmos	2
Uveitis and iridocyclitis	2
Corneal lesions	1
Strabismus	1
Retinoblastoma	1
Microcephaly	<1
Toxoplasmosis	<1
Others	<1
	100

EPIDEMIOLOGY

In Western countries, serious eye defects in children are rare, occurring in 3–4 children per 10 000 births.[112,320] Epidemiologic data for the UK are obtained from three sources: notification of congenital eye malformations during the first week of life, registration on form BD8, which is completed by a consultant ophthalmologist in respect of every blind and partially sighted child, and educational sources. BD8 registrations provide the best available data on causes and prevalence of visual handicap, and these are summarised in Table 15.2. Retrolental fibroplasia accounts for a much smaller proportion than was the case 25 years ago (although there may be a recent increase) and there has also been some decline in congenital rubella.

The number of children registered as visually handicapped is larger than the number attending special schools for the partially sighted or blind. This is because some attend normal school and many others have an additional handicap which is of greater educational significance than the visual defect, so that some other type of school is more appropriate. Additional handicaps are common in blind and partially sighted children[112] (Table 15.3). Many of

Table 15.3 Presence of additional handicaps in new registrations during 1973–74. (From DHSS (unpublished data) presented by S. Fine.[112])

	Blind	Partially sighted	Total
Hearing loss	8	6	14
Subnormality	53	33	86
Physical handicap	46	47	93
Epilepsy	7	12	19
Language disorder	1	5	6
Behaviour disorder	—	3	3
No. of handicaps	115	106	221
No. of affected children	100	94	194
Total children	217	315	532
% of affected children	46	30	36

the conditions responsible for eye damage also cause mental retardation or cerebral palsy. The combination of deafness and blindness is described on p. 302. Behaviour disorders include tedious repetitive speech, withdrawal, aggression and 'blindisms' such as head-banging, rocking or eye-poking.

EYE DISORDERS

Group 1—Eyes look abnormal to simple inspection

CATARACT

There are many types of cataract but the ability to distinguish these is not necessary for the paediatrician. They may range in size from tiny opacities to total obstruction of vision. The pupil is described by the parent as hazy or milky but this appearance may only be easily visible in certain lighting conditions. Early and reliable detection is best accomplished by looking at the pupil through an ophthalmoscope held about a foot away from the child with the lens set on $+1-+3$.

In about one-third of cases cataracts are inherited as isolated defects, and the inheritance may be dominant, recessive, or sex linked. Examination of other family members may be helpful. The numerous causes of cataract are summarised in Table 15.4. Most of these are very rare, but when cataract coexists with other defects or anomalies, these disorders must be considered since many have important genetic implications.[310]

Sometimes vision can be improved by dilating the pupil with atropine, but when the vision is seriously impaired, current opinion is that surgical treatment should be attempted in the first months of life whenever possible, because irreversible amblyopia (p. 115) develops very rapidly in untreated cases.[117] Urgent referral to an ophthalmologist is therefore recommended whenever cataract is suspected in infancy. After surgery, the aphakia (absence of lens) leaves the child severely hypermetropic, and this may be

Table 15.4 Some important causes of cataract.

Inherited recessive, dominant, sex-linked forms
Idiopathic
Congenital infections
   rubella
   cytomegalovirus
   toxoplasmosis
Chromosome disorders, e.g. Down's syndrome
Metabolic disorders, e.g. galactosaemia, galactokinase deficiency,
                     hypoparathyroidism, Lowe's syndrome
Dysmorphic syndromes
   Hallermann–Streiff
   Marinesco–Sjogren
   Myotonic dystrophy
Miscellaneous
   post-inflammatory
   associated with lens dislocation, glaucoma, retrolental fibroplasia, etc.

---

corrected by spectacles or contact lenses. Advances in contact lens technology are mainly responsible for the improved results of early surgery.

There are particular difficulties in the treatment of rubella cataracts, whose removal may cause a viral endophthalmitis. Virus can be grown from the lens up to the 3rd year of life, and this may be useful in cases where a diagnosis of rubella syndrome is strongly suspected but serological proof has been incomplete.

CORNEAL OPACITIES

These are less common than cataracts. Various inherited anomalies of the cornea may occur. Some mucopolysaccharidoses cause corneal clouding but other features are usually apparent. Corneal scarring due to gonococcal ophthalmia neonatorum, trachoma or vitamin A deficiency are now rare in Western countries but are a major cause of blindness worldwide.

MICROPHTHALMIA

Microphthalmia or 'small eye' may be associated with other developmental defects such as coloboma, or with intrauterine infections. Occasionally it may be recessively inherited. The eye is hypermetropic.

CRYPTOPHTHALMOS

This means 'hidden eye'. The palpebral fissure is absent and there are often defects of the anterior part of the eye. There may be associated abnormalities of the ear, genitalia, etc.

GLAUCOMA

Infantile glaucoma (buphthalmos) is rare, but rapid diagnosis and referral are important since it is one of the few paediatric eye disorders where effective treatment is possible. It may be unilateral or bilateral. It presents in the first year of life, with any of the following: large eye, corneal clouding, excessive tears (epiphora), and photophobia. The corneal diameter is usually greater than 12 mm (normal < 11 mm). Buphthalmos may be an isolated anomaly or a secondary phenomenon associated with a variety of other eye diseases.

ANTERIOR CHAMBER CLEAVAGE SYNDROME

This is a group of disorders caused by faulty cleavage between iris and cornea during embryological development. Various abnormalities of the lens, cornea and iris may be seen, and there may be facial anomalies, defective teeth, mental retardation and myotonic dystrophy. The syndrome is inherited as a dominant with very variable expression.

ALBINISM

This is a disorder of the melanin pigmentation system, caused by defective conversion of tyrosine to melanin.[217] There are oculocutaneous and ocular forms. The overall incidence is around 1 in 20 000. In the oculocutaneous forms, there is decreased pigmentation of hair and skin, pale iris and a red reflex from the eye due to transillumination through the iris, poor visual acuity which is worse for distant than for near vision, nystagmus, squint and photophobia. Binocular vision does not usually develop. There is an increased risk of skin tumours. Two main types and several rare variants are known. The inheritance is recessive. Ocular albinism is less common and the abnormality is confined to the eyes. Inheritance is as an X-linked recessive.

There is no specific treatment for albinism but sun-screen lotion and tinted spectacles can be provided. The visual and cosmetic handicaps combine to make this a particularly distressing disorder.

NYSTAGMUS

Congenital nystagmus must be distinguished from nystagmus caused by severe visual defects which prevent development of visual fixation.[77] Congenital nystagmus begins within the first few months of life. It is sometimes familial. Typically it is horizontal in all positions of gaze. Cases with vertical, rotary or compound nystagmus require further investigation. Visual acuity may be impaired but often is surprisingly good. Near vision is often better than distant vision. There is no sensation of apparent movement (oscillopsia). There may be associated head nodding movements.

UNUSUAL DISORDERS OF EYE MOVEMENT

Coarse bobbing movements of the eyes, fluttering, and an overshoot on lateral gaze, followed by several very large amplitude jerks ('ocular dysmetria') are occasionally seen in children with severe brain damage, and are thought to indicate disruption of the pathways controlling eye movement.[126] Occasionally such movements are mistaken for minor seizures. Oculomotor apraxia is an interesting disorder in which the child has difficulty in initiating tracking movements of the eyes and learns to overcome this problem by a jerk of the head. It can be an isolated disorder or may occur in association with brain damage or storage diseases.

ANIRIDIA

In this condition the iris is rudimentary rather than totally absent.[311] There may be associated refractive errors, photophobia and glaucoma. It may be inherited as a dominant. In sporadic cases (i.e. the parents are not affected) there is a strong association with an abnormal chromosome and the development of Wilms' tumour. Regular urine testing for blood, and six-monthly IVPs or ultrasound scans of the kidney should be continued until the age of 4 years.

Group 2—Mass behind the lens

In these conditions, the ease with which the mass can be seen is variable: the presenting features may be the mass itself, abnormal vision or squint.

RETROLENTAL FIBROPLASIA

A few years ago this was among the commonest causes of childhood blindness. In the seventies there was a substantial decline in the incidence, but with the increasing survival of extremely low birthweight babies the incidence is rising again. Although the development of this condition is probably related in some way to the oxygen sensitivity of retinal vessels in the premature infant, there are other factors which are not yet fully understood.[312,313]

All grades of severity are seen, and early changes sometimes regress and disappear. Proliferation of blood vessels, and fibrous tissue are the main features. In the most severe cases, the eye is small and a mass of whitish tissue can be seen behind the lens. Retinal detachment and glaucoma may complicate the picture. As this is primarily a disorder affecting sick premature infants, additional handicaps such as spastic diplegia and mental retardation are common.

RETINOBLASTOMA

This tumour may present with a squint or as a retrolental mass. Some cases are familial with dominant inheritance and these may be bilateral. A deletion of chromosome 13 has been described in association with retinoblastoma. Treatment with radiotherapy may be successful, but enucleation of the eye is often needed. Genetic counselling and, where appropriate, examination of relatives must be arranged.

TOXOCARA

This is a rare infection which may cause an inflammatory mass and mimics retinoblastoma.

NORRIE'S DISEASE

This is a rare sex-linked recessive disorder in which there are bilateral retinal masses, sometimes associated with mental retardation and deafness.

Group 3—Child's visual behaviour is abnormal but the eyes appear normal to inspection

REFRACTIVE ERROR

Every child whose vision is suspect must have a refraction, since refractive errors such as high myopia are easily overlooked in the pursuit of more exotic disorders. There is an increased frequency of myopia in premature infants, particularly those with retrolental fibroplasia; and also in those with albinism, Down's syndrome, muscular dystrophy and myotonic dystrophy.

Myopia occurring as an isolated disorder may either present in infancy ('congenital' myopia) or later in childhood (acquired myopia). The latter is uncommon before the age of 3, but the incidence increases steadily through the school years. Acquired myopia is more common in academically successful children. Very severe myopia is occasionally complicated by retinal detachment. There is no evidence for the old belief that children with high myopia need to 'rest their eyes'.

Refractive errors are also found in association with dislocation of the lens, for example in Marfan's syndrome and homocystinuria.

RETINAL DEGENERATIONS

This is a mixed group of disorders, some of which are very rare. The commonest is *Leber's amaurosis*, a recessive disorder which presents early in infancy with a severe visual deficit. The appearance of the retina is unremarkable in the early stages, but the electroretinogram is abnormal. There are often associated cerebral and renal defects, and this diagnosis should be considered in any infant with normal appearance of the eyes on funduscopy, visual defect and other neurological handicap.[77,314] It should not be mistaken for cortical blindness because of the genetic implications.

Retinitis pigmentosa is a degenerative disorder affecting the rods first, and the cones in the later stages. Pigment is deposited in clusters which resemble a bone corpuscle. It seldom presents before adolescence. The first complaint is usually poor vision in dim illumination. There is increasing constriction of the visual fields, with preservation of a central tunnel of vision. There are several types and the disorder can be inherited as a dominant, recessive or sex-linked trait. Rarely, retinitis pigmentosa is associated with a variety of other abnormalities (e.g. Usher's, Laurence–Moon–Biedl syndromes). A similar retinal degeneration occurs in juvenile Batten's disease ('neuronal ceroid lipofuscinosis'), and visual deterioration and school failure may be the first sign of this disease. Other associated diseases include Refsum's disease and abetalipoproteinaemia.

OPTIC ATROPHY

This condition is recognised by the abnormal pallor of the nerve head, which is of normal size and contour. The normal disc is quite pale in infants and diagnosis may be difficult. The electroretinogram is normal but there may be a fall in amplitude and an increase in the latency of the cortical visual evoked response.

Optic atrophy may occur as an isolated disorder, with dominant or very rarely recessive inheritance, and begins insidiously in infancy or childhood. Leber's optic atrophy (not to be confused with Leber's amaurosis) is a distinct entity in which there is sudden loss of vision with signs of optic neuritis occurring in the second or third decades. The inheritance is complex and expert genetic advice is desirable. Other important causes include papilloedema with secondary optic atrophy, craniopharyngioma, optic nerve glioma and hypertensive encephalopathy. It is essential to eliminate these possibilities when there is no obvious cause for the optic atrophy. Lastly, optic atrophy may often be found in association with hydrocephalus, cerebral palsy, microcephaly, non-accidental injury, cerebral storage disorders, hereditary ataxias and demyelinating diseases. It is doubtful whether optic atrophy in the absence of other evidence of cerebral damage should ever be attributed to perinatal hypoxia, and the diagnosis of isolated 'congenital' optic atrophy should never be made.

OPTIC NERVE HYPOPLASIA

Distinguished from optic atrophy by the small size of the disc, this may be unilateral or bilateral. It is frequently associated with absent septum pellucidum and hypopituitarism. The combination is called septo-optic dysplasia, and should be considered in cases of blindness with short stature.

COLOBOMA

A congenital defect affecting the eyelid, iris, retina or optic nerve. It may be an isolated defect or be found in association with other anomalies. Dominant inheritance has been observed in some cases.

CONGENITAL INFECTIONS

Details of the eye defects associated with congenital infections are given on p. 220.

CORTICAL BLINDNESS

This is among the commonest causes of severe visual handicap in childhood in the Western world, but because it is usually associated with other equally severe handicaps, it is under-reported. Most often the infant is first seen because of obvious and severe developmental delay and assessment reveals abnormal visual behaviour. Sometimes the parents become concerned about the child's vision before they realise that he has other problems as well. Ophthalmic examination reveals normal light reflexes, clear media and healthy fundi. Refractive error must be excluded. The ERG is normal. The VER may be, but is not always, abnormal. CT scan may show abnormalities in the region of the occipital cortex.

Most of these children are severely mentally retarded and many have cerebral palsy, and investigation is directed towards determining the cause. Occasionally cortical blindness may occur as a more discrete entity following severe cerebral damage such as anoxia or hypoglycaemia. The associated mental handicap is likely to be the limiting factor in the child's progress and therapy and education must be planned accordingly. Those working with the child should have some knowledge of the problems of 'normal' blind children. Over the first few years, it may become apparent that the child does have some vision. A characteristic feature is that the parents report apparent fluctuations in visual competence and may be uncertain as to the exact extent of his visual handicap.

DELAYED VISUAL MATURATION

This presents in the first two months when the parents realise that the baby lacks normal visual alertness and following, but gradually it becomes obvious that the infant can see. Later evaluation shows normal vision and no evidence of serious mental or any other handicap, though some of these babies seem rather slow. The cause of the condition is unknown. Diagnosis is made by the elimination of other more serious problems, and the ERG and VER are usually normal.[315]

DEVELOPMENT OF THE VISUALLY HANDICAPPED BABY

It is frequently the mother who first diagnoses visual impairment in her baby when she fails to elicit eye contact. The importance of vision in bonding was discussed on p. 29. The baby's first handicap may be the failure to establish this emotional bond.[316] The mother may feel rejected by the baby's inability to respond to her approach, as well as being frankly repelled if the eyes are physically unattractive. The baby may produce a smile at 6–8 weeks to his mother's voice, but it is unpredictable, and only gross physical stimuli such as ticking reliably elicit a smile. Between $2\frac{1}{2}$ and

6 months the sighted child learns to discriminate his mother's face from unfamiliar faces. The visually handicapped baby has to learn a similar discrimination by voice and by tactile exploration of the face, and his smile is less regular and consistent. However, his auditory and tactile senses are sufficiently developed for him to protest at being held by a stranger, not very much later than would a sighted child.

The visually handicapped baby will 'freeze' when he hears a sound and, at 2 months, there may be a reflex movement of the eyes towards the sound. This reflex movement does not reward him with an interesting spectacle and therefore disappears, so that by 5–6 months there is no movement of the eyes towards a sound. Because he cannot watch his hands, he does not learn to bring them together in the midline and the hands frequently are held immobile at shoulder level. Skilled use of finger–thumb opposition is often delayed and instead raking movements of all four fingers are used to search for objects.

The concepts of object and person permanence are very difficult to grasp; he has to master the association between voice and person, and between sound and sound maker. Reaching for a sound source begins in the last quarter of the first year, some 4–5 months later than the visually-directed reach of a sighted child. Reaching is followed by an increased urge to mobility in pursuit of sound. Person permanence may be demonstrated by extension of the arms towards the mother upon hearing her voice, creeping towards her, or by using the word 'Mama'. The delay in achieving all these milestones may lead to an incorrect label of mental retardation and further rejection by the mother.

The early language development of a baby experiencing normal care may not be markedly different from that of a sighted child, although vocalisation and babble are often diminished. The inability to explore and master the environment and the need to make a tactile search of new objects, delay the acquisition of vocabulary and of the more complex forms that involve the relationships of two concepts. The stage of echolalia may be prolonged, and the child may echo whole sentences without understanding their meaning. The use of 'I' is delayed, since he takes longer to become aware of himself as a person. Later, language skills may become as sophisticated as those of a sighted person though concepts of colour, width, depth, speed, etc. may present difficulties for a very long time.

These children frequently develop mannerisms such as eye-poking, eye-rubbing, and rocking; these are known as 'blindisms'. They should be regarded as a form of deviant development in a child who has failed to overcome the enormous problems of congenital visual impairment. Neither blindisms nor the patterns of delayed development outlined above should in themselves be regarded as evidence of associated mental retardation. The Reynell–Zinkin scales provide data on the developmental milestones of visually handicapped infants.[317] Table 15.5 summarises some simple developmental advice which should be made available to parents.

Table 15.5 Early intervention—advice for parents. (Modified from Hunt, with permission.)

Developmental stage	Features	Implications for intervention
Attachment	Lack of eye to eye regard and smiling to face. 'Stills' when listening—not extend arms to be lifted. Seen as unresponsive	Baby reported as 'good baby'. Left to lie without human contact. Worker can act as ambassador for the baby, interpreting his behaviour and needs to the parents. Plenty of physical contact is desirable
Midline handplay	Midline handplay gives knowledge of their position in space—a pre-requisite to reaching out. Blind child often has 'dead hands' remaining in fetal position	Aid baby identify his hands, e.g. stirrup bells on each wrist, alternatively bring hands together around squeaky toy. Encourage 'clap hands' lap-play
Reaching on sound cue	Sighted baby 'visually insatiable'—reaches and obtains objects at 4 months extending his knowledge and becoming an active agent on the world. Blind baby rarely reaches to sound before 9 months limiting his world to his body. Beginnings of 'blindisms'	Make sounds meaningful. Bring baby to source of sound. Aid reaching to sound. Stop rocking and eye poking at onset
Feeding and chewing	Resistance to spoon, new flavours and chewing without introduction that sight and imitation brings	Introduce new flavours early. 'Teach' chewing by reward producing foods (crisps, crackers)
Creeping and crawling	Directed mobility unlikely before reach on sound-cue established. Bottom-shuffling and crawling backwards common	Incentive for mobility lacking. 'Lure' creep or roll to accessible known sound (parent's voice, favourite sound toy). Bells, etc., on shoes/socks encourage mobility
Speech and language	Without vision, lacks shared frames of reference via pointing, imitation or preverbal gestural communication. Sounds produced lack communicative function. Echolalia may start and persist	Imitate and reward sound production. Keep up 'running commentary' around infant about what he's doing and ongoing events to coordinate sounds with meaning. Play with familiar household objects and action rhymes important

Management

There is some evidence that early intervention programmes based on an appreciation of the handicap of poor vision can substantially improve development, increase parental confidence, and minimise the emergence of blindisms and other behaviour problems.[316] The parents should always be given adequate counselling including genetic advice,[318] and suitable literature. These duties will normally be shared between the ophthalmologist, the paediatrician and either the peripatetic teacher of the blind and/or a developmental psychologist.

EDUCATION

Because visual handicap is rare in childhood, it is difficult for the education authority to provide viable local units; thus residential units serving a wide area were for many years seen as the only answer to this problem. Residential schooling for very young children is now less popular. Instead, a peripatetic teacher of the blind, provided either by the local authority or the Royal National Institute for the Blind advises the parents on methods of helping the preschool child at home. Many severely visually handicapped children may be able to attend and enjoy a normal nursery or nursery school.

Prior to school entry, the child may be seen by a specialist educational psychologist for assessment. Several I.Q. tests (e.g. the Williams) are available for the visually handicapped. Prolonged observation in a nursery or assessment unit is often the most effective way to decide about a child's future school placement. The child's intellect, his ability to make use of his residual vision, the wishes of the family, and his long term prognosis determine whether he should be placed in normal school, partially sighted unit, or school for the blind.

Recent improvements in this area of education include better optical aids, closed-circuit television, the Optacon machine (Fig. 15.1), good illumination, reading material prepared in very large type, and well designed desks at a comfortable angle. With this modern equipment, many more children can make good use of their residual vision and, provided the teacher is appropriately advised (Table 15.6), some will progress well in ordinary school. Braille, of course, remains an essential method of reading for the most severely handicapped, provided that their intelligence is in or near the normal range. Tape recorders and teaching machines are also widely used.

Mobility training is an essential part of the curriculum. As the child matures he learns to travel outside the school, first under supervision and then on his own. The long cane is widely used, and has yet to be displaced by more sophisticated electronic or ultrasonic devices. The length of the cane is chosen so that the tip just touches the ground one pace ahead of the user.

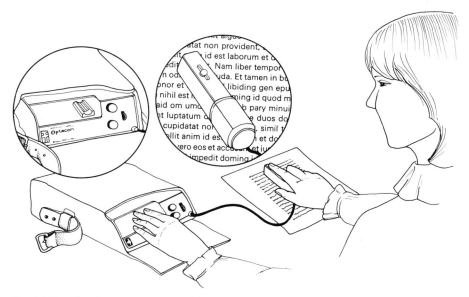

Fig. 15.1   The Optacon is operated by a small hand-held camera which the user moves over the printed text; the index finger of the left hand simultaneously reads the raised shapes of the letters as the camera scans them. Considerable skill is required on the part of the user who needs to undergo training. (Courtesy of Telesensory Systems.)

Table 15.6   Integration of visually handicapped child into normal school—simple advice for teachers.

Good lighting conditions
Adequate type size in books
Should be allowed to approach wall display materials
Use of felt-tip pens for writing
Writing on shiny blackboards is hard to read
Needs extra time to inspect objects, books, etc.
May have difficulty judging distances, stairs, ball games, etc.

Education of the visually handicapped in the UK is in a state of change at present,[320] for several reasons, including the fall in birth rate, the decline of retrolental fibroplasia, the increasing survival of children with very severe brain damage associated with cortical blindness, and the trend towards integration of the less severely handicapped into normal school.[319] Some teachers fear that their schools will be left only with mentally handicapped blind children, and the expertise needed to teach visually handicapped children of normal intelligence will be lost.

Employment for the visually handicapped school leaver, particularly in times of high unemployment, presents great problems. Some will overcome their handicap and succeed in a variety of occupations, and a few will take on the traditional occupations of the blind such as piano tuning. Unfortunately many will be virtually unemployable on the open market. Details of facilities for the adult blind are obtainable from the RNIB.

THE DEAF–BLIND CHILD

This devastating combination of handicaps is most frequently seen in the rubella syndrome, though this is becoming less common and is potentially preventable. Other rare causes include Usher's syndrome, Refsum's disease, congenital malformation syndromes, perinatal disorders, and acquired deafness in a blind child. The rarity of the double handicap makes management difficult since few education authorities have enough cases to justify provision of a specialist unit. In addition, these children may also suffer from mental retardation, cerebral palsy, or epilepsy.

Early management combines elements of the care outlined previously for both deaf and blind children.[321] Predictable daily routines of daily management, the development of the senses of touch and smell, and the encouragement of movement are vital. Communication is the greatest problem. Paget–Gorman or British Sign Language for the deaf may be used; the latter is now thought to be more suitable by many teachers. The child uses touch to 'read' the signs and the teacher helps him to make them himself by positioning his hands. The manual alphabet is used as soon as the child can master it.

Although this double handicap presents the parents with enormous problems, improved teaching methods give more hope for future development and communication and the parents should be encouraged to contact the relevant voluntary society for information and assistance (p. 492) and to purchase the useful book by Freeman (p. 495).

Chapter Sixteen
Cerebral Palsy

'Cerebral palsy' (CP) is an inclusive term for a number of disorders which share common problems of diagnosis and management.[322] It is not a single or specific condition and it would be more accurate to speak of the cerebral pals*ies*. Cerebral palsy is defined as 'a persistent but not necessarily unchanging disorder of posture and/or movement, due to a non-progressive lesion of the brain, acquired during the stage of rapid brain development'. When the effects of a progressive brain lesion, such as hydrocephalus or a tumour, are arrested or reversed by treatment, the child may be left with a non-progressive neurological deficit and such cases may conveniently be grouped with the cerebral palsies. The period of most rapid brain development is the first two or three years of life, although there is no exact age at which the above definition ceases to be applicable.

Although in some respects it is a useful concept, the term cerebral palsy is the cause of much confusion both among doctors and parents. There are several reasons for this.

1   The definition includes an enormous range of problems, from a minimal hemiplegia which has negligible effects on the child's life, to severe quadriplegia associated with profound mental handicap.

2   The layman's term for any child with CP is 'a spastic' but in fact the spastic type is only one form of CP.

3   To most laymen and many doctors, cerebral palsy is synonymous with perinatal brain damage, but often this is not the cause, or is only one of many contributory factors.

4   Many children with CP are mentally handicapped, but by definition the term refers only to the motor deficit; CP, however severe, is not incompatible with a normal intellect.

5   Although the underlying brain lesion is non-progressive, the movement disorder evolves over time and the final picture of, for example, athetosis may not be fully developed for some years. The movement problems exhibited by the infant or young child are often hard to classify into the traditional categories of CP.

6   Children in whom the main motor problem is hypotonia or ataxia are usually mentally retarded. Some doctors label these as having CP, while others regard them as primarily mentally handicapped with secondary motor delay.

7   There is little correlation between the nature of the cerebral insult and the severity or type of CP. The only exception to this is kernicterus, which is almost invariably followed by athetosis.

CLASSIFICATION

Cerebral palsy is usually classified according to the predominant neurological abnormality (e.g. spasticity) and the distribution of the abnormality (e.g. hemiplegia), as shown in Table 16.1. No two authors agree on the exact classification of CP. Some do not recognise the categories of rigidity or dyskinesia. There is no precise differentiation between diplegia with severe arm involvement and quadriplegia. Mixed forms with features of both spasticity and dyskinesia are common. The hypotonic and ataxic forms are not easily defined and therefore their prevalence varies substantially in published series.

As an alternative, the following simple classification is useful. It emphasises firstly the nature of the cerebral lesion and secondly the presenting features and functional problems of the child.

1. Unilateral, focal damage to an otherwise normal brain.   This appears to be the situation in most children with spastic hemiplegia. The upper motor neurone signs and the functional motor problems are mainly confined to the limbs on the affected side and the child's early motor development, though obviously characterised by asymmetry, passes through an essentially normal sequence.

2. Bilateral, widespread or generalised damage to a previously normal brain or abnormal development of the brain, indicated by bilateral motor abnormalities.   These children are further divided into two groups:

Table 16.1 Terminology used in cerebral palsy.

Term	Meaning
Spastic	In spastic cerebral palsy the dominant features are those of an upper motor neurone lesion with classic signs of pyramidal tract involvement; increased muscle tone of clasp-knife type, weakness, brisk reflexes, extensor plantars
Hemiplegia	There is an upper motor neurone lesion of the face, arm and leg, on one side of the body
Diplegia	There is upper motor neurone involvement of all four limbs but the legs are affected substantially more than the arms. Arm signs may range from severe to minimal. Diplegia may be symmetric or asymmetric
Quadriplegia or tetraplegia	These terms should be used to imply approximately equal involvement of legs and arms. It also may be symmetric or asymmetric
Paraplegia	There is involvement of the legs only. Pure paraplegia is suggestive of a spinal lesion rather than cerebral palsy
Double hemiplegia	Many cases described as quadriplegia are actually double hemiplegia. They are usually severely retarded and often epileptic. There is a pseudo-bulbar palsy (involvement of speech and swallowing musculature) due to bilateral upper motor neurone lesions
Monoplegia	There is involvement of one limb only. This is rare; usually there is a minimal hemiplegia
Rigidity	In rigidity, there is increased tone throughout the range of movement. This is often found in quadriplegic cases with severe mental handicap.
Dyskinesia	In dyskinesia, the dominant features are caused by damage to basal ganglia and extrapyramidal pathways. There are involuntary movements and changes in muscle tone, which usually involve the whole of the body though there may be some asymmetry. All motor activities including speech are affected. Dyskinesia and spasticity often occur together
Athetosis	Slow writhing movements of limbs, best seen on approach to an object when there is extension and fanning of the fingers and extension of the wrist
Chorea	Quick jerky movements of the limbs
Dystonia	Slow writhing movements of trunk and proximal limb muscles
Ataxia	Early hypotonia with very delayed walking. Gait is broad-based, and there is marked inco-ordination, tremor and titubation of the head
Hypotonia	There is diminished tone, persisting beyond the early months of life, caused by abnormality of the central nervous system. (Hypotonia due to lesions of the *lower* motor neurone is not cerebral palsy.)

1   Those with prominent pyramidal lesions, causing spasticity of variable severity, and/or extrapyramidal involvement, causing dyskinesia with or without rigidity. Often, pyramidal and extrapyramidal lesions coexist, but one or other is dominant. In contrast to the first group, these children tend to have more extensive abnormalities of early motor development. Their early motor progress is often very slow, and associated handicaps are more common and often more severe. This group includes the classic spastic diplegia (Little's disease), athetosis, the spastic and rigid quadriplegias and double hemiplegia.

2   Those whose pyramidal and extrapyramidal signs are minimal or absent. The main motor problem in infancy is usually hypotonia, but ataxia may appear later. The vast majority of these children are mentally retarded and this is often the presenting complaint. Their motor development is slow, but usually follows a fairly normal pattern. Eventually, all but the most severely retarded will walk and in later life any residual movement disorder may be of small importance and may disappear entirely. It is questionable whether the term 'cerebral palsy' should be used to describe such cases (*see* p. 383).

Incidence

Figures for the incidence of CP vary widely, because of the terminological difficulties described above.[323] In addition, there is no single system for reporting cases and the completeness of case finding is very variable. Estimates range from 1 to 4 per 1000 births in Western countries. There is some evidence that the incidence has fallen in recent years, but this trend is now levelling off. In Sweden, for example, the rate has fallen to 1.3 per 1000 children and remains around that figure. Non-specific improvements in socioeconomic conditions, general health and health care account for some of the decline. Better neonatal care probably accounts for the decrease in classic spastic diplegia (Little's disease) among prematures, although the exact factors which brought this about are not clear. Undoubtedly the elimination of rhesus disease is responsible for the disappearance of kernicterus as a cause of athetoid CP. Neonatal intensive care has certainly improved the survival of sick, low birthweight infants, at the cost of some increase in the number of handicapped survivors.[324] Intensive obstetric monitoring and intervention saves lives, but sometimes the very effectiveness of intervention salvages severely brain-injured babies who otherwise would have died. As a result of these changes, many clinics have an increasing proportion of children with profound and multiple handicap.

It will not be easy to achieve any further fall in CP rates. Improvements in obstetrics and in the care of low birthweight infants will undoubtedly continue but unexpected events such as prolapsed cord and neonatal meningitis can probably never be totally prevented. Furthermore, in most of the cases not directly associated with adverse perinatal events, the aetiology remains obscure and is not preventable by present means.

HEMIPLEGIA

This is probably the commonest type of CP now seen in the Western world. It may be congenital or acquired as a result of trauma, infection, or a vascular accident.

Congenital hemiplegia: early development

Most commonly, congenital hemiplegia is first suspected between 3 and 6 months when the parents observe asymmetry of hand function, but there is often a delay before they are sufficiently certain to seek advice. The affected hand shows a relative poverty of movement and is frequently tightly fisted (Fig. 16.1). Asymmetry of lower limb movement may not be so apparent at this stage though there may be a slight difference in reciprocal kicking, observed most easily while the baby has his bath. The hemiplegic leg extends when he is pulled to sitting (Fig. 16.2). Quite commonly, even the most meticulous examiner will find only minimal signs in the leg at this stage.

By the first birthday the hemiplegia is more obvious. In mild or doubtful cases the classical neurological signs of increased tone and reflexes may be

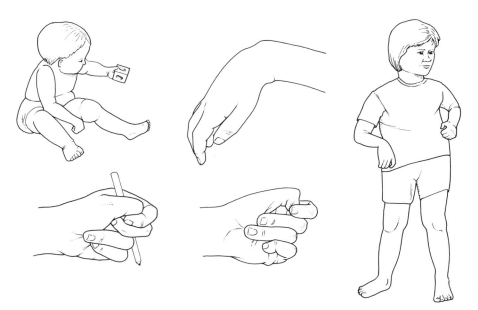

Fig. 16.1   The hemiplegic hand—variations in posture.

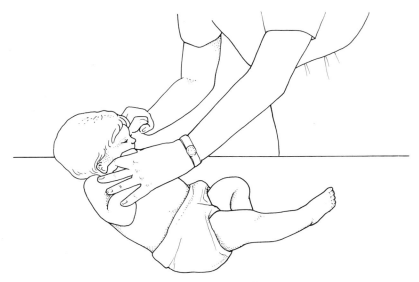

Fig. 16.2   Hemiplegia—note asymmetry of legs when pulled to sitting.

confirmed by asymmetry of the parachute response and the placing reaction (Fig. 16.3). Sitting and crawling are not very much delayed, but the mean age of walking is some 2–3 months later than the normal. Some hemiplegic children are also bottom-shufflers (p. 58) and these walk several months later than normal shufflers.

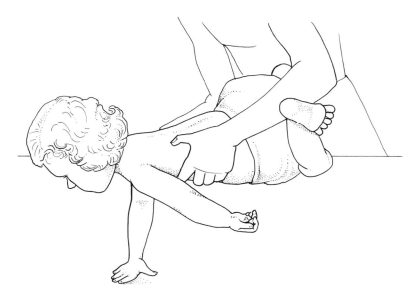

Fig. 16.3   Parachute reaction in hemiplegia.

When walking begins, the toddler's frequent falls and natural broad-based gait may rather obscure the abnormality in the hemiplegic limb but limp, spasticity and weakness gradually become more obvious, and this may create a mistaken impression of deterioration.

UPPER LIMB FUNCTION

The functional disability in the arm and hand may be categorised as follows:
1 Independent use of the hemiplegic hand.
2 Used as an active assistant to the normal hand.
3 Limited use, mainly for stabilisation and fixation.

The repertoire of hand skills in the normal baby is limited and the disability caused by a hemiplegic hand may not be very apparent in the first year. Because more is expected of the toddler and older child the problems become more evident in the second and third years, although in fact use of the upper limb is probably increasing over this period. As the child grows, the relative dwarfing of both arm and leg become more apparent and the later significance of a handicap which looks rather trivial in a 9-month-old baby should not be underestimated.

Hemiplegics are not all the same and observation reveals a number of different postures and strategies of hand use.[325] Many children have some tendency to hyperextend the wrist and fingers on approach to an object, suggesting that there is some dyskinesia. Some cortical sensory loss occurs in many cases and may be as important a cause of disability as the motor deficit.

Fig. 16.4 Right hemiplegia demonstrated by asking the child to run.

Associated movements are a common additional handicap in hemiplegia. When the child makes a movement with his normal limb, the hemiplegic limb makes postural changes which are not fully under its owner's control. This can be demonstrated by asking the child to run around a chair (Fig. 16.4) or undertake an activity needing intense concentration.

HEMIPLEGIA IN OLDER CHILDREN

In some cases a very mild congenital hemiplegia may be overlooked until 4 or 5 years of age and even then may only be revealed by a careful neurological examination. These cases are occasionally first diagnosed when referred for clumsiness or educational problems.

Acquired hemiplegia

The sudden occurrence of hemiplegia in infancy or childhood is well recognised. Some cases present with convulsions followed by hemiplegia, others with only a paralysis. There are many causes of this clinical picture which is often called the acute infantile hemiplegia syndrome (Table 16.2). Parents understand this event best if it is described as a stroke. Acquired hemiplegia may also result from trauma, intracranial infection or tumour.

In most cases of childhood stroke, language may be lost temporarily if the dominant hemisphere is involved, but permanent aphasia is rare. The

Table 16.2   Causes of acquired hemiplegia in childhood.

Infection
meningitis
encephalitis
Trauma
accidental
non-accidental
Space-occupying lesions (tumour, abscess)
Vascular disease
cerebral haemorrhage due to
vascular malformations
bleeding disorders
arterial occlusion:
direct injury to carotid
other trauma
homocystinuria
moya-moya
sickle-cell disease
emboli from heart disease
unknown
hypertensive encephalopathy

transfer of language to the undamaged hemisphere is not without cost; non-language functions are often impaired and there is a fall in I.Q. Although clearly this is related to lateralisation of function in the hemispheres, the traditional explanation that functions are 'transferred' is now known to be an oversimplification.[326,327] Rehabilitation of these children follows essentially the same pattern as for congenital hemiplegia.

Atypical hemiplegia

Some of the children who acquire a label of 'hemiplegia' have a variety of handicaps, of which hemiplegia is only one, and not necessarily the most important. They are often microcephalic, mentally retarded, mildly ataxic and may have a disproportionate delay in speech development. Assessment often reveals mild pyramidal signs on the apparently normal side, and sometimes the designation of double hemiplegia is more appropriate in that it draws attention to their multiple problems. In such cases the cause is more likely to be a diffuse or bilateral lesion than a single area of focal damage.

Other handicaps in children with hemiplegia

Speech and language development may be a few months delayed compared to the norm, but this is rarely a major problem. The mean I.Q. of children with hemiplegia is about 20 points lower than the norm, but in many cases the I.Q. is average or above average. Specific learning disabilities are also said to be more common. Right hemiplegia is slightly commoner than left. There is conflicting evidence on the differences in I.Q. and in the pattern of psychological deficits between right and left hemiplegia. Although there probably are some differences which are of considerable academic interest,[474] they are not sufficiently reliable to be useful in clinical or educational prediction.

DISORDERS OF SPECIAL SENSES

A routine check of hearing and vision should be made, but serious disorders are not commonly associated with hemiplegia. Hemianopia may occur; it is not easy to demonstrate in young children and a true field defect is probably less common than an attentional defect, but the distinction is mainly of academic interest and the educational significance is the same.

EPILEPSY

Throughout life there is an increased risk of epilepsy associated with hemiplegia. Published figures of 20–50% are rather high in the light of recent experience, because the increasing sophistication of developmental diagnosis brings to light a relatively larger proportion of children with very mild hemiplegia.

The risk of developing epilepsy is related to the severity of the neurological deficit, and is probably higher with acquired than with congenital hemiplegia. It has been suggested that an EEG should be performed in all cases of hemiplegia and that prophylactic anticonvulsants should be prescribed if the EEG shows 'epileptic' features even if the child has never had a fit. There is little to commend this approach; although there are statistical correlations in a large group of children between EEG abnormalities and the future occurrence of epilepsy, these are too unreliable to be used in the individual child. Furthermore, the first fit may occur at any time in childhood or in adult life, and many children, even those with very abnormal EEGs never have a fit at all. However, a few children develop severe epilepsy, often focal in onset with secondary generalisation, and this may be very difficult to control with anticonvulsants. Very rarely, such cases may benefit from hemispherectomy.

Causes and pathology

Although there may have been a history of minor abnormalities of pregnancy or birth, and the birthweight may have been above the mean, it is usually impossible to know the precise cause of a congenital hemiplegia. On occasion neonatal fits, either unilateral or bilateral, may have occurred, but are more likely the effect of, than the cause of the lesion. CT scanning often shows evidence of infarction of all or part of one cerebral hemisphere, with shrinkage due to atrophy and compensatory mild enlargement of the lateral ventricle (Fig. 16.12).[328] Sometimes a porencephalic cyst may form. Occlusion of the middle cerebral artery, or one of its branches, presumably causes these features, but both the reason and the time of its occurrence are usually obscure. A few cases of hemiplegia are caused by the Sturge–Weber syndrome and other malformations.[329]

Acquired hemiplegia may result from an obvious cerebral lesion but usually detailed investigation is necessary, since there are many possible causes as outlined above; however the majority of cases remain unexplained.

Differential diagnosis of hemiplegia

The current enthusiasm for early diagnosis of CP results in referral of some children with very minimal degrees of asymmetry. Some of these show the pattern described as *preferred head turning*.[330] This is probably an extreme variation of the normal asymmetry which can be detected in most babies. In most cases the right side is favoured. There is asymmetry of the skull (plagiocephaly) and the head is persistently turned to one or the other side, occasionally to the extent that a sternomastoid tumour is suspected. The fist

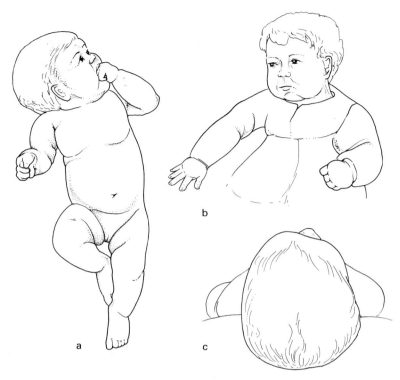

Fig. 16.5 **a** Typical trunk, lower limbs and occiput-upper limb posture in a 6-month-old baby. **b** Asymmetry of upper limb posture at 6 months. Child turns to sounds on right only. **c** Prominent left brow when seen from above. (Courtesy of Robson[330].)

on the occiput side is closed and movement in that limb is diminished (Fig. 16.5). There may, in addition, be a mild postural scoliosis. For the first few months, walking is asymmetrical (Fig. 16.6). All these signs gradually disappear.

Erb's palsy is occasionally mistaken for hemiplegia, but the physical signs in the arm are those of a lower motor neurone lesion and the leg is normal. Very rarely, lower motor neurone signs in the arm may be combined with spasticity of one or both legs: this combination suggests a cervical cord injury. Underdevelopment of one or both legs, sometimes associated with talipes and perhaps some sensory loss, may be indicative of *spinal dysraphism* (p. 369). *Old poliomyelitis* causes wasting with loss of reflexes, but in neglected cases where there are contractures and perhaps a vague history, the distinction from upper motor neurone lesions may not be as easy as it sounds.

Other causes of asymmetry of limb appearance and function include isolated deformities, such as bowing of the tibia, Poland's anomaly,

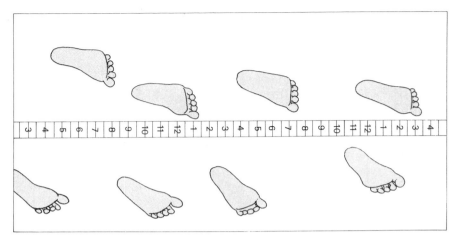

Fig. 16.6 Asymmetry of gait—footprints show line of march. (Courtesy of Robson[330].)

Sprengel's shoulder, and hemihypertrophy. The latter may be associated with aniridia (p. 294), Russell–Silver syndrome and Beckwith's syndrome. Provided one is aware of their existence, none of these should provide any diagnostic difficulty.

Orthopaedic disorders, such as congenital dislocation of the hip and rotational deformities (p. 58) sometimes cause confusion. Congenital dislocation of the hip is detectable by neonatal screening, using the manoeuvres described by Barlow and Ortolani, but some cases are missed by even the most expert examiner.[331] Beyond early infancy, the screening tests are unreliable, but there is usually other evidence of dislocation. Thigh abduction is limited, there is shortening of the leg on the affected side, and the femur can be moved up and down like a piston.[332] If the diagnosis is missed in the first year, the child presents with abnormal gait. The foot on the affected side is placed flat on the ground, and the opposite knee is flexed to make up for the shortening of the affected leg. When the dislocation is bilateral these signs are absent, but there is a lumbar lordosis and abduction may be reduced.[333,334]

Note that congenital dislocation of the hip does *not* cause substantial delay in walking. If a child presenting with delayed motor development is found to have dislocated hips, neurological disease should be suspected: cerebral palsy, spinal cord disorders, or muscle disease.

THE SPASTIC AND DYSKINETIC CEREBRAL PALSIES

This group of conditions is characterised by evidence of bilateral brain damage or disorder. Although there are cases with only minimal involvement, a substantial and persistent impairment of motor function is more usual and there are often multiple additional handicaps. In the majority of cases it is possible to identify the insult which caused the cerebral damage, though some are the result of unexplained genetic or prenatal factors.

Movement patterns in CP change continually over the first few years of life. It is extremely difficult to predict whether the child will eventually suffer from the spastic, dyskinetic or mixed form. The situation is further complicated by the lack of universally agreed description and interpretation of the abnormal movement patterns. For these reasons, the early evolution of the spastic and dyskinetic CPs will be considered together and the distinctive features of each type in the older child will then be described.

Early evolution of cerebral palsy

It is often said that there is a 'silent' period in the first few months following neonatal brain injury, during which the signs of CP are not detectable. In fact, subtle signs are often observed, though their interpretation can be extremely difficult.[335] There is usually some poverty of spontaneous movement and such movement patterns as are present are limited and stereotyped. Visual following, facial expression and 'turn-taking' behaviour in response to social stimuli are also often reduced. Motor milestones are delayed. Tone is variable; it is sometimes diminished and there may be marked head-lag, but the tendon reflexes are brisk and sustained ankle clonus may be present. Some infants may show marked spasticity from a very early stage, and extensor hypertonus affecting trunk and neck muscles is an important sign. Monitoring of the head circumference may reveal a fall-off in growth, suggestive of secondary microcephaly due to diminished growth of a brain severely damaged by anoxia, infection or other insults. Microcephaly is often associated with failure to thrive, which may be attributed both to brain damage and also to diminished food intake caused by impaired sucking and swallowing.

The physical signs of CP may be difficult to demonstrate in the first few months but they gradually become more obvious during the second half of the first year. There are three main features:[68,322,337]

1　Abnormalities of tone.
2　Delays in appearance of the normal postural reactions and therefore in motor milestones.
3　Persistent abnormal patterns of movement.

ABNORMALITIES OF TONE

Postural tone is often low in the period immediately following brain injury but gradually increases and eventually spasticity becomes apparent. The neurophysiology of spasticity in CP is complex and not fully understood. The loss of inhibitory mechanisms which normally control the excitability of motor neurones, and abnormal excitability of the gamma stretch-receptor system play an important role. There is a disturbance of reciprocal innervation (p. 51) which impairs the control of fine and complex movements and gives rise to apparent weakness. Superimposed on this abnormal postural tone is the effect of various reflexes described below, which cause sudden changes in tone; this phenomenon is particularly apparent in dyskinetic CP. In some babies, tone is increased in all positions, but in others it may be apparently reduced in the supine position but increased on vertical suspension or with sudden movements. It follows that a 'spastic' baby can be floppy and the fact that spasticity cannot be detected in all muscle groups at all times in CP (as it can in people with upper motor neurone lesions acquired later in life) is the source of much confusion and wrong diagnosis in CP.

DELAYS IN MOTOR DEVELOPMENT

These are usually apparent by 6 months of age. There is a poverty of normal spontaneous movement and such movements as are present are slow in initiation and execution, and stereotyped in pattern. The normal postural reflexes do not appear at the usual time and marked head-lag, delays in rolling over and in sitting are usually found. The parachute reactions develop slowly between 6 and 24 months; in the most severe cases they may never be more than fragmentary. Similarly, the Landau reflex is delayed. In infants with marked spasticity, extensor hypertonus may obscure the normal response and even leads occasionally to the erroneous diagnosis of advanced motor development! When hypotonia predominates, the infant may collapse into an inverted U shape (Fig. 16.7). This is not specific to CP and may occur in any condition associated with weakness or hypotonia of trunk musculature.

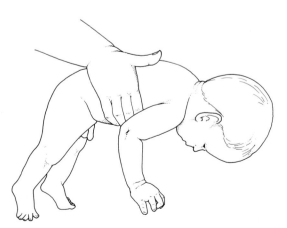

Fig. 16.7 Landau reaction in cerebral palsy.

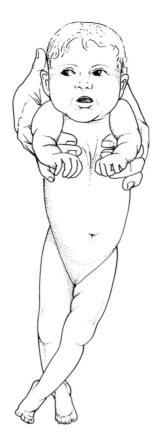

Fig. 16.8 Baby of 4 months with spastic tetraparesis in vertical suspension.

In the vertical position, the ability to weight-bear which is seen in the normal infant is impaired. Some evidence of a normal supporting reaction is seen by 12–15 months of age in infants whose predominant problem will be spasticity. In these babies there is often slight flexion of the hips and knees, equinus at the ankles and scissoring (Fig. 16.8). The placing response is not easily demonstrated. In infants who are destined to be dyskinetic, the supporting reaction may appear even later, at 18–27 months. These infants are more likely to be hypotonic when held vertically. There is little or no equinus and no scissoring, but the placing reaction is easily elicited. The 'slipping through the hands' sign (Fig. 16.9) characteristic of hypotonia may be present.

In the more severely affected cases, a pathologically intense positive supporting reaction is elicited as soon as the infant is held in vertical suspension or when the feet touch a surface. Tactile and proprioceptive stimuli cause reflex extension of the legs, back and neck, and adduction and internal rotation of the legs. This is called a 'dystonic reaction' by some authorities.

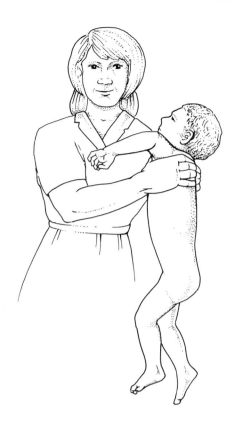

Fig. 16.9 When the hypotonic child is held up with an adult's hands under his armpits, his arms slide up and he 'slips through the hands'.

PERSISTENT ABNORMAL PATTERNS OF MOVEMENT

One of the most important diagnostic features of severe spastic and dyskinetic CP is the way in which a single movement sets off a complete stereotyped total body pattern—the baby with CP cannot make isolated discrete movements. The abnormal reflex patterns of movement are not merely due to retention of primitive reflexes; they are patterns which are never seen in the normal infant. These unwanted reflexes often become less powerful as the child matures and in the older child they may be quite difficult to demonstrate. In the most severely affected cases powerful abnormal patterns may persist throughout life.

The Asymmetric Tonic Neck Reflex (ATNR) is a reflex derived from proprioceptive receptors in the neck. Turning the child's head to one side will increase extensor hypertonus on the side to which the head is turned, (i.e. the face side) and flexor hypertonus on the occiput side (Fig. 16.10). It is usually stronger when the head is turned to the right. In the normal infant the ATNR is never obligate, i.e. the pattern may be imposed momentarily by

Fig. 16.10   Obligatory asymmetric tonic neck reflex.

turning the baby's head, but he can immediately break out of the pattern. In CP the ATNR is commonly obligate, i.e. the baby cannot escape from the pattern even when struggling. The ATNR persists for longer and is stronger in dyskinetic CP.

The ATNR causes marked asymmetry which is important in relation to scoliosis and hip dislocation, and it severely restricts the development of visually directed reaching and grasping.

The Symmetric Tonic Neck Reflex (STNR) and Tonic Labyrinthine Reflexes (TLR).   The STNR is a proprioceptive reflex derived from neck receptors. It is evoked by flexion or extension of the neck. When the neck is extended, the arms extend and the legs flex. Neck flexion has the opposite effect. The TLR is derived from stimuli originating in the labyrinths which monitor the position of the head in space. The effect of the TLR is to increase extensor

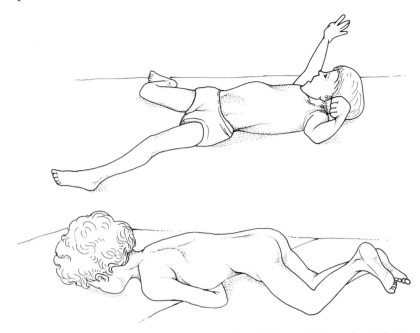

Fig. 16.11 Abnormal movements patterns, the STNR and TLR. (*Above*) Severe athetosis—extensor hypertonus in the supine position.
(*Below*) In spastic quadriplegia, there is total flexion of the head in the midline which causes difficulty in breathing in the prone position.

tone in supine and flexor tone in prone. The effects of these reflexes are illustrated in Fig. 16.11 but, in practice, their relative contribution is often very difficult to unravel.

Spastic diplegia

This was first described by Little in 1806. There is a strong association with abnormalities of pregnancy and delivery, and in particular with prematurity.[338] There has been a marked reduction in the incidence of classic Little's disease in recent years, which can probably be attributed to improvements in perinatal care, although it has not been possible to isolate one particular factor which is responsible. Probably better resuscitation, early feeding and controlled oxygen therapy have all played a part. However, the importance of perinatal factors should not be exaggerated,[19] since some cases of spastic diplegia are undoubtedly due to prenatal problems and in a minority of these the disorder is recessively inherited.

In the first 2 or 3 years of life, the child shows abnormalities of tone and reflex patterns, dystonia and delayed appearance of postural reflexes, as described above. He is frequently very irritable and difficult to handle. This phase merges into one in which spasticity alone is the most striking feature so that the child is no longer dominated by abnormal reflex patterns. The more rapidly this process happens, the better the prognosis. In some cases, usually those with very severe cerebral damage, profound hypotonia persists for many years and may be so severe that muscle disease is suspected. The history, upper motor neurone signs and associated mental handicap reveal the correct diagnosis. Such cases are sometimes called 'atonic diplegia'.

The extent of upper limb involvement is very variable: one side is often more severely involved than the other. Increase in tone and reflexes may be noted. Even in cases where these signs are minimal, careful observation of play and manipulation often reveals exaggerated grasp and release, and slowness of finger movements. A variable degree of dyskinesia may be present. In older children the tests described on p. 478 can be used to demonstrate these points. When upper limb involvement is severe, the terms quadriplegia or 'double hemiplegia' may be preferred. If there is no evidence of upper limb involvement, the term 'paraplegia' is more accurate. Although a pure paraplegia of cerebral origin can occur, it is rare and the possibility of a spinal lesion should always be considered (Fig. 16.12). To determine the level of the lesion, other evidence pointing to brain damage should be sought, such as impairment of intellect and speech, the presence of epilepsy and a history of cerebral insult. If none of these are found, a more detailed neurological assessment and perhaps a myelogram may be needed to exclude a spinal lesion (Table 16.5).

EARLY MOBILITY

Some children with mild diplegia may shuffle or roll; others progress by 'seal walking' (Fig. 16.13). Mild diplegias on average sit 2 months, stand 5 months, and walk 10 months later than the normal. In more severe cases, progress often seems very slow in the first 2 years but then continues steadily, reaching a plateau around the age of 7–8 years. The probability of eventual independent walking and crutch walking can be predicted by the age of 3 years,[339] using the criteria shown in Table 16.3.

The stance and gait of a diplegic are determined by the degree of spasticity and weakness in the lower limbs.[68] There is usually some undergrowth of the pelvis and legs and muscle bulk is diminished. There is flexion, adduction and internal rotation at the hips, flexion at the knees, and equinus and inversion of the feet (Fig. 16.14). Frequently contractures develop in these positions.

In order to walk, the child has to make excessive compensatory movements of the relatively uninvolved upper half of the body to maintain balance. He cannot shift his weight easily from one leg to the other. He may solve this difficulty by leaning the trunk backwards to raise one leg and

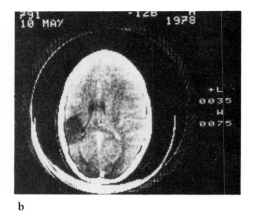

a

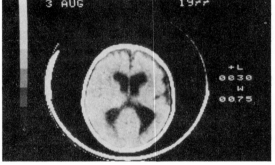

b

c

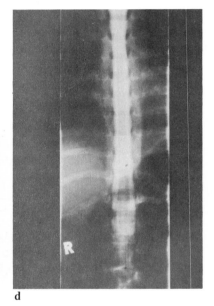

d

Fig. 16.12 a Mild spastic diplegia and severe mental handicap with cortical blindness, cause unknown; bilateral cortical atrophy and ventricular dilatation. **b** Severe right hemiplegia and focal epilepsy; left hemisphere atrophy and infarction. **c** Mild left hemiplegia. Right hemisphere infarction with ventricular dilatation. **d** Paraplegia possibly caused by shaking. Myelogram showing atrophy of spinal cord at T4.

bring it forward; the body is then thrown forwards to transfer his weight. Alternating sideways trunk flexion is the preferred mode of progression for some children. The pattern of spasticity leads to a tiptoe gait with the body weight on the inside of the foot, scissoring due to adduction and inwards rotation of the thighs, thoracic kyphosis and lumbar lordosis.

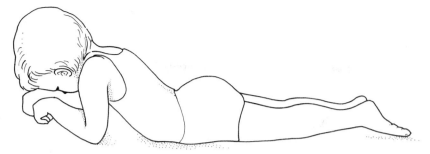

Fig. 16.13   Spastic diplegia—'seal walking'.

Table 16.3   Prognosis for ambulation in spastic diplegia. (From Beals.)

Severity Index (SI): motor age in months at chronological age 3 years
Range: 0–36
Examples:
    Motor age = 9: assume sitting position unassisted, sit for 5 minutes, stand holding
    onto rail
    Motor age = 10: roll, creep and sit, pull to stand
    Motor age = 12: walk with one hand held

Prognosis
    SI ⩾ 12 ∼ Free ambulation by age 7 years
    SI ⩾ 9 ∼ Ambulation ± crutches
    SI < 10 ∼ Free ambulation rarely achieved

Quadriplegia and double hemiplegia

Severe rigidity or spasticity affecting all four limbs is described variously as quadriplegia or double hemiplegia. Although it is possible to distinguish spastic or rigid quadriplegia from double spastic hemiplegia (Table 16.1), in practice such refinement is of doubtful importance. In many respects the features are similar to those of diplegia, but upper limb involvement is severe; the child's arms are inwardly rotated, the elbows are either extended or tightly flexed, and the hands are often fisted (Fig. 16.15). In many of these children, the severe motor disorder is associated with profound mental handicap and often other disabilities such as cortical blindness or epilepsy (which is often of the myoclonic type and responds well to clonazepam).

CAUSES

These include abnormal brain development, intrauterine damage or very severe perinatal or postnatal brain injury (p. 228). Microcephaly is commonly associated with these disorders (p. 215).

Fig. 16.14 Gait of spastic diplegic child. Note the position of the hands, lordosis, inwards rotation of the thighs and inability to place the heels on the ground.

Dyskinetic cerebral palsy—athetosis

The term 'dyskinesia' includes athetosis, chorea, and dystonia; but athetosis is usually the most striking clinical feature and this term will be used in the following discussion. Athetosis is nearly always caused by either perinatal anoxia or kernicterus.[340] Rarely, it is the end result of encephalitis, and occasional cases of prenatal or genetic origin have been described.[341]

In athetosis, there are violent and extreme fluctuations of tone, so that hypertonia and hypotonia may both be found in the same patient within moments of each other. In pure athetosis the basic postural tone is low, but a mixed picture of spasticity and athetosis is more commonly found. The ATNR plays a prominent part in these unwanted movement patterns. The head turns, the face grimaces, and the arms, trunk and legs execute bizarre writhing movements, which are usually bilateral, though there is often some asymmetry. True hemiathetosis is rare. All of the abnormal movements disappear in sleep.

In the early years, head control is poor and postural reflexes are very late to appear.[450] The child learns to make use of those abnormal patterns which are under some degree of voluntary control. He may use the ATNR pattern to turn towards and grasp an object, but the grasp is weak and objects are released too early and without voluntary control. There is often a back-handed grasp with hyperextension of the fingers (Fig. 16.16).

Fig. 16.15   Spastic quadriplegia.

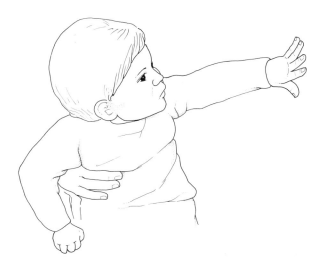

Fig. 16.16   Athetosis—a back-handed attempt to grasp an object with extension-abduction of fingers.

Athetoid movements in the upper limbs may appear between 1 and 3 years or even later on occasion. Their early appearance is indicative of *less* severe athetosis, since the more severe cases have little or no useful hand function in the first two years. A degree of ataxia is often superimposed on the athetosis. The young athetoid child may be able to sit on the floor with extended and abducted legs, but he cannot sit alone in a chair; he either collapses forward with total flexion or falls backwards in total extension. It may take years to achieve standing and walking and in some cases this is never possible. The athetoid walks with hyperextended hips and knees and an exaggerated high stepping gait, and leans backwards, extending the shoulder girdle and trunk, to reinforce extensor tone and prevent a sudden collapse into flexion.

Independent walking and improvement in speech may be achieved as late as the early teens but the most severely afflicted cases will require an electric wheelchair and an alternative means of communication. Fortunately some control of eye movements is often preserved and this may provide at least the ability to give a yes/no response. Adults with severe athetosis face particular problems of independence and social contact since the bizarre involuntary movements, together with incomprehensible speech, frequently lead the general public to regard them as mentally retarded or ill. Later in life, they may suffer from degenerative joint disease, particularly affecting the cervical spine, because of the constant abnormal movements.

Other handicaps

SPASTIC DIPLEGIA AND QUADRIPLEGIA

Intelligence may be normal even in severe cases, but in general there is a reduction in intellect which is proportional to the severity of the physical handicap. Learning disabilities of all kinds may occur. Bilateral upper motor neurone lesions cause a pseudobulbar palsy and therefore swallowing, chewing and speech may be affected and dribbling is a continuing nuisance. Epilepsy is said to occur in one-fifth of cases of diplegia and in a higher proportion of quadriplegics, but is seldom a major problem. As in hemiplegia, the EEG is of dubious value in predicting the development of epilepsy in the individual child and 'prophylactic' anticonvulsants are not indicated for children who have never had fits. Sensorineural hearing loss is unusual in spastic diplegia, although the incidence of conductive hearing loss due to secretory otitis is at least as high as in normal children.

There is a high incidence of eye defects including uniocular and alternating squint, and refractive error. Cataract, retinopathy and retrolental fibroplasia should be excluded by the ophthalmologist. Cortical visual defects of varying degree are common. In some cases other disturbances of eye movement are seen (p. 293) including an inability to initiate smooth following movements, so that the child has to move the whole head in order to track a moving object. This is a form of oculomotor apraxia (which may also occur as an isolated disorder). Dysconjugate movements and an unusual coarse fluttering of the eyes are also seen occasionally and these are sometimes mistaken for minor epilepsy.

ATHETOSIS

Mental retardation of variable degree is common but intelligence is preserved more often in the face of severe physical handicap than in other kinds of CP, and the head circumference is often normal, reflecting the localised nature of the brain damage. Dysarthria and severe delays in speech development are common. Approximately one-fifth of cases have high-frequency deafness. In cases due to kernicterus, loss of upward gaze and dental enamel hypoplasia are also seen. Epilepsy is relatively rare. Subluxation of joints may occur because of the continual movements, but for the same reason contractures are rare. Orthopaedic surgery is rarely helpful in athetosis.

Causes of severe cerebral injury

Perinatal problems are by far the most important cause of the bilateral cerebral palsies. Severe anoxic–ischaemic injury and the complications of extreme prematurity are the most important, but hypoglycaemia, neonatal meningitis, kernicterus and many others account for some cases. The commonest pathological findings are summarised in Table 16.4.

There are probably many prenatal factors which predispose an infant to the development of CP following an episode of anoxia. Mothers of CP infants have a poorer reproductive history than controls, as measured by fertility, fetal loss, toxaemia, bleeding and abnormalities in other siblings. Prematurity itself is not a random occurrence but is related to many social and

Table 16.4   Sequelae of hypoxaemic–ischaemic injury. (From work of Volpe.[342])

Lesion	Distribution	Pathological findings	Sequelae
Neuronal necrosis (hypoxaemia)	Cortex, especially hippocampus; cerebellum; thalamus; brain stem nuclei	Neuronal death, sclerotic microgyria	Quadriplegia, hemiplegia, ataxia, retardation, fits
Status marmoratus (hypoxaemia)	Caudate, putamen, globus pallidus, thalamus	Neuronal death, astrocytic gliosis, hypermyelination (often other hypoxaemic lesions)	Choreoathetosis
Watershed infarction (ischaemia)	Arterial border zones	Necrosis of cortex and subcortical white matter (often hypoxaemic lesions as well)	Neonatal: hip–shoulder pattern of weakness Later: focal deficits including ? associative functions
Periventricular leucomalacia (ischaemia)	Periventricular white matter in end-artery zones	Necrosis of white matter, cavitation, widening of ventricles; may be associated hydrocephalus	Spastic diplegia of prematurity

medical factors. Obstetric accidents and sometimes mismanagement may be contributory factors but should not too readily be assumed to be the complete explanation for CP.[19] In some cases, the perinatal history is normal or reveals only trivial problems. It is most unwise to assume that minor events such as a forceps delivery are the cause of the handicap. Other possibilities should be considered, such as cerebral malformation, an abnormality of neuronal migration, a congenital infection, a metabolic defect, or some other slowly progressive disorder (see below). Dysmorphic features sometimes provide valuable evidence of abnormal fetal development dating from early in pregnancy. Some of these prenatally determined cerebral palsies are inherited, and inappropriate genetic advice is inevitable if too much emphasis is placed on perinatal problems. There are no exact figures for the risk of recurrence in cases that cannot be explained by perinatal events, but for parents who have one child affected by unexplained spastic diplegia, the recurrence risk may of the order of 1 in 10. Spastic diplegia also occurs as a feature of several syndromes (*see* below).

PERINATAL BRAIN INJURY

Cerebral anoxia and hypoperfusion are the two most damaging aspects of perinatal brain injury. Severe asphyxia in the full-term baby is followed by a characteristic series of events.[342] In the first few hours, the baby is hypotonic and often unresponsive. This phase is followed by increasing irritability and frequent seizures. Then, on the 2nd and 3rd day there may be either steady deterioration, a rapid return to normal tone and behaviour, or an increase in tone—often associated with bulbar palsy. Skilled neonatal intensive care increases survival in these cases, and may minimise further brain damage, but it cannot reverse damage which has already occurred. Prolonged hypotonia is an ominous sign, whereas a rapid return to normal tone is associated with a better prognosis. Prolonged need for tube feeding (longer than one week), apnoeic attacks, apathy, fits, hypothermia, high pitched or 'cerebral' cry and vomiting are all bad prognostic signs associated with death or future severe handicap. The features of brain injury due to causes other than hypoxia and hypoperfusion are similar but their evolution differs according to the nature of the insult. It is never possible to be certain that a baby will be handicapped and quite severe neurological signs may subsequently resolve.

In premature infants it is probably the complications rather than prematurity itself which cause handicap. In these infants the signs of brain injury are seldom so clearly differentiated. Many of the features regarded as sinister in the full-term baby have less significance in the premature. Information about adverse events such as recurrent prolonged apnoeic spells not responding to stimulation is necessary in assessing the likely outcome. Intraventricular haemorrhage has been demonstrated by ultrasound to be very common and is not necessarily followed by handicap.

Some dilatation of the ventricles may also occur but it is not yet clear whether this should necessarily be regarded as hydrocephalus, and the extent to which it is followed by permanent disability is still in doubt.

KERNICTERUS

Kernicterus is a syndrome of neonatal neurological dysfunction caused by the deposition of bilirubin in the basal ganglia. It is usually seen between 2 and 5 days of age. There is apathy and hypotonia, interspersed with spasms and episodes of opisthotonus. In full-term babies, kernicterus very rarely occurs with bilirubin levels below 329 μmol/l, but sick premature infants may suffer damage at lower levels. The commonest cause of severe hyperbilirubinaemia used to be rhesus incompatibility, but this has now been almost eliminated in developed countries, and ABO incompatibility and a variety of hereditary disorders such as G6PD deficiency have become relatively more important.

Kernicterus has a high mortality, and handicap is common in the survivors. The usual picture is of athetoid CP. Kernicterus is the only neonatal cerebral insult in which the pattern of future handicap can be predicted with some confidence.

Minor degrees of neonatal jaundice, in the absence of associated neurological dysfunction, should not readily be accepted as the cause of CP, deafness or any other handicap.

POSTNATAL CEREBRAL DAMAGE

This rarely leaves the child with CP alone; there is more often a degree of mental handicap as well. A list of the more important postnatal causes of brain damage is given on p. 228.

Differential diagnosis

Variations in normal motor development in the first 12–15 months of life are common and it may be extremely difficult to distinguish these from cerebral palsy. A firm diagnosis of CP should not be made until it is clear that the abnormal signs are permanent.

Tip-toe gait is seen both in normal children and also in the mentally retarded and autistic. In many cases, careful observation shows that they are capable of walking with a plantigrade foot and the tendo-Achilles tightness can be overcome by steady pressure. Tendon lengthening in these cases is seldom indicated and may have adverse effects. Genuine congenital tightness of the TA in the absence of neurological disorder also occurs, although the explanation is obscure, and surgical treatment may then be necessary.

Miscellaneous disorders.   It is worth re-emphasising that CP is not in itself a diagnosis and is not always caused by perinatal brain damage. Intrauterine infections, unexplained abnormalities of neuronal development and migration and genetic factors must be considered. Motor disorder is a feature of

Table 16.5 Differential diagnosis of cerebral palsy.

Normal variations in motor development:
Hypertonia and dystonia
Hypotonia—bottom-shufflers
Preferred head-turning

Static disorders:
Dysmorphic syndromes
   congenital infections (spasticity)
   Cornelia de Lange (hypertonicity)
   Cockayne (ataxic gait and/or spasticity)
   Sjögren–Larsson (spastic diplegia)
   Marinesco–Sjögren (ataxia)
   ataxia-telangiectasia (ataxia and choreoathetosis)
   incontinentia pigmenti (spasticity)

Static motor defects:
   congenital chorea
   familial tremor
   paroxysmal choreoathetosis
   stiff-baby syndrome

Biochemical disorders:
Homocystinuria (variable; often asymmetric spasticity)
Untreated PKU (spasticity)
Hartnup disease (intermittent ataxia)
Lesch–Nyhan syndrome (choreoathetosis)
Propionic acidaemia (intermittent athetosis)
Metachromatic leukodystrophy and other lysosomal storage disorders
Abetalipoproteinaemia

Neurodegenerative disorders:
Familial spastic paraplegia
Behr's syndrome (spasticity ± optic atrophy)
Leber's disease (spasticity ± eye defects)
Devic's disease (spasticity ± eye defects)
Spinocerebellar degenerations (ataxia)
Mitochondrial cytopathy (mixed myopathic and pyramidal signs)

Neurosurgical disorders:
Slow-growing gliomata and other tumours (brain or spinal cord)
Atlanto-axial and foramen magnum disorders (spinal cord compression-spasticity)
Spinal dysraphism
Hydrocephalus

many dysmorphic syndromes and other specific diseases (Table 16.5). In many of these the motor deficit is progressive but deterioration is so slow that they masquerade as CP. These conditions should be recognised because of their implications for treatment and genetic counselling. For practical purposes, however, management is often identical to that of CP, except that the expected rate of deterioration must be considered before embarking on orthopaedic procedures.

Minimal cerebral palsy. In a few so-called 'clumsy' children (p. 398), careful neurological examination reveals mild but definite 'hard' signs of minimal spastic diplegia and/or dyskinesia. The term 'minimal cerebral palsy' should be reserved for these cases and should not be applied to those children who have only soft signs.

INVESTIGATIONS

Cerebral palsy is essentially a clinical diagnosis and investigation can make only a limited contribution unless unusual causes or conditions are suspected. In some cases of hemiplegia, skull X-ray shows that on the side of the lesion the cranial cavity is smaller, the skull is thicker and the petrous ridge is elevated. The air spaces of the frontal sinus and temporal bone are enlarged. These changes develop slowly. A CT scan is useful both to delineate the extent of the lesion, and to rule out very rare progressive or treatable causes, such as tumours, angiomas, etc.

The yield of plain skull X-rays and CT scanning[328] is small in cases with spastic diplegia and quadriplegia and in athetosis. Malformations, ventricular dilatation, cerebral atrophy or more rarely unexpected evidence of congenital infection may be detected but the abnormalities found are rarely helpful in further management and are not specific enough to assist in genetic counselling.

HYPOTONIC AND ATAXIC CEREBRAL PALSIES

These present different problems of diagnosis and management from those seen in spastic and dyskinetic cerebral palsies.

Ataxic cerebral palsy

In the neonatal period these babies are usually floppy and inactive. In infancy motor and speech development are slow and hypotonia is usually persistent, and it may be impossible to distinguish these children from others with central hypotonia (*see* below). Walking may begin as late as the 3rd or 4th year and the child may show a persistent fear of falling, so that he walks with hands held out for many months before achieving independent

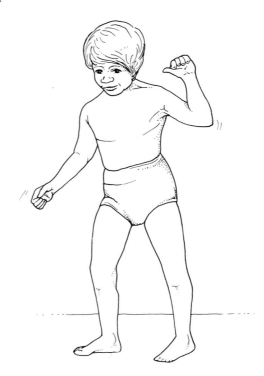

Fig. 16.17   Ataxia—broad-
based gait; exaggerated
balancing movements of
hands.

walking (Fig. 16.17). Exaggerated balancing movements of the arms are
often seen. The classic signs of a cerebellar lesion may be found, with the
exception of nystagmus which is rarely seen.[77,345]

Many of these children are mentally handicapped and it may be difficult
to decide whether the child shows simple motor delay, with the normal
toddler phase of a broad-based unsteady gait prolonged by the retardation,
or whether the term 'ataxic cerebral palsy' is applicable. Probably this term
should be reserved for those cases with unequivocal cerebellar signs. It is
rare that one can make a sufficiently precise diagnosis to be of value in
genetic counselling, and often the point is somewhat academic, but it
causes confusion among parents and therapists and largely explains the
wide differences in the incidence of ataxic CP quoted by various authors.

The prognosis for ataxic CP depends more on the extent of any
associated mental handicap than on the cerebellar disorder itself.

CAUSES

Most cases are of prenatal origin and are probably due to malformation of
the cerebellum and its connections. Congenital cytomegalovirus infection
occasionally causes a pattern of multiple handicap in which ataxia
predominates. Postnatal cases may result from meningitis, encephalitis,

encephalopathy, trauma or tumours. Ataxic diplegia is the commonest motor handicap associated with hydrocephalus. There is a rare form of atypical ataxia which is recessively inherited; the condition has been given the name of 'dysequilibrium' syndrome.

There are many causes of acquired ataxia and a number of slowly progressive syndromes which appear at various ages throughout childhood (Table 16.5). It may sometimes be difficult to distinguish these from non-progressive ataxic cerebral palsy and a full neurological evaluation is essential.

Hypotonic cerebral palsy

This category of cerebral palsy is so difficult to define that it may be better to avoid the term altogether, and instead regard hypotonia as a problem requiring differential diagnosis.

Hypotonia may present in the neonatal period as the 'floppy baby syndrome' or at any time in infancy, when hypotonia is usually associated with a presenting complaint of delayed milestones. It is convenient to divide the causes of hypotonia into normal variation (*see* p. 56), central causes, and peripheral causes.

HYPOTONIA OF CENTRAL ORIGIN

Many babies with perinatal brain injury pass through a period of hypotonia before spasticity or dyskinesia become apparent. This is most marked immediately after the cerebral insult, but may persist for many months. Usually muscle tone is variable and dependent on handling and posture. Tendon reflexes are brisk. Knowledge of the causative event, the variations in tone and the presence of an obligatory ATNR clearly indicate a central cause for the hypotonia.

Global mental retardation is the other major central cause of hypotonia. There is no difficulty in recognising the child with a dysmorphic mental handicap syndrome, but children of normal appearance may cause confusion. Unlike the primarily brain injured group described above, these infants are usually hypotonic in all positions. There is often an increased range of passive movement. Tendon reflexes are variable. The ATNR may be elicited more easily than normal up to the age of 8 or 9 months but is seldom obligatory and one rarely sees the abnormal total movement patterns which occur in severe spastic or dyskinetic cerebral palsy. There is some limb activity and weakness is not an important feature.

These children show extreme motor delay rather than persistent abnormalities of posture or movement which are the hallmark of CP, and are better described as having mental retardation with associated hypotonia and motor delay. The diagnosis depends on recognition of the delayed intellectual, communicative and social development. Some of these children will later be found to be ataxic, but it may be impossible to recognise these during the first year of life.

Causes.   The differential diagnosis is essentially that of mental retardation (p. 196). Disorders of aminoacid and organic acid metabolism should be excluded. A CT scan may reveal cerebral malformations such as absence of the corpus callosum. It should be remembered that the Prader–Willi syndrome which can be associated with profound hypotonia is easily overlooked in infancy (p. 210).

HYPOTONIA OF PERIPHERAL ORIGIN

There are numerous disorders of the anterior horn cell, peripheral nerve (lower motor neurone), muscle end-plate or muscle. Werdnig–Hoffman disease (p. 373) is by far the commonest of these. Congenital myopathies and myasthenia are very rare. Infants with peripheral hypotonia show severe weakness. They are unable to support their limbs against gravity or withdraw from a painful stimulus. The ATNR cannot be elicited. In Werdnig-Hoffman disease tendon reflexes are absent. Social responsiveness and intellectual development are usually unimpaired, except in a few of the rare myopathies.

Werdnig–Hoffman disease can usually be recognised clinically and, if it can be excluded, the statistical probability in the hypotonic child is strongly in favour of a central cause, since the many forms of mental retardation are commoner than congenital myopathies or neuropathies.

There are several uncommon disorders of connective tissue which cause laxity of joints.[454] These children are not necessarily hypotonic but they have a markedly increased range of passive movement which can be mistaken for hypotonia. Three of these—Larsen, Ehlers–Danlos and Marfan syndromes—are described briefly in Appendix 1.[454]

MANAGEMENT OF CEREBRAL PALSY—GENERAL PRINCIPLES

Most children with CP are multiply handicapped and require multidisciplinary assessment and care.[347] Table 16.6 summarises the numerous aspects of management. Parents must receive adequate explanation of the nature of CP and the associated handicaps, and genetic advice is offered where appropriate. For most children an attitude of cautious optimism is justified, but in those with profound and multiple handicap, the goals of management are of necessity limited. At the same time, hope of progress must not be destroyed. Professional staff have to disregard their own feelings of helplessness about such cases and should share the parents' pleasure in every small step forward.

Table 16.6 Management of cerebral palsy.

Accurate diagnosis
Counselling of parents
   on diagnosis and prognosis
   genetic advice
Guidance from therapists
Psychological assessment
Help with behaviour problems
   (prevention and treatment)
Educational advice
Nursery and school placement
Respite care
Special equipment
Financial support
Introduction to voluntary societies
Dental care (fluoride, dental hygienist)
Ophthalmic examination
Hearing test
Orthopaedic supervision
Immunisation

Early management

Inevitably, modern neonatal intensive care, with its emphasis on high technology, sometimes results in the survival of a handicapped infant who otherwise would have died. The parents may have serious reservations about the wisdom of having saved the baby's life, but seldom find it possible to express their resentment to the doctors and nurses who fought so hard to save him. They may find it very hard to love and care for the baby. Neonatologists now recognise the importance of early bonding and the dangers of 'bonding failure' (p. 28), and parents are given every encouragement to participate in the care of even the smallest or sickest babies. The care and empathy of the paediatric staff and mutual support by other parents during these difficult weeks have a considerable effect on the parents' ability to cope with any subsequent handicap.[348] Bonding failure is not a problem beyond the neonatal period, but otherwise the same points may be made about postnatally acquired handicap.

The initial follow-up care of a potentially handicapped infant should ideally be the responsibility of the paediatrician who cared for the child in hospital. It is quite unacceptable for this to be delegated to a succession of inexperienced junior staff. A referral to the physiotherapist may be appreciated; she can counsel the parents on various aspects of handling and management and is able to support them during this period of great anxiety.

Parents in Western society are well aware of the effects of brain damage and are often more realistic than their doctors. It is futile to pretend that all is well when a child is showing obvious signs of cerebral damage, and most parents prefer an honest appraisal of the situation.

Early recognition by developmental surveillance

Surveillance of babies who have suffered a cerebral insult is the commonest way in which the more severe cases of CP are diagnosed. In this situation a high index of suspicion is easily maintained. Many cases of hemiplegia and some of diplegia are first recognised by the parents. In the absence of a known cerebral insult or early parental suspicion, early recognition of CP by developmental surveillance is extremely difficult. There is wide variation in normal milestones, and a number of infants show unusual patterns of movement, such as hypotonia, irritability, persistent primitive reflexes, and hypertonia with dystonic posturing and scissoring (p. 56), yet eventually are perfectly normal.

The belief that early diagnosis is beneficial results in referral of numerous infants who turn out to be normal, but there is in fact no clear evidence that early recognition of cerebral palsy is rewarded by a substantially better outcome. Furthermore, although some cerebral palsies are of prenatal origin, the inheritance of these can rarely be established with sufficient precision to be useful in genetic counselling. If there is no history of cerebral insult, and the parents are not worried, a few months' further observation is often the wisest course of action when abnormalities of motor development are suspected.

The role of the therapists

The following discussion is oriented specifically to cerebral palsy, but similar principles apply to other physical handicaps. It is vital that therapy should be planned with specific goals in mind; for example, prevention of deformity, attainment of a good sitting posture, or independent walking. Both short term and long term goals should be set. Positioning and mobilisation in general follow the normal sequence of development, although it is quite unnecessary to insist that the child passes through each stage in turn (Fig. 16.18); for example, it may be desirable to provide a means of mobility for a child who cannot even sit on his own.

In an effective multidisciplinary team the occupational therapist and physiotherapist work so closely together that their separate roles cannot be clearly identified. The occupational therapist is usually better trained to advise on equipment such as wheelchairs, seating and bathing equipment, and on play materials and activities, whereas the physiotherapist is more expert in the handling and mobilisation of the child.

The primary goals of therapy are to enable the physically handicapped child to make maximum use of the movements under his control, and to prevent deformity. Many have questioned whether physiotherapy 'works'.

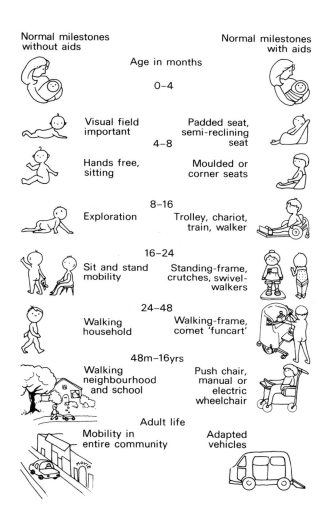

Fig. 16.18 Planned mobilisation for children with physical handicaps.

It is doubtful whether even the most skilled or intensive therapy can significantly change the neurophysiological functioning of the damaged brain, and few therapists would now claim to 'cure' cerebral palsy. However the therapist is much more than a mover of limbs; she is responsible for supervising the child's total physical management and mobilisation, and in addition frequently becomes the family's main confidante. It will probably never be possible to evaluate the effectiveness of individual physiotherapy treatments, but the value of the service as a whole is beyond question.

There are numerous systems of physical treatment for children with cerebral palsy.[349] The system devised by Vojta involves a series of reflex trigger zones to stimulate movement patterns. The Kabat method of proprioceptive neuromuscular facilitation (PNF) aims at increasing power of a movement by giving the child kinaesthetic sensation of that movement.

The Peto system is a unique approach in which children are treated by one person, called a conductor, who is trained in both therapy and education. The children carry out all movements themselves, while vocalising their activities together. This is believed to give mastery over essential movements and encourage independence.

The contribution of the Bobaths to the understanding of CP deserves particular mention. Their neurodevelopmental therapy is now widely used throughout the world. A detailed description of the principles and practice of this method will be found elsewhere,[68] but the techniques can only be mastered by practical experience. The approach is based on the reduction of unwanted and abnormal movements by means of reflex inhibiting patterns, and the facilitation of normal postural and balance reactions. The Bobath method was elaborated and modified by Finnie to produce an excellent approach to all aspects of daily management. Her book is essential reading for all those involved with cerebral palsied children.[350]

The simplest physiotherapy technique is passive stretching, which is intended to reduce the risk of contracture. This seems to be effective in some situations. However, although the term 'contracture' implies a true *reduction* in length, *unequal growth* may be the cause of many contractures and in these stretching is unlikely to be effective. Similarly, night splints are recommended by some authorities to prevent progressive deformities but the results seldom justify the effort involved in preparing and fitting them each night.

Whichever system of treatment is adopted, the need for, and frequency of regular therapy sessions should be reviewed at intervals.

SITTING AND STANDING

The young child with powerful abnormal reflex patterns is very difficult to handle. He does not easily adapt his body posture to normal cuddling or nursing. When distressed or angry, he may go into extensor spasm associated with spasm of hip adductors, a movement which often seems to be the only one under voluntary control and therefore his only means of protest. This behaviour is minimised by correct handling (Fig. 16.19). Seating similarly should be arranged to take account of abnormal movement patterns. Prone lying over a wedge and side lying are useful alternatives to the supine position (Fig. 16.20). Regular changes of position are desirable to reduce the risks of deformity and contracture.

Devices such as the standing frame and prone board (Fig. 16.21) are a useful intermediate stage in mobilisation, giving the child experience of the upright posture. Even for severe cases who will never walk, they are valuable in preventing deformity, and have the additional advantage of freeing the hands for play activities. Provided the child is placed in a symmetrical posture, early standing may be beneficial: early weight-bear-

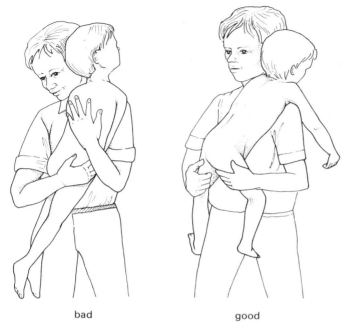

bad   good

Fig. 16.19   An example of good and bad handling. (Reproduced from Finnie[350] by permission.)

ing probably improves the development of the acetabulum and reduces the risk of dislocation. In the school-age child, a good stable seat, with the feet firmly on the floor or if necessary on a box, and a table at the correct height, are vital (Fig. 16.22); these simple measures are too often neglected, with detrimental effects on the child's mastery of writing and drawing.

MOBILITY

The physiotherapist may provide a variety of aids for the child who is beginning to walk. Firm boots help to maintain a plantigrade foot in the spastic child, and give a stable base for the ataxic. Modern boots such as 'Piedro' look smart and are far more socially acceptable than the old-fashioned surgical boots. Modern plastics allow the quick construction of lightweight splints which can be worn inside the boot to help maintain the feet in good position. Calipers are no longer popular for children with cerebral palsy, since they are heavy and do not usually improve the gait sufficiently to justify their weight and inconvenience. (They are of course essential in many other physical handicaps, for example lower motor neurone lesions, spina bifida and traumatic paraplegia.) Crutches, tripods, walking frames, swivel-walkers and sticks all have their uses. A lightweight

Fig. 16.20 Side-lying board.

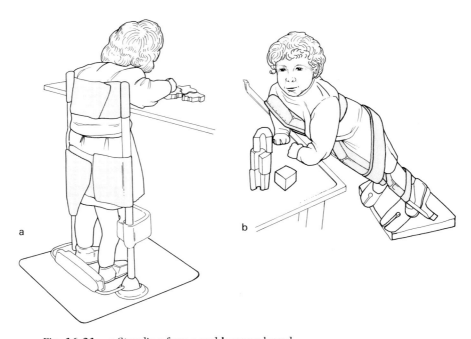

Fig. 16.21 **a** Standing frame and **b** prone board.

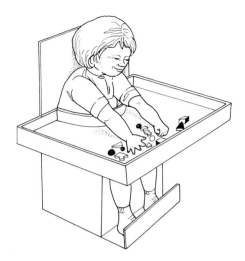

Fig. 16.22   Integral seat and table.

helmet may reduce the amount of trauma to the head if the child falls frequently, for example in ataxic CP.

A child's pushchair should be individually selected, since slight differences in design can have a surprising effect on the posture of a physically handicapped child. For the severely handicapped child, the 'Orthokinetic' chair offers a unique range of adaptations and functions. All physically handicapped children, except for the most severely retarded, want to walk and every effort should be made to achieve this, but when progress is slow there should be no hesitation in providing a wheelchair if it will give the child more freedom and independence. There are many carts, toys and 'fun cars' on the market which may provide great pleasure and increased mobility (Fig. 16.23), but they should be sanctioned by the therapist before purchase, since some of them encourage bad posture.

WHEELCHAIRS

In talking to parents about mobility it is vital to make the distinction between (1) walking as performed under the direction of the physiotherapist in perfect conditions, (2) walking within the home, (3) walking confined to short distances in the local community, and (4) walking as the main means of mobility in adult life. Most parents will appreciate that the child may function well as a walker at one of these levels, but may also need a wheelchair for independent mobility.

The child who has not achieved useful independent walking by the early teens is unlikely to do so thereafter. Too often, futile physiotherapy continues up to school-leaving age. At some point in the early teens, or perhaps earlier, the doctor, therapist and family must together consider

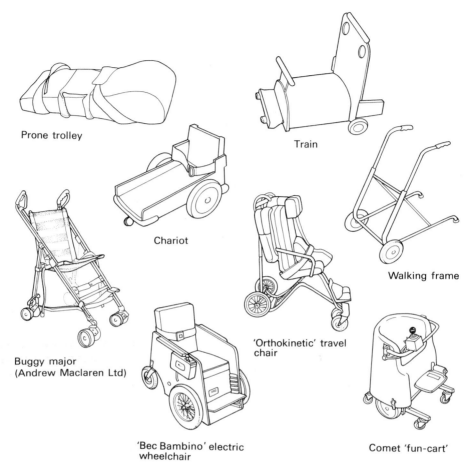

Prone trolley

Train

Chariot

Walking frame

Buggy major
(Andrew Maclaren Ltd)

'Orthokinetic' travel
chair

'Bec Bambino' electric
wheelchair

Comet 'fun-cart'

Fig. 16.23 Aids to mobility.

whether treatment should rather be directed towards achieving maximum wheelchair independence, perhaps using an electric wheelchair.

The paediatric team should collaborate with the officer from the local Artificial Limb and Appliance Centre (ALAC) in wheelchair selection and a special wheelchair clinic is a good way of developing expertise.[351] The wheelchair must be selected with the same care as one would prescribe a drug (see Fig. 16.24). Too often, children are given chairs that are the wrong size or inadequately modified for optimum posture and prevention of deformity. The DHSS will provide a hand-propelled wheelchair for home use and another for school. They will provide one electric wheelchair, for indoor use only. These can be operated even by retarded children if their mental age is at least $3\frac{1}{2}$–4 years. Individually designed switches may be needed to operate the chair for some severely handicapped children (Fig. 16.25).

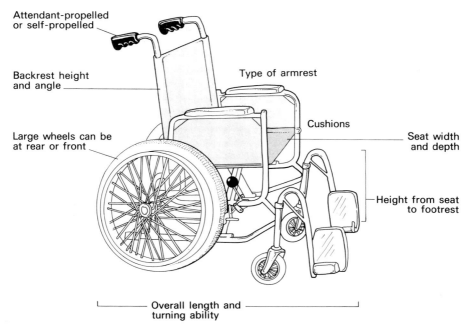

Attendant-propelled
or self-propelled

Backrest height
and angle

Type of armrest

Cushions

Large wheels can be
at rear or front

Seat width
and depth

Height from seat
to footrest

Overall length and
turning ability

Fig. 16.24   Points in the selection of a wheelchair.

Outdoor chairs with a range of several miles and even kerb-climbing ability
are now available and the mobility allowance may be used for the purchase
of such items, or local charities may be persuaded to donate them.

ACTIVITIES OF DAILY LIVING

The occupational therapist selects suitable activities and equipment to
improve hand function. She can guide the parents in the choice of toys from
a toy library in order to develop co-ordination and control of hand and
finger movements. Advice on activities of daily living, modifications to
eating utensils, techniques of dressing and equipment for bathing (for
example a bath-seat or hoist) are all the responsibility of the occupational
therapist (Fig. 16.26). There are also exciting developments in electronic
toys and computers (p. 494).

The role of orthopaedic surgery

Most paediatricians know their CP patients and families well and can make
informed guesses about future progress, but few have the expertise of an
orthopaedic surgeon in assessing muscle and joint movement and deformity.[352] Conversely, few orthopaedic surgeons are familiar with the
complex neurodevelopmental patterns of CP, or with the assessment of the

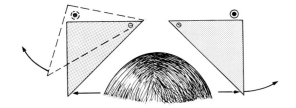

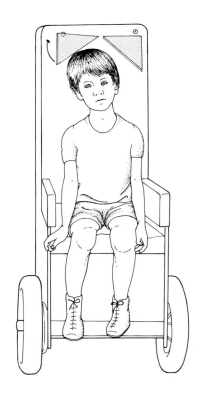

Fig. 16.25 A head-switch for a child with severe spastic quadriplegia.

associated intellectual and emotional handicaps. The best results are obtained if all CP children are seen regularly at a combined paediatric/orthopaedic clinic, where expertise can be shared and developed.

Because CP is so variable in its manifestations and in the changes over time, the results of surgery are hard to assess. Improvements in skills, or in the appearance of the limb certainly occur but it is difficult to balance the often small gains achieved against the risks and discomforts of surgery. It may be useful to summarise here some general points about orthopaedic surgery.

1   Surgery is most likely to be useful in spastic cerebral palsy.

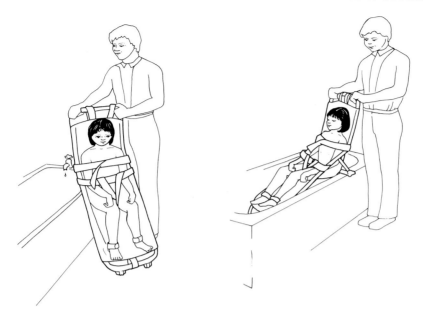

Fig. 16.26 The Orthokinetic bath care chair. An example of special equipment to help with the needs of daily living. (Courtesy Muscular Dystrophy Group.)

2 Functional improvement is more likely to follow surgery to the lower limb than to the upper limb.
3 The functional goal of each procedure should be clearly defined.
4 Surgery should not be undertaken without the availability of a planned intensive physiotherapy programme to obtain maximum benefit.
5 Surgery does not accelerate neurological maturation.
6 Fixed deformities should be corrected before tendons are transferred.
7 Tendons should be transferred before arthrodesis of joints is performed.
8 Wherever possible the effects of a proposed operation should be mimicked by the use of a cast or splint.
9 Orthopaedic procedures often cause a temporary setback in the development of the child with CP. It may take up to a year for the full benefits to be realised.

ORTHOPAEDIC ASPECTS OF HEMIPLEGIA

A limp and asymmetry of leg length are usual in hemiplegia, and there is a compensatory scoliosis which in itself is rarely a major problem. The limp is due to spastic weakness rather than the difference in leg length and many children do not find a shoe raise very helpful; however, occasionally this does have a significant effect on walking and is worth a trial. Firm supporting boots and sometimes a light plastic splint may improve gait, particularly when the child is first walking.

Tightness of the tendo-Achilles with limited dorsiflexion is the commonest orthopaedic problem in hemiplegia. In assessing the range of dorsiflexion, the foot must be held in the inverted position, to avoid movement at the subtalar and midtarsal joints. Steady pressure should be applied to overcome spasticity, otherwise the degree of fixed deformity will be overestimated. Dorsiflexion is measured with the knee both flexed and extended, to distinguish between tightness of the gastrocnemius muscle (which crosses the knee joint) from tightness in the soleus (which does not).

Physiotherapy may help to prevent or delay tendo-Achilles contracture. It is essential that the parents learn the techniques since they must be applied frequently if they are to be effective. The need for surgical treatment can sometimes be postponed by applying a series of plaster casts. Each time the plaster is re-applied, usually at 5–7 day intervals, dorsiflexion is increased and held until the cast is dry. If the ankle cannot be dorsiflexed with the knee flexed or extended, a tendo-Achilles lengthening may be needed. If the ankle can be dorsiflexed with the knee flexed but not when it is extended, the tightness may be confined to gastrocnemius and this muscle may be lengthened by various means. Other surgical procedures to the lower limb are rarely needed in cases of hemiplegia. Hip subluxation and dislocation are uncommon. Hyperextension of the knee is occasionally a problem.

Assessment of the upper limb for surgery is difficult. Ability to use the hemiplegic hand improves with increasing maturity and the results of surgery are therefore not easy to judge. A deficiency of cortical sensation in a hemiplegic hand often limits the possibilities of improvement. Although sensations of hot, cold and pain are generally preserved, cortical sensation as revealed by two-point discrimination and stereognosis is often severely impaired.

In the UK most surgeons adopt a very conservative attitude to upper limb surgery in CP patients. In one series only 4% of cases were considered suitable for hand surgery. The techniques of tendon transfer developed for polio victims have not been nearly so successful in CP. The cortical control of individual muscle groups is very variable and EMG studies show how apparently identical cases may differ widely in their abnormal spontaneous electrical activity and in their response to attempted movement. Some authors feel that EMG assessment improves preoperative case selection and planning, but this procedure is not in general use.

Assessment of the upper limb with a view to surgery should be shared with the physiotherapist and occupational therapist. The main points can be summarised as follows:

1 Fixed deformities are commonly found at elbow and wrist, but do not necessarily limit performance and may not require correction.

2 The power of the wrist, finger and thumb extensors and flexors is

assessed with the wrist held flexed and extended. When there is severe flexion deformity of the wrist and fingers and the flexors and extensors have neglible voluntary movement, little functional improvement can be expected from surgical procedures although the cosmetic appearance may be improved in various ways.

3   Where some activity can be demonstrated in wrist flexors and extensors but extension is very weak, and sensory impairment is not severe, tendon transfer from flexor to extensor groups may be considered.

4   The common 'thumb in palm' deformity has been variously treated by correction of the thumb adductor contracture or by procedures involving the extensor pollicis tendons.

With the possible exception of **4**, upper limb surgery in children is seldom considered before the age of 8 or 9 years. Operations for cosmetic indications should only be performed if the patient is enthusiastic about the possible improvement in appearance. Before performing an operation for functional improvement, one must ask, what will the patient be able to *do* after surgery which he cannot do now?

SURGERY IN SPASTIC DIPLEGIA

Surgery seldoms converts a non-walking to a walking child, although children with moderately severe diplegia may progress from standing to walking, following release of hamstring contractures. In milder cases, once the child is mobile an improvement in gait may be obtained by surgery in carefully selected cases. Occasionally, an operation may be needed to allow comfortable sitting in a wheelchair. The more severely handicapped diplegics and quadriplegics are at risk of hip dislocation, which is discussed below.

Flexion and adduction contractures of the hip are caused by tightness of the iliopsoas or adductor muscles, and these may require release. Some surgeons transfer the adductor origin posteriorly, thus increasing extensor power. Rotational deformity affecting the femur may need correction by osteotomy. Knee contractures may also need surgical treatment. Egger's operation in its original form consisted of weakening the hamstrings by transferring their insertion proximally from below the knee to the femoral condyles. Various modifications of this procedure are adopted depending on the degree of weakening required. If the hamstrings are weakened excessively the knee may become hyperextended (back knee, genu recurvatum). Children with diplegia, like those with hemiplegia, commonly need treatment for fixed deformity at the ankle. In some cases gait and foot comfort are improved by subtalar or triple arthrodesis.

When planning surgical procedures in spastic diplegia it must be remembered that deformity at the hip, knee and ankle are all interrelated. Thus a tendon lengthening at the ankle may increase knee flexion.

Hamstring release may cause increasing lumbar lordosis in the presence of untreated hip flexion deformity. There is some controversy over the exact order in which surgical procedures should be performed, but correction of proximal deformities before distal is generally a logical and successful approach.

With the exception of operations designed to protect the hips from dislocation, surgery should if possible be deferred until the child reaches a plateau of motor development and preferably is old enough to cooperate with postoperative rehabilitation. Case selection is difficult: the gains may only be modest, and operations done too early may need to be repeated or revised.

PREVENTION OF DEFORMITY IN THE SEVERELY HANDICAPPED

The child with severe spasticity or rigidity is liable to develop deformities, and hip dislocation is the most serious of these as it may cause severe pain and misery, and nursing care and perineal hygiene become very difficult.[353]

Children with very severe CP tend to adopt an asymmetric posture giving rise to the 'windswept hip' appearance (Fig. 16.27). This posture is part of a total pattern of movement and must be treated as such. The

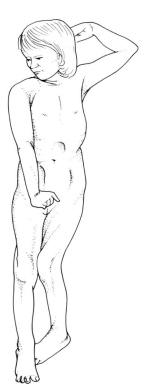

Fig. 16.27 The 'windswept' hip deformity: right leg abducted, left leg adducted.

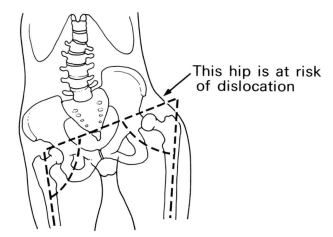

This hip is at risk
of dislocation

Fig. 16.28 Pelvic obliquity in
the windswept hip deformity.

adducted hip is at greater risk of dislocation (Fig. 16.28). There is also a
danger of scoliosis and this may be very difficult to prevent. Plastic jackets
may help but must be close fitting and need regular replacement as the child
grows. They have to be worn continually to be useful. For these reasons,
they are often not tolerated by either child or parents. Careful positioning
using moulded seat inserts and a variety of other devices (Fig. 16.29) and
frequent changes in posture help to minimise these risks.[354] The hip joint is
at risk of subluxation and dislocation in an upwards and backwards
direction, because of the imbalance between the hip adductors and flexors
on the one hand, and the gluteal abductors and extensors on the other. In
subluxation, at least part of the head of the femur is congruent with the
acetabulum; in dislocation, congruence is totally lost.

The mean age of dislocation of the hip in CP is 7 years. It can occur,
though rarely, after the age of 12 years or as early as 6 months, when it may
be mistaken for congenital dislocation. Indeed, on occasion dislocation of
the hips may be the presenting feature of spastic diplegia which should be
easily recognised because of the flexed and adducted position of the hips.
The X-ray may show a small upper femoral epiphysis and a shallow sloping
acetabulum in early cases, but these changes are less marked when the
dislocation occurs later in childhood.

Subluxation and dislocation of the hip usually occur slowly over a
period of months or years and are always associated with a moderate or
severe limitation of abduction. Once subluxation has begun, it is likely to
progress to dislocation unless prevented by effective physiotherapy or
surgery. If there is radiological evidence of progressive subluxation, surgical
procedures such as adductor tenotomy (perhaps combined with anterior
obturator neurectomy) may be necessary. When the windswept deformity
is mild, it may be advisable to carry out these procedures initially only on
the adducted hip, but a careful watch must be kept on the other side which

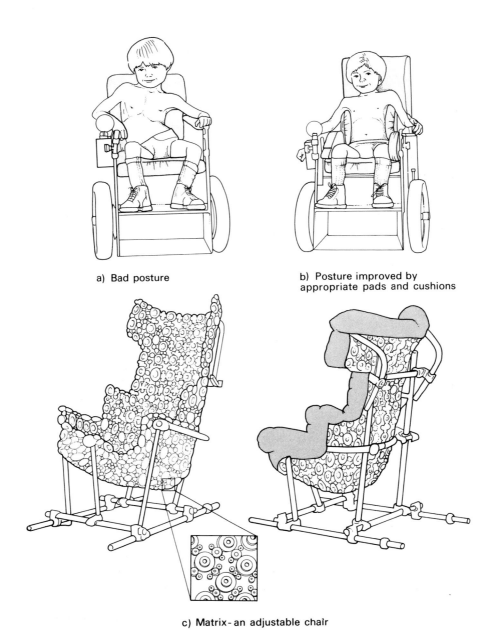

a) Bad posture

b) Posture improved by appropriate pads and cushions

c) Matrix- an adjustable chair

Fig. 16.29   Prevention of deformity—two examples.

may later also begin to sublux. If subluxation progresses in spite of these measures, further surgical procedures may be needed.

Once the hip has become dislocated, the orthopaedic surgeon is faced with an extremely difficult problem. For the older non-ambulant patient with a painful dislocation, proximal femoral resection appears to be the best option. The results of osteotomy and soft tissue releases are disappointing in terms of functional improvement.[478]

Often it is the most severely disabled children with a poor prognosis for ambulation who require surgery to the hip. It should be made absolutely clear to the parents in such cases that the surgery is intended to prevent painful dislocation, rather than to increase the probability of walking, and that the prevention of dislocation is a worthwhile goal in a profoundly handicapped child.

Fixed deformity may be somewhat easier to prevent in children with central hypotonia (p. 333) but very handicapped immobile children may develop contractures and scoliosis and a few of those who lie with their hips widely abducted may develop anterior dislocation of the hip.

Medical treatment of CP

Drugs. Spasticity can be reduced by baclofen. This drug acts at spinal level and is valuable where severe spasticity is causing painful spasms or serious functional problems in mobility or dressing.[355] Baclofen is supplied as 10 mg tablets but young children may require a much smaller dose initially, perhaps 1.25–2.5 mg twice daily, and a pharmacist should be asked to prepare capsules containing weighed portions of the drug. The dosage is monitored by clinical response and is gradually increased as necessary. A dose of 30 mg daily is seldom exceeded in children. Side-effects include mild drowsiness, which is usually transient. Theoretically, baclofen is epileptogenic but this has not been a problem in practice. Overdosage causes excessive hypotonia. No serious long term problems have emerged but it is advisable to withdraw therapy occasionally to determine whether the child still requires it.

Diazepam is also used in severe spasticity but because its action is central, it tends to cause an unacceptable degree of drowsiness before adequate muscle relaxation is achieved. Clonazepam is useful for myoclonic epilepsies in CP and relaxation and sedation may be an added bonus. Many other agents have been tried to reduce the unwanted movements in dyskinetic CP but none has been sufficiently effective to justify regular use.

Surgery. Stereotactic brain surgery has been recommended by a few neurosurgeons, to reduce spasticity and eliminate unwanted movements. Occasional good results are obtained but the procedure has many potential hazards and is only performed in carefully selected cases.

Communication

An increased emphasis on the importance of communication has been one of the few significant advances in the management of CP in the past decade. The speech therapist should advise the parents on all aspects of communication, including the non-verbal systems such as Bliss symbolics (p. 263). In addition, she can often help with difficulties in feeding and swallowing.

Assessment of intelligence

Much can be learned from the parents' observations but, inevitably, the greater the physical handicap the more limited is the child's repertoire of responses. A psychologist who is familiar with the problems of communicating with young physically handicapped children can carry out a formal I.Q. test using items selected from standard test batteries.[356] So long as some form of response can be elicited from the child, even if it is only a 'yes/no' response or eye-pointing, a fair estimate of I.Q. can be obtained (Fig. 16.30). In the same way a speech therapist can estimate verbal comprehension by using the Reynell test. In interpreting the results to the parents, it is perhaps wiser to err on the side of cautious optimism, since the child's ultimate

Fig. 16.30 Psychological assessment. A boy with no speech and severe athetosis points to the 'odd man out'. (Courtesy of L. Gardner, The Spastics Society.)

attainments may be much better than one would have dared to predict in the first 2 or 3 years of life.

Many children with hemiplegia or mild diplegia integrate readily into normal school and they should not be recommended for special education simply on the basis of the physical handicap. Apart from the increased incidence of learning problems, children with CP in normal schools have a number of minor problems, particularly with sporting and handicraft activities, and are likely to be slow in dressing after games, etc. A nursery school placement is often helpful; usually the choice lies between normal school and a school for the physically handicapped. Integration into normal school may be possible even for children with severe physical handicap provided that the lay-out and design of the school are suitable and the staff are enthusiastic.

Even the most severely handicapped child has a right to education. Many schools for the mentally or physically handicapped have a 'special care' area catering for the needs of profoundly brain-damaged children and will accept them at the age of 3 or even earlier, thus reducing the burden of care on the parents.

Common management problems

FEEDING PROBLEMS

Failure to suck. Following severe brain damage, there may be total inability to suck or swallow in the early months of life. Tube feeding may be the only means of maintaining life in such cases and this raises difficult ethical problems. However, if the parents wish, they can manage this at home. Many mothers are capable of learning not only the feeding techniques but also how to insert and secure the tube. The dietician can advise on the composition of feeds.

Tongue thrusting, gagging and choking.   These occur particularly in children with severe bilateral brain damage causing pseudobulbar palsy. Each feed is a prolonged and frustrating affair. The speech therapist and physiotherapist may be able to suggest helpful feeding positions and techniques. Desensitisation of the overactive mouth reflexes is popular with some therapists.

Vomiting and regurgitation are common in cerebral palsy. The causes include excessive air swallowing, the mother's determination to improve on an often very small intake of food, spasm of abdominal muscles, extensor spasticity, anticonvulsant drugs, etc. A barium swallow sometimes reveals a degree of oesophageal reflux. Sandifer described a syndrome consisting of bizarre movements in association with oesophageal reflux, probably in response to the pain caused by the acid stomach contents.[357] His cases occurred in normal children, but these movements are also seen in some cases of cerebral palsy and may even be mistaken for epilepsy.

Small frequent feeds, and thickening of the feeds with cereal or Nestargel may reduce regurgitation. Surface-active agents such as Gaviscon, or the antiemetic metoclopramide can be tried, but the latter should be introduced in small dosage because of the risk of extrapyramidal side-effects. Drugs which reduce spasticity (p. 351) also seem to make feeding easier. Rarely surgical reconstruction of the gastro-oesophageal junction may be justified.[471]

Rumination, the deliberate regurgitation of stomach contents for pleasure, is an occasional problem in mentally retarded children, whether or not they have cerebral palsy. It can be reduced by giving less fluid with meals, smaller more frequent meals, and provision of other activity at times when rumination is likely to occur. Occasionally more drastic behavioural measures may be needed (p. 161). The problem can be a major nuisance to the household; the child always smells of vomit and ruins the carpets and furniture.

DRIBBLING

Difficulty in swallowing, poor head control, and weakness of the jaw and facial muscles contribute to this intractable problem which is distressing both for the child and his parents.[358,359] Devices to support the chin, and behavioural training have not been very successful. Transplantation of the salivary ducts to the posterior part of the pharynx has been tried, but the results are disappointing. Temporary relief (for special occasions) may be obtained with atropine tablets (0.6 mg). Although it is difficult to prevent dribbling, it is at least possible to prevent soreness of the chin and neck by use of a silicone barrier cream, and 1% hydrocortisone is effective in treating areas of inflammation caused by constant soaking in saliva.

CONSTIPATION

Constipation is often more of a worry to the parent than a problem to the child, though it probably can cause pain and muscle spasm when severe. Contributing causes include small food intake, highly refined foods with little bulk, weakness and spasticity of abdominal muscles, and associated mental handicap. If treatment is needed, a glycerine suppository may suffice. Failing this, a stool softener such as lactulose should be tried before more powerful purgatives such as Senokot.

CRYING, SCREAMING AND SLEEP DISTURBANCE

Crying, screaming and sleep disturbance seem more common in cerebral palsy than in other handicaps. There may well be a neurological basis for these problems, though this is unproven. Other possible contributing factors include inability to change position when uncomfortable, a feeling of insecurity due to absent postural mechanisms, discomfort due to extensor spasms or reflux oesophagitis, and even painful subluxation or dislocation of the hip. The severely physically handicapped child may be unable to play and therefore becomes bored and demands constant attention. Handicapped children are not immune from ordinary paediatric problems such as otitis media and urinary tract infection. Management of sleep problems is discussed on p. 162.

CHILBLAINS AND COLD INJURY

These are associated with poor circulation and diminished muscular activity. In very cold weather children with severe cerebral palsy may develop quite severe cold injury to the hands and feet, with cyanosis and oedema which may take several days to resolve.

GROWTH

Growth is usually impaired in cerebral palsy. There is dwarfing of the affected limbs and pelvis, and in hemiplegia asymmetry of the face and skull may also occur. This is partly due to the brain damage; both motor and cortical sensory pathways seem necessary for normal growth. In severe cases, reduced food intake also contributes to growth impairment.

The adult with severe CP

At the end of their school career children with CP may be able to obtain further tuition and assessment at colleges and special centres. Only a few will be able to progress to higher education or to compete for work in the open market; in most cases the multiplicity of handicaps makes this impossible. Voluntary organisations, notably The Spastics Society, have shown how the imaginative design and construction of living accommodation can give the adult disabled more satisfying lives, with an acceptable degree of independence. Advances in electric wheelchair design, legislation about wheelchair access to public buildings and modified control systems in cars together allow a greater degree of mobility than ever before. Nevertheless much remains to be done and parents should be encouraged to give their support to one of the voluntary organisations active in this field.

Chapter Seventeen
Neural Tube Defects and other Motor Disorders

Spina bifida is the commonest malformation of the central nervous system.[360,363] It results from a failure of the neural folds to close, a process which is normally complete within 28 days of conception. The classification of neural tube defects is illustrated in Fig. 17.1. The clinical problems of spina bifida occulta are quite distinct from those of the cystica form and are described separately (p. 369). Anencephaly is a lethal malformation and is not discussed in detail here.

Encephaloceles account for only a small proportion of neural tube defects. They may occur anywhere along the midline of the skull but usually are located in the occipital region (Fig. 17.2). There is often other evidence of cerebral malformation, and serious neurological deficits and mental handicap are common. Other malformations may occur, notably in the Meckel syndrome (encephalocele, cystic kidneys, exomphalos, etc.) which is important because of its recessive inheritance.

SPINA BIFIDA CYSTICA

The neurological effects of the spinal lesion vary from a negligible deficit to total paraplegia (Fig. 17.3). The majority of children with myelomeningocele also have hydrocephalus, caused by the Arnold–Chiari malformation.

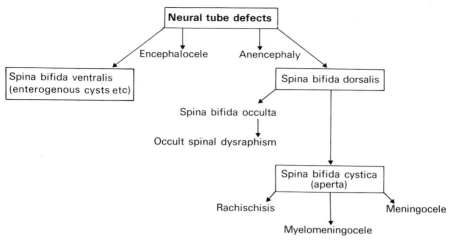

Fig. 17.1 Classification of neural tube defects.

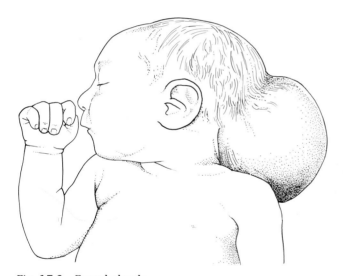

Fig. 17.2 Encephalocele.

This consists of prolongation of the cerebellar vermis and displacement of the fourth ventricle and medulla into the upper cervical canal. The CSF pathways may be interrupted by deformities of the aqueduct at the level of the fourth ventricle or around the brainstem. Other malformations are often found in the cerebral cortex. Spina bifida is associated with an increased risk of other anomalies, including heart and bowel defects, cleft palate, etc.

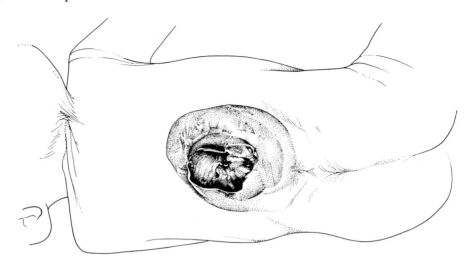

Fig. 17.3   Myelomeningocele.

EPIDEMIOLOGY, AETIOLOGY AND GENETICS

Neural tube defects are commoner in females than males. Many anencephalics and some cases of spina bifida are spontaneously aborted. The overall incidence in the UK is around 3 per 1000 births. There are international geographic variations in incidence, ranging from nearly 1 per 150 births in parts of Northern Ireland and Wales to less than 1 in 1000 in Los Angeles. The incidence is higher in social classes 4 and 5. People emigrating from high-incidence areas continue to be at high risk.

The cause of neural tube defects is unknown. Genetic factors contribute but the inheritance does not follow simple mendelian patterns and is assumed to be linked with a strong environmental contribution. The nature of this is uncertain, but various foodstuffs and toxins have been suspected. The association with low social class suggests a link with poverty and poor diet (p. 368).

PRELIMINARY MANAGEMENT

When a baby is born with spina bifida, it is necessary to tell both parents, as soon as possible, that there is a serious problem affecting the back. It is usually better for the parents to see and hold the child, since their fantasies about the malformation are often worse than the reality. Often transfer to a regional centre is desirable for detailed assessment. Prior to this, the lesion is covered with a gauze swab soaked in sterile saline and covered with plastic film to reduce evaporative heat loss. The GP should be informed. The father and, if possible, the mother should accompany the baby. Whatever management policy is adopted the mother should live in the ward at least for a day or two to gain confidence in handling the child before he is allowed to go home.

ASSESSMENT

The presence and extent of hydrocephalus, cranial nerve palsies, and other defects are noted. The most important task is to assess the level at which normal spinal cord function ceases (Fig. 17.4). Sensory level can sometimes be determined by response to pin-prick. Muscle power can be assessed according to the ability to contract with and against gravity. There may be complete or incomplete paraplegia, or less often some spasticity may be found. Rarely, there is marked asymmetry of the lesion and of the neurologic deficit. It is important to exclude movements caused by reflex withdrawal from painful stimuli; these are mediated through peripheral

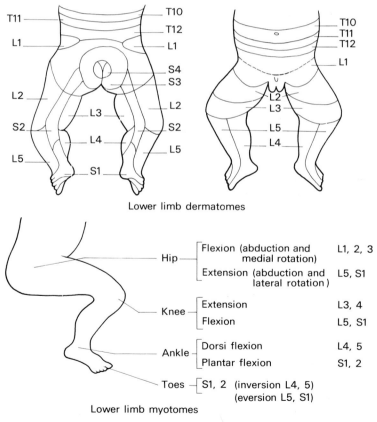

Lower limb dermatomes

Hip	Flexion (abduction and medial rotation)	L1, 2, 3
	Extension (abduction and lateral rotation)	L5, S1
Knee	Extension	L3, 4
	Flexion	L5, S1
Ankle	Dorsi flexion	L4, 5
	Plantar flexion	S1, 2
Toes	S1, 2 (inversion L4, 5) (eversion L5, S1)	

Lower limb myotomes

Fig. 17.4 Neonatal assessment—dermatomes and myotomes. (Redrawn from Brocklehurst[360] by permission.)

nerves and spinal cord and do not imply the presence of intact pathways between brain and spinal cord. Anal tone and bladder function are also assessed.

SELECTION FOR TREATMENT

Without treatment there is a high death rate; only 20% of babies survive two years. With closure of the back lesion and treatment of the hydrocephalus, a majority of babies survive, but for many children the quality of life is appalling. Most centres now try to select children for operative treatment,[362] using criteria such as those outlined in Table 17.1. Nevertheless, these decisions can be very difficult. Babies who are treated conservatively receive nursing care, are fed orally on demand, but are not tube fed or given antibiotics. Parents may wish to care for the child at home, perhaps using the hospital ward for short periods of respite. A hospice approach akin to that provided for dying adults, has been suggested. Heavy sedation is prescribed by some doctors to reduce suffering and to hasten the demise of severely handicapped babies. The point at which this becomes morally unacceptable is an individual judgement.

Because of antenatal screening and the policy of selection which is now followed in many centres, there is a decline in the number of children afflicted with the severe problems of total paraplegia and there are now relatively more cases with only mild or moderate handicap.

Table 17.1   Spina bifida: adverse prognostic signs used in selection for treatment.

Clinical features
There is no lower limb movement under normal upper motor neurone control (i.e. there is a paraplegia from L1 downwards)
There is clinically established hydrocephalus at birth (enlarged skull circumference)
There is an associated lumbar kyphosis or severe scoliosis
There are serious congenital malformations in other systems
The general neurological state of the infant is poor (from birth trauma or anoxia)

Radiological features
Spine
    eversion of pedicles
    kyphosis
    hemivertebrae
    double ribs
    absent ribs

Skull
    craniolacunae
    shallow posterior fossa
    eversion of petrous temporal bones
    enlargement of foramen magnum

Treatment

Spina bifida is a complex problem, and is best managed in centres which can accumulate and share experience. Combined clinics facilitate clinical decision-making and reduce the amount of time spent by the family in visiting hospital.

CLOSURE OF THE BACK

The operation is usually performed within 48 hours of birth.

HYDROCEPHALUS

The ventricles are enlarged in most cases of spina bifida. The cause of the hydrocephalus is the Arnold–Chiari malformation (see above). Diagnosis is usually easy, but CT scan or ultrasound are useful to demonstrate ventricular size and cortical thickness. A head circumference more than 2 cm above the 90th centile and a cerebral mantle thickness of less than 1 cm are both associated with low intellect in most but not all survivors; around 20% of such cases may achieve an I.Q. of 80 or more. However, cortical thickness of less than 5 mm is rarely associated with normal intellect.

Medical treatments include acetazolamide, which is of only transient benefit; isosorbide, a sugar derivative, has an osmotic effect and may at least delay the need for surgery; and head-wrapping, now largely abandoned.

Surgical treatment involves the insertion of a shunt to reduce CSF pressure. Prior to this procedure a ventricular tap is performed to estimate CSF protein and exclude infection. The shunt system consists of a ventricular catheter, a valve which opens at a preset CSF pressure (usually 50–70 mm H_2O) and has a non-return action, and a distal catheter. The latter drains either to the right atrium or to the peritoneal cavity (each has its advocates). The Holter valve is placed subcutaneously on the side of the head. In the Pudenz system the valve is an integral part of the distal catheter. For peritoneal drainage, a Raimondi catheter, reinforced to prevent occlusion, is used. A reservoir may be included in the system to allow access to ventricular CSF for diagnostic treatment. Whichever system is used, the parents should understand the principles involved and should have clear instructions as to whether, and how often, they should pump the valve.

Complications of shunt surgery are very common. Over half of all patients require at least one revision and up to a quarter have one or more infections. Malfunction and infection are the main problems. The shunt may become disconnected (visible on X-ray) or obstructed either at proximal or distal end. A shunt placed in the right atrium will gradually move up to the superior vena cava as the child grows. Thrombi are then more likely to develop around the tip. A few surgeons routinely replace the shunt when the tip reaches the vena cava but most wait until problems occur. Abdominal contents may block a peritoneal catheter at any time.

Shunt malfunction may present as a sudden catastrophic loss of consciousness, or more usually with variable and often non-specific features of raised intracranial pressure, including drowsiness, vomiting, headache, squint, ataxia, or deterioration in performance or personality. Other childhood illnesses may have very similar symptoms and whenever there is any doubt the child must be admitted for observation. Some diagnostic assistance may be obtainable by pumping the valve, depending on the system used. If the valve is easily depressed but slow to fill, the obstruction is likely to be proximal; conversely if the valve is hard to depress the blockage is distal. This manoeuvre is not totally reliable and the response to pumping may feel normal even when the system is obstructed. Blockage of the ventricular catheter sometimes occurs when the tip impinges on the wall of the ventricle as it shrinks in size, causing repeated cycles of deterioration needing emergency treatment. In some children, CSF drainage may reduce the pressure to too low a level, evidenced by a very sunken fontanelle and general misery and malaise.

In older childen with chronic raised intracranial pressure, there may be papilloedema or optic atrophy, a 'crackpot' sound on percussing the skull, and evidence of suture spreading on skull X-ray. CT scan, isotope studies and pressure readings may be useful in difficult cases.

Infection of the shunt may cause either ventriculitis, with signs similar to those of meningitis, or septicaemia, with fever, anaemia and splenomegaly. Septicaemia is usually caused by *Staphylococcus albus* (epidermidis). Antibiotics are given under the guidance of the microbiologist and neurosurgeon. Shunt revision is usually needed.

Convulsions occur in about 30% of children with treated hydrocephalus.[364] Repeated revisions probably increase the risk. EEG abnormalities around the catheter site suggest that focal scarring may give rise to an epileptic focus.

Less common complications include (1) shunt nephritis, which may cause symptoms suggestive of infection, but is sometimes only recognised by the finding of haematuria and proteinuria; (2) pulmonary emboli and pulmonary hypertension; (3) subdural haematoma, probably caused by rapid decompression of the ventricles by the shunt, with rupture of the bridging veins between brain and skull; (4) skin necrosis over the valve; and (5) perforation of blood vessels or other organs by the catheter.

Hydrocephalus will arrest spontaneously in most cases, presumably because a balance is achieved between production and absorption of CSF. The shunt is usually left in place at least until the child is beyond 5 years of age. Measures of head circumference over a long period, and isotope studies help to decide when arrest has occurred.

ORTHOPAEDIC MANAGEMENT

When intensive management of spina bifida was first introduced, the goals of orthopaedic surgery were independent mobility and normal function. Results were often poor, repeated operations were needed, and intellectual handicap limited the effectiveness of the surgery. Most surgeons now adopt a more conservative approach.

An early orthopaedic assessment is essential. Foot deformities, fixed flexion deformities of knee or hip, and hip dislocation may all improve with regular stretching and splintage without surgery. By the 2nd birthday the child's intellectual and motor limitations can be assessed. Realistic goals should be set which can be achieved by a minimum of surgery. Where the neurological deficit is mild, the child may need only short calipers, splints or special footwear. For the more severely affected children, early mobility may be achieved by a variety of means (*see* p. 337). Later, walking with the aid of long calipers is encouraged, but eventually many children find that a wheelchair gives them far more mobility and freedom. Nevertheless, some attempts at walking should continue if possible to reduce disuse osteoporosis and the risk of ischial pressure sores, and to improve bladder drainage.

OPERATIVE PROCEDURES

Hip.   In carefully selected cases iliopsoas transfer is performed for dislocation of the hip, but sometimes this is best left alone, and flexion or adduction deformity treated by simple tenotomy.

Knee.   Release of flexion deformity is useful, as fixed flexion makes fitting of calipers difficult. Hamstring transfer may help, but the loss of active flexion can result in a stiff, straight knee which can be a nuisance when sitting. Osteotomy for correction of deformity is best deferred until maturity.

Foot.   If the child will be able to stand or walk, the aim is to produce a plantigrade foot on which the child can weight-bear without developing pressure sores. This may be achieved by soft tissue releases in many cases.

Spine.   Kyphosis and scoliosis sometimes cause rapidly progressive deformity. Bracing is not usually successful and may cause pressure sores. Surgical treatment involves an extensive operation and is only justified if the deformity is causing functional disability or pain.

COMPLICATIONS OF PARAPLEGIA

Pressure sores usually occur in anaesthetic skin overlying a bony prominence and subjected to repeated pressure or friction. Inadequate footwear, together with uneven weight-bearing due to deformity may cause severe sores on the sole or toes. A full thickness sore on the heel is a very serious problem and may be almost impossible to cure. Prolonged sitting, particularly in wet nappies, may cause ischial tuberosity sores which may only heal with a prolonged period lying prone. Prevention of pressure sores requires constant vigilance, by parents and by the child as soon as he is old enough. Regular inspection of feet (including use of a mirror to see the soles) and of the buttocks is vital. The child must be moved regularly, and must learn to change position in bed or wheelchair. Calipers, the edges of plaster casts, and friction of heels on bed sheets are potential causes of sores. The latter can be prevented by use of a fleece. Cold injury is another hazard which can be avoided by use of fleece-lined boots; playing in snow is hazardous. Scalds from radiators or hot water bottles are also easily acquired.

Pathological fractures are liable to occur in spina bifida children. Osteoporosis due to disuse, lack of pain, and immobilisation in plaster contribute, together with metabolic bone disease in children with advanced renal problems. The history of injury is often trivial or absent and the signs are often suggestive of infection—fever, redness, and high white count. At first X-ray changes may be minimal, though new bone formation is visible within four or five days. Healing is rapid but may be associated with increased deformity. The minimum treatment needed to maintain alignment is recommended.

BLADDER AND URINARY TRACT

In the normal bladder, continence is maintained by the tone of the pelvic floor muscles which keep the bladder neck elevated. The exact role of the internal sphincter is uncertain. The external sphincter is regarded as a second line of defence. During micturition the sphincters relax, the bladder neck descends and the detrusor muscle contracts to empty the bladder (Fig. 17.5). The neurologic control of the bladder is complex and incompletely understood. There is a sympathetic component from T12–L1 which is responsible for contraction of the proximal sphincter region and also inhibits contraction of the detrusor; some sympathetic fibres also arise from S2–4. The parasympathetic fibres from S2–4 initiate contraction of the detrusor.

In spina bifida there may be varying combinations of upper and lower motor neurone lesions. The bladder may be small and empty by reflex action, or capacious with dribbling and incomplete emptying: the exact picture depends on the relative involvement of detrusor, sphincters and pelvic floor. All babies with spina bifida have an IVP and a micturating cystogram before discharge. Many centres now perform a detailed urodynamic study, i.e. a micturating cystogram combined with a bladder pressure study. This gives information about bladder capacity and outline, pressure

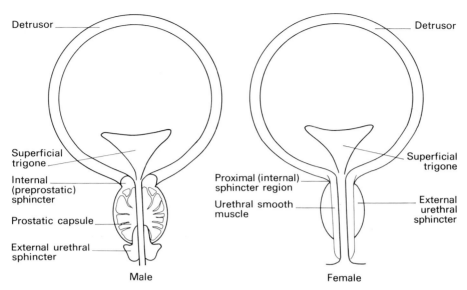

Fig. 17.5 Functional anatomy of the bladder.

changes during micturition, the completeness of emptying and the presence of reflux.

Management. The aims are to preserve renal function and avoid upper urinary tract damage; to obtain efficient bladder emptying to reduce the risk of infection; and to achieve continence. All children with bladder problems need regular urine examinations which can be performed by the parents, GP, or school nurse, using standard dipstick tests for bacteriuria and pyuria, and dipslides for culture when indicated. Opinion is divided on the value of continuous prophylactic antibiotics. Symptomatic infections should of course be treated. A positive culture in the absence of symptoms does not necessarily require antibiotics and certainly one should avoid exotic and potentially toxic antibiotics in this situation. Renal function is checked at intervals and it may be necessary to repeat the urodynamic studies. The need for repeated IVPs can be reduced by the use of ultrasound and isotope renography. These are done annually until age 5 and 2-yearly thereafter.

In about half of children with spina bifida, manual expression of the bladder is possible. Parents are taught how to do this prior to discharge. Outflow obstruction at the internal sphincter can sometimes be improved by phenoxybenzamine (an alpha-receptor antagonist). A spastic external sphincter may be divided surgically via an endoscope. Diazepam relaxes the external sphincter and has a similar effect. Urethral dilatation may also improve bladder emptying. If poor emptying and ureteric reflux persist in spite of these measures, ureteric reimplantation may be required. Continence may be achieved, rather suddenly in some children, between the ages of 3 and 7. Up to this time nappies and manual expression are usually acceptable. Penile appliances can be fitted at the age of 5, or earlier in some cases. These are very successful but need careful supervision to avoid ulceration, sores and leakage. A satisfactory urine collecting system for girls has not yet been invented. An indwelling catheter, made of silastic, can be used successfully for long periods. A small catheter (12–22 F), with the balloon inflated as little as possible, can be left in place for several weeks. Orchitis and epididymitis are occasional complications. Again, opinions differ about the value of prophylactic antibiotics.

In many cases, the technique of first choice, even in very young children, is now intermittent catheterisation, performed by the parents and later by the child; this has significantly improved continence for patients with a neuropathic bladder.[365] The catheter is inserted, using a mirror if necessary, with clean but non-sterile technique every 3–4 hours. Drugs such as propantheline, imipramine, or the new agent oxybutynin, can be used to increase the functional bladder capacity, and ephedrine increases tone in the bladder outlet. These drugs can also be used when approaches other than intermittent catheterisation are used.

Diversion of the urine was at one time a very popular procedure but there are numerous long term complications and there is a danger of progressive deterioration in renal function. Three methods are available: an ileal loop, a ureterostomy, or diversion into a colonic conduit. An important complication of urinary diversion is discharge from the isolated bladder, often mistaken for vaginal discharge. It is treated by bladder washouts; occasionally cystectomy is needed.

For those who cannot achieve continence by other means, the implantation of an artifical sphincter is a promising technique, though the device is expensive and is only available in a few centres, in the UK.

BOWEL

The aims are to avoid excessive constipation and maintain continence. Constipation can often be controlled by a sensible diet, and by bulk additives such as bran or methylcellulose. Powerful purgatives should be avoided if possible. A glycerine or Dulcolax suppository inserted in the morning may initiate a bowel movement and the child may then be clean all day. Disposable enemas have similar effects though there may be some leakage for a time. A few children require manual removal. A colostomy is rarely necessary.

GENERAL PROBLEMS

Families with spina bifida children have the same problems and need the same support services as those with other handicaps (p. 147), but because of the medical complexities of the disorder they are likely to spend much more time at hospital, both in clinics and as inpatients. The financial burdens of frequent travel, often to a regional centre, should not be forgotten.

Prognosis

This depends on the selection policy applied at birth. Treatment of all infants in the 1960s produced a very high proportion of children with total paraplegia, gross spinal deformity, chronic renal problems, and mental handicap. Average I.Q. was in the dull normal or ESN(M) range, with a scatter from the profoundly handicapped to the superior intelligence range. The need for orthopaedic and urological procedures and shunt revisions resulted in some children undergoing twelve or more operations. The more selective policy now adopted in most centres results in 50–60% of children being rejected for treatment and most of these die in the first 12–18 months. The five-year survival rate of those treated is probably around 60–70% and it is hoped that not more than one-third will have moderate impairment and two-thirds will have minimal problems or be essentially normal. The exact incidence of sexual dysfunction is not yet known[366] but this is undoubtedly a major problem (p. 151).

Prevention

GENETIC ADVICE

All parents who have had a child with a neural tube defect should be offered genetic counselling. Recurrence risks are shown in Table 17.2. If the affected child had spina bifida, then about two-thirds of the recurrence risk is for spina bifida, one-third for anencephaly, and vice versa. The occasional occurrence of a recessive disorder such as Meckel's syndrome should be remembered.

Table 17.2 Estimated recurrence risks for spina bifida or anencephaly or both.

Family history	Estimated risk
One sib affected	1 in 20
Parent and sib affected/two sibs affected	1 in 8
Three sibs affected	1 in 5
One sib and second-degree relative affected	1 in 11
One sib and a third-degree relative affected	1 in 14

ANTENATAL DIAGNOSIS

Alpha-fetoprotein (AFP) is the major protein of fetal serum. In pregnancy small amounts are found in the mother's blood. The level is raised in any condition in which fetal membranes are exposed to the amniotic fluid. Measurement of AFP can therefore be used for antenatal diagnosis of neural tube defects,[367] but the level is also raised in many other conditions (exomphalos, congenital nephrosis, Turner's syndrome, cystic hygroma, bowel defects, urethral valves, and missed abortion). AFP levels change throughout pregnancy and for proper interpretation of results the gestation must be accurately known. Serum levels only constitute a screening test, because the levels found in abnormal pregnancy overlap the normal range. Borderline or elevated levels are checked by AFP measurement in amniotic fluid, which is very reliable. If available, ultrasound examination of the fetal head and back is performed. (Parents do not usually understand that the latter is a more skilled and complex procedure than routine ultrasound measurement of the fetal head and, having seen the technique on TV programmes, feel bitter that their baby's lesion was 'missed'.)

Screening by measurement of maternal serum AFP is not foolproof. It is most likely to be positive when the baby is anencephalic or has a severe spinal lesion which would not be likely to be treated surgically when current criteria are applied. Some babies with mild or moderate lesions will be missed. Furthermore amniocentesis has a small but definite complication rate. It is thought that these disadvantages together with the cost do not necessarily justify a screening programme except in areas of high incidence.

If the fetus is found to have a neural tube defect the parents will be offered a termination. Antenatal screening should not normally be undertaken if the parents are morally opposed to termination of pregnancy, and this view should be (but often is not) elicited *before* screening blood samples are taken.

Other possible indicators of neural tube defects are being examined, notably acetylcholinesterase in amniotic fluid; this is more specific than AFP.

PRIMARY PREVENTION

The association between spina bifida and low social class suggested to Smithells and his colleagues[361] that dietary factors might be important. They found that vitamin supplements before and around the time of conception appear to substantially reduce the risk of a neural tube defect in babies born to mothers who already have one affected baby. Folic acid is suspected to be the crucial vitamin. Final proof is not yet available and the ethical problems of further research are considerable, but it seems sensible to advise the mothers of affected babies to take vitamin supplements when further conception is planned.

SPINA BIFIDA OCCULTA

Minor degrees of spina bifida occulta affecting the lower lumbar and sacral vertebrae (usually L5 or S1) are extremely common and, in the absence of any other features, are unlikely to be of clinical or genetic significance.

Occult spinal dysraphism

A number of developmental defects may affect the spinal cord, causing slowly progressive damage.[77,368] These include diastematomyelia (a cartilaginous or bony spur in the spinal canal), intraspinal dermoid, lipoma or haemangioma. With these there is always spina bifida occulta and often the X-ray also shows widening of the spinal canal. In most but not all cases, an invaluable clue to the presence of the disorder is provided by a cutaneous lesion over the lower spine. This may be a tuft of hair, a lipoma or naevus, or a dermal sinus (not to be confused with a dimple).

The clinical features of these defects include asymmetric wasting or weakness of one or both legs, foot and hip deformities, and bladder dysfunction.[369] These may be present in infancy or may appear and progress insidiously. Any child with complaints affecting the legs or bladder must have a careful examination of the lower spine, and a plain X-ray. If the cutaneous features mentioned above are found, the child should be referred for a paediatric neurosurgical opinion, however trivial the presenting complaint may be. If treatment is deferred until the neurological or bladder signs are obvious, the results of surgery are disappointing. These lesions are genetically related to spina bifida cystica and the genetic advice should be the same.

DUCHENNE MUSCULAR DYSTROPHY

This is the commonest and best known of the inherited disorders of muscle.[370] It is transmitted by an X-linked gene and is therefore confined to males. The incidence is of the order of 1 per 3000 male births. The onset is insidious. First symptoms are most often noted between 2 and 4 years but the delay before diagnosis is often as long as 3 years. An abnormal gait, frequent falls, and difficulties on steps are the commonest complaints. About half of these children are late in walking although muscular dystrophy accounts for less than 1% of all late-walking males.

The waddling gait is associated with a lumbar lordosis and toe walking. The child is never able to run or hop normally. Even small steps present problems. Gower's manoeuvre (p. 76) is an indication of proximal muscle weakness and is not diagnostic of muscular dystrophy. Examination shows the typical firm enlargement of the calf muscles (pseudohypertrophy) which is often noted by parents (Fig. 17.6), and the child may complain of painful muscles when tired. Tendon reflexes are usually absent, with the exception of the ankle jerk which may be brisk.

Associated problems include a mild reduction of intellect; the I.Q. curve in Duchenne muscular dystrophy shows normal distribution but the mean is shifted downwards by about 15 points. There is no deterioration in mental capacity as the disease advances. In some of these children with mild global developmental delay, a speech problem may be the presenting feature. Cardiac involvement is common but there is rarely clinical evidence of this in the early stages.

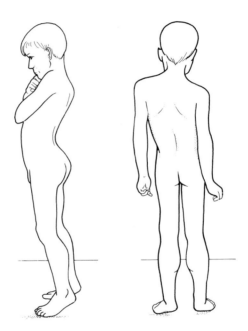

Fig. 17.6 Enlarged calf muscles in a child with Duchenne muscular dystrophy.

Once the diagnosis has been considered there is no difficulty in confirming or excluding it, for the CPK is massively elevated to 50 or 100 times normal, even before symptoms appear. Confirmation of such a serious diagnosis by biopsy is highly desirable (p. 378).

Management

There is no treatment or cure for the underlying disease, but counselling and family support are invaluable as in all handicaps. The parents may wish to meet other afflicted families, perhaps through the Muscular Dystrophy Group.

GENETIC ADVICE

There is some urgency about the early diagnosis of muscular dystrophy since this may avoid the birth of further affected siblings.[371] Neonatal screening has been advocated by some authorities, but the number of cases prevented each year would be very small, and the idea has not been widely accepted. Some cases are due to new mutations rather than a transmitted gene, so it cannot be assumed that the mother is necessarily a carrier unless another member of the family is also affected. Estimation of CPK levels in the mother and other family members may help to give an estimate of the risks in further pregnancies. Carrier detection and genetic counselling in muscular dystrophy are difficult, and families should be referred to a centre which deals with this problem regularly.

SCHOOL

Both the progressive nature of the disease and the statistical association with mild intellectual deficit should be explained to the educational psychologist. Neither necessarily precludes normal schooling and each case must be considered individually.

SUBSEQUENT PROGRESS

As with cerebral palsy, children with muscular dystrophy should be reviewed regularly in a combined clinic with the physiotherapist and orthopaedic surgeon. While the child is ambulant, contractures and deformities are not a major problem, although some tightness may develop in hip flexors and the tendo-Achilles. The physiotherapist must instruct the parents in passive exercises through a full range of movement. The child should spend some time lying prone, for example to watch television. Night splints for the ankles may be helpful.

Loss of ability to walk occurs between the ages of 7 and 13. Immobilisation even for short periods may cause permanent loss of ambulation. When it is apparent that walking is about to become impossible, it may be prolonged by the use of leg calipers, preceded if necessary by the release of contractures at hip, knee and ankle.[372] Rapid mobilisation and intensive postoperative physiotherapy are essential for success.

The child eventually becomes wheelchair-dependent and there is then a very high risk of rapidly progressive contractures and deformities (Fig. 17.7). In particular scoliosis is a major problem and can be prevented or at least reduced by a moulded spinal jacket. This needs to be checked regularly with a scoliosis film taken with the jacket in position. Boots and correctly placed footrests on the wheelchair keep the feet at 90°. Swivel supports for

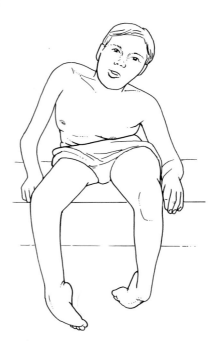

Fig. 17.7   A teenager with advanced muscular dystrophy. (Courtesy of Dubowitz[370].)

the arms reduce fatigue. There should be no hesitation in providing an electric wheelchair to prolong independence.

Most children with muscular dystrophy die of respiratory infection in their late teens or early 20s.

Muscular dystrophy—other forms

The Becker form of muscular dystrophy is clinically similar to the Duchenne type but usually has a later onset, is less severe and progresses more slowly. It is X-linked.

Limb girdle dystrophy is inherited as an autosomal recessive and may therefore be seen in females. The range of severity and rate of progression is wide.

Facioscapulohumeral dystrophy affects muscles of the shoulder girdle and face, but seldom presents before adolescence.

The rigid spine syndrome is probably a form of myopathy or muscular dystrophy. There are some features suggestive of Duchenne dystrophy but the main problem is shortening of extensor muscles of the spine together with contractures of other joints, particularly the elbows.

Some infants who are weak from birth and have dystrophic changes on muscle biopsy are categorised as congenital muscular dystrophy, although there is not always deterioration and some cases improve over the early years. Contractures are common and some cases may present as arthrogryposis (p. 378). Management is essentially as for spinal muscular atrophy with particular attention to releasing the contractures by physiotherapy and/or surgery.

THE SPINAL MUSCULAR ATROPHIES

This is a group of hereditary conditions in which progressive muscular atrophy and weakness occur in association with chronic degeneration of the anterior horn cells.[370] Heart muscle is not involved and intellect is preserved. Traditionally three types are recognised, although there is some debate about the genetic and clinical validity of these divisions.

Severe (Werdnig–Hoffman disease).   The onset may be *in utero* with diminished fetal movements or may be in the early months of life. Sometimes it may begin quite acutely. There is severe generalised hypotonia and paralysis; any movement is confined to ankles, forearms and hands. Tendon jerks are absent. Sucking and crying are weak, but the facial expression is often normal. Mild contractures may occur particularly at the shoulders. Death is almost invariable before the 1st birthday.

Intermediate.   Usually these children learn to sit, but cannot take weight in the legs and do not learn to stand or walk. There is usually fasciculation and atrophy of the tongue, and the parents may notice a tremor in the hands. This group presents the most difficult management problems. Respiratory insufficiency, flexion contractures and scoliosis are common. The length of survival depends mainly on the degree of respiratory muscle involvement but many cases survive to adult life.

Mild (Kugelberg–Welander).   Walking is achieved usually without undue delay, but mild proximal muscle weakness is noted. These children are easily mistaken for early cases of Duchenne muscular dystrophy. A tremor of the outstretched hands is commonly seen. The weakness is usually static and ambulation is not lost.

The CPK may be raised in the intermediate and mild types, but is often normal. The definitive tests are EMG, nerve conduction and muscle biopsy, and the latter should always be performed.

Management

There is no specific treatment for any of the forms of spinal muscular atrophy.

GENETIC COUNSELLING

With the exception of a few cases of the mild type which may have dominant inheritance, spinal muscular atrophy is transmitted as an autosomal recessive. Within a family, cases are usually, but not always, of similar severity.

PHYSIOTHERAPY

In the severe form, early death cannot be prevented by any supportive measures. In the intermediate type, regular supervision is essential, as with Duchenne muscular dystrophy. A spinal jacket should be supplied before scoliosis has become apparent, and if necessary more aggresive measures such as spinal bracing or a plaster jacket may be used. In some cases surgery has been attempted to prevent rapid progression of scoliosis, but results have been somewhat disappointing.

Even very weak children may be able to use calipers if the hips are supported by a pelvic band. Walking may then be achieved with crutches or a rollator, but even if this is not possible, the children enjoy the upright posture, and it probably helps to prevent deformity. A good time to introduce calipers is at school entry at 3 or 4 years of age. Most of these children should start at a school for the physically handicapped where regular and intensive physiotherapy supervision is available. There is no intrinsic reason why they should not attend normal school, but adequate physiotherapy and medical support would be essential for successful integration.

CONGENITAL MYOPATHIES

This group of rare disorders is distinguished by the presence of structural changes in muscle. Many can only be recognised by electron microscopy and clinical distinction between the types is rarely possible. The presentation may be as a 'floppy infant', or with muscle weakness at any age. The clinical course may be static, progressive or improving. Some cases have had ocular muscle involvement, and others dysmorphic skeletal features such as scoliosis, foot deformities, high palate and long thin facies. There are also many metabolic muscle diseases, but all are very rare.

Mitochondrial myopathies[373] are a particularly interesting group, and are probably rather more common than the other myopathies. Many

Table 17.3   Mitochondrial cytopathy: a multisystem disorder.

Myopathy, often progressive
Ptosis
Ophthalmoplegia
Pyramidal signs
Ataxia
Pigmentary retinal degeneration
Sensorineural hearing loss
Variable I.Q.
Cardiac conduction defects
Various endocrine defects
Nephropathy
'Ragged red' fibres on muscle biopsy

---

clinical features have been described, affecting both muscle and other systems (Table 17.3). It is likely that this group of conditions is not homogenous, but the unifying feature is the consistent finding of various mitochondrial abnormalities on electron microscopy. This diagnosis should be considered in any child with muscle weakness, especially that affecting limb girdle, neck flexor or ocular muscles, particularly when there are other systemic abnormalities. An unusual mechanism of inheritance has been postulated.[459]

Muscle weakness and myotonia

Myotonia is a state of unwanted sustained contraction of voluntary muscle. This may be manifest by difficulty in relaxing the grip on an object, stiffness after immobility or in response to a fright, or prolonged closure of the eyes after crying. Eye movements may be affected. Myotonia can be demonstrated by percussing (with a hammer or finger) on the tongue or thenar eminence: this manoeuvre produces a groove or dimple. EMG produces a characteristic response; when the needle is inserted or the muscle is tapped, there is a spontaneous burst of activity which on the loudspeaker sounds like a dive bomber.

Dystrophia myotonica

This is not a rare disease but the diagnosis is often long delayed. The classic form is not seen in paediatric practice. The features are wasting of facial muscles and sternomastoids, myotonia, cataract, frontal baldness, testicular atrophy, diabetes, cardiac involvement, retardation and progressive muscle weakness.

The disorder may present in infancy, with hypotonia, swallowing difficulty, respiratory failure, talipes and a history of hydramnios. There is facial weakness involving eyes and mouth. The congenital form is nearly always transmitted by the mother who usually shows the typical expressionless face and inability to close the eyes tightly enough to bury the eyelashes. Mental retardation is common. The early features slowly improve but later there is progressive deterioration as in the adult form. In childhood the diagnosis may be made because of facial weakness and scoliosis, or on the basis of the family history. Mental handicap may be noticed before the muscle disorder.

MANAGEMENT

Myotonia can be relieved by procainamide, prednisone or quinine, but the myotonia is seldom the main problem and may not justify treatment. There is no specific treatment for the other features of the disease. As deterioration is very slow, educational placement should be based on assessment of the child's current functional handicaps.

General anaesthesia can result in sudden death, possibly because of the cardiac involvement. There may also be respiratory insufficiency. This risk must be explained to parents and teachers, and a Medic-Alert bracelet is an additional safeguard.

Dystrophia myotonica is inherited as an autosomal dominant but there is marked variation in severity, so that a very mildly affected parent may have a severely handicapped child. Careful family studies and expert genetic advice are essential.

Miscellaneous neuromuscular disorders

MYASTHENIA GRAVIS

In myasthenia, muscles fatigue excessively after repeated muscle activity and recover with rest. There are three forms. A transient type is seen in infants born to myasthenic mothers. There is a very rare congenital form, and a commoner juvenile type. In the latter (which affects girls more than boys), there is weakness of eye muscles, and ptosis. Sometimes facial muscles, swallowing, speech or limbs are also involved. Pharmacological management using anticholinesterase drugs is usually effective. Steroids are occasionally useful and thymectomy improves some cases.

NEUROPATHIES

Numerous rare inherited disorders of peripheral nerve have been described. Early features include abnormal gait, foot deformity (pes cavus, hammer toes), clumsiness, thickening of peripheral nerves, etc. There may sometimes be mixed upper and lower motor neurone signs. There are also several conditions in which the dominant feature is lack of normal pain sensation.

The Guillain–Barré syndrome of acute infectious polyneuritis is commoner than the inherited neuropathies. Even after severe paralysis in the acute phase, recovery (although slow) is often complete or nearly so.

POLYMYOSITIS AND DERMATOMYOSITIS

These uncommon inflammatory diseases may cause severe disability, in particular muscle contractures and weakness. Additional problems are caused by the side-effects of the steroids needed to control the disease. Physiotherapy throughout the often prolonged course is essential to minimise eventual handicap.

POLIOMYELITIS

The polio virus attacks the anterior horn cell resulting in flaccid paralysis which may be focal, patchy or total. There is associated weakness, wasting and loss of tendon reflexes, but no sensory loss or intellectual deficit. The onset is usually with a meningitic illness, fever, headache, neck stiffness and abnormal CSF. In the UK, this is now a rare disease. More commonly an immigrant child presents with features of old polio. Usually the diagnosis is obvious, because of the asymmetric distribution of weakness in association with lower motor neurone signs. However, when the history is vague and the paralysis extensive, it may be surprisingly difficult to rule out other causes of lower motor neurone dysfunction.

Polio is preventable by immunisation and has virtually disappeared from Western countries. The WHO is working to eradicate it worldwide.[460] Every parent should be encouraged to accept immunisation against polio even if they reject the injectable vaccine for diphtheria, pertussis and tetanus. For an immigrant child visiting his family in a developing country, the risk of contracting polio is high and every effort should be made to encourage immunisation before travel.

REHABILITATION

In the early stages, respiratory care, together with prevention of contractures and deformities, are the priorities. This is followed by mobilisation and physiotherapy. Calipers are used where necessary. Tenotomies and muscle transplants may restore lost movements.[461] For the severely disabled, environmental control systems and specially adapted transport may be needed.

ARTHROGRYPOSIS

This rare congenital disorder is not a single entity. It is characterised by multiple joint deformities, which are a manifestation of intrauterine disease affecting anterior horn cell, nerve or muscle.[374] The main findings are featureless extremities, with absence of normal skin creases and deep skin dimples; rigidity of joints, due to short tight muscles and capsular contractures; dislocation of joints, particularly hip or knee; and muscle abnormalities. Intellect is usually normal.

Forcible stretching or manipulation is not effective and may produce fractures. Early surgical release, followed by appropriate splintage and physiotherapy, is the treatment of choice. Tendon transfers may replace ineffective muscles. An early consultation with an orthopaedic surgeon with experience of arthrogryposis is essential.

MANAGEMENT OF NERVE AND MUSCLE DISORDERS

INVESTIGATION

For suspected disorders of muscle, nerve or anterior horn cell, there are three standard investigations.

1   Measurement of creatine phosphokinase (CPK), an enzyme which leaks into the blood from damaged muscle. CPK is always elevated in Duchenne muscular dystrophy and in many other conditions, but a normal CPK does not exclude muscle disease. The estimation is technically demanding and borderline results should be rechecked by an experienced technician who does the test regularly. The CPK can be elevated following intramuscular injections or vigorous exercise.

2   Electromyography (EMG) and nerve conduction studies are useful to localise a disorder of nerve, muscle or anterior horn cell, although normal results do not completely eliminate the possibility of a neuromuscular disorder. Considerable expertise is needed for reliable interpretation of EMG results in young children who cannot fully cooperate.

3   Muscle biopsy is essential for definitive diagnosis. Since the advent of needle biopsy this has become a very minor procedure but it should only be performed in a centre with full facilities for processing and examining the specimen by all available techniques including electron microscopy.

TREATMENT AND THERAPY

Although numerous neuromuscular syndromes are now recognised, very few are treatable. The main justification for accurate diagnosis as far as the individual patient is concerned is for genetic counselling and to give some idea of prognosis where possible. There is always a danger that the child with the fascinating rare disease will be less well cared for, in terms of general support and services, than the child with non-specific handicap. Frequently his follow-up is at a major referral centre many miles from where he lives, and as a result there is little contact with the school, and information is not made available to his teachers, or to the community services.

Physical management of these children must take into account the natural history of their disease, but this often evolves slowly and is unpredictable. It is essential to prevent contractures and deformities, to have a planned programme of mobilisation, and to undertake regular surveillance in a combined paediatric and orthopaedic clinic, so that progressive deformities such as scoliosis can be recognised early. Children with neuropathies or insensitivity to pain present additional problems; they are liable to injuries, ulcers and burns which may heal very slowly, and protective footwear and constant supervision are necessary.

MISCELLANEOUS MOTOR DISORDERS

Congenital limb deficiencies

The limbs develop between the 4th and 8th weeks of gestation. Agents which cause limb deficiencies must exert their effects within this period. The best known teratogenic agent is thalidomide, which caused an epidemic of limb defects between 1959 and 1962. With this exception, congenital limb deficiencies are rare.[333,334]

There are numerous classifications of limb defects. The one illustrated in Fig. 17.8 is useful, though some defects are unclassifiable whichever system is used. In practice, the commoner defects continue to be identified by descriptive clinical terms (Table 17.4, Fig. 17.9).

In congenital absence of the fibula (fibular hemimelia) the affected leg is shortened, with an equinovalgus deformity of the foot. The tibia is bowed in an anteromedial direction with a skin dimple at the apex of the bow.

Several abnormalities of the femur are recognised including congenital short femur and proximal femoral focal deficiency. The thigh is short, flexed, abducted and externally rotated; it tapers towards the knee. There may be associated fibular hemimelia. Bilateral femoral defects lead to dwarfing.

In congenital absence of the radius (radial hemimelia) the forearm is shortened, the ulna is bowed radially and the hand is deviated. The most severe defects are those in which the entire limb is absent (*amelia*) or there is only a rudimentary hand or foot attached directly to the trunk (*phocomelia*): these defects are often bilateral, and sometimes all four limbs are involved.

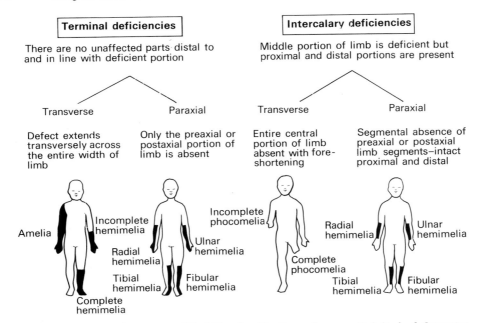

Terminal deficiencies
There are no unaffected parts distal to and in line with deficient portion

Intercalary deficiencies
Middle portion of limb is deficient but proximal and distal portions are present

Transverse — Defect extends transversely across the entire width of limb

Paraxial — Only the preaxial or postaxial portion of limb is absent

Transverse — Entire central portion of limb absent with fore-shortening

Paraxial — Segmental absence of preaxial or postaxial limb segments—intact proximal and distal

Amelia

Incomplete hemimelia

Radial hemimelia

Tibial hemimelia

Complete hemimelia

Incomplete phocomelia

Ulnar hemimelia

Fibular hemimelia

Radial hemimelia

Complete phocomelia

Ulnar hemimelia

Tibial hemimelia

Fibular hemimelia

Fig. 17.8 The Frantz–O'Rahilly classification of congenital limb deficiencies (Courtesy JAMA).

Table 17.4 Definitions of limb reduction defects.

Term	Meaning
Amelia	Complete absence of a limb
Hemimelia	Absence of the major portion of a limb
Phocomelia ('seal-limb')	Terminal portion (hand and foot) attached directly to trunk
Acheiria	Absent hand
Apodia	Absent foot
Adactylia	Absent digit
Aphalangia	Absent phalanx
Ectromelia	Absent radial side of arm or tibial side of leg

MANAGEMENT

As these defects are so rare, it is essential to obtain advice from a referral centre specialising in them. The child should be assessed by an orthopaedic surgeon, orthotist, paediatrician, occupational therapist and physiotherapist. The parents should be given an explanation of the problem, and a preliminary plan of management, as soon as possible. All children with limb defects must have a complete general examination, since some (particularly

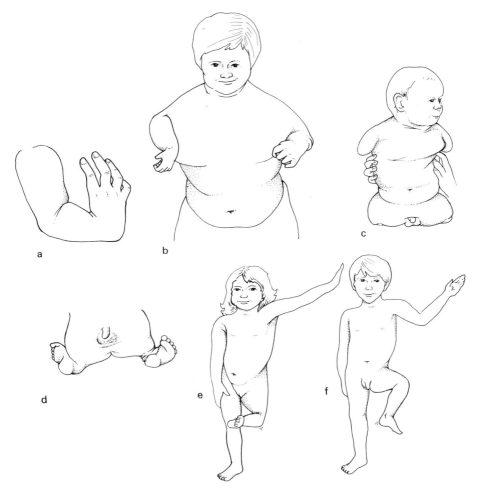

Fig. 17.9   Examples of congenital limb defects. **a** Radial hemimelia; radial deviation of hand, short forearm, bowed ulna, absent thumb and first metacarpal. **b** Bilateral upper limb phocomelia; hands attached directly to trunk. **c** Lower limb amelia; lobule of fat at site of lower limb attachment, wide pelvis due to subcutaneous fat accumulation. **d** Lower limb phocomelia; a deformed foot attaches directly to trunk. **e** Tibial hemimelia; severe flexion contracture and webbing at knee. **f** Proximal femoral focal deficiency; thigh is short, flexed, abducted and externally rotated. Soft tissues taper towards the knee.

radial defects) may be part of a recognisable syndrome with genetic implications, and there is a high incidence of other anomalies such as congenital heart disease, renal disorders, or cleft palate. Vision and hearing should be checked.

Children with congenital absence of radius or fibula, femoral defects, or similar problems, will require careful and prolonged follow-up by a paediatric orthopaedic surgeon and an orthotist. The timing and planning of surgical procedures requires expert judgement.

Management of phocomelia and amelia depends entirely on the distribution of the defects and on the function of the remaining parts. Only general principles can be given here. Digits, however rudimentary, should never be amputated since the child may learn to make use of them. The child without arms should be encouraged to use his feet, mouth and chin for function. The physiotherapist and occupational therapist may be able to help with simple adaptations of toys, feeding equipment, clothing, etc. A helmet should be supplied for an armless baby when he starts to walk, as he cannot save himself when he falls.

Babies with upper limb deficiencies can be assessed for a prosthesis when they can sit at around 6–8 months (Fig. 17.10). Initially this is mainly for cosmetic reasons, though it may also help the baby to accept the use of the apparatus as part of normal life. A functional prosthesis can be used at about 2 years, but the more sophisticated devices powered by electricity or gas pressure are seldom useful until the child is older. In spite of dramatic advances in bioengineering, an upper limb prosthesis is still a poor substitute for even a rudimentary limb that has sensation. A child may only use his prosthesis under pressure from adults and may function better without it.

Children with severe lower limb defects have problems in acquiring sitting balance. A 'bucket' seat may help to overcome this (Fig. 17.10). Later, various forms of swivel walker or a cart may be used until the child is old enough to walk using an orthotic appliance.

Acquired paraplegia

Fortunately this is rare. The more important causes are listed in Table 17.5. The problems arising from loss of sensation and bladder dysfunction have much in common with those of spina bifida and only a few additional points need be mentioned here. More detailed accounts of the rehabilitation of paraplegia victims will be found elsewhere.[334,375]

Long term goals for mobility depend on the level of the lesion. If this is above T8, the child is unlikely to achieve independent walking that will be useful in adult life, whereas if it is below T10 this may be possible using long leg calipers and crutches. Prevention of deformity is an important goal of management. In particular, contractures of hip flexors and of the tendo-Achilles can occur very rapidly. Scoliosis is very common and a brace or jacket should be supplied *before* it develops. Calipers not only assist standing and mobilisation but protect against trauma and fractures of the lower limbs.

After an acute lesion of the spinal cord an indwelling catheter is usually required, but later an 'automatic bladder' develops. Reflex bladder contrac-

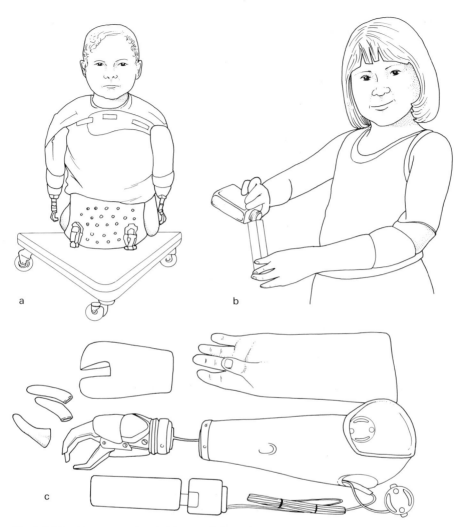

Fig. 17.10 Equipment for children with limb defects. **a** 'Bucket' trolley, **b** artificial limb in use, **c** detail view of limb. (Courtesy of H. Steeper, Roehampton Limb Fitting Unit.)

tion can often be initiated by stimulating the skin of the lower abdomen. Intermittent self catheterisation may be useful until the automatic bladder is established.

In the early stages after acute spinal injury, the lower limbs are often flaccid, but gradually spasticity develops and may become extreme. This may give rise to functional problems and uncomfortable spasms, which are often precipitated by urinary infections. Baclofen is sometimes helpful in the reduction of spasticity and spasm (p. 351).

Table 17.5   Causes of paraplegia in childhood.

Poliomyelitis
Neural tube defects
Accidental trauma (perinatal or postnatal)
Non-accidental injury (shaking)
Compressive lesions
    tumour (commonest: secondary neuroblastoma)
    abscess
    tuberculosis
    angioma
    cysts
Transverse myelitis
Foramen magnum and atlanto-axial anomalies

Acquired cerebral injury

Head injury, intracranial infection, and metabolic disturbances are important causes of acquired cerebral damage; the extent and speed of recovery from these disorders is unpredictable. Even after prolonged coma a child may recover essentially normal functioning and personality. Improvement in both motor and intellectual function may continue for at least a year. Common sequelae include motor deficits such as spasticity, with a risk of deformities similar to those seen in cerebral palsy. Intellectual impairment is related to the duration of post-traumatic amnesia and is usual if this was longer than three weeks, but unusual if less than two weeks. Personality changes such as irritability, poor concentration, unprovoked aggression, and poor impulse control are less closely related to the severity of injury; they can sometimes be attributed to the non-specific effects of illness, hospitalisation and intellectual impairment, but there is little doubt that acquired brain damage is associated with an increased incidence of various behavioural and personality problems (p. 392). These are not easily eliminated by any form of medical or psychological treatment, and may pose difficult management problems for parents and teachers. It should also be remembered that behavioural and psychosocial problems may have been present *before* the brain damage occurred and, in the case of head injury, may indeed have contributed to it.

The risk of post-traumatic epilepsy is greater if a fit occurs within the first week after brain injury, or there is a depressed fracture, an intracranial haematoma, or post-traumatic amnesia lasting for longer than 24 hours.[423] In these cases anticonvulsant prophylaxis is recommended for a period of 1–2 years. No comparable data are available on the risk of late epilepsy or the need for anticonvulsant prophylaxis following other forms of cerebral damage.

Achondroplasia

This is a disorder of cartilage formation which results in severe disproportionate dwarfism.[333,334] It occurs in about 1 per 30 000 births and is
dominantly inherited, with 80–90% of cases arising from a new mutation.
The limbs are very short in comparison to the trunk, and the adult height
seldom exceeds 100 cm. Bowing of the legs and hip flexion deformities are
common. The middle finger is short and is widely separated from the ring
finger, giving rise to the so-called 'trident hand' appearance. The head is
large and looks hydrocephalic and the ventricles are often slightly enlarged;
in a few cases true hydrocephalus develops. Thoracolumbar kyphosis,
lumbar lordosis and scoliosis are common and may lead to root compression or spinal cord damage, and progressive paraplegia. The latter may also
result from abnormalities at the foramen magnum. Regular follow-up to
detect neurological complications at an early stage is essential. Life
expectancy is limited by the neurological and cardiopulmonary complications of the spinal deformity.

Achondroplasia is only one of the many syndromes of short-limbed
dwarfism, which have many clinical features in common. An accurate
diagnosis in all such cases is essential if serious errors of genetic counselling
are to be avoided. Referral to a centre with clinical and radiological
expertise in these rare disorders is advisable. If this is not possible for any
reason, clinical photographs and X-rays (taken post mortem if necessary)
should be obtained and sent for expert comment.

Osteogenesis imperfecta

The incidence of this disease is about 1 per 20 000 births. The main clinical
and radiographic features[376,462] are summarised in Table 17.6. The disease
may present with multiple fractures at birth or with fracture caused by
trivial injury at any time in early life. The traditional distinction between a
severe recessively inherited 'congenital' form and a milder dominantly
inherited 'tarda' form is no longer accepted. It is now known that there are
several types including a dominantly inherited form with blue sclerae; a
second form, probably also dominant, but usually caused by a new
mutation, characterised by pale blue or white sclerae and progressive severe
deformity and dwarfing; and several rare recessive forms. The age of
presentation is variable in the two dominant forms, and does not appear to
be a distinguishing feature between them.

These children suffer from repeated fractures which often cause severe
deformities, particularly affecting the lower limbs. In the more severely
affected cases weight-bearing and walking may be impossible since they
inevitably cause further fractures, and other means of mobility must then
be provided (p. 341). Plastic orthoses can give some support and protection
and, recently, inflatable orthoses have been introduced. An important

Table 17.6   Features of osteogenesis imperfecta.

Hypoplasia and weakness of bone with multiple fractures
Narrow shafts of long bones, flaring at ends
Rapid healing of fractures with extensive callus
Honeycomb pattern in bones which have fractured
Broad skull; Wormian bones
Platybasia
Concave deformity of vertebrae
Scoliosis beginning in childhood
Joint laxity and easy bruising
Soft discoloured teeth
Deafness in 2nd and 3rd decade
Blue sclerae (see text)
High metabolic rate with elevated thyroxine
Heat intolerance
Risk of hyperpyrexia with anaesthesia
Chest infections potentially serious

advance has been the development of the extensible intramedullary nail which is inserted into the bones of the leg and extends as the bones lengthen with growth. This device controls fractures and prevents deformity, though it does not necessarily improve the prospects of independent walking.

There are numerous practical problems in the everyday care of children with osteogenesis imperfecta and parents should be encouraged to join the Brittle Bone Society which is a valuable source of information.

Chapter Eighteen
Learning Disabilities

Every school-teacher has experience of children who, in spite of normal intelligence, fail to make progress in one or more areas of learning. Since there is often no apparent reason for the child's failure, it is assumed that he must have some intrinsic deficit in cerebral or psychological function and as a result a medical opinion is requested. Problems with reading, writing, spelling and arithmetic are most commonly the cause of referral for expert advice, but this probably merely reflects the natural preoccupations of parents and teachers. Undoubtedly, if society gave a higher priority to athletic, musical or creative skills, children would be referred for failure in these areas. Other problems commonly observed in the classroom include 'clumsiness' and 'hyperactivity'. In this chapter, the problems of all these children will be described as 'learning disabilities'. This term, which was first used by Kirk in 1963, has the merit of making no implicit assumptions about the nature of the child's difficulties;[377] it merely recognises that he has a problem.

The concept of learning disabilities includes almost every form of behavioural aberration which has ever irritated a teacher or worried a parent.[378] Terminology generally reflects the orientation of the researcher involved; doctors use neurological words, psychologists try to define processes, and educators focus on learning and classroom behaviour. The terminology is indeed so confusing that one author invented a 'do-it-your-self terminology generator' (Table 18.1)!

Many of the labels used to describe learning disabilities are qualified by the word 'developmental'. The implication is that the child's problems are caused by some ill-defined delay or anomaly in brain maturation and that as the child matures he will grow out of his disability. The first of these

387

Table 18.1   Fry's do-it-yourself terminology generator. (From Fry (1968) Copyright 1968 International Reading Association, reprinted by permission.)

Directions: select any word from Column 1. Add any word from Column 2, then add any word from Column 3. If you do not like the result, try again—it will mean about the same thing.

Qualifier	Area of involvement	Problem
Minimal	Brain	Dysfunction
Mild	Cerebral	Damage
Minor	Neurological	Disorder
Chronic	Neurologic	Dis-synchronisation
Diffuse	CNS	Handicap
Specific	Language	Disability
Primary	Reading	Retardation
Disorganised	Perceptual	Impairment
Organic	Impulse	Pathology
Clumsy	Behaviour	Syndrome

assumptions cannot easily be tested; the second is not justified since, although the more florid problems often do decrease with age, residual difficulties and secondary handicaps may persist through the teens and into adult life.

PREVALENCE OF LEARNING DISABILITIES

Figures for the prevalence of learning disabilities vary widely in different studies, both because of genuine variations and more importantly because of the difficulties of definition. Probably between 3 and 10% of children have some form of learning disability. In all studies, boys are affected more often than girls.

HISTORICAL BACKGROUND

The origins of the various definitions and terminology used in this field are best appreciated in their historical context.[377,378] There have been two general lines of inquiry. Firstly, behavioural and learning problems are observed in adults with documented brain damage. It is tempting to deduce that similar functional problems in children might also be attributable to areas of brain damage or dysfunction. Secondly, it is known that severe brain damage in infancy can cause severe handicap; therefore, minor brain damage might cause minor handicaps such as learning disabilities. Both assumptions are plausible but are not necessarily correct.

Effects of focal brain lesions

The Scottish ophthalmologist, Hinshelwood, was the first to write extensively on reading disorders. Word blindness was first described in 1877, and the term 'dyslexia' was introduced some nine years later. Hinshelwood and his contemporaries were impressed by the apparent similarity between the specific reading deficits seen in adults with localised brain lesions and the 'developmental' problems of children. More recently, further evidence has been produced; for example Luria, a Russian neuropsychologist, showed that sharply demarcated brain lesions caused by war injuries could affect isolated aspects of reading, writing or calculation skills.

Since focal brain lesions can cause reading difficulties in adults, it is not surprising that a search for focal brain lesions in children with learning disabilities was initiated. This search still continues today although to date it has been largely unsuccessful; and terms borrowed from adult 'lesion' neurology such as 'dyslexia', 'dysgraphia', 'dysphasia' and 'dyspraxia' are firmly established in the literature of learning disabilities.

Damage or dysfunction?

DOMINANCE AND DOMINANCE FAILURE

In 1925, Orton, an American neurologist, proposed that the brain defects of learning-disabled children were functional rather than structural. This hypothesis was based on studies of cerebral hemisphere specialisation and dominance. The idea was that the child, in learning to read or write, has to concentrate on left hemisphere images and suppress those in the right. If for some reason the left hemisphere is unable to establish this dominance over the right, confusion and delay results, a situation called strephosymbolia ('twisted signs'). Orton described six syndromes which he attributed to dominance failure; these were: developmental dyslexia; developmental dysgraphia; developmental word deafness; developmental motor dysphasia; true childhood stuttering; and developmental dyspraxia. Orton and his followers developed a system of remedial education based on his hypothesis. Although Orton himself did not in fact regard the production of hemisphere dominance as a primary goal, the assessment and development of dominance has become a major preoccupation of many remedial educationalists. More recent evidence suggests that this is a misguided and naive view.

Dominance refers to the concept of lateralised specialisation of hemisphere function; laterality describes the *observed preference* of an individual for use of one or other limb, eye or ear. The dominant hemisphere is the one responsible for speech and language, and this is usually the one controlling the preferred or more skilled hand. However the situation is considerably more complicated that was realised at the time when Orton introduced his hypothesis,[379,380] as the following observations show.

1   Many left-handers have a left hemisphere localisation of language, while others seem to have bilateral representation.

2   In children who sustain injury to the dominant hemisphere temporary aphasia may occur, but the speed of recovery suggests that the other hemisphere already has a store of linguistic information: it does not have to relearn language from the beginning. This take-over of language functions occurs at the expense of other cognitive processes.[326,327]

3   The dominant hemisphere is only dominant for linguistic functions. The so-called minor hemisphere may be superior in spatial and complex visual functions and in some musical skills.

4   There are anatomical asymmetries in the size of the language areas of the temporal lobe and in the pyramidal tracts,[393] but these do not always correlate with observed dominance or preference.

The clinical assessment of laterality is exceedingly difficult.[10] Even for the simplest task, that of determining handedness, different results may be obtained by asking the subject which is his better hand, observing his preferred hand for writing, and administering a set of specialised laterality tests. Similarly, footedness for hopping and for kicking may be different. Eye and ear preference are at least partly dependent on handedness, and also on peripheral defects such as refractive errors, amblyopia, or mild middle-ear disease.

The extensive literature on laterality and dominance does not reveal any reliable correlation with learning disabilities. The distinction between familial and non-familial left-handedness, rate of development of hand preference, and the significance of 'crossed laterality' (i.e. handedness different from foot or eye preference) have all been studied extensively but, although there are often statistical links with learning disabilities, the relationships are too fragile to be of much clinical value.

Much further research is needed in this field and at present it is hardly justifiable for either paediatrician, psychologist or educationalist to devote time to the detailed assessment or remediation of laterality.

DIFFUSE BRAIN DAMAGE

Another hypothesis to explain the existence of learning disabilities was the concept of 'diffuse' brain damage. In 1918, an epidemic of encephalitis lethargica occurred in Europe and the USA. Although intellectual function as measured by I.Q. was not substantially reduced, many of the survivors were found to have significant behavioural problems, such as 'hyperactivity' and distractability. Similar behaviour was observed in soldiers who had sustained head injuries in World War One. These findings suggested a

Table 18.2 Behavioural characteristics of brain damage as described by Strauss and Werner.

Description	Behaviour
Forced responsiveness to stimuli	Any passing stimulus, however irrelevant, captures the child's attention
Pathological fixation	A tendency to fixate on a simple task for an excessive time
Disinhibition	Excessive attention to stimuli which elicit motor activity; 'hyperactivity'
Dissociation	Inability to comprehend a pattern as a whole; failure to integrate activities, leading to a general disorganisation

link between behavioural disturbances and brain damage, although no consistent anatomical localisation of these effects could be found.

In the 1940s Strauss and Werner, recognising the similarities between the behaviour of some retarded children and that of brain-damaged adults, suggested that behavioural disturbance in children might be the result of non-specific brain injury, caused for example by 'multiple small haemorrhages scattered throughout the brain'. They regarded learning disabilities as an inevitable consequence of four behavioural characteristics of brain-injured children (Table 18.2); conversely, they claimed that this behaviour pattern was diagnostic of brain damage. Although it is now clear that much of their theorising was naive and often wrong, Strauss and Werner made a great contribution to education, for their ideas encouraged a more constructive and less critical attitude to children with school problems.

Minimal brain damage and dysfunction

From these earlier observations on the apparent links between brain pathology and behaviour, the concept of minimal brain dysfunction (MBD) was developed and has given rise to a vast literature and a fair amount of 'neuromythology'.[467] In the early 1960s, Clements and Peters in the USA, and Bax and MacKeith in the UK investigated the problems of MBD and it rapidly became a popular concept. For the paediatrician it offered an explanation for many puzzling clinical phenomena, while for the child psychiatrist it provided an incentive to look more carefully at a child's instrinsic difficulties, instead of attributing all problems to psychodynamic factors.

At present there are two distinct theories. One is that minimal brain damage is a mild form of severe brain damage, caused by similar insults of lesser degree.[468] This idea was introduced in the 1950s, first by Lilienfeld and Parkhurst, and was developed by Pasamanick and Knobloch. They suggested that, since severe cerebral insults are known to cause major handicaps such as cerebral palsy, lesser handicaps might well be caused by minor perinatal brain injuries. The term 'continuum of reproductive wastage' was introduced to describe the full range of disorders from death, through cerebral palsy, to learning disabilities, which might result from perinatal brain damage.[381]

Alternatively, the term 'minimal brain dysfunction' may be preferred and the disorder may be viewed as a distinct entity involving an altered capacity for arousal, with impairment of attention control and stimulus filtering, possibly based on genetically determined neurotransmitter abnormalities. The name of Wender is particularly associated with this view.

The term minimal brain dysfunction is now commonly used to describe the supposed behavioural syndrome, irrespective of its possible aetiology. Exact definition is elusive, but the following is based on a recent study of MBD: 'A childhood disorder characterised by deficits of attention and impulse control associated with disorders of perception, motor function or cognition, in the absence of cerebral palsy or frank mental retardation'. No-one doubts that there are children who have such problems in various combinations, but there is considerable doubt as to whether they cluster together to form a meaningful syndrome.[382] Firstly, the number of symptoms suggestive of MBD in individual children forms a continuous distribution curve from none to numerous; there is no 'hump' as one would expect if MBD were a separate entity. Secondly, although the *overall* incidence of psychological disorders is increased after *proven* brain injury, there is no clear-cut pattern of disorder, and therefore there is no reason to think that a definable pattern of disorder should follow *unproven subclinical* brain damage (*see also* p. 8). Thirdly, the notion of attention deficits or 'hyperactivity' as a unifying factor in MBD is not supported by detailed studies, as discussed below (p. 399). Lastly, 'soft' neurological signs (p. 75) have been used as a clinical marker for identification of MBD, but although they are commoner in young children with learning difficulties than those without, these differences largely disappear by the age of 10 years and the association between soft signs, hyperactivity and learning problems are weak, while those with perinatal disorder are weaker still.

Although direct evidence is still scanty,[384] there is undoubtedly some biological contribution to the symptoms of MBD; environmental experiences and opportunities for learning are not a sufficient explanation in themselves. The male preponderance, and the association with chromosome defects and minor physical anomalies support this view (p. 74). Nevertheless, the reasons why an individual child should have severe developmental problems are usually quite obscure. There may be a genetic component to the inheritance of 'talents' (e.g. maths, music, sports) or lack of them, independent of I.Q. Perhaps a minority have a pathological basis for their problems, such as brain damage or abnormal development of cerebral functions.

In the present state of knowledge, the MBD concept is unsatisfactory since there are no common aetiological or diagnostic factors, no obvious clustering of the various symptoms into behavioural syndromes, and no universally effective method of treatment. Kirk's suggestion of the term 'learning disability' was prompted by an increasing distaste for unsubstantiated, unhelpful, and potentially damaging medical labels, and this term will be used in the remainder of this chapter.

MODERN IDEAS ABOUT LEARNING DISABILITIES

The information-processing approach

Much of the modern psychological research on learning disabilities has ignored the issues of brain damage and of the localisation of function, neither of which are directly relevant to educational management. Analysis of the means by which the human brain processes information has been a popular and profitable area of enquiry.[385] According to the information-processing approach, sensory inputs are transformed, rearranged, checked against stored memory, retrieved and used in a sequence of ordered stages which can be represented in the form of a flow-chart (Fig. 18.1). The schemes which result from this approach have the great merit of concentrating detailed attention on the child's difficulties and they are a rich source of hypotheses for remedial teaching and further research. There is, however, very little evidence that the various stages have any independent existence at the neurophysiological level. Furthermore, remedial programmes designed to overcome deficiencies in the processing of

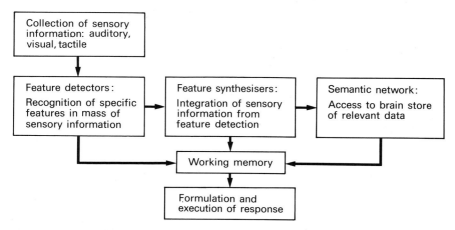

Fig. 18.1 A simple flow-chart of human information processing.

auditory or visual information have proved very disappointing and they do not give better results than the direct teaching of the skill which is lacking.

Emotional and environmental influences

There can be no doubt that learning disabilities may lead to emotional disturbances, including depression, social isolation and even school-phobia, but it is not clear whether learning disabilities can actually be caused by emotional disturbance. Factors such as family strife, a marital breakdown or death of a near relative sometimes seem to account for a generally poor performance in school, accompanied perhaps by day-dreaming, school refusal or disruptive classroom behaviour. In these circumstances, a psychiatric assessment may be helpful. However it is more difficult to explain a learning disability affecting only one or two areas of learning on this basis.

Poor attendance at school may well be a contributory factor to the development of a learning disability. In many cases poor attendance is due to emotional rather than organic causes. School refusal may develop because the child dislikes the teacher, or is bullied, or has no friends. He may be reluctant to leave home because of family disturbance, or one parent, usually the mother, may use minor ailments as an excuse to keep the child home to alleviate her own loneliness. When learning disabilities and school avoidance are associated, the relationship is seldom a simple one of cause and effect.

The skill and personality of the teacher are clearly of major importance, yet they are often discounted both in research studies and in clinical assessment. Every parent knows how a child's demeanour, behaviour and progress can change dramatically when he enters a new class with a new teacher. Children generally strive to please their teacher but if their efforts do not seem to be appreciated and encouraged, or, worse still, are met with ridicule, many simply stop trying. Much depends on parental support. Numerous indices of parental interest such as the display of a child's work on the walls at home, discussions about homework, educational and cultural outings, all correlate with academic progress. Until very recently, parents were commonly discouraged from helping their children to master essential skills such as reading, for fear of 'confusing' them. As a result, a valuable resource was wasted. Special schools, particularly those for the severely mentally handicapped and now many normal schools have begun to involve parents more extensively in the child's education and this practice receives official encouragement in the Warnock Report.

Outstanding educators such as Holt, who based their work on detailed classroom observation, have outlined many of the ways in which children fail in school, and these insights into the origins of learning disabilities deserve wider recognition than they have received.[386,387] Holt described how the child who is struggling to master the intricacies of reading or arithmetic experiences anxiety and tension if he is not succeeding, and may adopt a variety of strategies to conceal lack of understanding from his teacher. If fundamental principles are not mastered, and the child's problems are not recognised, he becomes more and more confused as the complexity of work increases. His mistakes become more and more bizarre. Eventually he admits defeat, his lack of progress is recognised, and a learning disability is diagnosed. The remedial teacher usually has to return to the most basic principles of the subject, which the child has never grasped.

The widespread belief of parents that some schools are better than others has received experimental confirmation in many studies.[10] Rather surprisingly, school size and class size do not have much effect on educational outcome. Factors which do correlate with higher attainment include the use of praise in the classroom, feedback to pupils about their behaviour and performance, the extent of pupil involvement in lessons, good working conditions, opportunities for children to take responsibility, and well organised lessons. All of these factors are within the power of any school to modify and improve. Although most research studies have looked at overall educational outcome, it would be surprising if the incidence of learning disabilities did not also show some correlation with good educational practices.

There are wide variations in the ages at which children are first suspected to have a learning disability, depending perhaps on the approach of the school, the availability of remedial teaching and the awareness of teachers. Too often, a child's total lack of progress is attributed to developmental variations, laziness, lack of motivation or disinterested parents. The first two years of schooling may slip by without any action being taken. The role of screening in the early identification of learning disabilities is discussed on p. 407.

TYPES OF LEARNING DISABILITY

Reading disability

Reading is a highly complex skill whose acquisition is very poorly understood. The representation of speech sounds by alphabetic symbols is a difficult concept for a child to grasp, since speech is not perceived as a series of discrete segments. Some children never learn to make the fundamental distinction between a letter and a word. Statements in many baby books like 'A is for Apple' can easily create confusion. Reading may be taught using 'Look and Say' methods, in which the child learns to recognise whole patterns rather than individual letters; or by phonic methods, which require him to sound out and blend the components of each word. To become a competent reader the child must acquire some skill in both techniques, and has to become familiar with the many words which do not conform to phonic rules. He then has to remember each word for long enough to absorb the meaning of a whole sentence.

It is difficult to define the point at which reading becomes 'automatic' but when this point is reached the child can begin to enjoy reading as a pleasurable activity rather than a chore. Automatic reading of print, like the reading of music, can only be achieved by practice, but the amount of practice which can be supervised by a class teacher is very limited, and there is increasing evidence that parental help is invaluable.

Reading can be broken down into a number of hypothetical component skills; for example, distinguishing the print from the background, scanning from left to right, seeing the letters in sequence, matching the print pattern to stored word memories,[388] etc. There have been many attempts to assess readiness for reading by assessing these various functions, and encouraging their maturation where appropriate, but in fact there seems to be little correlation between readiness for reading as measured in this way, and the child's actual progress when he begins to read.

Reading failure is the commonest learning disability seen in clinical practice, though this is probably because reading is fundamental to progress in nearly all other school subjects, and illiteracy is rightly perceived as a greater handicap than poor handwriting, poor spelling, or difficulty with numbers. It is commoner in children of low I.Q. and of low social class, and in late-born children of large families. There is also a correlation with speech problems in earlier childhood. Reading failure is associated with a substantially increased incidence of antisocial behaviour, aggression and delinquency. Since reading skill is correlated with intelligence, there is an excess of dull children with reading problems. These are said to have general reading backwardness. There are also some children whose reading attainments are substantially below what would be expected on the basis of their intelligence; these are said to have specific reading retardation.* The distinction is useful since there are some important differences between the groups (Table 18.3).

Table 18.3   General reading backwardness and specific reading retardation.

	General reading backwardness	Specific reading retardation
Sex ratio	Male = Female	3 males to 1 female
Neurological disorder	+ + +	+
Other developmental problems	Numerous	Speech and language only
Social disadvantage	+ + +	+

* The statistical details of this distinction are discussed in detail by Rutter.[11]

Table 18.4   Features characteristic of 'dyslexia'. (Miles 1983.[390])

Early difficulties in learning to read
Slowness in reading
Problems with reading aloud
Bizarre spelling
Difficulty distinguishing b and d
Weakness with arithmetic
Confusion with sequences
(reciting tables or months of the year)
Left–right confusion
Positive family history

The term 'dyslexia' has been widely used to describe the problems of children with severe difficulties affecting not only reading, but also spelling and sometimes arithmetic; the word is derived from the Greek 'lexis' (language), *not* the Latin 'lego' (I read).[389,390] Undoubtedly, there are children who display a particular and striking pattern of learning difficulties (Table 18.4) which extends beyond the mastery of reading. Some authorities, notably Critchley,[391] maintain that dyslexia is a definite neurological entity, and it is claimed by Miles and others that the problems listed in Table 18.4 occur together sufficiently often to justify its recognition as a distinct syndrome. Others argue that these features can occur singly or in any combination and it may be that the dramatic cases of 'dyslexia', which come to expert attention by reason of their severity, represent the extreme end of the distribution curve of learning disability rather than a separate entity. The issue is still controversial and it is uncertain whether children with a dyslexic pattern of difficulties require, or benefit from, a style of teaching which differs from that needed by children with less specific forms of reading retardation.

There are some superficial similarities between childhood dyslexia and the problems seen in adults with parietal lobe lesions, and the demonstration of a neurological basis for dyslexia would be the best way of establishing it as a discrete entity. Considerable interest was aroused when abnormalities of neuronal architecture in the cortical areas concerned with reading were found at autopsy in one dyslexic young man, but unfortunately this finding was of uncertain significance as he also suffered from epilepsy.[392,393] Further neuropathological studies will be of great interest; until these are available the possible organic basis of reading problems must remain conjectural.

There is a vast literature on all aspects of dyslexia and reading difficulties, including eye movement control, hemisphere asymmetry, visual perceptual function, transfer of information between auditory and visual channels and so on. There are two major problems of interpretation in these studies. Firstly, it is uncertain whether the control group should consist of normally-reading children of the same age, or younger children with the same level of reading ability as the children with reading problems. Secondly, when abnormalities are demonstrated in the poor reading group, there is no way of deciding whether they are the cause of the problem, or merely a secondary consequence of it.

Specific reading retardation is unlikely to be a single condition and is probably caused by both genetic and environmental factors. There is substantial evidence for a genetic component: reading problems are commoner in males and tend to cluster in families, and there is an association with impulsivity and other behavioural and temperamental characteristics which are known to have a genetic component.

Spelling, writing and arithmetic

In comparison with reading, the acquisition of these skills and disabilities affecting them have received much less attention. Spelling difficulties are often associated with reading retardation but the association is by no means invariable. Writing may be impaired by motor problems, such as excessive involuntary movement, but this is seldom the complete explanation. A demonstration of a child's incoordination or choreiform movements, using the neurodevelopmental examination techniques, may at least clarify the problem for his teacher. Much is made of immature or unusual pencil grips in the genesis of writing problems, but many adults hold their writing implements in a variety of unorthodox grips and yet can write without difficulty. The occupational therapist may be able to offer useful suggestions for the child who finds writing difficult.

Specific retardation in arithmetic may also occur but these children are seldom referred for medical assessment. While there are undoubtedly wide variations in the ability to handle mathematical concepts, the quality of teaching in this subject often leaves much to be desired, and this is an area where few parents feel competent to help, in contrast with the situation with reading. The observations of Holt reveal the enormous difficulties experienced by some children with this subject.

Motor disability ('clumsiness')

Orton included developmental apraxia in his list of clinical syndromes associated with hemisphere imbalance, but the current interest in the subject was revived by Walton in 1962, and Gubbay (1963) with publications on *The Clumsy Child*. The 'clumsy child' is one who has difficulty in learning and performing *motor* tasks which his peers acquire without apparent effort.[394,395] Some children who are clumsy have other developmental problems, such as reading retardation or poor handwriting. Secondary phenomena are also frequent, such as depression, loneliness, lack of friends, psychosomatic complaints, and school avoidance. The term 'clumsiness' is often used to describe those children who simply have an excess of natural exuberance (the 'bull in the china shop' syndrome) or have no concept of danger, or are restless, naughty and distractable in the classroom, but this is an inaccurate use of the term. If the term 'clumsiness' is to retain any useful meaning, it should be strictly reserved for *motor* problems. By analogy with the terminology used for reading problems, the term 'specific motor disability' might be more satisfactory, but it is not in general use at present. The concept of a clumsy child *syndrome* which includes numerous other learning disabilities is as unsatisfactory as that of 'minimal cerebral dysfunction'.

Tentatively, several subgroups of clumsy children may be recognised. Developmental dyspraxia implies a difficulty in organising and executing a series of skilled purposeful movements, even though the peripheral neurological pathways appear to be intact. Some of these children also have delayed speech development with dyspraxic features; this is not unexpected since speech is itself a complex movement (p. 243). Other children may have little or no dyspraxia, but have excessive unwanted movements, such as tremor at rest or on action, or choreiform movements. Although it may be tempting to regard these as a minimal form of choreoathetoid cerebral palsy, the physical signs often resolve with maturation and this term should therefore be avoided. There are yet other children who appear to be weak and to fatigue very easily, but investigation reveals no evidence of any neurological disorder. Intelligence and achievements in academic work may be anywhere within the normal range. A degree of motor clumsiness is often found in children of generally low ability and is therefore often reported in ESN(M) schools. It might be anticipated that a standard I.Q. test would reveal a higher score on items that are dependent on language than on those that require visual and motor 'performance' skills, but this is not always found. Furthermore, large verbal-performance discrepancies are common in the population at large and therefore this finding has to be interpreted with caution.

Clumsiness, like reading retardation, probably has many causes. Normal variation alone undoubtedly accounts for some cases, but others seem too severe to be easily explained on this basis alone. Children who were very small-for-dates or suffered prolonged postnatal malnutrition tend to be more clumsy than suitably matched controls. There is little evidence of focal lesions in the great majority of cases. Temperamental variations such as excessive timidity and lack of opportunity to play and practise motor skills may also contribute.

Hyperactivity

Strictly speaking, hyperactivity is a behaviour pattern rather than a learning disability, but the two often appear to be associated.[11,396] The term hyperactivity is commonly used as a synonym for naughty, restless, or overexuberant; any young child confined in inadequate accommodation may seem hyperactive to his parents. It is also sometimes applied to the aimless and exasperating repetitive activities of mentally retarded children and to the irritability induced by some anticonvulsant drugs such as phenobarbitone.

There are certainly children of normal intelligence and an unusual temperament which is recognisable from infancy in many cases, by the excessive irritability, colic and sleep disturbances. Some such children are reported to have needed only 3–4 hours sleep per night by their 1st birthday. Motor milestones are often achieved very early. In early and mid-childhood, hyperactivity and motor restlessness are accompanied by impulsivity, lack of awareness of danger with failure to learn from previous painful experiences, a low tolerance of frustration and a short attention span. This picture is much commoner in boys than girls.

Although the description given above suggests that hyperactivity is a definite entity, there has been much debate as to whether this is actually so.[397] Much of the difficulty derives from the problems of measuring hyperactivity. Numerous techniques have been used and they often correlate rather poorly with each other. Thus a child may appear hyperactive on one measure, but not on another. There is, however, probably a small group of truly hyperactive children who are hyperactive in all situations, have a borderline or low I.Q., make poor peer relationships and have a high incidence of psychiatric disorder.[468] These children have a rather poor prognosis for educational progress and adjustment to adult life. This condition has been called pervasive or generalised hyperkinesis. The much larger group of children who acquire the label of hyperactivity are hyperactive only in certain situations; these have an I.Q. within the normal range and as a group they are not so clearly demarcated from others with learning and psychiatric problems.

In the present state of knowledge, it seems worth recognising that some children genuinely have problems of attention and impulse control. Attempts should be made to define the situations in which this problem particularly occurs, and associated learning difficulties should be investigated. It must be remembered that psychosocial factors interact with the inherited temperamental characteristics of the child; and on this basis appropriate help is organised for the child and family. Whether or not one regards hyperactivity as a definite entity, it is in itself a fairly unhelpful diagnostic label.

CAUSES OF HYPERACTIVITY

A strong genetic contribution to hyperactivity is suggested by the persistence of the personality trait from early infancy onwards, and by the association of hyperactivity with minor physical anomalies (p. 75). With the possible exception of the rare cases associated with temporal lobe epilepsy, there is little evidence that the syndrome is caused by brain damage, but there may be neurophysiological abnormalities; for example, a disorder of monoamine metabolism has been postulated. Minor defects of vision or hearing may impair concentration in school and present as 'hyperactivity'. The possibility of lead intoxication should be considered, particularly in the mentally handicapped child with pica, but in practice this seems to be a rare cause. Undoubtedly environmental factors contribute to the extent and severity of the problem (p. 30), and there are also wide variations in adult tolerance of behaviour disorders.

The bright child

It is unfortunate that for some children high intelligence can actually be a disability.[463] Around $2\frac{1}{2}\%$ of children have I.Q.s in the range of 130–150. A very small number have an I.Q. substantially higher than this, and can be regarded as exceptionally gifted or 'genius'. Bright children are more likely to come from upper class homes, and contrary to popular belief, tend to be physically large and healthy.[398] They may come to professional attention because the normal school curriculum is intolerably slow-moving and boring to them. Usually teachers recognise that the child is bright, but do not appreciate how bright. The presenting problems include behaviour disorders, truancy, neurotic and personality problems, and even poor academic performance. They are often aware of their superior intelligence, and react either by deliberately underachieving to retain peer approval, or become immersed in subjects such as mathematics or science, sometimes to the exclusion of more 'normal' activities. Children who have adequate stimulation at home may cope well with their frustrations, although the label of 'gifted' often adds to their problems when conferred by parents who are concerned for the child to make full use of his talents. Hypersensitivity to criticism, and perfectionism may be observed in such cases.

Paradoxically, recognition and management of bright children is far inferior to that provided for the mentally handicapped. Parents who recognise their children's needs for a more demanding curriculum often find that the educational authorities, though sympathetic, are unable to help because resources are inadequate. The normal school finds these children disruptive and difficult. If they are promoted ahead of their peers, they lack the social maturity to enjoy the company of the older children. Unless special provision can be made by the school or the parents, their talents are likely to be wasted.

PAEDIATRIC ROLE IN LEARNING DISABILITIES

A detailed paediatric assessment is neither necessary nor feasible for all children with learning disabilities, although a check of vision and hearing

Table 18.5   Some causes of learning difficulty in schoolchildren.

Common causes
Vision and hearing defects
Limited intellect: mild mental handicap
Lack of family support
Poor teaching
Poor motivation
Non-specific ill-health
Irregular school attendance

Uncommon causes
Petit mal epilepsy and status
Anticonvulsant medication
Intracranial space-occupying lesions:
   hydrocephalus
   craniopharyngioma
   other tumours
Degenerative brain disease, e.g. Batten's disease, SSPE
Motor disorders presenting as 'clumsiness'
   mild cerebral palsy
   Duchenne muscular dystrophy
   hereditary ataxias
   spinal cord tumours
   benign spinal muscular atrophy

should always be arranged. Paediatric consultation may be requested merely to exclude organic disease or to assess the relative importance of biological, familial and educational contributions to the child's problems. In the more complicated cases a multidisciplinary assessment may be invaluable.

Many rare neurological conditions may present as clumsiness or school failure (Table 18.5) but the latter is usually global rather than specific to certain tasks and often there is actual loss of previously acquired skills as opposed to failure to make progress. Other features such as visual failure, fits or movement disorders may provide additional clues to the presence of progressive disease. Untreated petit mal is an important cause of poor school progress. However, progressive neurological diseases are a rare cause of learning disability and the fear of overlooking one of them should not be allowed to dominate clinical judgement.

Paediatric assessment

The history should include a list of those things which the child cannot do; equally important is to list the skills that he does have. Whatever his deficiencies may be, the existence of some well developed skills is useful evidence against a major disorder of the nervous system. In addition, the effect of the child's shortcomings on his everyday life, his family and his peers should be assessed. Is he happy?; is he worried about his supposed disability?; does he have friends?; does he like going to school?; how do his family feel about him? If the child presents with a psychosomatic or behavioural complaint, the relationship of his emotional troubles to the learning disability may not be immediately apparent and there are usually other family or personality problems which confuse the issue.

Physical examination is usually unrewarding. Minor dysmorphic features should be noted in view of their known association with hyperactivity. In cases of clumsiness a detailed neurological examination may be necessary and the neurodevelopmental examination provides a useful way of demonstrating movement problems caused by minimal cerebral palsy, muscle disease, etc.

Psychological assessment

Learning disabilities are predominantly an educational problem and in school-age children assessment and remediation are largely the responsibility of the educational psychologist. There is a strong correlation between intelligence as measured in standard I.Q. tests, and academic progress. Nevertheless, while some children of normal or above average I.Q. fail in school, others of very limited intelligence do surprisingly well, presumably because of such factors as good teaching, strong motivation and effective family support. It is therefore useful to assess the I.Q. of a child with a learning disability, to eliminate subnormal intelligence as the cause of his problems; however, intelligence testing does not elucidate the other factors which may be responsible, nor does it help directly in remediation. The psychologist's assessment will usually include an I.Q. test, measures of attainments (reading, writing, arithmetic, etc.), other tests designed to explore the child's difficulties in more detail, and consultation with teachers and parents.

Management

Simple counselling is often all that is needed. The parents are told that there is no serious disease of the nervous system, that the child's problems are real and not imaginary or due to naughtiness, and that the clinical picture of learning disability is well recognised. Parents find it oddly reassuring that the doctor 'has seen it before'. They are relieved to learn that constitutional factors are involved and that the problem is not their fault.

A common reason for referral of children with learning disabilities is a conflict between parents and the school over the management of the child's difficulties. Sometimes the paediatrician can act as mediator, and a brief conference at the school, involving parents, doctor, teacher, and psychologist is invaluable in improving communication and mutual confidence between family and school. A demonstration of soft signs elicited by the neurodevelopmental examination may help teaching staff to understand the nature of the child's problems.

School placement.   The new Education Act (p. 153) recognises that children who are failing in school require expert and individualised tuition, whether their difficulties are due primarily to low I.Q. or to a 'learning disability'. This specialised help can be provided within ordinary school, if resources are adequate, and both parents and educators are increasingly reluctant to segregate children with problems in special schools. The need to distinguish between children who are 'intrinsically dull' and those who have 'learning disabilities' would lose some of its urgency if it is accepted that most children with borderline–low I.Q.s need not be transferred to ESN(M) school but can be educated within the normal school. Nevertheless, the distinction does exist and it is important to assess with particular care those children who have so much difficulty in mastering skills which others acquire without effort.

Intervention programmes may be designed and executed at school, at home or at a Child Development Centre. Learning disabilities are best regarded as educational problems and their management should be based at school whenever possible. Regular visits to a hospital centre are time-consuming and expensive for parents and add an unjustified and potentially damaging medical element to the disability (*see* p. 4). Many ingenious remedial schemes have been devised for learning-disabled children, but their effectiveness is not known. Merely giving a child individual and sympathetic attention has a powerful (and valuable) placebo effect, known in educational research as the Hawthorne effect, and this must be separated from the benefit of the programme itself.

Remediation of learning disabilities should be geared to the teaching of those specific skills which are deficient rather than to the development of hypothetical psychological processes such as perception. There is, however, no clear guidance as to whether it is better to develop a child's strengths and interests, or to try and overcome his deficiencies. This decision should be made for each individual; every programme should have clearly defined goals and a limited duration, followed by review, otherwise there is a danger that it may continue for months or years without demonstrable benefit, but at considerable cost in time and money.

Reading.   Many remedial programmes have been devised to help the child with reading difficulties. Specific 'perceptual training' programmes such as that devised by Frostig have proved to be no more effective, and possibly less effective, than the direct teaching of reading. There is no conclusive evidence that any one method of teaching reading is superior, although some authorities feel that for children with dyslexic-type difficulties it is essential to use a carefully planned programme which emphasises the correspondence between sounds and letters.[389] Whatever view is taken one may well suspect that the skill and enthusiasm of the teacher is of primary importance.

Although short term gains can be made with most reading programmes, the long term results in general have been disappointing. There is increasing evidence that the involvement of parents in reading practice at home is beneficial,[399] and when the parents are keen to help, the technique of 'paired reading' provides a system of practising which avoids tension between parent and child.[400]

Writing and arithmetic.   The occupational therapist may be able to offer useful suggestions for the child who finds writing difficult. Comfortable seating at the correct height, allowing the feet to be put firmly on the floor or on a footrest is the first essential, while non-slip mats and thick pencils may also be helpful. For the more severely affected, whose output of imaginative ideas is severely restricted by inability to write or calculate quickly, a tape recorder, typewriter or calculator may be invaluable. Schools are increasingly sympathetic to the use of such devices.

Clumsiness.   The occupational therapist and physiotherapist may be able to help the clumsy child, and their advice is often appreciated since physical education and the study of movement have a low priority in most schools and few teachers have any knowledge of remedial techniques in this field. The occupational therapist's particular skill lies in her ability to separate everyday motor tasks, for example doing up buttons, into their component parts which the clumsy child can learn at his own speed. Simple activities of this nature have an additional spin-off effect in that the child's self-confidence and independence improve. It should be emphasised again that there is no evidence that the teaching of motor skills will have any directly beneficial effects on *other* learning disabilities such as reading.

Hyperactivity.   In many cases parents only require reassurance that they are managing the child correctly, and are not making the situation worse by their actions. A simple energy-consuming activity, which can be shared between parent and child, such as swimming, is sometimes surprisingly effective in restoring a deteriorating relationship. If treatment seems essential, amphetamine-like stimulant drugs such as methylphenidate may have a paradoxical calming effect. Some children tolerate this well; their hyperactivity decreases dramatically and their learning may also be improved. Others seem superficially quieter, but develop a zombie-like depressed affect which is usually intolerable as far as the parents are concerned. Some children seem totally unaffected by the drug. Hyperactive children who are also mentally handicapped do not often do well on stimulant drugs, but occasional successes justify a trial of therapy. An important side-effect is anorexia followed by diminished growth, although catch-up growth is seen when the drug is stopped. This should be done once or twice a year. Careful monitoring of growth is essential. A few children develop tics.

Many parents and teachers are quite disturbed by the prospect of manipulating behaviour by means of drugs. Their fears must be acknowledged and a plan agreed for a short therapeutic trial of fixed duration. The drug is then withdrawn and it immediately becomes obvious whether the effects have been beneficial.

The initial dose of methylphenidate is $\frac{1}{4}$ of the 10 mg tablet in the morning, then a repeat dose at midday. Late afternoon or evening doses sometimes are helpful but more often seem to be ineffective or even have adverse effects. The dose is increased slowly. Further benefit is rarely seen beyond 20–30 mg per day. Sedatives, major tranquillisers (e.g. haloperidol) and lithium carbonate have all been used in the treatment of hyperactivity, but their side-effects are considerable, and their effectiveness limited. Sulthiame is occasionally useful but has many side effects, similar to those of acetazolamide (p. 476). It is wise to obtain the advice of a child psychiatrist if contemplating the use of any of these drugs.

Hyperactivity has also been treated by psychotherapy and family therapy, with rather disappointing results. Behavioural methods, though time-consuming, appear to be helpful, if only in increasing the adults' ability to cope with the child. Whatever approach is adopted, the school must be involved, since the teachers must carry out any behavioural treatment and can help in assessing the effectiveness of drug therapy.

Management of sleep problems is discussed on p. 162.

Unorthodox medicine.   Much publicity has been given to the possible role of food allergy as a cause for hyperactivity and learning difficulties. Feingold introduced a diet which excludes all artificial colouring agents, and also some naturally occurring substances. Although convincing benefit has not been demonstrated in controlled trials, there may conceivably be a small subgroup of children who do benefit.[401] Many parents are convinced that this diet does help, and since the only easily available alternative is the use of stimulant drugs, there seems no reason to discourage them from experimenting.

Evening primrose oil has recently been recommended for hyperactive children. It is a source of essential fatty acids which are precursors of prostaglandins. There is however no conclusive evidence that abnormal prostaglandin metabolism is responsible for hyperactivity.

SCREENING IN SCHOOL—
THE SCHOOL ENTRANT EXAMINATION

In many schools the traditional annual medical inspection of all children has been abandoned. A detailed examination of all school entrants at age 5, and follow-up examinations only of selected children, are now more usual. The following discussion is confined to screening examinations, although the school medical officer has, of course, many other duties.

In modern Western society most children are relatively healthy, and by the age of 5 few important medical problems remain undetected. The 5 year examination may, however, reveal defects such as undescended testicle, inadequately treated asthma or extreme short stature. Most congenital heart defects are recognised in infancy. Two that may easily be missed are atrial septal defect (ASD) and coarctation of the aorta: ironically, neither of these are likely to be recognised at the school examination. Diagnosis of the first calls for careful auscultation for wide fixed splitting of the second heart sound; diagnosis of the second calls for measurement of blood pressure (palpation of the femorals is unreliable). The former is difficult, while the latter, for good reasons, is not part of most routine school examinations.

Detailed assessment of developmental status is undertaken in many school medical examinations, using the neurodevelopmental techniques described previously[402] (p. 75). The object of this examination is to identify children liable to have learning difficulties in school. Several authors have claimed that it is possible to do this with a fair degree of accuracy. Not surprisingly, the results of neurodevelopmental examination correlate better with motor problems (clumsiness) than with other learning disabili-

Table 18.6   The problem of educational screening. (*See* Lindsay and Wedell[404] for critique of original data.)

Educational screening test at age 5	Reference test: educational problems at age 7		Totals
	Present	Absent	
Failed	30	30	60
Passed	70	870	940
Totals	100	900	1000

Sensitivity = 30% (30/100)
Specificity = 97% (870/900)
Positive predictive value = 50% (30/60)

Interpretation
The test correctly classified 900 (870 + 30) of 1000 children = 90% *but* only half the children failing the screening test had problems at age 7 and the screening test only revealed one-third of children destined to have problems at age 7.

ties. Educationalists also have devised a variety of screening tests, with broadly similar aims.

All of these screening procedures can achieve a respectable level of prediction when large groups of children are considered and the results are expressed as a correlation coefficient between predicted and actual outcome.[403] However, when sensitivity and specificity are examined (Table 18.6), it is clear that even the best of these tests misclassifies substantial numbers of children. Many educationalists believe that this problem is not due to poor design or administration of neurodevelopmental screening tests, but to the intrinsic impossibility of predicting how a child's abilities may change under the influence of experiences yet to come. They argue that teachers should have the primary responsibility for identifying problem children, by continuously monitoring their progress in achieving educational goals.[404] Furthermore, the detection of potential school problems is of no value unless some form of educational intervention such as remedial teaching is available.

Chapter Nineteen
Non-accidental Injury

CLASSIFICATION AND CAUSES

The dramatic and horrific injuries which are found in some cases of child abuse represent one end of a continuous spectrum of maltreatment.[405,406] In the majority of children referred for suspected non-accidental injury (NAI), it is the circumstances and significance of the injuries rather than the actual physical damage which cause concern. Furthermore, the severity of the injury does not always correlate with the extent of the psychological disturbance which precipitated it.

It has been estimated that there are at least 3000 serious cases each year in England and Wales, of which 10% will be fatal. The number of less serious cases is unknown, since there are no exact definitions. Although the following distinctions are somewhat artificial, it may be useful to outline four categories of maltreatment, of increasing severity. In addition, some rather more unusual and specific syndromes are listed, and will subsequently be discussed in more detail.

1   Carelessness about domestic safety, casual attitudes to matters of general health, immunisation, etc., and incompetence and inadequacy in dealing with ordinary child-rearing problems are all extremely common. These difficulties may only come to be regarded as a form of maltreatment when a crisis such as an accident occurs.

2   Neglect, poor physical care, and unresponsiveness to the infant's needs, may cause serious impairment of both physical growth and development.

3   Physical injury may be inflicted on the child on one or more occasions, often as a result of uncontrollable parental anger. These outbursts may be, but are not necessarily, associated with evidence of the more chronic problems outlined in 1 and 2, above.

4   Physical injury occurs together with severe neglect and emotional

409

abuse which is persistent, deliberate and prolonged. The nature of the injuries may suggest that they have been inflicted in the most sadistic ways. Distorted ideas of what constitutes acceptable behaviour and discipline are often found in these parents.

SPECIFIC SYNDROMES OF ABUSE

5   Sexual abuse.
6   Non-accidental poisoning.
7   Munchausen's syndrome by proxy.
8   Bizarre life-styles, diets, etc.
9   Excessive punishment as a cultural phenomenon.
10   Sophisticated abuse.

Causes of child abuse

There are three components to child abuse: (1) the personality and background of the parents, (2) the temperament, behaviour and health of the child, and (3) the crisis which precipitates the injury or other event that finally brings the child to professional attention.

THE PARENTS

Although the risk of child abuse is higher where the parents are young, single, unsupported, and of low social class, it certainly is not confined to such people. The most important factor is the parents' own experiences of childhood and parental care and a high proportion of abusing parents have themselves been 'in care'. Young people deprived of love throughout their childhood, and perhaps exposed to repeated violence, seek desperately for a satisfying adult relationship, but often they make emotional demands of each other that neither can fulfil. Pregnancy is either unplanned and unwanted, or planned for poor reasons (*see* p. 27). Their concept of normal infant behaviour and responsiveness is often seriously distorted. If the baby fails to live up to their expectations, he is liable to be rejected or maltreated. There is often a preoccupation with naughtiness, discipline and punishment. Resentment that the baby has irrevocably changed the parents' life-style, or disturbed a fragile relationship sometimes contributes. The circumstances which lead to child abuse inevitably overlap with those that predispose to behavioural and developmental disorders (p. 42).

THE CHILD

The child makes an active contribution to the relationship with his parents, and there are undoubtedly temperamental differences between children which influence this (p. 30). Aggression, hyperactivity and similar traits which can put the child at greater risk of physical abuse may be, but are not necessarily, inherited; they may have been caused by prolonged emotional abuse. Children who have been premature, ill or abnormal in any way, or are of the 'wrong' sex, are more likely to be abused. Handicapped children may suffer NAI but this happens less often than one might expect, probably because these families receive a great deal of practical support and professional supervision. One child in a family may become the 'scapegoat' and suffer severe abuse while other children remain unscathed, but this is probably rather uncommon and in general, all children, even those not yet born, of abusive parents should be regarded as being at some risk.

THE CRISIS

This is commonly a trivial incident in itself, such as the child's persistent crying, vomiting or soiling, superimposed on a background of increasing parental fatigue, illness, irritability or depression.[408] The child's crying may interfere with the parents' sexual activity, or alcohol may be the factor which provokes serious injury. The risk of physical maltreatment is increased by the absence of any escape route for the strain of caring for a child. Abusive parents often have little support from their parents and relatives, and have few friends to whom they can turn in a crisis.

CLINICAL FEATURES

NEGLECT AND FAILURE TO THRIVE

Inadequate weight gain is a common manifestation of incompetent and inadequate parental care. Linear growth may also be impaired. Feeding and management difficulties are often recognised by the health visitor, but when the baby is admitted to hospital for observation organic disease is quickly excluded, and the baby feeds well and gains weight.[409] A striking feature of these cases is that often the mother has not herself sought help in spite of the baby's alarmingly low weight. These mothers usually admit to feelings of depression and low self-esteem, and were ambivalent or negative about the pregnancy—these features help to confirm the diagnosis.

There is often evidence of poor care, such as dirty clothes and extensive napkin dermatitis. In the most severely neglected cases, the baby appears quiet, apathetic, and developmentally retarded. He may even be hypothermic, and cold injury, with oedematous, discoloured feet, has been described in such cases.

Failure to grow is most commonly a problem of infants, but older children may also be affected, though usually the environment is more obviously abnormal. The mechanism of the failure to thrive is mainly a deficiency in caloric intake due to poor feeding practices, coupled with the baby's apathy and lack of interest in food, but growth hormone secretion may be depressed in some cases; this recovers very rapidly (24–48 hours).

PHYSICAL INJURY

Skin trauma.   This is by far the commonest manifestation of maltreatment. Bruises, lacerations, wheals, burns and scalds occur in infinite variety. The head and face are most frequently the target. Bruising over the cheek, eye or ear may be caused by the palm, fist or fingers. A torn frenulum of the lip and lacerations in the mouth can be caused by blows or by violent feeding of a reluctant child. On the trunk, patterns of bruising may correspond to the position of finger tips, when the child is shaken. The age of a bruise is occasionally an important issue. A yellowing bruise is at least 24 hours old, but even a forensic specialist may be unable to make any other reliable judgement as to the age of a bruise.

More bizarre marks often can be explained only by the use of an implement to strike the child. Scalds on the back or on the buttocks and perineum are unlikely to be accidental. Burns also must be viewed with suspicion. Cigarette burns are deep circumscribed lesions which may be found anywhere, but most often on the arms. Deep burns on the buttocks may be caused by placing the child on a hot radiator to dry wet nappies. Marks caused by tying the child's ankles together, and penile injuries due to ligatures to stop wetting are among the more bizarre injuries which are sometimes seen. Human bite marks may have sexual connotations; at the very least they indicate a lack of restraint in play.

Bone and joint injuries.   Ten to twenty per cent of fractures in young children are due to non-accidental injury. They are often caused by jerking or twisting a limb. Ribs may be broken by direct trauma. Metaphysial injuries with small chips of separated bone are easily missed on X-rays. Some bony injuries with haematoma formation may be mistaken for infection, particularly as fever and leucocytosis may occur.

Head injury and neurological damage.   These are the most serious of non-accidental injuries. The skull may be fractured by a direct blow and unexplained skull fractures in infancy should always arouse suspicion. Features said to be suggestive of non-accidental injury include multiple and depressed fractures, fractures wider than 3 mm, occipital bone injury, and associated brain injury. Often, however, no bony injury is detectable and there may be no external marks of violence at all. The damage is more often caused by violent shaking, which tears the bridging veins between brain and skull to produce subdural bleeding;[410] it also causes innumerable small intracerebral haemorrhages and perhaps disrupts neural pathways. It is possible that shaking can cause apnoea and convulsions and perhaps sudden infant death.[411] Undoubtedly it is a major cause of subdural haemorrhage and haematoma. Shaking may also cause fractures of the vertebrae and spinal cord injury.[412,413]

Subdural haematoma may present with the symptoms and signs summarised in Fig. 19.1. When this diagnosis is suspected, referral to a paediatric neurosurgical unit for CT scanning is far preferable to diagnostic needling of the subdural space by inexperienced operators. Most of the children have serious residual damage, due to the underlying brain injury rather than the haematoma. Mental handicap of all degrees, epilepsy, and cerebral palsy are common sequelae. It is very probable that some cases of unexplained mental handicap are caused by shaking. The shaking may cause such damage that no further brain growth occurs and these children are eventually undistinguishable from those with microcephaly due to other causes.[414]

Damage to the eyes is very common in association with head trauma, and retinal haemorrhages are a valuable diagnostic clue. There may also be retinal detachment, vitreous haemorrhage, optic atrophy and cataract.[415] Deafness is less well documented than visual handicap, but probably may occur.

Smothering with a pillow to stop crying is another form of abuse which may present as a sudden infant death or 'near-miss'. Some parents do not appreciate how dangerous this can be. Drowning 'accidents' in the bath are also suspect; the child may have been immersed deliberately.

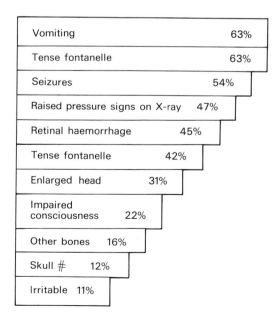

Vomiting	63%
Tense fontanelle	63%
Seizures	54%
Raised pressure signs on X-ray	47%
Retinal haemorrhage	45%
Tense fontanelle	42%
Enlarged head	31%
Impaired consciousness	22%
Other bones	16%
Skull #	12%
Irritable	11%

Fig. 19.1 Features of subdural haematoma and effusion. (Modified from Till[410].)

Other injuries.   Severe neck, chest or abdominal injuries occur, sometimes with remarkably little external evidence of trauma, even when caused by a punch or kick.

All who work with young children need to be on the alert for unusual behaviour and personality disturbances which might indicate maltreatment. Nevertheless, it must be recognised that children are very variable in their responses to new situations and therefore observations must be made with care and interpreted with caution. Even children who have been severely injured may greet their parents with enthusiasm and affection and may be distressed by their departure. These children seldom cringe away from their parents, though inexperienced staff often imagine that an abused child should do so. More expert observation may reveal deficiencies in the parent–child relationship but these will rarely be obvious to the casual onlooker (*see also* Chapter 3).

Reactions to separation can also mislead. Young children may greet their parents in hospital with hostility and this is a normal reaction, interpreted as anger at being 'abandoned' by the parent. After a few days, despair or quiet bewilderment may be noted and mistakenly regarded as 'settling down'. If the parents are confused by these reactions, it is easy for staff to interpret the disturbed relationship as evidence of previous abuse. Conversely, some children who have been neglected or had numerous care-givers are indiscriminately friendly to all adults; but so are some children from normal homes. Gross apathy and 'frozen watchfulness' are more obviously abnormal. The former is perhaps the end result of frustrated attempts at communication (p. 30); the latter may be due to fear of abuse, but sometimes a staring expression may be a sign of organic brain injury.

Diagnosis

The features which suggest that an injury is non-accidental are now well known. The appearance, severity or distribution of the injuries is not compatible with the story given, or perhaps no explanation at all is offered for an obviously serious and painful injury. Serious damage is attributed to trivial trauma— 'he rolled onto the floor' or 'his brother banged the baby's head with his feeding bottle'. There is often a delay between the time of injury and the request for medical help. The story changes each time the parent is interviewed.

With some injuries, notably unexplained subdural haematoma, the association with abuse is so strong that the presumptive diagnosis must be non-accidental injury. Whatever the injuries, it is usual to undertake a skeletal X-ray survey, and if there is bruising or bleeding, coagulation tests must be performed.*

The parents' behaviour may also arouse suspicion. Parents who have maltreated their child are often 'difficult', aggressive, tense and irritable, particularly when interviewed by inexperienced doctors. The degree of concern shown over the child's symptoms or injuries may be inappropriately high or low. They are liable to complain excessively or abscond if kept waiting in hospital casualty departments. Some react in the opposite way, being unusually quiet and compliant. The pattern of visiting the child after admission to hospital may be erratic and should always be recorded in the nursing records. It must also be remembered that most parents are now well aware of 'baby battering' and even innocent people may act strangely if they feel they are under suspicion.

Whenever maltreatment is suspected, informal enquiries are made with the health visitor, GP and the nursery or teaching staff. The local non-accidental injury register, maintained by the Social Services department, is inspected to see if maltreatment has been suspected previously.

Diagnostic errors

Professional awareness of child abuse is now so high that there is a real risk of overdiagnosis. It is essential to rule out genuine medical causes for the lesions which have caused concern. For example, bruising may be the first sign of leukaemia or a bleeding disorder. Some children really do 'bruise easily' and numerous bruises on skin, back and other parts of the body are commonplace in normal children. A 'black eye' may be the presenting feature of a retro-orbital tumour, such as a secondary deposit from a neuroblastoma. Both the scars of infected insect bites, and a BCG vaccination have been mistakenly identified as cigarette burns. Even a Mongolian blue spot has been misdiagnosed as extensive bruising. Fractures might be due to bone cysts or osteogenesis imperfecta. There are innumerable organic causes of failure to thrive, while in many cases of poor weight gain neither a physical nor an emotional cause can be found. The children of potentially abusive parents are not immune from organic disease!

One particular cause of poor weight gain deserves mention. Inadequate supply of breast milk usually results in an obviously hungry, angry baby, but sometimes the infant becomes quiet and sleepy very rapidly and his mother assumes he is satisfied.[416] Some apparently sensible and competent mothers have been deceived by this situation—particularly those who are determined that child-rearing is a 'natural' process. 'Underfeeding' at the breast is not necessarily a sign of maltreatment.

---

* A prothrombin time and platelet count are not adequate, since they do *not* exclude all clotting defects, notably haemophilia.

Management

Responsibility for the management of child abuse rests ultimately with the Social Services. It should always be remembered that it is the social worker who is most likely to be publicly reprimanded and humiliated if a serious error of judgement is made.

When maltreatment is suspected it is usual to admit the child to a paediatric ward. It is far better that the child should be admitted with the parents' cooperation, for if they refuse a decision will have to be taken, often on flimsy evidence, as to whether a Court Order is justified. The main provisions of the law regarding child abuse are summarised in Appendix 6. If the injuries are serious there is no difficulty, but often they are trivial in themselves and concern centres on the significance of the injuries rather than their severity in medical terms; this situation arises most commonly with bruising. The parents may then be persuaded to allow admission to exclude bleeding diseases, but this is often a transparent subterfuge which will not deceive the parents. It is usually better for the doctor who first sees the child to express concern about the bruises and their origins in a non-committal way, thus leaving more room for manoeuvre for the person who will have to interview the parents in more detail.

It is never easy to confront parents with the suggestion that the child's injuries could not have occurred by accident. This task should be undertaken by one, experienced doctor. A judgemental and accusing attitude is never constructive, but on the other hand the parents must be in no doubt about what is being suggested. One person must be seen to be in charge of the clinical problems and he must see the parents frequently, at least until follow-up decisions are made. This is equally important when the problem is one of neglect or failure to thrive rather than physical injury.

When maltreatment is suspected, a case conference is arranged by the Social Services. This is attended by the social worker, paediatrician, GP, health visitor, and often by an NSPCC officer also. In addition a police representative may be invited (see below).[407] The administrative work of arranging a conference, and the professional time involved, together make case conferences an expensive undertaking, but no better solution to the problem of managing child abuse has yet been devised. Until recently, parents were invariably excluded, but it is now recognised that in some circumstances their attendance for at least part of the conference can be constructive. The conference has two main advantages: firstly the sharing of information, and secondly the sharing of the responsibility for decisions which are often extremely difficult. The decisions which have to be made are (1) has maltreatment occurred and if so, what type of maltreatment (p. 414)?; (2) should the child's name be placed on the register of children 'At Risk' of non-accidental injury? If so, should the parents be told of this decision? (it is usual to do so unless there are good reasons to the contrary); (3) should the child be permitted to return home? (4) who is to be the 'key-worker'—the person primarily responsible for supervising the case? The conference will normally express an opinion about the desirability of police intervention, though the police are not bound to accept this view.

In the majority of cases, the child is returned to the parents. Various forms of practical help may be needed; rehousing or a nursery placement for example. The child may need to be physically examined at intervals. These measures may help to prevent further injury, which is the first goal of treatment. Parents in this situation are often under great strain, not only because of the circumstances which caused the original incident, but also because they feel themselves to be 'on probation' and live in constant fear that the child may acquire a genuine accidental injury, which may be misinterpreted as abuse. Improvements in the parents' competence in handling the child and in their affection for him and often for each other are also desirable, but this cannot always be achieved even with the most expert social casework or psychiatric treatment. When it would be unsafe to return the child to his parents, an alternative home needs to be found. Factors which help in assessing the risk are summarised in Table 19.1.

Table 19.1   Child abuse. Parental factors which indicate a high risk of further injury. (Kempe and Kempe.[405])

Mental illness
Criminal activity
Past history of abuse
Low self-esteem, social isolation, depression
Multiple life stresses
Violent temper
Unrealistic expectations of child's behaviour
Harsh punishment of child
Child perceived as difficult, provocative
Rejection, lack of bonding

An unsuccessful application to the Court for a Care Order is likely to make the social worker's subsequent task more difficult, but in spite of the parents' natural resentment and perhaps their triumph at defeating 'the system' this is not an unmitigated disaster. An appearance in Court emphasises that society regards child abuse as a very serious matter and this lesson may give the child a measure of protection.

A hospital ward is not a good place for a healthy child, particularly if he is already deprived of a stable home life. Childrens' homes or foster parents are the main options. It is always necessary to balance the risks of further injury against the damaging effects of separation. The prognosis for abused children in long term care is poor and when it is clear that the child cannot go back to his parents, early adoption is desirable. The Children's Act (1975) gives priority to the needs of the children rather than to the rights of the parents. Unfortunately there are still many borderline situations where there are grave misgivings about the child's safety at home, yet the final removal of parental rights is hard to justify or accomplish. Sometimes these families can be helped by more intensive treatment in residential facilities.

POLICE INVOLVEMENT

It is quite rightly an offence to injure a child, and it is inevitable that the police should take an interest in child abuse. In many districts, there is a good working relationship with the police, and many senior officers show admirable discretion in their handling of these cases. An experienced policeman has a very different approach to interviewing from that of a doctor, and when it is obvious that non-accidental injury has occurred, his findings may be invaluable. Sometimes, a parent will readily acknowledge that the child has been 'battered', but will accuse another person of having perpetrated the injuries.

From the point of view of treatment, it may not be vital to know which member of a stable couple inflicted the injuries; however, if any other person (for example, an ex-boyfriend, aunt or childminder) is accused, grave errors may result if the police do not investigate the matter thoroughly and promptly. It is naive to say, as some have suggested, that it does not matter 'who did it'. Whether or not a child can be returned home safely is often dependent on whether the person responsible still lives under the same roof or visits the family. In these circumstances, a case conference must be arranged with minimum delay, or alternatively the police should be asked to make preliminary enquiries before the conference.

Prosecution and imprisonment seldom aid the rehabilitation of parents who have abused their children. Where persons other than the parents have caused injury, there seems little justification for treating this crime differently from an assault on an adult. There may be occasions when prosecution of a parent has some therapeutic benefit—some people feel that they must 'pay the price' for the serious offence they have committed. Fortunately the courts usually take a compassionate view of the stress which resulted in a parent injuring his or her child.

Prevention

Observations made in pregnancy, labour, and in the first few weeks of life (Table 19.2) can predict with a fair degree of accuracy that a child is at risk of maltreatment.[417] The health visitor, social worker, and GP should be notified of high-risk families and extra support and supervision should be discreetly offered. Some form of escape from potential crises needs to be devised; this may be a telephone number of a professional worker or a friend, or a nursery placement, or even an offer to admit the baby to a childrens' ward for one or two nights. Parents who visit their GP or more

Table 19.2   Prediction of child abuse.

---

*Antenatal**
Negative memories of childhood
Denial of pregnancy
No plans for baby
Loneliness and isolation
Fear of labour
Bad social conditions

Labour and Delivery
Not wanting to hold baby
Hostile remarks about baby
Disappointed over baby's sex

Postnatal
Avoids handling or eye contact
Finds feeding and changing unpleasant
Angered or distressed by baby's crying
Disparaging remarks about baby
Father jealous of baby

---

* *See* p. 30.

often hospital casualty departments, with trivial complaints or unreasonable demands, may be uttering a 'cry for help', realising that they are on the verge of injuring the child. The question, 'Are you ever afraid you might hurt your baby?' is a useful probe when this is suspected. Some may confess to this fear but those who realise the strength of their own emotions are probably less likely to actually harm the child. Over-reaction by doctor or social worker in this situation may be very damaging.

Where the risk or suspicion of maltreatment is very high, the more intensive measures outlined above should be considered at an early stage. On rare occasions, care proceedings have been initiated at or even before birth of a subsequent child of known abusive parents.

Prognosis

About 10% of families who seriously injure a child are regarded as 'untreatable' and the child has to be permanently removed. Of the remainder, about half may improve with help and increasing maturity. In a substantial minority, there is insufficient justification to remove the child and expose him to the hazards of long term care or legal battles over adoption, yet the family remains chaotic and disturbed. For these children, the future is uncertain at best. The most serious physical consequences of abuse are those arising from neurological injury. A high proportion of these are permanently handicapped with mental retardation, cerebral palsy, epilepsy, visual defect, etc.

SPECIFIC SYNDROMES OF CHILD ABUSE

Sexual abuse

Although few paediatricians in the UK have much experience of this problem, studies in the USA suggest that it is common.[418] Three forms are distinguished:

1   Paedophilia involves non-violent genital manipulation of a young child.
2   Violent molestation and rape.
3   Incest is the most important form of sexual abuse and the one which most often remains undiagnosed for years. Father–daughter incest accounts for three-quarters of cases; the remainder include mother–son, father–son, mother–daughter, brother–sister and grandchild–grandparents. Incestuous activities may begin well before adolescence. As with other forms of child abuse, incest occurs in all races and social classes, but predisposing social and psychological factors are not the same as those causing physical injury.

Most cases of sexual abuse are first reported to the police, Social Services or the NSPCC. The paediatrician may occasionally be asked to provide facilities for the child to be examined for genital or other injuries and for venereal infection, perhaps under sedation or anaesthesia. The advice of a child psychiatrist may be needed.

There is more concern over the possibility that incest may be the well-concealed cause of more commonplace complaints which usually have a psychological basis—abdominal pain, headaches, anxiety, school failure and so on. An account of overt sexual activity is rarely obtained from a pre-adolescent child, but is unlikely to be fabricated. On the other hand, it is not unknown for adolescents to invent such accusations. Adolescent behaviour disorders, particularly mother–daughter estrangement, or the sudden assumption of domestic duties by a teenage daughter are said to be additional clues. As was the case when physical abuse was first clearly identified as a major problem, it is likely that sexual abuse will be discovered more frequently in the next few years.

The initial management of sexual abuse involves the protection of the child from further exploitation while a case conference is arranged. The subsequent care of the child and family is discussed elsewhere.[418]

Non-accidental poisoning; Munchausen's syndrome by proxy

The deliberate administration of drugs or other substances (e.g. salt) to children is an unusual form of child abuse.[419,420] Admission to hospital is precipitated by symptoms such as vomiting or coma. Repeated episodes of poisoning may occur while the child is in hospital. Once suspected, diagnosis is aided by careful recording of all parental visiting, and by toxicological screening of blood and urine.

Some parents probably administer drugs as a form of assault on the child, whereas in others the motivation seems more subtle. In Munchausen's syndrome by proxy, parents fabricate illnesses in the child rather than in themselves.[421] This may be achieved by the use of drugs, such as hypnotics or hypoglycaemics, or by other means, such as the addition of blood to the child's urine. There may be a history of convulsions, never observed by an independent witness. The mother perpetrates these acts more often than the father; she may have a nursing or other medical background, or have some personal experience of illness, and tends to be of higher intelligence and stronger character than the father. Sometimes her own physical symptoms have been ignored or dismissed. She is often very solicitous of the welfare of her own and other children in the hospital, and enjoys being resident in the ward.

Although experience is limited, the risk of further episodes of poisoning or fabrication seem high, and the child may need to be removed from the family, but confrontation sometimes brings the problem to an abrupt halt.

Bizarre life-styles and diets

Severe malnutrition, in some cases with the features of kwashiorkor, may be caused by adherence to diets totally unsuited to growing children.[422] Motivation for use of these diets and the strange life-styles which accompany them, may be based on distorted ecological or religious ideals.

Excessive punishment

Corporal punishment is now regarded as unacceptable by a majority of Europeans, but this view is not universally held. A 'good hiding' is not incompatible with parental love and the circumstances must be considered carefully before deciding that child abuse has occurred.

Sophisticated abuse

Subtle emotional cruelty, rejection, unfavourable comparison with siblings, and delegation of child care duties to a series of carelessly-selected child minders or au-pairs occur in many families and undoubtedly are the cause of many behavioural, psychosomatic and developmental problems. In the long run, this kind of abuse may well be as damaging as physical battering.

Epilepsy is commoner among handicapped children than in the normal population.[423] It may be a trivial problem, or a major handicap in its own right. Because the association between seizures and brain disorder is well recognised, overdiagnosis and overvigorous treatment may cause further iatrogenic handicaps. Many other physiological and pathological phenomena may give rise to 'funny turns' and they should not automatically be assumed to be epileptic just because the child is handicapped.[435]

FITS AND EPILEPSY

A fit is a clinical event in which there is a sudden disturbance of neurological function, in association with an abnormal and excessive electrical discharge of cortical neurones. Fits and epilepsy are not synonymous. In epilepsy there is a *tendency to recurrent fits* due to some abnormality in the brain itself, although events outside the nervous system may act as the trigger that determines the occurrence of a fit at any particular moment.

Fits are not the only cause of disturbed neurological function. Sudden changes of cerebral blood flow, oxygenation, or glucose supply, may all produce an alteration of consciousness or motor function, which may be mistaken for a fit, and to complicate matters further, they may actually culminate in a fit, with a brief episode of stiffening (the 'tonic' phase), followed by some 'clonic' jerks. It may be very difficult to differentiate fits from other causes of 'funny turns', particularly if the attacks terminate with a tonic/clonic episode. The events which are observed *during* the various types of attack may be very similar: the brain has only a limited repertoire of responses to acute insults. For this reason, great importance is attached to the events occurring immediately *before* and *after* the period of dramatic neurological disturbance, as will be seen in the subsequent sections.

Causes of epilepsy

Genetic predisposition and cerebral lesions both contribute to the development of epilepsy. In addition, there are numerous secondary factors which may determine whether, and when, a fit occurs. The underlying pathophysiological events of epilepsy are discussed in detail elsewhere.[424]

GENETIC FACTORS

Family studies show, without doubt, that there is an inherited component in some forms of epilepsy, although this is less important than in many other common disorders. The waveforms seen in the EEGs of children with some types of epilepsy, for example petit mal and benign focal epilepsy, may also be found in recordings from their relatives who never have seizures. Thus it is the tendency to a particular type of electrical discharge which is inherited, and other factors determine whether or not clinical attacks occur.

The brain must also have some mechanisms which inhibit the propagation of unwanted electrical activity, otherwise seizures would be universal and continuous. Probably there is also an hereditary component to these inhibitory mechanisms, which would explain why some people with abnormal EEGs do not have fits.

CEREBRAL LESIONS

Epileptic activity may originate in damaged areas of the brain, usually in the cortex, and rarely, if ever, in the brainstem. The damage may be focal or diffuse. The site, nature and rate of evolution of the lesion all affect the likelihood of seizures, as well as the underlying level of genetic predisposition. In children, the cortical abnormality is commonly focal brain injury, as may occur in cerebral palsy, or a diffuse abnormality of brain architecture, as in some forms of mental handicap. More rarely, a degenerative process or a metabolic abnormality such as an aminoaciduria, may be responsible. Tumours account for only a tiny proportion of cases.

PHYSIOLOGICAL AND PSYCHOLOGICAL FACTORS

These may be regarded as secondary, in that they do not themselves provoke fits, but they may explain why fits occur at a particular time.

Sleep and arousal.   There is a close relationship between epilepsy and sleep. Some seizure types occur predominantly during sleep, others very rarely. Abnormal EEG activity is often only manifest during sleep. Fits occur most often soon after going to sleep, and just before and just after awakening. The frequency is probably greater after sleep deprivation, and this is a means of revealing EEG abnormalities which are not usually apparent.

Excitement and anxiety also influence seizure frequency. Boredom and excessive stress both increase the number of fits, and interesting steady activity has the opposite effect. Some children only have fits under conditions of extreme excitement, for example on Christmas Eve or the first day of a holiday. Others have fits when intensely stimulating activity suddenly stops: presumably this phenomenon is related to levels of arousal in the brain. Also, anxiety leads to hyperventilation and mild hypocapnia (low CO_2) which itself lowers seizure threshold (p. 458).

BIOCHEMICAL EFFECTS

Female sex hormones change the seizure threshold, and fits occur in some women only at the time of menstruation (catamenial epilepsy). Electrolyte imbalance, low blood sugar or calcium, alcohol, and some drugs, such as phenothiazines, which are mildly epileptogenic, provide other examples.

TRIGGER FACTORS SPECIFIC TO INDIVIDUALS

There are many kinds of reflex epilepsy, in which seizures only occur in response to a specific stimulus. The best known is photosensitive epilepsy ('TV epilepsy') but there are many other triggers, such as reading or music; these are all much less common than the photosensitive type.

THE PHENOMENON OF 'KINDLING'

In animals, repeated electrical stimulation of the brain initially produces no effect, but gradually seizures of increasing intensity and duration develop. The stimulus strength required to produce them declines, until eventually spontaneous fits occur. This model suggests that each time a fit occurs, the electrical discharges spread with greater ease as if the brain is 'learning' to have fits. Thinking parents sometimes ask whether each fit makes subsequent ones more likely: tentatively, the answer is that this may be so; the implications for early effective treatment are obvious.

Classification

The International Classification of 1969 is widely used, although several attempts have been made to improve it. It is a convenient system, but does not imply that the seizure types classified together have similar aetiologies; in many cases these are unknown.

In this classification, which is shown with a few modifications in Table 20.1, the essential distinction is between generalised and partial seizures. The former are believed to have an onset somewhere deep in the central ('centrencephalic') areas of the brain and to involve both hemispheres simultaneously and symmetrically. Partial seizures on the other hand have a focal onset; the electrical discharges may be confined to one area throughout or may spread to involve both hemispheres resulting in a generalised fit—this is called secondary generalisation. This simple distinction is undoubtedly naive but is nevertheless of some clinical value.

Table 20.1   Classification of epilepsy.

Generalised epilepsies
Infantile spasms
Myoclonic epilepsies (also called petit mal variant, minor motor epilepsy, Lennox–Gastaut syndrome)
Classic 'petit mal' absences
Major epilepsy (grand mal)
   primary idiopathic
   secondary to diffuse brain disease
   generalisation of a partial seizure

Partial epilepsies
With elementary symptomatology and (usually) without impaired consciousness
   Jacksonian seizures
   adversive seizures
   epilepsia partialis continua
   benign focal epilepsy
With complex symptomatology and (often) with impaired consciousness (also called temporal lobe epilepsy and psychomotor epilepsy)
Both the above may spread and develop into a generalised seizure

Miscellaneous
Photosensitive epilepsy has much in common with the generalised epilepsies
Other reflex epilepsies

Note   Febrile convulsions are *not* classified as epilepsy

Prevalence

Prevalence figures can never be completely accurate because misdiagnosis is common; epilepsy may be concealed because of the stigma associated with it; the incidence is age-dependent; and authors differ on definitions. Overall, the prevalence is probably around 0.5% (1 in 200). In the severely mentally handicapped, about a third have epileptic seizures at some time during childhood. In the mildly handicapped, the figure is probably 3–6%. Cerebral palsy is such an imprecise term that data are unreliable. Published prevalence figures suggest that between 20 and 60% of cases have epilepsy, but many of these series are biased towards severe cerebral palsy and the true prevalence may even be below 20%. The commonest types of epilepsy are grand mal and 'temporal lobe' epilepsy. Classical petit mal and myoclonic epilepsies are relatively rare. Febrile convulsions occur in from 3 to 6% of all children.

THE GENERALISED EPILEPSIES

Infantile spasms

This form of epilepsy begins in the first year of life with a peak around 4–6 months. It is commoner in males. A family history of the disorder is very rarely obtained and there is no striking increase in the familial incidence of other types of epilepsy. The attacks consist of sudden, violent symmetrical contraction of muscles, usually affecting the flexor groups. The trunk, neck, and limbs flex and stiffen, the hands clench, and there may be a cry and a change in facial expression. Occasionally extensor spasms predominate. The episodes are often mistaken for colic or a startle reflex.

Infantile spasms are of serious significance, because developmental regression and subsequent handicap are commonly associated. The child may lose motor skills and becomes irritable and withdrawn, and many months may elapse before any recovery or developmental progress is seen. In about two-thirds of cases, these attacks occur in a baby who is either already suspected to be handicapped because of previous cerebral insults or has some clearly identifiable neurological lesion. These are described as 'symptomatic'. In the remainder, the 'cryptogenic' group, they occur in a previously normal child.

In the symptomatic group, the insult may be perinatal anoxia, hypoglycaemia or meningitis, or an intrauterine infection. Untreated phenylketonuria may be responsible but is of course very rare because of universal screening. Cerebral malformations and tuberose sclerosis (p. 217) are important causes. Aicardi's syndrome consists of spasms, agenesis of the corpus callosum and atrophic defects in the choroid. It is confined to females and has a very poor prognosis. The problem of pertussis immunisation as a cause of infantile spasms is discussed on page 229. The term 'West's syndrome' refers to spasms, retardation and the EEG patterns of hypsarr-hythmia (*see* below) but is now seldom used.

INVESTIGATION

In clinical examination particular attention is paid to head circumference and shape, dysmorphic features, fundi, and skin naevi. The parents should be questioned and examined for stigmata of tuberose sclerosis. Infantile spasms are one form of epilepsy in which the EEG is invaluable. There is gross disorganisation and continuous abnormal discharges are seen: the pattern is called hypsarrhythmia, though this term is often used, incor-rectly, for the clinical syndrome. Some children have records with periods of more normal activity interspersed with the hypsarrhythmia, but this seems to have little influence on prognosis. The EEG usually improves with treatment but deteriorates with clinical relapse. A few cases whose attacks resemble infantile spasms have normal EEGs and these have a good prognosis. A CT scan is a valuable investigation and often reveals an underlying cerebral malformation or signs of tuberose sclerosis (p. 217). Aminoacid studies and tests for congenital infection may be indicated.

TREATMENT

This is controversial. There is no doubt that ACTH or steroids improve the EEG and often control the spasms, but their effect on the ultimate degree of handicap is questionable.[425,426] It is also uncertain whether ACTH is superior to oral prednisolone. At present, it is usual to give the child the benefit of the doubt and prescribe ACTH. Opinions differ as to whether cryptogenic and symptomatic cases should be treated in the same way.

There is no evidence that high steroid doses are superior to low doses, or that long courses confer additional benefit, and no detailed studies on alternate-day therapy. There is a very high incidence of serious complica-tions of ACTH therapy, including severe hypertension, hypokalaemia and infection. A dosage of 20 units/day for 2–3 weeks seems to be adequate. Prednisolone 1 mg/kg/day is an acceptable alternative both for initial treatment and for relapses. Nitrazepam, often in low dosage (1.25–2.5 mg b.d.) is very effective in controlling the spasms and may do so more rapidly than ACTH. Some authors are reluctant to use this as initial therapy, arguing that the effect of ACTH is then harder to monitor; but since ACTH is dangerous therapy and its benefits are dubious, it seems preferable to start nitrazepam at the time of diagnosis, together with a short course of ACTH.

PROGNOSIS

This is poor. In the symptomatic group there is a very high risk (80–90%) of subsequent mental handicap and cerebral palsy. The spasms cease, usually

Table 20.2   Infantile spasms—poor prognostic factors.

Delayed development before onset
Neurological abnormality
Radiological studies abnormal
Symptomatic aetiology
Perinatal abnormality
Other seizure types before spasms
Seizures concomitant with spasms
? Long delay before ACTH therapy (cryptogenic cases only)

---

by the 2nd birthday, but other seizure types may appear. The cryptogenic group do rather better, with 30–50% making a full recovery. Table 20.2 summarises prognostic factors.

GENERAL MANAGEMENT

In view of the grave prognosis outlined above, management of infantile spasms involves much more than medication. Some optimism is justified in the cryptogenic group, and even in the symptomatic group recovery is not unknown. The visible developmental disintegration that affects the more severe cases is an appalling experience for parents. Careful judgement is needed about the introduction of physiotherapy and supporting services, but most parents will eventually want to do something active to help the child's recovery. With the obvious exception of tuberose sclerosis, it is usually possible to predict a low recurrence risk in subsequent children. Nevertheless, intense anxiety is usual as later children reach the age at which the spasms began and this needs sympathetic handling.

Myoclonic epilepsies of early childhood

This is a mixed group containing both idiopathic and symptomatic seizures. They have in common an early onset (1–6 years), a strong association with organic brain disease or damage, and often an EEG superficially similar to classical petit mal but with more irregularity and a slower rate of spike-wave discharge. Several clinical seizure patterns occur. In some cases, the myoclonic epilepsy is preceded by infantile spasms, which may indeed simply be myoclonic epilepsy with onset in infancy.

The terminology of myoclonic epilepsy is confusing. Included in this group are a number of overlapping disorders, such as petit mal variant, atypical petit mal, Lennox–Gastaut syndrome, and minor motor seizures. O'Donohoe, in his monograph, justifies the grouping of all these under the heading of 'myoclonic epilepsies'.

The child with myoclonic epilepsy may have several seizure types including atypical absences, with clouding rather than loss of consciousness, atonic-akinetic attacks in which sudden falls occur with immediate recovery, or there may be only head-dropping, and myoclonic flexion jerks. Generalised grand mal seizures may also occur and, if they are the presenting feature, the nature of the epilepsy may not be immediately recognised. Rarely, minor epileptic status, lasting hours or days may occur.

CAUSES OF MYOCLONIC EPILEPSIES

As with infantile spasms, a variety of cerebral insults is responsible for the secondary group. Myoclonic epilepsy is often associated with severe cerebral palsies or mental handicap. Some rare degenerative disorders (SSPE, storage disorders, Lafora body disease) may present with myoclonic epilepsy. In the idiopathic group, genetic and other unknown factors are presumably responsible.

DIAGNOSIS

The atonic-akinetic attacks are easily recognised but, if they are not the dominant features, classic petit mal or grand mal may be suspected. The EEG findings are usually helpful. There is often excess slow activity, and there are spike-waves and multiple spike complexes, with a rate of 1.5–2.5/second (*see* petit mal, p. 430). These abnormalities are usually present between seizures but occasionally prolonged or ambulatory recording may be required. The EEG may show characteristic patterns in the rare degenerative diseases.

PROGNOSIS

This is a serious form of epilepsy, and prognosis for future intellectual development is guarded, particularly in secondary cases. Good prognostic features are normal development prior to onset of epilepsy, older age of onset, and quick response to treatment. Children with myoclonic jerks but no other seizure types may also have a better prognosis.

MANAGEMENT

Benzodiazepines are often effective in the myoclonic epilepsies. Clonazepam is probably the drug of choice if it can be tolerated. Sodium valproate may also be useful. Ketogenic diet, ACTH and many other drugs have all been used in resistant cases, which unfortunately are common. A protective helmet is essential for children with atonic-akinetic attacks if they do not respond quickly to treatment. Many of these children have other handicaps and need supporting services.

Classic 'petit mal'

The adjective 'classic' is used here to emphasise the points of differential diagnosis discussed below. Classic petit mal is mainly a disorder of childhood, occurring between 4 and 12 years of age. It is commoner in girls. In contrast to myoclonic epilepsies, petit mal is rarely associated with organic brain damage or with physical or mental handicap. Petit mal attacks have a sudden onset and termination. There is no warning. Normal activity ceases, the eyes stare and may drift up , and the lids flicker. Pulling at clothes, chewing movements and urinary incontinence may occur. There are usually many attacks each day, but the duration is seldom more than 20–30 seconds. A minority of cases also suffer from other types of seizure, particularly grand mal.

CAUSES

The typical EEG abnormality is inherited, though the exact mode of transmission is disputed. Unknown additional factors determine whether epilepsy develops.

DIAGNOSIS

The differential diagnosis from myoclonic epilepsy and temporal lobe attacks is summarised in Table 20.3. The distinction is not always easy. Therapists and others who work with handicapped children often suspect petit mal, on the basis of attention lapses, staring, or changes of muscle tone. Petit mal is actually rarely associated with handicap; if there are genuinely absences or jerks, a myoclonic epilepsy is more likely. The diagnosis in these cases can be difficult and a period of observation may be preferable to immediate treatment. Teachers of normal children also request medical advice for suspected petit mal, but many of these turn out to be daydreamers (p. 458).

   The child should be asked to hyperventilate for 20–30 deep breaths; this will often elicit an attack. The EEG is usually diagnostic, with a spike-wave complex in both hemispheres at 3/second, both with clinically obvious attacks and in bursts between attacks, but occasionally the inter-ictal record is normal, and prolonged or ambulatory recording is needed.

EDUCATIONAL EFFECTS

Frequent petit mal attacks cause serious disruption of learning. It is probable that bursts of spike-wave in the EEG, even without apparent clinical manifestations, interrupt the child's concentration. Unrecognised

Table 20.3   Comparison of three seizure types with similar clinical features.

	Classic petit mal	Myoclonic epilepsies	Temporal lobe epilepsy
Age of onset (years)	4–12	1–6	Any time in childhood
Association with other handicaps	Rare	Common	Minority of cases
Frequency of attacks	Often many per day—dozens or hundreds	Very variable	Variable, rarely more than 3–4 per day
Duration of attacks	Rarely more than 30 secs	Very variable	Often > 30 secs, may be several minutes
Aura	No	No	Common
Behaviour during attacks	Cessation of activity, stares: mumbling, fiddling: rarely more complex behaviour	Atypical absences, often with clouding of consciousness: atonic attacks, myoclonic jerks	Various meaningless activities, often complex
Recovery	Sudden and complete	Depends on duration and type	Gradual, often post-ictal confusion, headache
EEG	3 per sec spike-wave during attacks and often between attacks	1.5–2.5 per sec spike-wave polyspikes, irregular slow activity	Temporal spikes between attacks

petit mal is a rare but important cause of school failure (p. 402). With treatment, however, progress should be satisfactory and special schooling arrangements should not be needed.

TREATMENT

Ethosuximide and sodium valproate are both highly effective in the treatment of petit mal. They may be given together in resistant cases. Sodium valproate is more expensive, but has the advantage of also providing protection against grand mal attacks. Clonazepam is also very effective. Acetazolamide alone or with ethosuximide may be useful. Drugs used for treatment of temporal lobe attacks are not generally effective in petit mal.

PROGNOSIS

If the EEG is classic, the response to treatment is good, and no other seizure types occur, the outlook for remission of the petit mal before adult life is excellent. There is, however, a significant risk that grand mal seizures will develop later.

These terms are often used as if synonymous, but they are in fact distinct entities.[77] Petit mal status is simply a series of classic absences occurring in such rapid succession as to form a continuous attack. Minor epileptic status includes conditions of diverse aetiology in which there is confusion, apparent intellectual deterioration and myoclonic twitches, with a variety of EEG changes. Management of both disorders can be difficult and the advice of a paediatric neurologist is desirable.

Grand mal epilepsy

To the layman, grand mal is 'typical' epilepsy. It is the commonest type of epilepsy in children. There may an aura or an onset in one side or limb, in which case the diagnosis is a partial seizure with secondary generalisation; but the generalisation may occur so rapidly that the focal onset is not apparent. In some cases there is no warning at all; in others, parents suspect that a fit is imminent because the child becomes irritable and behaves badly. At the onset of the attack, there is sudden loss of consciousness, and the child falls. There is a brief rigid (tonic) phase followed by violent jerking (clonic phase). Tongue-biting and incontinence may occur but are not necessary for the diagnosis, nor are they diagnostic of epilepsy. Cyanosis and noisy breathing are common. At the end of the attack, the child is limp; the pupils may be dilated for a short time; a post-ictal sleep and a headache on waking are usual. Plantars are often extensor, and the child may take some hours or even many days to recover fully; in particular, a slight ataxia often disappears very slowly, raising fears of a progressive lesion or drug intoxication. Status epilepticus consists of a series of tonic-clonic attacks without recovery of consciousness between seizures.

Primary grand mal is caused by an inherited predisposition, whose nature is unknown (p. 423), in combination with other cerebral disturbances or lesions. Even in the secondary cases, caused by diffuse disease or a focal lesion, it is likely that genetic factors contribute.

Prolonged attacks are so dramatic that the diagnosis is seldom in doubt, but a history suggestive of the various 'trigger' factors should be sought. Brief attacks are more commonly misdiagnosed and many alternative possibilities must be considered.

In physical examination, the skin should be inspected carefully for evidence of neurocutaneous syndromes. Blood pressure should be measured; hypertensive encephalopathy is a rare but treatable cause of fits, and if missed the consequences are serious (p. 296). The yield of plain skull X-rays in childhood epilepsy is very low, and it can be argued that if any X-ray is indicated, a CT scan is a more profitable investigation. It is usual to check for hypocalcaemia and renal failure. There is little point in measuring blood glucose except during a fit.

The EEG during attacks is dramatic with multiple spike discharges but it is rare for a fit to occur during recording. Between attacks the EEG may be normal or may show spikes or spike-wave complexes, which are sometimes identical to those seen in petit mal. In secondary cases there may be more extensive abnormal discharges, and, if the grand mal attacks are associated with myoclonic epilepsy or focal seizures, the EEG patterns associated with these conditions will be found.

Since there are innumerable causes of secondary grand mal epilepsy, the extent of investigation must depend on the clinical situation. The clinician and the parents often share the unspoken fear of a brain tumour, but these account for only a tiny minority of grand mal fits.

MANAGEMENT

Primary grand mal is more responsive to treatment than the secondary forms. There is a remarkable absence of properly designed trials of anticonvulsant therapy in the literature, and guidance on the choice of drug is anecdotal. As a first choice, one might select sodium valproate if the epilepsy appears to be primary or to arise from diffuse brain disease, and carbamazepine if a focal origin is suspected. Other potentially useful drugs are phenobarbitone, phenytoin, primidone, and clonazepam, alone or in limitless combinations of dubious efficacy but undoubted toxicity.

This is the most alarming form of epilepsy and adequate counselling of both parents and nursery or school staff is essential.

PROGNOSIS

Primary grand mal starting in mid-childhood (after 4–5 years) and responding quickly to drug treatment has a good prognosis. Early onset is usually associated with secondary forms of epilepsy with a worse outlook. Focal seizures with secondary generalisation are discussed below.

PARTIAL (FOCAL) SEIZURES

These begin in localised areas of the brain and the features depend on the particular site involved. The underlying lesion may be a cerebral scar caused, for example, by perinatal trauma or anoxia, meningitis, prolonged febrile fits or a valve inserted for hydrocephalus. Focal motor fits are common in cerebral palsy. Congenital malformations may be responsible, such as cysts, angiomas or haematoma. Tumours are a very rare cause.

Fits with elementary symptomatology

Motor or sensory symptoms confined to one side appear at the start of the attack. Secondary generalisation may occur almost instantaneously, after some seconds, or not at all. Focal motor fits may result in transient weakness or paralysis of the affected side, initially with hyporeflexia. Although this classic Todd's paralysis is said to last for 24 hours at most, careful examination may reveal residual neurological signs for some days after an attack.

The term Jacksonian epilepsy should only be used when there is a classic Jacksonian 'march' of symptoms, with clonic movements beginning distally and spreading proximally; this can only be recognised in a minority of cases.

Adversive seizures

This is a fairly common seizure type, certainly more common than the classic Jacksonian attack. There may be a brief warning, which the child can recognise. The head, eyes, and sometimes trunk rotate away from the side of the epileptic focus. Consciousness is usually lost and the child may fall. There may be secondary generalisation, but most adversive seizures are brief and recovery is rapid. It is not known whether the attacks originate in the frontal or temporal lobe.

TREATMENT AND PROGNOSIS

Treatment is the same as for benign focal epilepsy (see below), but adversive seizures are more difficult to control, and the prognosis for full recovery is more guarded.

Benign focal epilepsy of childhood

This is also called Rolandic or Sylvian epilepsy. It is a commmon condition with a male predominance, starting usually between 7 and 10 years. The attacks occur mainly during sleep, with jerking of one side of the face and sometimes also the limbs of that side. Speech is impossible because of salivation and facial movements but the child usually wakes and is aware of the attack. These seizures are easily mistaken for grand mal but the distinction is important because benign focal epilepsy has an excellent prognosis.

DIAGNOSIS

The EEG shows spikes over the Sylvian region, on one or both sides. These spikes may only appear during sleep in some cases. Benign focal epilepsy has a strong genetic component and is not particularly associated with handicap or brain damage. Although the focal features are alarming, if the seizure type is recognised, a CT scan is not necessary in the typical case.

TREATMENT

Most cases respond well to carbamazepine; a few require this drug combined with phenytoin. Clonazepam may also be effective. Most children with benign focal epilepsy are free of fits by their middle teens.

Epilepsia partialis continua

In this rare form of epilepsy there is a focal motor seizure lasting for hours or even days. It is often associated with progressive brain disease.

Fits with complex symptomatology

This cumbersome title is useful for purposes of classification, but these attacks are better known as psychomotor fits or temporal lobe epilepsy. It is a common seizure type and is often very difficult to control. The onset may be at any time in childhood, but the diagnosis is often overlooked in the very young who cannot describe their subjective experiences adequately.

The temporal lobe forms part of the brain 'circuit' known as the limbic system, which integrates autonomic and emotional functions, and is also closely connected with the sense of smell. The complexity of these functions accounts for the wide variety of clinical phenomena in temporal lobe epilepsy. Temporal lobe attacks usually begin with a brief subjective experience known as the 'aura'. There may be an unpleasant epigastric sensation, a nasty smell or taste, complex auditory or visual hallucinations or distorted perception, a feeling of 'having been there before' (déjà vu), a disturbance of speech, vertigo, tachycardia; or one of many other similar experiences. Often consciousness is disturbed and the child behaves strangely, sometimes performing complex actions in a disjointed fashion. He may mumble or talk repetitive nonsense, and is likely to be rather aggressive and confused. Secondary generalisation may occur causing a grand mal seizure. At the end of the attack, recovery is gradual and there may be post-ictal confusion, sleepiness and headache.

A variety of behavioural and personality disorders may be associated with temporal lobe epilepsy. Hyperactivity and outbursts of rage both occur, but they are more common in children whose epilepsy is associated with other evidence of brain injury and it is not certain how closely they are related to the epilepsy itself. Some children become more irritable and overactive prior to a fit, with a remarkable personality improvement after the attack. A reciprocal relationship between fit frequency and behaviour disorder is so dramatic in a few cases, that the complete abolition of seizures by medication makes the child's behaviour intolerable.

Episodic undesirable behaviour is commonly suspected to be a manifestation of temporal lobe epilepsy. The distinction is not always easy but, in a behaviour disorder, episodes are usually precipitated by some environmental trigger, however trivial; behaviour is not bizarre or stereotyped; and there is no post-ictal confusion or headache. If the child has a past history of a cerebral insult and/or a temporal lobe EEG abnormality, it is tempting to attribute his bad behaviour to an organic brain lesion, but there is little evidence to justify this unless he also experiences definite and discrete temporal lobe fits. A trial of medication may be justified in such cases, but is rarely helpful, and certainly a diagnostic label of epilepsy should be avoided.

Personality disturbances of all kinds are more common in children with epilepsy than in the general population, but there is no specific pattern and no such thing as an 'epileptic personality'. Temporal lobe epilepsy is, however, associated with an increased incidence of psychiatric illness in adult life. There is a tendency for patients with left hemisphere lesions to develop psychotic illnesses, while right-sided lesions predispose to neurotic and depressive disorders.

Although the EEG more often reveals temporal spikes during sleep, temporal lobe fits are rare in sleep and it is almost unknown for them to occur exclusively in sleep. (Pavor nocturnus (p. 460) is often the cause of episodic strange behaviour at night.)

CAUSES

Like other focal seizures, temporal lobe epilepsy may arise from any localised cerebral lesion and can occur in association with other handicaps. Mesial temporal sclerosis caused by prolonged convulsions in infancy accounts for some cases and epilepsy due to this lesion has a better prognosis. A congenital hamartomatous malformation is found in some cases treated surgically. Tumours are a rare cause in childhood. Genetic predisposition does not play a large part in temporal lobe epilepsy, except in its association with febrile convulsions and therefore mesial sclerosis.

DIAGNOSIS

The distinction between temporal lobe epilepsy, classic petit mal, and myoclonic epilepsies, is summarised in Table 20.3. Migraine is discussed on p. 456. The EEG during an attack shows multiple discharges over the affected lobe. Rarely, however, the attacks arise in deep structures and recording over the surface of the scalp does not show any abnormality; thus a normal EEG, even during an attack, does not completely rule out the diagnosis.

Between attacks, only about a third of cases show temporal spike discharges in the EEG, but the yield is at least doubled if recordings are made during sleep. A CT scan is indicated if there are other neurological signs or symptoms, and in resistant cases.

TREATMENT

Even with the most careful management, temporal lobe epilepsy may fail to respond to anticonvulsant therapy. The drug of first choice is carbamazepine. Phenytoin is the usual second choice, and the combination may be tried if neither is effective on its own. Primidone, phenobarbitone, sodium valproate, acetazolamide and clonazepam may also be tried in resistant cases, although it is unusual to obtain good control with any of these when a combination of phenytoin and carbamazepine has failed.

PROGNOSIS

A rapid response to therapy is an encouraging sign.[427] Intellectual retardation and resistant fits indicate that prognosis for recovery and adjustment in adult life should be guarded. Table 20.4 summarises prognostic factors in temporal lobe epilepsy.

Table 20.4   Prognosis of temporal lobe epilepsy. (Lindsay *et al.*[427])

Long term outlook
One-third independent: free of fits and off drugs
One-third independent: on anticonvulsants
One-third dependent on parents or in long term care

*Adverse features**
I.Q. below 90
Onset of fits before 28 months of age
Five or more grand mal fits
Temporal lobe fits at least once per day
Left-sided focus
Hyperkinesis
Outbursts of rage
Need for special school

Positive features
One or more first-degree relatives with epilepsy
Epilepsy *not* caused by meningitis, head injury or epileptic status

---

* Four or more adverse features indicate a poor prognosis for independence.

REFLEX EPILEPSIES

Of these, photosensitive epilepsy is by far the commonest.[428] It usually begins between the ages of 6 and 15. The usual stimulus is the normal flicker of the TV screen (black and white or colour), not a fault in the set. The flicker becomes a more potent stimulus with close proximity. Some children have a compulsion to come close to the set, presumably finding the sensation pleasant. Occasionally, other sources of flicker, such as sunlight through trees or fast flashing lights at a disco may cause attacks. The EEG shows a dramatic response to flicker. Treatment is summarised in Table 20.5.

Table 20.5   Advice and treatment for photosensitive epilepsy.

Watch TV from at least 3 m
Room should be well lit
Let someone else adjust set if possible
Cover one eye with hand if forced to approach set
Polarised sunglasses in bright sunlight
Cinema is safe: small risk in discos
If above advice not effective: sodium valproate

Rarely, other stimuli such as patterns, reading, music, arithmetic or immersion may cause fits. Fits evoked by sudden noise or touch occur in children with severe organic brain damage and in Tay–Sachs disease. Some children appear to deliberately elicit reflex seizures by various manoeuvres. This 'self-induced' epilepsy is more likely to occur in retarded children.[429]

FEBRILE CONVULSIONS

Unlike epilepsy, febrile convulsions are seldom a significant handicap in themselves, and for a fuller discussion the reader is referred to general paediatric texts. A brief summary is given in Table 20.6. Three aspects are of particular significance in the context of handicap. Firstly, febrile fits may be prolonged (febrile status) and are then a potential cause of handicap. They may be one cause of temporal lobe epilepsy, although they are probably only responsible for a minority of cases. Prolonged unilateral febrile fits may also result in a permanent hemiplegia (the HHE syndrome—hemiconvulsions, hemiplegia and epilepsy) but this is a rare cause of the acute infantile hemiplegia syndrome (p. 310). Secondly, they are more frequent and more severe in children with pre-existing handicap. As implied in Table 20.6, febrile fits in handicapped children have a substantial risk of recurrence and

Table 20.6   Febrile convulsions—a summary of available data.

Definition: a fit associated with fever, and not caused by central nervous system infection
Incidence: 3–6% of childen have at least one febrile fit
Sex: Boys slightly outnumber girls
Age range: 6 months–5 years
Peak age: 13–15 months in girls; 15–18 months in boys
Type of seizure: Usually brief (1–2 minutes), generalised, tonic-clonic, with postictal sleep. May be severe, i.e. prolonged (>15 minutes) or unilateral, or repeated within 24 hours

Causes
(1) Fever due to respiratory infections, otitis media, gastroenteritis, Shigella diarrhoea, Roseola infantum, urine infection, etc
(2) Together with genetic predisposition: 10–20% of relations have some convulsive disorder

Risk of recurrence
One recurrence 33%
More than one 17%
Predictive risk factors:
Onset before age 1 year
Family history of non-febrile seizures
Pre-existing neurological/developmental disorder
Persistent post-ictal neurological disorder

Risk of subsequent afebrile seizures and epilepsy
Overall risk 3%
No predictive factors—risk 1%
1 predictive factor—risk 2%
2/3 predictive factors—risk 10%
Risk of epilepsy in children *without* febrile fits 0.5%
Predictive factors
    family history of non-febrile seizures
    pre-existing neurodevelopmental abnormality
    severe first febrile seizure
Seizure types
    no predominance of any type in children who develop epilepsy

---

Note   The EEG is of negligible value in predicting either recurrence risk or the risk of later epilepsy.

of later epilepsy.[430,431] Thirdly, developmental disorders later in childhood are often attributed to 'brain damage' caused by febrile fits. In fact it is more likely that in most cases, the occurrence of febrile fits is a reflection of pre-existing neurological impairment rather than its cause.[77]

MANAGEMENT

The immediate control of fits is discussed on p. 449. Febrile fits are terrifying and parents usually think that the child is dying, but a study of nearly 2000 children with febrile fits revealed no deaths or severe sequelae directly related to the fits.[431] A calm attitude is reassuring. Clear instructions on future prevention and management, including fever precautions (fans, tepid sponging and antipyretics) are essential. Parents should be told how long to wait before summoning an ambulance if the child does have another fit: most febrile fits last for less than five minutes, so they can be told to call for help if the attack has not stopped by then. (The post-ictal sleep usually lasts longer than this; the difference between the fit and the sleep must be explained.) Immunisation is discussed on p. 148.

The prescription of prophylactic anticonvulsants is controversial.[432] The general principles discussed below (p. 447) are applicable to febrile fits and no exact rules are possible. There is no direct evidence that prophylaxis reduces the risk of epilepsy developing later, though the phenomenon of 'kindling' suggests that this is possible. An acceptable compromise is to offer anticonvulsant therapy after the first seizure if several high-risk factors are present, but only after the third or fourth in other cases. Sodium valproate and phenobarbitone are both satisfactory but the latter probably has more behavioural side-effects. Phenytoin is probably less effective. Therapy is continued until 3 years of age, or for a minimum of one year. An alternative is to provide the parents with an emergency anticonvulsant; this avoids the use of prolonged medication for what is essentially a benign disorder. Phenobarbitone is not effective as a short term treatment unless a substantial loading dose is given. Rectal diazepam or paraldehyde are both suitable, although experience with the former is still limited in the UK.

NEONATAL FITS

Diagnosis and management of neonatal fits are discussed elsewhere.[424] For the developmental paediatrician, it is worth noting that early neonatal fits (0–72 hours) are of serious import and the risk of subsequent handicap is substantial, but fits occurring in the 2nd week are often associated with hypocalcaemia and have a much better prognosis.

THE EEG

Most parents and many doctors regard this investigation with awe. It is thought to hold the answers to all questions relating to brain damage, funny turns, and even intelligence and personality. The impressive machinery, the apparently chaotic tracing and the incomprehensible nature of many reports all enhance the magic. Other fantasies and fears about EEGs are common: some parents even confuse it with electric shock therapy. It is most important to tell the parents the limitations of the investigations, and the decisions which will be based on it, otherwise they will live in an agony of suspense awaiting the (often irrelevant) results.

When an EEG is requested the procedure should be explained beforehand. If the parents are anxious they will be less able to calm the child. Handicapped children may need heavy sedation (trimeprazine 2–4 mg/kg 90 minutes beforehand) even though this makes interpretation more difficult. The seizure discharge seen in primary generalised epilepsies may be reduced by drugs and, if possible, the EEG should be performed before-starting treatment. Focal spike discharges are less likely to be affected. It is dangerous and unnecessary to withdraw therapy suddenly for performance of an EEG, but details of therapy must be available to the recordist.[449]

THE EEG REPORT

Numerous authoritative writers on epilepsy have stressed that the diagnosis of epilepsy depends on the history, yet many doctors continue to regard the EEG report as the final court of appeal. The EEG is invaluable in confirming a clinical suspicion of petit mal or myoclonic epilepsy, infantile spasms, or benign focal epilepsy. It may be helpful in the diagnosis of temporal lobe epilepsy or grand mal, but it may be normal in both conditions. Furthermore, spike or spike-wave discharges may occur in normal children who have never had fits and must never be taken as firm evidence of epilepsy when the clinical history is equivocal.[433,434] Other non-specific abnormalities (excessive slow activity, unusual responses to hyperventilation or drowsiness, etc.) have a statistical correlation with epilepsy and are often reported as 'an abnormal record compatible with epilepsy'—but even normal records are compatible with epilepsy!

The EEG does *not* predict the future occurrence of epilepsy in normal or in handicapped children. It is of very limited value in non-epileptic conditions such as behaviour disorders, mental handicap or clumsiness. It may be reported as immature, abnormal or even epileptiform but this information is rarely of clinical value. It is not a reliable way of distinguishing organic brain disease from 'minimal brain dysfunction'. Certain rare disorders have specific EEG patterns; for example, SSPE, Batten's disease and petit mal or minor motor epileptic status.

SPECIAL EEG INVESTIGATIONS

When there are serious doubts about the nature of a child's attacks, the EEG can be recorded continuously, for days if necessary, by radiotelemetry or by a portable cassette recorder (Fig. 20.1). Simultaneous video-recording may be invaluable. These investigations are not used as extensively as they could

Fig. 20.1 Ambulatory EEG monitoring using the Medilog recorder. (Courtesy of Oxford Medical Systems.)

be and many children are subjected to unnecessary treatment instead of accurate diagnosis.

MANAGEMENT OF EPILEPSY

An accurate diagnosis is the first essential, and the many other causes of 'funny turns' must always be considered. When uncertain, it is usually better to admit the fact and await events than to make a wrong diagnosis of epilepsy. Once the diagnosis is established, adequate explanation must be given. To the layman, epilepsy can seem as disastrous a diagnosis as mental handicap. It may be thought to imply madness, brain damage, and violence, and these misconceptions are not confined to the uneducated.[436,437] The literature produced by various voluntary societies may be useful. The onset of epilepsy in a previously handicapped child does not always create such alarm, as many parents know of the increased risk, but they may still have an exaggerated idea of its significance.

Starting treatment

Children with petit mal or myoclonic epilepsy have usually had many attacks before the diagnosis is made, and there is seldom any reason to delay treatment. Isolated grand mal fits present more of a problem. The diagnosis may be in doubt if the history is vague. Some children may have a single seizure due to a combination of circumstances—for example fatigue, overexcitement and a family quarrel occurring simultaneously. Anticonvulsants should rarely be commenced after a single seizure and, if potential trigger factors can be identified, a 'wait and see' policy can be recommended with confidence and is usually welcomed by the parents. There are particular problems with undiagnosable 'funny turns' in toddlers; but follow-up shows that these have a good prognosis. Many severely handicapped children have sudden outbursts of crying, unexplained staring, or occasional jerking movements. None of these should be regarded as epileptic without prolonged observation. Nothing will be lost by waiting a little and many chidren will be saved from unnecessary treatment.

PARENTS' VIEWS ON TREATMENT

A definite policy should be agreed with the parents at the start of treatment. They must understand the reasons for treatment and its minimum duration. If the parents decide that they 'do not agree with drugs' they will not give them. If they are worried about the fits and want treatment, they can be relied on to give it regularly, but if they are more afraid of the side-effects (real or imagined), compliance is likely to be poor. Treatment is neither totally safe nor always effective, and if there is parental resistance to medication, this should usually be accepted. Sometimes the fits never recur and the parents are vindicated!

Public awareness of drug side-effects has increased dramatically in recent years and people no longer believe in medical omniscience. Most parents prefer to know the side-effects of the drugs prescribed for their child. They believe (correctly) that all drugs have side-effects, and feel much happier if they know what to expect. I usually tell parents the main unwanted actions of the drug(s), describe the excellent safety record of anticonvulsants, and invite them to phone me if they suspect any problems. This offer is very rarely used or abused, but certainly gives the parents confidence to commence treatment. It also acts as a safety mechanism for early detection of serious side-effects.

Epilepsy is a chronic disorder and the patient's records rapidly become incomprehensible. Parents can help by keeping a record of seizure frequency themselves, perhaps using a diary. (An excellent diary is provided free by the makers of sodium valproate.) A tabular record greatly simplifies management; one can see at a glance what changes in therapy have been made, and why (Fig. 20.2). The burden of frequent outpatient or clinic visits can be reduced by judicious use of the telephone and by agreeing in advance whether, and how much, the parents can adjust dosage themselves. It is unreasonable for parents to waste half a day just to report that a child is well and seizure-free. The most important factor in the successful management

Name	F — 8 —				Date of First Visit	10. XII. 79				EEG	13. XII. 79	Focal spikes L. fronto-temporal
D of B	6. XI. 74				Diagnosis (i) Type	Adversive seizures				EEG		
No.	H19 --------				Diagnosis (ii) Aetiology	C.T. → small area cortical dysplasia				EEG		

	Weeks Since Seen	No. of fits					Drug 1			Drug 2			Drug 3			Investigations			Comments	Next Visit
Date		g.m.	p.m.	partial	myo	other	Name	Dose	Level	Name	Dose	Level	Name	Dose	Level					
14.12.79	1			4 in past week			pt	200 stat 100 on	—							c.T.	FBC	Ca LFT v/e	Entered in Trial — drew phenytoin. (pt)	3
2.1.80	3			6			"	"	✓ 4.7 mg/ml										4 dose → 125 → 150 (phone)	3
23.1.80	3			1			"	150 on	✓ 14.2 mg/ml										no toxic symptoms	2
6.2.80	2			0			"	150 on											well	4

Fig. 20.2 A tabular record for use in epilepsy clinics.

of epilepsy is continuity of care by one interested doctor. Some children, particularly those with temporal lobe epilepsy, have intractable seizures and these particularly need to be cared for by one person, if only to avoid multiple or ill-judged changes of medication.

EFFECTS OF EPILEPSY ON THE CHILD

Parents often believe that emotional upsets or tantrums may precipitate further fits, so they relax their previous levels of discipline, and behaviour problems may result. The constant fear that the child may die in a seizure also changes their attitude towards him. An additional, often unrecognised, source of transient behaviour disorder is hospitalisation. Many of the problems seen in children with seizures, and attributed to the fits or the drugs, may simply be a reaction to the experience of being in hospital, and occur after admission for numerous other reasons.

It is traditional to counsel parents that their epileptic child should not become 'overexcited and overtired' and that teenagers should not consume 'much alcohol', but imprecise advice of this kind raises more questions than it provides answers and simply creates anxiety. Some degree of 'overprotection' is inevitable if the child is epileptic. Advice depends on the type of seizure and on the success of therapy, but the only activities which need to be banned are usually cycling on busy roads, unaccompanied swimming[438] (Table 20.7) and (in the older age group) rock climbing, caving and similar activities. In general, the child should be able to lead an essentially normal life unless he has frequent uncontrollable fits.

EDUCATIONAL PROBLEMS

Children with epilepsy are more likely to suffer from educational problems, including poor progress particularly in reading, lack of attention, and

Table 20.7   Advice for epileptic children on swimming and bathing.

Many more deaths occur in the bath than while swimming
Water in bathtub should not be more than 7.5 cm deep
Young children should not bath alone
Older children should not lock the bathroom door
Showering while sitting in the bath with the drain open is safe
Showering while standing in a glass-enclosed shower cubicle is not advised
It is safe to sit on a low stool in the shower cubicle
Occasional seizures: child may swim with lifeguard or competent swimmer available. Diving is forbidden
Frequent seizures: child may swim at shallow end only with immediate and constant individual surveillance

behaviour disorders.[423,439] Partial epilepsies, particularly of left-sided origin, seem to be the type most often associated with educational failure, but subclinical spike-wave discharges, as in untreated petit mal, also disrupt learning.

Several factors may account for these observations. Firstly, the cerebral lesion which gives rise to the epilepsy may also interfere with learning. Secondly, there is some evidence that anticonvulsant drugs impair concentration. There is a suspicion that phenytoin, and perhaps phenobarbitone and primidone are the main offenders, and carbamazepine appears to be relatively innocuous in this respect, but this is a very difficult area of research. Thirdly, there are subtle social and emotional changes both in the child's view of himself and in the way others treat him. Epilepsy worries even the most enlightened of teachers, and often lower standards of behaviour and achievement are set for the epileptic child. When an epileptic child is failing in school, several possibilities should be considered, including underlying progressive brain disease, inadequate control of fits, drug intoxication, excessive time off school, and unrelated problems such as hearing loss. When these have been eliminated, it is often best to insist that the epilepsy be treated as a side-issue and the problem be assessed on its educational aspects alone. Rarely, when school failure and uncontrollable fits coincide, a transfer to a special school for epileptics can be arranged. These schools have a high staff:child ratio and constant medical cover. Often the relaxed atmosphere where fits are accepted as a fact of life, combined with a regular life-style and reliable drug administration, produce a marked improvement even without changes of medication.

The paediatrician must decide with the parents what information should be given to the child's headteacher. The vast majority of parents accept that the school needs to know about the child's epilepsy. Most headteachers will cope very well with an epileptic child, provided that they know exactly what to expect, and precisely what to do in the event of a seizure. They also need to know what activities are forbidden, particularly in sports and swimming. All this information should be provided in unambiguous terms in a letter to the headteacher, with copies to the schooldoctor, the GP and the parents. This simple manoeuvre makes it quite clear that responsibility for the child's wellbeing is shared with the paediatrician and is a great help in integrating the epileptic child into normal school. The ability of a teacher to cope with an epileptic child in the class is very dependent on the support and leadership of the headteacher.

When epilepsy appears in a previously handicapped child, school problems are usually less evident, because teachers in special schools are much more familiar with epilepsy and do not find it so alarming. Nevertheless advice and clinical details should still be made available to the headteacher.

Treatment

There is a vast literature on the pharmacology of anticonvulsant drugs, and this section offers only a brief summary of the most important practical points.

DRUG LEVELS

Techniques for the measurement of anticonvulsant levels have revolutionised both basic knowledge and clinical management. For all drugs, there is a dose-response curve (Fig. 20.3). With very low levels the effect is negligible. At high levels, little extra therapeutic effect is gained by further increases in dosage, but there is often a rapid increase in toxicity. The therapeutic range lies between these extremes, and here an increase in dose (or blood level) increases the response. In some cases seizures may be abolished with levels at the low end of the range, whereas others may only respond to high levels. The change in blood level of a drug, when the dose is altered, depends on its protein-binding and metabolism. In some cases, for example sodium valproate, the changes are reasonably predictable and blood levels reflect dosage. This is not true of all drugs; if there is an upper limit to the body's ability to metabolise the substance, then, when that limit is reached, a small increase in dose will cause a large rise in blood level. The main example of this is phenytoin.

The metabolism and excretion of most anticonvulsants is very slow and blood levels fall only gradually. The half-life of a drug is the time taken for the level to fall by one half. It is usually possible to precribe anticonvulsants at intervals equal to the half-life, which in practice may mean only once or twice a day. Rarely, thrice-daily dosage does seem to improve seizure control; perhaps seizures in these patients are only controlled when their levels are at the top of the dose-response curve.

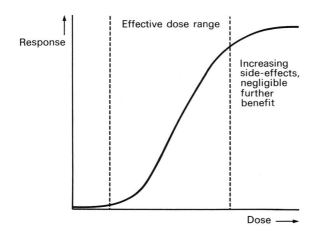

Fig. 20.3 The dose-response curve. Relationship between the dose of a drug and the clinical effect.

Availability of drug level monitoring makes it possible to obtain maximal therapeutic benefit from a drug before concluding that it is ineffective. Sometimes standard dosage fails to produce the maximal permissible levels and cautious increases in dose can be made without fear of serious overdosage. Before this facility was available, patients with resistant seizures often received three or four different drugs, all at ineffective doses and with inadequate blood levels. The advantages of monotherapy—one drug at a time, properly monitored—are now beyond question.

INTERACTIONS

Anticonvulsants interact with each other, with other drugs, and with endogenous substances. This happens in many ways. The most important in this context are liver enzyme induction and inhibition, and competition for binding sites on plasma proteins. Many drugs cause enzyme induction— they stimulate the production of the liver enzymes which detoxify them; the result is a fall in the blood level of any drugs metabolised in this way. The interactions which are most significant in paediatrics are summarised in Table 20.8.

Table 20.8   Interactions of potential importance in children and teenagers.

Carbamazepine, phenytoin, phenobarbitone, primidone (all enzyme inducers); usually reduced levels when combined
Sodium valproate increases free phenytoin levels; toxicity occurs at lower phenytoin levels
Sulthiame raises phenobarbitone and phenytoin levels by inhibiting metabolism
Enzyme-inducers accelerate metabolism of oral contraceptives; risk of pregnancy
Cotrimoxazole and isoniazid elevate phenytoin levels
Aminophylline reduces phenytoin levels
Major tranquillisers are epileptogenic

INDICATIONS FOR MEASURING DRUG LEVELS

It is not necessary to measure levels in every patient. Small children dislike venepunctures and the need for a blood level should always be considered critically. Saliva levels avoid this problem but are not widely available. Phenytoin levels are so unpredictable that they must be checked regularly, and always rechecked after adjusting the dose (allowing adequate time to reach a new equilibrium, which may take two weeks). The other anticonvulsants in common use generally produce acceptable blood levels if the recommended dose per kg is administered, and levels need to be measured only in the situations summarised in Table 20.9.

Table 20.9 Indications for measuring drug levels.

All patients on phenytoin
Doubtful compliance
Uncontrolled seizures
High doses, or previous levels near toxic range
Suspected toxic effects
Severely handicapped children—toxicity hard to recognise
Multiple drug therapy
Prior to discontinuation of therapy
Other systemic disease (liver, kidneys, etc.)

Note   When arranging venepuncture for drug level, check whether blood alkaline phosphatase and calcium levels are also needed.

METABOLIC BONE DISEASE

Enzyme-inducing anticonvulsants accelerate vitamin D metabolism[440] and long term therapy may cause osteomalacia and bone pain which may easily be overlooked, particularly in the handicapped. Inadequate exposure to sunlight in institutionalised children exacerbates this problem. Routine prophylaxis with vitamin D is not recommended but, in children on long term drugs, the calcium and alkaline phosphatase levels should be checked annually.

CHOICE OF DRUG

This has already been discussed for each type of epilepsy. Carbamazepine, sodium valproate and ethosuximide can be regarded as first line drugs, and clonazepam may be a first choice in some cases of myoclonic epilepsy. Phenytoin, with its long list of side-effects and need for monitoring, should be kept in reserve, and phenobarbitone also is now relegated to a second-line position, because it often causes behavioural disturbance. It is desirable to consider the clinical features and EEG to determine what type of epilepsy the patient has, and to select an appropriate drug for that type; but there are surprisingly few controlled drug comparisons, and evidence of the relative efficacy of even first-line drugs in different types of epilepsy is largely anecdotal. Essential pharmacological data on anticonvulsants are summarised in Appendix 3.

Emergency treatment of fits

This is identical whether the fits are of febrile origin or are epileptic. The majority of seizures are of brief duration. The only treatment needed is to protect the child from injury and safeguard the airway. The semi-prone or prone positions are safest. If the fit lasts longer than a few minutes, treatment is needed: intravenous diazepam is ideal but rectal administration is also effective. The safest treatment for use by parents is probably rectal paraldehyde. If the child has frequent fits which are not well controlled by anticonvulsants, the parents may feel happier if they can take immediate action themselves; this is particularly so in rural areas remote from emergency services.

Seizures not responding to these measures or recurring rapidly constitute epileptic status. The management of this emergency is discussed elsewhere.[423,424]

Drugs used in epilepsy

SODIUM VALPROATE

Sodium valproate has been available in the UK since 1975 but there is already an extensive literature on its efficacy and safety. Most children tolerate it well, and most of the side-effects are transient and minor. The main concern has centred around a serious and often fatal syndrome of liver damage and encephalopathy and, as this has inhibited many doctors from using this valuable drug, it merits a detailed description. About 50 cases have been reported. Almost all have been in children with pre-existing severe neurological or developmental disorder as well as epilepsy, and usually valproate has been administred in combination with at least one other anticonvulsant. This syndrome usually occurs within the first few months of therapy, and there is a prodromal phase of gastrointestinal disturbance and drowsiness. In several instances, two cases have occurred in the same family, raising the possibility that the predisposing factor is an unrecognised metabolic disorder.[469]

This problem cannot be anticipated by outpatient monitoring of liver function tests, although it seems reasonable to perform these prior to treatment to avoid giving the drug to children with pre-existing hepatic disease. The best protection is probably to warn the parents of this extremely rare complication and to see the child at once if the prodromal features appear. As this problem does not appear to have been reported in otherwise normal children treated for febrile fits or uncomplicated epilepsy, these precautions are reserved for handicapped children.

CARBAMAZEPINE

First used for trigeminal neuralgia, this is now one of the most valuable anticonvulsants available. There were a few early reports of aplastic anaemia, but these have never been confirmed. Unlike many other drugs it has little depressant or sedative action, and possibly a slight alerting action.

CLONAZEPAM

Although a very effective anticonvulsant, success with this drug has been limited for two reasons. Firstly, a wide variety of behavioural disturbances occur; some of these are all too obvious but often they are more subtle and may only be apparent in retrospect when the drug is withdrawn. This problem can be reduced, but not eliminated, by building up the dose very slowly. Secondly, after a few weeks or months of good control, seizures often recur, and the dose has to be increased, with more risk of behaviour change.

There is no 'correct' dose of clonazepam, and it can be increased at least up to the level shown in Appendix 3 (p. 476), but some seizures are

Table 20.10   Risk of relapse when stopping anticonvulsants.

Risk increased by
Mental handicap
Other neurological disease
Early (< 2 years) age of onset of fits
Difficulty in controlling seizures: large number of seizures
Need for high blood levels of drugs
? Abnormal EEG

Overall relapse rate: 10–30%
Range from 5 to 80%, dependent on number of risk factors
Half of all relapses occur in first 3 months
Three-quarters occur in 1st year

---

controlled on tiny doses. When this happens the parents should be told that relapse may occur and that they can increase the dose by 0.125 mg ($\frac{1}{4}$ tablet) increments every few days if necessary. Blood levels are technically difficult to measure and their value is not established.

Clonazepam has been outstandingly effective in myoclonic epilepsies, especially in association with severe handicap. Like diazepam, it has the additional benefit of reducing spasticity. In normal children side-effects are too common for it to be a first choice but it should certainly be tried in difficult cases.

ETHOSUXIMIDE

This has a long and excellent safety record in the treatment of petit mal. It is cheaper than sodium valproate; its main disadvantage is that it provides no protection against the grand mal fits which may occur in this disorder.

PHENOBARBITONE

This is a very cheap and effective drug, but it has a tendency to cause irritability and behaviour change, and probably impairs learning. For these reasons it is less popular now as a first-line drug, but its bad reputation may be a little exaggerated and it should certainly be tried when necessary.

PHENYTOIN

Because of its numerous side-effects, and the need for regular monitoring of blood levels, phenytoin should not be prescribed for children as a first choice. Perhaps its greatest value is in partial seizures resistant to carbamazepine alone, but it is sometimes effective in other seizure types when other agents have failed.

PRIMIDONE

Primidone is metabolised to phenobarbitone and phenylethylmalonamide. It is occasionally effective where other drugs have failed.

Stopping treatment

Most children and parents naturally want to stop taking medication if possible.[441] It is reasonable to try withdrawing treatment if the child has been free of fits for a prolonged period, perhaps two years if the seizures were few in number and easily controlled, and up to five years with the most severe problems. Medication should be reduced slowly (1–3 months) to avoid the risk of withdrawal seizures.

The probability of relapse can be predicted to some extent (Table 20.10). Opinions differ as to the predictive value of the EEG at the time of stopping the drugs, but in practice the over-riding factor is the need to give the child a trial off medication and the EEG result does not substantially alter this decision. Evidence is also equivocal about the significance of puberty as a cause of increased fit frequency, but perhaps a more important factor is the teenager's desire for a driving licence as soon as he is 16 years old. Freedom from seizures (on or off drugs) for three years is essential before a licence is granted. Thus it may be more sensible to discontinue medication at age 12 than at 14 so that, if relapse occurs, three fit-free years can still be attained by the age of 16!

The resistant case

When a child with epilepsy fails to respond to therapy with first one and then two drugs, in spite of good compliance and therapeutic blood levels, the following routine is suggested:

1   Review the diagnosis. The child may not have epilepsy at all. The epilepsy may be of a different type from that first suspected.

2   Is there an underlying focal lesion? Consider a CT scan to exclude this. Is there any evidence of a degenerative or progressive neurological disease?

3   Examine the child's seizure diary. Have the various drug changes made any significant difference to the seizure frequency? If in doubt, consider admission and withdraw one drug at a time, slowly. Some children actually improve when this is done; many are certainly no worse. A new drug can then be introduced. This procedure avoids the common error of treating a child with three or four drugs of which only one may be exerting any therapeutic effect. Very few patients experience better control on three drugs then they did on two. Occasionally, a ketogenic diet may help.[424]

4   When the diary shows that fits cluster at a particular time of day, a change in dosage times may help, particularly with drugs that have a short half-life.

5   In some children, notably those with complex partial seizures, full control cannot be achieved even with the most meticulous care. The possibility of neurosurgical treatment should be considered, and advice obtained from a centre specialising in epilepsy surgery.

Genetic advice

Many parents worry about the inheritance of epilepsy, but adequate counselling is rarely provided. When the epilepsy is caused by a known neurological disorder, genetic guidance is dependent on the nature of the

Table 20.11   Genetic advice for parents of a child with epilepsy.

Condition	Genetic implications
Grand mal	Risk to siblings and offspring $1:25$ One close relative also affected $1:15$ Parent also affected $1:10$ Presence of 3 per sec spike-wave in EEG increases risk $1\frac{1}{2}$–$2 \times$
Petit mal	Risk to siblings and offspring $1:25$ Parent also has epilepsy (petit mal or grand mal) $1:10$
Temporal lobe epilepsy	Risk is low unless epilepsy caused by febrile fits
Febrile fits	Risk to siblings $1:6$ Risk of siblings developing epilepsy is much smaller
Photosensitive epilepsy and benign focal epilepsy	Risk to siblings and offspring $1:30$

underlying disease or malformation.[442] The transmission of most forms of idiopathic epilepsy is not fully understood but empiric risks are available. The figures in Table 20.11 give an approximate guide; several more detailed accounts are available. [443] The risks quoted are for clinical epilepsy. The incidence of EEG abnormalities is much higher.

The teratogenic effects of anticonvulsants have been extensively investigated. There is a small increase in the risk of malformations in children born to epileptic mothers and, possibly, epileptic fathers.[444] It is still uncertain whether the cause of this increase is the epilepsy itself or the use of anticonvulsants, but the use of the latter is undoubtedly preferable to uncontrolled epilepsy. Phenytoin in particular may cause growth deficiency, facial anomalies, digit-nail hypoplasia, and possible oro-facial clefts and heart defects. Neural tube defects in association with maternal valproate therapy have been reported recently.

NON-EPILEPTIC 'FUNNY TURNS'

Numerous disorders present as transient disturbances of behaviour or consciousness.[423,435] Handicapped children are by no means immune from any of these conditions, but they are at particular risk of being wrongly diagnosed as epilepsy. It would be no exaggeration to say that the more precise diagnosis of the conditions which mimic epilepsy would make a substantial contribution to the prevention of unnecessary handicap. It must be re-emphasised that many of the conditions discussed below may terminate with loss of consciousness and may even provoke a fit. The events preceding and following the fit must be ascertained with as much care as those occurring during the attack.

Breath-holding attacks and reflex anoxic seizures

Breath-holding spells are common (5%) in normal children and also occur in the mentally handicapped though no prevalence figures are available.[445] They mainly affect the toddler age group, but I have seen typical spells in a 10-month-old mentally handicapped baby. The attacks are probably physiologically related to reflex anoxic seizures and fainting which occur in older children; 17% of breath-holding infants develop syncopal attacks in adolescence.

There is nearly always a precipitating event such as fear, trauma, frustration or temper but in some children the trigger event may be so trivial that it is not observed, and it is in these cases that misdiagnosis is more likely. In the most familar form (type I, blue breath-holding), the child usually cries, then stops breathing and becomes cyanosed, limp and unresponsive. There may be a brief tonic phase and some clonic movements. Recovery is rapid and complete. These spells are caused by cerebral hypoxia. The probable mechanism is that crying causes hypocapnia which reduces cerebral blood flow, apnoea causes hypoxaemia, and respiratory spasm (Valsalva manoeuvre) reduces cardiac output. Reflex anoxic seizures are also known as white breath-holding or breath-holding type II. The child becomes deathly pale, rather than cyanosed. The mechanism is cardiac slowing or even asystole, mediated vagally. They are usually precipitated by an unpleasant stimulus such as pain, but the breath-holding is not always obvious to an observer. The onset can be more sudden and dramatic than in the more familiar cyanotic type I spells. A febrile illness may be an additional provocative factor. Both groups can often be shown to have an abnormally sensitive oculocardiac reflex. Firm pressure on the eyeballs induces cardiac slowing and may elicit a typical attack. This can be demonstrated (by expert technicians) during simultaneous EEG/ECG recording (Fig. 20.4).

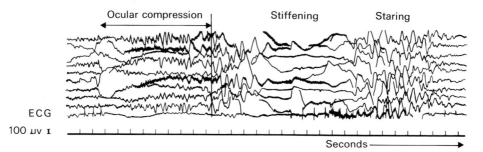

Fig. 20.4 Simultaneous EEG and ECG during and after ocular compression in a child with reflex anoxic seizures. Asystole lasted for 13 seconds, with flattening of the EEG for 7 seconds during the tonic seizure. The heart restarted 4 seconds before the high voltage slow activity which accompanied a blank stare (anoxic absence). (Courtesy of Stephenson[445].)

It is widely taught and believed that breath-holding spells are used by the child to manipulate his mother. It is true that she may relax discipline for fear of provoking them and it may be helpful to deal with any serious behaviour problems. However the attacks may occur when the child is playing on his own, and they undoubtedly have a physiological basis.

Treatment is very rarely needed, though it is said that the attacks can be abolished with atropine sulphate (10 μg/kg 6-hourly). This treatment is likely to be worse than the condition, which is harmless in spite of its alarming presentation. It is doubtful whether a slap or other painful stimuli are helpful. The child should be left lying flat, in the semi-prone position. If he is picked up and held vertical, cerebral blood flow is reduced further and it seems that the attacks then last longer and recovery is delayed.

Fainting

If a child faints during prolonged standing, for example in school assembly or waiting in the queue for an immunisation, the diagnosis is rarely difficult, but some faints occur without apparent external reasons. There is usually, but not always, a preliminary warning of light-headedness or dizziness (not vertigo). Incontinence, tongue-biting and even a brief tonic-clonic episode can occur and recovery can be quite prolonged. It is then easy to mistake a faint for epilepsy. If the events preceding the 'blackout' offer no clue, it is worth enquiring about the child's personality. 'Very sensitive', 'squeamish', 'fussy', 'anxious', 'tense', or 'nervy' are all adjectives which are often used to describe children who faint frequently. The parents' own view of what caused the attack may also be useful.

Other syncopal attacks

Syncope may also occur in association with prolonged coughing and with micturition. Both are rare in children. Occasionally a child becomes pale and looks vacant after prolonged vomiting; this is also probably vagally mediated.

Migraine

Common migraine consists of recurrent episodes of headache and nausea or vomiting.[77] In classical migraine these features are preceded by focal neurological disturbance. The headaches are often unilateral. In young children the history is often difficult to elucidate, because they cannot localise their pain, and abdominal discomfort may be the main complaint. For this reason there are no exact prevalence figures for preschool children. Migraine certainly occurs in the mildly mentally handicapped and probably in all other forms of handicap as well.

A convenient, though undoubtedly oversimplified, explanation of migraine is that an initial phase of vasoconstriction causes cerebral ischaemia, producing the focal features, and reactive vasodilation then causes the headache. The trigger for the individual attack may be emotion, anxiety, hyperventilation, hormonal changes or occasionally minor trauma to the head. Migraine caused by the last of these can produce considerable diagnostic confusion. The role of foods and food allergies is still uncertain but 'exclusion' diets appear to have some effect on the frequency of attacks.[464]

Focal features are related to the vascular territory involved. They include hemiparesis, hemisensory disturbances, ophthalmoplegia, vertigo, visual defects, speech involvement, and drowsiness with mental confusion. In these cases the distinction from partial seizures may be difficult, particularly if the child is seen after the attack is over. The evolution of the attack is usually somewhat slower than in epilepsy. The headache occurs early in the attack, whereas in epilepsy the headache is post-ictal. Migraine attacks last longer than epileptic seizures but post-ictal sleep may confuse the issue. The child with migraine usually retains some degree of rational action and rarely shows the bizarre behaviour of psychomotor epilepsy or becomes unconscious. A positive family history of migraine is important and, in its absence, the diagnosis must be made with extra caution.

The relationship between migraine and epilepsy is uncertain. They may occasionally coexist, raising the remote possibility of an angioma and justifying a CT scan. Migraine may also provoke a seizure, though this is rare. When there is clinical difficulty in making the distinction, the EEG is unlikely to clarify the situation as it may also be abnormal in migraine. Also controversial are the links (if any) between migraine, recurrent abdominal pain with vomiting, travel sickness, and 'abdominal epilepsy'. These are discussed elsewhere.[77] The main point to be made here is that, in these disorders, EEGs, anticonvulsants and talk of epilepsy are more likely to create iatrogenic handicap than to alleviate the child's symptoms!

There is an atypical form of migraine whose aetiology is unknown; it is characterised by very severe pain behind the eye associated with tears, and stuffiness of the nostril. Attacks last for 30–60 minutes and come in groups lasting for a few weeks, separated by long periods of remission, hence the alternative name, 'cluster headaches'.

TREATMENT

Emotional disturbance and anxiety, particularly about school, may be amenable to simple advice and discussion, and this, coupled with reassurance that the attacks are not of sinister significance, may be all that is needed.

Most cases of childhood migraine only require symptomatic treatment, such as paracetamol and perhaps an antiemetic such as metoclopramide. Ergotamine by nebuliser is occasionally useful, particularly in 'cluster headache'. Children whose attacks are frequent and disabling or who have alarming focal features may need prophylactic therapy. The most satisfactory drugs seem to be propranolol or pizotifen. The need for prophylactic therapy should be reviewed every 3–6 months. It seems reasonable to discontinue therapy slowly (over a few weeks); although there is no sound evidence for this, parents and child find this procedure less alarming than a sudden halt.

Hypoglycaemia

Hypoglycaemia in paediatrics[77] is most often encountered in the following situations: (1) the neonate, (2) numerous rare metabolic and endocrine disorders, usually presenting early in life, (3) insulin overdosage in diabetic children, and (4) ketotic hypoglycaemia. Only the last of these merits any discussion here. Ketotic hypoglycaemia occurs between 1 and 6 years of age, often in small, thin children after a period of fasting—it therefore usually presents early in the morning. Attacks are generally infrequent and recovery is usual even without treatment with intravenous glucose. This is a fairly common disorder which is often misdiagnosed as epilepsy.

Whatever the cause, significant hypoglycaemia presents with drowsiness, listlessness, staring, or coma. Fits are common but not invariable. A transient squint may be noted. The sweating and tachycardia seen in adults are unusual in children. Provided that *all* children with unexplained coma or fits have a blood glucose estimation *during* the episode, the diagnosis presents no problem. Retrospective diagnosis is more difficult, and is discussed in more detail in general paediatric texts.

Children are often suspected of having hypoglycaemia as a cause of more trivial and usually non-specific symptoms. Apparent recovery with a biscuit or sweet drink is often taken as proof but this is unwise, for often these children are simply responding to attention or diversion and their symptoms have an emotional basis. If doubt remains after a careful history, arrangements should be made for the child to be seen immediately next time an attack occurs.

Emotional causes of 'funny turns'

Emotional problems are responsible for many funny turns both in normal and handicapped children. They are by no means confined to disturbed children or to unhappy families. Diagnosis may be complicated because hyperventilation—a common response to anxiety—may provoke seizures and possibly migraine in susceptible subjects.[446]

Whenever a 'funny turn' does not obviously belong in any of the categories described in this chapter, emotional factors should be considered. Examples include recent separation or other family disruption; bereavement or illness in family or friends; school problems, particularly academic failure; and *relative* school failure, in that the child is failing to live up to high standards set by his parent or, more often, himself. Any of these, even the last, may be particularly distressing to a child who is unable to communicate his feelings because of mental or physical handicap. Lack of friends, social isolation and depression should be enquired for in teenagers, particularly the mildly mentally handicapped. The presenting complaint may be 'absence attacks' due to day dreaming (p. 430), or outbursts of overactivity or aggression (p. 435). Functional abdominal pain may cause inexplicable misery, pallor and restlessness in young or non-communicating children.

Hyperventilation is a very frequent manifestation of anxiety. It takes only a few deep breaths to produce alkalosis, hypocapnia and cerebral vasoconstriction. The symptoms are light-headedness or dizziness (*not* vertigo), non-specific visual disturbance ('eyes go funny'), a feeling of vague respiratory difficulty, tachycardia, tingling around the mouth and in the extremities, and general anxiety. Gross, dramatic and prolonged hyperventilation with tetany as described in most textbooks, is relatively rare and represents only the tip of the iceberg of this syndrome. Most children do not have such dramatic features and only a few symptoms may be recognised. If the overbreathing is not observed and described spontaneously by the parent, the diagnosis is easily missed. Hyperventilation is not as common in children as in adults, where it has been described as the most underdiagnosed condition in medicine; however, it is not rare, and may masquerade as asthma, faints, fits, cardiac arrhythmia, or stridor, as well as less specific funny turns whose features make no sense until this diagnosis is considered.

Cardiac disorders

Cardiac arrhythmias are less common in children than in adults, but the possibility should be considered in any child who has loss of consciousness associated with exercise. Resting and exercise ECG recordings may be necessary; sometimes only a prolonged ambulatory record reveals the diagnosis. Aortic stenosis and coronary ischaemia can also occur in children.

The hypercyanotic spells of Fallot's tetralogy are easily recognised if the defect has already been diagnosed, but can cause confusion if the murmur sounds trivial and the child is only minimally cyanosed between spells. Similar attacks can occur in other conditions, for example progressive pulmonary hypertension associated with a shunt in Down's syndrome.

Behavioural disturbances

Infantile masturbation occurs mainly in little girls. The child looks red in the face and perspires, while making violent rocking movements. Apart from checking for sources of perineal irritation such as pinworms or chemical irritation (bubble-bath, etc.), no treatment other than distraction and rearrangement of routine is necessary or effective. The activity is quite harmless and eventually subsides. It should not be confused with epilepsy at any age since rocking movements have not been described as a seizure manifestation.

Rocking, hand-flapping, eye-poking, head-banging and other self-stimulating behaviours are discussed on pp. 165 & 298. They are only likely to be mistaken for seizures by those unfamiliar with childhood handicap, but occasionally a sudden break in the activity, associated with a staring expression, may raise the question of absence attacks. Usually they turn out to be a purely behavioural phenomenon.

Tics

These are sudden, quick and repetitive circumscribed movements which serve no purpose, such as blinking, facial grimacing, throat-clearing, head-shaking and sudden limb movements. They seldom present diagnostic problems but are occasionally confused with myoclonic jerks, absence attacks, or chorea (p. 466). With careful observation the distinction is usually easy; the child will often reproduce the tic in the clinic.

Emotional disturbances may underline some tics. In general the prognosis for recovery is good. Treatment is difficult. The family should ignore the tic as far as possible. The behavioural method of 'massed practice' may help; the child repeats the tic voluntarily and deliberately for five-minute periods several times a day, from 2 to 3 weeks. If the tic is complex, attention is concentrated initially on the eye-blink.

The Gilles de la Tourette syndrome consists of severe vocal and body tics, together with coprolalia (explosive utterances of obscene words). It is uncertain whether it should be regarded as a separate entity or an extreme form of tic. It may be precipitated by methylphenidate (p. 406). Haloperidol sometimes helps.

Sleep disturbances

Simple nightmares are commonplace but night terrors (pavor nocturnus) are less well known and are sometimes mistaken for nocturnal temporal lobe epilepsy.[447] They occur in deep sleep: the child wakes, looking terrified; he may get out of bed seeming dazed and confused, but goes to sleep again quickly. Unlike nightmares, night terrors are not recalled when he awakes next morning. They are not associated with emotional disturbance. Diazepam 2 mg at bedtime helps, but is rarely needed.

Narcolepsy is rare in children, but the characteristic symptom of repeated episodes of irresistible sleep is unlikely to be missed, though is sometimes attributed to excessive late TV viewing! There may be associated cataplexy—a sudden loss of muscle tone causing a fall without loss of consciousness. Diagnosis and treatment are discussed in detail elsewhere.[447] Children who sleep very poorly at night due to chronic upper respiratory obstruction (p. 286) may sleep at odd times during the day.

A few myoclonic jerks at the onset of sleep are a normal phenomenon.

Vertigo

Vertigo is often confused with dizziness. The distinction is made by asking the patient if the sensation was 'like being on a roundabout' and whether it had a definite direction. If the answer to both questions is in the negative, the unpleasant sensation was probably not vertigo.

Benign paroxysmal vertigo is an unusual disorder affecting mainly young children.[77] The attacks of vertigo are sudden and severe but rarely last more than a couple of minutes. There may be pallor, vomiting, sweating, and nystagmus. Consciousness is seldom impaired. The child is frightened and remains still, unable to move. Recovery is rapid and complete. The diagnosis is easy if the child can describe his symptoms but is more difficult in the very young. There is no treatment, but the prognosis is excellent. The cause is unknown, though it may possibly be associated with middle-ear disorders in some cases.

Vertigo can also be a manifestation of complex partial seizures, posterior fossa lesions, and Menière's disease, but these are unlikely to cause confusion.

APPENDICES

One
Miscellaneous disorders causing neurological handicap

Abetalipoproteinaemia (Bassen–Kornzweig disease) Coeliac-like syndrome in first year of life. Sensory ataxia. Retinal degeneration with abnormal ERG. Acanthocytes (burr-like projections on red cells). Low cholesterol. Recessive. Treatment with vitamin E may arrest progression.

Adrenoleukodystrophy ('Schilder's disease') Demyelinating disease; onset may be sudden, slowly progressive or fluctuating; spasticity, cortical blindness, seizures, psychiatric disturbance. Associated adrenal insufficiency which may be subclinical. Sex-linked recessive. Other forms of childhood demyelinating disease; may be similar or identical to multiple sclerosis.

Alexander's disease Onset first year. Macrocephaly. Seizures. Deterioration, early death.

Alpers' disease Ill-defined group of grey-matter degenerations. Seizures, often myoclonic; spasticity; mental deterioration. Mimic leukodystrophies.

Apert's syndrome Craniosynostosis, particularly of coronal suture. Syndactyly. Small nose. Narrow or cleft palate. Variable degree of mental handicap. Numerous other occasional anomalies. Dominant: most cases are new mutations.

Ataxia-telangiectasia syndrome (Louis–Bar syndrome) Progressive ataxia and involuntary movements, abnormal eye movements, IgA deficiency, respiratory infections, telangiectasia on conjunctiva, and later on nose, elbows, etc. Lymphoma. Poor growth. Variable mental handicap. Investigations; low IgA, elevated alphafetoprotein, abnormal sensitivity to radiation of cultured fibroblasts.[346]

Basal cell naevus syndrome Basal cell naevi in childhood; jaw cysts; abnormal teeth; mental handicap; numerous other features. Autosomal dominant.

Beckwith–Wiedemann syndrome (EMG syndrome—exomphalos, macroglossia, giantism) Birthweight averages 4 kg; rapid growth, severe neonatal hypoglycaemia, large tongue, omphalocoele, creases in ear lobules. Occasional hemihypertrophy, tumours. Mental handicap variable, possibly related to hypoglycaemia. Usually sporadic.

Behr syndrome   Bilateral optic atrophy, spastic diplegia, mental handicap; onset in early infancy, may remain static for many years. Autosomal recessive.

Blepharophimosis syndrome   Ptosis, widely separated inner canthi, short palpebral fissures. I.Q. usually normal.

Canavan's disease   Onset first few months. Delayed development, optic atrophy, hypotonia. Macrocephaly. Recessive.

Cockayne's syndrome   Onset at 2–4 years of age. Growth failure, deafness, retinal degeneration, photosensitive rash, etc. Deterioration in gait and intellect. Recessive.

Coffin–Lowry syndrome   Mental deficiency, coarse facies, large hands with tapering fingers, abnormal vertebrae. X-linked semi-dominant inheritance.

Congenital chorea   Choreiform movements commencing early in life, non-progressive, not associated with any other handicap. Can be recessive or dominant.[343]

Congenital insensitivity to pain   At least six separate conditions described, all very rare. Neuropathy; some have deafness and/or retardation. Indolent ulcers on fingers and feet. Variable progression and inheritance.

Cornelia de Lange syndrome   Pre- and postnatal growth retardation. Mental handicap (often severe). Bushy eyebrows meeting in midline. Thin lips with midline 'beak' of upper lip. Limb deficiencies, and hirsutism. Mild cases are difficult to diagnose with confidence. High risk of aspiration pneumonia in infancy, and of other infections. Sporadic; recurrence risk small. Various chromosome defects have been observed—significance is doubtful.

Crouzon's syndrome (craniofacial dysostosis)   Craniosynostosis, hypoplasia of maxilla, parrot-like nose, shallow orbits, abnormal teeth, deafness. Mental handicap not a major feature. Dominant, with variable expression. Shallow orbits may be the only feature. May be new mutation.

Dandy–Walker syndrome Hydrocephalus and cystic dilation of the fourth ventricle associated with obstruction of the outlet foramina. Large, sometimes transilluminable posterior fossa. Other cerebral malformations. Congenital heart disease. Sporadic or recessive.

Devic's disease (neuromyelitis optica) Optic neuritis and transverse myelitis causing paraparesis, occurring together or in succession.

Dystonia musculorum deformans Variable onset, rarely before age 3. Bizarre posturing of feet, wrist, neck, trunk. Involuntary movements increasingly severe. Early stages easily mistaken for hysteria. Recessive form (mainly Jews); dominant form—all races. Stereotactic surgery may help.

Ectodermal dysplasia Abnormalities of sweating, nails, hair and teeth. Hyperthermia, which may cause mental retardation. Language defect. Several forms with variable inheritance.

EEC syndrome Ectrodactyly (limb reduction defects), ectodermal dysplasia, cleft lip and palate. Abnormalities of teeth, hair, occasional deafness. Intelligence usually normal or near normal. Autosomal dominant.

Ehlers–Danlos syndrome Hyperextensible joints and skin, easy bruising, slow wound healing with tissue paper scars, subcutaneous mobile nodules, fragility of blood vessels. At least eight types known, with variable severity and inheritance.

Facio-auriculo-vertebral anomalad Synonyms: first and second arch syndrome, Goldenhaar's syndrome. Asymmetric or unilateral anomalies of mouth, face, pinna, inner ear, hemivertebrae. Dermoid cysts of eyes. Microphthalmos. Mild mental handicap. Usually sporadic.

Familial dysautonomia (Riley–Day syndrome) Virtually confined to Jews from Eastern Europe. Disorder of autonomic nervous system. Neonatal problems. Absent tears. Unstable blood pressure and temperature control. Dysphagia. Psychomotor retardation. Corneal ulcers. Reduced pain sensitivity. Anaesthesia hazardous. Recessive. Several other forms of indifference to pain.

Familial myoclonus epilepsy Onset in mid-childhood. Severe myoclonic epilepsy. Dementia. Recessive. (Several other syndromes including myoclonic epilepsy are known.)

Fanconi's syndrome Small stature, microcephaly, mental handicap, thumb and other limb abnormalities, pancytopenia, skin pigmentation. Poor growth and tendency to infections. High risk of leukaemia. Autosomal recessive.

Friedreich's ataxia   The commonest hereditary spinocerebellar degeneration. Ataxia, speech defect, pes cavus (may be presenting feature and only sign for many years), kyphoscoliosis, dysmorphic appearance, wasting of small muscles, intellectual deterioration, cardiac defects, diabetes. Recessive form begins around 10–12 years, dominant form onset around aged 20.

Hallermann–Streiff syndrome   Small stature, micrognathia, small nose, cataract and microphthalmos, hypoplasia of skin, hair and teeth. Variable intellect, may be normal or retarded. Probably dominant; most cases are new mutations.

Hallervorden–Spatz disease   Foot deformity, abnormal gait, rigidity, athetosis, intellectual deterioration, dysarthria.

Hartnup disease   Intermittent cerebellar ataxia and other personality and behavioural changes. Retardation variable. Photosensitive rash. Aminoaciduria. Defective transport of tryptophan and other neutral aminoacids.

Huntington's chorea   About 5% of cases begin in childhood. Rigidity. Reduced movements. Chorea. Dementia. Seizures (may be main symptom). Ataxia. Rapid deterioration. Dominant.

Hypoparathyroidism   Cataract, photophobia, ridging of teeth, tetany, fits, extrapyramidal disease, mental deterioration.

Incontinentia pigmenti   Bullous skin lesions in infancy progressing to variable hyperpigmented areas. Fits; mental handicap; eye, teeth and hair defects. Genetics uncertain.

Klippel–Feil syndrome   Low posterior hairline, short neck, limited neck movements, fusion of cervical vertebrae. Scoliosis. Sprengel shoulder (abnormal and high scapula). Deafness. Renal anomalies. Synkinesia. Ptosis. Duane's syndrome. Abnormal hands. Cleft palate.

Larsen's syndrome   Multiple joint dislocation, shortened nails and metacarpals, flattened facies, foot deformities. Normal intellect. Inheritance uncertain.

Laurence–Moon–Biedl syndrome   Obesity, polydactyly, mental deficiency, retinitis pigmentosa, hypogonadism. Autosomal recessive.

Leber's disease Sudden loss of vision usually in 2nd decade, but may present in early childhood; cerebellar signs, spasticity, seizures, mental handicap. Sex-linked.

Leigh's disease (necrotising encephalomyelopathy) Early onset. Hypotonia with brisk reflexes. Abnormal eye movements. Elevated lactic and pyruvic acids.

Lesch–Nyhan syndrome A sex-linked disorder of hypoxanthine metabolism. Excessive production of uric acid. Psychomotor retardation in 1st year, extrapyramidal movements in 2nd year, progressive spasticity later in life. Severe involuntary self-mutilation (this does not respond to behavioural methods of treatment; restraint, toothguards and similar measures are necessary). Renal disease and gouty arthritis. Mental retardation variable, not severe. Diagnosed by serum uric acid or (better) by uric acid:creatinine ratio in urine.[344]

Lissencephaly ('smooth brain') Microcephaly, small mandible, odd facies, severe retardation. Cerebral malformation without normal convolutions. Can be recessively inherited.

Lowe's syndrome (oculocerebrorenal syndrome) Severe psychomotor retardation; hypotonia; glaucoma and/or cataract; aminoaciduria. Sex-linked recessive.

Maple syrup urine disease Severe form causes respiratory difficulty, abnormal muscle tone and rapid deterioration in neonate. Some untreated patients survive with severe psychomotor handicap. Urine has characteristic smell. Recessive. Dietary treatment is possible though very demanding. High risk of overwhelming infection.

Marfan's syndrome Tall stature with span greater than height, arachnodactyly, joint laxity, scoliosis, narrow face, upwards dislocation of lens, myopia, aortic valve abnormalities, dissecting aneurysm of ascending aorta. Normal intelligence. Autosomal dominant with variable expression. Can be mistaken for homocystinuria. (Marfanoid body build also seen in normals, particularly in Negroid subjects.)

Marinesco–Sjögren syndrome Cerebellar ataxia, weakness, cataracts, scoliosis. Autosomal recessive.

Megalencephaly Large head due to hamartomatous malformation of brain without hydrocephalus. Psychomotor retardation, occasionally progressive. Fits. Other congenital anomalies. Probably sporadic in most cases. Occasional reports of dominant or recessive inheritance.

Menkes' disease (kinky hair disease) Seizures and rapid psychomotor deterioration in early infancy. Sparse, short lightly pigmented abnormal hair. Abnormal copper metabolism. X-linked recessive.

Moya-moya syndrome An angiographic diagnosis; dilatation of small blood vessels forming a collateral circulation in association with carotid occlusion.

Multiple lentigines syndrome (leopard syndrome) Multiple 1–5 mm dark skin lesions; pulmonary stenosis; deafness; variable retardation. Dominant.

Noonan syndrome Short stature, mild mental handicap, epicanthic folds, eye defects, webbed neck (similar to Turner's syndrome), pectus excavatum, pulmonary stenosis, undescended testes. May occur in both sexes. Can be confused with XO/XY mosaic. Inheritance uncertain.

Paroxysmal choreoathetosis Sudden onset of dystonia, and abnormal postures, often precipitated by movement. Autosomal dominant.

Pelizaeus–Merzbacher disease Early onset of psychomotor regression. Trembling eye movements. Ataxia. Slow progression. Sex-linked recessive and dominant forms.

Poland's anomaly Unilateral hypoplasia or absence of part of the pectoralis muscle, sometimes also involving the breast; there may be underdevelopment of a hand.

Propionic acidaemia (ketotic hyperglycinaemia) Episodic vomiting, ketosis and lethargy. Mixed pyramidal and extrapyramidal signs. Neutropenia. Several other conditions produce episodic metabolic acidosis (methylmalonic, isovaleric, and lactic acidaemias).

Pseudohypoparathyroidism (Albright's hereditary osteodystrophy) Short stature, obesity, mental defect. Hypoplasia of teeth enamel. Short 4th and 5th metacarpals. Calcification in basal ganglia; variable hypocalcaemia.

Robin anomalad (Pierre Robin syndrome) Mandibular retrognathia, glossoptosis, cleft palate. Limb anomalies. Cardiovascular defects. Various eye disorders including Stickler syndrome (q.v.). Intellect usually normal. Respiratory difficulties in infancy—may need nursing in prone position.

Rubinstein–Taybi syndrome   Broad thumbs and toes, maxillary hypoplasia and down-slanting palpebral fissures, short stature. Head is often small. Testes are undescended. No clear inheritance pattern; recurrence risk is small.

Russell–Silver syndrome   Low birthweight, short stature, skeletal asymmetry, small face with appearance of large head, tendency to hypoglycaemia, early psychomotor retardation but I.Q. may be normal. Sporadic.

Seckel syndrome   Also known as 'bird-headed dwarf'. Severe growth deficiency. Microcephaly and mental handicap. Prominent beaked nose. Joint dislocation. Probably autosomal recessive.

Sjögren–Larsson syndrome   Spastic diplegia, mental retardation, ichthyosis, thin brittle hair, short stature. Autosomal recessive.

Smith–Lemli–Opitz syndrome   Pre- and postnatal growth deficiency, psychomotor retardation, failure to thrive, microcephaly, ptosis, syndactyly of 2nd/3rd toes; male has cryptorchidism, hypospadias. Autosomal recessive.

Sotos' syndrome (cerebral giantism)   Excessive growth, advanced bone-age, large hands and feet, macrocephaly, mild to moderate mental handicap, poor coordination, seizures. No endocrine abnormality established. Most cases sporadic.

Sprengel deformity   Congenital upward displacement of the scapula.

Stickler syndrome (hereditary arthro-ophthalmopathy)   Flattened facies, palatal clefts, small jaw, hearing loss, severe myopia, retinal detachment, cataract, tall thin build, hyperextensible joints, severe arthropathy, vertebral dysplasia, scoliosis. Autosomal dominant.

Stiff-baby syndrome   Attacks of stiffness precipitated by surprise or minor physical contact. Can be mistaken for spasticity. Abnormal muscle activity abolished by diazepam. Probably dominant.

Subacute sclerosing panencephalitis (SSPE)   Slowly progressive degenerative brain disease caused by previously acquired measles infection. Presents with intellectual deterioration, myoclonic jerks, occasionally major fits. Typical EEG features. Raised measles antibody titre in CSF. No established treatment; interferon under trial.

Treacher–Collins syndrome   Synonyms: mandibulofacial dysostosis,

Franceschetti–Klein syndrome. Antimongoloid palpebral fissures, hypoplasia of cheek and maxilla, small mandible, coloboma of lower eyelid, malformed external ears, conductive deafness, cleft palate; numerous other rare anomalies; intellect usually normal. Autosomal dominant, 60% of cases are fresh mutations.

Urea cycle disorders   Includes argininosuccinic aciduria, citrullinaemia; several other forms of hyperammonaemia. Clinical features variable; may be abnormal pale brittle hair; seizures; retardation; episodic headache, vomiting and stupor. Aminoacid studies and ammonia levels before and after protein loading for diagnosis.

Van der Woude syndrome (Lip-pit–cleft lip syndrome)   Small pits in lower lip, dental abnormalities, cleft lip with or without palate. Autosomal dominant.

Vater association   Vertebral defects, anal atresia, tracheo-oesophageal fistula. Radial and renal dysplasia. Cardiac defects, single umbilical artery. Many other defects described.

Williams' syndrome   Growth deficiency, mild-to-moderate mental handicap, anteverted nostrils, prominent lips with open mouth, aortic stenosis and other heart defects, variable hypercalcaemia in infancy.

Wilson's disease   Disorder of copper metabolism. May present as acute or chronic liver disease or hemolytic anemia. Kayser–Fleischer ring of corneal pigment. Neurological symptoms (dysarthria, drooling, tremor, various involuntary movements) are very rare before age 10–12. Recessive. Treatment with chelating agents.

Zellweger syndrome   Hypotonia, severe mental handicap, large liver with cirrhotic changes, albuminuria, many other defects described. Breech presentation, early failure to thrive, early death. Can be mistaken for Down's syndrome. Autosomal recessive.

Two
Lysosomal Storage Diseases

Disease	Enzyme defect	Age of onset, and racial predilection	Clinical features
Glycogenoses			
Type II (Pompe)	Acid α-1, 4 glucosidase	Usually early infancy	Muscular weakness, hypotonia, cardiomegaly, CNS involvement
Sphingolipidoses			
Gaucher (Type 1)	Glucocerebrosidase	Variable; Ashkenazy Jews	Hepatosplenomegaly, bone and lung disease, CNS not involved; raised acid phosphatase
Gaucher (Type 2)	Glucocerebrosidase	1st year	Regression, spasticity,
		All races	hepatosplenomegaly, rapid deterioration
Gaucher (Type 3)	Glucocerebrosidase	Childhood	As 2 but slower course
Niemann–Pick (5 Types)	Sphingomyelinase	Type 1- First year; Jewish	Hepatosplenomegaly, failure to thrive, CNS involvement; variant forms with later onset
Farber (lipogranulomatosis)	Ceramidase	1st year	Painful joint swelling, hoarse cry, feeding problems, mental deterioration
Fabry	α-galactosidase		Painful crises (intense burning), punctate purple skin lesions, renal disease, sex-linked
GM1 gangliosidosis (Infantile type)	β-galactosidase	Soon after birth; All races: Commoner in Malta	Severe early CNS involvement and dysmorphic features
(Juvenile type)	β-galactosidase	1–2 years	Motor and mental deterioration; fits

473

Disease	Enzyme defect	Age of onset, and racial predilection	Clinical features
GM2 gangliosidosis (Type 1—Tay–Sachs)	Hexosaminidase-A	3–6 months; Ashkenazy Jews	Motor weakness, violent startle reaction to sound, mental and motor deterioration after 1 year, doll-like appearance, cherry-red spot, blindness, macrocephaly, death by 3 years
At least two other types		Later onset	Similar findings
Krabbe (Globoid cell leukodystrophy)	Galactosylceramide β-galactosidase	All races; 1–6 months; May begin much later	Irritable, stiffness, fever, vomiting, rapid deterioration, decerebrate, blind. Raised CSF protein. Often small head
Metachromatic leukodystrophy Infantile form	Arylsulfatase A	1–4 years	Gait disturbance, variable mixture of upper and lower motor neurone signs, mental regression, optic atrophy
Juvenile form	Arylsulfatase A	4–21 years	As above, plus early emotional and learning problems
Mucopolysaccharidoses Type 1 (Hurler)	α-L-iduronidase	6–12 months	Rapid early growth then severe dwarfism, coarsening of features, mental and motor deterioration, restricted joint mobility, kyphosis, corneal clouding, deafness, cardiac failure, hepatosplenomegaly, death by 10 years
Type 1 (Scheie)	α-L-iduronidase	Early childhood	Similar but milder, intelligence often preserved

Disease	Enzyme defect	Age of onset, and racial predilection	Clinical features
Type II (Hunter)	Iduronate sulfatase	2–6 years	Similar to Hunter but milder; clear cornea; no kyphosis; X-linked
Type III (Sanfilippo) (several types)	Several enzyme defects are known	1–3 years	Clear cornea, mildly dysmorphic, mental and motor deterioration
Type IV (Morquio) and Type VI (Maroteaux–Lamy)	Several enzyme defects are known	1–3 years	Severe short stature, cloudy cornea, intellect preserved
Mucolipidoses (4 types)			
Type I	Not fully characterised	Early childhood	Mild Hurler-like features
Type II (I-cell disease)	Not fully characterised	Infancy	Hurler-like
Type III (Pseudo–Hurler polydystrophy)	Not fully characterised	Slower onset	Hurler-like
Type IV	Not fully characterised	Infancy	Corneal clouding
Other oligosaccharidoses			
Fucosidosis	α-L-fucosidase	Infancy or early childhood	Variable;
Mannosidosis	α-Mannosidase	Infancy or early childhood	Hurler-like features;
Aspartylglycosaminuria	N-aspartyl-β-glycosaminidase	Finland	Retardation; Dysmorphic features
Neuronal ceroid-lipofuscinoses			
Batten's disease(s); Amaurotic familial idiocy	Classification as LSD uncertain; enzyme deficiency not established. Diagnosis by electron microscopy of skin biopsy and exclusion of other LSDs	Depends on type: any time in childhood	Seizures, retinal degeneration, neurological deterioration (mental and motor), abnormal EEG response to flicker, abnormal VER and ERG
Several types, including Jansky–Bielschowsky and Spielmeyer–Vogt			
Kufs		Adult form	

Three
Prescribing Data for Anticonvulsants

Drug and presentation	Initial dose	Usual dose range (mg/kg/day)	Approximate half-life hours	Number of doses/day	Therapeutic range μg/ml	μMol./L
Phenobarbitone (15, 30, 60 mg tabs.) 15 mg/5 ml elixir.	Single loading-dose of 2 × maintenance 5–10/mg/kg/day; increase slowly (every 3–4 days)	3–6 (rarely up to 8)	40–70	1 or 2	15–30	65–130
Primidone (250 mg tabs 250 mg/5 ml suspension)		10–25	10–12	2	8–12 (measure phenobarb.) level as well	37–55
Phenytoin 25, 50, 100 mg caps. 30 mg/5 ml suspension chewable tabs. 50 mg.	Single loading-dose of 2 × maintenance	5–8 (rarely 10–12); dose/kg inversely related to bodyweight	Depends on blood concentration (*see* text)	1 or 2	5–20	20–80
Carbamazepine (100, 200, 400 mg tabs. 100 mg/5 ml syrup)	Start with ¼ maintenance; increase over 3 wks.	15–20	5–27	2–4	6–12	25–50
Ethosuximide (250 mg tabs. 250 mg/5 ml syrup)	Start with lowest dose; increase every 7 days.	15–40	30	1–2	40–100	283–708
Sodium Valproate (200, 500 mg tabs: 'enteric' 100 mg chewable tabs. 200 mg/5 ml syrup)	Start at 10 mg/kg/day and double after 1–2 weeks.	10–60	4–14	1–3	50–100	300–600
Clonazepam (0.5, 2 mg tabs.)	See text	0.01–0.3	20–40**	1–4	(Difficult assay of doubtful clinical value, rarely used except for research.)	
Clobazam (10 mg caps.)	¼–½ maintenance	0.3–0.7	8 (?)**	1–3	(as for clonazepam)	
Nitrazepam (5 mg caps)	1.25 mg at night only.	1.25–15 mg (total dose per day)	20(?)**	1–3	(as for clonazepam)	
Acetazolamide (250 mg tabs.)	¼–½ maintenance	125–750 mg (total dose per day).	4(?)	2–3	(as for clonazepam)	
Drugs for emergency control of seizures						
Diazepam 10 mg/2ml amp. 10 mg/2ml amp. (in emulsion) rectal tubes 5 mg, 10 mg.	—	i) Single dose: 0.1–0.3 mg/kg iv. ii) Infusion: 0.1–0.3 mg/kg/hour. iii) Rectal dose: 5 mg <age 3y 10 mg >age 3y.	variable: Clinical effect is <60 mins.	—	—	—
Paraldehyde (5 cm³ ampoule)	—	Single dose: i) 1 ml/year of age i.m. ii) 0.3 ml/kg in equal volume of mineral oil per rectum.	—	—	—	—
Chlormethiazole Solution for infusion, 8 mg/ml.	—	Infusion: 5–10 mg/kg/hour.	3–4 hours	—	—	—

Ideal sample time	Transient and dose-related side-effects	Other side-effects	Comments
Unimportant	Drowsiness, ataxia, nystagmus, irritability, hyperactivity.	Skin rashes. Can precipitate porphyria.	
Trough*	Drowsiness, giddiness, nausea.	Rash (often transient). Oedema, thirst, polyuria, megaloblastic anaemia.	Metabolised to phenobarbitone and phenylethylmalonamide.
Trough*; peak† (3–9 hrs. after dose) to confirm toxicity	Nausea, nervousness, poor sleep, unsteadiness, drowsiness, nystagmus, ataxia. Long term—gingival hyperplasia, hirsutism, coarsening of features.	Rashes, arthropathy, hepatitis, lupus, blood disturbances, lymphoma-like syndrome.	Complex relationship between dose and blood level (see text).
Trough*	Dizziness, drowsiness, diplopia, dry mouth, nausea, diarrhoea, hyponatraemia, oedema.	Rashes, blood disturbances, hepatitis.	
Unimportant	Drowsiness, headache, depression, euphoria, ataxia, nausea.	Skin rashes, (?) blood disorders.	Administer with food.
Peak (2–3 hrs. after dose)	Gastro-intestinal disturbance, behavioural changes, thrombocytopenia and bruising. Tremor and (?) encephalopathy.	Weight gain, partial alopecia, curly hair, pancreatitis, liver damage (see text).	Administer with food if G1. side-effects occur. Once-daily dose effective in spite of short half-life.
—	Fatigue, hypotonia, behavioural changes, hypersecretion of saliva and bronchial mucus.	—	i) Tolerance after 1–6 months is common. ii) Temporary cessation of therapy may restore effect. iii) Sudden halt may cause withdrawal fits.
—	as for clonazepam	—	As for clonazepam. New drug for epilepsy; information limited.
—	Minor drowsiness, hypotonia	—	Monitor dose by clinical response.
—	Gut disturbance, thirst, headache, drowsiness, paraesthesiae, hyperpnoea, excitement, visual disturbances.	Bone marrow depression, rashes, renal calculi, hearing loss.	
—	Sedation, hypotonia, (may mask meningism) apnoea, phlebitis (local action).	—	i) Rectal solution for parents to use. ii) Apnoea risk with rectal route is minimal. iii) Use emulsion preparation in dextrose (not saline) for infusion. iv) Oral diazepam not a useful anticonvulsant.
—	Respiratory depression.	Sterile abscesses with i.m. injection.	i) Rectal route suitable for home use. ii) Does not degrade modern plastic syringes if used quickly. iii) Limited shelf life. iv) Keep out of light.
—	Respiratory depression. Hypotension. Headache. Fever. Phlebitis.		

Four
The Neurodevelopmental Examination

The items described here are those which the author has found most useful. No attempt to give exact norms will be made; these vary between authors, and between study populations. It is essential to accumulate experience of norms by repeated performance of the examination. See references.[90,91,92,383,394,395]

SUPPRESSION OF HEAD MOVEMENTS

The child is asked to eye track a moving object, moving his eyes only and keeping his head still.

RAPID TONGUE PROTRUSION

The child is asked to rapidly protrude and withdraw his tongue. The speed of execution and overflow movements, grimacing, etc. are noted.

TONGUE PLACING

The child is asked to place tip of tongue at varying points on upper and lower lips, indicated both by touch and by examiner demonstrating.

BUILD STEPS WITH SIX 2.5 CM CUBES

THREAD BEADS ON A SHOELACE

FINGER–THUMB TEST

The child is asked to tap the thumb successively against each fingertip, going from index to little finger and back; this should be done as fast as possible.

HAND PATTING

Palmar surface of one hand patted against dorsum of other hand. Should be performed as fast as possible, each hand in turn.

PRONATION–SUPINATION

The palm and the dorsum of the hand alternatively are placed on the thigh, just above the knee, and the child is asked to change from one to the other as fast as possible (tests speed and smoothness of pronation and supination).

PIANO PLAYING MOVEMENTS

Hand placed on table, the child asked to raise and lower each finger in turn (similar to playing scales on a piano).

FINGER–NOSE TEST

Performed as in classical neurological examination.

GRAPHAESTHESIA TEST

Figures are written on child's palm (using a blunt instrument such as an orange stick). Circle, cross, H, T, S are easiest. Size of figure should be varied, decreasing if child is competent. Can be combined with classic two-point discrimination test if the child is sufficiently capable.

TEST FOR CHOREIFORM MOVEMENTS

See Fig. 4.7.

STANDING ON ONE LEG

HOPPING ACROSS THE ROOM

WALKING HEEL TO TOE ALONG A STRAIGHT LINE

WALKING ON THE HEELS

CATCHING AND DRIBBLING A BALL

DRAWING A MAN

Five
Whooping Cough Vaccine for Handicapped Children— Advice for Parents*

Whooping cough is always an unpleasant disease. The 'whoop' may last for many weeks or even months. It is frightening and exhausting for both parent and child. Complications are uncommon; brain damage and even death, though rare, happen occasionally.

Whooping cough vaccine is usually given with diphtheria and tetanus vaccines (the 'triple' injection) and polio vaccine by mouth (sometimes on a sugar lump or with syrup). Three doses are needed to get the best protection. Since whooping cough is most serious in young babies, it is best given in the first year of life, but it can be given any time up to the 6th birthday. It is an effective vaccine: although it does not give perfect protection against the disease, it does reduce the risk of developing it, and also the severity if the child does get an attack.

Whooping cough vaccine probably can cause fits and brain damage. The risk of this happening is about 1 in 300 000 doses. It is very difficult to give exact figures for the frequency of whooping cough and its complications, but almost certainly death and severe complications from the disease are more common than complications of the vaccine.

The Government experts advise that whooping cough vaccine should not be given if the child suffers from fits or has any form of brain damage. This advice seemed sensible when it was first issued and it is still followed by most doctors. It was based on the commonsense argument that, if the vaccine can cause fits or brain damage, it would be better not to give it to children who already have those problems. However before the present scare began, many handicapped children received the vaccine and there was no convincing evidence that complications were more likely in those children.

Many parents of handicapped children feel that they would rather take the tiny risk of immunisation than watch the child suffer with whooping cough. Many paediatricians now believe that this is a sensible attitude. They feel that the danger of complications when a handicapped child develops whooping cough is probably greater than the risk of immunisation. We share this view and are willing to arrange whooping cough immunisation in most cases.

The Government guidelines may eventually be changed, but until they

---

* This information sheet is offered to parents who enquire about pertussis immunisation.

are, a doctor who gives whooping cough vaccine to a handicapped child may be criticised if any complication should occur. Some doctors may therefore ask a parent to sign a form to confirm that they were in possession of these facts before the vaccine is given.

The other aspects of Government advice should still be followed; if there is a severe reaction to any dose, no further whooping cough vaccine should be given. It is now known that allergy, asthma and eczema are *not* reasons for refusing whooping cough vaccine.

If the child has had one or two doses of triple vaccine in the past but has not completed the course because of illness or other reasons (except of course bad reactions), he can complete his three injections at any time. He does not have to start again with the first one.

SUMMARY

Most paediatricians now believe that whooping cough vaccine is worth-while for normal healthy children. If your child has had fits, or suffers from any form of handicap or brain damage, and you would like him to have the vaccine, please consult your paediatrician.

Six
Child Care Legislation

CARE PROCEEDINGS—CHILDREN AND YOUNG PERSONS ACT 1969

There are various grounds under which Care Proceedings may be taken. Evidence has to be provided to the Juvenile Court. In the first four instances below, this is done by the Social Services Department or Police; in the fifth by the Education Department; and in the last by the Police or the Social Services Department. Evidence must be provided on one of the following grounds.

1 The proper development of the juvenile is being avoidably prevented or neglected, or that his health is being avoidably impaired or neglected, or that he is being ill-treated.

2 It is probable that the above condition will be satisfied because the condition is or was satisfied in the case of another child or young person who is or was a member of the household.

3 The juvenile is exposed to moral danger.

4 The juvenile is beyond the control of his parent or guardian.

5 He is of school age (1944 Education Act) and is not receiving efficient full-time education suitable to his age, ability and aptitude.

6 He is guilty of an offence (excluding homicide).

The Court may make one of the following.

A Place of Safety Order. This is usually an emergency procedure to enable a child to be removed from home to a safe place, or to enable a child to remain in a safe place (e.g. a hospital) where there is a probability that the child will be removed home by a parent. The Order is granted by a Magistrate, at the Juvenile Court in working hours or at his home.

Evidence can be presented by anyone who has an interest in the child. In practice this is usually a Social Worker or Police Officer.

If an Order is made, it lasts for between 8 and 28 days. The Police may only ask for 8 days. At the end of this period of time either the Order lapses and the Child must be returned to the parents, or the matter must go to the Juvenile Court for further evidence to be presented for Care Proceedings.

The decision of whether to present evidence for a Place of Safety Order (except in an emergency) and subsequently for Care Proceedings is often discussed and taken at a Case Conference. The final decision to present the evidence in whatever way is felt best, remains the responsibility of the Social Services Department.

An Interim Care Order (up to 28 days) if the Court is uncertain whether a full Care Order is justified. At the end of this time, the matter returns to Court.

A Supervision Order.   In this case, the child remains at or returns home. The Social Worker is required to provide guidance and assistance and the juvenile or the child's family have to accept visits. If the situation changes or there is further evidence of concern, the Social Worker may return to Court to present evidence to vary the Order to a Care Order.

A Full Care Order.   For juveniles who are the subject of Care Orders, the Social Services Department is responsible for deciding where the child will live and go to school, and for making plans for his future. A Care Order lasts until 18 years of age (19 years if made at 16 or 17 years of age); unless the Court removes the order or the child is adopted. A child can return home 'on trial' while remaining the subject of a Care Order.

A Wardship Order (Guardianship of Minors Act 1971).   In practice Wardship is used where other legislation is not appropriate or applicable. Wardship is a special process whereby the Courts can protect minors against injury of any kind, if they think such protection is necessary. The child's welfare is the first and paramount consideration. The applicant can be anyone with a 'sufficient interest' in the child.

The Court has custody over the child and grants care and control to another person (often the local authority). No important steps can be taken in the child's life without the Court's consent. The first hearing is usually before a Registrar, followed by a second final hearing before the Judge. In a dire emergency, there can be an application for an injunction without notice to the other side, to a Judge.

VOLUNTARY CARE—SECTION 2 CHILD CARE ACT 1980—RECEPTION INTO CARE

A local authority must receive a child into care if the child is under 17 years and it appears that:
—the child has no parent or guardian
—the child has been and remains, abandoned
—the child is 'lost'
—his parents are, for the time being or permanently, prevented by mental or bodily disease or infirmity or other incapacity or any other circumstances from providing for his proper accommodation, maintenance and upbringing
and
intervention is necessary in the interests and welfare of the child.

The local authority has no right to keep the child if the parent wishes to have the child back. However, when a child has been in care for six months or more, the parent must give the local authority 28 days notice of the wish to have the child back.

The Social Services Committee may pass a *resolution* by which *it takes over the parental rights and duties* in respect of the child. This may be in the following circumstances.

1   The parents are dead and there is no guardian.

2   The parent

—has abandoned him,

—suffers a permanent disability, making him incapable of looking after the child,

—suffers from a mental disorder rendering him unfit to have the care,

—is of habits or mode of life to be unfit to have the care,

—has failed consistently, without reasonable cause, to discharge the obligations of a parent as to be unfit to have the care.

3   A Resolution is in force under 2 in relation to one parent who is or is likely to become a member of the household comprising the child and the other parent.

4   Throughout the 3 years preceeding the resolution the child has been in the care of the Local Authority.

If the parent objects to the Resolution being made, the local authority goes before the Juvenile Court for the Resolution to be upheld or otherwise. A parent may object and the matter go to a Juvenile Court at any time a Resolution is in force.

CHILDRENS' ACT 1975

This has been implemented in stages. The Act makes numerous amendments relating to adoption, care and fostering. It emphasises the principle of 'the best interests of the *child*', and the rights of parents are no longer the over-riding factor in decision-making.

Seven
Equipment for Developmental Paediatrics

1. Box of miscellaneous toys (for siblings etc).
2. Box of 8 2.5 cm cubes (2 each of 4 colours).
3. 3-piece form board and 12 piece form board.
4. Colour sorting task (e.g. peg board).
5. Set of small dolls (pipecleaner or similar), with table, chairs, etc.
6. Black cloth (for object permanence test).
7. Action toys (e.g. wind-up animal, musical box).
8. Small sweets (Smarties).
9. Selection of children's books (e.g. Ladybird Series).
10. Paper and pencil or felt-tip pen.

STANDARDISED TESTS AND DEVELOPMENTAL CHARTS AVAILABLE TO DOCTORS

Griffiths Mental Development Scales (Test Agency).
Reynell Language Scales (NFER).
Lowe and Costello Symbolic Play Test (NFER).
Denver Developmental Screening Test (Test Agency).
The PIP (Parental Involvement Project) Developmental Charts (Hodder & Stoughton).
Gunzberg Progress Charts (MENCAP).
From Birth to 5 years by Dr Mary Sheridan (NFER).
Egan 'Bus-Puzzle' test (E.J. Arnold).

EQUIPMENT FOR HEARING TESTS

Noise Makers. Cup and spoon, tissue paper, selection of squeakers; musical boxes, etc., drums, cymbals and rattles (Manchester or Nuffield type).

Toys for cooperative hearing tests. E.g. bricks, marbles, together with suitable container; peg board, etc.

Set of toys. Kendall toy test material or similar. Suitable items include: fish, dog, cat, house, horse, mouse, car, bus, coat, cup, bed, sock, book, chair, girl, boy, bird, duck, gun, ball, shoe.

Pictures can also be used (e.g. those supplied by LDA) or the Michael Reed Test (RNID).

The Stycar Hearing Test (NFER) includes pictures but these are somewhat dated.

Other essential equipment.   Portable free-field audiometer, pure tone audiometer, sound-level meter, impedance equipment, otoscope with pneumatic speculum.

EQUIPMENT FOR VISION TESTS

Minimum visible tests: hundreds and thousands, saccharin tablets, cake decorations, sweets, Smarties.

Sheridan Graded Ball Tests (available in Stycar Vision Tests—NFER).

Small interesting toys and pictures

Stycar five-letter test, and/or Sheridan–Gardner Letter Test.

Other items
Snellen Chart,
Colour Vision Tests (Ishihara, City University, Guys'),
Torch, ophthalmoscope, and eye patch,
Maclure Test Types for children (Clement Clark).

USEFUL ADDRESSES

NFER (National Foundation for Educational Research).
Nelson Publishing Company Limited, Darville House, 2 Oxford Road, East Windsor, Berkshire SL4 1DF.
The Test Agency, Cournswood House, North Dean, High Wycombe, Bucks.
E.J. Arnold Educational Equipment, Parkside Lane, Leeds LS11 5TD.
Hodder and Stoughton Educational, Mill Road, Dunton Green, Sevenoaks, Kent.

AUDIOLOGICAL EQUIPMENT

P.C. Werth Ltd., 45 Nightingale Lane, SW12.
Castle Associates, Redbourne House, North Street, Scarborough.
Amplivox Limited, 9–13 Grosvenor Street, London, W1.
Peters Limited, Weeks Lane, Dromfield, Sheffield.

LDA (Learning Development Aids) (Picture Clues No. 57 is ideal), Park Works, Norwich Road, Wisbech, Cambridge.

VISION TESTING EQUIPMENT

Keeler Limited, 21–27 Marylebone Lane, London, W1.
Clement Clarke International Limited, 15 Wigmore Street, London, SW1.

Eight

Audiological Assessment—A Checklist for Parents

(Courtesy of Dr. B. McCormick, Dept. of Audiology, General Hospital, Nottingham.)

Can your baby hear you?

Here is a checklist of some of the general signs you can look for in your baby's first year

Tick if
Response
Present

SHORTLY AFTER BIRTH

Your baby should be startled by a sudden loud noise such as a hand clap or a door slamming and should blink or open his eyes widely to such sounds.

BY 1 MONTH

Your baby should be beginning to notice sudden prolonged sounds like the noise of the vacuum cleaner and he should pause and listen to them when they begin.

BY 4 MONTHS

He should quieten or smile to the sound of your voice even when he cannot see you. He may also turn his head or eyes towards you if you come up from behind and speak to him from the side.

BY 7 MONTHS

He should turn immediately to your voice across the room or to very quiet noises made on each side if he is not too occupied with other things.

BY 9 MONTHS

He should listen attentively to familiar everyday sounds and search for very quiet sounds made out of sight. He should also show pleasure in babbling loudly and tunefully.

488

BY 12 MONTHS

He should show some response to his own name and to other familiar
words. He may also respond when you say 'no' and 'bye bye' even when he
cannot see any accompanying gesture.

Your health visitor will perform a routine hearing screening test on your
baby between seven and nine months of age and will be able to help and
advise you at any time before or after this test if you are concerned about
your baby and his development. If you suspect that your baby is not hearing
normally either because you cannot place a definite tick against the items
above or for some other reason then seek advice from your health visitor.

Dr McCormick reports that in Nottingham earlier diagnosis has been
achieved by the use of this checklist, together with:
1 Regular in-service training for health visitors;
2 Early audiological assessment of high risk babies (p. 106);
3 A policy of open access to the audiology centre for parents concerned
about their child's hearing.

Nine
Written Reports for Parents —
a Sample Letter

Dear Ms Smith

Vanessa Smith 30.1.1982

I promised to let you have a brief summary of our discussion about Vanessa.

You listed your main concerns as (1) her eyesight, (2) slowness in developing normal movement, (3) you were uncertain about her general intelligence, but felt that she is mentally handicapped..

I understand that Dr B. was concerned about her when she was first born, and that he has told you about her chromosome problem, which is most probably the cause of her slow development. As you do not yourself have the chromosome defect, it is unlikely to affect any future children you may have, but this can be checked during pregnancy if necessary.

At present, Vanessa obviously has more vision than you thought 6 months ago, and we found that she could recognise faces, and toys at a distance of 3–4ft. She could reach for objects about 1–2″ across provided they were brightly coloured and moving. Her concentration is very brief and it is therefore difficult to be certain exactly how much she sees. I could find no sign of any cataract or other eye disease. I agree with you that she has good hearing, though we will need to do further tests to be sure it is completely normal.

She is now able to sit without support though is still a little unsteady, and is just beginning to crawl. I think that the general pattern of the movements is normal, but it is of course many months behind for her age.

She shows some understanding of simple things, e.g. recognises you, her feeding bottle, and preparations for meal times. She can imitate clapping, and enjoys simple games. Even so, in general, I thought that her development was not what I would expect for a child of this age; she behaves like a much younger baby and I agree that she is mentally handicapped.

In summary, I think that her apparent poor vision is more likely to be caused by her generally slow development, and not by any disease of the eyes. It is quite common for babies who are backward in their development to have more problems in learning to make use of their eyesight than their hearing. As they get older, it becomes obvious that the vision is improving. Even so, we must rule out simple things such as severe short-sight, and I will arrange for her to have an eye examination.

I think you are looking after her very well, and I agree with the physiotherapist that we should do everything possible to help you with her development. As we discussed, a good child minder will be the first step as you have to continue working. We are supplying you with a chart to record Vanessa's progress, and have suggested a useful book for you to buy.

As you know, we recommend a full immunisation programme, and

Vanessa should receive fluoride drops for her teeth—you can get these at the clinic.

We discussed the following other points: (1) In keeping with the 1981 Education Act, I am sending a copy of this letter to the Education Office, for their information—they need take no action as yet; (2) Our social worker will contact you to discuss allowances and to tell you about the various societies for children with handicaps; (3) the main person for you to contact if you have any problem is your physiotherapist.

Your next appointment is enclosed.

Yours sincerely,

NOTES

1   With practice, this type of letter can be dictated in about 10 minutes. It is time consuming for the medical secretary, but it avoids the need for numerous letters to different professionals, except in the occasional case where a brief covering note is needed to fill in technical data or delicate family problems.
2   There is no doubt that such letters are very much appreciated by parents.
3   It is imperative to exercise care in the selection of vocabulary, both non-medical and technical. The social class and educational background of the parents must be considered.
4   The letter should only include information previously discussed; it must not be used to make up for deficiencies or omission of important information at the actual consultation.
5   As far as possible, the letter should always contain some optimistic points in the history and prognosis. Emphasise what can be done to help the child, as well as the extent of the problem.

Ten
Useful Addresses

A list of the voluntary organisations concerned with handicap should be kept in every Child Development Centre.

1 An up to date list is available on request from:
The National Children's Bureau (address below).

2 All types of social and medical organisations are described in: The Sunday Times Self-Help Directory (1983), Granada Publishing Co. in conjunction with Times Newspapers.

3 The King's Fund Directory is now out of date but a new edition is anticipated:
King's Fund Centre, 126 Albert Street, NW1 (01-267 6111).

4 'Voluntary Organisations':
Voluntary Council for Handicapped Children, National Children's Bureau.

Organisations concerned with specific handicaps

Association For All Speech Impaired Children, 347 Central Market, Smithfield, London EC1A 0NH (01-236 3632/6487).

Association for Spina Bifida and Hydrocephalus, Tavistock House North, Tavistock Square, London WC1H 9HJ (01-388 1382).

Association of Parents of Vaccine-Damaged Children, 2 Church Street, Shipston-on-Stour, Warwicks, CV36 4AP (0608-61595).

British Dyslexia Association, Church Lane, Peppard, Oxon RG9 6JN (049-17 699).

British Epilepsy Association, Crowthorne House, New Wokingham Road, Crowthorne, Berks (03446-3122).

Brittle Bone Society, 112 City Road, Dundee, DD2 2PW (0382-67603).

Downs Childrens Association, Quinborne Community Centre, Ridgeacre Road, Quinton, Birmingham B32 2TW (021-427 1374).

Friedreich's Ataxia Group, 12c Worplesden Road, Guildford, Surrey (0483-503133).

Gifted Children's Information Centre, Hampton Grange, 21 Hampton Lane, Solihull, W. Midlands (021-705 4547).

Hyperactive Children's Support Group, 59 Meadowside, Angmering, Littlehampton, West Sussex.

Muscular Dystrophy Group of Great Britain, Nattrass House, 35 Macaulay Road, Clapham, London SW4 0QP (01-720 8055).

National Association for Deaf/Blind and Rubella Handicapped, 311 Grays Inn Road, London WC1X 8PT (01-278 1000).

National Association For The Education Of The Partially Sighted, East Anglian School, Church Road, Gorlstone-on-Sea, Great Yarmouth (0493-62399).

National Association for Gifted Children, 1 South Audley St., London W.1. (01-499 1188).

National Deaf Children's Society, 45 Hereford Road, London W2 (01-229 9272).

National Physically Handicapped and Able Bodied, 42 Devonshire Street, London W1N 2AP (01-637 7475).

National Society for Autistic Children, 276 Willesden Lane, London, NW2 5RB (01-451 3844/5).

National Society for Mentally Handicapped Children (MENCAP), 117–123 Golden Lane, London EC1Y 0RF (01-253 9433).

National Society of Phenylketonuria and Allied Disorders, 26 Towngate Grove, Mirfield, West Yorkshire. (0924-492873).

Royal National Institute for the Blind, 224 Great Portland Street, London, W1N 6AV (01-388 1266).

Royal National Institute for the Deaf, 105 Gower Street, London WC1E 6AH (01-387 8033).

Scottish Society for the Mentally Handicapped, 13 Elmbank Street, Glasgow G2 4PB (041-226 4541).

Spastics Society, 12 Park Crescent, London W1N 4EQ (01-636 5020).

Spinal Injuries Association, 5 Crowndale Road, London NW11 1TU (01-388 6840).

Tuberose Sclerosis Group, Church Farm House, Church Rd., North Leigh, Oxfordshire (0993-881238).

Organisations concerned with handicap in general

British Sports Association for the Disabled, Stoke Mandeville Sports Stadium, Harvey Road, Aylesbury, Bucks HP21 8PP (0296 84848).

DHSS (Department of Health and Social Security), Alexander Fleming House, Elephant & Castle, London, SE1 6BY (01-407 5522).

Handicapped Adventure Playground Association, Fulham Palace Playground, Bishops Avenue, London, SW6 6EA (01-731 2753).

Invalid Children's Aid Association, 126 Buckingham Palace Road, London, SW1W 9SB (01-730 9891).

Lady Hoare Trust for Physically Disabled Children, 7 North Street, Midhurst, West Sussex, GU29 9DJ (073-081 3696).

National Association for the Welfare of Children in Hospital, 7 Exton Street, London SE1 8UE (01-261 1738).

National Children's Bureau, 8 Wakley Street, London EC1V 7QE (01-278 9441).

Royal Association for Disability and Rehabilitation (RADAR), 23–25 Mortimer Street, London, W1N 8AB (01-637 5400).

SPOD (Sexual Problems of the Disabled); 286, Camden Road, London N7 0BJ (01-607 8851-2).

Scottish Information Services for the Disabled, Claremont House, 18/19 Claremont Crescent, Edinburgh EH7 4QD (031-556 3882).

Voluntary Council for Handicapped Children, National Children's Bureau, 8 Wakley Street, London EC1V 7QE (01-278 9441).

Financial help and advice

Social Services (for advice on statutory allowances).

The Family Fund, Beverley House, Shipton Road, York YO5 1UY (0904-29241).

Mobility Allowance Unit, DHSS, Norcross, Blackpool, Lancs.

Motability, The Adelphi, John Adam Street, London WC2N 6AZ (01-839 5191). (Advice on best use of mobility allowance for vehicle purchase).
Network for the Handicapped (Legal Advice):
Bedford House, 35 Emerald Street, London WC1N 3QL (01-504 3001).
Guide to Benefits for Handicapped Children and their Families:
Disability Alliance, 25 Denmark St., London WC2 8NJ.

Adoption and Fostering

British Agency for Adoption and Fostering, 11 Southwark St., London SE1 1RQ. (01-407 8800).

Education

Local Education Authority.
National Bureau for Handicapped Students, 40 Brunswick Square, London WC1N 1AZ (01-278 3459).
Pre-School Playgroups Association, Alford House, Aveline Street, London SE11 5DJ (01-582 8871).
Toy Libraries Association, Seabrook House, Wyllyotts Manor, Darkes Lane, Potters Bar, Herts EN6 5HL (0707-44571).
Advisory Centre for Education (ACE) (free information and advice service) 18 Victoria Park Square, London E.2. (01-980 4596).
For a list of private sector schools:
Schools, Truman and Knightley, 78 Notting Hill Gate, London W8. (01-727 1242).

Aids and Equipment

Social Services.
All voluntary organisations dealing with specific handicap.
Disabled Living Foundation, 346 Kensington High Street, London W14 8NS (01-602 2491).
Medicalert Foundation, 11/13 Clifton Terrace, London N4 3JP. (01-263 8597).

Activities

Some voluntary organisations arrange holidays for handicapped children.
Riding for the Disabled, Avenue R, National Agricultural Centre, Kenilworth, Warwickshire (0203-56107).
The Uphill Ski Club (c/o Spastics Society).
British Society of Music Therapists, 69 Avondale Avenue, East Barnet, Herts.

Information on Electronics and Microcomputers
Special Education Microelectronics Resource Centres (SEMERCs)

Bristol SEMERC, Faculty of Education, Bristol Polytechnic, Redland Hill, Bristol B56 6U2.

Manchester SEMERC, Manchester College of Higher Education, Heathersage Road, Manchester M13 0JA.

Newcastle SEMERC, Newcastle Polytechnic, Coach Lane Campus, Newcastle upon Tyne NE7 7XA.

Redbridge SEMERC, Dane Centre, c/o The Teachers' Centre, Melbourne Road, Ilford, Essex 1G1 4HT.

Eleven
Books for Parents of Handicapped Children

The following is a small selection of books which can form the nucleus of a parents' library in the Child Development Centre. Numerous leaflets and booklets, together with more comprehensive lists of suitable books, are obtainable from the major voluntary organisations.

Help Starts Here. (1976) A booklet produced by the National Childrens Bureau with useful factual information.

Carr, J. (1980) *Helping your Handicapped Child*, Penguin Books. This gives a sensible introduction to behaviour modification concepts for parents.

Newson, E. & Hipgrave, A. (1982) *Getting Through to your Handicapped Child*, Cambridge Educational. Sensible advice on many aspects of handicap.

Richards, M. (1980) *Infancy (a 'Life-cycle' book)*. Harper and Row, New York. A useful outline of modern ideas of early child development, in non-technical language.

Cunningham, C. & Sloper P. (1978) *Helping your Handicapped Baby*, Human Horizons Series, Souvenir Press.

Jeffree, D.M., McConkey, R. & Hewson, S. (1977) *Let Me Play*, Human Horizons Series, Souvenir Press.

Kiernan, C., Jorden, R. & Saunders, C. (1979) *Starting Off*, Human Horizons Series, Souvenir Press.

Russell P. (1978) *The Wheelchair Child*, Human Horizons Series, Souvenir Press.

Cunningham, C. (1982) *Down's Syndrome, An Introduction for Parents*, Human Horizons Series, Souvenir Press.

Finnie N. (1974) *Handling the Young Cerebral Palsied Child at Home*. William Heinemann, London.

Laidlaw, M.V. & Laidlaw, J. (1980) *Epilepsy Explained*. Churchill Livingstone, Edinburgh.

Fraiberg, S. (1977) *Insights from the Blind*, Human Horizons Series, Souvenir Press.

Bloom, F. (1978) *Our Deaf Children*. Old Woking, Gresham Books.

Blumberg, T. (1980) *The Challenge for the family of a child born deaf*. William Heinemann, London.

Freeman, T. (1975) *Understanding the Deaf/Blind Child*, Heinemann Health Books. Heinemann, London.

Jeffree, D.M. & McConkey, R. (1976) *Let Me Speak*. Condor Books. Souvenir Press.*

* Authors of the Parent Involvement Project (PIP) charts (p. 232).

References

1. Holt, K.S. (1977). *Developmental Paediatrics.* Butterworths, London.
2. Drillien, C.M. and Drummond, M.B. (1977). *Neurodevelopmental Problems in Early Childhood.* Blackwell Scientific Publications, Oxford.
3. Gordon, N. (1979). Labels—Advantage or Disadvantage? *Developmental Medicine and Child Neurology* **21**, 106.
4. Tuckett, D. (Ed.) (1976). *An Introduction to Medical Sociology.* Tavistock.
5. Shearer, A. (1981). *Disability—Whose handicap?* Basil Blackwell Publisher, Oxford.
6. Goffman, E. (1963). *Stigma—Notes on the Management of Spoiled Identity.* Pelican Books, Harmondsworth.
7. Guralnick, M.J. and Richardson, H.B. (1979). *Pediatric Education and the Needs of Exceptional Children.* University Park Press, Baltimore.
8. Mitchell, R. (1973). Defining medical terms. *Developmental Medicine and Child Neurology* **15**, 279.
9. Sheridan, M. (1969). Definitions relating to developmental paediatrics. *Health Trends.* **1**, August 4th.
10. Rutter, M. (Ed.) (1980). *Scientific Foundations of Developmental Psychiatry.* Heinemann, London.
11. Rutter, M. and Hersov, L. (Eds) (1976). *Child Psychiatry.* Blackwell Scientific Publications, Oxford.
12. Scott, H. (1976). Outcome of very severe birth asphyxia. *Archives of Disease in Childhood* **51**, 712.
13. Orgill, A.A. *et al* (1982). Early development of infants 1000 g or less at birth. *Archives of Diseases in Childhood* **57**, 823.
14. Davies, J.A. and Topping, J. (1981). *Scientific Foundations of Paediatrics.* Heineman, London.
15. Werner, E., Bierman, J.M. and French, F. (1971). *The children of Kauai: A longitudinal study from the prenatal period to the age of 10.* University of Hawaii Press, Honolulu.
16. Falkner, F. and Tauner, J.M. (Eds) (1979). *Human growth, Volume 3: Neurobiology and Nutrition,* pp. 481–514. Baillière Tindall, London.
17. Neligan G.A. *et al* (1976) *Born too soon or born too small?* Clinics in Developmental Medicine no. 61. Spastics International Medical Publications/Heinemann Medical, London.
18. Neligan, G.A., Prudham, D. and Steiner, H. (1974). *The Formative years.* Published for the Nuffield Provincial Hospitals Trust by Oxford University Press.
19. Illingworth, R.S. (1979). Why blame the obstetrician? *British Medical Journal* **1**, 797.
20. Sheridan, M.D. (1975). *Childrens' developmental progress: From birth to 5 years.* NFER, Windsor.
21. Newson, E. (1976). Parents as a resource in diagnosis and assessment. Early

management of handicapping disorders. Associated Scientific Publishers. *IRMMH Review of research and practice* **19**, 105.

22. Hart, H., Bax, M. and Jenkins, S. (1978). The Value of a Developmental History. *Developmental Medicine and Child Neurology* **20**, 442.

23. Carey, W.B. (1982). Validity of parental assessments of development and behaviour. *American Journal of Diseases of Children* **136**, 97.

24. Roberts, C.G. and Khosla, T. (1972). An evaluation of developmental examination as a method of detecting neurological, visual and auditory handicaps in infancy. *British Journal of Preventive and Social Medicine* **26**, 94.

25. Reynell, J. (1976). Early education for handicapped children. *Child Care, Health and Development* **2**, 305.

26. Clark, A.D.B. (1973). The Fred Esher Lecture—The prevention of sub-cultural subnormality. *British Journal of Mental Subnormality* **19**, 7.

27. Tizard, J. (1960). Residential Care of Mentally Handicapped Children. *British Medical Journal* **i**, 1041.

28. Donachy, W. (1976). Parent participation in pre-school education. *British Journal of Educational Psychology* **46**, 31.

29. Clark, M.M. and Cheyne, W.M. (1979). *Studies in pre-school education.* Scottish Council for Research in Education. Hodder & Stoughton Educational, Sevenoaks.

30. Soboloff, H.R. (1981). Early intervention. *Developmental Medicine and Child Neurology* **23**, 261.

31. Wright, T. and Nicholson, J. (1973). Physiotherapy for the spastic child: an evaluation. *Developmental Medicine and Child Neurology* **15**, 146.

32. Rutter, M. (1980). The long term effects of early experience. *Developmental Medicine and Child Neurology* **22**, 800.

33. Clark, A.M. and Clark, A.D.B. (1976). *Early experience: Myth and evidence.* Open Books, London.

34. Rutter, M. (1972). *Maternal deprivation reassessed.* Penguin Books, Harmondsworth.

35. Lamb M.E. (1983). Early Mother–Neonate contact and the Mother–Child relationship. *Journal of Child Psychology and Psychiatry* **24**, 487.

36. Sandberg, E.C. and Jacobs, R.I. (1971). Psychology of the Misuse and Rejection of Contraception. *American Journal of Obstetrics and Gynaecology* **110**, 227.

37. Lewis, E. (1979). Mourning after a Stillbirth or Neonatal Death. *Archives of Disease in Childhood* **54**, 303.

38. Trevarthen, C. (1974). Conversations with a 2 month old. *New Scientist*, May 2nd, 230.

39. Richards, M. (1980). *Infancy: world of the newborn.* Harper & Row, New York.

40. Trevarthen, C. (1974). In *Language and Brain; Developmental Aspects*, (Ed. Lenneberg, E.H.). *Neurosciences Research Program Bulletin* **12**, 570.

41. Shaffer, H.R. (Ed.) (1977). *Studies in mother–infant interaction.* Academic Press, New York.

42. Dunn, J. (1977). *Distress and comfort.* Fontana Books, London.

43. Rutter, M. (1982). *Temperamental differences in infants and young children.* Ciba Foundation Symposium No. 89. Pitman Books, London.

44. Pollak, M. (1979). Housing and mothering. *Archives of Disease in Childhood* **54**, 54.

45. Wolkind, S. (1981). Depression in mothers of young children. *Archives of Disease in Childhood* **56**, 1.

46. Coleman, J. Wolkind, S. and Ashley, C. (1977). Symptoms of behaviour disturbance and adjustment at school. *Journal of Child Psychology and Psychiatry* **18**, 201.

47. Kalverboer, A.F. (1975). *A neurobehavioural study in pre-school children.* Clinics in Developmental Medicine no. 54. Spastics International Medical Publications/Heinemann Medical, London.

48. Newson, E. (1978). Unreasonable care: the establishment of selfhood. In *Human Values: Lectures of the Royal Institute of Philosophy*, Vesey G. (Ed.); Harvester Press.

49. Shepherd, M., Oppenheim, B. and Mitchell, S. (1971). *Childhood Behaviour and Mental Health.* University of London Press, London.

50. Crystal, D. (1981). *Clinical Linguistics.* Disorders of Human Communication (3). Springer Verlag, Berlin.

51. Crystal, D. (1976) *Child Language, Learning and Linguistics.* Edward Arnold, London.

52. Martin, J.A.M. (1981). *Voice, Speech and Language in the Child; Development and Disorders.* Disorders of Human Communication (4). Springer-Verlag, Berlin.

53. Collis, G.M. and Schaffer, H.R. (1975). Synchronisation of visual attention. *Journal of Child Psychology and Psychiatry* **16**, 315.

54. Snow, C.E. and Ferguson, C.A. (Eds) (1977). *Talking to Children.* Cambridge University Press.

55. Blakemore, C. (1977). *Mechanics of the Mind.* Cambridge University Press.

56. Moscowitz, B.A. (1978). Learning to speak. *Scientific American* **239**, 84.

57. Cromer, R.F. (1981). In *Language Intervention Series, Vol. 6: Early Language, Acquisition and Intervention.* Schiefelbusch, R.L. and Bricker, D.D. (Eds). University Park Press, Baltimore.

58. Bernstein, B. (1970). *Class, Codes and Control*, Vol. 1. Routledge & Kegan Paul, London.

59. Serpell, R. (1976). *Culture's Influence on Behaviour.* Methuen, London.

60. Hinde, R.A. (1972). *Non-Verbal Communication.* Cambridge University Press.

61. Hopkins, B. and Kalverboer, A.F. (1983). Symposium on Mother Infant Interaction (Four papers). *Journal of Child Psychology and Psychiatry* **24**, 113.

62. Turner, J. (1975). Cognitive development. Methuen, London.

63. Brazelton, T.B. (1973). *Neonatal behavioural assessment scale.* Clinics in Developmental Medicine, Vol. 50. Spastics International Medical Publications/Heinemann Medical, London.

64. Dunst, C.G. (1980). *A clinical and educational manual for use with the Uzgiris and Hunt scales of infant psychological development.* University Park Press, Baltimore.

65. Darvey, C. (1977). *Play.* Fontana Books, London.

66. Goodnow, J. (1977). *Childrens' Drawing.* Fontana Books, London.

67. Illingworth, R.S. (1980). *The development of the infant and young child; normal and abnormal*, 7th edn. Churchill Livingstone, Edinburgh.

68. Bobath, K. (1980). A neurophysiological basis for the treatment of cerebral palsy. Clinics in Developmental Medicine, no. 75. Spastics International Medical Publications/William Heinemann, London.

69. Robson, P. (1970). Shuffling, hitching, scooting, or sliding: observations in 30 otherwise normal children. *Developmental Medicine and Child Neurology* **12**, 608.

70. Haidvogl, M. (1979). Dissociation of Maturation: A distinct syndrome of delayed motor development. *Developmental Medicine and Child Neurology* **21**, 52.

71. Symposium (1977). Common Orthopedic Problems. *Pediatric Clinics of North America* **24**: 4.

72. Jolly, H. *et al* (1977). Charing Cross Hospital Child Development Centre. *Child: Care, Health and Development* **3**, 425.

73. Court, S.D.M. (Chairman) (1976). *Fit for the Future: Report of the Committee on Child Health Services.* HMSO, London.

74. Bond, J.V. (1981). Community Paediatric Service and Child Development Centres, *British Journal of Hospital Medicine* **25**, 164.

75. Brimblecombe, F.S.W. (1974). The Exeter project for handicapped children, *British Medical Journal* **4**, 706.

76. Goddard, J. and Rubissow, J. (1977). Meeting the needs of handicapped children and their families—the evolution of Honeylands. *Child; Care, Health and Development* **3**, 261.

77. Clifford-Rose, F. (Ed.) (1979). *Paediatric Neurology.* Blackwell Scientific Publications, Oxford.

78. Cooper, N.A. and Lynch, M.A. (1979). Lost to follow-up: A study of non-attendance. *Archives of Disease in Childhood* **54**, 765.

79. Townsend, P. and Davidson, N. (1982). *Inequalities in health—The Black Report.* Penguin Books, Harmondsworth.

80. Lobo, E. (1978). *Children of immigrants to Britain.* Hodder and Stoughton, Sevenoaks.

81. Egan, D.F. (1969). *Developmental screening 0–5 years.* Clinics in Developmental Medicine, no. 30. Spastics Society/Heinemann Medical, London.

82. Sheridan, M. (1975). The Stycar Language Test. *Developmental Medicine and Child Neurology* **17**, 164.

83. Gordon, N. (1976). *Paediatric Neurology for the Clinician.* Clinics in Developmental Medicine, nos. 59/60. Spastics International Medical Publications/Heinemann Medical, London.

84. Smith, D.W. (1982). *Recognisable patterns of human malformation,* 3rd Edn. W.B. Saunders, Philadelphia.

85. McKusick, V.A. (1978). *Mendelian inheritance in man.* Johns Hopkins University Press, Baltimore.

86. Königsmark, B.W. & Gorlin, R.J. (1976). *Genetic and Metabolic Deafness.* W.B. Saunders, Philadelphia.

87. Marden, P.M., Smith, D.W. and McDonald, M.J. (1964). Congenital anomalies in the newborn infant. *Journal of Pediatrics* **64**, 357.

88. Touwen, B.C.L. (1979). *Examination of the child with minor neurological dysfunction.* Clinics in Developmental Medicine, no. 71. Spastics International/Heinemann Medical, London.

89. Rutter, M., Graham, P. and Yule, W. (1970). *A Neuropsychiatric Study in Childhood.* Clinics in Developmental Medicine, nos. 35–36, Spastics International, Heinemann Medical, London.

90. Ingram, T.T.S. (1973). Soft signs, *Developmental Medicine and Child Neurology* **15**, 527.

91. Peters, J.E. *et al* (1975). A special neurological examination of children with learning disabilities. *Developmental Medicine and Child Neurology* **17**, 63.

92. Henderson, S.E. and Hall, D.M.B. (1982). Concomitants of Clumsiness in Young Schoolchildren. *Developmental Medicine and Child Neurology* **24**, 448.

93. Hinchcliffe, R. and Harrison, D. (1976). *Scientific Foundations of Otolaryngology*. Heinemann Medical, London.

94. Newby, H.A. (1979). *Audiology*, 4th edn. Prentice Hall, New Jersey.

95. Whetnall, E. and Fry, D.B. (1964). *The Deaf Child*. Heinemann Medical, London.

96. Bove, C.F. and Flugrath, J.M. (1973). Frequency components of noise makers for use in paediatric audiological evaluations. *The Volta Review* **75**, 551.

97. Nolan, M. and Tucker, I.G. (1981). *The Hearing-Impaired Child and the Family*, Human Horizons Series. Souvenir Press.

98. The ACSHIP Report, Chairman, Ballantyne, J.C. (1981). *Report of the Advisory Committee on Services for Hearing Impaired People*. DHSS.

99. Yeates, S. (1981). *Development of hearing*. MTP Press, Lancaster.

100. Rutter, M. and Martin, J.A.M. (Eds) (1972). *The child with delayed speech*, Clinics in Developmental Medicine no. 43. Spastics International/Heinemann Medical, London.

101. Taylor, I.G. (1964). *The neurological mechanisms of hearing and speech in children*. Manchester University Press.

102. Dieroff, H.G. (1980). The efficiency of subjective audiometry. *Audiology* **19**, 94.

103. Martin, F.N. (1978). *Pediatric audiology*. Prentice Hall, New Jersey.

104. Flood, L.M. *et al* (1982). Assessment of hearing using the post auricular myogenic response. *British Journal of Audiology* **16**, 211.

105. Sanders, J.W. (1975). Impedance measurement. *Otolaryngologic Clinics of North America* **8**, 109.

106. Symposium (1981) Pediatric Otolaryngology. *Pediatric Clinics of North America* **28**: 4.

107. Martin, J.A.M. and Moore, W.J. (1979). *Childhood deafness in the European Community*. Commission of the European Communities, HMSO (EUR 6413).

108. Bennett, M.J. and Lawrence, R.J. (1980). The Auditory Response Cradle. *British Journal of Audiology* **14**, 1.

109. Boothman, R. and Orr, N. (1978). Screening for Deafness in the First Year of Life. *Archives of Disease in Childhood* **53**, 570.

110. Brooks, D.N. (1977). Auditory Screening—Time for reappraisal. *Public Health* (London) **91**, 282.

111. Cashell, G.T.W. and Durran, I.N. (1974). *Handbook of orthoptic principles*. Churchill Livingstone, Edinburgh.

112. Smith, V. and Keen, J. (1979). *Visual handicap in children*, Clinics in Developmental Medicine, no. 73. Spastics International/Heinemann Medical, London.

113. Wybar, K. and Taylor, D. (Eds) (1979). *Paediatric Ophthalmology*. Marcel Dekker, New York.

114. Robb, R.M. (1981). *Ophthalmology for the pediatric practitioner*. Little Brown, Boston, Mass.

115. Tyler, C.W. (1982). Assessment of visual function in infants by evoked potentials. *Developmental Medicine and Child Neurology* **24**, 853.

116. Eggers, H.M. and Blakemore, C. (1978). Physiologic basis of anisometropic amblyopia. *Science* **201**, 264.

117. Taylor, D. and Rice, N.S.C. (1982). Congenital cataracts, a cause of preventable child blindness. *Archives of Disease in Childhood* **57**, 165.

118. Trevor-Roper, P.D. and Curran, P.V. (1984). *The Eye and its Disorders*, 2nd edn. Blackwell Scientific Publications, Oxford.

119. Graham, P.A. (1974). Epidemiology of strabismus. *British Journal of Ophthalmology* **58**, 224.

120. Hilton, A.F. and Stanley, J.C. (1972). Pitfalls in testing childrens' vision by the Sheridan–Gardner single optotype method. *British Journal of Ophthalmology* **56**, 135.

121. Ingram, R.M. (1980). The possibility of preventing amblyopia. *Lancet* 1, 585. (See also papers by Ingram (1979) in *British Journal of Ophthalmology* **63**).

122. Peckham, C. *et al* (1978). Vision screening in children tested at 7, 11 and 16 years. *British Medical Journal* **1**, 1312.

123. Banks, J.L.K. (1974). Eye defects of mentally handicapped children. *British Medical Journal* **2**, 533.

124. Hall, S.M. *et al* (1982). Vision screening in the under fives. *British Medical Journal* **285**, 1096.

125. Taylor, D. (1978). The assessment of visual function in young children. *Clinical Paediatrics* **17**, 226.

126. Wybar, K. (1976). Disorders of ocular motility in children. In *Medical Ophthalmology*, Rose F.C. (Ed.). Chapman & Hall, London.

127. Sheridan, M. (1976). Manual for the Stycar Vision Tests. NFER, Windsor.

128. Sheridan, M. (1973). The Stycar 'Panda' Test for children with severe visual handicaps. *Developmental Medicine and Child Neurology* **15**, 728.

129. Sonksen, P.M. (1982). Assessment of vision for development in severely visually handicapped babies. *Acta Ophthalmology* (Copenhagen) (Suppl.) **157**, 82.

130. Atkinson, J. *et al* (1981). Does the Catford Drum Give an Accurate Assessment of Acuity? *British Journal of Ophthalmology* **65**, 652.

131. Rosner, J. (1978). The random dot E stereo test. *Journal of the American Optometry Association* **49**, 1121.

132. Dobson, V. (1978). A behavioural method for efficient screening of visual acuity. *Investigative Ophthalmology and Vision Science* **17**, 1142.

133. Tyler, C.W. (1979). An electronic sweep technique for pattern evoked visual potential. *Investigative Ophthalmology and Vision Science* **18**, 703.

134. Carr, R.E. and Siegel, I.M. (1982) *Visual electrodiagnosis testing; a practical guide for the clinician.* Williams and Wilkins, Baltimore.

135. Mandola, J. (1969). The role of colour vision anomalies in elementary school achievement. *The Journal of School Health* **39**, 633.

136. Bacon, L. (1971). Colour vision defect—an educational handicap. *Medical Officer* **125**, 199.

137. Voke, J. (1978). Colour vision defect—occupational significance and testing requirements. *The Journal of the Society of Occupational Medicine* **28**, 51.

138. Kessler, J. (1977). What can be done for the colour blind? *Annals of Ophthalmology* **9**, 431.

139. Howland, H.C. and Howland, B. (1974). Photorefraction. *Journal of the Optical Society of America* **64**, 240.

140. Kaakinen, K. (1978). Screening by simultaneous photography of corneal and fundus reflexes. *Acta Ophthalmologica* **57**, 161.

141. Fletcher, C.M. (1973). *Communication in medicine.* Nuffield Provincial Hospitals Trust.

142. Appelton, C. (1978). Help for parents of the handicapped. *British Medical Journal*, **1**, 1348. (*see also* ibid **2**, 352.)

143. Bicknell, J. (1983). The psychopathology of handicap. *British Journal of Medical Psychology* **56**, 167.

144. Olshansky, S. (1962). Chronic sorrow: a response to having a mentally defective child. *Social case work* **XLIII**, no. 4.

145. Fox, A.M. (1974). *They get this training but they don't really know how you feel.* National Fund for Research into Crippling Diseases, London.

146. Kew, S. (1975). *Handicap and family crisis.* Invalid Childrens' Aid Association/Pitman, London.

147. Fox, A.M. (1977). Psychological problems of physically handicapped children. *British Journal of Hospital Medicine* **17**, 479.

148. Lieberman, S. (1979). *Transgenerational family therapy.* Croom Helm, London.

149. Evans, E. (1976). Grief reaction of parents of the retarded. *Australian Journal of Mental Retardation* **4**, 8.

150. Joint Statement (1968) Doman-Delacato Treatment of Neurologically Handicapped Children. *Developmental Medicine and Child Neurology* **10**, 243.

151. Clarke, G.A. (1983). The mobility allowance. *New Law Journal* **133**, 147.

152. Symposium (1982). Oral Health. *Pediatric Clinics of North America* **29**: 3.

153. Robinson, R.J. (1981). The whooping cough immunisation controversy. *Archives of Disease in Childhood* **56**, 577.

154. Dudgeon, J.A. (1977). Measles and rubella vaccines. *Archives of Disease in Childhood* **52**, 907.

155. Wolkind, S. (Ed.) (1979). *Medical Aspects of Adoption and Foster Care*, Clinics in Developmental Medicine, no. 74. Spastics International/Heinemann Medical, London.

156. Trower, P. (1982). Social skills training. *British Journal of Hospital Medicine* **27**, 608.

157. Spence, S.H. (1983). Teaching Social Skills to Children. *Journal of Child Psychology and Psychiatry* **24**, 621.

158. Department of Education and Science (1978). *Warnock Report on Special Educational Needs.* HMSO, London.

159. Joint Circular from DES and DHSS; DES (1983) *Assessments and statements of special educational needs (Education Act 1981).*

160. Rosenbloom, L. (1980). Should handicapped children attend ordinary schools? *Archives of Disease in Childhood* **55**, 581.

161. Ross, A.O. (1981). *Child behaviour therapy.* J. Wiley, Bristol.

162. Carr, J. (1980). *Helping your handicapped child.* Penguin Books, Harmondsworth.

163. Hill, P. (1982). Behaviour modification with children. *British Journal of Hospital Medicine* **27**, 51.

164. Yule, W. and Carr, J. (Eds) (1980). *Behaviour modification for the mentally handicapped.* Croom Helm, London.

165. Seidel, U.P. *et al* (1975). Psychological disorders in crippled children. *Developmental Medicine and Child Neurology* **17**, 563.

166. Reid, A.H. (1980). Psychiatric disorders in mentally handicapped children. *Journal of Mental Deficiency Research* **24**, 287.

167. Spencer, D.A. (1976). New long stay patients in a hospital for mental handicap. *British Journal of Psychiatry* **128**, 467.

168. Singh, N. (1982). Self injurious behaviour. In *Advances in Paediatrics*, **28**, 377. Yearbook Medical Publications, Chicago.

169. Comley, J. (1975). *Behaviour modification with the retarded child.* William Heinemann, London.

170. Douglas, J. and Richman, N. (1982). *Sleep management manual.* Institute of Child Health, London.

171. Richman, N. (1981). Sleep problems in young children. *Archives of Disease in Childhood* **56**, 491.

172. Editorial (1980). Children and lead, some remaining doubts. *Archives of Disease in Childhood* **55**, 497.

173. Bicknell, J. (1975). *Pica, a childhood symptom.* Butterworths, London.

174. Tait, T., Brookes, M. and Firth, H. (1976). Sleep problems in mental subnormality. *Nursing Mirror*, **143**, 69.

175. Leading Article (1980). Sterilisation of mentally retarded minors. *British Medical Journal* **281**, 1025.

176. Shennan, V. (1976). *Help your child to understand sex.* National Society for Mentally Handicapped Children, London.

177. Vogel, F. and Motulsky, A.G. (1979). *Human Genetics.* Springer-Verlag, Berlin.

178. Symposium (1978). Medical Genetics. *Pediatric Clinics of North America* **25**: 3.

179. Editorial (1977). Diagnostic amniocentesis in early pregnancy. *British Medical Journal* **1**, 1430.

180. Gordon, I.R.S. and Ross, F.G.M. (1977). Diagnostic radiology in paediatrics. Butterworths, London.

181. Pembrey, M.E. (1979). Genetic registers. *Archives of Disease in Childhood* **54**, 169.

182. Wilson, J.M.G. and Jungner, G. (1968). *Principles and practice of screening for disease*, Public Health Papers, no. 34. WHO, Geneva.

183. Rose, G. (1978). Epidemiology for the uninitiated; screening. *British Medical Journal* **2**, 1417.

184. Cochrane, A. and Holland, W. (1969). Validation of screening procedures. *British Medical Bulletin* **27**, 3.

185. Gesell, A. (1950). *The first 5 years of life.* Methuen, London.

186. Rogers, M.G.H. (1968). Risk Registers and Early Detection of Handicaps. *Developmental Medicine and Child Neurology* **10**, 651.

187. Report of a Working Group (1981). *Early detection of handicap in children.* WHO, Geneva.

188. Leaver, J.M., Alvik, A. and Warren, M.D. (1982). Prescriptive screening for

adolescent idiopathic scoliosis: A review of the evidence. *International Journal of Epidemiology* **11**, 101.

189. Holt, K. (1974). Screening for disease in infancy and childhood, *Lancet* **2**, 1057.

190. The Royal College of General Practitioners (1982). *Healthier children—thinking prevention.* Report no. 22.

191. Hart, H. *et al* (1981). Use of the child health clinic. *Archives of Disease in Childhood* **56**, 440.

192. Curtis-Jenkins, G.H. *et al* (1978). Developmental surveillance in general practice. *British Medical Journal* **1**, 1537.

193. Richards, M.P.M. (Ed.) (1974). *The Integration of a Child into a Social World.* Cambridge University Press.

194. Frankenburg, W.K. *et al* (1981). The newly abbreviated and revised Denver Developmental Screening Test. *Journal of Pediatrics* **99**, 995.

195. Bryant, G.M. *et al* (1979). Standardisation of the Denver test for Cardiff children. *Developmental Medicine and Child Neurology* **21**, 353.

196. Jaffe, M. *et al* (1980). Use of Denver Developmental Screening Tests in infant welfare clinics. *Developmental Medicine and Child Neurology* **22**, 55.

197. Craft, M. and Craft, A. (1978). *Sex and the Mentally Handicapped.* Routledge & Kegan Paul, London.

198. Gostin, L. (1982). A review of the Mental Health (Amendment) Act. *New Law Journal*, **132**, 1127.

199. Gostin, L. (1982). Mental Handicap Policy in Great Britain: The Advent and Demise of the Institution. *Mental Handicap* **10**, 39.

200. Simon, G.B. (1980). Modern Management of Mental Handicap. MTP Press, Lancaster.

201. Wilson, J. (1972). Investigation of Degenerative Disease of the Nervous System. *Archives of Disease in Childhood* **47**, 163.

202. Menkes, J.H. (1974). *Textbook of Child Neurology.* Lea and Febiger, Philadelphia.

203. Kirman, B. and Bicknell, J. (1975). *Mental Handicap.* Churchill Livingstone, Edinburgh.

204. Reed, E.W. and Reed, S.C. (1965). *Mental Retardation: A Family Study.* W.B. Saunders, Philadelphia.

205. Berg, J. and Kirman, B.H. (1959). Some Aetiological Problems in Mental Deficiency. *British Medical Journal* **2**, 848.

206. Mittler, P. and Dejong, J.M. (Eds) (1981). *Frontiers of Knowledge in Mental Retardation,* (2 vols). University Park Press, Baltimore.

207. Mackay, R.I. (1982). The Causes of Severe Mental Handicap. *Developmental Medicine and Child Neurology* **24**, 386.

208. Costess, H. *et al* (1981). Pathogenic Factors in Idiopathic Mental Retardation. *Developmental Medicine and Child Neurology* **23**, 484.

209. Smith, G.F. and Berg, J.M. (1976). *Down's Anomaly.* Churchill Livingstone, Edinburgh.

210. Duncan, S.L.B. (1978). The Problems of Prenatal Screening Programmes for Down's Syndrome in Older Women. *Journal of Biosocial Sciences* **10**, 141.

211. Curtis, B.H., Blank, S. and Fisher, R.L. (1968). Atlantoaxial Dislocation in Down's Syndrome. *Journal of the American Medical Association* **205**, 464.

212. Park, S.C. *et al* (1977). Down's Syndrome with Congenital Heart Malformation. *American Journal of Diseases of Children* **131**, 29.

213. Cunningham, C. (1982). *Down's Syndrome, An Introduction for Parents*, Human Horizons Series. Souvenir Press.

214. Haka-Ikse, K., Stewart, D.A. and Cripps, M.H. (1978). Early Development of Children with Sex Chromosome Aberrations. *Pediatrics* **62**, 761.

215. Ratcliffe, S.J. *et al* (1982). Klinefelter's Syndrome in Adolescence. *Archives of Disease in Childhood* **57**, 6.

216. Berry, C. (1981). X-linked Mental Retardation. *Archives of Disease in Childhood* **56**, 410.

217. Stanbury, J.B., Wyngaarden, J.B. and Fredrickson, D.S. (1978). *The Metabolic Basis of Inherited Disease*. McGraw Hill, Maidenhead.

218. Salmon, M.A. (1978). *Developmental Defects and Syndromes*. H.M. & M, Aylesbury.

219. Danks, D.M. *et al* (1979). Diagnosis of Malignant Hyperphenylalaninemia. *Archives of Disease in Childhood* **54**, 329.

220. Holm, V.A., Sulzbacher, S. and Pipes, P.L. (1981). *Prader–Willi Syndrome*. University Park Press, Baltimore.

221. Palmer, S.K. and Atlee, J.L. (1976). Anaesthetic Management of Prader-Willi Syndrome. *Anesthesiology* **44**, 161.

222. Report on Obesity (1983). *Journal of the Royal College of Physicians* **17**, 5–65.

223. Day, R.E. and Schutt, W.H. (1979). Normal Children with Large Heads: Benign Familial Megalencephaly. *Archives of Disease in Childhood* **54**, 512.

224. Lorber, J. and Priestley, B.L. (1981). Children with Large Heads. *Developmental Medicine and Child Neurology* **23**, 494.

225. Bell, W.E. and McCormick, W.F. (1978). *Increased Intracranial Pressure in Children*. W.B. Saunders, Philadelphia.

226. Palmer, P. *et al* (1982). Developmental and Neurological Progress of Preterm Infants with Intraventricular Haemorrhage and Ventricular Dilatation. *Archives of Disease in Childhood* **57**, 748.

227. Levene, M.I. and Starte, D.R. (1981). Posthaemorrhagic Ventricular Dilatation in the Newborn. *Archives of Disease in Childhood* **56**, 905.

228. Dennis, M. *et al* (1981). The Intelligence of Hydrocephalic Children. *Archives of Neurology* **38**, 607.

229. Till, K. (1975). *Paediatric Neurosurgery*. Blackwell Scientific Publications, Oxford.

230. Monaghan, H.P. (1981). Tuberose Sclerosis. *American Journal of Diseases of Children* **135**, 912.

231. Williamson, W.D. *et al* (1982). Symptomatic Congenital Cytomegalovirus. *American Journal of Diseases of Children* **136**, 902.

232. Stagno, S., Pass, R.F. and Alford, C.A. (1982). Perinatal Infections and Diagnostic Difficulties. In *Medical Virology* (de la Maza L. and Peterson E., Eds). Elsevier, Amsterdam.

233. Bell, W.E. and McCormick, W.F. (1975). *Neurologic Infections in Children*. W.B. Saunders, Philadelphia.

234. Dudgeon, J.A. (1976). Infective Causes of Human Malformations. *British Medical Bulletin* **32**, 77.

235. Saigal, S. *et al* (1982). Outcome in Children with Congenital Cytomegalovirus Infection. *American Journal of Diseases of Children* **136**, 896.

236. Hanshaw, J.B. (1982). Deafness, Cytomegalovirus and Neonatal Screening. *American Journal of Diseases of Children* **136**, 886.

237. Mandell, G.L., Douglas, R.G. and Bennett, J.E. (1979). *Principles and Practice of Infectious Diseases*. John Wiley and Sons, Bristol.

238. Miller, E., Cradock-Watson, J.E. and Pollock, T.M. (1982). Consequences of confirmed maternal rubella at successive stages of pregnancy. *Lancet* **2**, 781.

239. Chess, S. (1977). Follow-up Report on Autism in Congenital Rubella. *Journal of Autism and Childhood Schizophrenia* **7**, 69.

240. Wilson, C.B. (1980). Development of Adverse Sequelae in Children Born with Subclinical Congenital Toxoplasma Infection. *Pediatrics* **66**, 767.

241. Fleck, D. (1981). Toxoplasmosis. *Archives of Disease in Childhood* **56**, 494.

242. Wright, J.T. *et al* (1983). Alcohol and the Fetus. *British Journal of Hospital Medicine* **29**, 260.

243. Walsh, M.P. (1979). Screening for Neonatal Hypothyroidism. *British Journal of Hospital Medicine* **21**, 28.

244. Price, D.A. *et al* (1981). Congenital Hypothyroidism: Neonatal Screening. *Archives of Disease in Childhood* **56**, 845.

245. Grant, D.B. and Hulse, J.A. (1980). Screening for Congenital Hypothyroidism. *Archives of Disease in Childhood* **55**, 913.

246. Miller, D.L. *et al* (1981). Pertussis Immunisation and Serious Acute Neurological Illness in Children. *British Medical Journal* **282**, 1595.

247. Rutter, M. (1980). Raised Lead Levels and Impaired Cognitive Functioning: A Review of the Evidence. *Developmental Medicine and Child Neurology* **22** (Suppl) 1, 1–6.

248. Chisholm, J.J. and Barltrop, D. (1979). Recognition and management of children with increased lead absorption. *Archives of Disease in Childhood* **54**, 249.

249. Lingam, S. *et al* (1982). Value of computerised tomography in children with non-specific mental subnormality. *Archives of Disease in Childhood* **57**, 381.

250. Baraitser, M. (1980). Clinical genetics: (i) Down's Syndrome, (ii) Mental retardation. *Hospital Update* (i) **6**, 1021, (ii) **6**, 1103.

251. Bicknell, J. and Morley, R. (1979). A district based mental handicap service. *Apex* **6**, 4, 4–7.

252. Geschwind, N. (1976). Selected papers on language and the brain. Reidel, Boston.

253. Geschwind, N. (1979). Specialisations of the Human Brain. *Scientific American* **241**, 158.

254. Stevenson, J.E. and Graham, T.J. (1975). Prevalence of behaviour problems in three year old children. *Journal of Child Psychology and Psychiatry* **16**, 277.

255. Butler, N.R., Peckham, C. and Sheridan, M. (1973). Speech defects in children aged 7 years: a national study. *British Medical Journal* **1**, 253.

256. Wyke, M.A. (Ed.) (1978). Developmental dysphasia. Academic Press, New York.

257. Morley, M.E. and Fox, J. (1969). Disorders of articulation: theory and therapy. *British Journal of Disorders of Communication* **4**, 151.

258. Bishop, D.V.M. (1979). Comprehension in developmental language disorders. *Developmental Medicine and Child Neurology* **21**, 225.

259. Neilson, P.D. and O'Dwyer, N.J. (1981). Pathophysiology of dysarthria in cerebral palsy. *Journal of Neurology, Neurosurgery and Psychiatry* **44**, 1013.

260. Worster-Drought C. (1956). Congenital Suprabulbar paresis. *Journal of Laryngology* **70**, 153.

261. Meyerson, M.D. and Foushee, D.R. (1978). Speech, language and hearing in Moebius syndrome. A study of 22 patients. *Developmental Medicine and Child Neurology* **20**, 357.

262. Ferry, P.C., Hall, S.M. and Hicks, J.L. (1975). Dilapidated speech: developmental verbal dyspraxia. *Developmental Medicine and Child Neurology* **17**, 749.

263. Sommerlad, B.C. (1978). Cleft lip and palate. *British Journal of Hospital Medicine* **19**, 28.

264. Edwards, M. and Watson, A.C.H. (Eds) (1980). *Advances in Management of Cleft Palate*. Churchill Livingstone, Edinburgh.

265. Williams, A.J. *et al* (1981). The Robin Anomalad. *Archives of Disease in Childhood* **56**, 663.

266. Pigott, R.W. (1975). The technique of recording nasal pharyngoscopy. *British Journal of Plastic Surgery* **28**, 26.

267. Ellis, R.E. and Fleck, F.C. (1979). *Diagnosis and Treatment of Palato-Glossal Malfunction*. Monograph 2, with British Journal of Disorders of Communication; College of Speech Therapists.

268. Dalton, P. and Hardcastle, W.J. (1977). *Disorders of fluency*. Edward Arnold, London.

269. Kolvin, I. and Fundudis, T. (1981). Elective mutism. *Journal of Child Psychology and Psychiatry* **22**, 219.

270. Silva, P.A. (1980). Prevalence, stability and significance of developmental language delay in preschool children. *Developmental Medicine and Child Neurology* **22**, 768.

271. Klackenberg, G. (1980). What happens to children with retarded speech at 3? *Acta Paediatrica Scandinavica* **69**, 681.

272. Stevenson, J. and Richmond, N. (1976). The prevalence of language delay in a population of three year old children and its association with general retardation. *Developmental Medicine and Child Neurology* **18**, 431.

273. Woods, B.T. and Teuber, H.L. (1978). Changing patterns of child aphasia. *Annals of Neurology* **3**, 273.

274. De Negri, M. (1980). Some critical notes about the epilepsy aphasia syndrome in children. *Brain and Development* **2**, 81.

275. Deonna, T., Fletcher, P. and Voumard, C. (1982). Temporary regression during language acquisition. *Developmental Medicine and Child Neurology* **24**, 156.

276. Maccario, M. *et al* (1982). Developmental dysphasia and EEG abnormalities. *Developmental Medicine and Child Neurology* **24**, 141.

277. Pollak, M. (1972). *Today's three-year-olds in London*. William Heinemann, London.

278. Rutter, M. and Schopler, E. (Eds) (1978). *Autism: a reappraisal of concepts and treatment*. Plenum Press, New York.

279. Vilensky, J.A. *et al* (1981). Gait disturbances in patients with autistic behaviour. *Archives of Neurology* **38**, 646.

280. Delong, G.R., Bean, S.C. and Brown, F.R. (1981). Acquired reversible autistic syndrome in acute encephalopathic illness in children. *Archives of Neurology* **38**, 191.

281. Wing, L. and Gould, J. (1979). Severe impairments of social interaction and associated abnormalities in children: epidemiology and classification. *Journal of Autism and Developmental Disorders* **9**, 11.

282. Wolff, S. and Barlow, A. (1979). Schizoid personality in childhood; a comparative study of schizoid, autistic and normal children. *Journal of Child Psychology and Psychiatry* **20**, 29.

283. Wing, L. (1981). Asperger's syndrome: a clinical account. *Psychological Medicine* **11**, 115.

284. Ratcliff, S.G. (1982). Speech and learning disorders in children with sex chromosome abnormalities. *Developmental Medicine and Child Neurology* **24**, 80.

285. McLaughlin, J.F. and Kriegsmann, E. (1980). Developmental dyspraxia in a family with X-linked mental retardation. *Developmental Medicine and Child Neurology* **22**, 84.

286. Hauser, S.L. *et al* (1975). Pneumographic findings in infantile autism. *Brain* **98**, 667.

287. Student, M. and Sohmer, H. (1978). Evidence from auditory nerve and brainstem-evoked responses for an organic brain lesion in children with autistic traits. *Journal of Autism and Childhood Schizophrenia* **8**, 13.

288. Darby, J.K. (1976). Neuropathologic aspects of psychosis in children. *Journal of Autism and Childhood Schizophrenia* **6**, 339.

289. Cooper, J. *et al* (1979). Developmental language programme: results from a five year study. *British Journal of Disorders of Communication* **14**, 57.

290. Wood, D. *et al* (1980). *Working with under fives.* Grant McIntyre/Blackwell Scientific Publications, Oxford.

291. Bruner, J. (1980). *Under fives in Britain.* Grant McIntyre/Blackwell Scientific Publications, Oxford.

292. Wing, L. (1981). Management of early childhood autism. *British Journal of Hospital Medicine* **25**, 353.

293. Conference Report (1980). *Autism—The Way Ahead.* National Society for Autistic Children.

294. Musselwhite, C.R. and St Louis, K.W. (1982). *Communication programming for the severely handicapped.* College Hill Press, San Diego.

295. Blissymbolics: Bliss Communication Research Centre, South Glamorgan Institute of Higher Education, Western Avenue, Llandaff, Cardiff, CF5 2YB.

296. Latham, C. (1983). *Communication Systems.* Available from: Graves' Medical Library, Holly House, 220 New London Rd., Chelmsford, CM2 9BJ.

297. Paget-Gorman, Centre for the Deaf, Keeley House, Keeley Street, London, WC2.

298. D'Souza, S.W.D. *et al* (1981). Hearing, speech and language in survivors of severe perinatal asphyxia. *Archives of Disease in Childhood* **56**, 245.

299. Abramovich, S.J. *et al* (1979). Hearing loss in very low birthweight infants. *Archives of Disease in Childhood* **54**, 421.

300. Gold, T. (1980). Speech production in hearing impaired children. *Journal of Communication Disorders* **13**, 397.

301. Quigley, S.P. *et al* (1976). *Syntactic structures in The Language of Deaf Children.* Institute for Child Behaviour and Development, Urbana, Illinois.

302. Baraitser, M. (1980). Clinical Genetics; Deafness. *Hospital Update* **6**, 853.

303. Bicknell, D.J. (1974). Communication with the deaf mentally handicapped in hospital. *Proceedings of the Royal Society of Medicine* **67**, 1029.

304. Denmark, J.C. (1971). Developmental Disorders of Communication with special reference to deaf children with additional handicaps. *British Journal of Disorders of Communication* **6**, 113.

305. Sadé, J. (1979). *Secretory otitis media and its sequelae*, Monographs in Clinical Otolaryngology, no. 1. Churchill Livingstone, Edinburgh.

306. Paradise, J.L. (1981). Otitis media during early life: how hazardous to development? A critical review of the evidence. *Pediatrics* **68**, 869.

307. Cantekin, E.I. *et al* (1983). Lack of efficacy of a decongestant–anti-histamine combination in otitis media with effusion. *New England Journal of Medicine* **308**, 297.

308. Shah, N. (1971). Use of grommets in glue ears. *Journal of Laryngology and Otology* **85**, 283.

309. Brown, M.J.K.M. *et al* (1978). Grommets and glue ear. *Journal of the Royal Society of Medicine* **71**, 353.

310. Kohn, B.A. (1976). Differential diagnosis of cataracts in infancy and childhood. *American Journal of Diseases of Children* **130**, 184.

311. Shannon, R.S. *et al* (1982). Wilms' Tumour and aniridia. *Archives of Disease in Childhood* **57**, 685.

312. Silverman, W.A. (1982). Retinopathy of prematurity. *Archives of Disease in Childhood* **57**, 731.

313. Alberman, E. *et al* (1982). Visual defects in children of low birth weight. *Archives of Disease in Childhood* **57**, 818.

314. Vaizey, M.J. (1977). Neurological abnormalities in amaurosis of Leber. *Archives of Disease in Childhood* **52**, 399.

315. Mellor, D.H. and Fielder, A.R. (1980). Dissociated visual development. *Developmental Medicine and Child Neurology* **22**, 327.

316. Sonksen, P.M. (1979). Visual handicap and development. In *Paediatric Ophthalmology*, Wybar, K. and Taylor, D. (eds). Marcell Dekker, New York.

317. Reynell, J.R. and Zinkin, P. (1975). New procedures for assessment of children with severe visual handicaps. *Child: Care, Health and Development* **1**, 61.

318. Baraitser, M. (1981). The genetics of blindness. *Hospital Update* **7**, 516.

319. Jamieson, M. *et al* (1977). *Towards integration. A study of blind and partially-sighted children in ordinary schools.* NFER, Windsor.

320. Vernon, M., Department of Education and Science (1972). *Report of the Committee on the Education of the Visually Handicapped.* HMSO, London.

321. McInnes, J.M. and Treffry, J.A. (1982). *Deaf-Blind Infants and Children.* Open University Press, Milton Keynes.

322. Ingram, T.T.S. (1966). The neurology of cerebral palsy. *Archives of Disease in Childhood* **41**, 337.

323. Kiely, J.L. *et al* (1981). Cerebral palsy and newborn care. *Developmental Medicine and Child Neurology* **23**, (3 articles) 533–8, 650–60, 801–6.

324. Stanley, F.J. and Atkinson, S. (1981). Impact of neonatal intensive care on cerebral palsy in infants of low birthweight. *Lancet*, **2**, 1162.

325. Scrutton, D.R. (1976). The physical management of children with hemiplegia. *Physiotherapy* **62**, 285.

326. Bishop, D.V.M. (1981). Plasticity and specificity of language localisation in the developing brain. *Developmental Medicine and Child Neurology* **23**, 251.

327. Robinson, R.O. (1981). Equal recovery in child and adult brain? *Developmental Medicine and Child Neurology* **23**, 379.

328. Koch, B. *et al* (1980). Computerised tomography in cerebral palsied children. *Developmental Medicine and Child Neurology* **22**, 595.

329. Christensen, E. and Melchior, J. (1967). *Cerebral Palsy—Clinical and Neuropathological Study.* Clinics in Developmental Medicine, no. 25. The Spastics Society/Heinemann Medical, London.

330. Robson, P. (1964). Persistent head turning in the early months; Some effects in the early years. *Developmental Medicine and Child Neurology* **6**, 82.

331. Frankenburg, W.K. (1981). To screen or not to screen: Congenital dislocation of the hip. *American Journal of Public Health* **71**, 1311.

332. Lloyd-Roberts, G.C. and Ratliff, A.H.C. (1978). *Hip Disorders in Children.* Butterworths, London.

333. Lovell, W.W. and Winter, R.B. (Eds) (1978). *Pediatric Orthopaedics.* J.B. Lippincott, Philadelphia.

334. Sharrard, W.J.W. (1979). *Paediatric Orthopaedics and Fractures.* Blackwell Scientific Publications, Oxford.

335. Ellenberg, J.B. and Nelson, K.B. (1981). Early recognition of infants at high risk of Cerebral Palsy. *Developmental Medicine and Child Neurology* **23**, 705.

336. Keats, S. (1965). *Cerebral Palsy.* Charles C. Thomas, Springfield, Illinois.

337. Paine, R.S. (1963). The evolution of infantile postural reflexes in the presence of chronic brain syndromes. *Developmental Medicine and Child Neurology* **10**, 345.

338. O'Reilly, D.E. and Walentynowicz, J.E. (1981). Aetiological factors in cerebral palsy. *Developmental Medicine and Child Neurology* **23**, 633.

339. Beals, R.K. (1966). Spastic paraplegia and diplegia. *Journal of Bone and Joint Surgery* **48a**, 824.

340. Polani, P.E. (1959). The natural clinical history of choreoathetoid cerebral palsy. *Guy's Hospital Reports* **108**, 32.

341. Gordon, N. (1980). Choreoathetosis of genetic origin. *Developmental Medicine and Child Neurology* **22**, 521.

342. Volpe, J.J. (1976). Perinatal hypoxic ischemic brain injury. *Pediatric Clinics of North America* **23**, 383.

343. Sleigh, G. and Lindenbaum, R.H. (1981). Benign non-paroxysmal familial chorea. *Archives of Disease in Childhood* **56**, 616.

344. Nyhan, W.L. (1976). Behaviour in the Lesch-Nyhan Syndrome. *Journal of Autism and Childhood Schizophrenia* **6**, 235.

345. Sauner, G. (1979). Non-progressive ataxic syndromes. *Developmental Medicine and Child Neurology* **21**, 663.

346. Jason, J.M. and Gelfand, E.W. (1979). Diagnostic considerations in ataxia telangiectasia. *Archives of Disease in Childhood* **54**, 682.

347. Holt, K.S. (1965). *Assessment of Cerebral Palsy* (2 vols). Lloyd Luke, London.

348. Dammers, J. and Harpin, V. (1982). Parents' meetings in two neonatal units: a way of increasing support for parents. *British Medical Journal* **285**, 863.

349. Shepherd, R. (1980). *Physiotherapy in Paediatrics.* Heinemann, London.

350. Finnie, N.R. (1974). Handling the young cerebral palsied child at home. Heinemann, London.

351. Holt, K.S. *et al* (1972). Childrens' wheelchair clinic. *British Medical Journal* **4**, 651.

352. Samilson, R.L. (Ed.) (1975). *Orthopaedic aspects of cerebral palsy*, Clinics in Developmental Medicine, nos. 52–3. Spastics International/William Heinemann, London.

353. Moreau, M. *et al* (1979). Natural history of the dislocated hip in spastic cerebral palsy. *Developmental Medicine and Child Neurology* **21**, 749.

354. Scrutton, D. (1978). In *Care of the Handicapped Child*, Apley, J. (Ed.), Clinics in Developmental Medicine no. 67. Spastics International/Heinemann Medical, London.

355. Milla, P.J. and Jackson, A.D.M. (1977). A controlled trial of Baclofen in cerebral palsy. *Journal of International Medical Research* **5**, 398.

356. Mittler, P. (Ed.) (1973). *The Psychological Assessment of Mental and Physical Handicaps*. Tavistock.

357. Werlin, S.L. *et al* (1980). Sandifer Syndrome. *Developmental Medicine and Child Neurology* **22**, 374.

358. Harris, M.M. and Dignam, P.F. (1980). A non-surgical method of reducing drooling in cerebral palsied children. *Developmental Medicine and Child Neurology* **22**, 293.

359. Rapp, D. (1980). Drool control. *Developmental Medicine and Child Neurology* **22**, 448.

360. Brocklehurst, G. (Ed.) (1976). *Spina bifida for the clinician*, Clinics in Developmental Medicine no. 57. Spastics International/Heinemann Medical, London.

361. Smithells, R.W. *et al* (1981). Apparent prevention of neural tube defects by periconceptional vitamin supplementation. *Archives of Disease in Childhood* **56**, 911.

362. Lorber, J. and Salfield, S.A.W. (1981). Results of selective treatment of spina bifida cystica. *Archives of Disease in Childhood* **56**, 822.

363. Frank, J.D. and Fixsen, J. (1980). Spina bifida. *British Journal of Hospital Medicine* **24**, 422.

364. Hosking, G.P. (1974). Fits in hydrocephalic children. *Archives of Disease in Childhood* **49**, 633.

365. Scott, J.E.S. and Deegan, S. (1982). Management of neuropathic urinary incontinence by intermittent catheterisation. *Archives of Disease in Childhood* **57**, 253.

366. Dorner, S. (1976). Adolescents with spina bifida. *Archives of Disease in Childhood* **51**, 439.

367. Wald N.J. and Cuckle H.S. (1980). Alpha fetoprotein in the antenatal diagnosis of open neural tube defects. *British Journal of Hospital Medicine* **23**, 473.

368. Guthkelch, A.N. (1974). Diastematomyelia with median septum. *Brain* **97**, 729.

369. Borzyskowski, M. and Nevill, B.G.R. (1981). Neuropathic bladder and spinal dysraphism. *Archives of Disease in Childhood* **56**, 176.

370. Dubowitz, V. (1978). *Muscle Disorders in Childhood*. W.B. Saunders, Philadelphia.

371. Dubowitz, V. (1976). Screening for Duchenne Muscular Dystrophy. *Archives of Disease in Childhood* **51**, 249.

372. Gardner-Medwin, D. (1979). Controversies about Duchenne Muscular Dystrophy (ii). Bracing for ambulation. *Developmental Medicine and Child Neurology* **21**, 663.

373. Egger, J., Lake, B.L. and Wilson, J. (1981). Mitochondrial cytopathy. *Archives of Disease in Childhood* **56**, 741.

374. Williams, P. (1978). Arthrogryposis. *Orthopedic Clinics of North America* **9**, 1.

375. Guttmann, L. (1976). *Spinal cord injuries.* Blackwell Scientific Publications, Oxford.

376. Symposium on Osteogenesis Imperfecta (1982). *Clinical Orthopaedics and Related Research* **159**.

377. Levine, M.D., Brooks, R. and Shonkoff, J.P. (1980). A paediatric approach to learning disorders. John Wiley, Bristol.

378. Farnham-Diggory, S. (1978). *Learning Disabilities.* Fontana Open Books, London.

379. Touwen, B.C.L. (1972) Laterality and dominance. *Developmental Medicine and Child Neurology* **14**, 747.

380. Bishop, D.V.M. (1980). Handedness, Clumsiness and Cognitive Ability. *Developmental Medicine and Child Neurology* **22**, 569.

381. Pasamanick, B. and Knobloch, H. (1960). Brain damage and reproductive casualty. *American Journal of Orthopsychiatry* **30**, 298.

382. Schmitt, E.D. (1975). The minimal brain dysfunction myth. *American Journal of Diseases in Children* **129**, 1313.

383. Stott, D.H., Moyes, F.A. and Henderson, S.E. (1972). *A Test of Motor Impairment.* NFER, Windsor.

384. Towbin, A. (1971). Organic causes of minimal brain dysfunction. *Journal of the American Medical Association* **217**, 1207.

385. Lindsay, P. and Normand, D. (1977). *Human Information Processing.* Academic Press, New York.

386. Holt, J. (1969). *How Children Fail.* Pelican Books, Harmondsworth.

387. Holt, J. (1970). *How Children Learn.* Pelican Books, Harmondsworth.

388. Haber, R.N. and Hershenson, M. (1973). *Psychology of Visual Perception.* Holt Saunders, New York.

389. Benton, A.L. and Pearl, D. (Eds) (1978). *Dyslexia: an Appraisal of Current Knowledge.* Oxford University Press.

390. Miles, T.R. (1983). *Dyslexia: the pattern of difficulties.* Granada, London.

391. Critchley, M. (1970). *The Dyslexic Child.* Heinemann, London.

392. Galaburda, A.M. and Kemper, T.L. (1979). Cytoarchitectonic abnormalities in developmental dyslexia; a case study. *Annals of Neurology* **6**, 94.

393. Galaburda, A.M. and Geschwind, N. (1981). Anatomical Asymmetries in the Adult and Developing Brain and their implications for function. *Advances in Pediatrics* **28**, 271.

394. Gordon, M. and McKinlay, I. (Eds) (1980). *Helping Clumsy Children.* Churchill Livingstone, Edinburgh.

395. Gubbay, S.S. (1975). *The Clumsy Child.* W.B. Saunders, Philadelphia.

396. Barklay, R.A. (1981). *Hyperactive children—a handbook for diagnosis and treatment.* John Wiley/Guilford Press, New York.

397. Rapoport, J.L. and Ferguson, H.B. (1981). Biological validation of the hyperkinetic syndrome. *Developmental Medicine and Child Neurology* **23**, 667.

398. Burt, C. (1975). *The Gifted Child.* Unibooks/Hodder and Stoughton, London.

399. Tizard, J., Schofield, W.N. and Hewison, J. (1982). Symposium on reading; collaboration between teachers and parents in assisting children's reading. *British Journal of Educational Psychology* **52**, 1.

400. Morgan, R. and Lyon, E. (1979). Paired reading—a technique for parental tuition of reading retarded children. *Journal of Child Psychology and Psychiatry* **20**, 151.

401. Taylor, E. (1979). Food additives, allergy and hyperkinesis. *Journal of Child Psychology and Psychiatry* **20**, 357.

402. Jaffa, E. (1977). Learning disorders in young schoolchildren. *Public Health, London*, **91**, 237.

403. Bax, M. and Whitmore, K. (1973). Neurodevelopmental screening—the school entrant medical examination. *Lancet* **2**, 368.

404. Lindsay, G.A. and Wedell, K. (1980). The early identification of educationally 'at risk' children. *Remedial Education* **15**, 130.

405. Kempe, R.S. and Kempe, C.H. (1978). *Child Abuse*. Fontana Books, London.

406. Lee, C.M. (Ed.) (1978). *Child Abuse: a reader and sourcebook*. Open University Press, Milton Keynes.

407. Arthur, L.J.H. *et al* (1976). Non-accidental Injury in Children: What we do in Derby. *British Medical Journal*, **1**, 1363.

408. Lynch, M.A. (1975). Ill health and child abuse. *Lancet* **2**, 317.

409. O'Callaghan, M.J. and Hull, D. (1978). Failure to thrive or failure to rear? *Archives of Disease in Children* **53**, 788.

410. Till, K. (1968). Subdural haematoma in infancy. *British Medical Journal* **3**, 400.

411. Caffey, J. (1972). On the theory and practice of shaking infants. *American Journal of Diseases of Children* **24**, 161.

412. Caffey, J. (1974). The whiplash shaken infant syndrome. *Pediatrics* **54**, 396.

413. Swischuk, L.E. (1969). Spinal cord trauma in the battered child syndrome. *Radiology* **92**, 733.

414. Oliver, J.E. (1975). Microcephaly following baby battering and shaking. *British Medical Journal* **2**, 262.

415. Harcourt, R.B. and Hopkins, B. (1971). Ophthalmic manifestations of the battered baby syndrome. *British Medical Journal* **3**, 398.

416. Evans, T.J. and Davies, D.P. (1977). Failure to thrive at the breast. *Archives of Disease in Childhood* **52**, 974.

417. Frommer, E.A. and O'Shea, G. (1973). Antenatal identification of women liable to have problems in managing their infants. *British Journal of Psychiatry* **123**, 149.

418. Morazek, P.P. and Kempe, C.H. (1981). *Sexually abused children and their families*. Pergamon, Oxford.

419. Rogers, D. *et al* (1976). Non accidental poisoning. *British Medical Journal* **1**, 793.

420. Watson, J.B.G. *et al* (1979). Non accidental poisoning in childhood. *Archives of Disease in Childhood* **54**, 143.

421. Meadow, R. (1982). Munchausen Syndrome by proxy. *Archives of Disease in Childhood* **57**, 92.

422. Roberts, I.F. *et al* (1979). Malnutrition in Infants receiving cult diets: A form of Child Abuse. *British Medical Journal*. **1**, 296.

423. Laidlaw, J. and Richens, A. (1976). *A Textbook of Epilepsy.* Churchill Livingstone, Edinburgh.
424. O'Donohoe, N.V. (1979). *Epilepsies of Childhood.* Butterworths, London.
425. Harchovy, R.A. (1980). A controlled study of ACTH therapy in infantile spasms. *Epilepsia* **21**, 631.
426. Riikonen, R. and Donner, M. (1980). ACTH therapy in infantile spasms: side effects. *Archives of Disease in Childhood* **55**, 664.
427. Lindsay, J. *et al* (1979). Outcome of temporal lobe seizures. *Developmental Medicine and Child Neurology* **21**, (i) 285, (ii) 433, (iii) 630.
428. Jeavons, P.M. and Harding, G. (1975). *Photosensitive Epilepsy,* Clinics in Developmental Medicine, no. 56. Spastics International/Heinemann Medical, London.
429. Andermann, K. *et al* (1962) Self induced epilepsy. *Archives of Neurology* **6**, 63.
430. Nelson, K.B. and Ellenberg, J.H. (1978). Prognosis in children with febrile seizures. *Pediatrics* **61**, 720.
431. Nelson, K.B. and Ellenberg, J.H. (1976). Predictors of epilepsy in children with febrile seizures. *New England Journal of Medicine* **295**, 1029.
432. Addy, D.P. (1981). Prophylaxis of febrile convulsions. *Archives of Disease in Childhood* **56**, 81.
433. Lerman, P. and Kivity-Ephraim, S. (1981). Focal epileptic EEG discharges in children not suffering from clinical epilepsy. *Epilepsia* **22**, 551.
434. Cavazzuti, G.B. *et al* (1980). Longitudinal study of epileptiform EEG patterns in normal children. *Epilepsia* **21**, 43.
435. Rabe, E.F. (1974). Recurrent paroxysmal non epileptic disorders. *Current Pediatric Problems* **4**, 3.
436. McGuckin, H.M. (1980). *Changing the world view of those with epilepsy.* Advances in Epileptology, 11th Epilepsy International Symposium (Eds Canger, R. *et al*). Raven Press, New York.
437. Ward, F. and Bower, B.D. (1978). Social aspects of epilepsy in childhood. *Developmental Medicine and Child Neurology* **20**, Supplement 39.
438. Livingston, S. *et al* (1980). Drowning in epilepsy. *Annals of Neurology* **7**, 495.
439. Trimble, M.R. (1980). Anticonvulsant drugs and cognitive abilities. In *Advances in Epileptology.* (*See* reference 436.)
440. Morijin, Y. and Sato, T. (1981). Factors causing rickets in institutionalised handicapped children on anticonvulsants. *Archives of Disease in Childhood* **56**, 446.
441. Emerson, R. *et al* (1981). Stopping medication in children with epilepsy: Predictors of outcome. *New England Journal of Medicine* **304**, 1125.
442. Baraitser, M. (1981). Clinical genetics: epilepsy. *Hospital Update* **7**, 139.
443. Jennings, M.T. and Bird, T.D. (1981). Genetic influences in the epilepsies. *American Journal of Diseases of Children* **135**, 451.
444. Dietrich, E. *et al* (1980). Congenital anomalies in children of epileptic mothers and fathers. *Neuropaediatrie* **11**, 274.
445. Stephenson, J.B.P. (1978). Reflex anoxic seizures. *Archives of Disease in Childhood* **53**, 193.
446. Langford, W.S. (1937). Anxiety attacks in children. *American Journal of Orthopsychiatry* **7**, 210.
447. Fenton, G.W. (1975). Clinical disorders of sleep. *British Journal of Hospital Medicine* **14**, 120.

448. Herrnstein, R.J. (1983) I.Q. encounters with the press. *New Scientist* 28th April, p. 230.

449. Montagu, J.D. and Rudolf, N. (1983). Effects of anticonvulsants on the EEG. *Archives of Disease in Childhood* **58**, 241.

450. Foley, J. (1983). The athetoid syndrome. *Journal of Neurology, Neurosurgery and Psychiatry* **46**, 289.

451. Young, A.B., Reid, D. and Grist, N.R. (1983). Is cytomegalovirus a serious hazard to female hospital staff? *Lancet* **1**, 975.

452. Bergman, A.B. (1982). Use of Education in Preventing Injuries. *Pediatric Clinics of North America* **29:2**, 331.

453. Huizing, H.C. and Reyntjes, J.A. (1952). Articulation Curves. *Laryngoscope* **62**, 521.

454. Mckusick, V.A. (1972). *Heritable disorders of Connective Tissue.* C.V. Mosby, St. Louis.

455. Beeley, L. (1981). Adverse Effects of Drugs in the first trimester of pregnancy. *Clinics in Obstetrics and Gynaecology* **8:2**, 261.

456. Tizard, B. *et al* (1983). Language and Social Class: is verbal deprivation a myth? *Journal of Child Psychology and Psychiatry* **24**, 533.

457. Hitchings, V. and Haggard, M.P. (1983). Incorporation of Parental Suspicions in Screening Infants' Hearing. *British Journal of Audiology* **17**, 71.

458. Miles, R.N. and Hosking, G.P. (1983). Pertussis: should we immunise neurologically disabled and developmentally delayed children? *British Medical Journal* **287**, 318.

459. Egger, J. and Wilson, J. (1983). Mitochondrial Inheritance in a mitochondrially mediated disease. *New England Journal of Medicine* **309**, 142.

460. Sabin, A.B. (1980). Vaccination against poliomyelitis in economically underdeveloped countries. *Bulletin of the World Health Organisation* **58(1)**, 141.

461. Huckstep, R.L. (1975). *Poliomyelitis.* Churchill Livingstone, Edinburgh.

462. Smith, R., Francis, M.J.O. and Houghton, G. (1983). *The Brittle Bone Syndrome.* Butterworths, London.

463. Freeman, J. (1983). Emotional problems of the Gifted child. *Journal of Child Psychology and Psychiatry* **24**, 481.

464. Egger, J. *et al* (1983). Is migraine food allergy? *Lancet* **2**, 865.

465. Evans-Jones, L.G. and Rosenbloom, L. (1978). Disintegrative Psychosis. *Developmental Medicine and Child Neurology* **20**, 462.

466. Tizard, B. *et al* (1983). Childrens' questions and adults' answers. *Journal of Child Psychology and Psychiatry* **24**, 543.

467. Rutter, M. (1981). Psychological sequelae of brain damage in children. *American Journal of Psychiatry* **138**, 1533.

468. Rutter, M. (1982). Syndromes attributed to minimal brain dysfunction in childhood. *American Journal of Psychiatry* **139**, 21.

469. Symposium on Sodium Valproate (1983). *British Journal of Clinical Practice* Supplement 27.

470. Hagberg, B. (1978). Severe mental retardation in Swedish children. In *Major Mental Handicap,* Ciba Foundation Symposium no. 59, p. 29. Elsevier Excerpta Medica, North-Holland.

471. Byrne, W.J. *et al* (1983). A diagnostic approach to vomiting in severely retarded patients. *American Journal of Diseases of Children* **137**, 259.

472. Kennedy, E. (1977). *On Becoming a Counsellor.* Gill and Macmillan, London.

473. Hersen, M. and Barlow, D.H. (1976). *Single-case Experimental Designs.* Pergamon, Oxford.

474. Kiessling, L.S., Denckla, M.B. and Carlton, M. (1983). Evidence of differential hemisphere function in children with hemiplegic cerebral palsy. *Developmental Medicine and Child Neurology* **25**, 727.

475. Simeonsson, R.J., Cooper, D.H. and Scheiner, A.P. (1982). Review and analysis of the effectiveness of early intervention programmes. *Pediatrics* **69**, 635.

476. Jones, M. (1983). *Behaviour Problems in Handicapped Children.* Human Horizons Series, Souvenir Press.

477. Hall, S.M. (1983). Congenital toxoplasmosis in England, Wales, and Northern Ireland: some epidemiological problems. *British Medical Journal* **287**, 453.

478. Sherk, H.H., Pasquariello, P.D. and Doherty, J. (1983). Hip dislocation in cerebral palsy. *Developmental Medicine and Child Neurology* **25**, 738.

479. Peckham, C.S. *et al.* (1983). Cytomegalovirus infection in pregnancy: preliminary findings from a prospective study. *Lancet* **1**, 1352.

480. Touwen B.C.L. (1976). *Neurological Development in Infancy.* Clinics in Developmental Medicine no. 58. Spastics International Medical Publications.

Index

519

SOCIAL SCIENCE LIBRARY

Manor Road Building
Manor Road
Oxford OX1 3UQ
Tel: (2)71093 (enquiries and renewals)
http://www.ssl.ox.ac.uk

This is a NORMAL LOAN item.

We will email you a reminder before this item is due.

Please see http://www.ssl.ox.ac.uk/lending.html
for details on:

- loan policies; these are also displayed on the notice boards and in our library guide.

- how to check when your books are due back.

- how to renew your books, including information on the maximum number of renewals.
  Items may be renewed if not reserved by another reader. Items must be renewed before the library closes on the due date.

- level of fines; fines are charged on overdue books.

Please note that this item may be recalled during Term.